THE POPULATION OF TROPICAL AFRICA

The Population of Tropical Africa

Edited by John C. Caldwell and Chukuka Okonjo

LONGMANS

LONGMANS, GREEN & CO. LTD.

74 Grosvenor Street
London, W.1

P.O. Box 1176
Freetown

P.O. Box 2051
Accra

LONGMANS OF NIGERIA, LTD.

P.M.B. 1036
Ikeja

P.M.B. 5197
Ibadan

P.O. Box 425
Enugu

Longmans of Kenya Ltd.
P.O. Box 18201
Nairobi

Longmans of Zambia Ltd.
P.O. Box 886
Lusaka

Longmans of Uganda Ltd.
P.O. Box 3409
Kampala

Longmans of Malawi Ltd.
P.O. Box 468
Limbe

Longmans of Tanzania Ltd.
P.O. Box 3043
Arusha

Associated companies, branches and representatives throughout the world

First published 1968
Second impression 1968

Printed in Great Britain by
Lowe & Brydone (Printers) Ltd. London

THIS WORK FORMS A
RECORD OF THE FIRST
AFRICAN POPULATION
CONFERENCE SPONSORED
BY THE UNIVERSITY OF IBADAN
IN CO-OPERATION WITH
THE POPULATION COUNCIL
AND HELD AT THE
UNIVERSITY OF IBADAN
NIGERIA 3–7 JAN 1966

Preface

Except for the introductory chapters, this work comprises the papers presented at the First African Population Conference, held at the University of Ibadan in Ibadan, Nigeria, from 3rd to 7th January 1966. The Conference, a major event in the study of African population, stirred interest in demography throughout the universities of half the continent and beyond. By bringing together for the first time a large number of people in the field, it served as a forum for the presentation of the results of new research. The focus was on university research and teaching, with emphasis mainly on countries where English is an official or institutional language, although all of Africa was under consideration. The subject matter was confined to tropical Africa, with Africa north of the Sahara and south of the Tropic of Capricorn serving only for comparison.

A sense of completeness nevertheless pervaded the Conference because those countries of tropical Africa where English is used as the medium of instruction within the universities represent almost half the population of the continent. In addition to a considerable number of persons working outside the continent on aspects of Africa's demography, almost everyone engaged in population research in each discipline of every university within the area concerned was able to attend.

By early 1966, when the Conference met, most tropical African countries had completed the major analyses of their 1960 censuses, and most had begun preliminary discussions of plans for the 1970 censuses. Thus, one of the purposes of the Conference was to examine the experience and research findings since the last round of censuses in order to help guide substantive and administrative decisions prior to the next one.

The editing of the papers collected in this work has necessarily entailed much compression and deletion, particularly of the speeches by the Discussion Leaders, the ensuing discussion, the Oral Statements, and certain tables, diagrams, and highly specialized papers. The complete collection, which runs into a great many volumes, will be retained in bound typescript by the Centre for Population Studies at the University of Ibadan.

The major aim of the Conference was to increase understanding of tropical African population phenomena and trends. The need for such a conference had been felt for some time, but it became possible to fulfil this need only when The Population Council of New York generously offered to support it. The services of its two experienced consultants, Dr Dudley Kirk and Dr John F. Kantner, and the rôle as host of the University of Ibadan, notably its Centre for Population Studies and its Vice-Chancellor, Dr Kenneth Dike, greatly contributed to the success of the Conference.

It is hoped that the aim of the Conference is furthered by this publication of almost the complete proceedings, a project to which The Population Council again contributed greatly.

J. C. Caldwell
C. Okonjo

Contents

PART 1 The Demographic Situation

THE MOVEMENT OF POPULATION, DENSITY, AND URBANISATION

PART 2 The Situation with regard to Population Growth and Economic Development

MAPS

MAPS

PART I
THE DEMOGRAPHIC SITUATION[1]

INTRODUCTION

J. C. Caldwell
Department of Demography, Australian National University, Canberra, Australia

In this work, attention is focussed on tropical Africa, the vast part of the continent that lies between the Arab world north of the Sahara and the racially mixed peoples of South Africa. This is the Black Africa of legend and of modern nationalism. Over most of it, the climate is hot, the people are poor, the economy is agricultural and the nations are new.

The existence of widespread poverty is not to be equated with a slow rate of change. Not only is the population growing rapidly, but the social structure and technology are changing at a pace that is in many ways startling. Old men in tropical Africa have seen the land of their birth, its society and its economy, transformed to a degree that no one in Europe has witnessed over a lifetime. Railway lines and roads have brought freight trains and lorries, towns have grown with commercial markets, tribal organization has been largely replaced by other forms of government, schools have transformed the rôle of children in the society and the land tenure system has buckled or broken under very great pressure. Not all these changes have brought proportional increases in happiness. Some have brought intractable problems, and most have led to an awareness that fuller lives are being lived in other parts of the world. Nevertheless, the attainment of better conditions in the future lies in an intensification of every one of these changes. However, it is to be hoped that with an increased understanding of them, the more severe strains upon individual Africans can be diminished, and some of their social and economic goals more easily attained.

Measuring the Population

An essential component of this increased understanding must be greater knowledge of demographic change. Demography is only just emerging from its heroic age in Africa. In many areas, views concerning number of inhabitants vary widely and great doubt surrounds the figures on fertility and mortality. At the political and administrative level the demand is increasing for statisticians and demographers to provide answers or at least unambiguous information to serve as a basis for proper policy decisions.

1. What is the number of people in each country and in its geographical subsections?
2. What are the current trends and levels of fertility and mortality? Is present population growth rapid? Is it likely to become too rapid?
3. How many people can the region absorb, and at what pace?
4. How is population being redistributed? Of what significance is the accelerating growth of urban population? Is planned internal migration from densely to sparsely settled areas a meaningful solution to fast population growth?

For the first time, a reasonably reliable answer now exists for most African countries to the first of these questions. Although we still know little about African population prior to this century, both Willcox and Carr-Saunders have interpreted the fragmentary data to suggest that African population has been growing quite rapidly for at least 100 years.[2] (A considerable component of this growth has been outside tropical Africa in Egypt for instance.) For the period 1850–1900, they suggest average annual growth rates for the whole continent of 0·7[3] or 0·5 per cent,[4] the former similar to rates in Belgium, Spain and Portugal during the same period. The average annual growth rate between 1900 and 1930 has been computed at 0·6 per cent[5] and that between 1930 and 1950 at 1·3 per cent.[6] The estimated rate for the 1960–62 period is 2·4 per cent for the whole continent, subdivided into 2·3 per cent for North Africa and 2·5 per cent for sub-Sahara Africa.[7] The age structure and contemporary rates of growth suggest that, on the whole, tropical African populations have exhibited considerable and accelerating rates of population growth since at least the beginning of the present century.

The Census

Satisfactory evidence to settle questions on rates of growth comes from expensive and well-administered censuses, surveys and registration systems. Mere inspection, even in these days of roads, motor vehicles and central administration, can lead to widely differing estimates, as is still the case in Ethiopia.[8] Censuses in small areas have been taken since the second half of the 19th century (beginning in Gambia, Lagos and Sierra Leone Colony in 1871),[9] but the type of census now advocated and described in the following papers, dates from the Second World War.[10]

The modern census still presents administrative problems and technical defects. Recent censuses have been better than earlier ones, not merely because of superior wisdom, techniques and administration, but because of decisions to spend much more money. To a considerable degree better results have to be bought. The average cost of British West African censuses in 1931 was a tenth of a penny per head of enumerated population. In 1948 East Africa spent 2*d* per head as compared with 1*s* 2*d* in Ghana in 1960 (Lury, ch. 4). The enumeration alone for the 1962 and 1963 Nigerian censuses cost two shillings per head (Udo, ch. 7), approximately the same as the whole Australian census programme. As income per head in Australia is much higher than in Nigeria, this shows that Nigerians have deliberately chosen to allocate more resources to census-taking than Australians.

The question of choice is strongly emphasized (Brass, ch. 2). Those advocating more complete censuses must show that the extra money is worth it. The same applies to allocation of administrative resources and professional experts. As with all governmental expenditure, the main criteria are the needs of the people and the government. A profile of the population describing its chief characteristics is a major need. Another need is to provide a kind of catalogue of settlement indicating where the inhabitants live and who they are. Demographic studies 'provide planning authorities with data they require to reach decisions based on rational choice' (Iro, ch. 46).

In the 'early 1960s . . . many newly independent states realized that information on the size, structure and rate of growth of their populations was seriously deficient' (Jupp, ch. 45). To improve this situation is difficult and expensive. In a developing country a census bears a heavy load because it is often the only vehicle for providing information that in advanced countries is collected through many different channels (Gil, Ghansah, ch. 10). The rôle of government, important everywhere in exercises of this kind, is of crucial significance in tropical Africa (Omaboe, ch. 3). In the census operation, shortages of personnel, transport and equipment develop that can be overcome only by utilizing, often at short notice, all the necessary specific skills and materials in the country. Furthermore, even the best censuses are not enough. In these times of rapid demographic change, one census, however good, is of very much less value than a series of censuses (Brass, ch. 2). Although work such as that published by Brass has greatly extended the information that can be derived from the usual census question on recent births or deaths, in the absence of vital registration systems, even a good single census reveals only limited information about the levels of mortality, fertility and natural increase.

One way out of the dilemma might seem to be the sample census, a recent practice in most francophone countries, where the full effort devoted to the best censuses is concentrated on intensive questioning of a representative sampling of the population at a fraction of the cost of a complete census (Clarke, ch. 27).

This was not, however, the general view of those who attended the conference, perhaps partly because few francophone demographers were present. It seemed to be the feeling that sample surveys yield a good measure of such demographic phenomena as levels of fertility and mortality, especially if a full census is used as a sampling frame, but that they are liable to substantial error in estimating total population figures and by their very nature are incapable of providing administrators with the catalogue of population and localities needed. For example, in the post-enumeration survey in Ghana, 10 per cent fewer people were enumerated than in the preceding full census, and less satisfactory age data were obtained. In general, a sample survey does not seem to arouse the same interest and concern among the populace as a full census does (Gil, Ghansah, ch. 10).

The greatest doubts about the efficacy of sample censuses are illustrated by an account of the 1956 Sudan census (Henin, ch. 12). In the Sudan, a full census was undertaken in the towns and a sample census in rural areas on the grounds that the former were by their nature heterogeneous and the latter homogeneous. But experience showed that the homogeneity of subsistence farming areas is now a myth and may always have been so.

Rural areas vary greatly in density of settlement and allied characteristics, and few are fully subsistent in their economy, being penetrated to different degrees by a cash economy. Also, the sample census probably faces greater difficulties than the full census in enumerating nomads. More serious is the fact that the sample census may not be markedly cheaper and certainly not nearly so cheap as originally expected.

The basic problem is that the rapidity of demographic and economic change so affects society that the original sampling frame is quickly outdated and invalidated. Supplementary data can correct this to a large extent but the work is often lengthy, and dissipates the original savings achieved by the use of the sample. In the Sudan this activity added an extra 20 per cent of work and expense to that planned for the census, so that in the Blue Nile Province, for instance, the cost of the sample amounted to three-quarters that of a full census.

In this volume, certain of the 1960 censuses are examined. One, the 1960 Ghana census, discussed in several papers (Omaboe, ch. 3, Gil, Ghansah, ch. 10, Owusu, ch. 11, Gil, ch. 13, Hilton, ch. 28, Owusu, Special Report 3), is judged by some to have been the most successful and is recommended as a model for the 1970 round (Blacker, Discussion Leader's Report 1).

In contrast, several Nigerian delegates analysed the 1962 and 1963 Nigerian census enumerations, emphasizing their weakness (Okonjo, ch. 6, Duru, ch. 5, Udo, ch. 7, Yesufu, ch. 8, Ogunlesi, ch. 9). The count in 1962, which enumerated some millions more Nigerians than expected, became a centre of political controversy and was declared void without the release of any figures. In 1963, another census, which was organized hurriedly, incorporated apparent safeguards but probably involved a greater expenditure per head than any other tropical African census. It has since been announced that 56 million persons were enumerated (as compared to the 38 million estimated, based on the 1952–53 census [11]) and one delegate states that the figure was probably over 60 million before it was scaled down prior to release (Udo, ch. 7). Few details of the 1963 census have yet been released but one matter on which participants in the controversy seem agreed is that it was probably in error by 10 million or more people, a margin of error greater than the total population of most African countries, and this in a direction that had hitherto been regarded as unlikely.

What went wrong? Perhaps the answer is that the population was *too* census-conscious. Census publicity is of great importance in countries where illiteracy is wide-spread, where the people are often suspicious of being counted (Udo, ch. 7), and where census-takers have long been suspected of being in league with tax-collectors. The importance of the pre-census publicity campaign and of the organized census night festivities in Ghana has been pointed out (Gil, ch. 10). But such measures can easily get out of hand in a country where different ethnic groups are competing, and especially where expenditure and political representation are related to the population numbers (Udo, ch. 7). These problems are unlikely to be transient in tropical Africa, especially if, as in 1962, voter registration cards are disbursed as an integral part of the enumeration. Possibly the danger of overcounts will be greater than that of undercounts in the 1970 census round in tropical Africa (Blacker, Discussion Leader's Report 1). In view of the fact that lack of definition, especially with regard to residence, can lead to an inflated count even where no fraud is attempted, the establishment of a permanent Census Commission charged with providing and publicizing adequate definitions might be in order (Ogunlesi, ch. 9).

Incorrect or controversial census results do cause problems. In Nigeria the 1962–68 National Development Plan has been left in a very precarious position because its targets were expressed in per capita terms or in population ratios. Many developmental indices, such as national income per head, depend on population estimates for their construction, and on a continuous series of such estimates to calculate their directions and rates of change. National income per head now appears to have fallen over the last fifteen years but, in fact, few Nigerians really believe this to have been the case (Yesufu, ch. 8).

Nigeria is not the only country that has felt or is likely to experience strains over census-taking. The 1963 Sierra Leonean census produced consternation among politicians because of the unexpectedly low population revealed and the questions it raised about the ethnic balance. But, and this is ultimately the important point, the Sierra Leonean Government has decided to proceed with publication and analysis, at the same time promising to hold another census soon.

The chief importance of such discussion is its bearing on the planning for the 1970 census round. Such planning has already begun in the Economic Commission for Africa (ECA, ch. 13 Annex, and Jupp, Oral Statement 2). Yet preparations for another census have not even started in those countries that led the 1960 round, such as the Sudan and Uganda where, if the governments intend to hold decennial censuses, their next census-taking should be in 1966 and 1967 respectively.

Pre-census mapping, possibly based on international standards, is already greatly needed (Brass, ch. 2, Lury, ch. 4, Duru, ch. 5, Clarke, ch. 27). In fact, pre-census planning, training and action not only should be moving faster than is the case but also should be treated as being as essential an aspect of the census as actual enumeration (Gil, ch. 13). It has been estimated (Gil, ch. 13) that the 1970 census round will require for its success 150 to 170 experts (three to five per country in the fields of statistics, demography, geography, machine processing, etc.). The need for a timetable of censuses and for manuals of instruction and procedures based on African standards and experience was pointed out (Gil, ch. 13). According to Gil money for censuses would be considered a worthwhile investment if censuses were regarded not as desirable though unique phenomena in their own right but as integral parts of developmental planning. Preliminary and precautionary steps, essential to a good census, Gil estimated would cost no more than about one-eightieth of likely census expenditure in Africa around 1970.

Data analysis and publication, not data collection, may be the main problem with censuses in contemporary Africa (van de Walle, ch. 1 and Brass, ch. 2). Not all information gathered is being published, and some that is published appears in a 'corrected' form that makes further analysis hazardous. Above all, existing data should be exhaustively and competently analysed, for analysis is very much cheaper than mounting vast census operations. Thus the training of high level personnel can effect very substantial economies.

Vital Rates

While censuses spread over the face of Africa, registration schemes do not, even though in most advanced societies they are as important as censuses in providing the complementary information necessary to measure demographic trends. Registering a vital event requires individual initiative and decision; it is very much more a sophisticated act than being enumerated by a census-taker. Registration usually develops because a society directly or indirectly imposes penalties for failure.

Registration is not unknown in tropical Africa, although nowhere does an effective, nationwide system exist. In some parts of Uganda, registration began as early as 1904, but even now it remains incomplete.[12] Registration areas exist in some towns such as Lagos (Ohadike, ch. 39). Ghana has 37 such areas covering a sixth of the country's population (Holzer, ch. 21), and plans to cover the whole country within five years (Owusu, Special Report 3).

Incomplete registration tends to lower the birth rate; incomplete census enumeration tends to raise it, and the registration of births from outside the census area or the exclusion of those from within raises or lowers the rate, depending on which is the more common occurrence. National registration systems are so expensive and the effectiveness of the coverage so dependent on the nature of the society and its stage of evolution that possibly the improvement of registration in tropical Africa should be dominated by non-demographic needs (Brass, ch. 2), with sample surveys used instead for estimates of vital levels (Brass, ch. 2, Heisel, ch. 14, Scott, ch. 15, Friedlander, ch. 22).

Sample surveys for determining vital rates are of two basic types: the retrospective survey, which aims at securing vital histories for either an indefinite or a specific period prior to the survey, and the survey composed of successive rounds, each like a small census. There is much to be said for the latter, since illiterate villagers are not asked to recall events in a specified unit of time but rather since the last visit. Of course persons who have been born and who subsequently die between successive rounds may be omitted. Also, in cases of uncertain age statement, the first method often yields better statistics on completed family size unless the rounds extend over a woman's full reproductive span (Pool, ch. 40).

The use of different survey and analytical techniques is necessary only because of defective data; if all births and deaths were reported correctly for a certain period, the problem would be solved (Brass, ch. 16). But in fact all births and deaths are not remembered, or at least not reported to the survey workers, and omissions become greater with time elapsed since the events. R. K. Som has been applying to African data correction methods developed in India, but Brass feels that these experiments have failed to make allowance for respondents mistaking the time scale used and that 'further exploration is certainly justified' (Brass, ch. 16). Brass also pointed out that his own analytical techniques have made it possible to attempt checks on fertility and child mortality but not on adult death rates or natural increase. However, if the inclusion of a question on the mortality of parents, as advocated by Clairin (ch. 19), is adopted, as in the 1963–64 inquiry in Chad, a way of examining adult mortality may be developed. Scott (ch. 15) advocated sampling to select unit areas, but complete enumeration within such areas, because problems of house and household and type and place of residence do raise awkward difficulties when sampling persons within areas.

There is, of course, a third method for determining the level of vital rates that depends neither on registration nor on sample survey data, and that, in fact, does not necessarily utilize data on births or deaths at all. This is stable population analysis, which begins with census age data, and which is justified by the fact that unchanging levels of fertility and mortality do over a period of time define a specific age structure for the community, the level of fertility being the dominant determinant. The temptation to use this method in tropical Africa is strong, for it is unlikely that secular change in fertility has been occurring. Again the problem is that age misstatement in the censuses, largely unintentional and unavoidable, leaves us uncertain as to the exact nature of the age structure.

Two good censuses, however, can determine the rate of natural increase for populations not greatly affected by migration, and the fixing of estimates for fertility and natural increase consequently yields a mortality estimate. However, it should be noted that the fertility component is the sum of the other two, and hence a small error in it can produce a proportionately larger one in the mortality estimate. One reason for urging early planning and sustained effort to ensure the success of the next census round is that such censuses will provide many tropical African countries with two reasonably good censuses only ten years apart, and so allow the construction of life tables to measure mortality directly.

If stable population techniques are used, and are guided by measures of fertility or mortality, problems arise, not merely because of insufficient knowledge of age structure, but because of inadequate data on fertility and mortality patterns by age. The latter is the more serious, especially as 'there is good evidence . . . that in many West African populations mortality at 1–4 years is very high relative to the level at under one year; the situation in East Africa is less clear' (Brass, ch. 16). Such a pattern would be abnormal only in the sense of experience elsewhere, particularly to the extent that such mortality has been summarized in the widely used United Nations Model Life Tables.[13] Although no adequate sets of tropical African life tables yet exist, the United Nations tables have now been joined by the Coale-Demeny sets,[14] which in the case of the North region tables 'incorporate such a pattern, although not with such extreme features as have been claimed for African mortality, and will often be the best for applications of quasi-stable population theory' (Brass, ch. 16).

The Demographic Picture

The kind of painstaking work briefly described above has already begun to yield dividends. Over the last few years both the Economic Commission for Africa and the African Demography project at the Office of Population Research at Princeton University have pieced together coherent pictures of population phenomena in tropical Africa. Demographers at the Ibadan Conference enjoyed for the first time the opportunity to compare the two pictures, one by ECA, one by Princeton. Kirk (Oral Statement 6) believed the two sets of results to be sufficiently similar to give rise to optimism and to show in general approximately where the truth probably lies. An analytical comparison follows.

The Princeton team (Coale, Lorimer, Brass, van de Walle, Demeny, Romaniuk, Heisel, Boute, nearly all of whom were at the conference) used 24 post-1950 censuses or surveys, in all cases employing two different methods for estimating fertility, noting that in nearly every case 'both methods were consistent' (Coale, ch. 17). Where stable population methods were used, evidence of age composition was supplemented by some other demographic index, such as infant mortality or rate of population growth, in choosing a suitable model.

The Economic Commission for Africa (ECA) presented its findings in a paper entitled 'Recent Demographic Levels and Trends in Africa' (ch. 13 Annex) and in Som's paper (ch. 18), which introduced some more recent work.

ECA's findings are for whole national areas, but Princeton's are for small regions. The Princeton group regards its most reliable work as that done on data provided by the francophone sample surveys and East African censuses where retrospective questions on the household history of fertility and mortality allowed the use of Brass's analytical techniques. They feel their least reliable estimates to be those for Nigeria, the Portuguese territories, Ghana, Senegal, Gabon, Southern Rhodesia, Zambia and the Sudan. Possibly the methods employed for those countries were similar to those usually utilized by ECA, for, if anything, the two sets of results show slightly more agreement in the cases of these countries than for the others.

Not all findings can be directly compared, usually because data are taken from censuses or surveys carried out at different times, but an analysis is possible of most of those findings in Coale's and Som's papers where the dates do coincide. In a few cases comparison cannot be undertaken because Princeton's findings are confined to only part of the national area.

As Princeton's estimates are on average higher for crude death rates and lower in the case of crude birth rates, their estimates of natural increase are usually below those of ECA. Of the seven direct comparisons of natural increase possible, the average difference is 0·5 per cent. ECA's rates are higher in five cases and Princeton's in two, ECA's exceeding Princeton's by an average of 25 per cent.

Several general points might be made before examining the actual estimates of fertility and mortality levels. First, our present knowledge of tropical African fertility and mortality patterns seemed inconceivable half a dozen years ago. Second, we have not as yet arrived at consensus. Even the two sets of crude birth and death rate estimates examined above vary by an average of over 10 per cent. (It is a courageous demographer who disputes a national crude birth rate of, for instance, 50 per 1,000 on the grounds that his analytical approach yielded a figure of 45 or 55 per 1,000.) The third general point is our lack of knowledge of fertility and mortality by age. This shows up in the fact that the age-specific birth rates quoted by ECA from INSEE for 15 francophone countries turn out to be the same distribution, but adjusted to an estimated total fertility rate.[15]

Fertility

Both ECA and Princeton depict a pattern for tropical Africa whereby crude birth rates range from a little above 30 to about 60 per 1,000 and total fertility rates from about 4 to 8. The Princeton group establishes an average crude birth rate of 49 per 1,000 and a total fertility rate of 6½ for all countries studied, and, as Coale comments, 'Only Latin America from Mexico to Peru and Brazil has fertility rates this high' (Coale, ch. 17). ECA gives a crude birth rate for the whole of Africa of 47 per 1,000 and claims this as the highest among the continents (ch. 13 Annex). R.K. Som gives a gross reproduction rate for the whole of Africa of 3·1 (ch. 18).

Thus fertility in tropical Africa is very high, if not quite uniformly so. According to Som, national fertility is highest in West Africa. According to the Princeton team, who used an approach involving analysis for smaller areas, the fertility of West Africa was exceeded by the population of a strip of East and Central Africa, clearly visible on Figure 1, stretching 2,000 miles from about 10° N in the Sudan to 20° S in Rhodesia and averaging something over 500 miles in width.

Fertility rates for the whole continent are, of course, computed only because work of different magnitude and quality is done for each country. For instance, in Ghana, crude birth rates of 50 and 51 have been estimated by Princeton and ECA respectively for 1960. Friedlander concluded from researches on certain towns in Ghana, where it might be noted urban-rural fertility differentials seem to prevail, that their crude birth rate was just under 50 per 1,000, but his technique for analysing the 1960 census age data produced a rate of 45 per 1,000 for the whole country (ch. 22).

Princeton and ECA computed total fertility rates for Ghana of 6·5 and 6·1, while Gaisie has estimated 6·7 (ch. 23). In Lagos, Nigeria, Ohadike pointed out that official registration figures suggest a total fertility rate exceeding seven, but women of 45 years of age and over in his survey average only 6·8 live births (ch. 39).

Fertility Differentials

The work of the Princeton group draws attention not merely to high fertility but to marked variations in the level of fertility, which is partly artificial but also partly real. The importance of Romaniuk's analysis of the Congo census is the demonstration that certain elements in modernization, such as the reduction of venereal disease and perhaps the greater stability of sexual relations, tend to raise the birth rate.

Some urban–rural fertility differentials do exist, an important point in view of the present increase in urban population and the rôle African cities play as centres exposed to strong non-African cultural forces. Crude birth rates appear to indicate substantial differentials in Congo (Kinshasha), Guinea and Mali, and lesser differentials in the Central African Republic and Senegal. Calculations based on completed family size in Ghana have shown urban fertility to be 10 per cent lower than that of rural areas (Gaisie, ch. 23). Such differentials may be related to delayed marriage in the towns. In Lagos urban-born females and males marry later than rural–urban immigrants (Ejiogu, ch. 33), and the age-specific birth rate is much lower for 15–19-year-old females in the large town of Sekondi-Takoradi than it is in smaller towns (Friedlander, ch. 22).

Other differentials are associated with education, income and to a lesser extent occupation and religion. Significantly lower fertility among wives in polygamous marriages in Congo (Kinshasa) and Guinea, may perhaps reflect the older age of wives in polygamous marriages: there is no difference in Lagos when age is standardized (Ohadike, ch. 39).

Marriage

Measurement of married condition is perhaps the most difficult of demographic investigations in tropical Africa. There are many variations in the method of signalizing traditional marriage. These include Western forms, which often have more legal force; traditional types and unstable unions of different degrees; and Moslem marriages. Survey workers are wise to follow such legal attitudes as are found in Ghana, namely that a marriage exists if the couple regards itself as married, irrespective of whether or what rites have been performed.

In Lagos age at marriage rises with city residence, education, adherence to Christianity and high occupational status (Ohadike, ch. 39). Ideal marriage age varies in the same way but always remains a little higher. Marriage instability, as measured by number of successive marriages, is highest among adherents of traditional religions and Islam and lowest among Catholics. The practice and advocacy of polygamy decline with increasing social status and education, but rise with age. (Although imported Christianity has not favoured polygamy, over a sixth of married Catholics and almost a quarter of married Protestants are found in polygamous marriage.)

To detect possible changes in vital rates, investigation of age at marriage is important.[16] In tropical Africa the vast majority of females 20–24 years of age are married, but the proportion of 15–19-year-olds married varies greatly, ranging, for national data collected by ECA from less than half to almost five-sixths. Ohadike finds that age at marriage of females is rising, with a narrowing age gap between spouses. A possible reason is his finding that the size of the gap is negatively associated with education. However, modernizing societies experiencing a reduction in the incidence of polygamy and unstable marriage are subject to considerable demographic pressures to narrow this age gap if universal or near universal female marriage is to be maintained.[17]

Sex Ratio at Birth

From more specialized work on births, Holzer contributes the information that his study of birth registration in Accra and Kumasi indicates ratios of 102·5 and 103·5 males per 100 females respectively, while analysis of the 1960 Ghana census data suggests ratios for the two towns of 100·7 and 103·6 (Holzer, ch. 21). By world standards these are low, and unlikely to have been reduced by a stronger tendency to register or enumerate females. Holzer also demonstrates a peak birth period for the two towns, that means a peak conception period during the cooler months following the rains, and a peak death period during the hotter months preceding the rains.

Mortality

When turning to mortality we are on weaker ground. Even in retrospective surveys, the outcome of a birth is usually still present in the household when the investigators arrive, but the outcome of a death never is. The Princeton group estimates crude death rates from about 15 per 1,000 to over 40, with half in the range from 26 to 33 (Coale, ch. 17). ECA's estimates stretch from 14 to 40 with over half between 19 and 30 (Som, ch. 18). Their regional estimates for 1956–60 are 29 for West Africa, and 22 for East and Southern Africa, a margin between West and East Africa that leads one to wonder whether mortality has been underestimated in the latter area. However, it should be added that Princeton concurs with this analysis, calculating crude death rates for Kenya, Uganda and Tanganyika of 18, 25 and 26 respectively, as compared with, for instance, 38, 36 and 33 for Guinea, Upper Volta and Dahomey respectively.

Princeton estimates a range in expectation of life at birth from under 30 to over 45 years (Coale, ch. 17). ECA suggests regional expectations of 35 years in West Africa and 42 years in East and Central Africa.

Princeton infant mortality estimates are from 100 per 1,000 live births to over 300, while 24 out of the 28 estimates given by Som fall in the range 100 to 225. Mortality at ages 1–4 is probably also very high, and in many areas equals infant mortality (Clairin, ch. 19). There are probably still parts of tropical Africa where not many more than half the children born survive to their fifth birthdays.

Despite the uncertainty about levels and trends, the conviction is widespread that death rates are falling, perhaps rapidly. Even before the arrival of antibiotics, modern health measures could do much to combat tropical disease, as is shown by the dramatic fall in European mortality in West Africa around the turn of the century.[18] Coale agrees that mortality is declining, perhaps rapidly, so that the apparent differences between Princeton's estimates of Kenyan and Tanganyikan mortality may only be a matter of census dates (Coale, ch. 17). It may now be a political necessity in tropical Africa to continue health work (Lucas, ch. 38), and most governments are spending around 10 per cent of their budgets on it (Caldwell, ch. 37). It is probable that death rates will decline quite rapidly, in spite of some doubt on the point,[19] and despite a very great shortage of doctors.[20]

Not much is known about mortality differentials to indicate the speed and direction of change. ECA has gathered material showing a very marked urban–rural differential in six out of seven tropical African countries for which data exist. In three, the urban crude death rate is around half the rural rate. This is only partly a product of the age structure of the immigrant towns. It is widely assumed in tropical Africa that the large towns are healthier because of public health measures, doctors and hospitals, as well as higher levels of education and income. For example, mortality is lower in Freetown than elsewhere in Sierra Leone, and Western Area of the country, where Freetown is located, contains one-eleventh of the total population but more than one-third of all hospital beds (Clarke, ch. 27).

According to Hilton, the 1960 Ghana census data show a male–female mortality differential favourable to males in the emigrant areas of northern Ghana. This can

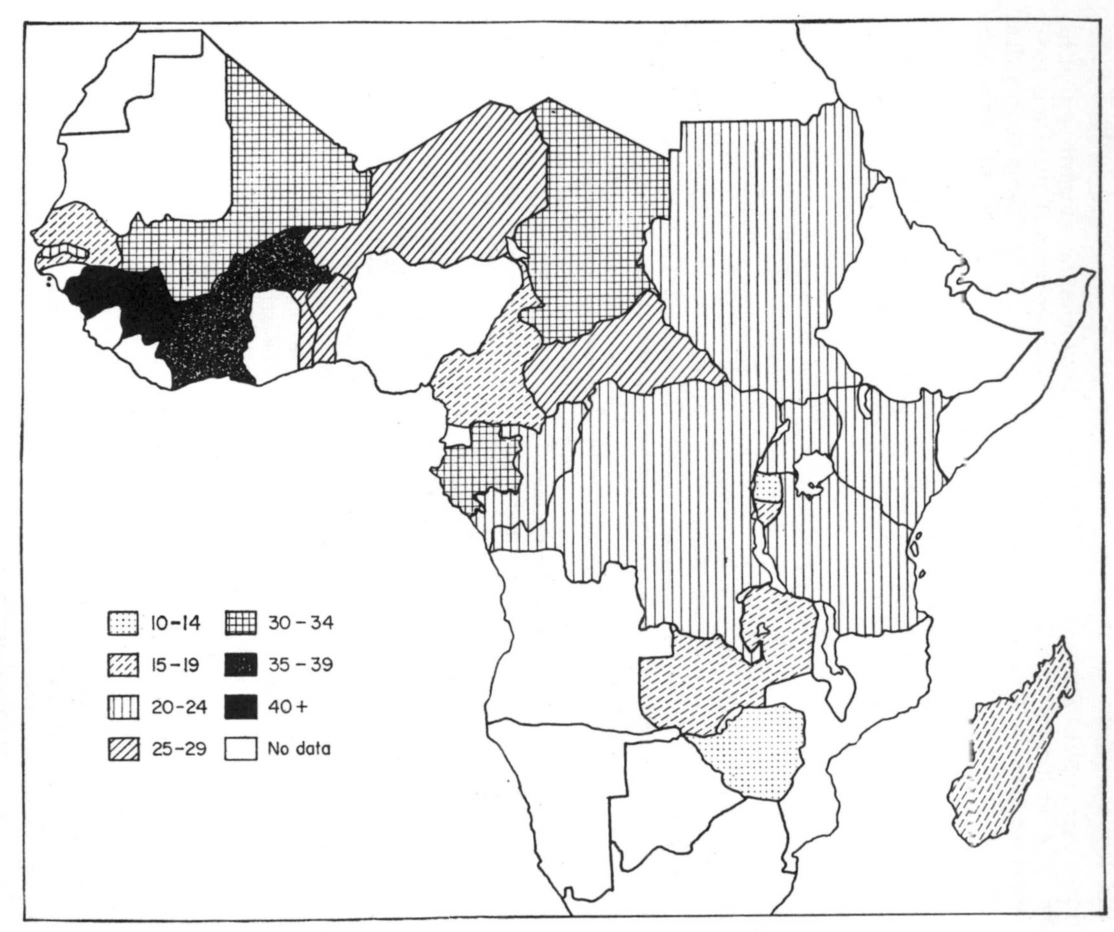

Map 1 Tropical Africa: estimated crude death rates (deaths per thousand inhabitants).

Source : R. K. Som, ch. 18 ; data as shown on Table 6.

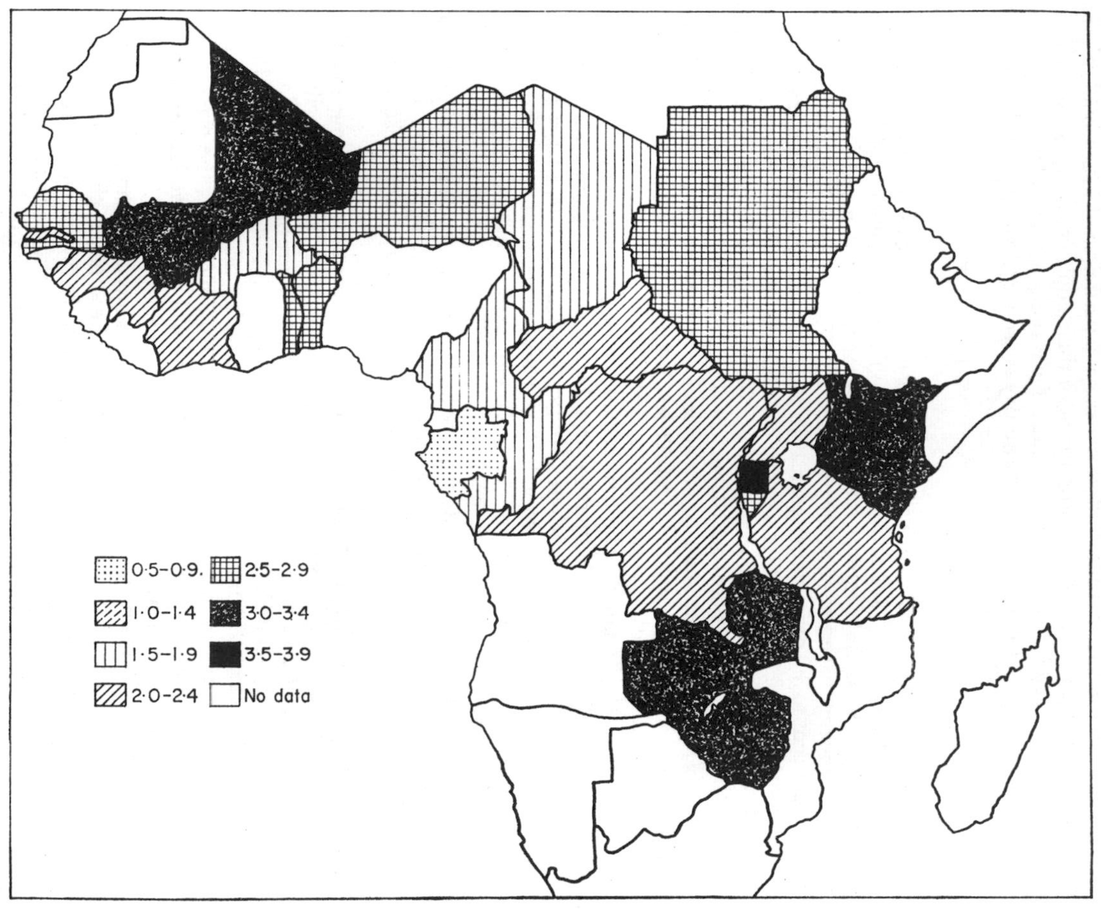

Map 2 Tropical Africa: percentage estimated rates of natural increase.

Source: R. K. Som, ch. 18; data as shown on Table 6.

be explained by the fact that most adult males have participated in seasonal migration, thus spending a considerable proportion of their adult years in the south with its better health facilities and generally more favourable environment, while their womenfolk remain in the north during the dry season and suffer from periods of recurrent hunger (Hilton, ch. 28).

Natural Increase

The deficiency in precise rates of natural increase puts African governments in an anomalous position. The 1970 census round should allow many countries to compute a reasonably accurate rate of intercensal growth, but it may be 1972 before many governments have the necessary detailed figures. Princeton's estimates range from 0·3 per cent to 3·0 per cent per year. Half the rates fall between 1·0 per cent and 2·7 per cent, and the modal rate is 1·9 per cent (Coale, ch. 17). ECA's rates are on the whole considerably higher and range from 0·6 per cent to 3·4 per cent. Half are found in the range 2·1 per cent to 3·1 per cent, and the modal rate is 2·5 per cent (Som, ch. 18). The natural increase of the major regions has been computed for 1956–60 by ECA as 2·3 per cent for West Africa, 2·4 per cent for East Africa and 2·2 per cent for Central Africa.

Two points might be noted. The first is that for most of the major countries of tropical Africa the rate of natural increase and the rate of population growth are not significantly different. In Ghana, where immigration has been on a large scale, the average annual rate of population growth might have exceeded natural increase by about 0·6 per cent between 1948 and 1960. In emigrant countries, such as Upper Volta, the opposite occurred though to a less extent. The second point, made by Ojo and others, is that the rate of population growth alone is not necessarily a socially or economically significant measure, unless the size of the base population and some estimate of the maximum population in terms of the existing economy are also kept in mind (ch. 32).

A far from simple but very pertinent question, is whether secular change in either mortality or fertility is under way, and, if so, whether this can be described as a 'demographic transition'. Stephens believes that population movements in Africa now are similar to those in Europe at the beginning of the Industrial Revolution.[21]

It is reasonably clear that mortality transition is taking place. Population growth figures suggest that mortality may well have been declining during the present century, with a marked steepening since the Second World War. Two factors indicate that mortality will fall further. One is the analogy with the dramatic drop in the death rates in recent years in many parts of Asia and Latin America because of the import and application of advanced medical technology. The other is that the mortality differentials described above also point in this direction. In the towns, where the cash economy is dominant, where social and economic change are greatest, and where there are more doctors and hospitals, death rates are indisputably lower. Not only is the proportion of urban population growing, but the kind of life now lived in the larger towns is perceptibly spreading not only to the smaller towns but also deep into what have been subsistence, rural fastnesses. In these areas not only are there improved medical facilities, but also a diminution in the prejudice against using them (Ojo, ch. 32).

It is equally clear that as yet no major fall in fertility has been experienced, but such movements may be afoot. Not to be overlooked is the potential for raising the birth rate that lies in the reduction of disease, especially venereal disease (Romaniuk, ch. 20, Yesufu, ch. 8). Also, there is some, but not conclusive evidence, that fertility might rise with a decline in polygamous and unstable marriages, a trend that apparently exists.

On the other hand, forces such as urban–rural fertility differentials, delayed female marriage and expansion of education may operate to lower the birth rate. Urban–rural fertility differentials do exist in some areas, perhaps most frequently associated with delayed female marriage; a spread and intensification of the way of life now experienced chiefly in the large towns may diffuse such patterns. Indeed the town population itself is increasing. Ohadike's work suggests that the expansion of education and a rise in living standards may tend to depress fertility (ch. 39). It might be noted that extended female education is hardly reconcilable with very early marriage.

But changes caused by such mechanisms are unlikely to be very great in the immediate future. Of more significance may be the pressures generated within the family and society by major mortality declines and consequent large increases in the numbers surviving from birth, and in the rate of population growth. The West never experienced the effect of a very sudden inflation in number of children surviving within the family. It is still a moot point whether pressures upon the family coupled with government action will act towards beginning a fertility transition. Experience elsewhere suggests that it might well (Kirk and Nortman, ch. 35), but, as yet, this is a matter for debate. Although it may be true that 'Throughout tropical Africa there is nothing that ranks as high as children in the estimation of the inhabitants' (Ojo, ch. 32), 'for the majority of persons, deeply-felt emotional factors in opposition to the idea of family planning are not at work, and, given sufficient education, the opening of sufficient [family planning] clinics and the ready availability of contraceptive devices, one might anticipate a significant expansion in use' (Daramola *et al.*, ch. 41). Similar findings have been reported from a study of the urban élite in Ghana.[22]

Certainly, rates of population growth in Africa now exceed those ever experienced in Europe during its demographic transition. ECA reports, 'The present rate of population growth in Africa is about twice as high as that in industrial Europe in the nineteenth century'. Coale comments, 'The recent experience of other developing areas suggests that tropical Africa is in the early phase of rapidly accelerating population growth. In some areas, for example Kenya and the Sudan, the rate of natural increase has apparently already reached about 3 per cent per year' (ch. 17).

Rapid population growth, and in particular high fertility levels, have their demographic as well as economic effects. The most notable is the distinctive age pattern. ECA has shown that in most tropical African countries more than two-fifths of the population is under fifteen years of age, a situation that 'involves a proportionately bigger investment in, and depreciation of, human capital'. It is possible that this may have been offset to some degree by the improvement in the health of the work force, which can thereby shoulder a somewhat larger burden (Ojo, ch. 32).

Aspects of the Population Pattern

The above is an outline of what is now known of the demographic forces operating within tropical Africa. What are the present and future implications of these forces for the people of the region?

PROJECTIONS

Surprisingly little work has been done on the projection of tropical African population, partly, admittedly, because of the lack of accurate estimates of fertility and mortality levels and patterns. The most significant recent attempt to assess present and likely future growth rates is that found in the United Nations' *Provisional Report on World Population Prospects as Assessed in 1963*[23] (and also under the heading of 'Demographic development strategy' in the article 'Recent Demographic Levels and Trends in Africa', *Economic Bulletin for Africa*[24]). Som points out that the former assessment estimated the 1960–63 rate of population growth in Africa at 2·5 per cent, lower than only that of Latin America, and indicates that in the years ahead Africa will probably outpace Latin America (Som, ch. 18). This potential for very rapid growth in Africa is a reflection of the fact that its fertility rates are on the whole the world's highest.

The assessment by the Economic Commission for Africa of the position up to 1980 is shown in the table below. The figures are for the whole continent. The fundamental assumption is that the pattern of mortality can be predicted reasonably accurately, but that fertility trends depend upon 'what is done about the birth rate', presumably largely by governments, in the sense of providing large-scale family planning facilities. The *neutral* projection for 1980 is a quarter larger again than the *highly effective* projection, the projection names referring to governmental intervention in the family planning field. However, even the latter implies an average population growth rate of 1·7 per cent during the 1960–80 period, almost double that found in the developed world.

Table 1

Africa: Population Growth according to Different Assumptions of Demographic Strategy, 1960–80[a]

Demographic strategy	Vital rate	Rate per 1,000 persons			Population		
		1960	1980	Average, 1960–80	1960[b] (millions)	1980[b] (millions)	1980 (index 1960=100)
Neutral	Birth rate	47	47	47			
	Death rate	23	15	19			
	Natural increase	24	32	28	257	447	174
Moderately effective	Birth rate	47	39	43			
	Death rate	23	15	19			
	Natural increase	24	24	24	257	414	161
Highly effective	Birth rate	47	25	36			
	Death rate	23	15	19			
	Natural increase	24	10	17	257	360	140

Source: (a) Unless shown otherwise, the material in the table is taken from UNITED NATIONS, ECONOMIC COMMISSION FOR AFRICA, 'Recent Demographic Levels and Trends in Africa', *Economic Bulletin for Africa*, Vol. V, January 1965, p. 78.
(b) UNITED NATIONS, *Demographic Yearbook, 1963,* New York, 1964, p. 142.

It might be noted first that the examples given by the United Nations of possible types of effective action are taken from outside tropical Africa, and second that almost a third of the 1960–80 period has already passed with little suggestion of decline in birth rates anywhere in the continent. In fact, the table suggests that moderately effective governmental intervention will be necessary merely to prevent a rise in the rates of natural increase. The 1960–80 average annual growth rates of 2·8 per cent, 2·4 per cent and 1·7 per cent for the *neutral, moderately effective* and *highly effective* projections can be compared, although not directly, with rates of 2·7 per cent, 2·5 per cent and 2·3 per cent given for the *high, medium* and *low* projections of the *Provisional Report on World Population Prospects.*

DENSITY

In the minds of most African administrators, a fundamental question is whether their countries are sparsely or densely settled, or, to use terminology still in constant political use even if largely out of favour with demographers, 'underpopulated' or 'over-populated'. In continental terms, Africa, with nine persons per square kilometre (23 per square mile), exhibits a settlement density comparable with that of the Americas but less than half that of the whole world, whose average is bolstered by the very great densities found in much of Asia and Europe (Som, ch. 18).

Total density figures, do not, of course, convey very much, because a good deal of land is permanently, or seasonally uninhabitable. Perhaps more important, a great deal of Africa is affected by a combination of insufficient or badly distributed rainfall and high low-latitude temperatures, so that effective moisture in the soil, namely that remaining after evaporation and other use, is deficient seasonally or for much of the year. Africa suffers, too, from a near absence of the great alluvial plains along riverine valleys, of the type that in Asia accommodate a large proportion of the population. Much of the soil is lateritic, with no counterpart to such cool temperate plains of fair to good soil quality as are found aoross northern Europe and in north-east China. Carrying capacities vary with technology and the quality of land; research demonstrates the optimum settlement density of one area of Zambia to be around eight persons per square mile (van de Walle, ch. 36).

The lessons of the developed world are not always as directly applicable as they might at first appear. For instance, parts of Mali, Niger and Chad are geographically similar to a stretch of northern Queensland in Australia, but while the population of the former area is poor, that of the latter area is comparatively well-off even in the developed world. If the Queensland area is to be considered, with an average of one person for several square miles, to be adequately populated for its type of cash economy, what relevance does its experience have to people already living at densities of up to five or even ten per square mile and practising subsistence food-cropping as well as stock raising?

However, perhaps the first step in mitigating the dangers of international comparisons of population density is to recognize that settlement densities are of two very different types, urban and rural, and that the level of urbanization varies markedly from one continent to another. This recognition has been accorded in Coale's map (Map 2, ch. 17) of population densities exclusive of the inhabitants of the larger towns. Som shows that settlement density in terms of arable land is probably about half the world average (Som, ch. 18), but, while such a man–land ratio is very much more realistic than that obtained by including all land, one must remember that even 'arable land' is a very heterogeneous commodity.

Is this underpopulation? Perhaps the question was not very relevant for the majority of the Conference delegates, as Commonwealth Africa does exhibit an overall population density equal to the world average (Caldwell, ch. 37). ECA states that, 'Except for a few regions (for example, most of the Nile River areas, some areas in the equatorial highlands, parts of West Africa and the islands in the Indian Ocean) there does not seem to be much pressure on land', but Som modifies this by adding 'as measured by the density of population in relation to the total land area' (Som, ch. 18). Many African governments with sparsely populated areas feel that population pressures can be relieved by redistribution of rural populations.[25] However, such redistribution is often expensive. Furthermore, it can be argued, as shown by van de Walle, that it is not absolute population size or density that adversely affects economic development, but the rate of population growth, an argument that is probably valid in rural, subsistence areas as well as in the urbanized, cash economy. (See Caldwell's Introduction to Part II, *The Population of Tropical Africa.*)

Nevertheless, population research workers in Africa are still, like the politicians, fascinated by the uneven pattern of settlement and the reasons for it. At the Ibadan Conference the subject was discussed by several delegates: Ominde (ch. 26), Clarke (ch. 27), Hilton (ch. 28), Agboola (ch. 29), Mortimore (ch. 30), Dema (ch. 31) and

Ojo (ch. 32). The most intensely farmed parts of Eastern Nigeria are more densely settled than the Low Countries (Dema, ch. 31), and two million people live in the Kano close-settled zone, a savannah area, at over 300 persons per square mile (Mortimore, ch. 30). In Kenya's Nyanza Province on the north-east corner of Lake Victoria, population density exceeds 500 persons per square mile in core areas and 1,000 persons in restricted districts (Ominde, ch. 26).

Even before colonization, areas of dense settlement existed beside sparsely settled areas, partly because of physical controls such as relief, rainfall, vegetation and the quality of the soil; of economic factors such as the mode of farming and the type of staple food grown (Clarke, ch. 27); and of social and political conditions, such as slavery, tribal warfare (Clarke, ch. 27), and government protection. In Nigeria, for example, strong government around Ilorin prevented the populace from being molested and their numbers increased considerably (Agboola, ch. 29).

More recently, colonial administration made it safer for migrants to travel outside their ethnic areas, and individual movement began from districts of low economic potential to those of greater promise (Prothero, ch. 25). Modern transportation, in the form of trains and lorries, gradually replaced human porterage and made communication and movement less difficult. As economic conditions altered and soils changed in relative value, migration began from areas of land deterioration and areas where a suitable cash crop has not yet been developed (Dema, ch. 31).

Now the pace of change is quickening in Africa, and perhaps the most obvious sign is the volume of migration. The migrants have been increasingly attracted to restricted areas, such as the mining fields and the large ports and other towns within the cash economy (Clarke, ch. 27). Sometimes the most densely populated area is also the most advanced economically, and, as in southern Ghana, grows in numbers disproportionately rapidly, both because it attracts immigrants and because lower levels of mortality result in higher rates of natural increase. Thus, migration movements have led more often to an increase rather than a decrease in the unevenness of the settlement pattern (Clarke, ch. 27). (See also the section on migration in the Introduction, pp. 20–22.)

FARMING

Tropical African land tenure systems and agricultural practices have been affected by social and economic change as well as by population pressures. The two fundamental aspects of traditional African farming have been the communal ownership of land, which was held by the whole tribe or smaller subsection and never became the sole property of a single family, and the system of shifting cultivation, which ensured adequate fallow for the poor, lateritic soils. Both have been distorted and are beginning to break under pressures exerted by the growth of rural population and the spread of the cash economy, with the accompanying, justifiable temptation to undertake cash-crop farming.

Cash-cropping, especially of such perennials as trees, exerts pressure toward freehold ownership of land, often in large quantities, and may eventually create a landless class (Ojo, ch. 32). Polly Hill, in her study of cocoa-farming in southern Ghana, has shown how indigenous farmers, bent on growing profitable cash crops, have been able to secure freehold land even where all land was tribally held and the tribal law on the matter was quite clear.[26] Ojo says of southern Nigeria, that the breakdown in traditional group farming methods is beginning now, as evinced by 'the ever-decreasing ability of obas and chiefs to organize free labour' (Ojo, ch. 32).

The decline of communal ownership, whatever may be the social effects, is not a bad thing agriculturally. Communal ownership may have reduced individual desire to increase the capitalization of the land (van de Walle, ch. 36). Neither freehold nor communal grants have always been established in the most efficient way, and as a result Africa suffers very greatly from the fragmentation of holdings (Dema, ch. 31). As population grows, it becomes incompatible with the fallow system, for, under the pressure of population, it is communal ownership and the consequent universal right of access to land that destroy the fallow. The basic problem is this increase in population pressure and the resultant shortening of the fallow period. Although much of tropical Africa appears to have surplus land, this is so only because of the vast amount of fallow needed to revitalize the soil after a comparatively short period of cultivation. As Hilton says of northern Ghana, 'This country takes decades to recover from exhaustion' (Hilton, ch. 28).

To date, living standards have been maintained in most tropical African rural areas because over a generation or two, the fallow land has been available for invasion and at the same time the introduction of new crops has raised productivity (van de Walle, ch. 36). But all over Africa the last great reserve of land, the tropical forest, is disappearing (Ojo, ch. 32). The maintenance of or even increase in living standards has not compensated for the increase in the use of soils. Communal ownership in the past has not bred the same intense love of one's land as has been the case in Asia, and land husbandry has suffered. The marginal productivity of the subsistence sector is very low (van de Walle, ch. 36), but, even in the sector where some cash income is earned, the rise in income has not usually been used to improve either the soil or the diets, for the money is used 'to satisfy other needs beside food, for example, clothing, building, education and medical care' (Dema, ch. 31).

Hilton describes in northern Ghana a cycle of soil use, exhaustion and, with luck, recovery (ch. 28). He points out that in North Mamprusi, and also apparently Frafra, shifting cultivation has given way to continuous cropping because of population pressure. He also cites examples of soil exhaustion being most extensive where population concentration has been greatest and of the disappearance of top-soil where farming has been most intensive. He describes the cycle in northern Ghana as the retreat of the farmers up the watersheds, erosion there, the breakdown of settlement into a patchy distribution, the disappearance of the population and the return of the bush.

Each area, and indeed each era, has its own variation of the settlement cycle. Generations ago, the slave trade led to depopulation in parts of West Africa, followed by an invasion of game, accompanied by tsetse. (Extraordinarily enough, modern forms of economic change have sometimes, it appears, had the same effect: 'After about 1907, pacification and increased commerce facilitated the spread of sleeping sickness away from the Volta.') However, by 1951 tsetse was being overcome, and in certain areas, 'control measures were followed by increased settlement' (Hilton, ch. 28).

What ensues has been described by the Food and Agricultural Organization as 'the already precarious ecological balance in some areas',[27] but this is not the whole story of agricultural change in contemporary tropical Africa. The arrival of cash-cropping has brought the possibility of great improvement in living conditions. Ojo emphasizes that every Nigerian farmer who wishes to improve his standard of living knows that he must find some cash crop he can successfully grow (ch. 32). Furthermore, where farms of large size can be formed or retained, the greater acreage can be related to higher dietary intakes by the farmer's family, better-than-average children's physique and a less-than-average tendency to emigrate (Dema, ch. 31).

Other improvements are possible. Around Kano the potential of certain soils can be reached when new crops more suited to them are introduced (Mortimore, ch. 30). Furthermore, much more first class agricultural labour is becoming available, partly because the reduction of disease has increased the number of healthy, active people (Ojo, ch. 32). But it arises also from the fact that economic advance has, rather inconspicuously and sometimes unwittingly, released rural labour in considerable quantities. It is not always appreciated how much work in African farming areas goes not into tilling the soil but into carrying water and wood. In some areas piped water or closer wells or bores and modern roads and lorries are now reducing these labour inputs.

Improvement in agriculture will bring anomalies. On the one hand, the use of fertilisers and other modern agricultural techniques means that less land will be needed per head of population. On the other hand, greater efficiency will reduce the proportion of the population needed in agriculture because, as argued by some, modern agricultural methods are at their most efficient when comparatively few people do the farming (Ojo, ch. 32).

According to Dema and many other Africans, the only ultimate solution, given tropical Africa's already substantial population, is industrialization in urban areas (Dema, ch. 31), a point of view accepted in the United Nations' survey, *Industrial Growth in Africa.*[28] Such industrialization would solve the problem of surplus labour by absorbing it, provided that population growth was not too rapid. More important, it would in the long run increase the supply of goods and services, thus providing a wealthier internal market for the farmers' produce as well as supplying them with many farming needs, such as machinery and fertilizers. Farms may ultimately be allowed to grow bigger, an important consideration in view of the suitability of tropical Africa for the production of tree crops that can probably be grown most profitably in holdings of vast size. Ojo believes that plantation agriculture in tropical Africa, whether carried out by population of foreign or of local origin, will inevitably lead to government intervention at least in questions of land tenure (ch. 32).

MIGRATION

The traditional answer to worsening farming conditions has been migration. In the past, and even nowadays, whole farming communities migrated. But today the migrant is more frequently an individual, usually a young male, who sets off, either temporarily or more permanently, for areas offering good economic prospects. Massive individual migration is not a recent phenomenon; migration from the Sudanic areas of West Africa south to the coast began long before 1931 (Hilton, ch. 28). It is not a simple case of sending and receiving areas. Northern Ghana in 1960 contained 41,000 residents who had come from the countries further north, while 116,000 persons originating there were to be found in the southern part of the country.

These movements indicate that a considerable amount of population redistribution is occurring (Mortimore, ch. 30). 'But it would be wrong to ascribe a close correlation between population density and migration, either in regions of departure or arrival' (Clarke, ch. 27). In fact, Clarke, in Sierra Leone, found that, as in Ghana, population concentration is occurring. However, Ominde's work in Kenya indicates a different pattern in that country, for 'interprovincial population movements are in the main from the more to the less developed parts of rural Kenya' (ch. 26). Ominde also shows that the immigrant provinces exhibit higher per capita incomes, citing especially the case of the White Highlands which attract immigrants both directly to the farms as labour and subsequently to the nearby towns that spring up in the area as a result of economic development.

The observation that 'Development is inseparable from large-scale movements from areas of less to areas of higher economic opportunity' (van de Walle, ch. 36) is probably especially true of Africa. But this does not mean that governmental schemes to achieve this end, especially in terms of the settlement of areas where the 'higher economic opportunity' would have to be created along with the settlement, would prove to be a wise investment. Apparently in Nigeria such schemes are regarded as too costly (Dema, ch. 31). In East Africa redistribution could be achieved effectively only with the lapse of sufficient time, but 'if the populations of these countries continue to grow at the rates they have been for the past decade there will not be time for these adjustments and redistributions' (Saxton, Serwadda, Saxton, ch. 42). It might be noted that individual migration from one's own community to another is much more a phenomenon of cultivators than of nomadic pastoralists.

Migration in Africa has been of various types (Prothero, ch. 25). Its nature is still undergoing change and it is becoming a more important element in African life. Van de Walle quotes Barber's[29] views that the division of labour between the sexes in Central Africa has allowed males to leave indigenous agriculture for extended periods without harm to productivity (van de Walle, ch. 36). Watson's[30] work supports this by showing that apparently up to 50 per cent of the males can be absent from the Mambwe village without any effect on total production (van de Walle, ch. 36). Such absence has often been periodic and has been facilitated by the seasonal nature of agriculture; in the dry season there may be little work to do and if few remain at home the available food will go further. Such movements reduce the size of the labour force in the emigrant areas but not necessarily the earning power of the population, for, the migrants' absence is often compensated for by the value of their remittances (Clarke, ch. 27). In recent times it has often been the seasonal migrants who have earned the cash that led to the purchase of bicycles, transistor radios, kerosene or sardines in the village.

Because of the sex differential in migration, sex ratios are widely used to measure the extent of immigration and emigration. Dema has demonstrated the cyclic effect of seasonal migration by showing that in a rural area of Eastern Nigeria the sex ratio climbed from 68 males per 100 females in April to 86 in August (ch. 31). Most of the seasonal migrants from this area go to other rural areas, with a different climatic régime to work as either tenant farmers or farm-labourers. Conversely, sex ratios are often high in immigrant centres. In some diamond-mining areas of Sierra Leone, Clarke reports over twice as many males as females (ch. 27). The extreme difference in the effect of migration upon the sex and age structure is illustrated in a comparison of two Sierra Leonean census districts: in the immigrant district, the proportion of males aged 15–54 to total population was 50 per cent; in the emigrant district it was only 18 per cent.

But this pattern is changing. In southern Ghana sex ratios are now really high only among migrant groups who have come long distances from the less socially and economically changed savannah lands. Clarke found evidence in the long-established iron-ore mine at Marampa that the sex balance can be restored even in mining centres (ch. 27). In Lagos, despite the fact that the city has recently been attracting migrants from greater distances than was previously the case, sex ratios among the immigrant groups have been consistently falling (Ejiogu, ch. 33). Family life is now the established migrant pattern in the city, even though migration, as shown by the fact that almost half the rural–urban immigrants in Lagos live in nuclear families, tends to break up the close residence of members of the extended family (Ejiogu, ch. 33).

Several points might be noted about the mechanics of the rural–urban and rural–rural migrant streams. In spite of the high sex ratios quoted, substantial numbers of females have been found in some migrant streams for a considerable period. In southern Ghana, women have participated in both short and long term movements to cocoa-growing areas since before the turn of the century. Both distance and social change affect the sex differential in the stream: the longer the journey or the more traditional the society, the higher in general are the migrant sex ratios. But the ethnic differences that have always prevailed in the attitude toward female migration are still factors in the sex composition of the migrant stream. Increasingly, the male preponderance in receiving areas can be explained largely in terms of the presence of seasonal or of more permanent male migrants who have preceded their families in order to find work and accommodation. It is widely accepted that long-term migrants will send for their families or their intended wives as soon as possible or return to their area of origin to secure a wife. Clarke tested the theory that regardless of the feeding of developing areas by mobile population, the existing pattern of population distribution reflects physical and historical influences: a coefficient of correlation of only 0 502 (ch. 27) between sex ratios and population densities in Sierra Leone confirms this hypothesis. But this correlation is well below that found in Ghana by Hunter.[31]

URBANIZATION

Although rural–rural migration is still the predominant form of migration in tropical Africa, as measured by the numbers involved, the most significant aspect of the migration pattern, in terms of implications for the future, is the movement into the new, fast-growing towns. Before this century, although village life was the normal condition for nearly all tropical Africans, some towns did exist. Some were set up by foreign traders and slavers, such as the Arab settlement of Zanzibar off the East African coast and the small settlements, often around forts, in West Africa. In Ghana there were settlements associated with defence and trade, refugee and 'spy' towns, and traditional capitals (Addo). One of the latter, Kumasi, had in the nineteenth century a population that made it a major centre even by mid-20th-century standards. In some areas, such as Ibadan in Western Nigeria, the predilection of the farming population for aggregating their dwellings produced large towns at an early date. It is possible that, in terms of their stage of economic development, the Yoruba of Western Nigeria are among the most urbanized people in the world (Prothero, ch. 25).

But, for much of tropical Africa, towns began to develop only with the arrival of territorial administrations and the penetration of commerce. In the rural hinterland small administrative centres have assumed trading functions and have developed into true towns (Clarke, ch. 27, Hilton, ch. 28, Mortimore, ch. 30). The interrelated penetration of commerce and communications has been particularly important. Ports came first, and in West Africa especially they have continued to be the dominant form of urbanization. The spread of railways, followed by roads and lorries and the consequent substitution of mechanical for human forms of transport were also vital. Although the first lorry used as far inland in Ghana as Bawku arrived in 1926, the real revolution dates only from the mid-1930s. By 1936 lorries were regularly calling at the Navrongo market, 400 miles inland, to trade in salt, fish, cattle and kola-nuts. Tamale, only 300 miles from the coast, was the first great northern lorry terminal, but by 1937 Bolgatanga and Bawku in the far north were taking a lot of its trade, and subsequently the Bawku market was to see lorries regularly from Niamey and even Gao, far to the north on the Saharan fringe.

Market towns have grown to supply local needs. Purchases are often made with cash remittances from distant areas, but the great impetus in many parts of tropical Africa has come with the spread of commercial agriculture, which provides the local population with more spending money and creates the need for facilities to remove the produce (Clarke, ch. 27). Small centres may with increasing urbanization become towns: 'In places like Bongo and Tongo a mission house, local authority office or market gives some appearance of a nucleus' (Hilton, ch. 28). In some areas the growth of towns and of a cash economy has arisen from mining activities. Since Independence, urban growth in national and regional capitals has been accelerated by an increase in administrative positions and diplomatic functions, the setting up of institutions such as universities and sometimes the encouragement of industry and commerce.

However, Africa is still the least urbanized continent, and tropical Africa is probably the least urbanized major region in the world. Only 9 per cent of Africa's people

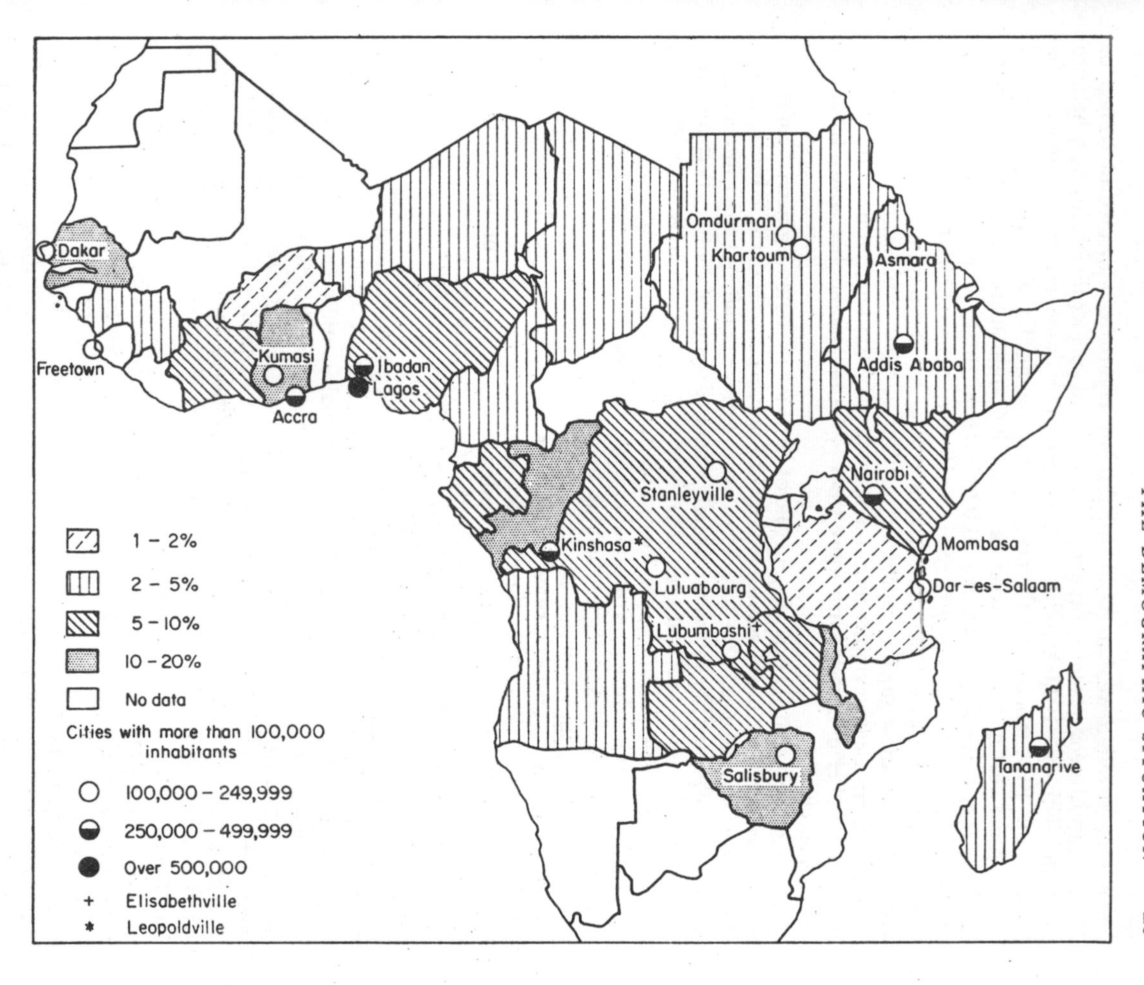

Map 3. Tropical Africa: percentage urban population and cities with more than 100,000 inhabitants.

live in centres with more than 20,000 inhabitants, compared with a world average of 21 per cent. Moreover, more of the 9 per cent live in smaller towns, for only half are in centres with over 100,000 inhabitants compared with five-eighths in the world as a whole. But ECA reports that the position is changing: Of 'the current increase of 7 million per year in Africa, at least one and a half million are being added to these big cities [i.e. those with more than 100,000 inhabitants].' This quickening in the urbanization process is almost universal. By 1960, one quarter of Ghana's population was in towns with over 5,000 inhabitants which developed rapidly between 1948 and 1960 when these towns absorbed two-fifths of the country's total population increase. Sierra Leone exhibits half this level of urbanization, but even there since 1927 the number of centres with more than 5,000 inhabitants has grown from 2 to 18 (Clarke, ch. 27).

Although, according to experts, the rôle of large towns in non-industrial countries may be suspect, these towns serve a variety of functions. Some of these functions are of economic significance in the long term even if they are difficult to fit into an economic balance sheet. The towns are usually major educational centres. Perhaps even more important is the fact that they are essential acculturation areas for social attitudes and economic skills of a type that must be acquired if economic development is to proceed rapidly. In terms of social change, they are the cutting edges of their countries to a more marked degree than has been the case in most Western countries. Mortimer analyses their function also in terms of their former defence rôle, when the town constituted the strong, protective nucleus and, if need be, a place for shelter. He also shows that the core of the relation of the modern town of Kano to its surrounding area is the exchange of firewood, household refuse, and sheep and goat manure (with the latter providing 'a significant proportion of the large fertilizer input required by the intensively cultivated soils'), for agricultural produce and the cloth woven in the rural households (Mortimore, ch. 30).

Town life is different from rural life in many ways other than occupation and residence. (Some of these differences are discussed in Part II where family and attitudinal change is treated.) Town life exists almost wholly within the cash economy: the rent of rooms averages over £3 per month in Lagos, a fact that compels considerable crowding (Ohadike, ch. 39). Sex differentials are reduced, at least as far as they are measured by attendance at schools (Ejiogu, ch. 33). Worldly success is attained and measured by very different criteria than in traditional society: in Lagos, 'There exists a marked relationship between socio-economic status, living conditions and educational attainment' (Ohadike, ch. 39).

Much of this urban growth has been possible only because of migration from the farming areas. Such migration is selective: Ejiogu showed for Nigeria what has also been established for Ghana,[32] that educated villagers are the most likely to migrate (ch. 33). Nevertheless, migrants' children are more likely to be put to work instead of enrolled in school on arrival in Lagos than children of the town-born. Migrants' wives often have real difficulty securing employment. Many migrants are young when they first reach town; some who come alone fall in the 10–14 age range. Most female migrants are married or 'potentially married' (Ejiogu, ch. 33), and many join menfolk already in the town.

However, migration is not a one-way process, and the volume of movement between countryside and town is very much greater than would explain urban growth if merely a single shift were involved. Ejiogu's study shows the large scale of the return movement to the villages and the fact that a very big fraction of returnees are those who have not lived in the town for very long. Most migrants intend to return to their rural origins in old age, and in fact older women often do so while their husbands are still living in the town, and are very likely to do so if they are widowed or separated (Ejiogu, ch. 33).

Part of the explanation for the quick return of some migrants to the village lies in the difficulty of securing employment in the city. In its rate of expansion the urban labour market in many countries is tending to lag behind the demands of rural–urban migrants. Unemployed Nigerian youths are sometimes sustained in town by remittances from their relatives' farms (Dema, ch. 31). The time may come when even educated young migrants may be forced back to the villages in considerable numbers (Ojo, ch. 32). 'Unemployment is now a feature of African cities. This is due in part to the slackening of foreign investment in recent years. New industries incorporate all the labour-saving devices of Western technology' (van de Walle, ch. 36).

Nevertheless, urban incomes are still on average well above rural incomes. For many Africans the town is the only place they know to earn cash. Nor do they spend all this cash in the towns; much flows, in the form of remittances or as goods taken back by the migrants, to distant villages. The cash that reaches the rural areas often establishes a demand for retail outlets there. This flow of cash, goods and migrants returning from the town to the villages is a vehicle of social and economic change. The mobility of Africans makes it most unlikely that modernized enclaves will develop within the continent except where these are associated with populations of foreign origin.

This discussion has not attempted to separate internal and international migration. The small area of many of the states today, coupled with the tradition of crossing frontiers in the past, has meant that for Africans at least the distinction has not been of great importance. This is passing because the new national states face both foreign exchange difficulties, which often dictate the control of remittances, and the demand by the internal electorate for protection against competition for employment (Caldwell, ch. 37). There have been increasing barriers to international movement, not all well publicized, and the process will probably continue. European and Asian immigration has been important, especially in East Africa, but, apart from Boute's work on the demography of the Indian population (ch. 24), the lack of current research in this field is evidence of a widespread conviction that the important population trends in the foreseeable future are likely to be those involving Africans.

Summary: Answering the Questions

1. *How many people are there?* The research reports presented at the Ibadan Conference show that the major outlines of demographic change in tropical Africa can now be distinguished, even if there is a certain blurring around the edges. With exceptions, such as Nigeria and Ethiopia, there is for most countries an estimate, probably of fair accuracy, of total population size.

2. *What is happening to the population?* Fertility is very high, and except among the Indo-Pakistani population of East Africa, and possibly in some of the towns, there is no evidence that it is falling or is about to fall. In most countries birth rates are over 45 per 1,000 and in many over 50 per 1,000, among the highest ever recorded in any part of the world. Those countries that appear to have birth rates below this level, may be suffering from either deficient statistics or high rates of venereal or other diseases, possibly abetted by a greater degree of instability of conjugal relations. In the long run, fertility change will depend on whether birth rates fall in the direction indicated by some of the fertility differentials examined. Social and economic change and more particularly governmental intervention in the family planning field aided perhaps by such fertility change will be the main determinants. Mortality has been high, although almost certainly below the level of fertility since at least the turn of the century. Tropical Africa has been slow to participate in the fall in death rates following the Second World War experienced in much of the developing world. But it is believed that such a decline is now occurring, and it may turn out to be quite steep. Probably most countries in tropical Africa now exhibit death rates below 35

per 1,000, and quite possibly the majority are below 30 per 1,000. Almost all governments and electorates are determined that the decline should continue.

The resulting rates of natural increase are already high and clearly could rise much higher. The majority, although there is some dispute here, are probably now above 2 per cent per annum and the highest are well over 3 per cent per annum.

The answer to the question posed at the beginning of this chapter about what is happening is, then, that population growth is now rapid throughout most, and perhaps nearly all, of tropical Africa, and that it is accelerating.

3. *How many people can be absorbed?* This has given rise to a debate that has not yet been resolved but there are many who hold that the appearance of easy absorption of population during the present century may be spurious. Much of the land is very poor, and, with the existing farming technology, the carrying capacity in some areas may already be exceeded by the population. The extra population has been accommodated by decreasing the fallow period to an extent that endangers long-term carrying capacity, because of failure to prevent erosion and to give sufficient time for full soil regeneration. New technology may overcome these difficulties, but its implementation depends upon increased wealth. Such discussion may miss the essential point: high rates of population growth, even in rural areas free from oppressive population pressures, reduce the rate of rise in individual living standards.

4. *How is population being redistributed?* Tropical Africans continue to be mobile and are probably becoming more so. The chief focus of the migration movement is shifting from mining, plantation and other cash-crop areas to the towns, which are growing very rapidly. Urban population is still relatively small, and the urban labour market is having some difficulty in expanding. Nevertheless, in the whole continent over a fifth of the population increase is flowing into the cities, and in at least one tropical African country, Ghana, almost half the increase has been added to towns of some size.

Footnotes

1. This survey is based primarily upon the papers presented to the First African Population Conference, University of Ibadan, Nigeria, 3–7 January 1966, and on the discussion arising from them at the Conference. Some reference is made to oral statements, discussion leaders' remarks or special reports which could not be included in this book although they are parts of the Proceedings of the First African Population Conference. These are available at the Centre for Population Studies, University of Ibadan.
2. A. M. CARR-SAUNDERS, *World Population: Past Growth and Present Trends*, Oxford, 1936, pp. 34–35.
3. WALTER F. WILLCOX, 'Increase in the Population of the Earth and of the Continents since 1650', in Walter F. Willcox (ed.) *International Migrations*, Vol. II, *Interpretations*, New York, 1931, p. 78.
4. CARR-SAUNDERS, *op. cit.*, p. 42.
5. *Ibid.* Willcox also produced an estimate for 1929, no higher than his 1900 estimate, and only a little below Carr-Saunders' figure for 1929. I have quoted only Carr-Saunders for the present century as he approximates closely to the subsequent United Nations series of estimates referred to here.
6. UNITED NATIONS, POPULATION DIVISION, DEPARTMENT OF SOCIAL AFFAIRS, *The Determinants and Consequences of Population Trends: A Summary of the Findings of Studies on the Relationship between Population Changes and Social Conditions*, New York, 1953, p. 11.
7. UNITED NATIONS, *Demographic Yearbook, 1963*, New York, 1964, p. 142.
8. FRANK LORIMER, WILLIAM BRASS and ETIENNE VAN DE WALLE, 'Demography', in ROBERT A. LYSTAD (ed.), *The African World: A Survey of Social Research*, London, 1965, p. 271.
9. R. R. KUCZYNSKI, *Demographic Survey of the British Colonial Empire*, Vol. 1, *West Africa*, Oxford, 1948, p. 1.
10. LORIMER, BRASS and VAN DE WALLE, *op. cit.*, p. 274.
11. According to the projections of the Federal Ministry of Health, Lagos, which were apparently the basis of estimates in the United Nations *Demographic Yearbooks* up to the 1963 issue.
12. LORIMER, BRASS and VAN DE WALLE, *op. cit.*, p. 277.
13. UNITED NATIONS, DEPARTMENT OF ECONOMIC AND SOCIAL AFFAIRS, *Manuals on Methods of Estimating Population, Manual III: Methods for Population Projections by Sex and Age*, New York, 1956.
14. ANSLEY J. COALE and PAUL DEMENY, *Regional Model Life Tables and Stable Populations*, Princeton University Press, Princeton, 1966.

15. The rates, quoted in ECA, 'Recent Demographic Levels and Trends in Africa', a paper read at the conference, are from INSEE, *Perspective de Population dans les pays Africains et Malàgache d'expression française, 1963*, and from national publications. The fertility distribution for the 15–19, 20–24, 25–29, 30–34, 35–39, 40–44 and 45–49 years of age groups is 17·1, 24·0, 21·6, 17·1, 12·3, 5·5 and 2·4 per cent respectively.
16. A. J. COALE and C. Y. TYE, 'The Significance of Age-patterns of Fertility in High Fertility Populations', *Milbank Memorial Fund Quarterly*, Vol. 39, October 1961.
17. J. C. CALDWELL, 'Fertility Decline and Female Chances of Marriage in Malaya', *Population Studies*, Vol. XII, No. 1, July 1963.
18. KUCZYNSKI, *op. cit.*, pp. 17–18.
19. See RICHARD W. STEPHENS, *Population Pressures in Africa South of the Sahara*, Washington, 1958, pp. 8–9.
20. FAO *Africa Survey*, Rome, 1962, p. 15.
21. STEPHENS, *op. cit.*, p. 41.
22. J. C. CALDWELL, 'Family Formation and Limitation in Ghana: A Study of the Residents of Economically Superior Urban Areas', paper delivered to the International Conference on Family Planning Programmes, Geneva, August, 1965, Population Growth and Family Change in Africa: The New Urban Elite in Ghana, Canberra, 1967.
23. UNITED NATIONS, *Provisional Report on World Population Prospects as Assessed in 1963*, New York 1964 (ST/SCA/SER.R/7).
24. UNITED NATIONS, ECONOMIC COMMISSION FOR AFRICA, 'Recent Demographic Levels and Trends in Africa', *Economic Bulletin for Africa*, Vol. V, January 1965, p. 78.
25. ECONOMIC COMMISSION FOR AFRICA, *Report on the Seminar on Population Problems in Africa* (E/CN. 14/186).
26. POLLY HILL, *Migrant Cocoa-farmers of Southern Ghana*, Cambridge, 1963.
27. *FAO Africa Survey*, *op. cit.*, p. 17.
28. UNITED NATIONS, ECONOMIC COMMISSION FOR AFRICA, *Industrial Growth in Africa*, New York, 1963.
29. W. BARBER, *The Economy of British Central Africa*, OUP, 1961.
30. W. WATSON, *Tribal Cohesion in a Money Economy*, Manchester, 1958.
31. J. M. HUNTER, 'Regional Patterns of Population Growth in Ghana, 1948–1960', in J. B. WHITTON and P. D. WOOD (eds.), *Essays in Geography for Austin Miller*, Reading, 1965.
32. J. C. CALDWELL, 'Migration', in WALTER BRIMINGHAM, I. NEUSTADT and E. N. OMABOE (eds.), *A Study of Contemporary Ghana*, Vol. II, *Some Aspects of the Social Structure of Ghana*, London, 1966.

1 The availability of demographic data by regions in tropical Africa

Etienne van de Walle
Princeton University, U.S.A.

The terms used in the title should be defined, so that its restricted perspective might be kept in mind. Data are said to be available when they have been published at least partially, even when their diffusion has been very limited. Demographic data considered here are only those concerning population movements, and specifically those types which are collected in statistically developed countries through vital registration used in conjunction with national censuses. Of course, the analysis of these data requires information on the numbers and structure of the population (for instance distribution by age and sex), and we shall discuss their availability as well. Because of circumstances specific to tropical Africa, vital registration does not yet play a large rôle in the gathering of data on fertility, mortality and migration. These will probably, for some time to come, continue to be collected mainly by means of retrospective questions included in self-contained, census-type surveys. This explains why, in the perspective adopted here, the knowledge of the absolute number of people in a country and of their exact geographical distribution is not accorded the highest priority, and why we are more interested in demographic inquiries on a sample basis than in full censuses. Indeed the former usually include more questions and yield more accurate information on such subjects as age distribution, fertility, mortality and migration. Finally we cannot deal adequately here with anthropological studies of these subjects (by case histories, etc.), although some of the most effective studies to date of migration in tropical Africa have been of that type.

The following regions of tropical Africa are considered:

1. *West Africa*: Mauritania, Senegal, Gambia, Mali, Niger, Portuguese Guinea, Guinea, Sierra Leone, Liberia, Ivory Coast, Upper Volta, Ghana, Togo, Dahomey and Nigeria.
2. *Central Africa*: Chad, Cameroun, Central Africa Republic, Spanish Guinea, Gabon, the Congos and Angola.
3. *East Africa*: Ethiopia, Somalia, French Somaliland, Kenya, Uganda, Tanzania, Rwanda, Burundi, Mozambique, Malawi, Zambia and Rhodesia.

This classification excludes North Africa (i.e. the countries bordering on the Mediterranean plus the Sudan and Spanish Sahara) as well as Southern Africa (i.e. the Republic of South Africa, South-West Africa, the High-Commission Territories, and Madagascar). Smaller islands far from the mainland (Mauritius, Fernando Po, etc.) are also excluded because their conditions are very different from those of the rest of tropical Africa.

Availability of Vital Registration

Besides fairly complete vital registration in some towns such as Lagos, there are a number of pilot projects aiming at giving accurate records of births and deaths in selected areas of certain countries. Perhaps the most ambitious of the kind is in Ghana where compulsory registration areas (in certain towns) cover about 12 per cent of the population. Such projects usually address themselves to a part of the population which is not representative of the country as a whole, and there is often little knowledge of the base population to which vital events are to be referred. Furthermore, many countries have had some fragmentary vital registration, sometimes for long periods in the past. This is for instance the case for Uganda, where registration of births and deaths goes as far back as 1904. In 1949, Kuczynski's evaluation was that 'the records are fairly complete in a number of *sazas* but quite inadequate in others.'[1] Possibly the coverage has since deteriorated. In the Congo (Kinshasa, formerly Leopoldville) at the time of the 1955–57 demographic inquiry, about 80 per cent of the births were registered. It may be said that the main value to demographers of vital registration, as it exists now, is not in enabling them to compute vital rates, but in helping interviewers to record accurate ages.

Censuses and Demographic Sample Inquiries

Ideally, the following items should be included in the collection of data aiming at assessing the vital trends from a census or a demographic inquiry:

1. a detailed age distribution by age and sex;
2. information on current (i.e. occurred during the 12 months preceding the survey) births by age of the mother;
3. information on current mortality by age and sex, and
4. information concerning the total number of children ever born and surviving to all women, by their present age.

One should add data on migration, but this topic is treated separately at the end of this paper.

We have classified the populations of tropical Africa in five categories. Each category refers to the relative completeness of the information which was collected on that population by censuses and sample inquiries available to date. Table 1 gives the results by regions.

CATEGORY A live in countries covered by surveys which include all the items enumerated above. They cover about 27 per cent of the population of tropical Africa. The whole array of information has been gathered in the demographic inquiries taken in ex-French territories by the Institut National de la Statistique et des Etudes Economiques.[2] For instance, the sets of questions asked in the 1961 Dahomey inquiry are typical.[3] Ages were gathered by single years, but published only by five-year groups.

There are three sets of questions relating to fertility by sex:

(a) to the heads of household: births in the compound[4] during the preceding 12 months;
(b) to women aged over 15 years:
  (i) their births during the last 12 months;
  (ii) the children ever born to them.

There are six sets of questions relative to mortality:

(a) to the heads of household:
  (i) deaths in the compound by age and sex during the last 12 months;
  (ii) children surviving or dead among those born during that period;
  (iii) (if no deaths during preceding 12 months) last death in the compound by age and sex.
(b) to women over 15 years of age, concerning their offspring (by sex):
  (i) total numbers surviving or dead;
  (ii) deaths during the preceding 12 months;
  (iii) dead or surviving children among those born during the preceding 12 months.

Very extensive and detailed questions of this kind clearly cannot be included in full censuses. However, similar sets have been asked in the 1955–57 Congo sample inquiry[5] and in the 1960 Ghana post-enumeration survey. The results of the latter are yet to be published. The Buganda Province (Uganda) supplementary census of 1959 included detailed questions on age.

CATEGORY B live in countries covered by surveys which include detailed investigation of fertility and mortality, but only incomplete information on age. They cover 21 per cent of the population of tropical Africa, but are typical of East Africa only. In Uganda, for instance, the supplementary sample census of 1959 (taken after a full census), included the following questions[6]: Births to adult women during the preceding 12 months; deaths in the household during the same period (without mention of age); children ever born and surviving to adult women, and finally, among the dead children, a distinction between those who were younger or older than one year at death. The value of this information would be considerably enhanced if it could be used in conjunction with information on age, but age is given only in the following classes: under age one, one to five years, six to 15 years, 16 to 45 years, over 45 years.[7] The reasons for the adoption of those age groups, instead of the more conventional ones ending with the digit 4 (5 to 14, 15 to 44) is not clear, but it has been a tradition in East Africa at least since the 1948 round of censuses. During the 1950s in the (then) Rhodesias and Ruanda-Urundi, age was given in physiological terms, such as 'women between puberty and menopause'.

CATEGORY C live in countries covered by surveys including detailed age distributions but only partial information about fertility and mortality. They cover seven per cent of the population of tropical Africa. All information has been gathered by full censuses taken in Portuguese Africa. These include a question to all women concerning the number of children ever born and surviving. The quality of the information is poor. The main interest of these data is that they constitute the longest series of full censuses held at regular intervals (1940, 1950 and 1960) in tropical Africa. The rates of intercensal increase which can be computed appear to be reliable.

CATEGORY D live in countries without fertility and mortality information (27 per cent of tropical Africa). To this category belong, for instance, the 1952–53 Nigerian full census (age by broad age classes) or the 1962 Liberian census (age by single years). Such censuses can yield practically no information on vital trends. Nevertheless, some brave efforts have been made to obtain fertility indices from such data.[8]

CATEGORY E live in countries where no systematic survey has ever been taken and form about 19 per cent of the population of tropical Africa. The largest *terra incognita* is Ethiopia.

It should be noted that the population estimates underlying Table 1 are subject to strong reservations, and that the table purports to give orders of magnitude only.

The following conclusions emerge from this classification in categories:

(a) There appears to exist serious demographic information from systematic census-type surveys, for almost half of the population of tropical Africa (Categories A and B).

(b) This information is the result entirely of sample surveys. At present, to get trustworthy results, questions relating to fertility and mortality must be so detailed, and include so many cross-checks, that their inclusion in a full census is impossible. Sampling thus is a way to solve 'the problems of how to collect

Table 1

Proportion of the population of tropical Africa by regions in categories for which the specified type* of demographic information is available (percentages)

Region	Category A	Category B	Category C	Category D	Category E
West Africa	32	—	1	63	5
Central Africa	71	—	17	1	11
East Africa	3	51	10	—	36
Tropical Africa	27	21	7	27	18

* Category A: Detailed information on age, fertility and mortality.
Category B: Incomplete information on age, detailed information on fertility and mortality.
Category C: Detailed information on age, incomplete information on fertility and mortality.
Category D: No direct information on fertility and mortality.
Category E: No information from systematic surveys.

demographic statistics efficiently, that is, how to attain high accuracy at a minimum cost'.[9]

(c) The authors from which the preceding quotation is borrowed, state the following about detailed reporting of ages: 'The greater the details of presentation the stronger the checks. In particular it is essential that ages be recorded in reasonable detail, whatever the errors and biases involved. . . . The detailed classification is required for any serious demographic studies.'[10] Thus the most interesting and thorough kind of analysis is possible only with data from Category A, that is, for about one-fourth of the population of tropical Africa. No such inquiry has yet been conducted in East Africa (except in Buganda).[11]

The insistence upon age recording must be explained in terms of the unsatisfactory quality of all the collected age distributions. Many inquiries have been organized on the underlying assumption that one could do no better than classify the population in very broad age classes. It might easily be asserted that more detailed age distribution can be obtained by graduation and that they may be less biased than those obtained by direct reporting, thus being sufficient for most purposes (school planning, estimates of the labour force, etc.). However, this is not true for demographic purposes (in the special sense which we accepted earlier). The main ground for requiring detailed age distributions, however biased they may be, is their use in conjunction with fertility and mortality data. Persons reported in an age group will be older on the whole than those in the preceding one, even if the scale is defective; this alone is invaluable in the study of an age-specific process, such as fertility or mortality. In the latter instance, age biases may affect in a similar way the reporting of living and dead, thus cancelling some part of the error when rates are computed. The comparison of current births and parity by age is a valuable tool for the study of fertility.

Publication of Demographic Data

In comparison with the demographic information on tropical Africa available only ten years ago, amazing progress has taken place. 'The fact is that, for the first time, sets of demographic data for some African countries are now emerging above the threshold of completeness and specificity required for critical evaluation and analysis.'[12]

Thus the collected data cover large parts of Africa, and are often very detailed. The wording of the questions and the techniques of fieldwork have often reached an advanced stage. For the time being, it seems that the most headway can be made, not by adding new information to that already collected, but by publishing extensively and evaluating critically that which has already been collected. Only through this long and unspectacular procedure will the data become available in the full sense. However remarkable the analysis made by various statistical offices—as for instance the Government Statisticians in Tanzania, Uganda and Kenya—there is also a great need of unadjusted data, so that one may evaluate the estimates and their possible bias. In that connection, the publication of obviously biased data is as essential as that of credible ones. Even trivial-looking tabulations may throw some light on the nature of the biases affecting the data. For instance, the sex ratio of children ever born increases significantly with the age of the reporting mothers in the Mozambique censuses and in the Niger Inquiry and this perhaps affords some insight into the type of differential omissions which occur. The same *Niger Inquiry Report* fails to publish the collected current mortality information (covering the preceding 12 months) because 'it appears clearly that deaths have been under-estimated'.[13] It is understandable that administrative reports hesitate to diffuse obviously false information, but the latter may be an indicator of not so obvious biases in plausible data. The INSEE publications have been fairly detailed, but nevertheless have published only a fraction of the collected information. For instance, the Dahomey report[3] published the answers to only two of the six questions on mortality which the schedule included. Again publication of data from the Congo sample inquiry has been interrupted from 1961.

It takes about one year to bring out the preliminary results of a survey in Category A, based on hand tabulations. Final publication has usually taken four to five years. Since the first such inquiry was taken in Guinea in 1954–55,[14] hardly enough time has elapsed to take stock and evaluate. The opportunities that Category A inquiries offer for cross-checking and analysis have not yet been exploited to the full. INSEE has a promising evaluation programme under way which should yield conclusions well before the 1970 round of censuses and inquiries.[15] Meanwhile some results which may very well be deceptive, such as age distributions and population growth rates, have already been used for planning purposes.

Surveys in Category B have been published fairly rapidly, since cross-tabulations here must be much less detailed. Usually they have not warranted separate publication, but have been diffused as articles, chapters in annual reports, or mimeographed sheets. In East Africa they have been published together with the census results. Critical evaluation of results has often been scanty.

Need for Further Research

This study of the availability of data would not be complete without an indication of the areas where further research is mostly needed. Although we are on the verge of getting a satisfactory picture of fertility and mortality by regions, we have hardly started to explore the possible causes of the differentials. In the case of fertility for instance, ways should be investigated for relating fertility to marital status, kinship systems, type of habitat, etc. Census-type inquiries are not particularly well suited for this type of research.

Thus there is a need for special studies supplementing the inquiries, and serving at the same time as a check of the demographic inquiries' accuracy and effectiveness. One example is the continuous observation of small areas. One such project at least (in Senegal) has reached an advanced stage.[16]

The study of migration has been somewhat neglected in demographic inquiries. Most Category A inquiries have included a question on place of birth, and the data have often been tabulated in terms of the place of residence. (Such tabulations have been done also for full censuses, for instance in Mozambique in 1950 and Ghana in

1960.[17]) The Dahomey report contains for instance the following type of information: Of a total of nearly 16,000 male residents aged 15 to 29 years who were absent from home (or 8 per cent of the age-group), some 27 per cent had left for the local *sous-préfecture*, 9 per cent for Cotonou, the national capital, 27 per cent for Ghana and 16 per cent for other foreign countries.[18] Other INSEE inquiries also contain detailed tabulations of this kind. The Upper Volta inquiry of 1960–61 included a special questionnaire on previous migrations (results not yet published). The methods of research appropriate to conditions in Africa must be investigated further.

Footnotes

1. R. R. KUCZYNSKI, *Demographic Survey of the British Colonial Empire*, Vol. II, Oxford, 1949, p. 272.
2. INSEE—Institut National de la Statistique et des Etudes Economiques (France). These inquiries were taken in collaboration with national statistical offices.
3. RÉPUBLIQUE DU DAHOMEY and INSEE, SERVICE DE COOPÉRATION, *Enquête démographique au Dahomey 1961*, Paris, 1964.
4. Compound: a free translation of the French *concession*.
5. The great interest of the Congo inquiry lies in its extensive use of vital registration as a cross-check. See RÉPUBLIQUE DU CONGO, BUREAU DE LA DÉMOGRAPHIE, *Tableau général de la démographie Congolaise*, Léopoldville, 1961.
6. UGANDA, STATISTICAL BRANCH, MINISTRY OF ECONOMIC AFFAIRS, *Uganda Census, 1959, African Population*, Entebbe, 1960.
7. Except in Buganda, where age was recorded in five-year groups.
8. Notably by UN demographers; see the fertility estimates for Nigeria in the *Demographic Yearbook 1963*. The present writer has indulged in a similar attempt, 'An Approach to the Study of Fertility in Nigeria', *Population Studies*, July 1965.
9. F. LORIMER, W. BRASS and E. VAN DE WALLE: 'Demography' in ROBERT A. LYSTAD (ed.), *The African World—A Survey of Social Research*, Pall Mall, London, 1965, p. 275.
10. *Op. cit.*, p. 282.
11. Results of the Kenya Census became available after this was written.
12. LORIMER, BRASS and VAN DE WALLE, *op. cit.*, p. 275.
13. RÉPUBLIQUE DU NIGER AND INSEE, SERVICE DE COOPÉRATION: *1960, Etude Démographique du Niger*, 2me Fascicule, Paris, 1963.
14. SERVICE DES STATISTIQUE AOF: *Etude démographique par sondage en Guinée 1954–1955*, I, Paris (no date).
15. See: INSEE, *Enquêtes démographiques récentes réalisées en Afrique Noire d'expression Française et à Madagascar: Tableau d'ensemble*. Paris (no date), mimeographed.
16. PIERRE CANTRELLE, *Etude démographique dans la région du Sine Saloum (Senegal)*, ORSTOM, Dakar-Hann, 1965.
17. CENSUS OFFICE, ACCRA, *1960 Population Census of Ghana*, Vol. III, 1965.
18. *Op. cit.*, pp. 281–83.

2 The improvement of the quantity and quality of demographic statistics

W. I. Brass
London School of Hygiene and Tropical Medicine, U.K.

The simplest way to prepare a paper on this topic would be to describe the statistics which ideally a demographer would like to have and to contrast them with the limited and deficient data which exist for tropical Africa. Such an account would be almost valueless because the gap between desire and possible achievement is too wide. When any project for the collection of population statistics is assessed in an African country one main question must first be considered. Will the economic and social value of the information collected repay the expenditure of scarce resources of money and skill or would it be better to use these for some other purpose? A general answer to the question is not possible, but I believe that no African country at the present time can afford more than a fraction of the expense which would be needed to establish an efficient and comprehensive system for the provision of demographic statistics.

My aim in this paper, therefore, is to outline briefly how cautious advances can be made from the present position by seeking the best demographic goods for the money that can be spent. What is written must necessarily be dogmatic and probably controversial because decisions between procedures have to be made by a balancing of advantages and shortcomings. I would rather be wrong, however, than vague or hesitant, because it is important to stress the necessity of choice. The discussion will be restricted to the collection and tabulation of basic demographic materials; although the use of these for economic, social and medical studies must be a major factor influencing decisions, data obtained primarily for such purposes will not be considered. Much thought has already been given to the subject of the paper and many words have been written on it or spoken at conferences; none of the suggestions here is in any way novel. My purpose is simply to provide a framework within which possible programmes can be assessed.

The fundamental requirement for national demographic studies is a profile of the main characteristics of the population—size, geographical distribution, sex and age divisions, employment and so on. Without such a profile there can be no adequate investigation or planning of community services (agricultural, medical or educational), of man-power, employment and skills, or of economic development and social welfare. It is essential for the assessment of human resources and needs. Many of these purposes can only be fully achieved if the statistics are known for quite small areas. The population profile can only be drawn, therefore, from a complete census in which every person is enumerated. Inquiries and surveys in which the size and characteristics of the population are estimated from data for a randomly selected sample have many advantages that will be indicated below, but they cannot efficiently provide information for small communities.

The first demographic priority for an African country is a complete enumeration of the population in all regions or as many as can reasonably be covered. The term *census* is now usually restricted to enumerations in which details for each individual are recorded separately. A census in this sense is necessary if any more than the minimum characteristics are to be recorded and has also great advantages for the control of fieldwork and the checking of errors. Most African countries, in my view, have reached a stage in their development where censuses of this kind are practicable. In others it may only be possible to afford a group enumeration in which the persons in small population units are counted according to their distribution by categories, e.g. numbers by sex in broad age groups. Valuable information can be obtained by such means but only, I believe, if the population units are kept small (e.g. households or some equivalent) and the results are skilfully checked and analysed.

The next step in order of importance, after a census or group enumeration has been carried out, is the institution of a regular series at moderate intervals, preferably not longer than ten years. Experience has shown in Africa as elsewhere that the first census is generally very deficient in completeness and accuracy. With repetition, however, design, organization, fieldwork and processing can all be improved; group enumerations can become censuses and coverage can be extended to difficult regions. Population characteristics change with time (in many African countries very rapidly) and information soon becomes out of date. I suggest also that, despite the other means of collecting relevant statistics considered below, series of censuses will, in African conditions, supply the best basis for estimating birth, death and particularly growth rates; the alternatives are too uncertain and/or costly in isolation, although they may provide strong support.

The primary statistics to be obtained in a complete census are of numbers, sex and age, residence and birthplace, and employment. In particular countries other information, for example on tribe, marital state, religion or education, may be equally important but attention will first be concentrated on the four headings listed.

Above all a census should be an accurate count of numbers; all else is subsidiary. It is clear that the coverage of many enumerations in Africa has been incomplete. We do not know whether this may have been due to the omission of whole villages, of households or of individuals; probably each played a part. The maximum effort must be applied to the specification and location by maps and listing, of the enumeration tracts, the dwelling units within them and the residents in these, even if other parts of the census thereby suffer. In some developed countries post-enumeration sample surveys are used to check the accuracy of recording and it has often been suggested that the practice should be adopted for poorer populations. Surveys of this type, however, are not efficient for detecting major defects in the listing of population units. Omissions of smaller units such as households may be noted but adjustments to totals can only be made effectively for large regions. To know data are in error is important, but the statistics will be used nevertheless when there are no others. The reduction of error is even more important and, in my view, the resources taken up by post-enumeration checks would be better used to this end.

Sex–age distributions are the crucial measures for economic and social planning and are also the key to the estimation from two or more censuses of birth, death and growth rates. Most Africans know their ages only very approximately and the reported distributions are obviously very distorted. One subsidiary but frustrating consequence that hinders the investigation of completeness is the impossibility of separating the effects of age misreporting and the omission of particular groups, such as young men. We have some idea but no certainty of the form of the age misstatements, and there are variations among populations. There is no satisfactory answer to this problem but some points should be made. The attempt to record age in years (and months for young children) is worthwhile in a census because the issue is brought more forcibly to the attention of the enumerators and because the pattern of distortion is more clearly seen. If age intervals are used, for example in group enumeration, they should not be too broad at least up to age 30 years. Wide intervals bounded by one and five years or an age taken to be puberty are particularly unhappy because of the known tendency to serious biases at these dividing points. Further research (which could be with samples of very modest size) on how best to link ages to social organization and calendars of events would be valuable. It would, however, be foolish to pretend that much increase in accuracy is possible at present except by searching questions put at lengthy interviews. Such procedures are hardly practicable in complete censuses but can be used in sample inquiries covering small percentages of the population, as indicated later.

In many African countries migration, from neighbouring territories or by internal movements to towns or more prosperous areas, is large and has important economic and social consequences. Direct measurement of gross and net effects is not practicable except in the crudest terms. The most useful statistics are obtained from questions at a census on residence and birthplace (perhaps tribe also), particularly when these are related to sex–age distributions in small areas. The pattern of migration is often complex; data from simple questions give only a partial picture and are not always easy to interpret. I do not think, however, that it is profitable to ask at a complete census those more elaborate questions about frequencies of movement, length of stay, etc., which are necessary for the full tracing of migration streams. Again, a more suitable scheme is a small sample survey.

The census is also the most convenient source of comprehensive statistics of the size, nature and distribution of the labour force. In framing questions about employment in Africa it is valuable for comparative purposes to follow the structure of the International Classification but categories must be subdivided and extended to suit local conditions. In particular some attempt should be made to separate casual and irregular work from more permanent labour.

The advantages of sample inquiries over complete censuses have often been stated. Only a fraction of the population is included and the cost can, therefore, be much lower. A smaller and better-trained staff can collect more detailed and accurate data, and control is closer. All these arguments are valid. Nevertheless they are offset in my view by limitations: sample inquiries do not give detailed statistics for small areas or sufficiently exact totals, even for much larger ones, which can be used for the estimation of population growth. Secondly, in sampling modest percentage errors in estimated numbers, large relative random variations result in the much smaller differences between totals at successive inquiries.

The main strength of a sample inquiry operates if it can be organized in conjunction with a complete census or enumeration, not as a subsequent check on coverage, but to supplement the basic information. It is wasteful to collect by a complete census, statistics of the distribution of characteristics which are required only for large populations particularly if lengthy questioning is necessary; adequate accuracy can usually be obtained with quite small samples. It is important to note that if a sample inquiry is divested of the functions that can better be performed by a complete census, its supplementary rôle can be achieved with much smaller numbers. Two of the basic types of data which can be sought in detail by a sample inquiry have already been mentioned, those of age distributions and migration. The age statistics are best used for the adjustment of reports from the complete census rather than independently; further study of how this can be done most efficiently is needed. No attempt will be made to list or consider the various kinds of information which might be collected by sample inquiries. Questions which attempt to extract data on vital events retrospectively fall into a special category and will be discussed with the other methods for determining current population changes.

In more developed countries statistics of births and deaths are obtained from vital registration in which the events are recorded as they occur. The relation of the events to the numbers of the population in relevant categories gives the measures of rates of change (births, deaths and growth) and also of fertility and mortality, which are used to trace demographic trends and as a basis for projection and planning. The remarks on the development of effective registration systems in African countries will be brief because I believe that improvements must be dominated by administrative needs and actions which are outside the control of the demographer. When birth and death certificates are essential in the social and economic organization of the community, for education, participation in adult life by voting, state support in old age, inheritance and so on, accurate registration will develop. The experience of some Asian countries such as India shows that this may take a long time. The demographer must be ready to take any opportunity to improve the scope and detail of the data and the extraction of the statistics as coverage improves, but he can initiate little that is fundamental.

These comments apply to country-wide registration. In recent years there has been much discussion and exploration of the proposal that vital events should be recorded in representative sample areas or communities. The aim is to achieve as nearly complete coverage as possible in these areas by the use of close and intensive checks which would be too expensive to apply on a national scale. These multi-check vital statistics inquiries incorporate some or all of the following procedures: registration by the established system or by special schemes with 'active' observers; listing of events in previous time intervals by periodic 'rounds' of questioning as frequently as four times a year; multiple recording of such events in the different 'rounds'; noting of pregnant women and seriously ill persons for subsequent determination of outcome; enumeration of the population at risk, at the start of the inquiry and at later stages to find changes; individual matching of events reported, by the various means to detect omissions. Notable studies of this type have been or are being carried out in Pakistan, Thailand, Morocco, Senegal and elsewhere.

Experience in such inquiries is only beginning to accumulate and there has been little time to digest it properly. I will give briefly my own views about the implications for Africa; there is not space to detail all the supporting reasons. Despite the very great efforts to achieve completeness of registration and periodical recording of events, deficiencies have remained substantial. Individual matching is very laborious and has a considerable margin of uncertainty. In order to obtain vital statistics of real value for the measurement of trends and the making of projections for planning purposes, very large samples are needed. One reason for this is the regional variation in many African countries which necessitates estimates for sub-populations. The major point, however, is that sample variabilities of birth, death and above all, growth rates, are very high; for trend estimation and projection it is necessary to include the variation from year to year, as well as among sample units in the assessment. We have little quantitative information about possible sample errors but may note, for example, the results from the Senegal study recently reported by Cantrelle; in each of the two areas within one region surveyed, of 34,000 and 18,000 inhabitants respectively, the natural increase estimated for 1963 and 1964 differed by nearly 10 per 1,000; the average level over the two years was higher in one area than the other by 12 per 1,000. These differences are very much too large to be accounted for by the hypothesis (sometimes made in this connection) of simple random sampling.

My conclusion is that the estimation of vital rates by multi-check inquiries, with sufficient accuracy to be useful, is too costly for African countries. The opinion is reinforced by the fact that vital rates alone, without much more information about patterns of fertility and mortality, are an unsatisfactory basis for population projections when demographic characteristics are changing rapidly—as may be the case in many parts of Africa.

In some countries, notably several of French expression in West Africa, data on births and deaths have been collected in sample inquiries of the census type. In these surveys questions have been asked about births and deaths in the previous year and also the total number of children born and died to each mother. Recently information about deaths of parents has also been recorded. The collection of these statistics can be relatively cheap, particularly if an inquiry is already planned to replace or supplement a complete census. The problem, of course, is the reliability of the reports of past events. However, a variety of internal checks and adjustments has been developed, dependent upon comparisons of the data for the previous year with the reports of births and deaths of children over the life of the mother, the examination of trends with age and time intervals, the use of quasi-stable population theory, etc. There is scope for further extension and improvement in questions and techniques of adjustment, e. g. by the breakdown of events by shorter periods than a year and the utilization of results on deaths of parents and perhaps of brothers and sisters. As stated above I consider that a series of complete censuses or enumerations is the most promising basis for the determination of growth rates in Africa. I believe that supplementary sample inquiries of the kind described are a powerful tool for extending the knowledge of fertility, mortality and natural increase quickly and relatively cheaply.

Special research surveys are of two main kinds, namely those concerned with the examination and assessment of demographic methodology and those seeking substantive results about the communities studied, although many combine the two purposes. The scale of such work will often be very different from the schemes discussed previously and valuable returns can be obtained from very small studies given sufficient imagination, ingenuity and understanding. For many years to come, a large part of the demographic knowledge which is derived in developed countries from censuses, registration and national surveys must in Africa be sought by small surveys; it is to be hoped that the number of these will increase rapidly with the establishment of new universities and research institutes and centres.

The possibilities for substantive studies are so wide that no brief account of problems and methods can be given. Arbitrarily I shall mention two which are of particular interest to me. There is strong evidence that the age pattern of child mortality differs in parts of Africa from the experience of countries with better statistics, in particular that death rates in the second and third years of life are extraordinarily high. Further knowledge about the causes of this phenomenon would be of the greatest value both for the planning of health measures and for improving techniques for the estimation of vital rates from limited data. Investigation is only practicable by means of small studies in which children with known birth dates are followed up over the first few years of life from a clinic or medical centre. Several surveys of this kind have been carried out. In some of them, unfortunately, the results have been less rewarding than they might have been because of unsatisfactory analysis of the data. For example, in the calculation of vital rates the age divisions have not been the most useful, and proper allowance has not been made for the children still alive and not exposed to risk for a full age interval. These defects could have been overcome with a very slight amount of skilled advice. A type of survey which has been surprisingly little exploited is that of social and economic differentials in fertility and mortality. Although reports of births and deaths in a previous period or maternity histories may have deficiencies for the estimation of absolute measures, biases in differentials are likely to be much less serious. In several sample inquiries, data have been collected which made some analysis possible of variations in vital rates by socio-economic characteristics, but the opportunities have not been properly exploited.

Important contributions to methodology, which would increase the accuracy and reliability of estimates of demographic measures for Africa, could be made by special studies. I am particularly anxious that some of the multi-check vital statistics surveys should be linked with procedures for collecting information by single round retrospective sample inquiries. The validity and efficiency of the techniques of correction and adjustment developed for the latter data could then be tested. It should also be possible to establish ages of persons in a small community fairly accurately by intensive questioning about relative dates of birth, social ceremonies, etc. With these as a yardstick, investigation could be made of errors in ages when various techniques of ascertainment were used, e.g. respondent's statement, enumerator's estimate from physical development, calendars of events. Other research which would be practicable on a small scale with close and repeated checking is on the nature of errors in retrospective reports of births and deaths, such as variations with the length of interval, age of respondent and number of events.

Great efforts have been made to design sound plans and organize efficient fieldwork for the collection of demographic statistics in Africa. It is, therefore, particularly unfortunate that much of the work has been wasted because the processing, tabulation and publication of the results have been slow, inaccurate and inadequate. Anyone who has studied reports of African censuses and sample inquiries must be aware of the many inconsistencies in the statistics, errors in calculations and limitations of the cross-tabulations presented. Too little attention has been paid to improving these phases of the operation. It is probably here that help from richer countries can be most useful, particularly with the spread of facilities for electronic digital computing. The successful planning of demographic surveys demands a close and extensive knowledge of the life of the population, which is not quickly or easily gained by visiting advisers, but the processing and compilation of data can be done elsewhere without raising problems of comparable difficulty.

The most fundamental way in which the quantity and quality of demographic data can be improved has not been considered in this paper because I assume it will receive adequate attention in other sessions. It must be mentioned, however, to preserve a proper balance. The collection, analysis and interpretation of population statistics requires even greater knowledge and skill in Africa than in developed countries; only if there are men well educated and trained in the different parts of the operation can advances be made.

3 The rôle of government in population census projects in Africa

E. N. Omaboe

Chief Statistician, Central Bureau of Statistics, Accra, Ghana

The right type of sponsorship for a population census is one of the most important of the factors that determine the success of national census enumerations. This fact is fully recognized all over the world, and the United Nations' *Principles and Recommendations for National Population Censuses* (Series M, No. 29) gives it pride of place in its list of features essential to national censuses.

Both past census counts and modern scientific population censuses have relied heavily on the sponsorship of governments for their satisfactory execution. It is now accepted that not only should governments sponsor national population censuses but they should also assume full responsibility for the operations. This is true of all countries, irrespective of their level of economic and social development. For the developing countries, however, there are other factors that make the active participation of governments in census enumerations inevitable. In Africa, for example, it is almost impossible for a successful population census to be conducted by any other organization without full government support.

Factors Involving Government Participation in Census Projects

It may be appropriate to list the factors that make government participation inevitable.

First, there is a need to provide a good legal basis for a census enumeration. Population census projects require legal definition of their scope and of the responsibilities of the organization charged with their execution. In some countries there is provision in the Constitution; in others a general Statistics Act provides the legal basis, while a few have to resort to *ad hoc* legislation for the purpose. But whatever the form of the provision, the fact remains that only the government is competent to promulgate laws of the nature required.

It is also necessary in any census project to safeguard the confidentiality of the information collected. This is done by enacting laws and regulations indicating for what purposes the data collected may be used and setting out the penalties to be imposed in the case of any unauthorized disclosure of information. In order to ensure this, the active participation of governments is needed, as only they can fix penalties and prosecute individuals in competent courts for contravening the laws.

Although it is necessary to pass laws to make it obligatory for individuals to provide the information required in a population census enumeration, it should be pointed out that the success of a population census hinges more on the understanding and voluntary co-operation of the population than on fear of the penalties imposed by law.

A second factor that forces censuses into the domain of governmental responsibility is cost; good censuses, conducted on modern scientific lines are expensive. The 1960 population census of Ghana, for instance, cost more than £396,000 (i.e. over 1*s* 2*d* per head). Similar costs have been encountered by all African countries that have tried to conduct population censuses in recent years.

In order to realize the importance of financial considerations in census enumeration as far as governmental sponsorship is concerned, one should not look only at the expenditure side. The benefits that flow from such expenditure have to be taken into account. The most important point in this connection is that the benefits of a population census are indirect. A population census provides a country with statistical data of an economic and social nature, essential for planning and other purposes before these result in real benefits to the country. Because it will not be able to obtain direct returns a non-government organization is unwilling to spend money on a population census. Governments, however, look upon this type of expenditure as a form of support service. The statistical information that flows from a population census is needed by governments to formulate and implement policies. In addition to this, it is the basic responsibility of a government to provide these data for all other establishments in the country—whether public, private or joint public–private—for their planning purposes.

The next factor to be considered relates to the administrative requirements of a census. A modern population census is a complex administrative project which requires extensive preparatory work for its successful implementation. To ensure this, all the resources of a country, human, financial, etc., have to be organized for the project.

In terms of human resources, a census requires enumerators and supervisors in the field as well as a large body of professionals and senior officers to plan and implement the project. In Ghana, for instance, the 1960 population census employed nearly 9,000 persons at the peak of operations. The recruitment of such a large body of able officers poses a complex problem that can be handled only by government with all its resources and power.

In Africa, because there is no other source of capable enumerators and supervisors, school teachers and certain other government employees must be heavily relied upon. The government, being the body responsible for teachers in almost all African countries, is the only authority able to marshall them.

Additional to the recruitment of the field force, the large scale and *ad hoc* nature of censuses necessitate either the establishment of an organization for the planning and execution of the project or strengthening the personnel of an existing statistical office. This can be done either by direct recruitment or by seconding officers from other government departments. The paucity in African countries of competent personnel for recruitment to senior posts makes secondment the only reasonable course of action, and only the government can order the secondment of officers to the census organization.

Another aspect, transport, is also vital. Census documents must be distributed, enumerators and supervisors conveyed to their respective enumeration areas and completed census schedules collected for processing at the census headquarters. In Africa, transport and communications are not very well developed. It is only governments that have adequate transportation resources and the necessary authority to commandeer vehicles for this purpose.

Even such a seemingly simple operation as the printing of the census schedules and manuals must be accorded high priority if printing is not to interfere with the time-table of census operations. The printing is normally handled by government presses. Only the government is in a position to insist it be done.

The Importance of Publicity

Mention should also be made of the publicity aspect of a population census. This is one of the most important factors that determine the success or failure of a population census, especially in Africa. Without the co-operation and understanding of the entire population, it will not be possible to execute a successful census. It has already been pointed out that a census requires a sound legal basis. This is necessary, among other reasons, to take care of the few individuals who may wish to frustrate the good intentions of the responsible authorities and agencies by refusing to provide the data needed or by illegally impeding the data collection process. In the final analysis, however, it is not possible to prosecute more than a few persons, and it is advisable to rely on educating the population about the objectives of the census, the part they are required to play and the benefits that are expected to accrue to them rather than on the force of the law.

This can be effected only through an extensive publicity programme. All modern communication media—radio, television, newspapers and periodicals—must be employed, as well as the traditional (e.g. the chiefs' 'gong-gong', durbars, and political and social welfare rallies). The only body that controls the publicity media and that is able to make full use of the information services is the government.

Financial and Administrative Implications

In the collection of the completed questionnaires and the processing and publication of the results, active participation of the government is necessary, because this stage requires the investment of human and financial resources normally in African countries far beyond the means of any body other than a government.

It is important to understand what governments should do and what they should not do in census enumeration programmes. By 'government' is meant the whole system of national governmental administration made up of the central, regional, and local governments. In a Federal type of government there is need for the closest form of co-operation between the Federal Government and the Regional Governments. Even where responsibility for the census is given to the different regional governments, it is necessary to maintain co-operation among them.

The most important rôle of governments in census enumeration in Africa is to provide the requisite legal basis for the operation and to establish or strengthen the governmental body charged with responsibility for the census. The latter may be done with technical assistance on a bilateral basis or through a multilateral technical assistance scheme such as the United Nations Technical Assistance Board, now expanded into the United Nations Development Programme.

The census-planning officers will advise the government on the required financial and human resources and propose a suitable time for the enumeration. It is not easy to obtain foreign financial aid for conducting a population census, and it is therefore the responsibility of the economic planning agency of the country, the financial ministry and the census authorities to determine the amount of the country's financial resources that can be allocated to the census project. Census expenditure will be spread over a number of years with a peak expenditure period coinciding with the year of enumeration. Governments should bear this fact in mind and not enter into any commitments until they are sure that they will be able to afford the total cost involved. There is nothing more disappointing and wasteful than having to alter or suspend census plans in midstream. The assurance of adequate funds for a number of years also enables the planners to provide a balanced census scheme—balanced in the sense that the various stages of census operation get their proper share of the budget. There have been in Africa certain statistical survey projects on which vast sums of money were spent in the collection of data that have subsequently been left unprocessed and unpublished.

Another important rôle for governments in census enumeration is to ensure that the project is accorded top priority. This is not difficult once the governments have realized the complex nature of the operation and are determined to do everything for the success of the scheme. If the government is not prepared to accept this, especially during the few weeks preceding the enumeration and at the time of the enumeration, then it must stop thinking in terms of a successful census.

It is also vital that the government should take certain decisions regarding the secondment of officers to the census organization, allowances to be paid to the census officials, etc. In all of this it may be found that current administrative practices and procedures have to be set aside. Red-tape must be cut to the minimum if a census is to succeed. Speed is essential in the planning and execution of a census project, and this requires that the government should be prepared to order short-cuts in certain administrative procedures.

In some countries the appointment of a Central Census Committee composed of those ministers directly responsible for services connected with the population census project (transport, finance, education, information, etc.) helps greatly to speed up matters. The advantage here is that all decisions taken by the Committee are implemented without delay because the ministers responsible are themselves members of the decision-making body. Subcommittees can be appointed to deal specifically with details.

The Importance of Co-operation and Goodwill

There are a few things against which governments must be warned. A population census cannot be undertaken if an atmosphere of controversy surrounds the project. Political, religious, tribal and other differences can wreck a population census. If the atmosphere is not conducive to the taking of a good census, it is advisable to postpone the project, perhaps even for a number of years, rather than to force it through and waste money.

The use of political rallies for publicizing census operations has been mentioned. This aspect of the work needs to be handled with great caution, especially in countries where political parties are likely to put partisan considerations above the national interest. It is the duty of the government to impress upon all political parties the need for raising the census project above the level of party politics. In this respect the ruling party must set a good example. Political parties can play useful rôles in ensuring the success of census projects. However, if doubts exist as to their sincerity, they should not be allowed to participate in the publicity campaign.

The government must take care lest its interest in the census should lead it towards interference with the technical planning and execution of the project and so affect the success of the census. Ministers have occasionally given wrong interpretations to questionnaire items, which can lead to much confusion and chaotic results. The technical planning staff should be given as much freedom as possible in the execution of the census scheme, but they should also consult with the government on important policy matters so that there is no danger of the government being kept in the dark.

The main attribute of governments which enables them to play important rôles in census enumeration is the authority and legal power that they wield. However, no census will succeed if governments rely upon this alone. In a census, goodwill and co-operation as well as sacrifice by the population count for very much, and the best that a government can do is to ensure that these prevail.

4 Population data of East Africa

D. A. Lury
University College, Nairobi, Kenya

Before 1948

The demographic information available on East Africa before the last two decades was surveyed exhaustively by Kuczynski (70). (Numbers in parentheses refer to bibliography at end of chapter.) His conclusion was (pp. 124–25):

> If one wanted to summarize the demographic position of British East Africa [Kuczynski included in this area Zambia, Malawi, and Somaliland in addition to the countries covered in the present note] in recent times all that one could say would be: Practically nothing is known of the population trend . . . there is no reason to assume that the total population in 1940 was any larger than in 1895 or that the total population in 1895 was much smaller than in 1875.'

The results of the recent censuses suggest that there was a more rapid growth in population from 1921 than Kuczynski, affected by inconsistencies in arguments put forward by some supporters of a high growth view, could accept. The results of the 1948 Census showed a population 26 per cent larger than the previous official estimate (79).

The 1948 Census

The organizers of the 1948 census were confronted by a situation with the following main features:

1. A population that could be divided into two groups: a small group of non-Africans and a much larger group of Africans.
2. Practically all non-African households contained at least one literate person (though the languages in which they were literate were not necessarily the official administrative language, English). Relatively few African households contained literate persons.
3. Non-Africans were more familiar with the idea of census taking and could provide reasonably accurate demographic information with little difficulty. In general, the Africans were likely to be more suspicious of census procedures and were in many cases unable to give accurate information directly (e.g. about age), even when they wished to co-operate.
4. Most of the non-Africans lived in towns, but the Africans were spread through the countryside.
5. The East African Statistical Department had central authority for the collection of statistics throughout East Africa (except in Zanzibar, but there it had an effective advisory rôle). Both the Department and the District Administrations through which it had to work for census purposes were not yet fully staffed after the 1939–45 war; but there was an effective channel of command, and the Director of the Statistical Department, C. J. Martin, was particularly concerned with demography.

The scheme devised to meet this situation is described by Martin (78). The main steps may be summarized:

1. A separate census was held on 25–26 February 1948, of non-Africans and persons living on their premises. In most cases the householder was expected to complete a detailed questionnaire without assistance, giving information about individuals.
2. A general census of Africans was held in August 1948, in which limited data were collected by enumerators on a 'hut' basis. This was 'completed within four days in districts including about 60 per cent of the total population' (74).
3. A sample census (10 per cent) of Africans was held subsequent to the general census, during which detailed information about individuals was collected by enumerators.
4. Special arrangements were made for Zanzibar and some other areas.

As J. G. C. Blacker has written (109): 'This census constituted a landmark, not only in the demography of the East African territories, but also in that of tropical Africa as a whole . . . Apart from the immediate value of the population figures obtained, the great achievement of the 1948 census was that it proved that the operation was possible.' Martin could write with justifiable pride (78): 'Those who doubted the wisdom of attempting to count about 3¾ million huts in 640,000 square miles had their doubts dispelled, and those who had stated dogmatically that a census was impossible were proved wrong.'

But the sequel was not so satisfactory. The results of the non-African census were reported in detail (4), (14), (24), but the published results of the African censuses were limited. Some analyses of the African general census were issued (3), (12), (25), but discussion of demographic characteristics in the light of the general and sample censuses taken together was limited to two sources, (13) and (81). No full official report was ever published.[1]

The nature of the questions asked at the 1948 census are shown in Annex I and a summary of the results is given in Annex II.

The Second Round of Censuses

There was a census of non-Africans and urban Africans in Tanganyika in 1952 (15), and a sample census of Nairobi in 1957–58 (122). But the second round of full censuses really started with the 1957 census in Tanganyika. It had become clear in preliminary discussions that it would not be possible to hold a census in 1958 for East Africa as a whole, and the original plan was for censuses to be taken in Tanganyika, Uganda and Kenya in 1957, 1958 and 1959 respectively. The time-table finally achieved was:

1957	Tanganyika	1959	Uganda
1958	Zanzibar	1962	Kenya

The basic organization of these censuses followed the procedures adopted in the 1948 census. The sampling techniques employed were in general an improvement, although in Tanganyika unfortunate decisions spoiled the original design (see (20), p. 11). Further, by the time the Kenya Census was taken, it was possible to modify the basic plan and remove the racial division. A census of all races was taken at the same time. Two forms were used, a simple form in rural areas and a detailed form in urban areas (the latter was also used for the relatively few non-Africans living in the countryside). The more detailed form was then used (with minor modifications) for a sample census of 10 per cent of rural Africans. Special arrangements were made for the Northern Province.

Detailed reports of the Tanganyika, Zanzibar and Uganda censuses have been published (16), (20), (27), (28), (32). Some of the data obtained during the Kenya census has also been published (6). The general reports on the African and non-African populations should be available soon.[2]

The nature of the questions asked at the censuses is shown in Annex I and a summary of the results is given in Annex II.

Brief Comments on the East African Censuses

The East African censuses were successful in obtaining reliable information on the basic demographic characteristics of the East African population, at a low cost. (The total expenditure in the second round of censuses was of the order of £200,000, so that the cost per head was around 0·16 shillings or *2d* sterling.) There is still the question of what is meant by 'reliable information', since the Reports rightly stress the many sources of error and the uncertainty of many of the resulting estimates. Basically the criterion of reliability is the growing confidence in the consistency and likelihood of the results that comes as one uses the figures. Blacker has expressed this well (109), pp. 59–60):

> 'Much has been said and written about the unreliability of East African census data. Such contentions undoubtedly contain a large measure of truth; anyone who has had to deal with census schedules at first hand must be all too acutely aware of the frequency of the mistakes made in their completion. . . . Yet, in the opinion of the writer, it is easy to exaggerate the general untrustworthiness of the data. For the fact remains that the figures do piece together into a reasonably coherent picture. Different estimates of the birth and death rates obtained by entirely independent means rarely differ by more than a few points, while the rates themselves are of about the level expected for countries in the state of development of East Africa at the present time. Finally, the rates of natural increase indicated by the birth and death rates correspond reasonably closely with the inter-censal rates of growth. Small discrepancies of course remain which cannot easily be accounted for (especially in the case of Tanganyika), but the general pattern which emerges is clear enough.'

Two criticisms may be noted. First, the data failed to provide detailed geographical information about the lower-level census areas. These areas had not been previously mapped and so far as the 1948 census is concerned it would, I think, be justifiable to reply that the organizers already had enough on their hands. And as already noted, the 1948 results were not fully reported in other respects. For Uganda in 1959, a density map showing *gombolola* (division) boundaries, which had not been previously available, was produced by the Survey Department on the basis of sketch maps made by the District Administration in the course of census organization. Morgan has prepared a map of locations for Kenya (88), and he and Shaffer have in course of preparation a monograph giving a sectioned map with fuller information.

A second criticism was that occupational or industrial information was not collected for the African population during the second Tanganyika and Uganda censuses. The number of questions that can be adequately handled even in a sample census is, of course, limited; and it was considered that information about the employed labour force, which was collected by governments annually as a separate exercise, could substitute for census information. A labour force budget using this approach has been made by Martin for East Africa (85). Nevertheless, further information in this field, particularly information about rural Africans engaged in non-agricultural self-employment, is clearly desirable and the results of the Kenya sample census in this respect are awaited with interest.

Fertility, Mortality and Rates of Growth

The main sources of information on vital rates in East Africa are Martin (81) and the reports of the second censuses, published or to come. Estimates of rates are summarized in Annex II. They show wide variation from area to area. Some census results have been foreshadowed on occasion by sample investigations. For example the low birth rate in Teso and the high rate in Kigezi reported in the Uganda census (27) were foreshadowed by Wilson and Watson (120) and Purseglove (101). The reasons for the wide range of rates require further elucidation, but specific reference may be made here to some sources (42), (56), (72), (103), (113).

Reference should also be made to discussions of the characteristics of the Asian community. The numbers involved are very small relative to the East African population as a whole. But the community is of demographic interest as an emerging group, because its structure is changing from one determined by migration to one with a more stable pattern. Study of the Asian community also provides an interesting comparison for use in studies of certain population groups in India. Reference should be made to (37), (38), (80) and (129).

Vital Statistics

Birth and death registration has been fairly effective for Europeans but of variable accuracy for Asians. In some areas, registration schemes for Africans have been in existence for a long time, but the results are worthless for demographic analysis. There is, however, growing concern about registration, and schemes have been discussed which combine publicity and pressure for registration and 'continuous enumerations' in sample areas. Martin has put forward a scheme (83), and he and Blacker have reported on developments in 1961 (41). Since then one series of enumerations has been made in three districts in Kenya. The potentialities of the procedures and the relevant priority to be attached to this type of operation are still under discussion.

Migration, Urbanization and Employment

Indigenous Africans are not required to fill in immigration forms, and the only Africans appearing in the regular migration statistics are sea and air travellers from abroad. The regular migration statistics are therefore relevant mainly to the study of the European and Asian groups and of the tourist trade.

Migratory movements affecting Africans are:

1. East Africans out of East Africa. The only substantial emigration has been to Northern Rhodesia and South Africa. This is discussed in (59).
2. Movement into East Africa from neighbouring countries. There has been substantial immigration from Ruanda and Burundi. The published census figures of persons born in those countries and enumerated by East African censuses are (in thousands):

	Tanganyika		Uganda	
	1948	1957	1948	1959
Ruanda	20	35	289	379
Burundi	90	122	57	139

This migration in relation to Buganda is extensively discussed in (104).

3. Movement from one East African country to another. This occurs on a limited scale. Figures at census dates of persons enumerated in other countries are (in thousands):

	Tanganyika 1957	Uganda 1959	Kenya 1962	Total
Tanganyikan tribes	—	35	19	54
Uganda tribes	11	—	17	28
Kenya tribes	17	80	—	97
Total	28	115	36	179

In addition there were 27,000 persons born on the East African mainland (mainly in Tanganyika) in Zanzibar in 1958.

4. Movement within each country. This is substantial and is a key feature of the economic and social structure. Southall (111) provides an excellent introduction to this subject.

The population of urban areas in East Africa is still relatively small—of the order of 5 per cent. The towns are centres of paid employment, and many of the studies of the fourth type of migration listed above discuss migration, urbanization and employment as related problems. The references are usually identifiable by title in the bibliography, but we may note here the studies by Elkan (43), (44) and Powesland (100), which stress employment and economic aspects; the series by Ominde (93), (97); and the studies by Southall and Gutkind (112), Wilson (119) and Leslie (73), which deal with more general urban problems, mainly from a sociological viewpoint.

Each of the mainland countries carries out an enumeration of employees, normally at annual intervals. Recent reports are cited at (8), (22) and (29).

Manpower and Education

In addition to the studies of actual employment referred to in the last paragraph, the East African countries have recently turned their attention to manpower problems in relation to economic development. References in the bibliography are (10) and (23). In addition to projections of requirements, these studies usually give information, not available elsewhere, about the existing employment situation.

Some information about education was obtained in the second round of censuses, and other regarding various aspects of the education systems (numbers of schools, teachers and pupils) is found in the *Annual Abstracts* of the three countries. Uganda and Kenya have recently had important Commissions of Inquiry into education and their reports, (9), (30), give further information and statistics. There is a good general survey in (64).

Two studies of 'élites'—Richards (105) and Goldthorpe (53)—should also be noticed.

Health

Teams from the World Health Organization have investigated tuberculosis, malaria, and nutrition, Professor J. N. P. Davies and others a special type of cancer. But perhaps the most important recent work has been on malnutrition and kwashiorkor, and in particular the activities of the Medical Research Council Infantile Malnutrition Unit at Mulago Hospital, Kampala (118).[3]

Concluding Comment

These brief notes have been prepared as an introduction and first guide to the studies listed in the bibliography. Although the information available is of variable quality and some of it is of a partial or uncertain character, it is clear that much useful work has been done. The foundations for a steady and sound expansion of demographic enquiries already exist.

Footnotes

1. 'The 1948 census material was unfortunately not written up because of the decision by the governments not to continue with the analysis owing to shortage of funds.' Martin in Foreword to (27).
2. They have appeared in the interval between the presentation and publication of this paper (130 and 131).
3. For a detailed bibliography of medical investigations see: LONGLANDS, B. W., *Bibliography of the Distribution of Disease in East Africa*, Makerere Library Publications No. 3, Makerere College, Uganda, 1965.

Subjects of Questions in East African Censuses 1948–62

ANNEX I

Question relating to:	1948 Census				1957 Tanganyika			1958 Zanzibar	1959 Uganda			1962 Kenya	
	Aug.	Aug./Sep.	Feb.	Feb.	Aug.	Aug./Sep.	Feb.	March	Aug.	Aug./Sep.	March	Aug.	Aug./Sep.
	African general	African sample	Non-African	Zanzibar	African general	African sample	Non-African	All	African general	African sample	Non-African	African general	Other and African sample
Name		×	×	×		×	×	×		×	×		×
Relation to h/h			×	×		×	×	×		×	×		×
Sex	×	×	×	×	×	×	×	×	×	×	×	×	×
Marital status	×	×	×	×			×				×		×
Age		a	×	×		a	×	a		b	×		×
Age groups													
Under 1	×				×				×				
1–5	×				×				×			×	
6–15	c				×				×				
16–45	c				×				×			×	
over 45	×				×				×				
Birthplace		×	×	×		×	×	×		×	×		×
Nationality/tribe	×	×	×	×	×	×	×	×	×	×	×	×	×
Religion		×	×	×		×	×			×	×		×
Race			×	×			×	×			×		×
Residence			×	×			×	×			×		×
Education		×				×				×			×

ANNEX I (*continued*)

Question relating to:	1948 Census				1957 Tanganyika			1958 Zanzibar	1959 Uganda			1962 Kenya	
	Aug.	Aug./Sep.	Feb.	Feb.	Aug.	Aug./Sep.	Feb.	March	Aug.	Aug./Sep.	March	Aug.	Aug./Sep.
	African general	African sample	Non-African	Zanzibar	African general	African sample	Non-African	All	African general	African sample	Non-African	African general	Other and African sample
Mother tongue							×	×			×		×
Housing			×	×			×	×			×		g
Infirmities		×	×	×									
Occupation		d	×	×		e		f			×		d
Occupational status			×				×				×		dg
Industry			×				×				×		dg
Period of work		f											
No. of wives						×							
Distance to work											×		
Members h/h absent							×				×		
Deaths in last year		×				×				×			

ANNEX I (*continued*)

Question relating to:	1948 Census				1957 Tanganyika			1958 Zanzibar	1959 Uganda			1962 Kenya	
	Aug.	Aug./ Sep.	Feb.	Feb.	Aug.	Aug./ Sep.	Feb.	March	Aug.	Aug./ Sep.	March	Aug.	Aug./ Sep.
	African general	African sample	Non-African	Zanzibar	African general	African sample	Non-African	All	African general	African sample	Non-African	African general	Other and African sample
Fertility questions to adult women only													
No. born alive		×	×	×		×	×	×		×	×		×
No. alive now		×	×	×		×	×	×		×	×		×
Still births		×	×	×				×					
Died under 1		×	×	×		×		×		×	×		
Died over 1		×	×	×		×				×	×		
Births last year		h				×	×	×		×	×		×

(a) Actual age if known, otherwise age group.
(b) Age in Buganda: as in (a) elsewhere.
(c) In Kenya groups for females were 6–13 and 14–45.
(d) Adult males only.
(e) Adult males: urban non-employees only.
(f) Urban areas only.
(g) Urban areas and non-Africans only.
(h) Not in Kenya.

ANNEX II

KENYA

1. Population by Province, 1948 and 1962 (in 000s)

Province	1948 total	1962			Increase (per cent)	1962 Density (a) (number per sq. mile)
		African	N-A	Total		
Nairobi E.P.D.	140	197	118	315	124	867
Central	1,395	1,910	16	1,925	38	173
Coast	501	643	85	728	45	25
Nyanza	1,867	2,993	20	3,012	61	312
Rift Valley	646	1,023	26	1,049	59	60
Southern	637	1,010	4	1,014	59	31
Northern	220(b)	588	2	590	—	5
Total (c)	5,406	8,364	270	8,634	60	38

(a) District range 3 to 689 (excluding Nairobi and Mombasa).
(b) Estimates prepared by District Commissioners.
(c) Excludes persons in transit (2,629 in 1959).

Sources: (5) and *Kenya Statistical Abstract 1964*, Table 12, and Kenya Statistics Branch.

N.B. It has not been possible to present figures for Kenya entirely in the same manner as those of Tanganyika and Uganda as the full Kenya Census reports have not yet been published. See footnote 2 to text.

2. 441,739 (or 5·3 per cent) Africans and 229,206 (or 85 per cent) non-African lived in Towns in 1962

Source: (7).

3. Age and Sex Distribution of African and Asian Populations, 1962

Age group	African and Somali		Asian	
	Male	Female	Male	Female
0–4	708·1	737·8	12·2	11·8
5–9	662·8	656·0	14·0	13·3
10–14	601·5	501·0	13·2	12·3
15–19	424·1	405·6	8·7	8·5
20–24	271·6	392·3	7·3	8·3
25–29	275·8	372·1	7·4	7·3
30–34	227·3	285·2	6·5	6·0
35–39	200·3	216·3	5·0	4·8
40–44	166·0	171·2	5·0	3·8
45–49	149·0	128·2	4·0	2·9
50–54	114·9	102·2	3·4	2·0
55–59	76·0	58·5	2·1	1·1
60 and over	228·6	178·7	3·2	1·8
Not stated	28·5	26·2	0·3	0·3
Total	4,134·6	4,231·3	92·4	84·2

Source: Kenya Statistical Abstract 1964, Table 17.

4. African Population: Main Tribes, 1962

Kikuyu	1,642,065
Luo	1,148,335
Luhya	1,086,409
Kamba	933,219
Kisii	538,343
Meru	439,921
Mijikenda	414,887
Kipsigis	341,771

Source: Kenya Statistical Abstract 1964, Table 16.

5. Fertility and Mortality Information derived from the 1948 Census

(a) LIVE BIRTHS

Age	Average no. per woman	Percentage distribution of women by no. of live births							
		0	1	2	3	4	5	6	7 or more
14–45	3·2	23	14	13	11	10	8	7	14
46 and over	5·3	12	5	7	9	10	11	10	36

(b) INFANT WASTAGE RATE per 1,000 live births to women 14–45.

Kenya	184
Central Province	130
Nyanza Province	228

Source: Summarized from Martin (81).

6. Rates from 1962 Census

(a) Birth rate (African): 50 per 1000
(b) Death rate (African): 20 per 1000
(c) Rate of natural increase (African): 30 per 1000

Source: (5).

7. African Age-specific Fertility Rates, 1962(a)

Age	Births per 1,000 women
15–19	141
20–24	304
25–29	301
30–34	243
35–39	196
40–44	138
45–49	36
Total fertility rate	6·8

(a) Provisional figures.

Source: Provisional census calculations (by permission of J. G. C. Blacker and A. T. Brough, Chief Statistician, Kenya).

8. African Migration: Percentage Analysis by Birthplace, 1962

Birthplace	Males	Females
Born in district where enumerated	84·7	88·8
Born elsewhere in Kenya	14·6	10·7
Born outside Kenya	0·7	0·5

Source: As 7 above.

TANGANYIKA

AFRICAN POPULATION

1. African Population by Region, 1948 and 1957

Region	1948	1957	Increase (a) (per cent)	1957 Density (b) (per sq. ml.)
Central	815,941	879,421	7·8	25·0
Eastern	908,662	1,039,791	14·4	25·1
Lake	1,844,950	2,228,485	20·8	57·5
Northern	584,993	758,960	29·7	22·9
Southern	914,049	1,008,046	10·3	18·1
S. Highlands	845,476	1,023,805	21·1	22·9
Tanga	547,212	671,381	22·7	48·0
Western	946,234	1,052,795	11·3	13·5
Total (c)	7,410,269	8,665,336	16·9	25·4

(a) District range from 18·2 to 93·4.
(b) District range from 2·8 to 229·3 (excluding Dar-es-Salaam).
(c) Including persons in transit.

Source: (20) pp. 14, 18, 21–24.

2. 276,362 (or 3·2 per cent) lived in 31 gazetted townships in 1957

Source: (20), p. 19. (Cf. Non-African (2) below: 2 gazetted townships were down-graded to minor settlements between the non-African and African censuses.)

N.B. See note on Kenya 2 above.

3. African Population by Sex and Age, 1957

Age group	NUMBERS ('000s)		PERCENTAGES		Sex ratio
	Males	Females	Males	Females	
0–4	760	752	18·2	16·7	101·0
5–9	586	582	14·1	13·0	100·6
10–14	490	509	11·8	11·3	96·2
15–19	422	469	10·1	10·4	89·9
20–24	370	431	8·9	9·6	86·0
25–29	325	382	7·8	8·5	85·0
30–34	280	328	6·7	7·3	85·3
35–39	234	273	5·6	6·1	85·7
40–44	190	222	4·6	5·0	85·5
45–49	152	167	3·6	3·7	90·6
50–54	119	128	2·9	2·8	92·9
55–59	90	95	2·2	2·1	94·3
60–64	64	69	1·5	1·5	93·7
65–69	44	46	1·1	1·0	95·2
70–74	26	29	0·6	0·6	90·9
75–79	13	14	0·3	0·3	95·9
Total (a)	4,165	4,498	100	100	92·6

(a) Smoothed and interpolated distribution.
(i) Figures may not always add to the totals shown on account of rounding.
(ii) Total population excludes persons in transit.

Source: (20) p. 30.

4. African Population: Main Tribes, 1957

Sukuma	1,093,767	Gogo	299,417
Nyamwezi	363,258	Ha	289,712
Makonde (a)	339,989	Hehe	251,624
Haya	325,539	Nyakyusa	219,678
Chagga	318,167	Luguru	202,297

(a) Includes the Matabwe.

Source: (20) p. 42.

5. Fertility and Mortality Information derived from the 1948 Census

(a) ESTIMATED AGE-SPECIFIC FERTILITY RATES

Age	Per 1,000 women
18–22	180
23–27	185
28–32	180
33–37	135
38–42	75
43–47	40

Weighted fertility rate 160 per 1,000.

(b) LIVE BIRTHS

Age	Average no. per woman	Percentage distribution of women by number of live births							
		0	1	2	3	4	5	6	7 or more
16–45	2·6	30	15	13	10	9	7	5	11
46 and over	4·4	17	9	10	9	9	9	9	28

(c) INFANT WASTAGE RATE: women 16–45 per 1,000 live births

Tanganyika	172
Lake Province	203

An infant mortality rate of 254 per 1,000 is also used in one calculation.

(d) BIRTH AND DEATH RATES

Birth rate:	maximum 44 per 1,000
Death rate:	25 per 1,000

Source: Summarized from Martin (81).

6. Estimates of Fertility, Mortality and Natural Increase, 1957

(a) CRUDE BIRTH RATE of 46 per 1,000
(b) TOTAL FERTILITY RATE of 5·6 live births per woman
(c) RELATIVE AGE-SPECIFIC FERTILITY RATES

Age	Observed	Graduated
15–19	0·025	0·025
20–24	0·047	0·048
25–29	0·043	0·043
30–34	0·031	0·032
35–39	0·028	0·026
40–44	0·020	0·020
45–49	0·006	0·006

(d) AVERAGE LIVE BIRTHS per woman

16–45	2·8
46 and over	4·6

(e) CRUDE DEATH RATE of some 24 or 25 (possibly up to 30) per 1,000
(f) DEATHS IN FIRST YEAR OF LIFE per 1,000 children were born to women 16–45: 192. (See discussion in Report on comparison of this figure with 5(c) above.)
(g) LIFE EXPECTANCY AT BIRTH: between 35 and 40 years
(h) NATURAL INCREASE
  (i) from intercensal growth: 1·75 per cent.
  (ii) from birth and death rates: 2·1–2·2 per cent.

Source: Derived from data given in (20).

7. Migration: Percentage Analysis by Birthplace, 1957

Birthplace	Males	Females
Born in district where enumerated	82·4	85·0
Born elsewhere in Tanganyika	13·8	11·6
Born outside Tanganyika	3·8	3·4

Source: (20) p. 57.

8. (a) Education: Percentage Distribution for Adults, 1957

Education	16–45		46 and over	
	Male	Female	Male	Female
None or not stated	74·3	91·6	86·9	96·1
Primary	18·2	7·0	8·5	2·8
Middle	4·5	0·7	1·4	0·3
Secondary	0·4	—	0·1	—
School Certificate	0·1	—	—	—
Bush or other	1·7	0·4	1·8	0·6
Koran	0·8	0·3	1·3	0·2

Source: (20) p. 69.

8. (b) Percentage of Population attending Primary and Middle Schools, 1957

Sex	8–11	12–15
Male	62	6
Female	40	2
Total	51	4

Source: (20) p. 71.

NON-AFRICAN POPULATION

1. Non-African Population in Census Years

	1913	1921	1931	1948	1952	1957
Asian	9,440	10,209	25,144	46,254	59,739	76,536
European	5,336	2,447	8,228	10,648	17,885	20,598
Other (a)	6,001	4,782	7,648	13,258	17,870	25,996
Total	20,777	17,438	41,020	70,160	95,494	123,130

(a) Mainly Arab.

Source: (16) p. 10.

2. 84,466 (or 68·6 per cent) Lived in the 33 Gazetted Townships in 1957

Source: (16) p. 7.

N.B. See notes on similar entries earlier.

3. Asian Population by Age and Sex, 1957

Age	Male	Female	Total	Per cent
0–4	6,007	5,788	11,795	15·5
5–14	10,525	9,929	20,454	26·9
15–59	22,324	19,122	41,446	54·5
60 and over	1,354	934	2,288	3·0
Total (a)	40,210	35,773	75,983	100·0

(a) Excludes 'Not Stated'.

Source: (16) p. 14.

4. The Crude Birth Rate for the Asian Population probably Ranged between 33 and 38 per 1,000

THE CRUDE DEATH RATE may have been between 8 and 11 per 1,000.
THE RATE OF NATURAL INCREASE was probably of the order of 2·6 per cent.

Source: (16) pp. 41, 42.

UGANDA

AFRICAN POPULATION

1. African Population by Province, 1948 and 1959

Province	1948	1959	Increase (a) (per cent)	1959 Density (b) (per land sq. ml.)
Buganda	1,302,162	1,834,128	40·9	114
Eastern	1,508,512	1,872,949	24·2	171
Northern	943,175	1,244,971	32·0	39
Western	1,163,706	1,497,510	28·7	87
Total (c)	4,917,555	6,449,558	31·2	84

(a) District range from 12·6 to 48·0 (excluding Mbale Township).
(b) District range from 15·8 to 259·4 (excluding Mbale Township).
(c) Excludes persons in transit (1,415 in 1959).

Source: (27) pp. 1, 16, 17.

2. 247,404 (or 3·8 per cent) of Africans lived in Towns, Peri-urban Areas, or Trading Centres

Source: (27) p. 17.

N.B. See notes on similar entries earlier.

3. African Population by Age and Sex, 1959

Age group	Males		Females		Total	
	'000	%	'000	%	'000	%
All ages	3,237	100·0	3,213	100·0	6,450	100·0
Under 1	122	3·8	121	3·8	244	3·8
1–4	439	13·6	437	13·6	876	13·6
5–9	443	13·7	427	13·3	871	13·5
10–14	344	10·6	337	10·5	681	10·6
15–19	282	8·7	294	9·2	576	8·9
20–24	259	8·0	293	9·1	552	8·6
25–29	258	8·0	281	8·7	539	8·4
30–34	232	7·2	242	7·5	475	7·4
35–39	204	6·3	204	6·3	408	6·3
40–44	177	5·5	168	5·2	345	5·4
45–49	149	4·6	130	4·1	279	4·3
50–54	114	3·5	94	2·9	208	3·2
55–59	80	2·5	70	2·2	150	2·3
60–64	60	1·9	52	1·6	112	1·7
65–69	35	1·1	29	0·9	64	1·0
70–74	22	0·7	17	0·5	39	0·6
75–79	11	0·3	9	0·3	20	0·3
80 and over	7	0·2	6	0·2	13	0·2

Source: (27) p. 22.

4. African Population: Main Tribes, 1959

Baganda	1,048,642	Lango	363,807
Iteso	524,716	Bagiou	329,257
Banyakore	519,283	Acholi	284,929
Basoga	501,921	Lugbara	236,270
Bakiga	459,619	Batoro	208,300
Banyaruanda	378,656		

Source: (27) p. 18.

5. Fertility and Mortality Information Derived from the 1948 Census

(a) ESTIMATED AGE-SPECIFIC FERTILITY RATES

Age	Per 1,000 women
18–22	155
23–27	210
28–32	220
32–37	200
38–42	155
42–47	55

Weighted fertility rate 170.
(Figures exclude Northern Province.)

(b) LIVE BIRTHS

Age group	Average no. of live births	Percentage distribution of women by number of live births							
		0	1	2	3	4	5	6	7 or more
16–45	2·7	30	15	12	10	8	7	6	12
46 and over	4·8	18	6	7	7	8	9	10	35

(c) INFANT WASTAGE RATE: per 1,000 live births to women 16–45

Uganda	200
Buganda	207 (a)
Western	182 (a)

(a) See note to (27) Table IV, 19.

(d) BIRTH AND DEATH RATES:

Birth rate		Death rate	
Uganda	42 per 1,000	*Uganda*	25 per 1,000
Buganda	30 ,, ,,	Buganda	at least 20 ,, ,,
Eastern	48 ,, ,,	Eastern	30 ,, ,,
Western	45 ,, ,,	Western	25 ,, ,,

Source: Summarized from Martin (81).

6. Estimates of Fertility, Mortality and Natural Increase, 1957

(a) CRUDE BIRTH RATE of 42 per 1,000
(b) AGE SPECIFIC FERTILITY AND TOTAL FERTILITY RATES

Age group	Buganda	Eastern	Northern	Western	Uganda
15–19	0·1607	0·1207	0·0935	0·1148	0·1252
20–24	0·2370	0·2292	0·2451	0·2874	0·2475
25–29	0·2157	0·2007	0·2418	0·2567	0·2252
30–34	0·1694	0·1650	0·1959	0·2415	0·1894
35–39	0·1057	0·0971	0·1895	0·1716	0·1335
40–44	0·0579	0·0472	0·0754	0·0624	0·0588
45–49	0·0254	0·0329	0·0105	0·0642	0·0338
Total fertility rate	4·8590	4·4640	5·2585	5·9930	5·0670

(c) AVERAGE LIVE BIRTHS per woman:

16–45	2·84
46 and over	4·85

(d) CRUDE DEATH RATE: 20 per 1,000
(e) INFANT MORTALITY RATE: 160 per 1,000 live births
(f) LIFE EXPECTANCY AT BIRTH: about 42·5 years
(g) RATE OF NATURAL INCREASE: about 2·2 per 1,000

Source: **Derived from (27), except for (f)—private communication, Uganda Statistics Branch.**

7. Education: Extent of Schooling by Sex and Age Group (Thousands)

Age group	Sex	Never at school	Up to 4 years	5–6 years	7–9 years	10 years and over
6–15	Male	365	273	50	12	1
	Female	442	150	19	3	—
16–45	Male	778	327	148	76	30
	Female	1,248	174	50	16	6
Over 45	Male	344	51	13	5	2
	Female	352	10	2	1	—
Total	Male	1,487	651	210	93	33
	Female	2,041	333	71	19	6

Source: (27) p. 32.

NON-AFRICAN POPULATION

1. Non-African Population in Census Years

	1921	1931	1948	1959
Asian		14,150	35,215	71,933
European	(1,269)	2,001	3,448	10,866
Other		1,116	2,302	3,801
Total	6,873	17,267	40,965	86,600

Source: (28) p. 10.

2. 68,585 (or 78.8 per cent) lived in Towns and Trading Centres and about 8,000 more lived in Peri-Urban Areas, in 1959

Source: (28) pp. 9, 10.
N.B. See note to (2)'s earlier.

3. Asian Population by Age and Sex, 1959

Age group	Male	Female	Total	Per cent
0–4	6,144	5,858	12,002	16·8
5–14	11,029	10,410	21,439	29·9
15–59	19,916	16,840	36,756	51·3
60 and over	952	448	1,400	2·0
Total (a)	38,041	33,556	71,597	100·0

(a) Excludes 'Not stated'.

Source: (28) p. 14.

4. The Crude Birth Rate for the Asian Population was between 35–40 per 1,000, probably Nearer 40 than 35

THE CRUDE DEATH RATE was of the order of 10 per 1,000
THE RATE OF NATURAL INCREASE had been of the order of 3 per cent per annum

Source: (28).

ZANZIBAR

Source for all information: (32).

Key to racial classification: A Afro-Arab
B Asian other than Arab
C European
D Somali and other

1. Population in Census Years

	1921–24	1931	1948	1958
A	202,665	219,867	247,687	279,935
B	13,772	15,246	15,892	18,334
C	272	278	296	507
D	88	37	287	335
Total	216,797	235,428	264,162	299,111

Density in 1958: 293·1 per square mile. (pp. 19, 22.)

2. Urbanization, 1958

	Zanzibar Island		Pemba Island	
	Urban population	Per cent of total	Urban population	Per cent of total
A	46,711	31·4	14,375	11·0
B	15,196	96·6	2,221	85·6
C	438	97·3	54	94·7
D	291	97·0	1	2·9
Total	62,636	37·9	16,651	12·4

(pp. 21, 22.)

3. Population by Age Group, Sex and Racial Group, 1958

Age group	A		B		C		D		Total	
	M	F	M	F	M	F	M	F	M	F
Under 1	4,985	4,760	273	247	4	3	4	1	5,266	5,011
1–4	14,721	14,894	876	903	24	16	4	5	15,625	15,818
5–9	20,577	19,962	1,326	1,352	16	14	6	4	21,925	21,332
10–14	11,066	8,321	1,202	1,149	6	7	8	1	12,282	9,478
15–19	10,677	15,758	1,024	961	14	2	29	9	11,744	16,730
20–45	61,671	53,931	3,148	3,205	142	126	191	23	65,152	57,285
46 and over	23,673	14,659	1,555	1,109	80	53	42	8	25,350	15,829
Not stated	156	124	2	2	—	—	—	—	158	126
Total	147,526	132,409	9,406	8,928	286	221	284	51	157,502	141,609

(p. 26.)

4. (a) FERTILITY. There is a 'marked fertility differential between the Afro-Arab populations of Zanzibar and Pemba Islands: while the crude birth rate in Pemba is unlikely to be much below 40 per 1,000, that in Zanzibar cannot be much above, and is more probably under 30 per 1,000; while the total fertility rate in Pemba is certainly over 4, and may be as high as 4½, that in Zanzibar is probably under 3½ . . . these differences are largely attributable to the remarkably low fertility of Afro-Arabs in Zanzibar Town.' (p. 55.)

(b) MORTALITY. 'Crude death rates of between 20 and 24 per 1,000 and life expectancies at birth of between 40 and 45 years in both islands may be accepted with tolerable degree of certainty.' (p. 60.)

Deaths under 1 year per 1,000 live births: Afro-Arabs

Zanzibar Island	157
Pemba Island	171

(p. 60.)

(d) RATE OF GROWTH. 'For Afro-Arabs in Zanzibar Island, all indices point to a rate of growth of rather less than 1 per cent per annum. . . . For Afro-Arabs in Pemba, all the indices . . . point to rates of growth of rather more than 1½ per cent per annum.' (p. 62.)

EAST AFRICA

1. Total Population (excluding Zanzibar)

June	Total		African		Asian and Arab		European	
	'000s	Per cent	'000s	Per cent	'000s	Per cent	'000s	Per cent
1948								
K.	5,399	30·3	5,240	29·9	128	56·4	31	67·4
T.	7,461	41·9	7,389	42·2	61	26·9	11	23·9
U.	4,942	27·8	4,900	27·9	38	16·7	4	8·7
E.A.	17,802	100·0	17,529	100·0	227	100·0	46	100·0
1964								
K.	9,104	34·4	8,832	34·0	223	51·6	49	62·8
T.	9,990	37·8	9,849	38·0	121	28·0	40	25·6
U.	7,367	27·8	7,270	28·0	88	20·4	9	11·6
E.A.	26,461	100·0	25,951	100·0	432	100·0	78	100·0

Africans formed 98·1 per cent of the population in 1964.

2. Characteristics of African Population (excluding Zanzibar)

	Annual rate of growth per cent	Proportionate age and sex division at census dates (per cent)					
		Male			Female		
		Under 16	16 and over	Total	Under 16	16 and over	Total
K.	3·00	26·5	22·9	49·4	24·7	25·9	50·6
T.	1·75	22·2	25·9	48·1	22·1	29·8	51·9
U.	2·50	21·9	28·3	50·2	21·6	28·2	49·8
E.A. (a)	(2·40)	(23·6)	(25·5)	(49·1)	(22·8)	(28·1)	(50·9)

(a) Weighted average using 1962 population figures as weights.

3. Estimates of African Population 1921–63 (Millions)

	1921	1931	1939	1948	1963
K.	3·8	4·1	4·8	5·7	8·8
T.	5·9	6·0	6·5	7·4	9·8
U.	3·4	3·6	4·2	4·9	7·2
Z.	0·2	0·2	0·2	0·3	0·3
E.A.	13·3	13·9	15·7	18·3	26·2

Source: (75).

BIBLIOGRAPHY[1]

OFFICIAL

East Africa

1. *East Africa Royal Commission 1953–1955 Report*, Cmd. 9475, London, 1955.
2. Despatches from the Governors of Kenya, Uganda and Tanganyika and from the Administrator, East Africa High Commission, commenting on the *East Africa Royal Commission 1953–1955 Report*, Cmd. 9801, London, 1956.

Kenya

3. '*African population of Kenya Colony and Protectorate*', *Geographical and Tribal Studies*, East African Statistical Department, 1950.[2]
4. *Report on the Census of the Non-Native Population of Kenya Colony and Protectorate, 1948*, Nairobi, 1953.
5. 'Population growth in Kenya, 1948–1962', *Kenya Statistical Digest*, *1*(*1*), September 1963.
6. *Kenya Population Census, 1962*; Advance Report of Vols. I and II, Jan. 1964. *Kenya Population Census, 1962*, Vol. I, July 1964. 'Populations of Census Areas by sex and age group', *Kenya Population Census, 1962*, Vol. II, March 1965. 'Populations of locations and county council wards by race, tribe and sex', Statistics Division, Ministry of Economic Development and Planning, Nairobi.
7. 'Population growth and urbanisation in Kenya', *Kenya Statistical Digest 2*(*3*), September 1964.
8. 'Reported employment and earnings in Kenya', Economics and Statistics Division, Ministry of Finance and Economic Planning, Nairobi, 1963.
9. *Kenya Education Commission Report*, S. H. OMINDE, Chairman, Part I, Government Printer, Nairobi, 1964, Part II, Government Printer, Nairobi, 1965.
10. C. F. DAVIS, *High-level manpower: requirements and resources in Kenya, 1964–1970*, Government Printer, Nairobi, 1965.

Tanganyika

11. *The population of Tanganyika*, prepared by I. B. TAEUBER, United Nations, New York, 1949.
12. '*African population of Tanganyika Territory*', *Geographical and Tribal Studies*, East African Statistical Department, 1950.
13. *Additional information on the population of Tanganyika*, prepared by I. B. TAEUBER, with the collaboration of C. J. MARTIN, United Nations, New York, 1953.
14. *Report on the Census of the Non-Native Population, 1948*, Government Printer, Dar-es-Salaam, 1953.
15. *Report on the Census of the Non-Native Population, 1952*, Government Printer, Dar-es-Salaam, 1954.

16. *Report on the Census of the Non-Native Population, 1957*, Government Printer, Dar-es-Salaam, 1958.

17. *Tanganyika: African Population Census, August 1957, Tribal Analysis*: Part I Territorial/Provincial/District, Part II Territorial Census Area, East African Statistical Department, 1958.

18. *Tanganyika: African Population Census, 1957*, Analysis by sex and age for Province, District, and Territorial Census Area, East African Statistical Department, 1958.

19. *Tanganyika: Population Census, 1957*, Analysis of total population; certain analyses by race and sex, geographical area, age, religion, and nationality, East African Statistical Department, 1958.

20. *African Census Report, 1957*, Government Printer, Dar-es-Salaam, 1963.

21. M. J. B. MOLOHAN, *Detribalization*, Government Printer, Dar-es-Salaam, 1959.

22. *Employment and earnings in Tanganyika, 1963*, Central Statistical Bureau, United Republic of Tanganyika and Zanzibar, Dar-es-Salaam, 1964.

23. *Survey of the high level manpower requirements and resources for the five year development plan, 1964/65 to 1968/69*, Manpower Planning Unit, Directorate of Development and Planning, Office of the President, United Republic of Tanzania, 1964.

Uganda

24. *Report on the Census of the Non-Native Population of Uganda Protectorate, 1948*, Nairobi, 1953.

25. *'African population of Uganda Protectorate', Geographical and Tribal Studies*, East African Statistical Department, 1950.

26. *Uganda: General African Census, 1959*; Vol. I, Population by sex and age group (adults/children) to PCA (i.e. Parish level); Vol. II, Population by tribe and sex, Part 1 Protectorate by counties, Part 2 Buganda by division (sub-county), Part 3 Eastern Province by division (sub-county), Part 4 Northern Province by division (sub-county), Part 5 Western Province by division (sub-county), East African Statistical Department, 1960.

27. *Uganda Census, 1959, African Population*, Statistics Branch, Entebbe, 1961.

28. *Uganda Census 1959, Non-African Population*, East African Statistical Department, 1960.

29. *Enumeration of employees, June 1963*, Statistics Division, Ministry of Planning and Community Development, Entebbe, 1964.

30. *Education in Uganda*, The Report of the Uganda Education Commission 1963, Government Printer, Entebbe, 1963.

Zanzibar

31. *Notes on the Census of the Zanzibar Protectorate, 1948*, Zanzibar, 1953.

32. *Report on the Census of the Population of the Zanzibar Protectorate, 1958*, Government Printer, 1960.

OTHER

33. ABRAHAMS, R. G., 'Kahama Township, Western Province, Tanganyika', in SOUTHALL, A. W. (ed.), *Social change in modern Africa*, London, 1961.

34. ADAM, V., 'Migrant Labour from Ihanzu (Tanganyika)', *Proceedings of the EAISR Conference, January 1963*, Pt. C, Kampala, 1963.

35. BARBER, W., *Some questions about labour force analysis in agrarian economies with particular reference to Kenya*, Discussion Paper No. 13, Centre for Economic Research, Nairobi.

36. BELSHAW, D. G. R., 'An outline of resettlement policy in Uganda 1945–63', *Proceedings of the EAISR Conference, June, 1963*, Pt. E, Kampala, 1963.

37. BLACKER, J. G. C., 'Fertility trends of the Asian population of Tanganyika', *Population Studies*, Vol. XIII, No. 1, July 1959.

38. BLACKER, J. G. C., 'Population Growth and Differential Fertility in Zanzibar Protectorate', *Population Studies*, Vol. XV (3), March 1962.

39. BLACKER, J. G. C., 'The Demography of East Africa', in RUSSELL, E. W., *The Natural Resources of East Africa*, Nairobi, 1962.

40. BLACKER, J. G. C., 'Population growth in East Africa', *Economic and Statistical Review*, E.A. Statistical Department, September 1963.

41. BLACKER, J. G. C. and MARTIN, C. J., 'Old and new methods of compiling vital statistics in East Africa', *International Population Conference, New York, 1961*, Union Internationale pour l'étude scientifique de la population, London, 1963.

42. BRASS, W., 'Differentials in child mortality by the marriage experience of the mothers in six African Communities', *International Population Conference, Vienna, 1959*, Union internationale pour l'étude scientifique de la population, Vienna, 1959.

43. ELKAN, W., 'An African Labour Force', EAST AFRICAN STUDIES, No. 7, Kampala, 1956.

44. ELKAN, W., *Migrants and Proletarians: Urban labour in the economic development of Uganda*, London, 1960.

45. ELKAN, W., 'Labour for industrial development in East Africa', in *Urbanization in African social change*, Edinburgh, 1963.

46. ETHERINGTON, D. M., 'Projected Changes in Urban and Rural Population in Kenya and the Implications for Development Policy', *East African Economic Review*, Vol. 1 (2), June 1965.

47. EVANS, W. J. M., 'A survey of a tropical area (Mlalo Basin, Tanganyika)', *Journal of the Royal Sanitary Institute*, 70 (5), September 1950.

48. GALE, G. W., 'Food Balance Sheets for the African populations of East Africa', Proceedings of a scientific conference on the Origin and Effects of Malnutrition in Man and Animals, *East African Medical Journal*, 37 (5), May 1960, Dar-es-Salaam, 1960.

49. FEARN, H., Population as a factor in land usage in Nyanza Province of Kenya Colony, *East African Agricultural Journal*, 20 (3), Jan. 1955.

50. GOLDTHORPE, J. E., 'Attitudes to the Census and Vital Registration in East Africa', *Population Studies*, Vol. VI (2), November 1952.

51. GOLDTHORPE, J. E., 'Population trends and family size in Uganda', *Proceedings of the World Population Conference, 1954*, Papers: Vol. VI, United Nations, New York, 1955.

52. GOLDTHORPE, J. E., *Outlines of East African Society*, Makerere University College, Kampala, 1962.

53. GOLDTHORPE, J. E., 'An African Elite: Makerere College Students 1922–1960', *East African Studies*, No. 17, Nairobi, 1965.

54. GOLDTHORPE, J. E. and WILSON, F. B., 'Tribal maps of East Africa', *East African Studies*, No. 13, Kampala, 1960.

55. GOUROU, P., 'Une paysannerie africaine au milieu du XXe siecle. Le Kikuyu et la crise Mau-Mau', *Les Cahiers d'Outre-Mer*, 7 (28), 1954.

56. GRIFFITH, H. B., 'Gonorrhea and fertility in Uganda', *Eugenics Review*, 55 (2), July 1963.

57. GULLIVER, P. H., 'The population of Karamoja', *Uganda Journal*, 17 (2), September 1953.

58. GULLIVER, P. H., 'Labour migration in a rural economy. A study of the Ngoni and Ndendeuli of Southern Tanganyika', *East African Studies*, No. 6, Kampala, 1955.

59. GULLIVER, P. H., 'Nyakyusa Labour Migration', *Rhodes-Livingstone Journal*, No. 21, March 1957.

60. GULLIVER, P. H., 'Land Tenure and Social Change among the Nyakyusa', *East African Studies*, No. 11, Kampala, 1958.

61. GULLIVER, P. H., 'The population of Arusha Chiefdom: a high density area in East Africa', *The Rhodes-Livingstone Journal*, No. 28, December 1960.

62. HEISCH, R. B., 'Survey of the Kerio Valley', *East African Medical Journal*, 27 (6), June 1950.

63. HOMAN, F. DEREK, 'Land consolidation and redistribution of population in the Imenti sub-tribe of the Meru (Kenya)', in BIEBUYCK, D. (ed.), *African Agrarian Systems*, London, 1963.

64. HUNTER, G., *Education for a developing region. A study in East Africa*, London, 1963.

65. ILLINGWORTH, S., 'Kenyans in Busoga', *Proceedings of the EAISR Conference, June 1963*, Pt. E, Kampala, 1963.

66. JOLLY, R., 'Stocks and flows in Uganda education; the links between education and manpower', *Proceedings of the EAISR Conference*, Pt. B, Kampala, 1964.

67. JOLLY, R. and RADO, E., 'Education in Uganda—reflections on the Report of the Uganda Education Commission', *East African Economic Review*, Vol. 1 New Series, 1964.

68. KAMOGA, F. K., 'Divorce and School Leavers in Buganda', *Proceedings of the EAISR Conference, January 1963*, Pt. B, Kampala.

69. KENDALL, H., *Town Planning in Uganda*, Government Printer, Entebbe, 1955.

70. KUCZYNSKI, R. R., *Demographic Survey of the British Colonial Empire*, Vol. II, East Africa etc., London, 1949.

71. LARIMORE, A. E., *The Alien Town*, Research Paper No. 55, Chicago: University of Chicago Department of Geography, 1958.

72. LAURIE, W., BRASS, W. and HOPE TRANT, *East African Medical Survey: a health survey in Bukoba District*, East African High Commission, 1954.

73. LESLIE, J. A. K., *A survey of Dar-es-Salaam*, London, 1963.

74. LORIMER, F., *Demographic information on Tropical Africa*, Boston University Press, 1961.

75. LURY, D. A., 'East African Population Estimates: Back Projections of Recent Census Results', *Economic and Statistical Review*, E.A. Statistical Dept., Nairobi, September 1965.

76. MALECHE, A. J., 'A study of wastage in primary schools in Uganda', *Proceedings of the EAISR Conference, December 1960*, Kampala, 1961.

77. MALECHE, A. J., 'Wastage among school leavers in West Nile 1959 and 1960', *Proceedings of EAISR Conference, January 1962*, Kampala, 1962.

78. MARTIN, C. J., 'The East African Population Census, 1948: Planning and Enumeration', *Population Studies*, Vol. III (3), December 1949.

79. MARTIN, C. J., 'Colonial statistics, A discussion opened,' by SEARLE, W. F., PHILLIPS, E. J. and MARTIN, C. J., *Journal of the Royal Statistical Society*, A113 (3), 1950.

80. MARTIN, C. J., 'A demographic study of an immigrant community: the Indian population of British East Africa', *Population Studies*, Vol. VI (3), March 1953.

81. MARTIN, C. J., 'Some estimates of the general age distribution, fertility and rate of natural increase of the African population of British East Africa', *Population Studies*, Vol. VII (2), November 1953.

82. MARTIN, C. J., *The collection of basic demographic data in under-developed countries*, Bull. International Statistical Institute 34 (3), 1954.

83. MARTIN, C. J., 'A method of measuring fertility in under-developed countries where birth registration is non-existent or defective', *Proceedings of the World Population Conference, 1954*, Papers: Volume IV, United Nations, New York, 1955.

84. MARTIN, C. J., 'Population Census estimates and methods in British East Africa', in BARBOUR, K. M. and PROTHERO, R. M., *Essays on African Population*, London, 1961.

85. MARTIN, C. J., 'The relationship of the labour force in East Africa to economic development', *International Population Conference, New York, 1961*, Union Internationale pour l'étude scientifique de la population, London, 1963.

86. MIDDLETON, J. F. N. and GREENLAND, D. J., 'Land and Population in West Nile District, Uganda', *Geographical Journal*, Vol. CXX (4), December 1954.

87. MORGAN, W. T. W., *Kenya: Population Distribution Map, 1962* (1 : 1 million), Department of Geography, University College, Nairobi, 1963.

88. MORGAN, W. T. W., *Kenya: Density of Population Map, 1962*, Department of Geography, University College, Nairobi, 1964.

89. MORRIS, S., 'Indians in East Africa', *British Journal of Sociology*, 7 (3), September 1956.

90. MUNGER, E. S., *Relational Patterns of Kampala, Uganda*, Research Paper No. 21, Chicago, University of Chicago, Department of Geography, 1951.

91. NHONOLI, A. M., 'An enquiry into the infant mortality rate in rural areas of Unyamwezi', *East African Medical Journal*, 31, 1954.

92. OGOT, B. A. and ODHIAMBO, T. R. (eds.), 'East African Brain Power', *East African Journal*, Nairobi, August 1965.

93. OMINDE, S. H., 'Movement to Towns from Nyanza Province, Kenya', in *Urbanization in African social change*, Edinburgh, 1963.

94. OMINDE, S. H., 'Problems of land and population in the Lake Districts of Western Kenya', *Proceedings of the Inaugural Symposium of the East African Academy*, Nairobi, 1964.

95. OMINDE, S. H., 'Population movement to the main urban areas in Kenya', *Cahiers d'Etudes Africaines*, 20, pp. 593–617.

96. OMINDE, S. H., 'Rural population patterns and problems of the Kikuyu, Embu and Meru Districts of Kenya', *Second Proceedings of the East African Academy* (in press).

97. OMINDE, S. H., *The ethnic map of the Republic of Kenya*, Department of Geography, University College, Nairobi, 1965.

98. PARK, G. K., 'The problem of late marriage of Kinga women', *Proceedings of the EAISR Conference*, July 1962, Kampala, 1962.

99. PERLMAN, M. L., 'Some aspects of marriage stability in Toro, Uganda', *Proceedings of the EAISR Conference*, Part I, December 1960, Part II, January 1962, Kampala, 1962.

100. POWESLAND, P. G. (ed. ELKAN, W.), 'Economic Policy and Labour', *East African Studies*, No. 10, Kampala, 1957.

101. PURSEGLOVE, J. W., 'Kigezi Resettlement', *Uganda Journal* 14 (2), September 1950.

102. RAO, G. RAGHAVA, 'Indian immigrants in Kenya—a survey', *Indian Economic Journal*, 4 (1), July 1956. For comment also see 4 (3) and 5 (2).

103. RICHARDS, A. I. and REINING, P. 'Report on fertility surveys in Buganda and Buhaya', in LORIMER, F. (ed.), *Culture and Human Fertility*, UNESCO, 1954.

104. RICHARDS, A. I. (ed.), *Economic development and tribal change: a study of immigrant labour in Buganda*, Cambridge (Eng.), 1954.

105. RICHARDS, A. I. (ed.), *East African Chiefs*, London, 1960.

106. ROBERTS, D. F. and TANNER, R. E. S., 'A demographic study of an area of low fertility in north-east Tanganyika', *Population Studies*, Vol. XIII (1), July 1959.

107. SCAFF, A. H., 'The re-development of Kisenyi (Kampala); progress report of the UN Urban Planning Mission to Uganda', *Proceedings of the EAISR Conference*, Part E, Kampala, 1964.

108. SILBERMAN, L., 'Social Survey of the Old Town of Mombasa', *Journal of African Administration*, 2, 1950.

109. SMITH, T. E. and BLACKER, J. G. C., *Population characteristics of the Commonwealth Countries of Tropical Africa.*

110. SOFER, C. *and* R. 'Jinja Transformed', *East African Studies*, No. 4, Kampala, 1955.

111. SOUTHALL, A. W., 'Population movements in East Africa', in BARBOUR, K. N. and PROTHERO, R. M., *Essays on African Population*, London, 1961.

112. SOUTHALL, A. W. and GUTKIND, P. C. W., 'Townsmen in the making', *East African Studies*, No. 9, Kampala, 1957.

113. TANNER, R. E. S., 'Sukuma Fertility; an analysis of 148 marriages in Mwanza District', *East African Medical Journal* 33 (3), March 1956.

114. TANNER, R. E. S., 'Fertility and child mortality in cousin marriages. A study in a Moslem community in East Africa (Pangani, Tanganyika)', *Eugenics Review*, 49 (4), January 1958.

115. TEMPLE, P. H., 'Kampala: influences upon its growth and development', *Proceedings of the EAISR Conference, June 1963*, Pt. B, Kampala, 1963.

116. TITMUS, R. M. (Chairman), *The Health Services of Tanganyika*, London, 1964.

117. TREWARTHA, G. T., 'New Population Maps of Uganda, Kenya, Nyasaland and Gold Coast', *Ann. Assn. Amer. Geog.* 47, March 1957.

118. TROWELL, H. C., DAVIES, J. N. P., and DEAN, R. F. A., *Kwashiorkor*, London, 1954.

119. WILSON, G., 'Mombasa—a modern colonial municipality', in SOUTHALL, A. W. (ed.), *Social change in modern Africa*, London, 1961.

120. WILSON, P. N. and WATSON, J. M., 'Two surveys of Kasilang, Erony', *Uganda Journal*, 20 (2), September 1956. See also correspondence in 21 (2), September 1957.

ADDITIONAL REFERENCES

121. *Medical and Health Services in Uganda* (Frazer Committee), Government Printer, Entebbe, 1956.

122. *Sample Population Census of Nairobi, 1957/58. An Experiment in sampling methods*, E.A. Statistical Dept.—Kenya Unit, June 1958.

123. ALLAN, W., *The African Husbandman*, Edinburgh, 1965.

124. OGOT, B. A., 'The movement of peoples in East Africa', in OGOT, B. A. (ed.), *East Africa past and present*, Paris, 1964.

125. DUNLAE, A. R., 'Mutala Survey of Bujenje', *Uganda Journal*, 29 (1), 1965.

126. MORRIS, H. F., 'Marriage and Divorce in Uganda', *Uganda Journal*, 24 (2), 1960.

127. SOUTHALL, A. W., 'On Chastity in Africa', *Uganda Journal*, 24 (2), 1960.

128. TURYAGYENDA, J. D., 'Overpopulation and its effects in Buhaea, Kigezi', *Uganda Journal*. 28 (2), 1964.

129. J. BOUTE, *La Démographie de la branche indo-pakistanaise d'Afrique*, Louvain–Paris, 1965,

130. *Kenya Population Census, 1962, Vol. III: African Population*. Statistics Division, Ministry of Economic Planning and Development, Nairobi, 1966.

131. *Kenya Population Census, 1962, Vol. IV: Non-African Population*. Statistics Division, Ministry of Economic Planning and Development, Nairobi, 1966.

Footnotes

1. For references to earlier publications see Kuczynski (70). I have not yet seen the papers of the 1965 Belgrade Conference and there are therefore no references to them. I have not seen items (47), (55), (91) and (114), which have been taken over from the useful annotated bibliography in Lorimer (74). General anthropological studies have been omitted.

2. It may be useful to add a note about this Department. The East African Statistical Department was set up in 1946 with offices in Nairobi and became a Department in the East African High Commission. Sub-offices were soon established in Dar-es-Salaam and Entebbe, and as the demand of the territorial governments expanded, the functions of these sub-offices increased. In 1957 separate Units were established in each of the three East African countries, but the Department remained in the High Commission as a whole, and there was still some central control and co-ordination. In 1961 the Department broke up, the Units transferring to the governments of the countries in which they were operating. The office dealing with East African affairs remained in the East African administration (now known as the East African Common Services Organization) and inherited the name of the East African Statistical Department. Earlier publications under that name are however, generally now available (if still in print) from the present statistics offices in the countries to which they refer.

5 Problems of data collection for population studies in Nigeria with particular reference to the 1952/53 census and the Western Region

R. C. Duru

Department of Geography, University of Lagos, Nigeria

The United Nations Draft Recommendation of 1960 defined a census of population as the total process of collecting, compiling and publishing demographic data pertaining at a particular time to all persons in a defined territory. It follows that unless the results of a canvas have been published, the census cannot be said to have been completed. The *1960 Draft Recommendations* go further to state that the essential characteristics of a census are universality, simultaneity, compilation of data by the individual, and precise definition of the territory covered. Without the compilation and publication of data by geographic areas and by basic demographic variables no census figures are available. The most recent census of Western Nigeria according with this definition was that taken in 1952–53.

Population studies in Western Nigeria call for three forms of data, namely up-to-date population data, vital statistics and migration figures. In Western Nigeria, there is no record of movements of persons into or out of the Region. The crude figures given in the published census are such that evaluation is almost impossible. Certain places are erroneously located in the existing maps. Names on some maps are those of villages that either have changed their names or are really parts of a major settlement group known by a different name.

Immense difficulties are encountered in the determination of such personal characteristics as age and educational status. The census authorities have so far excluded from their questionnaires some important types of questions relating to economic characteristics, household situation and social data. From the census questionnaire it is not possible to differentiate between the economically active and the economically inactive population. The list of occupations is grossly inadequate. There are no records for secondary occupation, time spent at work or gross income. The nature of family dependency, nuptiality and fertility as well as details of educational attainments cannot be deduced from the available censuses. Finally, such social data as physical and mental disabilities, migration, military service and family expenditures are not provided in the system of census-taking employed in the country.

There has been no systematic study of the limitations inherent in the censuses, hence in the Nigerian census reliance has been on methods found satisfactory in other countries. Despite increasing expenditure of time and money these have resulted in levels of accuracy that are generally below average. A fairly detailed study of the conduct of the census of 1952–53, which is still the principal source of demographic data in Western Nigeria, will serve to illustrate the problems faced in data collection in the Region.

The 1952 Census

The value of population statistics as a tool for planning administration and development seems to have been better appreciated since the Second World War. During this time a strong national consciousness developed among the peoples of Nigeria, partly due to the propaganda machinery of the government and partly due to the great trade boom in export commodities. After the war the boom continued, and return of the ex-servicemen strengthened the growth of national consciousness. By 1951, the nation was prepared for another census count.

Preparations for the 1952 census began in 1950. It was decided that the count should be simultaneous, not only to obtain figures that would refer to some specific point in time, but also to avoid counting persons twice or omitting them. However, the Government Statistician, designated Census Superintendent, found it impracticable to have a simultaneous count in the three regions of Nigeria, and the census was therefore held in three different periods of the year.

The Divisions of Brass, Degema, Ogoni, Opobo and Eket are the main areas where the deltaic and coastal creeks of Eastern Nigeria impose a grave handicap to the successful completion of census counts. The southern portions of Ahoada, excluding the metropolitan area of Port Harcourt and the south and south-eastern portions of Calabar Province, also involved difficulties. The rainfall figures for the month of June are as follows: Brass 27 inches, Degema 18 inches, Opobo Town 30 inches, Port Harcourt 13 inches and Calabar Town 16 inches. The number of rainy days in this area is above 20 in Brass, Degema and part of Opobo and Eket Divisions. Rain falls all the year round in this area but the fall does not exceed 2·5 inches in most areas in December and January. By February, however, the number of rainy days increases to five in most areas, and the monthly rainfall mean lies between 3·5 and 4 inches. Rains increase rapidly after March, and by the beginning of June the top layers of most clay loams or pure clay soils become water-logged and swampy in several districts. The roads are mostly loose surfaced and become impassable to motor vehicles. The Report in the *Census Bulletin* overlooked this fact but recorded a suspected overcount in Degema Division. It is easier in the Nigerian environment to detect a possible overcount than to estimate an undercount. In the Report it was held that the 50 per cent increase over the 1931 census figures noted in the Degema Division was not recorded anywhere else in the Region and that the figures were three times the size of those estimated.

Because of political disturbances in parts of Eastern Nigeria, no real counts were taken in 1931. Estimates and computations making use of the figures obtained in 1931 are likely to be erroneous. It was the opinion of the Government Statistician that the 1931 census was more likely to have been an undercount than an overcount. If estimates for the number of people in 1952 were based on 1931 figures, the fault of underestimation might be expected. Buchanan and Pugh stated that the apparent increase 'must be attributed in part to an underestimate of the 1931 population.'[1] In fact the Report issued on the 1952 census stated that 'the census has demonstrated that in 1952 when the region's population was estimated at 5·8 million, it must in fact have been about 7·8 million or 34 per cent more than had been thought.'

Poor communications in the riverine area of Nigeria militated against a complete count in 1952–53. In places it took two weeks to reach settlement sites within an enumeration area. Other small settlements, notably fishing hamlets, were completely omitted. Even though the count in most of the Rivers Province was taken in April, it was already difficult to travel from one place to another. The recount that was taken to confirm the claim that the figures were inflated in Degema showed a 4 per cent increase on the estimate as compared with the 22 per cent of the first count. The recount could itself have been an undercount. At the time of the 1952 census no air photo cover existed for Degema Division; indeed there were no accurate topographical maps nor was there a complete list of all villages and settlements for checking the completeness of the census count.

In the towns, where the difficulties of reaching remote hamlets and homesteads did not exist, counting was completed in one day with each enumerator counting about 1,400 persons. Because the 1952 census was the first real count in Eastern Nigeria, neither the enumerators nor the people counted appreciated the need for accuracy in giving absolute numbers and details of demographic characteristics. The value of the vital statistics so obtained varied, therefore, with the calibre of each enumerator as well as that of the persons being counted. The figures obtained for age were definitely of questionable accuracy. If this was the case in Eastern Nigeria, such data would have been much more questionable for Northern Nigeria.

This was probably why no attempts were made in the 1931 census to obtain details about age in number of years for Northern Nigeria. There people were classed simply as adults and non-adults. The 1952 census for Northern Nigeria was taken at a suitable time, namely July when, because of the rains, the grass on which the cattle feed was growing luxuriantly. This had the effect of keeping the rural population stationary to a great extent and of preventing the nomadic cattle-rearers from migrating into Eastern and Western Nigeria. But factors militating against the accuracy of population statistics were still numerous and in certain areas serious. The questionable figures obtained for Ilorin Province, which returned a conspicuously high figure, were accepted uncorrected. No sample or full-scale recount was undertaken. It was also impossible to obtain a reliable figure for the mobile family units of the cattle Fulani.

The people connected with this seasonal movement are mostly Fulani herdsmen; though Hausa migrant labourers are also involved. Substantial numbers of both groups move southwards during the long dry season. Not all the herdsmen travel as far as southern Nigeria. But migrant farmers find work in farm lands of southern Nigeria where they stay through the planting season, returning with the rains in time for the northern planting season. No official records exist as to the exact or estimated numbers of these migrants.[2]

The error in the north was probably one of deficit rather than excess. Despite the fact that 13,000 officers were used for the enumeration, the task of completing the count within the time limit was considerable. Some offices, like those in Bauchi and Yola, were poorly staffed, overworked, and faced with inadequate means of transportation to cover considerable distances, all of which made the counting very slow. Gross errors in the total numbers counted and deficiencies in the answers obtained almost certainly resulted.

In several Divisions, in the absence of enough educated people, semi-literate persons were drafted to assist the staff of local authorities. The employment of the staff of local authorities heightened the fear and suspicion in rural districts that the census was to be used to compile a new tax register. Most of the vast expanse of the Northern Region could not be reached by the publicity organization established by the Government Statistician in Lagos. In the case of the Eastern and Western Regions, the radio, press, mobile cinema, gramophones, posters and leaflets proved very effective. But in the Northern Region the effects of these could be felt to any degree of intensity only in districts immediately adjacent to each of the provincial administrative headquarters. Because most of the population of Northern Nigeria is illiterate, the newspapers, posters and leaflets conveyed little meaning to them. The impression lingered that the census was a device for registering more taxable adults, and, as a result, a number of adults were not counted.

However, it should be appreciated that the 1952–53 census was restricted to modest goals. It was not expected that with the available resources an accurate inventory of complete demographic statistics could be produced. The enumeration was of a *de facto* type, and in any given enumeration area only persons who were actually resident there on the day of the census were counted. If rigidly followed, this method has the advantage of preventing persons from being counted more than once, first in their houses or places of origin and again in their places of usual residence.

Another feature of the census was the distinction between African and non-African population. This division was made on the basis of approximate colour. White South Africans, for instance, were not regarded as 'Africans'. The reasons for the distinction were, one, to make it possible to employ the group count method, whereby only the name of the head of the household or the compound was recorded, and two, to provide a rough check for use by immigration officers. One cannot fail to wonder whether these reasons justify the distinction made. Presumably, the individual count method could apply equally well for African as for non-African population. Indeed, it would help check the known practice of inflating the number of wives and children, a fact that has reduced the accuracy of later censuses. However, it should be realized that the group count method was decided upon in recognition of the actual situation in parts of the country, where, for religious reasons, individual counts of wives in purdah could not be carried out. Again the use of the group count system for inflating the population figures was not foreseen during the census planning but subsequent censuses might be criticized for not discarding this defective system. The funds available for the census no doubt limited the number of enumerators that could be employed and this in turn limited the amount of detail that could be collected from each enumeration area. Households comprising non-African husbands and African wives were counted by the 'individual' method.

There were therefore two schedules. Each provided for the breakdown of data for households by sex, age, occupational group, tribal origin, literacy and religion.

Age and Sex Characteristics

It is usual to assist the analysis of population growth and population composition by constructing population pyramids from quinquennial age groups. This cannot be done with 1952–53 census data as the census gave figures for groups whose age class intervals vary from two years to well over 34 years. Figures were given for males and females but in the following form: Under 2, 2–6, 7–14, 15–49, 50 and over.

Comparative studies of demographic variables by regions can however be achieved. It is clear also that the nature of differences in the potential labour force and in fertility can be deduced from the proportions of people in the age group 15–49 years. By giving the age groups percentage values and depicting the situation on a micro-regional basis, a measure of a real differentiation can be achieved. Other areal correlations can be attempted by superimposing either a hypothetical age/sex pyramid or an age/sex pyramid constructed with mean values for the different age groups recorded throughout the region.

This type of demographic work provides reasonable material, subject to the following assumptions: one, that faults in the later censuses are in the same sense and form as in the 1952–53 census, and two, that the distortion seen in the classification of persons by sex and age is of uniform occurrence in each part of the region. There is usually under-reporting of males around 15 years of age but reliable reporting of females of that age, even though married girls sometimes raise their ages to the legal marital level. The result of this is an excess of females over males in the age group 15–49 as recorded in the census reports, and an excess of males over females in the reported age group 7–14. Older people in many rural districts exaggerate the number of years they have lived. This is so because the aged are exempt from taxation and also because in several areas village headship is based on seniority.

Ultimately, age and sex data could be improved if birth registration were extended to all parts of the Region, as has been the case in Lagos, so that exact birth dates would be known. Hospitals, maternity centres and voluntary organizations, notably missionary institutions that encourage the baptism of infants, provide useful records of dates of birth. These records, however, do not contain complete information about the dates of birth of all persons in any one geographic unit area nor do they contain the dates of birth of all persons in any one age group.

Occupational Structure

There are still no specific studies of the occupational structure and characteristics of the Nigerian population. The categories adopted for the purpose of the census were very broad. Six occupational groups for men and three for women were distinguished. These included for men: Agriculture and Fishing; Crafts; Trading and Clerical Work; Administrative, Professional and Technical Work; Other Occupations; and Other Males Not Working (including all boys under 15 years). They included for women: Agriculture and Fishing; Trading and Clerical Work; and Other Females including females in other occupations (and all girls under 15 years). Combinations of occupation created difficulties in determining the occupation to which some persons should be assigned.

Ethnic Groups

The 1952–53 census of Nigeria distinguished ten tribal groups. The other four columns in this section of the schedule recorded persons who belonged to the other tribes which are important in their Provinces but are not numerically large, for instance the Igbirra tribal group in Northern Nigeria, the Urhobos in Mid-Western Nigeria and the Ijaws in Eastern Nigeria. No other inventory for tribal origins of all Nigerian peoples exists anywhere. If the recording of tribal origins is to be attempted on a national scale, it would be proper if no individual tribe were to be left out irrespective of its size. The rate of dispersion of tribes provides a strong clue to the economic and cultural unity of the people. This is in contrast to the ancient migrations of persons from places within and without Nigeria to their present dwelling areas, which were accomplished in tribal and ethnic groups.

Figures quoted for each of the ten tribal groups were on a district basis. This creates the misleading impression that 'strangers' live in all parts of each district. The fact is, however, that in eastern Yorubaland, where most of the forest products, notably rubber and palm produce, come from, the 'strangers' are found mainly in rural communities living in camps as in eastern Ekiti and Owo Divisions of Ondo Province. In contrast, in the savanna open forest and western cocoa belt the 'strangers' live in the towns either mixed up with the local populations or in district settlements, the most notable of which is the 'Sabo' settlement.

Literacy

The attempt in the 1952 census to enumerate those who had reached at least Standard II and those who could write in Roman script yielded results which are unacceptable in several places. Standard II is attained after one has spent three to four years in a primary school. Nevertheless, the figures show that whereas a fairly large number of people in each settlement claim to have reached this standard of education at one time or another, only a small number of them can write a simple text or passage in Roman script. Although persons who have learnt to read and write can lose this ability as a result of lack of practice, the great demand for literate persons at this time makes it probable that the percentage of persons so affected was small indeed. Therefore the disparity between the two sets of figures—namely the number that had reached Standard II and over and the number able to write in Roman script—is due to the improper definition of the terms in the questionnaires, or to inaccurate enumerators, or provided by persons questioned. In some areas the number of people who are able to write in Roman script exceeds the number of people who have attained Standard II. In a majority of cases, however, the reverse is true. This variation in opposite directions clearly suggests that the meaning of the question was not properly explained to the people.

The table below provides an example of the disparity:

OWO TOWN

	Education (Standard II or over)	Literacy (able to write in Roman script)
Owo Town	3,576	797
Emine Ile	195	1
Amuerin	18	22
Isho	97	155
Yakoyo (Ife Division)	128	—

Source: (60).

Religion

Even though the schedule carried columns for recording the major religious groups, the final report omitted this valuable piece of information.

The Conduct of the 1952 Census

A census constitutes the total process of collecting, compiling and publishing demographic, economic and social data pertaining at a specified time or times to all inhabitants of a given administrative area. It is in fact a composite operation, but the different steps or series of steps constituting it are interrelated. Each of these steps needs to be carefully planned and meticulously carried out. Each census reflects the government's appreciation of the fact that population statistics serve as a tool for town and country planning, economic development and frictionless administration. The conduct of the census shows the degree of co-operation that the intellectuals and the politicians have accorded to each other and to the government. In the conduct of the census in Nigeria, the place of the politician, who is usually neither a civil servant nor a demographer, is particularly conspicuous. The politician plays a leading rôle in educating people in his constituency as to the value of the census. His interest is often not completely in the accuracy of statistical data as a tool for nation-building.

An objective approach to all the problems of census-taking is indispensable if an accurate assessment of the human resources of a country is to be obtained. How well this can be achieved rests to a great extent with the census staff.

Planning

The 1952–53 census of Nigeria was conducted by the Federal Department of Statistics, Lagos, under the direction of the Government Statistician. Regional census officers supervised the census in the Regions. The whole country was divided into census areas coinciding with administrative divisions; some towns were treated as census areas. These were further divided into census districts. A census supervisor who was responsible to a census officer was placed in charge of a team of enumerators drawn wherever possible from the areas in which they were to count people. Enumerators were reliable persons, mainly teachers and students from the neighbourhood. Census officers were District Officers. Some additional staff, such as divisional supervisors and temporary clerks, was engaged for administrative work. The census officers were charged with the duty of training their field staff of enumerators.

One unhappy fact was that the majority of staff used for the census was not well trained for the census-taking. Several of the District Officers who became census officers had no previous education on the statistical value of the census. Those District Officers, who were then charged with the responsibility of training the enumerators, were probably no better than their counterparts in Ghana, one of whom frankly confessed his limited knowledge of the subject in these words: 'Had I known before leaving London that I was to be placed in charge of the census, I would have spent part of my leave in study of the subject, more especially in consideration of those statistics which would be most accurately collected under the conditions . . .'

Thus, training was given to a considerable extent by untrained staff. The field staff was impelled not so much by an understanding of, or interest in, the job they were to undertake, as by the extra income that would accrue to them on the completion of the task. Speaking on the question of training, the Government Statistician stated that 'training was left to census officers and their methods varied with type of district. In some cases staff were brought to the centre; in others, they were trained in groups at outlying stations . . . No definite programme was laid down for training periods . . . Some Divisional Supervisors were sent to the Regional Census Office for training but it was generally considered that the handbook and instructions were inadequate. . . .' Not only were the census officers themselves badly trained but they also had their normal duties to attend to as District Officers, and several possessed little knowledge of the people and the land area to which they were assigned.

Conclusion

This paper has attempted to sketch the inadequacies of existing demographic data from Western Nigeria for work and research in population studies. Problems of planning, illiteracy, staff and physical conditions handicapped the collection of data. Furthermore the problems encountered in compiling a population inventory become all the larger when economic and social statistics are also required, as with geographic demography, to help explain areal variation in demographic characteristics.

Footnotes

1. K. M. Buchanan and J. C. Pugh, *Land and People in Nigeria*, London, 1955.
2. Details can be obtained from:
   (i) D. S. STENNING, *Savannal Nomads*, London, 1959.
   (ii) A. T. GROVE, *Land and Population in Katrine Province*, 1957.
   (iii) M. CHISHOLM, in *Nigerian Geographical Journal*, Vol. 7, No. 2, December 1964.

REFERENCES

BARBOUR, K. M., *Population in Africa—a geographer's approach*, Ibadan, March 1963.
BLACKER, J. G. C., *Stages of Population Growth*, 1947.
CHISHOLM, M., *Nigerian Geographical Journal*, Vol. 7, No. 2, December 1964.
COALE, A., 'Population and Economic Development' in P. M. HAUSER (ed.), *Population Dilemma*, 1963.
FEDERAL GOVERNMENT [of Nigeria] PRINTER, *Population of the Western Region of Nigeria—1952*, 1955.
FORDE, D., *The Yoruba Speaking Peoples of Western Nigeria*, 1951.
HAUSER, P. M. and DUNCAN, O. D. (eds.), *The Study of Population*, 1959.
IGUN, A. A., *The Census, Plans and Operations*, 1963.
LINDER, F. E., 'World Demographic Data' in P. M. HAUSER and O. D. DUNCAN, *op. cit.*
LORIMER, F., *Demographic Information on Tropical Africa*, 1961.
MABOGUNJE, A. L., *Yoruba Towns*, 1962.
NIVEN, C. R., 'Some Nigerian Population Problems', *The Geographical Journal*, 1935.
OKONJO, C., 'Patterns of Population Growth', *The Nigerian Journal of Economic and Social Studies*, Vol. 6, No. 1, 1964.
PROTHERO, R. M., 'The Population of Eastern Nigeria', *Scottish Geographical Magazine*, 1952.

6 A preliminary medium estimate of the 1962 mid-year population of Nigeria[1]

Chukuka Okonjo

Centre for Population Studies, University of Ibadan, Nigeria

Pre-Second World War Estimates

The size of the population of Nigeria, Africa's most populous country, has become since the middle of the 19th century a matter of great interest, not only to scholars and administrators but also of late to the Nigerian citizen. This interest in a best estimate of the population of the country has increased, especially on the part of the Nigerian citizen, since the preliminary figures of the November 1963 census became known. This census produced figures that were not acceptable to all the governments of the Federation and that have since become the subject of dispute and controversy.[2]

Estimates of the population of the largest region of the country—Northern Nigeria—exist as far back as the middle of the 19th century. Writing in 1854, Heinrich Barth estimated the population of Northern Nigeria at between 30 and 50 million.[3] Lugard accepted these estimates as being correct for the time in which they were made but put the 1900 population of Northern Nigeria at nine million. As Prothero has pointed out, acceptance of both these estimates would necessitate the postulation of extensive slaughter and depopulation in Northern Nigeria during the intervening 50 years.[4] Kuczynski was highly critical of Lugard's views and regarded such early population estimates as grossly exaggerated, doubting whether the population decreased very much in the second half of the 19th century.[5]

The best available estimates of the population of Nigeria for the first half of the 20th century are to be found in the census returns of the period. Censuses were taken in Nigeria in 1866, 1868, 1871 and thereafter every ten years up to 1931. Before 1911 the census area was made up of Lagos Island and small parts of the mainland. In 1911, 1921, 1931, the census area was extended to cover the whole country, but the figures obtained were based largely—as Kuczynski has remarked—on estimates and guesses. After the Second World War an attempt was made to improve on the poor state of knowledge of the population of the country and censuses were mounted in 1950, 1952–53, 1957, 1962 and 1963. The censuses of 1950 and 1957 were confined to Lagos only, while those of 1952–53, 1962 and 1963 were national censuses. The last two censuses, those of 1962 and 1963, differed fundamentally from former national censuses in that they were the first attempts at obtaining a truly national head count of the population. But the results of the 1962 census were rejected and never published, and the intrusion of politics into the 1963 count has probably made it difficult to derive any meaningful scientific results from data that might be published as a result of this census.[6]

In the 1911 census an attempt was made to estimate the total population of the country. In certain parts of southern Nigeria a house-to-house enumeration of the population was undertaken. But the proportion of inhabitants covered in this enumeration, excluding that of Lagos, was certainly less than one per cent of the population of southern Nigeria. The census returns of Northern Nigeria gave the total indigenous population, as on 2 April 1911, as 8,110,631. No details of how these returns were obtained were given at the time although Meek states that 'the 1911 census was . . . merely a rough estimate of population by sex.'[7] Adding to the figures for the north the 7,858,689 persons returned for southern Nigeria, we obtain a total estimated indigenous population of 15,969,320 for Nigeria. In the 1921 census the scope of the enumeration was extended. The count was taken in two parts—a township census confined to municipal areas, and a provincial census; fairly accurate information was obtained on the inhabitants of municipal areas. A total estimate of 8,368,512 persons was returned for southern Nigeria; of these 299,106 persons lived in the trust territory of Cameroons Province. For Northern Nigeria a total of 9,994,515 persons was returned. Adding to this the 261,663 persons in the trust territory of northern Cameroons, and the population of southern Nigeria, we obtain an estimate of the total 1921 population of Nigeria with the trust territory of the Cameroons as being 18,624,690 persons.

Although originally an all-inclusive census had been planned for the whole country in 1931, this scheme had to be modified by the Governor's orders in April 1930 to exclude the southern Provinces of the country. This was because disturbances in the Onitsha, Owerri and Calabar Provinces of Eastern Nigeria had interrupted the arrangements being made. The women in these areas feared that the attempt to enumerate them was a prelude to the introduction of taxation of women and an increase in the taxation of men. In 1931, an enumeration took place in fact only in Lagos and in five townships and 201 villages in Northern Nigeria. For some 96 per cent of the indigenous population of Northern Nigeria and 98·6 per cent of that of southern Nigeria the figures were obtained from existing records. The returns gave the population of the southern Provinces including the Colony as 8,493,247 persons and that of the northern Provinces as 11,434,924, giving a total of 19,928,171 persons for the whole country, including the mandated territory of the Cameroons. It is to be noticed that the 1931 total of 8,493,247 persons for the southern Provinces did not differ substantially from the 1921 figure of 8,368,512 persons.

The 1950–1953 Censuses

The Second World War interrupted the pattern of decennial censuses in the country, and no count was made in 1941. By the end of the decade, circumstances made evident the need for more recent data than that of the 1931 population census. The extension of the franchise and the introduction of planned programmes of economic expansion made it imperative for administrators and planners to have a more accurate knowledge of population distribution and movement in the country. In 1948, however, the Acting Government Statistician expressed the view that it might be politically impossible to take even a simple census of the country. Fortunately, this view was not held by his successor, and, after experience of the successful Lagos census of 1950, one for the whole country was planned. This census took place in Northern Nigeria in May, June and July 1952, in Western Nigeria in December 1952 and January 1953 and in Eastern Nigeria in May, June and August 1953.[8] The population of the country, excluding the trust territory of southern Cameroons, was given as 31,500,000, of whom 16,840,000 lived in Northern Nigeria, 6,087,000 in Western Nigeria, 7,218,000 in Eastern Nigeria and 272,000 in the capital, Lagos.[9]

In view of the fact that the 1952–53 census still seems to be the best available source of demographic information for contemporary Nigeria, it is advisable to examine critically the methods by which the census was carried out and the degree of accuracy claimed for the results. The method of counting used was the group count method of enumeration. The name of the head of each house or compound was recorded on a line of the schedule, while particulars of all members of the household were entered in appropriate columns. Generally enumerators were responsible for 1,500 persons in rural areas and 2,000 persons in urban areas. On the average there was one supervisor to each ten enumerators. Supervision was difficult and often impossible in the remote areas but elsewhere was considered good.

For Northern Nigeria the Government Statistician reported that some census officers 'estimated that the coverage was nearly complete, and most believed that the count must be more than 95 per cent accurate. There is no reason to suppose that half a million people were left out and an overall accuracy, therefore, of over 97 per cent may well have been attained.' This high level of estimated accuracy, as he further remarked, did not apply to Ilorin Province, where a serious undercount of the population must have amounted to more than 100,000 or about 20 per cent of the recorded population. In respect of twelve districts of Ilorin Province the census figure was 94,000 less than the 1951 'tax count' figure. Moreover, he felt that the tax figures tended to understate rather than overstate the population of the areas they covered. Many of the Cattle Fulani were probably missed, although the census figure for these nomads provided the most accurate assessment made up to that time. Considerable difficulty had been foreseen throughout the Region, he reported, in recruiting a sufficient number of competent field workers. In Bornu Province these difficulties were most severely realized. Certain parts of Bornu Emirate, which is more than three-quarters of the size of the Western Region, were extremely difficult of access. In these areas travelling teams were used, as it was not possible to provide separate enumerators for every village. The count in Northern Nigeria cost £39,000 or slightly more than 0·5*d* per person counted.

In Eastern Nigeria, with an expenditure of £44,000 or 1·3*d* per head for the count, the Government Statistician estimated that in total the figures were correct within three per cent. With few exceptions the census officers contended that the count was complete and the Government Statistician reported that this belief was substantially borne out by all the tests that could be applied. Yet the census was not conducted under auspicious circumstances. It was prefaced by the resignation of most of the members of the first elected government of the Region, in protest against the interpretation by the Governor of Eastern Nigeria of the provisions of the regional constitution. Particular difficulty was experienced in Eket and Degema Divisions. In Eket Division the newly formed District Council had just imposed an education rate, and this was regarded as a prelude to the introduction of taxation of women. Accordingly, protests against the census and the rate were made, including the destruction of the Council House. After a visit by the Resident of Calabar Province the division was counted, but it is most improbable that the count approached the three per cent accuracy claimed for the whole Region. In Degema Division the records showed signs of overcounting, indicating a 227 per cent increase over the estimated 1952 figures. A recount of about half the Division, enabled the figures to be adjusted to show only a 41 per cent increase on the estimate.

In Western Nigeria, which then included the two Provinces now constituting Mid-Western Nigeria and also the city of Lagos, a 95 per cent accuracy for the total population of the Region was claimed, with an expenditure of £31,000 or 1·2*d* per head of population counted. Some census officers, the Government Statistician reported, estimated a 90 per cent to 95 per cent count; others claimed a complete count. Undercounting, he suggested, certainly occurred in a few areas, especially where there were boundary or chieftaincy disputes. For reasons of this kind it was estimated that two quarters at Ede town were undercounted by about 12 per cent. The Region's population was found to be some 33 per cent higher than had been estimated.

The Government Statistician's claim of degrees of accuracy of 97 per cent or over for the census in Northern Nigeria, of 95 per cent for Western Nigeria and a margin of error of three per cent in Eastern Nigeria seems, however, not to be justified for the following reasons:

1. The degrees of accuracy quoted by the Government Statistician seem to imply that there was a systematic underestimation of the population in Northern and Western Nigeria. While there is independent evidence to suggest that this is true in the Western Region, he does not, except perhaps in the case of Ilorin Province, adduce evidence to support his contention in the case of Northern Nigeria. In view of the difficulties encountered in enumerating the population in some Provinces like Bornu, Adamawa, Niger and Sokoto, the returns for these Provinces are no better than informed estimates of the population. It might well be that there was an underestimation of the population of Ilorin Province. Evidence of the quality and size of the staff employed for the count seems to suggest that there could equally well have been an overestimation of the population of other Provinces, resulting in an overestimation of the total population of the Region.

2. The standard of literacy of the enumerators in Northern Nigeria was low, as is evidenced by the use of middle and elementary school boys on holiday as part of the field staff. Training was left to census officers who at the same time were carrying a full load of administrative work as District Officers of their Divisions. The most important training was that given to Supervisors who very often were solely responsible for the training of enumerators. Most enumerators found the book of instructions too complicated and evidently relied on the oral instructions given to them. Enumerators were employed in certain cases for periods up to four weeks and, especially in remote areas, had little supervision. They were paid £1 10*s* for their work and had little incentive to work conscientiously.

3. A comparison may be made of Northern with Western Nigeria, where training seems to have been more thorough and the field staff consisted mainly of teachers who were paid £2 for their work with bonuses being authorized for additional work. In the latter Region some census officers claimed only a 90 to 95 per cent count. It is difficult in these circumstances to accept the proposition that the Northern Nigeria census count, which had to deal with greater difficulties in organization and execution, could have attained a higher degree of accuracy.

4. Even in the Western Region, independent evidence seems to show that the degree of accuracy claimed for this census was exaggerated.[10] In Ibadan Province where the regional capital and the headquarters of the regional organization were situated, 'hundreds of hitherto unrecorded villages were found.' In certain areas of the province where adequate communications existed, undercounting as reported by the Government Statistician was of the order of 12 per cent. In other areas of the region, such as Urhobo Division, work was delayed by opposition to the census. Moreover a detailed examination of the names of villages as recorded in the census shows many omissions.[11] Therefore, it seems more reasonable to accept the lower limit of a 90 per cent degree of accuracy, quoted by some census officers for their areas, as being more indicative of the situation throughout the Region.

5. Neither does the margin of error claimed for the Eastern Nigeria census stand up to critical examination. Apart from local, but nevertheless serious, disturbances in Eket and Degema Divisions, the census took place at a time when there was political tension in the Region. In an area a substantial portion of which is heavily wooded, 'and the only sign that one is in the middle of a village may be a number of paths running into the bush and an occasional glimpse of a house roof, and it is not possible to find all the houses let alone their occupants without the full co-operation of the people,' this needed co-operation was not forthcoming.

6. A careful reading of the reports of the Government Statistician makes it clear that a strong association existed in the minds of the population in all parts of the country, and especially in the Eastern Region, between the census and a tax count.

7. Special difficulty was encountered in the riverine Divisions of Eket, Brass, Degema, Ogoni and Opobo and the southern parts of Ahoada Division. In these areas communications were poor, and the scattered settlements could be reached only by canoe. This is also an area in which considerable smuggling from Fernando Po exists and inhabitants traditionally arrange to be absent when there is a tax collection. With no aerial photographs of these districts available and no list of the villages, it must be doubted whether the count in these areas was anywhere near complete.

8. Finally, the censuses in the three Regions were not simultaneous and there were migrations of people during the period of counting, the scope and extent of which were unknown.

For these and other reasons we can conclude that while certain areas may have had as much as a 20 per cent undercount, it could not have been this high everywhere. On the other hand the margin of error could not have been as low as the 3 per cent claimed by the Government Statistician for Northern and Eastern Nigeria. This becomes clear in the light of the experience in the 1950 Lagos census. There, in order to achieve higher accuracy in the counting, and having the advantages of a better-educated public and an incomparably better communications system, each enumerator was limited to counting 500 persons, and 1·9*d* was spent per person counted. It would seem therefore that the results of the Western Region census are a better guide, and that the lower limit of 90 per cent accuracy given for parts of Western Nigeria indicates the relative accuracy of the censuses.[12] We can therefore reasonably conclude that while the censuses might not have given a figure within 8 per cent of the true total, they are unlikely to have been so far out as not to have given within 15 per cent, the true population of the country.

The 1962 and 1963 Censuses

By October 1960, when Nigeria became independent, it had become evident that the information obtained from the 1952–53 censuses was out of date and in many cases unsatisfactory. A comparison of the 1960 and 1948 censuses in Ghana suggested that there might well have been considerable undercounting of the population of Nigeria in the 1952–53 censuses. Accordingly, a comprehensive programme for a census in 1962 was mounted. The actual count took place from 13 to 27 May 1962. This census differed in many respects from the previous censuses. Some £1·5 million was voted for the exercise, approximately 8*d* per person to be counted. The census organization was in itself an improvement on former census organizations. By this time also, the country had become aware of the importance of censuses and thus favoured them more. In fact in certain areas there was over-enthusiasm for the census.

Ultimately political influences caused the rejection of the figures obtained in this census. Commenting on the results of the Eastern Nigeria census, Mr J. Warren, the Federal Census Officer, gave it as his opinion that, 'the figures recorded throughout the greater part of Eastern Nigeria, during the present census are false and have been inflated. The figures for the five Divisions, Awka, Brass, Degema, Eket and Opobo, which have recorded increases of over 100 and 120 per cent can certainly be rejected out of hand.'[13] With respect to Western Nigeria the Federal Census Officer reported that, 'of the 62 census districts . . . provisional total figures are available for only five, due in my view, to weakness in the census organization in the Region.'[14] On Northern Nigeria the Federal Census Officer made no adverse comments.

The Federal Census Officer's conclusions are by no means convincing for the following reasons:

1. The work of the census organization in the Western Region was from all available evidence the most thorough and efficient and produced more useful scientific data

than in the other regions. The 'weakness' referred to here cannot be attributed to the census organization but rather to administrative problems that followed the declaration of a state of emergency in the Region on 19 May 1962. As a result of the state of emergency the government of the Region was replaced, until 31 December 1962, by an administrator assisted by political commissioners and it was they who had general supervision of the census.

2. The Federal Census Officer seems to have taken it for granted that the 1953 census figures for the Eastern Region were substantially correct and that undercounting did not occur to any great extent in any of the Divisions of the Region.

3. The Federal Census Officer certainly underestimated the difference in enthusiasm for the 1952–53 census as compared with the 1962 census.

4. The Federal Census Officer does not seem to have taken into account the essential changes in boundaries and the shifts of population which had occurred between 1953 and 1962 in the five Divisions, Awka, Brass, Degema, Eket and Opobo.

5. The Federal Census Officer does not seem to have fully appreciated the difficulties encountered in the four creek Divisions—Brass, Degema, Eket and Opobo—during the 1952–53 census, which may have resulted in a serious undercount of their populations.[15] The month of June is one of the worst months to choose for a census in these areas. There are on average about twenty rain days yielding more than 20 inches of rainfall. Moreover, the area is poorly provided with communications and it takes as long as two weeks to reach some villages.

6. The Federal Census Officer does not seem to have fully understood the implications of the low male/female ratio in the 1953 census for Awka Division. A large number of men from this Division are away for most of the year as labourers in nearby towns. It should therefore not be surprising, in a situation in which such labourers were encouraged by their town and clan unions to have themselves and their families counted in their home towns, that Awka Division should show an abnormal increase of men.[16]

It may well be that in some areas in Eastern Nigeria there was an inflation of the population figures. But the magnitude of the population increases recorded are probably to be accounted for more by undercounting in 1953 than by overstatement in 1962. The evidence available certainly does not justify the Federal Census Officer's conclusion that the figures recorded for the greater part of Eastern Nigeria are false and have been inflated. It may also be that the figures for Awka, Brass, Degema, Eket and Opobo Divisions were quite defective. The probable degree of defectiveness does not, however, warrant the conclusion that they should be rejected out of hand. Indeed, the evidence suggests that the proper conclusion was that the magnitude of the increases in population over 1953 indicated the need for checking these figures and for a post-enumeration survey in these areas.

The experience obtained in the 1962 census was utilized in the 1963 census. The new census was supervised by a Census Board made up of Federal and Regional representatives working under the direction of the Prime Minister. For this exercise the sum of £2·5 million, or between 10*d* and 11*d* per head of population to be counted, was provided. The actual count took place from the 5 to 8 November 1963. The released preliminary figures gave the population of the country as 55·7 million, with 29·8 million in Northern Nigeria, 12·4 million in Eastern Nigeria, 10·3 million in Western Nigeria, 2·5 million in Mid-Western Nigeria and 0·7 million in the Federal territory of Lagos.[17] The results of this census have since then been the subject of controversy and the figures have not received wide acceptance either in Nigeria or in other countries.[18] (See Table 2 in the Annex.)

Lower and Upper Bounds to the 1962 Mid-Year Population of Nigeria

In view of the fact that the population figures given by the 1963 census seem to have doubtful scientific value, attempts have been made to estimate the population of Nigeria. Writing in 1965, Etienne van de Walle suggested that the 1963 figure of 56 million may have been an overestimate and that the real figure probably lay in the region of 40 to 45 million.[19] Mackintosh, writing in 1964, gave the population of Nigeria as 45 million with 22·5 million in Northern Nigeria, 12·5 million in Eastern Nigeria, 7·8 million in Western Nigeria, 1·8 million in Mid-Western Nigeria and 0·4 million in the Federal territory of Lagos.[20] Aluko quotes unofficial figures giving the population of Northern Nigeria as 21 million, that of Eastern Nigeria as 12·5 million, Western and Mid-Western Nigeria 9·5 million and Lagos 550,000.[21] This gives a total 1962 population of 43·55 million for the country.

A lower bound to the population of the country is given by the projections of the Federal Ministry of Health as shown in Annex Table 3. The 1962 mid-year population of the country is given as 36·475 million. This figure was reached by projecting the 1953 population of the country on the assumption of a 2 per cent per annum growth rate and that of the Federal territory of Lagos at a 4 per cent per annum rate. Recent research on vital rates in the country suggests that these rates of growth were too low.[22] The 1963 census results can be regarded as an upper bound to the population of the country. An upper bound lower than this can be obtained by considering the population that each enumeration area was supposed to contain during the 1963 census.

Each enumeration area in the 1963 census was supposed to contain not more than 400 persons. Where there were more than 400 persons in an enumeration area, census officers were instructed to break such enumeration areas into areas with less than 400 persons.[23] We have as yet not found any evidence to suggest that Federal Census Officers did not comply with these instructions. There were some 125,350 of these enumeration areas and 2,053 special areas. The distribution of the enumeration areas is shown in Annex Table 4.

With the recent experience of the 1962 census before them, it is difficult to believe that the Census Board and the United Nations demographic expert who advised them could have been so much in error in their preparations for the census as to underestimate the population they were about to count by as much as 5 million. If anything, the magnitudes shown in Annex Table 5 indicate that they must have expected a population of less than 50·7 million to be returned in the 1963 census. Projecting this figure backwards, and assuming a growth rate of 2·8 per cent per annum, we obtain an estimated population of 48·59 million as a lower upper bound to the 1962 mid-year population of Nigeria.

Centre for Population Studies—1962 Mid-Year Estimates of the Population of Nigeria

Before presenting the estimates of the 1962 mid-year population of Nigeria determined by the Ibadan Centre for Population Studies, it is necessary to give in detail the adjustments made in the areas of the various Divisions as compared with their areas during the 1952–53 census. For Northern Nigeria the changes which took place from 1954 to 1957 are listed in Annex Table 6.

Lagos was removed from the Western Region on 1 October 1954 to constitute the Federal territory of Lagos. Since then a new Mid-West Region has been created in 1962, including Benin and Delta Provinces. In Mid-Western Nigeria two new Divisions called Akoko-Edo and Isoko Divisions have been created from Afenmai and Urhobo Divisions. In Eastern Nigeria the changes which have taken place are listed in Annex Table 7.

Having made these necessary adjustments, we have projected the population of the various Divisions and Provinces using the growth rates shown in Annex Table 8. These we have described as the best available estimates of the mid-year 1962 population of Nigeria. We may summarize as follows: upper and lower bounds for the 1962 mid-year population of Nigeria may be taken as 48·590 and 36·475 million; the best available estimate of the 1962 mid-year population is 45·332 million. The distribution of this population is shown in Annex Table 9.

Footnotes

1. The projections given here of the 1962 mid-year population of Nigeria are the product of the extensive fieldwork of the staff of the Centre for Population Studies during the last two years. I wish to mention especially Messrs. Okorafor and Okoye, Research Assistants at the Centre, who, when I was otherwise engaged, led field teams to Eastern and Northern Nigeria. We are grateful to the Permanent Secretaries, Chief Statisticians and others of the Federal and Regional Governments for giving their time to help us with our inquiries and allowing us to interview officials. We wish also to thank all those in Native Administration, district, council, provincial and regional offices as well as private individuals, too numerous to mention here by name, who have helped us in our work. This research was made possible by a grant from The Rockefeller Foundation.
2. The figures were initially rejected by the Eastern and Mid-Western Regional Governments but later accepted by the Mid-Western Regional Government. The Northern and Western Regional Governments accepted them. The Eastern Nigerian Government challenged the acceptance of the figures by the Federal Government in the Federal Supreme Court but lost on the technical ground that the Supreme Court had no authority to entertain the suit.
3. HEINRICH BARTH, *Travels and Discoveries in North and Central Africa*, London, 1857.
4. R. MANSELL PROTHERO, 'The Population Census of Northern Nigeria 1952, Problems and Results,' in *Population Studies*, Vol. X, No. 2, London, November 1956, pp. 166–83.
5. R. R. KUCZYNSKI, *Demographic Survey of the British Colonial Empire*, Vol. 1, West Africa, London, 1948, p. 15.
6. This point will be further discussed in a forthcoming paper 'The Post-War Nigerian Censuses'.
7. C. K. MEEK, *The Northern Tribes of Nigeria*, Vol. II, p. 169.
8. Western Nigeria at the time of its census contained Benin and Delta Provinces (since 1962 constituted into Mid-Western Nigeria) as well as what is now the Federal territory of Lagos.
9. The results of this census are to be found in column 1 of Table 1 in the Annex. The Western Region as defined here includes Benin and Delta Provinces but not the Federal capital of Lagos. The total given here for Nigeria is the 1953 mid-year estimate.
10. From the census returns it was expected that some 170,000 six-year-old children would register for the free primary education scheme on its introduction in 1955. In the event some 392,000 registered. In 1956 and thereafter, enrolments steadied at about 230,000 or 35·3 per cent higher than would have been expected from the census returns.
11. Such an examination has been carried out for the Ishan area of Mid-Western Nigeria by the Centre for Population Studies. A comparison of the village lists of the 1963 and 1953 censuses also shows many omissions after allowance has been made for newly founded villages. Details of some such omissions will appear in the projected paper, 'The Post-War Nigerian Censuses'.
12. In Northern, Eastern and Western Nigeria there was approximately one census official to each 1,500 persons enumerated in rural areas, and one official to 2,000 persons enumerated in urban areas, as compared to one census official to 500 persons in the 1950 Lagos census. Costs were 0·5*d*, 1·3*d* and 1·2*d* per person enumerated for Northern, Eastern and Western Nigeria respectively compared with 1·9*d* in Lagos.
13. *Report of the Federal Census Officer, 18 July 1962:* Sections of this report were quoted in the *House of Representatives Debates:* 5 December 1963, pp. 2734–35. Mr J. Warren, the Federal Census Officer, was a lawyer by profession and before being appointed Federal Census Officer was Deputy Town Clerk in the Lagos Town Council.
14. *Ibid.*, p. 2735.
15. See p. 72 and paragraph 48 of the Census Report.
16. Some town and clan unions asked their members to proceed to their home towns for counting, with a threat of a heavy fine if they did not comply. In certain cases, where it was difficult for persons to go home, a list of such persons was compiled and sent to the home town for entering in the census lists.
17. The results of this census by Provinces and Divisions are to be found in column 2 of Table 1, which also shows the percentage increase of the 1963 recorded population over that of 1953, the annual percentage growth rate and the population density. Table 2 summarizes the position with respect to the Regions.
18. See Footnote 2.
19. ETIENNE VAN DE WALLE, 'An Approach to the Study of Fertility in Nigeria', *Population Studies*, Vol. XIX, No. 1, London, July 1965, p. 5.

20. J. P. MACKINTOSH, 'How Many Nigerians', *New Statesman*, London, 13 March 1964. It should be noticed that the total population for the Southern Regions and the Federal territory are together equal to that of the Northern Region. Mackintosh maintains here the political fiction of an equality of population between northern and southern Nigeria.
21. S. A. ALUKO, 'How Many Nigerians', paper prepared for the *Journal of Modern African Studies* 1965.
22. Various medical surveys report birth rates of between 50 to 60 per 1,000, while death rates range between 15 and 28 per 1,000. Greater detail on the pattern of birth and death rates in the country is expected from the country-wide demographic survey being mounted by the Federal Office of Statistics,
23. See Federal Census Office brochure *Instructions to Census Officers, Part 1, Census of Population 1963.*

Annex

Table 1

Centre for Population Studies

NIGERIA: POPULATION (1952 AND 1963), PERCENTAGE INCREASE, ANNUAL GROWTH RATE AND DENSITY BY REGIONS, PROVINCES AND DIVISIONS

NORTHERN NIGERIA

Provinces and Divisions	POPULATION		% Increase	Annual % growth rate	Area in sq. km.	Persons per sq. km.	Area in sq. mls.	Persons per sq. ml.
	July 1952	Nov. 1963						
Northern Nigeria	17,007,377	29,808,659	75·3	5·0	730,407	41	281,782	106
Adamawa Province	685,728	1,585,290	131·2	7·4	82,424	19	31,786	50
Division								
Adamawa	304,044	703,365	131·3	7·4	48,122	15	18,558	38
Muri	260,280	599,270	130·2	7·4	28,560	21	11,014	54
Numan	121,404	282,655	132·8	7·5	5,741	49	2,214	128
Bauchi Province	1,423,439	2,476,329	74·0	4·9	67,731	37	26,120	95
Division								
Bauchi	512,209	895,412	74·8	4·9	37,641	24	14,516	62
Gombe	476,844	841,217	76·4	5·0	16,806	50	6,481	130
Katagum	434,386	739,700	70·3	4·7	13,284	56	5,123	144
Benue Province	1,467,972	2,641,960	80·0	5·2	76,024	35	29,318	90
Division								
Idoma	318,821	497,953	56·2	3·9	9,651	52	3,722	134
Lafia	131,556	289,659	120·2	7·0	10,240	28	3,949	73
Nasarawa	162,303	324,517	100·0	6·1	14,425	22	5,563	58
Tiv	718,619	1,244,185	73·1	4·8	25,570	49	9,861	126
Wukari	136,673	285,646	109·0	6·5	16,137	18	6,223	46
Bornu Province	1,519,473	2,853,553	87·8	5·6	118,589	24	45,733	62
Division								
Bedde	45,064	94,343	109·4	6·5	5,186	18	2,000	47
Biu	164,621	270,810	64·5	4·4	10,165	27	3,290	69
Bornu	1,005,775	1,971,870	96·1	5·9	8,556	23	32,995	60
Potiskum	114,632	221,256	93·0	5·8	4,328	51	1,669	133
Dikwa	189,381	295,274	55·9	3·9	13,352	22	5,149	57
Ilorin Province	529,899	1,119,222	111·2	6·6	45,947	24	17,719	63
Division								
Borgu	75,740	106,991	41·3	3·0	28,285	38	10,908	10
Ilorin	398,569	901,416	126·2	7·2	10,798	83	4,164	216
Lafiagi	55,580	110,815	99·4	6·1	6,864	16	2,647	42

Table 1 (*continued*)

Provinces and Divisions	POPULATION		% In-crease	Annual % growth rate	Area in sq. km.	Persons per sq. km.	Area in sq. mls.	Persons per sq. ml.
	July 1952	Nov. 1963						
Kabba Province	661,387	1,280,143	93·6	5·8	28,402	45	10,953	117
Division								
Igalla	361,119	684,880	89·7	5·7	12,919	53	4,982	137
Igbirra	156,755	325,273	107·5	6·4	2,977	109	1,146	284
Kabba	110,281	180,037	63·3	6·1	9,467	19	3,651	49
Koton (Kwara)	33,232	89,953	170·7	8·8	3,044	30	1,174	77
Kano Province	3,820,348	5,774,842	51·2	3·6	43,123	134	16,630	347
Division								
Kano	3,396,350	4,958,396	46·0	3·3	33,536	148	12,933	383
Northern	423,998	816,446	92·6	5·8	9,587	85	3,697	221
Katsina Province	1,483,125	2,545,005	71·6	5·3	24,546	104	9,466	269
Division								
Katsina	1,483,125	2,545,005	71·6	5·3	24,546	104	9,466	269
Niger Province	715,169	1,398,527	95·6	5·9	74,333	19		
Division								
Abuja (including Lapai Emir)	101,408	141,124	39·2	2·9				
Bida	221,456	437,246	97·4	6·0	14,887	29	5,741	76
Kontagora	250,711	458,396	82·8	5·3	34,278	13	13,219	35
Minna	141,594	361,761	155·5	8·3	25,168	14	9,706	37
Plateau Province	824,700	1,367,448	65·8	4·5	29,229	47	11,272	121
Division								
Jos	246,406	457,759	85·8	5·5	3,877	118	1,495	306
Pankshin	279,003	372,637	33·6	2·6	9,496	39	3,662	102
Shendam (Low'd)	194,194	359,193	85·0	5·4	12,447	29	4,800	75
Southern (Akwanga)	98,152	177,859	81·2	5·2	3,410	52	1,315	135
Jos Township	6,945							
Sokoto Province	2,679,841	4,334,769	61·8	4·2	94,588	46	36,477	119
Division								
Argungu	170,603	293,985	72·3	4·8	8,702	34	3,356	88
Gwandu	488,898	847,765	73·4	4·9	19,482	44	7,513	113
Sokoto	2,020,340	3,193,019	58·0	4·0	66,404	48	25,608	125
Sardauna Province	313,667	878,271	180·0	9·1				
Division								
Gwoza	75,821	69,580	−8·2	−5·7				
Adamawa (For. Tr. Terr.)	237,846	808,691	240·0	10·8				
Zaria Province	869,244	1,553,300	72·7	4·8	45,747	34	17,642	88
Division								
Zaria	795,922	1,183,090	48·6	3·5	42,755	28		
Kaduna Township	38,794	149,910	286·4	11·9				
Jema'a	64,946	220,300	239·2	10·8	2,992	74	1,154	191

Table 1 (*continued*)

EASTERN NIGERIA

Provinces and Divisions	POPULATION		% Increase	Annual % growth rate	Area in sq. km	Persons per sq. km	Area in sq. mls.	Persons per sq. ml.
	Dec. 1952	Nov. 1963						
Eastern Nigeria	7,217,829	12,394,462	71·7	5·2	76,454	162	29,484	420
Calabar Province	1,540,091	3,023,784	96·3	6·5	16,194	187	6,245	484
Division								
Abak	233,361	355,724	52·4	4·0	908	392	350	1,016
Calabar	140,731	267,014	89·7	6·1	7,390	361	2,850	937
Eket	238,748	765,162	220·5	11·2	189	404	730	1,048
Enyong	175,849	271,673	54·5	5·2	2,523	108	973	279
Ikot Ekpene	282,736	440,082	55·7	4·2	1,180	373	455	967
Opobo	172,057	405,191	135·5	8·2	1,151	352	444	913
Uyo	296,609	518,938	75·0	5·3	1,149	452	443	1,171
Ogoja Province	1,082,211	1,602,533	48·1	3·8	19,409	83	7,485	214
Division								
Abakaliki	472,860	627,589	32·7	2·8	4,769	132	1,839	341
Afikpo	246,796	376,139	52·4	4·0	1,880	200	725	519
Ikom	45,760	69,797	52·5	4·1	2,391	292	922	757
Obubra	109,870	241,706	120·0	7·6	3,169	76	1,222	198
Ogoja	206,925	287,302	38·8	3·1	7,201	40	2,777	103
Onitsha Province	1,768,413	2,943,483	66·4	4·9	12,646	233	4,877	604
Division								
Awgu	150,868	212,805	41·1	3·3	1,099	194	424	502
Awka	295,048	694,396	135·4	8·2	1,740	399	671	1,035
Nsukka	449,345	689,353	53·4	4·1	3,407	202	1,314	525
Onitsha	466,193	797,386	71·0	5·2	2,982	267	1,150	693
Udi	406,959	549,543	35·0	2·9	3,418	161	1,318	417
Owerri Province	2,077,891	3,280,348	57·9	4·4	10,032	327	3,869	848
Division								
Aba	396,111	541,968	36·8	3·0	2,489	218	960	565
Bende	322,145	427,867	32·8	2·7	2,150	199	829	516
Okigwi	442,706	743,832	68·0	5·0	1,522	489	587	1,267
Orlu	356,256	665,665	86·9	6·0	1,058	629	408	1,632
Owerri	560,673	901,016	60·7	4·6	2,813	320	1,085	830
Rivers Province	746,645	1,544,314	106·8	7·0	18,172	85	7,008	220
Division								
Ahoada	286,225	506,577	77·0	5·5	5,186	98	2,000	253
Brass	126,954	309,716	144·0	8·6	8,687	357	3,350	925
Degema	117,903	400,740	240·0	21·4	3,241	124	1,250	321
Ogoni	156,717	231,513	47·7	3·7	1,048	221	404	573
Port Harcourt	58,846	95,768	62·7	4·7	10	924	4	23,692
WESTERN NIGERIA								
Western Nigeria	4,595,801	10,265,846	123·4	7·4	78,970	130	30,454	337
Abeokuta Province	629,830	974,866	54·8	4·0	11,062	88	4,266	229
Division								
Egba	393,800	629,565	59·9	4·3	5,469	115	2,109	299
Egbado	236,030	345,321	46·3	3·5	5,593	62	2,157	160
Colony Province	237,929	778,321	227·1	10·9	3,511	222	1,354	575
Division								
Badagry	65,594	122,159	86·2	5·7	742	165	286	427
Epe	59,938	130,395	117·6	7·1	1,675	78	646	202
Ikeja	112,396	525,767	367·8	14·1	1,094	480	422	1,246

Table 1 (*continued*)

WESTERN NIGERIA (*continued*)

Provinces and Divisions	POPULATION		% Increase	Annual % growth rate	Area in sq. km.	Persons per sq. km.	Area in sq. mls.	Persons per sq. ml.
	Dec. 1952	Nov. 1963						
Ibadan Province	1,649,926	3,326,647	101·6	6·4	11,723	284	4,521	736
Division								
Ibadan	796,942	1,258,625	57·9	4·2	5,759	219	2,221	567
Oshun	852,984	2,068,022	142·4	8·1	5,964	347	2,300	899
Ijebu Province	348,024	576,080	65·5	4·6	6,369	90	2,456	235
Division								
Ijebu	248,611	420,355	69·1	4·8	4,994	84	1,926	218
Ijebu-Remo	99,413	155,725	56·6	4·1	1,374	113	530	294
Ondo Province	945,440	2,727,675	188·5	9·7	21,165	129	8,162	334
Division								
Ekiti	327,363	1,418,114	333·2	13·4	5,446	260	2,100	675
Okitipupa	150,185	275,709	83·5	5·6	4,019	69	1,550	178
Ondo	243,099	536,374	120·6	7·2	6,859	78	2,645	203
Owo	224,793	479,478	121·3	7·3	4,841	103	1,867	266
Oyo Province	782,802	1,882,237	140·5	8·0	25,140	75	9,695	194
Division								
Ife	216,511	515,194	137·9	7·9	2,121	243	818	630
Ilesha	188,084	481,720	156·1	8·6	2,463	196	950	507
Oyo	377,867	885,323	134·3	7·8	20,555	43	7,927	112

MID-WESTERN NIGERIA

Provinces and Divisions	POPULATION		% Increase	Annual % growth rate	Area in sq. km.	Persons per sq. km.	Area in sq. mls.	Persons per sq. ml.
	Dec. 1952	Nov. 1963						
Mid-Western Nigeria	1,492,116	2,535,839	69·9	4·9	38,694	66	14,922	170
Benin Province	900,886	1,354,986	50·4	3·7	21,995	62	8,482	160
Division								
Asaba	212,382	315,998	48·8	3·6	3,151	100	1,215	260
Benin	292,081	429,907	47·2	3·5	10,372	41	4,000	107
Ishan	192,194	270,903	41·0	3·1	3,013	90	1,162	233
Afenmai	204,229	338,178	65·6	4·6	5,458	62	2,105	161
Delta Province	590,529	1,180,853	100·0	6·3	16,699	71	6,440	183
Division								
Aboh	130,121	178,154	36·9	2·9	2,212	81	853	209
Sapele Township	33,638	61,007	81·4	5·5	—	—	—	—
Warri	34,758	89,806	158·4	8·7	3,630	25	(1,400)	104
Warri Township	19,526	55,254	183·0	9·5				
Western Ijaw	82,809	231,746	179·9	9·4	6,096	38	2,351	99
Urhobo	289,677	564,886	95·0	6·1	4,761	119	1,836	309
Federal Territory of Lagos	272,000	665,246	144·6	8·2				

Table 2

NIGERIA: OFFICIAL POPULATION AND POPULATION DENSITY BY REGIONS, 1963

Region	Population	Area in sq. km.	Persons per sq. km.	Area in sq. mls.	Persons per sq. ml.
Northern	29,808,659	730,407	41	281,782	106
Eastern	12,394,462	76,425	162	29,484	420
Western	10,265,846	78,940	130	30,454	337
Mid-Western	2,535,839	38,679	66	14,922	170
Lagos	665,246	70	9,505	27	24,639
Nigeria	55,670,052	924,522	60	356,669	156

Table 3

NIGERIA: POPULATION ESTIMATES BY REGIONS, 1953–1962[1]

Region	1953	1954	1955	1956	1957	1958	1959	1960	1961	1962
Nigeria	31,557	32,149	32,753	33,368	33,995	34,634	35,284	35,091	35,752	36,475
Northern	17,153	17,472	17,797	18,128	18,465	18,808	19,158	19,514	19,877	20,275
Western	6,144	6,258	6,374	6,492	6,613	6,736	6,861	6,989	7,119	7,261
Eastern	7,229	7,363	7,500	7,640	7,782	7,927	8,074	8,224	8,377	8,545
Southern Cameroons	754	768	782	796	811	826	841			—
Lagos	277	288	300	312	324	337	350	364	379	394

1. Mid-year populations in thousands.
The population figures for the Regions have been projected at a rate of nearly 2 per cent per annum, the intercensal rate for the Northern Region (see Regional Reports). The rate of increase for the Federal territory of Lagos has been estimated at 4 per cent per annum.
Source: Federal Ministry of Health, Lagos.

Table 4

NIGERIA: DISTRIBUTION OF ENUMERATION AREAS IN THE 1963 CENSUS

Region	Non-special areas	Special areas[1]	All enumeration areas
Northern Nigeria	59,953	996	60,949
Eastern Nigeria	31,124	255	31,379
Western Nigeria	24,326	434	24,760
Mid-Western Nigeria	7,780	141	7,921
Lagos	2,167	227	2,394
Federal Republic of Nigeria	125,350	2,053	127,403

1. Special areas are places like markets and other public places. Allowing for 577,992 persons who were counted in the special areas and reckoning that each non-special area contained not more than 400 persons as given by the instructions, we obtain an upper limit to the population of Nigeria of 50,717,992, which would be distributed as in Table 5.

Table 5

NIGERIA: POSSIBLE DISTRIBUTION OF POPULATION ACCORDING TO ENUMERATION AREAS

Region	Possible total population in non-special enumeration areas[1]	Total population counted in special areas	Total estimated population
Northern Nigeria	23,981,200	148,242	24,129,442
Eastern Nigeria	12,449,600	187,834	12,637,434
Western Nigeria	9,730,400	193,631	9,924,031
Mid-Western Nigeria	3,112,000	34,847	3,146,847
Lagos	866,800	13,438	880,238
Federal Republic of Nigeria	50,140,000	577,992	50,717,992

1. Number of such areas × 400.

Table 6

BOUNDARY ADJUSTMENTS IN NORTHERN NIGERIA, 1954–1957

Area	Division and N.A. Area or District			
	Population	From	To	Date
Jema'a Emirate	64,969	Jema'a (Plateau)	Jema'a (Zaria)	1957
Jaba, Kagoro and Moroa districts	56,265	Zaria	Jema'a	1957
Gawun district	5,459	Abuja, Lapai Emirate	Minna, Gwari N.A.	1956
Aworo district	4,642	Kabba	Kwara	1954
Lokoja Town district	13,388	Igbirra	Kwara	1954
Kaduna Township	6,605	Zaria	Kaduna Capital Territory	1956
Kaduna Sabon Gari district (part)	36,042	Zaria	Kaduna Capital Territory	1956
Kaduna Sabon Gari district (part)	7,344	Zaria	Zaria, Igabi district	1956
Kaduna Sabon Gari district (part)	1,154	Zaria	Zaria, Chikum district	1956

Source: Report of the Constituency Delimitation Commission, 1958 (Chairman: Lord Merthyr), Lagos, 1958, pp. 17–23.

Table 6 (*continued*)

SUBSEQUENT BOUNDARY ADJUSTMENTS, 1958–63

Area	Province		
	From	To	Date
Dikwa and Gwoza districts	Bornu Province	Sardauna Province	1962
Mubi, Cubanawa, Madgali, Gashaka, Maubila, the United Hills and Chamba districts	Adamawa Province	Sardauna Province	1962
Dikwa N.A. area	Sardauna Province	Bornu Province	1962

Source: Report of the Constituency Delimitation Commission, 1964, Lagos, 1964, p. 5.

Table 7

BOUNDARY ADJUSTMENTS IN EASTERN NIGERIA, 1954–62

Division, Council, Clan or Village	Divisional and Council Area			
	Population	From	To	Date
Twelve villages	10,038	Uyo, Western Nsit District Council	Eket, Eket District Council	1954
Etchie Clan (part)	11,594	Aba, Southern District Council	Ahoada Etchie Rural District Council	—
Ifu Clan (part)	4,801	Bende, Elu Elu District Council	Ikot Ekpene, eastern Ibibio, Ikono District Council	1954
Two villages	391	Ikom	Calabar, Ejaghan Dusanga, Iyong-Iyong District Council	1956
One village	269	Ikom	Ogoja, Ogoja District Council	1957
One village	376	Degema	Brass	1957
Enna Clan	3,555	Enyong, Biase District Council	Afikop, Afikop District Council	1954
Aro-Ibo County Council		Enyong Division	Bende	
Eastern Ibibio Ikono County Council		Ikot-Ekpene Division	Enyong Division	
Abanyum Local Council		Obubra Division	Ikom Division	
Obudu Division		Ogoja Division		
Thirteen villages of Egbemua		Ahoada Division	Oguta County Council	1958
Oguta County Council		—	Owerri Division	1959
Mile 2 Diobu		Ahoada Division	Port Harcourt Municipality	

Sources: Report of the Constituency Delimitation Commission, 1958 and *Report of the Constituency Delimitation Commission, 1964*, Lagos, 1958 and 1964.

Table 8

CENTRE FOR POPULATION STUDIES ESTIMATES OF 1962 POPULATION BY PROVINCES AND DIVISIONS

Provinces and Divisions	POPULATION		% In-crease	Annual % growth rate	Area in sq. km.	Persons per sq. km.	Area in sq. mls.	Persons per sq. ml.
	July 1952	Mid-year 1962						
Northern Nigeria	16,884,072	22,027,096	30·5	2·7	730,407	30	281,782	78
Adamawa Province	771,877	901,469	16·8	1·6	82,392	11	31,786	28
Division								
Adamawa	389,905	418,268	7·3	0·7	48,104	9	18,558	23
Muri	260,280	326,186	25·3	2·3	28,549	11	11,014	30
Numan	121,404	157,015	29·3	2·6	5,739	27	2,214	71
Unstated	288							
Bauchi Province	1,423,825	1,884,668	32·4	2·8	67,706	28	26,120	72
Division								
Bauchi	512,209	707,566	38·1	3·3	37,627	19	14,516	49
Gombe	476,844	620,525	30·1	2·7	16,799	37	6,481	96
Katagum	434,386	556,577	28·1	2·5	13,279	42	5,123	109
Unstated	386							
Benue Province	1,455,175	1,979,093	36·0	3·1	75,995	26	29,318	68
Division								
Idoma	318,821	475,455	49·1	4·0	9,648	49	3,722	128
Lafia	131,556	198,822	51·1	4·1	10,236	19	3,949	50
Nasarawa	162,303	245,291	51·1	4·1	14,420	17	5,563	44
Tiv	718,619	869,871	21·0	1·8	25,561	34	9,861	88
Wukari	123,876	189,654	53·1	4·2	16,131	12	6,223	30
Bornu Province	1,330,506	1,818,198	36·7	3·2	118,545	15	45,733	38
Division								
Bedde	45,964	90,549	97·0	6·9	5,184	17	2,000	45
Biu	164,621	171,823	4·4	0·4	10,161	17	3,920	44
Bornu	1,005,775	1,413,167	40·5	3·5	85,526	17	32,995	43
Potiskum	114,632	142,659	24·4	2·2	4,326	33	1,669	85
Unstated	414							
Ilorin Province	530,595	930,913	76·0	5·7	45,929	20	17,719	53
Division								
Borgu	75,740	90,150	19·0	1·8	28,275	3	10,908	8
Ilorin	398,569	773,994	94·2	6·7	6,861	113	2,647	292
Lafia-Pategi	55,580	66,769	20·1	1·9	10,793	6	4,164	16
Unstated	706							
Kabba Province	663,639	829,659	25·0	2·4	28,391	29	10,953	76
Division								
Igalla	361,119	463,553	28·4	2·5	12,914	36	4,982	93
Igbirra	143,367	172,533	20·3	1·9	2,971	58	1,146	151
Kabba	105,639	131,368	24·4	2·2	9,464	14	3,651	36
Kwara	51,262	62,205	21·3	2·0	3,043	20	1,174	53
Unstated	2,522							
Kano Province	3,396,350	4,330,000	27·5	2·5	43,107	100	16,630	260
Division								
Kano	2,972,015	3,763,478	26·6	2·4	33,524	112	12,933	290
Northern	423,998	566,522	33·6	2·9	9,583	59	3,697	153
Unstated	337							
Katsina Province								
Division								
Katsina	1,483,125	1,868,738	26·0	2·4	24,537	76	9,466	197

Table 8 (*continued*)

Provinces and Divisions	POPULATION		% Increase	Annual % growth rate	Area in sq. km.	Persons per sq. km.	Area in sq. mls.	Persons per sq. ml.
	June 1953	1962						
Niger Province	715,728	1,000,329	39·8	3·4	74,305	13	28,666	35
Division								
Minna	147,304	210,792	43·1	3·6	25,159	8	9,706	22
Bida	221,743	295,140	33·1	2·9	14,881	20	5,741	51
Kontagora	250,711	363,782	45·1	3·8	34,265	11	13,219	28
Abuja	95,970	130,615	36·1	3·1				
Unstated								
Sardauna Province	687,146	867,052	26·2	2·4	Unknown			
Division								
Northern	246,974	300,231	21·6	2·0	,,			
Southern	174,970	166,341	−4·9	−0·5				
Dikwa	265,202	400,480	57·0	4·2				
Sokoto Province	2,680,333	3,347,673	24·9	2·2	94,552	35	36,477	92
Division								
Argungu	170,603	188,365	10·4	1·0	8,699	22	3,356	56
Gwandu	488,898	583,958	19·4	1·8	19,474	30	7,513	78
Sokoto	2,020,340	2,575,350	27·5	2·5	66,378	39	25,608	100
Unstated	492							
Zaria Province	870,508	1,111,184	27·7	2·5	45,730	24	17,642	63
Division								
Jema'a	121,201	175,076	44·5	3·7	2,991	59	1,154	152
Zaria	705,906	935,315	32·5	2·8	42,739	22	16,488	57
Unstated	797	793						
Kaduna Capital Territory	42,200	115,260	164·6	9·9	Not given			
Plateau Province	826,440	1,042,860	26·2	2·4	29,218	36	11,272	93
Division								
Akwanga	98,152	120,438	22·7	2·1				
Jos	253,351	326,041	28·7	2·6	3,875	84	1,495	218
Lowland	194,194	259,596	33·7	3·0	12,442	21	4,880	54
Pankshin	279,003	336,785	20·7	1·9	9,492	35	3,662	92
Unstated	1,740							
Eastern Nigeria	7,107,790	12,332,046	73·5	6·1	76,425	161	29,484	418
Abakaliki Province	828,000	1,189,649	43·7	4·0	9,814	121	3,786	314
Division								
Abakaliki	472,860	598,491	26·6	2·6	4,767	125	1,839	325
Afikpo	250,351	388,514	55·2	4·9	1,879	207	725	536
Obubra	104,789	202,644	93·4	7·3	3,168	64	1,222	166
Annang Province	443,150	748,676	68·9	6·6	2,087	359	805	930
Division								
Abak	233,361	438,639	88·0	7·0	907	483	350	1,253
Ikot Ekpene	209,789	310,037	47·8	4·3	1,179	263	455	681
Calabar Province	141,122	261,985	85·6	6·9	7,387	35	2,850	92
Division								
Calabar	141,122	261,985	85·6	6·9	7,387	35	2,850	92
Degema Province	117,527	304,025	158·7	10·6	3,240	94	1,250	243
Division								
Degema	117,527	304,025	158·7	10·6	3,240	94	1,250	243
Enugu Province	944,369	1,392,125	47·4	4·3	7,921	176	3,056	456
Division								
Awgu	150,868	299,298	98·4	7·6	1,099	272	424	706
Nsukka	449,345	652,444	45·2	4·1	3,406	192	1,314	497
Udi	344,156	440,383	28·0	2·7	3,416	129	1,318	334

Table 8 (*continued*)

Provinces and Divisions	POPULATION June 1953	POPULATION 1962	% Increase	Annual % growth rate	Area in sq. km.	Persons per sq. km.	Area in sq. mls.	Persons per sq. ml.
Ogoja Province	257,375	369,682	43·6	4·0				
Division								
Ikom	50,181	87,229	73·8	6·1	2,390	37	922	95
Obudu	57,602	89,992	56·2	5·0				
Ogoja	149,592	192,461	28·7	2·8				
Onitsha Province	740,890	1,470,969	98·5	7·6	4,720	312	1,821	808
Division								
Awka	294,810	664,208	125·3	9·0	1,739	382	671	989
Onitsha	446,080	806,761	80·9	6·6	2,981	271	1,150	702
Owerri Province	1,365,690	2,210,141	61·8	5·3	5,392	410	2,080	1,063
Division								
Okigwi	442,751	654,418	47·8	4·3	1,522	443	587	1,149
Orlu	356,211	632,680	77·6	6·4	1,058	598	408	1,551
Owerri	566,728	923,043	62·9	5·4	2,812	328	1,085	851
Port Harcourt Province	483,670	719,310	48·7	4·4	6,242	115	2,408	299
Division								
Ahoada	274,954	390,295	41·9	3·9	5,184	75	2,000	195
Ogoni	156,723	235,005	49·9	4·5	1,047	225	404	582
Port Harcourt	51,993	94,011	80·8	6·6	10	9,067	4	23,503
Umuahia Province	733,744	1,170,111	59·5	5·2	4,637	252	1,789	654
Division								
Aba	384,151	547,545	42·5	3·9	2,488	220	960	570
Bende	349,593	622,566	78·1	6·4	2,149	290	829	751
Uyo Province	924,923	2,186,656	136·4	9·6	6,714	326	2,590	844
Division								
Eket	248,786	729,835	193·4	12·0	1,892	386	730	1,000
Enyong	217,509	420,663	93·4	7·3	2,522	167	973	432
Opobo	172,057	468,973	172·6	11·1	1,151	407	444	1,056
Uyo	286,571	567,186	97·9	7·6	1,148	494	443	1,280
Yenogoa Province								
Division								
Brass	127,330	308,717	142·5	9·8	8,684	356	3,350	922
Western Nigeria	4,593,650	8,157,554	77·6	7·0	78,940	103	30,454	268
Abeokuta Province	629,830	898,579	42·7	3·8	11,058	81	4,266	211
Division								
Egba	393,800	558,952	41·9	3·7	5,467	102	2,109	265
Egbado	236,030	339,627	43·9	3·9	5,591	61	2,157	157
Colony Province	237,928	548,696	130·6	8·9	3,510	156	1,354	405
Division								
Badagry	65,594	114,723	74·9	5·9	741	155	286	401
Epe	59,938	104,825	74·9	5·9	1,674	62	646	162
Ikeja	112,396	329,148	192·8	11·4	1,094	301	422	780
Ibadan Province	1,649,926	2,572,889	55·9	4·7	11,719	220	4,521	569
Division								
Ibadan	796,942	1,115,203	39·9	3·4	5,757	194	2,221	502
Oshun	852,984	1,457,686	70·9	5·7	5,962	245	2,300	634
Ijebu Province	348,024	538,151	54·6	4·4	6,366	84	2,456	219
Division								
Ijebu	248,611	410,001	64·9	5·4	4,992	82	1,926	213
Ijebu-Remo	99,413	128,150	28·9	2·6	1,374	93	530	242

Table 8 (*continued*)

Provinces and Divisions	POPULATION		% Increase	Annual % growth rate	Area in sq. km.	Persons per sq. km.	Area in sq. mls.	Persons per sq. ml.
	Dec. 1952	1962						
Ondo Province	945,440	2,188,493	131·5	8·7	21,157	103	8,162	268
Division								
Ekiti	327,363	1,004,460	206·8	11·9	5,443	184	2,100	478
Okitipupa	150,185	220,648	46·9	4·0	4,018	55	1,550	142
Ondo	243,099	561,215	130·9	8·7	6,856	82	2,645	212
Owo	224,793	402,171	78·9	6·0	4,839	83	1,867	215
Oyo Province	782,502	1,410,744	80·3	6·0	25,130	56	9,695	146
Division								
Ife	216,551	383,037	76·9	5·9	2,120	181	818	468
Ilesha	188,084	321,396	70·8	5·5	2,462	130	950	338
Oyo	377,867	706,320	86·9	6·4	2,055	34	7,927	89
Mid-Western Nigeria	1,491,421	2,365,091	58·6	4·7	38,679	61	14,922	158
Benin Province	900,886	1,276,895	41·7	3·6	21,986	58	8,482	151
Division								
Asaba	212,382	280,411	32·0	2·8	3,149	89	1,215	231
Benin	292,081	464,533	59·0	4·7	10,368	45	4,000	116
Ishan	192,194	247,991	29·0	2·6	3,012	82	1,162	213
Akoko-Edo (Afenmai)	204,229	283,960	39·0	3·4	5,456	52	2,105	135
Delta Province	590,535	1,088,196	84·3	6·4	16,693	65	6,440	169
Division								
Aboh	130,127	165,283	27·0	2·5	2,211	75	853	194
Warri	54,284	116,805	115·2	8·1	3,629	32	1,400	83
Western Ijaw	82,809	172,332	108·1	7·7	6,094	28	2,351	73
Isoko (Urhobo)	323,315	633,776	96·0	7·1	4,759	133	1,836	345
Federal Territory of Lagos	267,407	450,392	68·4	5·5	70	6,435	27	16,681
Nigeria		45,332,179			924,452	49	356,642	127

Table 9

Centre for Population Studies Estimates, Distribution and Density of Population by Regions

Region	Population	Area in sq. mls.	Density per sq. ml.
Northern Nigeria	22,027,096	281,782	78
Eastern Nigeria	12,332,046	29,484	418
Western Nigeria	8,157,554	30,454	268
Mid-Western Nigeria	2,365,091	14,922	158
Lagos	450,392	27	16,681
Nigeria	45,332,179	356,669	127

With allowance for 11·7 per cent underestimate in the 1952–53 census figures, this would imply an annual growth rate of about 2·8 per cent per annum for Nigeria for the intercensal period.

7 Population and politics in Nigeria
(Problems of census-taking in the Nigerian Federation)

R. K. Udo

Department of Geography, University of Ibadan, Nigeria

In view of the wide range of topics which might properly come under the title of population and politics in Nigeria, it is necessary to start by stating precisely the scope of this paper. It is concerned primarily with the politics of the 1962 census and the factors leading to the re-count of 1963. Both enumeration exercises cost the country over £4 million and they engendered so much internal friction that the very survival of the Federation was threatened. The 1962 census was the second country-wide count in Nigeria and the first since independence.[1] It was cancelled after a heated and prolonged controversy which featured charges and counter charges that certain states had inflated their census figures. A new count was ordered in 1963 but when the figures were made public they were rejected by the Governments of Eastern and Mid-Western Nigeria. The Federal Government, together with the Governments of Northern and Western Nigeria, however accepted the census figures, whereupon the Eastern Nigerian Government took the Federal Government to court on the grounds that the handling of the census by the latter was 'unconstitutional, ultra vires and illegal'. The case was lost when the Federal Supreme Court ruled that it had no jurisdiction over the administrative function of the Federal Government and so the official figure for the population of Nigeria remains at 55·6 million.

It took the Census Board slightly over three and a half months from the close of enumeration before it announced the preliminary figures for the 1963 census. This delay, according to the Board, was occasioned by the fact that the census figures had to undergo a number of exhaustive tests to ensure their accuracy and acceptance. 'Without this thorough appraisal of the figures,' the Board argued, 'the Governments of the Federation and the general public will have little or no confidence in any population figures.' That was a true statement, but whatever the Board did to ensure accuracy, it does not appear that they achieved much and today there is a growing opinion in Nigeria and abroad that they returned an excessively high total figure. The growth rates implied by their figures are ridiculous and unrealistic. Since the number of immigrants into Nigeria during the last decade has been negligible, such growth rates can only be accounted for by a gross undercount in 1953 or a deliberate overcount in 1962. We cannot rule out the former completely but the mass of evidence provided by various incidents during and after the 1962 census suggest that there was large scale inflation in 1962 and also in 1963.

Yet the importance of an accurate and complete census for a developing country like Nigeria can hardly be exaggerated. A complete enumeration providing information on sex and age composition, the areal distribution of the population and movements of population is an important tool for social and economic research and is indispensable for planning purposes. An accurate count is also of great help in the allocation of parliamentary seats in a country like Nigeria where the basis of representation in parliament is population. Finally, a series of such censuses appears to provide the only major means of determining the growth rate of population in underdeveloped countries where there is a complete absence of vital statistics of births and deaths, except in a few urban centres. The problems and expense of collecting data on vital statistics are enormous and experience in other tropical countries shows that it will not be possible to rely on such a source for several decades.

We have so far touched upon a few questions which require closer examination at this stage. How did the Census Board come to the conclusion that without exhaustive and time-consuming tests of the census returns the general public and the Government of the Federation would have little or no confidence in any population figures? Did the Board actually carry out any tests and if so how did the Board account for the ridiculous growth rate suggested by the figures it accepted? Why did people who refused to be counted in 1952 decide to return inflated figures during the 1962 census thereby necessitating a second count, the figures of which were described by the Eastern Nigeria Government as 'worse than useless'. What could Nigeria or any of its districts gain by inflating its population? Finally what chances are there of obtaining a reliable census in the future?

Table 1 provides the basic information regarding the size of the land area, the total population and the number of seats allocated in the Federal Legislature to the various states making up the federation. A little calculation will reveal that Northern Nigeria is more than thrice as extensive as the other states put together and that its population both in 1953 and 1963 was more than half the population of the country. According to the 1962 estimates, however, the population of Northern Nigeria was slightly less than that of the other states combined. One important fact which is relevant to this study as indicated in Table 1 is that the basis of representation in parliament is population. This applies even to Northern Nigeria where the principle of one man one vote cannot be said to apply, since women may not vote in this state. It is true that in most democracies throughout the world, population is also the basis of representation but in Nigeria this fact has a special political implication which can only be appreciated after a clear understanding of the contemporary Nigerian political scene.

Table 1

The Population and Parliamentary Seats of the States of the Nigerian Federation

State	Area in sq. mls.	Population (in millions)			Representation in Parliament, based on census	
		1952/53	1962 est.	1963	1953	1963
Northern Nigeria	281,782	18·8	22·01	29·8	174	167
Eastern Nigeria	29,484	7·2	12·3	12·4	73	70
Western Nigeria	30,454	4·6	8·1	10·3	47	57
Mid-Western Nigeria	14,922	1·5	2·4	2·5	15	14
Lagos	27	0·23	0·45	0·7	3	4
Total	356,669	30·33	45·26	55·7	312	312

When the Premier of Eastern Nigeria and leader of the National Council of Nigerian Citizens (NCNC) rejected the 1963 census on behalf of his government and party, the Northern Peoples Congress (NPC) suggested that he did so because the figures published had thwarted his ambition to become the Prime Minister of the country. One implication of this suggestion is that the census figures, that is the size of the population of the various states, rather than the manifestoes and past records of the contesting parties, would decide who won the 1964 federal elections. This is precisely what happened and here lies the crux of the matter—the higher the population figure for a given state, the greater the number of seats allocated to it and this in Nigeria today means the greater the number of seats that will go to the governing party in that state. Such would not be the situation if all political parties campaigned on a national level and if some politicians were not obsessed by the desire to rule whether or not the people wanted them. The political creed of the NPC and its ally the Nigerian National Democratic Party (NNDP), which rule Northern and Western Nigeria respectively, is 'North for Northerners, East for Easterners, West for Westerners and the Federation for all.' One of the facts of Nigerian politics today is that the ruling party always wins in any election[2] and that it is becoming increasingly difficult, if not impossible, for a party to campaign for parliamentary seats in a state where it is not in power.

The Balance between North and South

Earlier population estimates, including that of 1948, had shown that there were more people in Northern Nigeria, than in the rest of the country. The first census in 1953 confirmed this. The political significance of population figures was however not exploited until 1949 when the drafting committee of the Macpherson Constitution proposed a federal system of government with a fairly strong central legislature and executive. The committee also proposed that the federal legislature be made up of 22 members from Eastern Nigeria, 22 from Western Nigeria and 30 from Northern Nigeria.[3] Northern Nigeria however insisted that since its population was greater than that of both Eastern and Western Nigeria combined,[4] its representation should at least be equal to the combined total of the Southern States. A select committee of the legislative council later decided that the North should have equal representation with the South and so when in 1952 the Macpherson Constitution came into effect with a federal legislature of 148 members, half of them came from Northern Nigeria.[5]

It is proper to point out that in the early 1950s, there was a considerable amount of distrust between Northern and Southern Nigeria and that this distrust tended to deepen with the approach of independence. It arose partly from cultural differences between North and South but particularly as a result of the fact that the North was far behind the South in the acquisition of Western education. A large part of the North is Muslim and the entire state is ruled by Muslim chiefs and so the Christian missions which built most of the schools in Nigeria could not readily establish many in the North. Their schools were therefore concentrated in the South and for a long time the Northern civil service was dominated by Southerners. This is no longer the case, since for political reasons the North prefers expatriates to Southerners. But fortunately for the North it had the largest population and, by virtue of the constitutional power due to its numerical superiority, could counter any unpleasant moves from the South.

In 1953 for instance, the North used its majority to throw out a motion by an Action Group parliamentarian demanding self-government by 1956. Northern leaders argued that they were not ready for independence in 1956. The key posts in the North were still manned by Southerners and expatriates and Northern politicians wanted time to catch up. But the stand taken by the North on the independence issue was not well received in the South; hence the unfortunate incident in which Northern parliamentarians were booed and insulted by angry Lagos crowds. This was followed by a riot in Kano in which many Southerners were killed.[6] When at last the British left for good, the North–South relation was far from normal. Many Southern politicians could not readily accept the fact that some of them who had been most vocal in the struggle for independence were to play second fiddle while the reins of power went to those who had delayed self-rule. They openly expressed the feeling that Northern politicians were reaping where they had not sown simply because the North had a greater population!

Although the North is gradually catching up with the South, there are still marked differences between the more accessible, better developed and more literate South and the North, which ironically had a more developed economic system before the establishment of British administration in Nigeria. In addition the distrust between North and South has tended to worsen after a short-lived 'independence truce'. Since the 1950s the North has dominated the federal legislature as a result of its numerical majority. Indications from a national census in 1962 that the population of the North was less than that of the South would be likely to upset the constitutional allocation of power under the then-existing political alignments in the country. This would please some Southern politicians, but it was unlikely to be acceptable to the North, the ruling party of which had persistently refused to extend its field of operation to other parts of the federation, being convinced that as long as the population of the North exceeded that of the South it could always gain enough seats to enable it to control the Federal Government. The political implications of the 1962 and 1963 enumerations must be seen against this background. It is also necessary to observe that Northern Nigeria can so far go it alone, if she wishes, in the federal legislature, but not so any of the other states.

The point has often been made that the larger population of Northern Nigeria is in keeping with the large territorial area of that state. This statement tends to ignore the fact that vast stretches of Northern Nigeria are virtually uninhabited and that in any case it does not follow that the most extensive state should be the most populous. The population of other states of the Western Sudan such as Mali, the Niger Republic, Chad and Upper Volta, show clearly that in the Sudan there is no relationship between the size of the territorial area and the population of a state.[7] It is possible to object that considerable parts of these other Sudanese states extend into the Sahara desert which is uninhabitable. But what of the entire French-speaking West Africa which is more than five times the size of Nigeria and yet is not as populous?

The Effect of Propaganda in the 1962 Census

The 1962 census was taken in May (13–31) under the direction of the Federal Census Office in the Ministry of Economic Development. Experience during the 1953 count had shown that many people associated the census with taxation and had therefore dodged the census officers. There were also superstitious fears in some districts of its being dangerous to reveal the size of one's family to a stranger. A pre-census campaign was therefore launched early in May 1962 with a view to educating the people on the significance of the census. It is necessary to examine the character of this campaign in order to appreciate its contribution in creating rather than solving a number of problems during the enumeration.

Looking back at the situation, it would appear that it was unfortunate to entrust the census campaign to the politicians. Everywhere the campaign was opened with radio broadcasts by political leaders. The national papers of May 1962 carried special census messages and in the churches the preachers did not forget to stress the importance of the census.[8] Ministers and parliamentarians from the federal and regional legislatures as well as many other lesser politicians went to their constituencies on 'census tours'. They stressed amongst other things that the census had nothing to do with taxation,[9] that social services to rural areas would be provided on the basis of population and that, in a reconstituted federal parliament, population would remain the basis of representation. In launching the census campaign at Enugu for instance the Eastern Nigeria Premier stressed that the census was very important because 'on it will be based future legislative representations, siting of industries and provision of amenities.'[10] It was also indicated at mass rallies as well as in the press and radio that the electoral register for the forthcoming federal election of 1964 would be prepared from the census returns[11] and voter's registration cards were actually given out in the process of enumerating the people.

All we can say today is that the census campaign was more than successful. People did not only make sure that they were not left out in the census but thousands saw to it that they were counted at least twice. In its editorial comment of 21 May 1962 the Federal Government daily paper, the *Morning Post*, observed as follows: 'The publicity campaign (of the census) was conducted in order to make sure that people will not be reluctant to enrol their names. But in fact we find that the position is the reverse; lots of people are treating the census with more enthusiasm than could have been imagined. People don't want to be left out. And as a result, we find enumerators being suspended in some parts of the country for listing down more names than they are expected to do.'[12]

The great emphasis placed on the claim that the material development of an area as well as the seats allocated to it in parliament would depend on the size of the population of the areas did great harm in that it occasioned a mass migration of people from their places of work to their natal villages. In spite of a series of warnings against migration, many people deserted towns like Kano, Aba, Enugu and Lagos to return to their natal villages to be counted. This was done to swell up the population of one's village of birth so as to ensure that it would not be overlooked when settlements were being scrutinized for the provision of electricity, postal services and many other 'good things of life'. Where people could not or decided not to travel home as did one clan union at Enugu, officials of the branch were sent home with a list of members of the clan resident in the township. The list was to be incorporated into the census returns and in this particular instance the enumerator was caught copying the list into his census book. The enumerator as well as the Union officials later appeared in court for the offence.[13] As a result of such 'census migrations' the data for many districts will be useless for the study of population movement, depopulation of rural areas or the growth of urban centres.

The case of the dishonest clan leaders indicates that some enumerators disregarded the instructions given to them that counting should be by sight, and even the Federal Government daily paper thought that such instructions should not be rigidly applied.[14] In those parts of Northern Nigeria where entry into the 'purdah' quarters was refused the question of counting by sight was completely ruled out. But in other parts where there was no such restriction, some enumerators merely relied on information provided by the heads of families. Yet it is a fact that there are numerous polygamous fathers who do not know how many children they have. Some heads of families returned figures which included sons and daughters who had migrated to work elsewhere.

In the heat of the census campaign, an administrative officer in Eastern Nigeria triumphantly announced the discovery of a village of about 20,000 people 'which has neither been registered for parliamentary elections, nor represented in any of Nigerian legislatures.'[15] This grand discovery was in Eket Division and was later cited by the Northern Peoples Congress to support their charge that Eastern Nigeria had inflated its figures. A few days after the census had started another fishing village with an estimated population of 1,000 is said to have been discovered in Uyo Province. This village was also alleged to have been left out during the 1953 census.[16] It is possible that many more villages were 'discovered' but is it a mere coincidence that these villages were discovered in a 'minority area'? During his census campaign tour of the minority areas the Eastern Premier had blamed the 'under-representation' of these areas in parliament on the people who, he claimed, had refused to be counted in 1953.[17] What if the people wanted to make up for the loss of 1953?

Inflation in the 1963 Re-count

According to the Eastern Nigeria Premier the rumpus over the 1962 census arose from the fact that the population of the South totalled a little more than that of the North; that when the North whose figure was the first to be announced over the radio realized this fact, it proceeded on a supplementary count which resulted in an addition of nine million people to the Northern Nigeria figures. At the same time the North accused the East of inflation, making special mention of the discovery of villages in Eastern Nigeria. This 1962 census controversy, as already pointed out, ended with the cancellation of the census. All the Governments of the Federation agreed to a new count and each of them gave an undertaking to ensure an honest and accurate count. The Prime Minister expressed the wish to see the count through as early as possible so that the figures could be used in delimiting constituencies for the 1964 federal elections.

In the re-count of 1963 which was to be supervised by a Census Board set up by the Federal Government, the census was to last only four days (5–8 November), unlike the 1962 census which lasted two weeks. There were 180,000 enumerators and supervisors as against 45,700 in 1962. These changes were directed at ensuring an honest and accurate count. An exchange of enumerators between the states was agreed upon and a team of women enumerators from Eastern Nigeria went to the North since men are never allowed into the purdah quarters. Later events were to prove that these as well as other precautions proved ineffective. This is not surprising: what is surprising is that the politicians agreed to trust each other in expecting that each Regional Government would ensure an accurate count. This was clearly the time for an impartial supervisor, as from the United Nations or the OAU, to have been invited to the scene. Indeed this idea had been put forward but those in authority decided to argue that such a move would portray the country to the outside world as incapable of carrying out such a basic exercise as census taking. Yet it was clear that in order not to expose itself as guilty of inflation in 1962, each Regional Government, and indeed each district, would ensure that the 1963 figures were not below those of the 1962 census. This is precisely what happened, and instead of a decrease, there was further inflation in some cases. Today, many of those who shouted down the 1962 figures believe that those figures were nearer the truth than the 1963 figures.

One of the most unfortunate episodes of the re-count in 1963 was that some census areas selected for sampling were disclosed long before the enumeration. Some members of the Census Board admitted that this could have afforded a great deal of opportunity for unfair practice. The important point is that as a result of this lapse, the main check against inflation was sabotaged long before the count. It is reported that at the close of enumeration in 1963, the total population of the country was put at about 60·5 million. After a few tests, the Census Board found itself 'unable to accept the actual population count for a number of census districts.' Further tests and checking finally brought down the figure to 55·6 million.

At this stage we can confirm that whereas there is evidence to support the conviction that the census figures were inflated, it is not yet possible to say how much more distorted figures in a given district were in comparison with those of other districts. But we know that a large number of census districts failed the basic tests applied by the Census Board. We also know that the scale of inflation was largest in the North, but the main point is that the figures for each state were inflated and for our purpose it is immaterial if some districts were more dishonest than others.

In justifying the figures for their states, some politicians concentrated on comparing the percentage increase for the various states. Thus one Northern legislator calculated that the difference between the 1952 and the 1963 figures gave the North 76 per cent increase, the West and Mid-West 110 per cent and Lagos 152 per cent. Apparently pleased with himself the man declared, 'Well ours is just 76 per cent whilst Lagos is 152 per cent, and yet the East is accusing the North.' He was of the opinion that Dr Okpara, the Eastern Nigeria Premier, also leader of the NCNC, failed to accuse Lagos because the NCNC had strong support in that city.[18] Such comments suggest ignorance or downright dishonesty; how could one compare the rate of increase of population in a fast-growing city like Lagos with that in a vast territory like Northern Nigeria which had lost a considerable number of people to Lagos since 1952? The argument by another Honourable Member that there was no fantastic rise in the figures for Northern Nigeria because 'the overall percentage of the majority of Northern Nigeria over the rest of the Southern provinces put together is 3·3 million in 1951, 3·3 million in 1962 and 3·8 million in 1964',[19] is similarly puerile.

The Effect of the Census on the 1964 Elections

During his formal rejection of the 1963 census figures, the Eastern Premier, an Ibo, singled out the North for criticisms. This brought about a fierce reaction from the floor of the Northern House of Assembly in its March 1964 session. A series of attacks were made by many members on Southern Nigeria but particularly on the Ibo people; and the President of the Federal Republic of Nigeria, also an Ibo, had his share of the diatribe. Speaker after speaker rose to demand the dismissal of Ibos from the Northern civil service, the confiscation of their landed property and the repatriation of all Ibos in the North. In reply to the various demands made by members, the Minister of Establishments and Training assured them that he would put their views to his government. He reminded the members that since 1955 the policy of his government with regard to employment has been 'Northerners first, Expatriates second and Non-Northerners third'.[20]

We have already observed that the substance of the speeches of these overzealous politicians suggests that they were both impulsive and not very well informed. Nevertheless their outburst had the desired effect. A number of Ibos were deprived of their landed properties and many of them had to leave the North.

In preparation for the 1964 Federal election, the Electoral Commission was directed to re-allocate parliamentary seats on the basis of the 1963 census. The total number of legislators was to remain at 312 as in the outgoing parliament. This explains why there was a decrease from 174 to 167 and from 73 to 70 in the number of seats allocated to Northern and Eastern Nigeria respectively even though their population had increased. In Western Nigeria the number of seats was increased from 47 to 57 to conform with the very large increase in the population of Western Nigeria suggested in the census. The North in spite of a loss of seven seats still had more than 50 per cent of the seats in the Federal Parliament. The official statement announcing the census figures had expressed the hope that Governments of the Federation would be in a position to review their plans for social development on the basis of the new census. The Eastern Nigeria Government has however refused to carry out such a review and recently when people from minority tribal groups in Eastern Nigeria complained that they did not get a 'fair share' in the 1965 scholarship awards, this government retorted that the awards were based on the 1953, not the 1963 census.

After formal acceptance of the figures for the 1963 census, it was possible to predict the results of the 1964 Federal election, the first to be conducted in Independent Nigeria. It was a straight fight between the Nigerian National Alliance (made up of the NPC and the NNDP, who believe in regional politics) and the United Progressive Grand Alliance (made up of the NCNC and the Action Group, who though still dominated by tribal loyalists had some semblance of a national outlook). At this time the NNA controlled the Northern and Western Legislatures while the UPGA controlled the Eastern and Mid-Western Legislatures. At the close of nominations each camp succeeded in returning through dubious manipulations a number of its candidates unopposed and a few days before the election the state of the parties was NNA 63, UPGA 15. Parties found it virtually impossible to campaign for votes in Regions where they were not in power. Naturally the complaints about such difficulties came more often from the NCNC and the Action Group which tried to capture some seats in Northern Nigeria, though not from the NPC or NNDP which are essentially Regional parties. There were however a number of smaller parties, allied to the NNA, in Eastern and Mid-Western Nigeria who experienced as much difficulty as the UPGA did in the North and West.

It was clear from the beginning that to form a government, the UPGA had to capture a considerable number of seats from the North, but they soon realized that it was impossible to campaign freely for votes. All over the Federation, there were reports of mass arrests, intimidation and imprisonment of political opponents. There were incidents of forcible prevention, by paid thugs, of political opponents from filing nomination papers. In the circumstances the UPGA demanded that the election be postponed. The Electoral Commission, however, decided to proceed with its arrangements for voting whereupon the UPGA ordered its supporters to boycott the election. The boycott was not effective except in Eastern Nigeria and the NNA was returned to power with the NPC winning 162 of the 167 seats in the North. The Head of State however refused to call on anyone to form a government, arguing that there was much evidence to show that the election was not free and fair. Then followed a five-day constitutional crisis which was resolved when the outgoing Prime Minister decided to form a 'broad-based' government consisting of representatives from various parts of the country. The significant point is that the result of the 1964 election was not a surprise to most Nigerians. It merely confirmed the political significance of the 1963 census.

Footnotes

1. By a strange coincidence the 1962 census started on the same day on which Western Nigeria plunged into what was to become one of the most prolonged and bitter crises in Nigeria.
2. The most extreme case was that of the recent Western Nigeria election when a party leader declared in a television broadcast that whether or not the people voted for his party, they were sure to win because they must rule.
3. There was no Mid-Western Nigeria at this time, and Lagos was part of Western Nigeria.
4. In 1948, the population of Nigeria was estimated at 23 million made up as follows: Northern Nigeria 13·5, Western Nigeria 4·4 and Eastern Nigeria 5·2 million.
5. M. Crowder, *The Story of Nigeria*, Faber and Faber, London, 1962, p. 250.
6. M. Crowder, *op. cit.*, p. 253.
7. **Area and Population of some West African States**

State	Area in sq. miles	Population in millions	Date	Density per sq. mile
Northern Nigeria	281,782	16·8	1952	59·7
Mali	460,617	3·4	1951	7·5
Niger	494,980	2·2	1951	4·4
Upper Volta	105,791	3·1	1950	29·5
French-speaking West Africa	1,831,272	17·4	—	9·6

8. The Nigerian *Daily Times* carried the following census item for about a fortnight prior to the Census Day—'Remember May 13 is Census Day. You should co-operate with census officials . . . This will help the Governments of the Federation to plan their (household members') needs—hospitals, school, roads, trade, employment and many good things of life.'
9. See 'Census is not tax' by the Western Nigeria Minister of Information, Nigeria *Daily Times*, 14 May 1962, p. 12. In Eastern Nigeria the Minister for Economic Development even threatened that anyone who refused to be counted would be liable to a fine of £100 or 12 months' imprisonment.
10. *Nigeria Outlook*, Enugu, 1 May 1962, p. 1.

11. Wraith, R. E., 'Effects (of the census) on Future Elections', Nigeria *Morning Post*, 15 May 1962, p. 5.
12. Nigerian *Morning Post*, Lagos, 21 May 1962, p. 5.
13. 'Census Officials to be tried', *Daily Times*, 17 May 1962, p. 2.
14. See the editorial comment of the Nigerian *Morning Post*, 21 May 1962, p. 2.
15. *Nigerian Outlook*, Enugu, 10 May 1962, p. 1.
16. Nigerian *Daily Times*, Lagos, 18 May 1962, p. 20.
17. *Nigerian Outlook*, Enugu, 3 May 1962, p. 1.
18. Northern Nigeria Legislature, Parliamentary Debates, House of Assembly, Daily Hansard, Third Legislature—Fourth Session (First meeting), Kaduna, 4 March 1964, p. 112.
19. *Ibid.*, p. 109.
20. Northern Nigeria Legislature, *op. cit.*, 12 March 1964, pp. 434–35.

8 The politics and economics of Nigeria's population census

T. M. Yesufu

School of Social Studies,
University of Lagos, Nigeria

Introduction

Nearly two years ago, Dr C. Okonjo expressed the hope of many, 'that the publication of the results of the 1963 census will allow far-reaching analysis of population development in this country.'[1] The hope remains unfulfilled: to statisticians and demographers this must be truly frustrating. And, in this era, when virtually all analysis that cannot be quantified is looked on with suspicion, if not downright hostility, the position is unenviable even for the economist. Nevertheless, it would be out of tradition and character if economists were to permit the absence of quantified details to deter them from wading into the census controversy.

But this paper is not an attempt at an economic 'analysis' of the census results as such, for the available information is inadequate for that. It merely attempts to recall part of the political controversy and to participate in some of the economic speculation surrounding the 1962–63 censuses of population in Nigeria.

The Politics of the Census

It is paradoxical that the Federal Minister of Economic Development in a statement in Parliament on 18 August 1962 felt constrained to emphasize that 'the conducting of a census in Nigeria is not a political matter.'[2] While acknowledging that the census would provide a basis for the distribution of seats in Parliament, the Minister considered it 'the least of the important reasons for which we in Nigeria conduct our census'.[3] Ultimately, however, it was upon the rock of politics that the 1962 census foundered, and, if the failure to produce the details of the subsequent re-count is any guide, the 1963 census has shared the same fate.

The degree of political importance placed upon a census in any country depends a great deal upon its political maturity, the nature of its constitution, the degree of social integration between the various people of the country and the state of the political parties and the balance of power between them. In a socially integrated country like the United Kingdom, with a unitary constitution, and with political parties drawing support horizontally from all parts of the country, the internal political consequences of a census, while not unimportant, are not of vital significance. In Nigeria, on the other hand, the federal character of the constitution, as well as the fact that political parties draw support largely from a single Region, are such that any large shift in the distribution of the population can have very important consequences for the interregional balance of power. For example, if the 1962 estimate of 11 million for the population of the Northern Region (instead of 22 million as given by the Minister of Economic Development as the preliminary figure[4]) had been substantiated, as against 12·5 million for the Eastern Region, control of the Federal Government would have passed from the Northern People's Congress (NPC) to the National Convention of Nigerian Citizens (NCNC).

This need to control or, at the least, participate in the Federal Government is of special, if not overriding, importance for a number of reasons. For example, the Federal Government is indisputably stronger than the Regions financially, and the latter depend upon federal sources for more than 63 per cent of their revenue.[5] The regional distribution and siting of projects under the Federal Government's development programme, in the context of Nigerian politics, are to a considerable extent determined by the dominant party in the Federal Cabinet or by the party affiliation of the Ministers charged with responsibility for particular portfolios. The allocation of funds from the financial pool and of federal grants (for example, for agricultural development) appears also to reflect, to some extent at least, the relative population of the Regions.

The attempts made originally to minimize the political importance of the census in Nigeria seem therefore to have been totally misguided. An acknowledgement of the political significance of the census might have assisted in overcoming some of the subsequent difficulties.

As it was, after the 1962 census the rumour of the 'discovery' in Eastern Nigeria of a village or town with a population of about 20,000 led to that Region's being accused of trying to dominate the Federation by falsifying the population figures. Simultaneously, there were reports of gross inaccuracies in recording the count in Northern Nigeria. A request in Parliament for the Minister of Economic Development to clarify the situation led to the eruption of the census volcano.[6] The Minister released the text of a report made to him by Mr Warren, the Federal Census Officer, in which the latter wrote that, 'the inescapable conclusion to be drawn from my investigations . . . is that figures recorded throughout the greater part of Eastern Nigeria during the present census are false and have been inflated . . . [and] there will be no alternative to conducting a complete re-enumeration in the majority of divisions in Eastern Nigeria.' As regards the West, the Census Officer reported that 'of the 62 census districts in Western Nigeria, provisional total figures are available for only five, due, in my view, to weaknesses in the census organization in the Region. . . .' The Minister added rather significantly that 'in respect of the Northern Region, no adverse comment of any kind has been made by the Federal Census Officer in his report.'[7]

The political consequences of this statement were cumulative. Two days later, a Member of Parliament, Mr D. N. Abii, demanded a full dress debate. On the defeat of his motion, several Members walked out of the House. The Prime Minister considered the matter so serious that he took the unusual step of openly rebuking the Minister of Economic Development in Parliament.[8] Referring to the embarrassment caused to him by the Minister's statement of 5 December and the subsequent walkout by some MPs, the Prime Minister added:

> 'While one may grant that the Minister had been provoked by recent criticisms that were often unfair, it must be said that his particular reaction to them on the occasion in question should have been more restrained.'

The Prime Minister went on to condemn the release by the Minister of the report of the Census Officer and the derogatory things said of some of the Regions.

The controversy did not abate, and ultimately the 1962 census was nullified. It was decided to undertake another in 1963, and the Prime Minister took over from the Minister of Economic Development the direct conduct of the census. The scrapping of the 1962 census was itself a sad comment on the capacity of the Federal Government, and should have called for a censure, if not resignation, of the government as a whole. But the government did not resign, and the Minister retained his office minus (temporarily) the control of the census.

If no one was satisfied, every one had reason to hope that the personal intervention of the Prime Minister would protect the new census from the political pitfalls of the census of 1962. This subsequent count, for which an elaborate census office was organized independently of the Federal Office of Statistics, was undertaken in November

1963. A United Nations' expert was recruited as an adviser. In order to avoid mutual inter-Regional recriminations and allegations, arrangements were made for the interchange of enumerators between the Regions. Yet the results turned out to be even more unacceptable to some Regions than those of the 1962 census. A court action by the Eastern Regional Government in regard to the census led to a confirmation of the legal authority of the Prime Minister, whose decision on the matter was therefore final. This action, however, only clarified the constitutional position; it did not and could not remove the political recriminations or the related doubts about the accuracy of the count.

How Reliable is the Census?

The debate about the census continues. Speculations regarding inaccuracies tended to be given credence by the failure, even two full years later, to publish the details of the population structure. Since the value of any comments must depend to a large extent upon the accuracy of the census results, a most important question at this stage, therefore, is whether the figure of 55·6 million can be regarded as correctly reflecting Nigeria's population.

One index by which the accuracy of the 1963 census could be checked is the rate of growth of the population. Usually a net rate of natural population growth above 3 per cent must be regarded as bordering on the abnormal. But Nigeria's 1962 census figure of 55·6 million, compared to the 1952–53 census figure, gives a growth rate much higher than this figure, as the following table illustrates.

Table 1

Rate of Population Growth by Regions, 1952–53 to 1963

Region	Population 1952–53 (in thousands)	Population 1963 (in thousands)	Ten-year increase (percentage)	Average annual growth rate (percentage)
North	16,840	29,809	77·0	5·9
East	7,218	12,394	71·7	5·4
West	4,595	10,266	123·4	8·3
Mid-West	1,492	2,536	70·0	5·4
Lagos	272	665	144·1	9·3
All Nigeria	30,417	55,670	83·0	6·3

The overall growth rate of nearly 6·3 per cent is obviously too high to be accepted with equanimity. Nevertheless, there are important arguments for resisting the temptation to reject the figures. For example, the rates of increase calculated above presume that the 1952–53 census was itself accurate. There is no reason to believe that this was so, for it was not a complete house-to-house enumeration, as was the 1963 census. The 1952–53 census figures were based partly on head counts and in some areas on estimates. Generally, people did not understand the meaning and purpose of a population census.

Many have argued that the 1963 figures were probably more accurate than either the 1952–53 census or that of 1962, because the 1963 census had a more elaborate organization, including the appointment of more enumerators, the interchange of census enumerators and officials between Regions, the participation of a UN adviser, coupled with the sheer fact that in 1963 everyone had become watchful for the falsification of results. In any case, a high rate of population growth is to be expected, not only in Nigeria but in most developing countries at the present time. For over 30 years, with the elimination of intertribal warfare, there has been relative peace and stability in Nigeria. There has been a definite improvement in sanitation and health facilities. More and better water-supply is provided by the country's development programmes. The control of malaria and the use of relatively cheap insecticides, vaccination and antibiotics are now widespread. Coupled with an improvement in educational standards, these factors have reduced the death rate dramatically.

On the other hand, except in a few urban areas such as Lagos and among the wage and salaried classes, marriage customs and sex relationships have hardly changed, and consequently the birth rate appears to have altered very little. Once more quantification is difficult because of the absence of birth and death registrations. Indeed some observers think there are grounds for believing that the birth rate is rising. Dr Okonjo, for example, appears to think this could be the case in Nigeria, due to the containment of venereal diseases and the gradual elimination of malaria with all its health complications.[9] Thus the trend is clear. Nigeria appears to have reached the second of the four of Karl Sax's stages of demographic transition—a high and stable (and possibly rising) birth rate, and a rapidly declining death rate.[10]

The experience of recent population censuses in some other countries appears also to have some relevance. For example, Ghana's census of 1960 gave her population as 6·7 million, an increase of 2·6 million or 63 per cent over a period of 12 years, compared with the recorded population in 1948 during the colonial era. A recent census of the Western Cameroon, carried out under French auspices, gave the population as 1·8 million.[11] This compares with the 753,000 credited to the territory, when it formed part of Nigeria, in the 1952–53 census. The new figure represents an apparent increase of 183 per cent, compared with about 83 per cent for Nigeria over approximately the same period. In contrast one may refer also to the recent censuses of Sierra Leone and Liberia which recorded significantly lower populations for the countries concerned than had been estimated from previous censuses.

All these experiences combined to cloud any analysis of current population censuses in Africa. They suggest very strongly that more studies and better data are required before definite and reliable conclusions can be reached. But, however suggestive they may be, they provide no argument for sustaining the results of the 1963 census in Nigeria. The rates of population growth shown in Table 1 are not only too high but are too mutually inconsistent to be easily explained away. True, the high growth rate for Lagos is accounted for partly by continuous immigration from the Regions. But the rate of 8·3 per cent for the Western Region is patently preposterous and out of tune with growth rates of less than 6 per cent in other Regions. It is highly suggestive of a widespread falsification of the population count. Even the 0·5 per cent by which the growth rate in Northern Nigeria is greater than the rate in the East and Mid-West is still too much to be explained by possible inter-Regional differences in socio-cultural background.

It behoves the Federal Government to carry out studies to test the consistency and correct the deficiencies of the 1963 census. For this purpose a post-enumeration survey of the population on a sample basis is overdue. This should be done, and the details of the 1963 census should be published without further delay. Failure to do this only adds to the current mystery and strengthens the stand of those who find it unrealistic to accept the 1963 figures as a true reflection of Nigeria's population.

Characteristics of the Population

In view of the absence of published details of the census, the official figures provide only very limited insight into the characteristics of the Nigerian population. The most obvious one is the wide divergence in Regional distribution and population density. The situation is revealed in the following table.

Table 2

Nigeria's Population Distribution and Density by Regions, 1963

Region	Area		Population		Density (persons per sq. mile)
	sq. miles	%	Total	%	
North	281,782	79·0	29,809,000	53·6	106
East	29,484	8·3	12,394,000	22·1	420
West	30,454	8·5	10,266,000	18·6	337
Mid-West	14,922	4·2	2,536,000	4·5	170
Lagos	27	—	665,000	1·2	24,639
All Nigeria	356,669	100·0	55,670,000	100·0	156

It is clear from the table that Northern Nigeria, with 79 per cent of the land area of the Federation has only 53·6 per cent of the population. In contrast, Eastern Nigeria with only 8·3 per cent of the land area has as much as 22·1 per cent of the population. The contrast in population density is consequently very great. Thus, whereas, as compared with the 1952–53 census, the other Regions have gained on Eastern Nigeria in total population, the East remains by far the most densely populated with a figure of 420 persons per square mile compared with 106 for the North and an overall average of 156.

Other characteristics of the population remain largely a matter of conjecture. With a rapidly declining death rate (at all ages) and a steady (and possibly increasing) birth rate, the base of the population pyramid is getting relatively wider. These changes, however, take place relatively slowly. Indeed, sample studies undertaken in 1963 by the National Manpower Board in certain towns throughout the Federation, indicated in many cases that the age and sex distribution of the population have not altered significantly since 1953. For example, whereas, at the 1952–53 census, the male population of Kano was 50·8 per cent of the total, the percentage based on the Manpower Board's sample of 1963 was 50·9. Similarly the ratios for Aba were 63·4 and 62·4 for 1953 and 1963 respectively.[12]

Using the 1952–53 ratios in the absence of other reliable indicators, therefore, the 1963 population of Nigeria may be analysed as follows.

Table 3

Nigeria's Population by Age and Sex 1963 (estimates only)

Age	Males (in thousands)	Females (in thousands)	Both sexes (in thousands)	Percentage of age groups
Under 2 years	2,973	3,095	6,068	11
2–6 years	4,940	4,746	9,686	17
7–14 years	4,780	4,072	8,852	16
15–49 years	12,686	13,869	26,555	48
50 years and over	2,074	2,435	4,509	8
All ages	27,453	28,217	55,670	100

Reference to the 1952–53 census figures, for example, will show that there are some variations in individual Regions from the above overall pattern. But these are minor. The important point at this stage is that, generally speaking, Nigeria's population is young. Thus 44 per cent of the population is below the age of 15 years in contrast to the more developed countries where the ratio is much lower; in the United Kingdom, for example, the corresponding age group constitutes only about 23 per cent of the population.

Table 3 also indicates that females on the whole outnumber males by about 2·2 per cent. The survival rate of the sexes probably differs significantly at different ages.

Other important characteristics of the population, such as the degree of urbanization, migration, size of families and occupational distribution, have not yet been published for the 1963 census. Because of momentous political changes and economic and social development, the 1952–53 census can now offer but a very poor guide in these matters. The inadequacies of even the above analysis of the 1963 population by age and sex on the basis of the 1952–53 census are too glaring to pass unnoticed. It is only a sense of desperation and the need to provide a basis for the comments that follow that justify making the attempt.

Some Economic Implications

The more one considers the economic importance of a census for developing countries, the more acute is the ineptitude of Nigeria for failing to undertake an accurate population count. The cost in terms of the country's international image and prestige cannot be measured in money. It is pertinent to recall that before the 1963 census Nigeria's position in the world's population schedule was thirteenth. The new population figures moved Nigeria into ninth position, and in the process she overtook France, the United Kingdom, Italy and West Germany. Nigeria not only still has the largest population in Africa, but also has increased the population gap from her nearest rivals, such as the United Arab Republic. As has been pointed out, 'Northern Nigeria alone has a bigger population than any African state, and the population of even the newest and smallest region, the Mid-West, exceeds that of a dozen African states.'[13]

Nigeria is likely to pay more for her membership in international organizations, because of the new population figure. Normally, contributions to the United Nations budget and that of other agencies is based upon the degree of the country's industrialization and national income. To the extent that some of these indices will be reflected in population size, it follows that Nigeria's international financial obligations will increase, not only absolutely, but relatively.

Internally, the most obvious economic aspect of the census was its financial cost. By December 1962, more than £1 million had already been spent in regard to the census for that year. But the view of the Federal Government appeared to be that the importance of a census was so great that no amount spent could be considered too much. Subsequently, a sum of £2·5 million was provided for the 1963 census.[14] There appears as yet to be no final official assessment of the actual expenditures, but there is little doubt that both the 1962 and 1963 censuses cost the Federal Government over £4 million. When the loss in production of the enumerators and other census officials, who had to absent themselves from their normal duties, is taken into account, the censuses may have cost Nigeria anything up to £5 million.

Of much more serious character, however, are the implications that the 1963 census figures have for development planning in Nigeria. The census makes completely irrelevant all the major assumptions and calculations upon which the 1962–68 National Development Plan is based. The Plan presumed a net population growth rate of about 2 per cent per annum, and programmed for a rate of economic growth of about 4 per cent per annum, on the basis of an annual investment of approximately 15 per cent of the national income.

If indeed Nigeria's rate of population growth is over 6 per cent per annum, it follows that per capita national income has been declining and will continue to decline by at least 2 per cent per annum, even if the economic growth rate of 4 per cent per annum were attained and maintained. It would follow also that to maintain whatever may be the prevailing level of per capita national income, Nigeria's economic performance must rise to a level of at least 6 per cent growth per annum. On the basis of existing assumptions (a capital/output ratio of 3·75 is assumed in the Plan), this would require an annual investment of nearly 25 per cent of the national income. Is this really possible? Israel, for example, has been able to attain one of the highest economic growth rates in the world (8 per cent) by investing 35 per cent of her national income. But Israel's per capita national income is about four to five times that of Nigeria. To the extent that savings (and therefore investment) is a function of income, it follows that Nigeria's capacity to attain an investment rate of the order indicated would be extremely unlikely. How unlikely may be understood from the fact that even under the current Development Plan, requiring an investment of 15 per cent of the national income, 50 per cent of the investment is expected to come from abroad. This means that it is not expected that Nigeria can save and invest much more than 7 per cent of its national income from its own resources. Thus, if the rate of investment is to be stepped up to 25 per cent, it means that the equivalent of 18 per cent of our national income must be sought from foreign sources, i.e. more than twice the current expectation. This would be clearly ridiculous since available evidence suggests that even the current expectations are not being fulfilled. The alternative, which is to invest about 16 per cent from the country's own resources, may be possible, but it would require grim determination and a machinery for effecting and mobilizing forced savings to an extent that no Nigerian Government in present circumstances would probably be willing to undertake.

It may be noted that the census also complicates the calculation of the national income itself, to the extent that the income derived from the subsistence sector of the economy is calculated by a quantification and evaluation of the average production per head of those concerned. Since this sector is still very important in the Nigerian economy,[15] it follows that, if the 1963 census is correct, the national income from the subsistence sector has until now been undervalued. But, since average incomes in this sector compare unfavourably with those from other sectors, there would (even if the undervaluation were corrected) still be a decline in the average national income per capita. Nigeria's gross domestic product during 1962–63 (at 1957 factor cost) has been estimated at £1,072·3 million.[16] If the speculated 1962 population of 42 million were accepted, the per capita national income would thus have been somewhat above £25. With the 1963 figure of 55·6 million the per capita national income is only about £19, compared with the 1957 estimate of about £29.

But, could the average national income (and so the standard of living) really have declined by over 30 per cent in eight years? A decline of that magnitude, bearing in mind prevailing low incomes, would show in declining standards of nutrition. But there is no evidence that this is the case. This, however, provides no comfort, since even with a lower population figure of 42 million, the downward trend in the per capita national income would still have been evident. It is equally clear that, at current living levels *vis-à-vis* existing incomes,[17] it would, as already indicated, be very difficult to achieve the 25 per cent savings required to sustain an economic growth rate which would arrest a decline (let alone permit the possibility of growth) in the per capita income in Nigeria.

Yet to continue with the existing plan without rethinking what this means for the population is to miss the fundamental purpose of planning. It follows that, if the

Governments do seriously accept the results of the 1963 census, the present Development Plan should not be merely reviewed but rather completely reformulated. There are in the Plan many programmes which are specifically tied to the population—for example, the improvement of the ratio of doctors to the population from 1 : 32,000 to 1: 10,000, or again the ratio of agricultural extension workers to the agricultural population. To take the former example, the 1963 population census result is such that even if the target for the training of doctors in the Plan were to be fulfilled it would now hardly be adequate to sustain the current ratio.

In any case, it is clear that to maintain the per capita income at its present apparent level of £20, on the basis of the assumed capital/output ratio of 3·75, the annual investment required in Nigeria would have to be at least £272 million. This contrasts with the existing average of £207 million (£132 million and £65 million in the public and private sectors respectively); it would represent a minimum increase of 24 per cent. To attain the 1957 level of £29 per capita would require an annual investment of about £408 million or more than a 90 per cent increase on the existing level of investment.

It is instructive to look at certain specific problems of special importance for the Nigerian economy that the results of the 1963 census illuminate with ominous clarity. These are educational planning and a national manpower policy.

The importance of education for Nigeria's development from the point of view of skill formation has received special attention in the last few years.[18] The Governments have, however, also accepted the expansion of education as a social obligation. The result is that, today, education constitutes the greatest single 'industry' in Nigeria (excluding agriculture) accounting for 113,297 out of 530,167 employed persons covered in the National Manpower Board survey of 1963.[19] This importance is reflected in the Development Plan 1962–68, in which £69·8 million, or 10·3 per cent of all expenditure under the Plan, is earmarked for education. During 1961–62 the recurrent cost of education to the Governments of the Federation was £24·4 million or 25 per cent of the total budget. The results of the census are such that these amounts now seem to be far from adequate to maintain the levels of education presumed in the Plan. In Northern Nigeria, for example, the Plan makes provision for an annual primary school enrolment of 720,000 new pupils by 1968, as compared with the 1962 level of 259,934. It was hoped that this would permit the primary school enrolment of about 28 per cent of the age group 6–7 years. With the census results taken at their face value, Northern Nigeria had, in 1963, about 8·8 million children in the age groups 7–14 years (or very roughly 1·3 million children at seven). With annual primary school enrolments running at 411,000, it follows that only 4·6 per cent of the relevant age group was at school, and to provide facilities for anything approaching 28 per cent would strain the Region's resources to the limit.

In Western Nigeria the annual primary school enrolment in 1963 was about 1·1 million. On the basis of the census, the appropriate age group would be of the order of 1·6 million. This means that, far from the current assumption, primary school education is still not universal in that Region. The relative position would be worse if the target enrolment of 1·5 million by 1968 in the Development Plan were adhered to. Thus, the Region requires to raise its expenditure on education by over 30 per cent to attain its relative (as distinct from its absolute) targets.

The manpower and employment implications of the census results are equally great. They raise the size of the country's potential labour force (aged 15 years and above) to over 31 million. This would mean that in 1963 there were about 1·8 million persons working or seeking employment in industry or other forms of wage employment.[20] Yet in that year the wage-earners in Nigeria numbered in fact about 1·2 million. This would, accepting the 1963 census figures, give an unemployment figure of about 600,000. On the basis of previous assumptions, it would require an outright investment of £12·4 million to generate a per capita income of £10 per month for these persons. The labour force situation would demand employment creation in the modern industrial sector at a rate of at least 500,000 per annum, compared with the performance of the economy of about 25,000 per annum within the last few years.

Of equal analytical and practical significance is the very uneven distribution of human resources between the various Regions. In comparison with other African countries, the population density in Eastern Nigeria is bordering on overpopulation. But, taking the country as a whole, it is significant, for example, that Nigeria has adequate productive land. Yet the uneven population density revealed by the census reflects to a considerable extent, the growing immobility of labour in the country, due to the Regionalist employment policies of the Governments. At present, Eastern Nigeria is not only overpopulated by comparison with the other Regions, but other available information indicates that it leads the country in education and training in skills. A summary of the National Register of Students for 1963–64 highlights this position. The following selected areas of study illustrate this.

Table 4
Registered Students in Institutions of Higher Learning by Region of Origin and Selected Fields of Study, 1963–64

Field of study	Students by Region of origin				
	North	East	West	Mid-West	Federal territory
Accountancy	3	107	47	25	3
Agriculture	15	127	49	12	—
Business administration	2	127	33	26	1
Botany	—	26	17	4	1
Education	42	215	110	40	5
Medicine	33	75	121	43	14
Veterinary medicine	—	165	16	3	—

Taking student registrations as a whole, persons of Eastern Region origin accounted for 2,356 or more than 50 per cent of a total of 4,534 registered in the senior category. It behoves all the Regions to relax their Regionalist employment policies. Otherwise, because of the fundamental importance of human resources for economic and social development, one of two things is likely to happen, either of which has grave political and economic consequences for the country as a whole. On the one hand, the disparity of economic development between Regions may widen still further than it is at present, to the relative advantage of Eastern Region because of its superiority in the availability of trained manpower. This may have the effect of accentuating Regional jealousies and exacerbating political dissension throughout the Federation. On the other hand, the population pressure in the Eastern Region (and subsequently in the Western Region) may become so great, manifesting itself in mass unemployment, that any continued failure of the Governments to liberalize their employment policies and permit a freer mobility of labour and settlement between the Regions would cause dissension. This dissension could be intra-Regional to start with, but it would sooner or later develop into a national issue; or it could, with political adroitness in the Region concerned, lead to a canalization of disaffection in that Region against the Federal and other Regional Governments.

Either way the country stands to lose economically. In the first case, the available high-level manpower is not distributed to the best advantage. While one Region has a relative oversupply of high-level manpower, the other Regions would still be handicapped by a relative shortage, which can be met only partly by substituting high-cost expatriate manpower. This particular aspect of the problem is likely to be accentuated by the new cry for a fair distribution of the national cake. In terms of employment, this implies that employment in the Federal Public Service and institutions should be filled on the basis of distribution between persons of various Regional origins in proportion to the population of the Regions concerned. Whatever may be the political attraction of the slogan, it is economically indefensible. It means that, because of considerations of Regional origin, an incompetent person could be recruited to fill a post for which a better qualified person was available. In some cases, vacancies would not be filled because of lack of qualified candidates from a particular Region. In either case, the whole economy suffers, through non-performance or inefficient performance of essential functions. And social discontent is generated on the part of those being discriminated against.

The second alternative, which means unemployment, would be a clear case of non-utilization of a valuable economic resource. The higher the rate of unemployment, the greater also is the pressure of the dependency burden upon those in employment—a burden which is already so much greater than in the developed countries because of the much higher proportion of persons below the legal working age, the absence of a national social security system, and the force of social obligations connected with the extended family system.

Conclusions

The above considerations have neither been exhaustive nor conclusive. Put together, they re-emphasize the one major question that underlines this paper—namely, how reliable was the 1963 census? The search for an answer has been complicated by a number of factors. First, there is no previous reliable census to provide a basis of judgement. Second, the figures of the annulled 1962 census differ too widely from those of the subsequent one held a year later. And third, the internal inconsistencies of the 1963 census (e.g. the differences in the rates of population growth between Regions) are too great to be ignored. Taken together, the evidence points clearly to inaccuracy in the census.

The failure of this first complete national census is one more price which Nigeria has had to pay for its constitutional structure and the nature of its party politics. But if the political problems have for the moment been contained or postponed, the economic implications of the census cannot be so easily ignored. The census has made irrelevant most of the basic assumptions and calculations of the Six-Year National Development Plan, such as the level of the national income and the rate of growth of the economy. The Plan needs to be reviewed immediately.

In general, the experience of Nigeria shows that in a developing country, even simple scientific processes such as a head count cannot be taken for granted. In particular, it suggests that in Federal states where regionalist feelings are strong, the political stakes of a census can be so high as to make the desirability of a statistically accurate count seem irrelevant. It has been suggested that, in such conditions, the best course would be to entrust the census to an independent body, such as a legally constituted but politically neutral body, or to the United Nations.

Footnotes

1. CHUKUKA OKONJO, 'Patterns of Population Growth', *The Nigerian Journal of Economic and Social Studies*, Vol. 6, No. 1, March 1964.
2. *Parliamentary Debates, House of Representatives*, 18 August 1962, columns 2356–58.
3. *Ibid.*, column 2356.
4. *Ibid.*, column 2359.

5. This percentage is for 1963 when, of total Regional revenues of £68,053,000, as much as £43,229,000 came from Federal sources (cf. *Digest of Statistics, 1964,* Federal Office of Statistics, Lagos, Table 11.2).
6. Parliamentary Question No. *0.781 by Mallam Ibrahim Na Maitama: cf. column 2732 in *Parliamentary Debates, House of Representatives*, 5 December 1962.
7. *Ibid.*, columns 2734–35.
8. *Parliamentary Debates, House of Representatives, 10 December 1962,* columns 2359–2860.
9. CHUKUKA OKONJO, *op. cit.*, pp. 18–22.
10. See ADAMANTIOS PEPELASIS, LEON MEARS, and IRMA ADELMAN, *Economic Development*, Harper, 1961, Chapter 3.
11. *West Africa*, 21 August 1965, p. 927.
12. Calculations based on *Population Census of Nigeria: (Summary of Tables),* Table 9, page 10, and on Table 8, *Urban Unemployment Survey, 1963* (Report submitted to the Seminar on Manpower Problems in Economic Development, 1964, by the National Manpower Board).
13. 'Nigeria's Population Explosion', *West Africa*, 29 February 1964.
14. For some official information on the cost of the census, see the statements of the Minister of Economic Development in *Parliamentary Debates of the House of Representatives*, 5 December 1962, columns 2735–36; and 9 January 1964, column 3233 and Answer to Parliamentary Questions 0·1218 of the same date.
15. Agriculture, which is still largely subsistence, accounts for about 70 per cent (78 per cent in 1953) of Nigeria's labour force and 56 per cent of the national income.
16. *Annual Abstract of Statistics, 1962,* Table 13.1.
17. For zonal breakdown of what it would cost to live with a minimum of decency as against current incomes, see Chapter 3 of the *Report of the Morgan Commission, 1964.* The Governments condemned this part of the Report. But all they succeeded in achieving was the chastisement of the innocent and unwilling bearer of bad news. Their inability to pay the minimum wages laid down by the Commission was not a valid argument against the findings of the Commission.
18. See the Ashby Report, *Investment in Education,* 1960, and the National Manpower Board, *Nigeria's High-Level Manpower 1963–68*, 1964.
19. *Nigeria's High-Level Manpower, 1963–68.*
20. For details of such calculations, see T. M. YESUFU: *Forecasting Nigeria's Manpower Needs: A note on Methodology,* submitted to the International Seminar on Manpower Problems, Lagos, 1964. (The papers of the Seminar are in the course of publication.)

9 Before and after a population census operation in Nigeria—a physician's experience

T. O. Ogunlesi

Department of Medicine, University of Ibadan, Nigeria

The experience described here relates to the National Population Census taken in Nigeria in November 1963. I was an observer in the pre-enumeration training given in Ibadan to district census officers and assistant district census officers in September 1963, and I took part in the actual enumerating and supervising in one particular census district during the four days of the counting in November. I have continued to be involved in the planning and execution of the post-census exercises that followed in a district where the University of Ibadan has a primary interest in various studies of the population. I wish to make it clear that my experience is limited to Ibarapa district only, and I make no claim for the generality of the situation in census districts in other parts of the country.

It was purely by chance that I was involved in the 1963 population census. The University of Ibadan launched its Community Health Project at Igbo Ora in Ibarapa district in February 1963, and it had been decided that one of the Project's first priorities in baseline studies would be to check the estimate of the population of the district derived from the 1952 census figures. The 1952 census showed the population figures for Igbo Ora town as 19,294 and for the whole district of Ibarapa as 51,494 (Table 1). On an estimated rate of growth of 3 per cent per annum, our provisional figures for 1962 were in the region of 25,000 for Igbo Ora and about 65,000 to 70,000 for the whole district. As a matter of fact, the Project's five-year budget, which was submitted to the Rockefeller Foundation in 1962, were based on these figures. The 1963 census suggested that, while our estimate of the Igbo Ora town population was a reasonable approximation, that of the district, which consists of towns, villages and hamlets, was off the mark by nearly 50 per cent, as shown in Table 1.

Some of the reasons why so much argument followed the announcement of the 1963 census results can be inferred from this table. The absence of any record of populations in the 1952 census for villages surrounding Igbo Ora, Eruwa, Lanlate, Tapa-Aiyete, Igangan and Idere that are now known to have been in existence long before 1952 suggests that the 1952 census was incomplete in this respect. Furthermore, if the 1963 figures for Eruwa, Tapa, Aiyete are reliable, then the omissions in the 1952 census must also include households and individuals in the towns and larger villages, apart from small villages and hamlets omitted in the more inaccessible areas. We intended to check the 1952 census figures for Ibarapa district by carrying out our own population census independent of any governmental system. The 1962 census had generated so much political heat that there seemed to be little chance late in 1962 of our gaining access to the detailed figures for Ibarapa district which we required. About the middle of 1963, however, while we were preparing for our independent census of the district, the Federal Government announced plans for another countrywide population census, and so we decided that it would be easier and better for us to collaborate with the national organization in the census operation in Ibarapa district.

Table 1

District	1952 census	1963 census
1. Igbo Ora	19,294	29,435
Igbo Ora villages	—	14,481
2. Eruwa	8,154	20,479
New Eruwa	2,034	2,107
Eruwa villages	—	9,010
3. Lanlate	4,874	11,982
Maya	—	605
Lanlate villages	—	14,431
4. Tapa	1,755	7,604
5. Aiyete	4,197	11,171
Tapa-Aiyete villages	—	4,101
6. Igangan	5,190	9,800
Igangan villages		5,756
7. Idere	4,235	5,300
Idere villages	—	395
Other villages	1,751	—
Total	51,494	137,542

The Nigerian Census, 1963: The Pre-Enumeration Stage

No uniform or rigid pattern can be laid down for planning a census. The 1963 Nigerian population census had everything in its favour except time. The political wounds caused by the abortive 1962 population census had not had a chance to heal. There had hardly been time for anyone, politician or non-politician, to digest the experience. Nigeria, however, was in a hurry for an answer to the question of total numbers. The previous census had been in 1952, and independence came in 1960. Therefore it was a job that had to be done quickly, 'rushed through' as one might say, and, in those circumstances, all the major elements necessary for the pre-enumeration stage were provided 'ready-to-wear' rather than 'made-to-measure'.

OPERATION COSTS

The four-day operation cost the country well over £2 million. From medical considerations, this is about as much as it costs to provide medical and health services for the whole of Western Nigeria for one year. We witnessed the breakdown of this large sum of money in Ibarapa district and the formula was much the same as for any other census district throughout the country. Each enumerator was paid £7 for the four days' work, each supervisor £9, each assistant district census officer £20, each district census officer £30. When one bears in mind that in Ibarapa district alone, there were 358 enumerators (excluding reserves), some 97 supervisors, two assistant district census officers and one district census officer, and that throughout the country, all census officials had to be issued with equipment for writing with census handbags, and to be paid allowances for travelling and transport (in some cases up to one shilling a mile), then it becomes easier to understand why the cost of a census can run into millions of pounds.

RE-DELIMITATION OF ENUMERATION AREAS

Resulting from experience of the 1962 census, in which enumeration went on for three weeks, the enumeration period for the 1963 census was reduced to four days, and the enumeration areas used for the 1962 census were broken up into smaller areas. In the 1962 census there were 18 enumeration areas in Igbo Ora town and altogether 97 enumeration areas in Ibarapa district. In the 1963 census, the corresponding figures were 62 and 358 respectively.

THE CENSUS QUESTIONNAIRE

The questionnaire used in 1963, though similar, was much simpler than the one used in 1962. The direct topics in the 1963 census were based on items relating to personal, cultural, social and economic characteristics only, namely name, sex, age, ethnic group (or nationality, if non-Nigerian), religion and occupation. The 1962 questionnaire contained items of literacy and educational characteristics, as well as columns for age-group and for exact age. In 1963 this was simplified to age (in years only). Total numbers (of the population, as well as of houses numbered during the census) were derived topics in both cases. Items relating to place of birth, relationship to head of house, or family or fertility data were not included either in 1962 or 1963.

PRELIMINARY TRAINING OF CENSUS OFFICIALS

The Regional census officer organized a training course lasting about a week, in September 1963, for some 200 district census officers and assistant district officers throughout the Western Region; presumably the same kind of training was organized in all the other Regions of the Federation. After this training, the district census officers in turn were instructed to organize the training of enumerators and supervisors in their respective census districts. Our Project staff took some part in the training of enumerators in our district, and we addressed supervisors and enumerators in Ibarapa district on the importance of the census and the need for complete and reliable information. We worked very closely with the district census officer (who was the Secretary to the District Council) and his two assistants (the Local Education Secretary and the Technical Officer responsible for the Council's works), and several of our Project staff served either as supervisors or enumerators. The majority of the enumerators and supervisors were teachers in primary schools in the district (Ibarapa district had at that time one secondary grammar school, two teacher-training colleges and 57 primary schools). A small number of the enumerators were students from the secondary school or teacher-training colleges. Practically all the census officials were recruited locally from those ordinarily resident in the district.

Most of the officials that we dealt with in Ibarapa were responsible, intelligent and hard-working people, capable of performing a good job, which most of them did, allowing for some of the circumstances surrounding the task itself. But the tools available to them were poor. They were, for instance, expected to assess age from inadequate local historical data. The very commendable effort of Professor Ajayi and Dr Igun, which led to the compilation in May 1962 of a list of historical events, partly filled the gap, but further work and a breakdown into more comprehensive local lists were needed. Some of the houses that the enumerators tried to number before the census were so complex in shape, size and location that even the definition of what constitutes a house, and how a house is to be differentiated from a compound were not easy questions to answer in rural areas. They were expected to map out on enumeration area description forms the boundaries of their respective areas. In fact, many villages and fairly large-size communities in Nigeria were not shown on any maps available in 1963. The Ibarapa Project had to commission aerial photographs of Igbo Ora and Eruwa in 1961 at a cost of £400 at the commencement of our operations in the district.

The task of dividing up census districts into enumeration areas of approximately 400 to 500 people each, and of making sure that each enumerator clearly knew the boundaries of his or her area was far more complex than was first realized, and there was hardly any time before the census for this task to be properly done. The delimitation of districts into fairly accurate enumeration areas is one of the crucial problems to be solved in any future population census in Nigeria. We found, for instance, in Eruwa and in Igbo Ora that the boundaries between the various wards in these rural towns varied according to whether the subject was tax collection or voting for local council elections. Some households in certain wards paid their taxes into wards different from those in which they were located physically, and consequently, for voting and census purposes, these households claimed to be in wards outside their physical location. The task of producing accurate and reliable diagrams of the 358 enumeration areas in Ibarapa district would take a lot more work than has been done to date, but first may well require the appointment of a delimitation commission to settle boundary disputes between various wards.

Yet another example may be quoted to illustrate the background to some of the arguments which followed the announcement of the 1963 census results. It was not always clear to enumerators whom to count or whom not to count in a particular house. More investigations are required into family and migration patterns to enable clear guide-lines to be provided for the future.

No doubt the same person was enumerated in several places during the four-day period; in Village A, because his father was born there (therefore he is a member of that family), in Village B, because his mother was born there (and therefore he is also a member of that family), in Village C, because that is where he lives and works from Monday to Saturday (or during the planting season), and in Town D, because he has built a modern house there (his ancestors came originally from there, and that is where he hopes to be buried).

The Enumeration Period

Four medical students and I, together with other Project staff, watched the actual enumerating and supervising during the four days, 5 to 8 November 1963. In addition to the census officials already described, there were some 30 inspectors in the district throughout the four days. They were observers drawn from the Northern and Eastern Regions, and they could choose any of the enumeration areas in the district during the four days of the count for a 'spot check' on what was actually going on in the area—one of the many checks and balances built into the census organization. Similar arrangements, I believe, were made in the other regions.

We listened to enumerators as they 'calculated' ages in some of the households by questioning people on local historical events. The results were very variable, and depended to a large extent on the intelligence and patience of the examiner. On the whole, we think that this method of age assessment constitutes a forward step, superior to guess work if properly applied. At the end of four days, the census books were collected and carried away.

After the Census

It might well be asked, and we were asked, what business doctors have to do with a population census. We explained to the people of the district at the time, particularly to the enumerators, that our work in the district had much to do with the census, and that if we were to make objective plans of medical care for the population, we needed to know how many people there were, where they lived, their names and addresses, sex, age, occupation and more. The information we gained has since been transferred to punch cards for analysis, and we have used the data in some of the following ways:

1. Permanent numbering of houses in December 1963 in seven large towns and villages in the district (Igbo Ora, Eruwa, Lanlate, Idere, Tapa, Aiyete, Igangan).
2. Registration of births and deaths in Igbo Ora (since November 1963).
3. Sociological studies—of family patterns, housing patterns, marriage, religion, rural industries, etc. (see BARBER, C. R., *Igbo Ora: a town in transition—a sociological study*, Oxford, 1965.
4. Health and morbidity surveys:
   - (i) Eruwa (1964 and 1965), measles and poliomyelitis vaccination trials on children;
   - (ii) Igbo Ora (1965), tuberculosis prevalence survey;
   - (iii) Idere (1965), tuberculosis prevalence survey;
   - (iv) Tapa (in progress), trial-survey for schistosomiasis prevalence.

In the course of these exercises and studies we have had cause to look for persons whose particulars were recorded in our Census Books, for houses and families similarly registered, as well as for deaths, births and migrants in this population. These efforts have brought us face to face with some of the irregularities and inaccuracies varying from minor, easily understood errors of recording by enumerators, e.g. 'X, aged under 1 year, occupation—farmer', to entire households of six or more persons whose names were not entered in the census books, and who claimed to have been present in the house during the census period. At the same time there are several names of persons in the books who cannot be traced in the houses to which they were supposed to belong. Some of the basic problems which we have encountered in the use of data recorded in the 1963 census of the district fall into three parts, and these have been described in detail elsewhere (OGUNLESI *et al.*, 'Demographic Concepts in Baselines for Health Studies of Human Population', *Journal of the Nigerian Medical Association*, 1965). They are problems of

- (a) identification of individuals, by names and addresses;
- (b) age assessment in an illiterate society;
- (c) social organization and family relationships.

Some of these problems came into bold relief quite recently during a survey carried out in Idere village near Igbo Ora by a group of American medical students on a study of tuberculosis prevalence in that population (August 1965). The method used was to carry out a tuberculin test on the whole population (5,000, 1963 census). In a preliminary check, some 10 per cent of this number were either unknown, had died or had migrated permanently from the village by August 1965. At the same time, however, an additional 10 per cent of the population was found to be present in the village (of all ages) whose names were not in the 1963 census records. The new census population, which formed the frame for this survey, was about the same size as the 1963 census population. About 65 per cent of this population turned up for the tuberculin injections. Practically all those who did not turn up (during the rainy season) were on their farms, these being a day's walk or more from Idere. Overt refusal amounted to less than 1 per cent. This experience, coupled with a similar experience in Igbo Ora earlier in the year in connection with a general medical survey of a random sample of the population, raises the question as to which population is the most appropriate frame for such survey work in rural communities, a *de facto* population, which is much easier to cope with, or a *de jure* population, which is what the census information provides, and which is more suitable for purposes of comparison with other studies of the same population. More studies are in progress on this question.

General Conclusions and Summary

The most important consideration, in any census plan, ought to be how to obtain the best value for money in social and economic terms, and this applies particularly to developing countries with very slender financial resources. Quite apart from direct answers to questions asked during a census, a good deal more that is of social and economic benefit can be derived from a census operation. We think, for example, that Ibarapa district probably got more out of the 1963 census than any other district in the country by obtaining from the census a system of house-numbering for its towns and villages. We think that census time offers the best opportunity for that kind of exercise. The same could be said of registration of vital events.

The climate of public opinion required for introducing universal registration of births is at its best at census time, and if it became generally known that the only proof of legal existence for a person and the passport to the enjoyment of legal rights and social benefits was a birth certificate, a new generation of citizens with birth certificates could be raised in ten years.

There is a strong case for a permanent Census Commission. It should take much longer than it did in 1962 and 1963 to prepare for the next Nigerian National Population Census, presumably in 1973, and a full-time Commission would have much to do between now and then. Time is needed to educate the public in the right kind of attitude to a population census.

The disadvantages of the present attitudes are obvious in the opposite kinds of reaction to registration when it is for social benefits as compared with when it is for tax assessment purposes. A favourable atmosphere for the universal registration of births, to begin with the next census, can be created during the intercensal period by linking the obligation to do so with social benefits such as entry into free primary schools, obtaining licences and passports, and registration of deaths with exemption from the tax roll, etc. The high investment of public funds in education, which is common to all regions of Nigeria, offers the best hope for a rise in the literacy rate, which should then facilitate obtaining answers to the questions: What is your name? Where do you live? How old are you? Where were you born? What do you do for a living?

10 Design and concepts of population censuses and sample surveys in a developing country—Ghana

B. Gil

International Labour Organization, Geneva

and D. K. Ghansah

Central Bureau of Statistics, Accra, Ghana

Introduction

The 1960 population census of Ghana followed the principles and recommendations of the United Nations with but a few adaptations to meet local requirements and conditions. It applied modern census techniques in all stages of the programme which on the whole turned out successfully. The entire programme is now being studied systematically, and the results of this study may be a valuable contribution to the knowledge of census-taking, not only in Ghana, but also in other areas in Africa and elsewhere at a similar stage of development. A full description of the 1960 census events and some evaluation of its methods and results are contained in the *General Report.*[1] Some highlights of the programme, relating mainly to the general problems of policy, administration and organization, are discussed in an article published recently in the *International Labour Review.*[2]

This paper deals with two technical problems, those of design and those of concepts, which are closely related one to another and which bear implications for a wide range of aspects of enquiry.

Census Design

THE HIGHLIGHTS OF THE DESIGN

The Ghana census was designed with the aim of achieving several objectives in one integrated programme. The design was dictated not only by the scientific–technical objectives but also by certain policy decisions and administrative–organizational requirements. These three categories of determinants bore their respective weights on the design of the census programme according to the then existing circumstances.

The programme was composed of several projects carried out either simultaneously or in succession in three main phases or field operations. Their integration one with another aimed at giving a complete picture of the population at a certain point of time or in a particular period. At the same time the main operations were basically independent one from another so as to make feasible a statistical appraisal of quality.

(a) *Main Census Enumeration:* The main census enumeration took place in March 1960 (reference date 20 March). This was a 100 per cent enumeration with a 'house' questionnaire containing 11 items which covered all but two of the basic items recommended by the United Nations, under four headings: geographic, personal, economic and educational characteristics. Indeed, the main questionnaire of the Ghana census was among the most extensive ones used in the 1960 censuses in various countries of the world.

(b) *Post-Enumeration Survey* (*PES*): Almost three months after the main census date (8 June 1960) the PES started and lasted for about six weeks. The PES had two types of objectives (listed here according to their statistical sequence and not necessarily their actual weight in the inquiry).

1. Collection of information for an Evaluation Study of the main census results. This study consisted of three projects:
   (i) Coverage of houses;
   (ii) Coverage of persons in houses;
   (iii) Errors of content.
2. A supplementary inquiry on topics that could not be included in the 100 per cent enumeration.

In carrying out the fieldwork different combinations of the above four projects were effected.

For the purpose of evaluating the coverage of houses (finding out houses missed or enumerated twice by the main census enumerator, vide project (b)1(i)), a special house listing was carried out in 5 per cent of main census enumeration areas (EAs), i.e. in 344 out of the total, 6,878 EAs. This was a one-stage sample design and took place in the first three days of the PES inquiry.

On the other hand, the fieldwork for the remaining three projects ((b)1(ii), (b)1(iii) and (b)2) was combined in one multipurpose re-enumeration of persons in a 5 per cent sample of the main census houses. The sample design was different from the one used for the house listing, as explained below. These three studies, though different in techniques and objectives of analysis, derive their information by the same method, namely enumeration of persons. Briefly, in order to evaluate the coverage of persons (persons missed or enumerated twice by the main census enumerator) one needs to list again all persons in a sample of census houses. Likewise, for the evaluation of content errors (accuracy of information recorded),[3] a re-interview of persons, using main census questions, had to be made.

The third project, Supplementary Inquiry, was essentially an extension of this latter interview.

This multipurpose re-enumeration and re-interview used a 'household' schedule containing 20 items or topics (some 40 questions). Nine of these were repeated from the main census while 11 were new items relating to: literacy and languages, migration, marital status and marriage, fertility and mortality, household and housing, and certain economic characteristics. This was a 'heavy' questionnaire, which normally needed 45 to 90 minutes of interviewing time to complete.

(c) *Field Reconciliation Check:* For purposes of census evaluation and in order to study methods and procedures so as to improve future inquiries, a third field operation, the Field Reconciliation Check, was carried out about a year later (the main part of it in March–August 1961). It covered less than 0·5 per cent of the main census houses and its specific task was to find out the reasons for the discrepancies between the main Census and the PES counts (i.e. the coverage error only; the plan for a field reconciliation of response discrepancies between the two main enumerations was given up after a field trial in September 1960).[4]

Thus, there were three field operations involving house visits, successively decreasing with respect to volume of work (the number of field workers being 10,000, 1,000 and 10 to 15 respectively) but increasing in requirements of quality (educational and statistical background of interviewers). Meanwhile, administrative and statistical controls were shifting from a decentralized to a strictly centralized control. In the main Census there was overall control by 736 Field Supervisors and 82

Census District Officers; in the PES by 82 and 40 respectively, with an indirect 'statistical' control by five senior officers from the Head Office in Accra; in the Field Reconciliation, overall (administrative and statistical) direct control was exercised by two senior officers from the Head Office.

The results obtained from the two main enumerations (Census and PES) were in part according to expectations and in part somewhat surprising. Contrary to the general opinion and experience in some other countries, the Ghana main Census achieved a better coverage than the PES. The PES as evidenced by the subsequent reconciliation checks showed, in comparison with the main Census, an under-enumeration of approximately 10 per cent.[5] With regard to content (accuracy of information recorded) it appears that in several respects the PES was of better quality than the main Census (e.g. in respect to information on place of birth, type of activity, and employment status, not to mention all the topics of the Supplementary Inquiry which were considered *a priori* 'unfeasible' for a 100 per cent enumeration). In certain other respects, such as information on age, the main Census on the whole gave perhaps a more accurate picture than the PES.[6]

Objectives of the Inquiries and Scope of the Subject Matter

In countries where no reliable data are collected on a current basis (e.g. through continuous registration) or periodically (sample surveys) the population census is obviously considered a good, and perhaps the only, opportunity to obtain information on a broader range of subjects than provided by the conventional census items. Where no good prospects exist for a population sample survey in the not too distant future, census planners can hardly resist the temptation to gather as much information as possible on the occasion of a population census. Such was in fact the attitude of the Ghana Census Office. As 12 years had passed since the previous count in 1948—which was considered poor not only in quality but also in quantity of information supplied—planners, administrators and research workers placed considerable hopes on the 1960 census. In addition, the Census Office felt that the interest of the policy-makers, who made the money and manpower available for the main enumeration, might lapse very soon after the total count had been completed, when only a few basic data had been made available. Also the Census Field Organization, which was built up with the temporary secondment of staff from other departments, could not be kept even on a reduced scale after the census. The sacrifices that other departments were making (some willingly and others not) in the generally favourable atmosphere of the decennial census had little prospect of being repeated for some time to come. Consequently, the census planners felt that this was the only opportunity to obtain much-needed information. For the same reasons, the PES was made a multi-purpose inquiry in respect to the objectives, i.e. combining the evaluation studies with the Supplementary Inquiry, and to the scope of the subject matter, i.e the Supplementary Inquiry extended over a variety of fields—demographic, social, economic, etc. In the given circumstances, whether through objective reasoning or partly also under the influence of subjective fears, one could hardly have decided otherwise. Today, after an appraisal of experience, one might decide to modify slightly the census design on certain points as described below.

PHASING OF INQUIRIES

In several developed countries, the Supplementary (sample) Inquiry is conducted almost simultaneously with or very close to the 100 per cent enumeration (e.g. in the censuses taken around 1960 in the USA, some European countries and Israel) while the re-enumerations for the purpose of content-error evaluation are entirely separate projects taking place often several months (three to six months in the USA) after the main census enumeration.

The integration of the Supplementary Inquiry with the 100 per cent enumeration presents certain statistical and economic advantages. The two sources offer the possibility of using the census items in the analysis of the sample items (without the need of re-enumeration). In addition, the separation of the evaluation inquiries from the above two enumerations has definite statistical and to some extent also organizational advantages:

1. The evaluation inquiry is made statistically independent of both the 100 per cent census and the supplementary sample enumeration and thus is more likely to give an unbiased estimate of the values required.

2. Different sampling techniques, and in general different statistical methods and procedures, can be used in the evaluation inquiry from those employed in the supplementary enumeration, without complicating either of the inquiries.

3. The evaluation inquiry fieldwork can be better organized in view of its smaller size as compared with the supplementary enumeration.

The Ghana phasing was quite different and perhaps somewhat unique. It resulted from the decision to combine the Supplementary Inquiry with part of the evaluation inquiry rather than with the main Census. Several reasons dictated this approach. First, technically and organizationally, there was no possibility of combining the supplementary enumeration with that of the main Census, or of conducting the two within a short period of each other. Whereas an attempt was made to keep the main census as simple as possible the Supplementary Inquiry was much more complex. Also the limited organizational potentialities dictated the need to separate the dates of the two enumerations as widely as possible. There were even proposals to postpone the Supplementary Inquiry for another year or more, but this was rejected in view of the temporary nature of the Field Organization and for other reasons.[7]

On the other hand, the merging of the evaluation re-interview with the supplementary enumeration appeared to offer several advantages such as a reduction in the number of field operations, which always presented organizational problems, and in the number of house visits (problems of contact) and finally a reduction of costs.

TIMING

In Ghana, the main census was fixed to take place in the dry season in order to find most farmers at home and to ensure a better coverage. This season, however, is the one of lowest economic activity. This shortcoming in the main census date was compensated for by the fact that the Supplementary Inquiry, which also recorded economic data, took place at the beginning of the rainy and busier farming season. This resulted in an interval of about three to four months between the census date and that of the evaluation field inquiry. On the other hand, for purposes of comparability a date as close as possible to that of the main census, say an interval of not more than one month, would have been preferable. The long interval, as well as the change in the level of economic activity, brought about considerable population movements which impaired the evaluation study involving e.g. difficulty in matching names recorded in the main census with those in the PES. On the contrary, for at least certain items of the Supplementary Inquiry, namely those relating to the economic characteristics an even more distant date, say one in the middle of the peak farming season, would have been preferable. It follows that the timing of the two inquiries (i.e. supplementary and evaluation) should be determined by their different statistical objectives.[8]

SAMPLE SIZE

For the Supplementary Inquiry Ghana considered a 5 per cent sample of the population desirable (in fact 5 per cent of main census houses). Since the re-enumeration for purposes of evaluation was combined with the former, in order not to complicate the operation, it too covered the same population. At a later stage the evaluation study was limited to a sub-sample of one-fifth of the former (i.e. to 1 per cent of the main census houses) which was considered an appropriate size for the purposes. However, even this proved to be too large for an intensive inquiry, and consequently another, smaller sub-sample of less than 0·5 per cent of census houses (in 59 EAs) was selected. This latter restriction was dictated partly by financial reasons but mainly by the shortage of qualified and reliable staff who were required at the same time for the processing of the main census and post-census Supplementary Inquiry data. The urgency of these latter tasks outweighed the importance of the evaluation studies.

SAMPLING UNIT

For the Supplementary Inquiry, Ghana applied a two-stage sampling design in order to decrease the sampling error. The first-stage units consisted of 868 census EAs. Being 'clusters' of houses or compounds these units were subject to large sampling errors. On the other hand, they were less exposed to a bias because their boundaries were marked on maps and systematically described by physical or other clear features. In the second stage, a sample of houses and compounds recorded in the main census was selected from the 868 EAs. The census houses were often described in an unreliable manner, particularly in rural areas using as an 'address' the name of the 'head of house' (i.e. the house owner, if living in the same house, or the oldest person in the house). While such an 'address' was quite an efficient aid to the main-census enumerator in ensuring coverage of his area, it resulted in a bias of under-enumeration when used subsequently by the PES interviewer. In some cases, the PES enumerators dealt with only one of the structures making up the census house or compound, e.g. the one in which the census 'head of house' lived at the time of the PES (leaving out other structures bearing the same name).

It follows that in enumerations, or re-enumerations, in which identical units are aimed at, e.g. for matching purposes in coverage evaluation studies, sampling units which ensure best identification in the field should be preferred. Houses or compounds are less reliable than continuous areas with boundaries marked and described on maps. The increase in variance due to this type of cluster sampling is much smaller than the enumerator/interviewer's variance in the definition of house or compound.

CONCLUSIONS

Differences between developed and developing countries, with respect on the one hand to the objectives of the Supplementary Inquiry and on the other to resources (financial, organizational and technical), determine a different phasing and timing of the various census projects. An appraisal of the Ghana census programme confirms its basic feasibility. However, in order to avoid in future the shortcomings experienced in 1960 such as under-enumeration in the Supplementary Inquiry and the difficulties of comparability in the evaluation studies a few modifications in the plan appear advisable:

1. The double-coverage evaluation field inquiries (house listing and listing of persons in houses) should be combined in one operation and carried out as soon as possible after the main census. To ensure an unbiased estimate, both coverage inquiries should be made entirely independent from the main-census enumeration.

2. The Supplementary Inquiry should be conducted in a season showing a different level of economic activity, and possibly with different techniques and better qualified staff than the main census. At least a part of the content-evaluation re-enumeration should be integrated with the supplementary enumeration. These need not

necessarily be designed as statistically independent from the main-census enumeration. On the contrary, coverage control devices and values drawn from the main-census enumeration should be applied as far as possible to obtain at least an equivalent coverage as in the main census and to avoid significant under-enumeration.
3. In deciding on the most appropriate type of sampling unit, one which decreases the chances of bias, rather than one which decreases the sampling error should be preferred.

The Concepts

INTERNATIONAL AND LOCAL CONCEPTS

As a rule, international concepts, namely those recommended by the United Nations, should be used. With a few exceptions, Ghana used the concepts recommended by the UN (e.g. the concepts of place of birth, usual residence, locality, economic activity and even house and household). These required a few adaptations in order to define their meaning more clearly in the African environment. For example, in defining a 'house', the UN definition was adapted to include the African compound. In defining a 'household', the words 'sleeping under one roof and eating from the same pot' were used in place of the UN definition relating to persons:

(a) jointly occupying the whole or part of a housing unit; and
(b) sharing the principal meals.

Alteration of the definition, from experience in Ghana, did not alter the meaning. On the contrary, it aimed at the same meaning but with variables better reflecting local practice and above all local language-interpretation. Both definitions reflect common provisions for basic 'living needs' and often a 'common budget to a greater or lesser extent' (*UN Principles and Recommendations*, pp. 11–12).

The doubts raised by certain social scientists in Ghana as to the meaningfulness in an African environment of the international concept of 'household' proved to be unfounded. The data obtained have a real meaning and are very useful for socio-economic analysis.

The application of international concepts (with adapted definitions where necessary) does not minimize the importance of certain local concepts for the study of specific local features. For example, the 'extended' family as conceived in Africa should not be confounded with the 'biological' family mentioned in the UN recommendations and based on Western family patterns. This latter family nucleus usually comprises parents and their unmarried children living in one household. The UN recommendation states that 'a household can consist of more than one family but a family cannot be composed of two or more households'. In contrast, the African family may comprise several households living even in separate houses or compounds, and sometimes even a whole village consists of one family. The 'extended' family has a deep sociological and sometimes even an economic meaning. It can and should be studied by a separate set of concepts and methods without confusing it with, or replacing it by, the international concept of household. Both concepts have their specific values.

We find another example of how the two types of concepts should be distinguished and studied in the sphere of relationship to head of family or household. In Ghana, and in several other African countries, common speech does not distinguish between direct descendants and other relatives, e.g. between own children and children of brothers or sisters, all being considered sons and daughters. Similarly, there is a 'small' father and a 'big' father and cousins are also called brothers and sisters. In order to study the household pattern in the PES the international concepts of relationship were used and clear distinctions were made between direct descendants and other relatives. In fact it is the strict application of international concepts and definitions in respect to intra-household relationships that enables us to study the Ghana household structure (see Table 1). The African concepts definitely have their relevance. For example, in the classification of relationships in an African household or family it may be very useful, even indispensable, to make more detailed distinctions, such as between paternal and maternal relatives.

Table 1

Persons Aged 15 Years and Over by Relationship to Head of Household, Ghana PES, 1960

Relationship to Head	Both sexes	Males	Females
All relationships:			
Absolute numbers	3,730,300	1,884,540	1,845,760
Percentages	100·0	100·0	100·0
Head	43·2	64·0	22·0
Husband/wife	22·4	0·4	44·8
Father/mother	1·5	0·1	2·9
Brother/sister	5·3	7·0	3·6
Sister's son/daughter	1·8	2·0	1·7
Brother's son/daughter	1·3	1·8	0·8
Son/daughter	12·2	12·9	11·5
Son's/daughter's child	1·3	1·1	1·5
Son's wife/daughter's husband	1·4	0·1	2·8
Other relatives of head	3·4	2·0	4·8
Relatives of head's wife/husband	1·3	0·9	1·6
Non-relatives, e.g. guests, lodgers	4·9	7·7	2·0

Finally, an example should be given in the field of economic activity. The existence in certain areas of some sort of subsistence economy, a high percentage of family workers in agriculture, and a large proportion of women engaged in, mainly 'petty', trading call for special studies. This, however, does not prevent the use of modern labour force concepts in definition of the activities of the population of working age in Africa. The application of this concept in Ghana proved, with but one or two changes, to be appropriate. At the same time, inquiries into specifically local problems would be very useful, even indispensable, for a fuller understanding and interpretation of data obtained using the labour force concept. These as a rule should be undertaken separately, though a combined study should in certain cases not be excluded. For example, in the Ghana census the concept of caretaker in agriculture (a type of farmer-tenant) was introduced in the classification by employment status and thus provided quite interesting results when cross-classified by other variables e.g. sex, age, country of birth, occupation, industry, etc.

CENSUS AND SAMPLE SURVEY CONCEPTS

Another aspect to consider is when and where the various types of concept should be applied. When social scientists of different disciplines discuss census questionnaire contents, arguments arise as to what is meaningful from the point of view of a given scientific field and what is appropriate to a given type or method of inquiry. In the preparatory stages of the Ghana census and the PES such exchanges of views took place among the members of the advisory committee, representing various branches of social science: demographers, sociologists, economists, administrators and census organizers. For example, with respect to the basic nucleus of enumeration, four concepts were discussed: house/compound, household, 'biological' family and 'extended' family. It would not be difficult to identify the protagonists among the committee members of each of the above types of enumeration units. The Census Office finally decided to use the house/compound concept in the main Census and the household concept in the PES.

The house/compound concept had the advantage of a somewhat more reliable definition than the household or family concept in that the former had a physical delineation, though this was not always discernible in the field.[9] The house/compound concept was considered likely to give better coverage, which was one of the primary objectives of the main census. In addition, it is not entirely void of statistical relevance for certain administrative and physical planning purposes. The advantages of the household concept for purposes of analysis of the PES data were: international comparability, economic relevance, and to some extent, socio-demographic meaningfulness. In addition, the definition of the household was more precise than the various definitions of 'family'. The definition of the household could be uniformly applied to the whole country, while that of 'family' might have required different definitions to suit family patterns in various tribes and areas. The complexities of such a study might even have required specifically designed small-scale inquiries. Had the PES questionnaire not been loaded with so many topics of socio-demographic and economic relevance one might perhaps have tried in Ghana a combined household/family study similar in method, although different in concept, to that recommended by the ECE for the 1960 European censuses. However, even the 5 per cent PES sample in Ghana might have been too large for such an inquiry.

Likewise, in respect to occupation, a simple and straightforward question was used in the main census, while a somewhat more complex one was used in the PES. In the main census, occupation was recorded only in respect of employed persons and the question related to the work the person performed *most of the time* during the reference month (the month preceding the census date). Thus, unemployed persons were not asked about previous occupation though this was a departure from the UN recommendations; nor was a 'secondary' occupation recorded in respect of persons performing two jobs. Both these items were included in the PES.

On the other hand, for the measurement of the economically active population, the concise labour force concept was uniformly applied both in the main census and in the PES. The United Nations' definition was fairly strictly applied in the matter of employed and unemployed persons, i.e. the two categories of which the economically active population consists. Farmers were included among the employed even if they did not satisfy the minimum requirement of working for at least one day during the month preceding the census date. This was important because the census was taken in the 'off-season'; at the same time this approach can also be regarded as consistent with the United Nations recommendations that 'the employed comprise all persons . . . who are at work or who have jobs during the specified period.' The farmers being 'absent' temporarily only by reason of the off-season were, therefore, qualified for inclusion among the economically active population. They should perhaps have been more conveniently recorded and classified under a category 'off-season', had such a category been in the questionnaire, but for reasons of simplicity only the two main categories were specified, employed and unemployed.

Following strictly the UN recommendations, the only persons considered as family workers and included among the economically active population were those who 'did a specified minimum amount of work' during the reference month. The 'off-season' rule was not applied in respect of family workers in order not to inflate the economically active figures. This ruling is sometimes disputed, and at the Belgrade Conference one of the participants[10] proposed applying, as an exception for family workers, a reference period of one year, while for all others a shorter period, say of one month or week, should be used. Such an approach, however, would not only complicate the inquiry but also tend to an overestimation of the economically active population, apart from giving data which would in part refer to one month and in part to one year and, therefore, be hard to interpret. Obviously, both approaches present disadvantages and the worst would be a combination of the two. A better solution would be to collect data in at least two seasons, one of high-activity and one of low-activity. This was done in Ghana, and the data obtained are enlightening (see Tables 2 and 3).

Table 2

Percentage Distribution (of Persons Aged 15 Years and Over) by Type of Activity, Ghana, 1960

MAIN CENSUS AND PES COMPARED (PROVISIONAL)

Type of activity	Census			PES		
	Total	Males	Females	Total	Males	Females
All types of activity	100·0	100·0	100·0	100·0	100·0	100·0
Economically active, total	(73·0)	(89·1)	(56·6)	(78·1)	(89·2)	(66·8)
Employed	68·6	83·3	53·7	76·3	86·7	65·7
Unemployed	4·4	5·8	2·9	1·8	2·5	1·1
Not economically active, total	(27·0)	(10·9)	(43·4)	(21·9)	(10·8)	(33·2)
Homemaker	18·4	0·6	36·7	13·2	0·2	26·5
Student	4·0	6·0	1·8	4·3	6·6	2·0
Vocational trainee	0·3	0·5	0·1	0·4	0·6	0·2
Disabled	4·0	3·3	4·7	3·7	3·0	4·4
Other	0·3	0·5	0·1	0·3	0·4	0·1

Table 3

Percentage Distribution (of Persons Aged 15 Years and Over) by Employment Status, Ghana, 1960

MAIN CENSUS AND PES COMPARED (PROVISIONAL)

Employment status	Census			PES		
	Total	M	F	Total	M	F
All categories of employment status	100·0	100·0	100·0	100·0	100·0	100·0
Employer and own account worker	63·5	55·5	76·2	59·0	53·3	66·7
Caretaker in agriculture	1·9	3·0	0·3	2·0	3·3	0·1
Employee	19·3	29·1	3·6	17·3	28·4	2·4
Apprentice	1·9	2·6	0·8	2·0	3·0	0·7
Family worker	13·4	9·8	19·1	19·7	12·0	30·1

The percentage of economically active (employed and unemployed) among adult males was almost the same (89 per cent) in both the main census and the PES (there was only a shift from unemployment to employment). On the other hand, among adult females, the percentage of economically active, rose from 56·6 per cent (employed, 53·7 per cent; unemployed, 2·9 per cent) to 66·8 per cent (employed, 65·7 per cent; unemployed, 1·1 per cent), i.e. a 10 per cent increase matched by an identical decrease in the percentage of home-makers (from 36·7 per cent in the main census to 26·5 per cent in the PES). A similar change can be seen in the percentage of family workers (a rise from 19·1 per cent in the main census to 30·1 per cent in the PES; see Table 3).

One final example might be mentioned to support the application of unambiguous definitions. Ghana used the international definition of unemployed with only a slight modification to suit local conditions. The UN defines the unemployed as persons 'not working and seeking work'. The Ghana definition was: 'persons who did not work . . . and had no fixed job and who were looking for work by visiting employment offices, writing applications, etc.' On the other hand, persons able to work and unemployed, but 'not looking actively' for work, either because they did not want to work or because they had given up the idea of being able to find work, were considered as 'voluntarily unemployed' and, consequently, classified among the not economically active. This definition has been objected to in one of the background papers prepared by the Economic Commission for Africa for the use of the Working Group on Census of Population and Housing.[11] A suggestion was made (later endorsed by the Working Group)[12] that only two criteria should be applied, i.e. 'available for work' and 'desire for work'. The criterion 'actively looking for work' should be replaced by a modification which would 'include in the unemployed category persons not seeking work for specified valid reasons.' This modification was proposed on the grounds of alleged difficulties in most African countries, particularly in rural areas, in manifesting an active search for work because of 'lack of adequate employment opportunities, lack of well-developed organisation of the labour market, etc.' However, the lack of such facilities does not justify abandonment of the criterion demanding manifest proof of the 'desire to work'. In Ghana labour market conditions in great part are similar to those in other African countries. Ghana should, therefore, have obtained an inflated number of 'voluntarily' unemployed. In fact, the total number recorded by the census was negligible: males 2,675 and females 1,414, as compared with the unemployed category, males 109,093 and females 54,550 showing incidentally identical ratios for both sexes.

CONCLUSIONS

International concepts can and should as a rule be applied in developing countries. The main problem in their application is to find an adapted definition or a local language-interpretation to convey the correct meaning; such adaptations should be based on reliable tests and factual evidence and no concept should be rejected or changed because of alleged difficulties or apparent lack of feasibility. Likewise, specifically local concepts have their relevance and should be studied side by side with the international ones; in some cases special inquiries would be advisable for this latter type of concept.

Simplicity and unambiguity of definition are always advisable and, in 100 per cent enumerations, indispensable. Higher accuracy is obtained by simplification of questions rather than by their elaboration. More complex concepts can be studied in sample surveys and some specific ones in very small and special inquiries.

Footnotes

The views expressed in this paper are those of the authors and do not necessarily reflect those of the agencies with which these authors are associated.

1. B. GIL and K. T. DE GRAFT-JOHNSON, *1960 Population Census of Ghana*, Volume V, *General Report*, Census Office, Accra, 1964.
2. B. GIL and E. N. OMABOE, 'Population Censuses and National Sample Surveys in Developing Countries', *International Labour Review*, Volume 92, No. 3, September 1965.
3. Only part of this large complex of errors was included in this project and more precisely only those

referred to as 'observational' errors, i.e. errors in respondent's reply and in the recording by the enumerator/interviewer (for an exact definition of such errors see *Evaluation and Research Program of the U.S. Censuses . . .* 1960, U.S. Bureau of the Census, Series ER60, Nos. 1–6). Other content errors (committed in processing, transcribing, etc.) have been studied separately; see publication under footnote 1.

4. *General Report, op. cit.*, p. 377.

5. Some of the causes of under-enumeration are given in the *General Report, op. cit.*, Chapters 26–28; others are still under study. Briefly, the following were the main reasons (not necessarily in order of importance):

(a) Movement of population between the main Census and the PES.

(b) Changes in house vacancies; during the PES farmers went to live on their forest farms and in the outlying villages and so they were omitted from the PES re-enumeration; on the other hand, houses vacant during the main census were not always recorded by the census enumerator and consequently were not always included in the re-enumeration sample.

(c) The PES interviewer tended to underestimate the 'house' boundaries. For example, he included in the PES only the household under whose head the census house was listed.

(d) Flexible or moveable reference date (persons were included in the PES only if they slept in the house the night before the interviewer's visit).

(e) Greater emphasis on content (accuracy of replies) than on coverage.

(f) Tiredness on the part of the interviewers and population.

6. Mainly due to differential under-enumeration by age, i.e. to coverage errors in the PES which are not revealed by the content-error evaluation relating to response and recording errors.

7. *General Report, op. cit.*, p. 315, sec. 22.2.1.

8. In this respect the conditions differ between developing and developed countries. In the latter countries there are other opportunities (e.g. current or periodic sample surveys and continuous registrations) to measure changes in economic activities and related factors. In developing countries in view of the absence of such opportunities the supplementary post-census enquiry becomes the only one.

9. As mentioned before, the shortcomings in this respect were one of the causes of an under-count in the PES re-enumeration.

10. MILENKO BAN, 'Les Aides Familiaux et la Définition de la Population Active', *United Nations World Population Conference, Belgrade, 1965*, B11/I/F/496.

11. *Some Problems of Enumerating Economic Characteristics of the Population in African Censuses*, UN Economic Commission for Africa, E/CN.14/CAS. 4/CPH/3, 18 May 1965.

12. *Report of the First Working Group on Censuses of Population and Housing*, Addis Ababa, 21–29 June 1965 UNECA, E/CN. 14/CAS. 4/CPH/11.

11 Taking a population census in tropical Africa

D. J. Owusu
Census Office, Accra, Ghana

Importance of Censuses to Tropical African Countries

The importance of censuses to government has long been recognized. Where the administrative branch of government formerly took censuses for military and taxation purposes, it now takes them for other reasons, such as to decide on the allocation of various social services. For example the census gives an estimate of the number of children in different age groups by regions through the whole country, information essential for the provision of schools, teachers and equipment.

To provide houses for the people is one of the problems facing all African countries. To be able to do this effectively, estimates have to be made of present population, natural increase of population, internal migration and changes in family pattern, all of which are provided by the census.

National electoral distribution is based upon the population distribution of the country involved. Since the war, most African countries have gained their independence and established national governments. These governments rely on population data to compile electoral rolls used in the administration of the nation.

Population censuses provide the frame for other statistical surveys. This is important in Africa where the development of statistics is still in its infancy.

PRE-COLONIAL COUNTS

Population counts are not new to tropical Africa. There is evidence that before the arrival of Europeans, some African countries conducted population counts. These counts were carried out for military and taxation purposes at such times as the chiefs felt them to be necessary. Heads of families were instructed to drop into receptacles, articles such as grains of wheat or cowries according to the number of their people. Different articles were used for each sex, for instance wheat for males and cowries for females. Simple though these counts may have been, they show the cleverness of the tribal chiefs.

COLONIAL COUNTS

During the colonial era, population censuses in African countries were taken by the Colonial Administration in the same years in which the metropolitan countries took theirs. For instance, when a census was taken in the United Kingdom, censuses were conducted in all the British Colonies. Thus, after the 1871 censuses in St. Mary's Island (Gambia), Lagos and the Colony of Sierra Leone, censuses became routine in these three areas and were subsequently taken at ten-year intervals. Ghana's first official population count was in 1891, and was followed by censuses at ten-yearly intervals until 1931. Uganda and Northern Rhodesia had their first counts in 1911, followed by censuses in 1921 and 1931.

An interesting aspect of these early censuses in the colonies is that there was no legal provision made for most of them, including the 1871 censuses of Lagos and Sierra Leone, the 1891 census of the Gold Coast, the Uganda enumerations of 1911 and 1921 and the 1911 censuses in Kenya and north-eastern Rhodesia. However, *ad hoc* ordinances were promulgated for censuses in Sierra Leone from 1881 to 1931, in Lagos from 1890 to 1901 and in the Gold Coast for 1911 and 1921. From 1911 general census ordinances were enacted for some colonies, as for the censuses of 1911 in southern Nigeria (including Lagos), of 1921 and 1931 in Nigeria (including Lagos), of 1931 in the Gold Coast, and of 1921 and 1931 in Northern Rhodesia.[1]

IMPORTANCE OF EARLY COUNTS

These counts were very simple, and only totals of men, women, children and in some cases taxpayers were given. In spite of this the methods used have some value to the modern African demographers. Studying the design and shortcomings of these early counts will help in understanding the difficulties involved and in planning better population censuses.

Essential Features of a Modern Census

The United Nations document *Principles and Recommendations for National Population Censuses* states, 'A census of population may be defined as the total process of collecting, compiling and publishing demographic, economic and social data pertaining at a specified time or times to all persons in a country or delimited territory.'[2] The essential features of the modern census are government sponsorship, defined territory, universality, individual units, compilation and publication. These features will be discussed in the light of African experience.

1. GOVERNMENT SPONSORSHIP

A national census is the responsibility of the central government because, apart from the fact that it has the administrative machinery and financial resources to undertake such a difficult task, it has also the power to enact the necessary laws to facilitate the smooth taking of the census.

2. DEFINED TERRITORY

'The coverage of a census operation should relate to a precisely defined territory.' This is important when comparison is to be made with previous or future censuses. At the moment almost all the African countries have well-defined territories. However, when we come to consider regions, districts and towns within a particular country, we find that in some cases the boundaries are not defined and where they are defined, they keep on changing, thus making future comparison virtually impossible.

3. UNIVERSALITY

'The enumeration should include every member of the community within the scope of the census without omission or duplication.' Some of the past population counts in Africa were not censuses, since only adults, taxpayers or males were counted.

4. SIMULTANEITY

'The total population enumerated should refer to one well-defined point of time.' Most of the information would be difficult to compare and meaningless unless it referred to a given moment. Therefore, not only the Census Day or Census Night should be fixed but also the hour.

5. PLACE REFERENCE

This is a special factor which should be considered one of the essential features of a population census in Africa. Like the time reference just discussed, the place reference should refer to a specific place where each person stayed at a particular point of time. For it is most likely that an error associated with the place of enumeration can easily arise. In Africa, and in other places of the world where the canvasser method is used, enumeration does not take place in one day but continues for about two or three weeks. During this period, the population cannot be brought to a standstill. People have to move from place to place for business or social purposes. Therefore, if the actual place of reference at a point in time is not defined this may lead to double enumeration or total omission of persons, such as pedlars, who move from one locality to another. For example, in the 1960 Ghana Population Census, the enumerator was instructed to enumerate only persons who slept in a given house on census night.

6. INDIVIDUAL ENUMERATION

In most of the past population censuses in Africa, the enumerator was instructed to enter on his questionnaire the numbers of males and females, children and adults, married and single persons, i.e. what we may term 'group enumeration'. Group enumeration, concerned with summarized information about a group of people, makes it impossible to relate one characteristic to another, such as marital status to age, and thus deprives us of an important element of statistics. Group enumeration, according to the United Nations definition, is only a count and not a census.

7. COMPILATION AND PUBLICATION

It is not enough to invest large sums of money in collecting census data, as has happened in the past censuses of some countries. According to the United Nations, a census is not complete unless the data collected are compiled and published by geographic areas and by basic demographic variables.

Post-Enumeration Survey

It is now an accepted fact that the best planned and organized census cannot be free from errors. Consequently census planners in countries such as the United States, Britain and Yugoslavia have, since 1950, carried out post-enumeration surveys to check the accuracy of the main census. The aim of the survey is to estimate the magnitude of the errors involved and the circumstances under which these errors came about, so that the planners can improve upon the methods in future censuses.

In Africa, where statistical services are backward, additional information may be needed for other fields of administration. Because collection of this additional information may be time-consuming and costly, it is advisable to gather this on a sample basis. The best enumerators can be put on this job, and, therefore, the quality of information obtained may be very high. Ghana, in her 1960 Population Census Programme, conducted a Post-Enumeration (5 per cent sample) Survey.

Main Conditions Necessary for the Success of a Census in Tropical Africa

The considerable benefits which nations derive from use of the data collected have led to emphasis being placed on the careful planning of censuses. According to the United Nations:

> 'The careful planning of a census is of prime importance both for statistically advanced countries and for those with less statistical experience. A census is a complete operation in itself, consisting of a complex series of closely interrelated steps which must be carefully planned in advance so that a proper and uninterrupted sequence can be maintained. A small oversight in planning may lead to serious defects and inefficiencies. All censuses cannot follow a fixed and uniform pattern, but the following list containing the most common major elements of a census plan is an illustration of the points to be considered in planning a census.'[3]

Since the list of operations is very long, only the main items will be mentioned. These include the legal aspect, finances, the time-table of operations, head office administration, field organization, preparation of questionnaires and enumeration documents, field tests, publicity, enumeration procedure, post-enumeration checks, compilation and tabulation. As regards these international standards, procedures, techniques and concepts, it must be realized that not all of them will suit African conditions without some modification. A few of these concepts and procedures will be discussed in the light of African experience.

STRONG GOVERNMENT SUPPORT

It is an accepted fact that national governments must sponsor the taking of censuses in their respective countries. However, in Africa this has a special meaning. The government must not only sponsor but also take direct responsibility for the census. Even though there may be a statistical office entrusted with this job, and the necessary laws have been enacted, the responsibility of directing the census operation should be entrusted to a committee with executive powers. All Ministries should be made to feel that the census is a co-operative project. It is interesting to note that the Central Census Committee of the 1960 Ghana Population Census included four Cabinet Ministers and six Regional Commissioners with cabinet rank. As a result the Committee was highly authoritative and gave strong backing to the Census undertaking. Because it represented the Cabinet, it could guide policy as well as implementation.

If the government has charge of the census, provision of a sufficient number of competent personnel is facilitated and priority is more readily obtained for essential services such as printing, transport and communications.

For example, during the 1960 Ghana Population Census the Census Office, in addition to mobilizing government and local authority vehicles, succeeded in securing the services of an aircraft belonging to the Ministry of Defence. The Head Office must be in close contact with field officers and, since in some areas it takes hours to get a telephone call through, census calls must be given priority. Priority crossing must be given at ferries too.

Division of Country into Enumeration Areas

After the necessary legal backing, money and government support have been acquired, the work for the enumerators should be set out. If each enumerator is supplied with a map showing the important boundaries and routes in his Enumeration Area (EA) and a list of its localities, there should be few areas which might be regarded as a 'no man's land'. Though this operation may seem ambitious and expensive, the advantages derived from it are worth the effort and expense involved. The EA maps could be used in future censuses and other statistical surveys.

PROBLEMS ASSOCIATED WITH THE DIVISION OF THE COUNTRY INTO ENUMERATION AREAS

Difficulties encountered in such an undertaking in tropical Africa are related to transport, terrain, and area and population distribution. Most parts of Africa are covered with thick forest and savannah lands that can be reached by motor transport during the dry season only because of floods during the rainy season. In some areas the population is sparsely distributed. The area to be surveyed is vast and it is not easy to define the scattered population by modern locality concepts. Therefore, this operation should start early, say one-and-a-half or two years before the census.

Contents of Questionnaires

The content of a population census questionnaire can be divided into two broad groups; questions relating to the demographic and social characteristics of the population and questions relating to the economic characteristics. The United Nations Statistical Office has compiled a list of questions to be asked, from which a judicious selection of topics of relevance to the country must be made. Basic information such as sex, age, birthplace, education, economic activity and occupation must be collected. Additional information will depend on money and time available and the specific needs of the country conducting the census. Because the majority of the population of tropical Africa is illiterate, even the collection of information on such simple questions as age, education and type of activity may present problems.

POPULATION

There are two concepts of the definition of persons to be enumerated. A *de jure* count is the enumeration of persons who usually reside in a given place, and a *de facto* count is the enumeration of persons physically present at a specific place on census night. Each of these two concepts has its advantages and disadvantages. The *de facto* count is simple because the enumerator just has to count people who spent census night at a given place. However, the *de jure* count may be more suitable for administrative and planning purposes such as taxation, housing and education, because the number of people who normally live in a place is more meaningful than the number who are physically present at a moment in time. In adopting the *de facto* count, the organization taking the census will have some difficulties in enumerating the floating population and people may forget where they spent census night if enumeration drags on for a long time. In spite of this, the *de facto* count is simple and unambiguous. Which of these two concepts is adopted will depend upon the needs of the country conducting the census.

AGE

There are many people in Africa who do not know their age. This is because compulsory registration of vital events, like births and deaths, is restricted to small sections of the country. In Ghana, for instance, vital registration is compulsory only in 37 registration areas and this in 1960 covered about 16 per cent of the population. Few people have birth certificates to remind them of their dates of birth.

Second, a greater part of the population of tropical Africa being illiterate, few see the importance of age in their everyday life, and most do not bother to find out their ages. This is the reason why in past censuses in Africa, the census-takers usually chose to use broad age groups, e.g. below 1 year, 1–14, 15 and over, in order to conceal misstatements in age. 'Even then misstatements still appeared. For example, in the 1948 census of the Gold Coast (Ghana), the proportion of children under 1 year was given as 8·2 per cent—an obvious over-statement.'[4]

Since misstatements in ages are bound to appear in both single and broad age groups it is better to ask questions in single years. The data obtained can be smoothed by using several methods of refinement recommended by the UN. A question on age 'last birthday' should be asked. There is no point in asking for 'date of birth' because a greater part of the population do not know it; 'age last birthday', however, can be worked out by recourse to national historical events, local events, family age relationships etc. These were precisely the methods Ghana used in the 1960 Population Census. In the census education, through the radio, newspapers, talks etc., the topic of age was one of the most publicized items. Teachers were trained to find the ages of their school children. School children in turn were to help their parents estimate their own ages.

The enumerators were instructed during the training period to use this order of preference: birth or baptismal certificates, national historical events, local events and facial appearance.

EDUCATION

This is an item that is likely to give all countries in tropical Africa some difficulty as far as the formulation of relative questions is concerned. Should a question be based on literacy or on actual attendance at regular schools? In a review on the check of consistency of reports on school attendance between the Census and the Post-Enumeration Survey of the 1960 Ghana Population Census, the authors of the Census stated, 'There is quite a high degree of consistency between the Census and Post-Enumeration Survey reports with respect to those who had "never attended school" 94·7 per cent of the males and 98·3 per cent of the females gave in the PES replies identical to those in the Census.'[4] In view of this high degree of consistency between the two reports with respect to the 'never attended school', the questions on literacy and regular school attendance should be included in the main census questionnaire. There should not be any fear that it will cause ambiguity in the minds of the respondents or of the enumerators. If the level of school attendance is required this will be asked of persons who attended regular school only.

TYPE OF ACTIVITY

This is one of the items which needs modification to suit conditions in tropical Africa, where most of the working population are employed in agricultural activities. Many people will describe themselves as unemployed if enumeration takes place in the dry season, when most farmers will not be doing any work on the farms. Therefore, it is necessary to choose a reference period during which information obtained on the working population will be typical of the year. In the 1960 Population Census in Ghana, 'employed' persons were those who worked during the month preceding the census date for even only one day or for a few hours daily.[4] 'The essential modification of the concept consisted in the consideration of all "job holders" as employed.'[4] This means that those who did not work during the reference period but had a job from which they were temporarily absent, e.g. farmers in off-season, workers on leave, temporary lay-off workers etc., were described as employed.

VOTERS' LIST

Some countries compile the voters' list by including in the census questionnaire a question related to the age at which one can vote. The chances of such a question inflating the census figures are great. Persons who will reach the age of voting in a year or two, often claim to have reached that age. There is also the tendency for unscrupulous enumerators to inflate the adult population in areas that share their political beliefs. This will eventually lead to suspicion among local people and lack of confidence in the declared figures for certain areas.

Training and Testing

The period for training should be long enough to allow for adjustments to be made in the various aspects of the programme and for the questionnaire, field organization, methods of enumeration, and effectiveness of publicity to be tested and, where necessary, modified before the actual census.

TRAINING OF STAFF

In tropical Africa it is very difficult to obtain personnel who have already been trained in census techniques. Therefore as soon as a census head office is established, the senior officers start training long before the census is taken, preferably for about 18 to 24 months. These officers in turn train their subordinates. After the training of the personnel required in the head office, the whole census operation can start.

The enumerators and supervisors should be conversant with all aspects of the census. After a long period of training and testing the best enumerators and supervisors can be selected. It is advisable to train more persons than are actually needed in order to allow selection. The training can be carried out in several short sessions over a long period or concentrated in a few long sessions.

PUBLICITY

The history of past censuses in Africa reveals that these counts were sometimes connected with the levy of taxes, so that people sometimes fled their villages during census counts. This fear has to be removed by educating them to realize that present-day censuses are not connected with taxes. They must be told that information derived from the census will assist planning in the field of education, health and social welfare services, housing, employment, etc.

The census education programme also aims at enlightenment of the public on certain census concepts like age, birthplace, level of education, type of activity, occupation, industry, etc., and on the replies to be given to certain questions so that the people will be ready to answer when the census enumerator visits their houses.

Enthusiasm must be inspired in the enumerators, field-workers and census staff to encourage them to take pride in the success of the census.

The 1960 Ghana Census organizers named their extensive programme census *education* and not census *publicity*. It was defined as 'a systematic programme of education on census features operating in widening circles; more specialized information for smaller and more educated classes and more elementary knowledge for the broader masses of the population.'

The schools can be used to educate the masses. First the teachers will teach the school children who will in turn teach their parents and other adults in the community. News about the census can be spread through the rural areas by organizing country-wide mass education by the appropriate Government Departments such as the Department of Social Welfare and Community Development. This department can reach the rural population, using mobile vans, giving talks about the importance of the census, and subsequently explaining the questionnaire and helping to find answers to questions like age, occupation, etc. Other media such as the press, radio and television may be used to similar effect.

CONTROL SYSTEMS

In every census or statistical operation, there are bound to be errors from the beginning of the operation to the processing and compilation. But the magnitude of the error is what matters to the statistician. Therefore, at every stage of a census operation elaborate controls for checking the quality and quantity of work being performed must be worked out. The rules or instructions must be written in a simple language so that the officer or clerk implementing them will understand them and once laid down, must be strictly followed. It is the quantity control that will enable the organizers to know whether plans are proceeding according to time-table and whether they have to make adjustments as they go along.

CLERICAL PROCESSING

There are four main methods of processing census data. These are: simple hand count, punch card, mark sensing and the computer.

Now that the computer is becoming available in African countries, we should make good use of it as it affords larger scope for complicated tabulations. Since it is able to produce complicated tables, it saves time otherwise used to copy this information on to working sheets before being typed or sent for printing. With the computer, the tabulation sheet can come out of the machine ready for photographing and the preparation of plates for printing.

When the computer cannot be used the conventional electronic machines may be used. It must be realized that there is always a difficulty in securing personnel to work on these complicated machines. However, every effort should be made to secure the services of a foreign expert who will teach the local people. It does not pay to send the punch cards outside for an expert to tabulate, as the local people will be deprived of the opportunity of learning. Also, if there is an error, it makes checking from the original documents impossible.

Conclusion

It will be in the interest of African Governments to establish permanent Demographic Divisions or Departments in the appropriate Ministry dealing with statistics. Since 1960 various African countries have taken population censuses. The local people have in the process acquired a good knowledge of the techniques of population studies. It will be a great loss if offices that were entrusted with the taking of censuses are dissolved after the analysis of the census data with the necessity of re-establishment for another census. If the offices were made permanent, members of the staff could be sent overseas or to local universities or establishments offering demographic studies to learn more about the relevant techniques, so acquiring experience that will be of immense help during future censuses.

Footnotes

1. *1891 Census Report of the Gold Coast Colony.*
2. R. R. KUCZYNSKI, *Demographic Survey of the British Colonial Empire*, Vols. I and II, London, 1948.
3. United Nations, *Principles and Recommendations for National Population Censuses* (St./STAT/SER.M/27). Subsequent quotations are also from this source.
4. *1960 Population Census of Ghana*, Vol. V, *General Report*, Accra, 1964.

12 Second thoughts on Sudan's population census[1]

Roushdi A. Henin

Economics Department, University of Khartoum, Sudan

The following are no more than some scattered ideas, which may be found useful when the 1970 population census is taken in Sudan. The reader should therefore be warned that he must not expect to find in the following paragraphs an account of the limitations of the first population census in 1955/56 and consequently a list of suggestions on how the next census should be conducted. Those who carried out the 1955/56 census are possibly more aware than others of the limitations of this first attempt, because most of these limitations came to the surface as the census operation progressed from the preparatory stage to the writing of the final report.

It is not of course claimed that those who took the Sudan 1955/56 census are more capable of doing this than others. They are perhaps better equipped because they lived through the battle. A population census in a country like the Sudan with one million square miles can justifiably be compared to a battle because the country is far from homogeneous, and the lessons learned from one area could not be applied in another. It is from this heterogeneity of the components of the Sudan population that different experience was acquired in the different areas, and it would be advisable to profit from lessons learned in this first attempt. This is mentioned because there is a tendency for each group of census-takers to start from scratch and not to make use of material left behind by its predecessors.

Furthermore, it is essential to extend this principle to other countries. Experience gained by different countries in Africa should be pooled and made available for all of them, because African countries, with some few exceptions, do not have long-established traditions of census-taking.

No doubt, sampling censuses may continue to be found preferable to full counts in many parts of Africa for some time to come. Information about sampling techniques, sampling fractions and sampling errors might be found very useful by countries just about to embark on a sampling census. Further, a good part of Africa is still nomadic, and enumerating nomadic populations has always been a difficult task. Any pooling of information in this field becomes very important. Information on enumeration techniques and difficulties encountered by one country may help another in perfecting these techniques so that the least amount of bias is introduced. Information on sampling errors from one country may be of use to the planners of a census in another country, putting them e.g. in a better position to decide on the most suitable sample size.

The value of co-operation can be extended in other directions. International classification lists of occupations and other characteristics of the population such as marital status, provided by the specialized agencies of the United Nations, are no doubt very useful. Nevertheless, countries in Africa might find it very difficult to adhere strictly to these standard lists. Further, production of such lists to suit the condition of one country is a lengthy and costly business, both in terms of time and resources. In the circumstances, improving a list supplied by a neighbouring country might be better than producing a completely new one.

The sharing of experience in tabulating census results, especially with regard to population characteristics peculiar to African conditions, such as tabulations by tribe, language, marital conditions, mode of life, and fertility and mortality patterns, is doubly important. For example, one country may find it useful to know to what extent data on polygamy or frequency of marriage has been found reliable, and how far such data may be related to fertility differentials.

With these points in mind, we can proceed to discuss some of the lessons gained from the Sudan's first population census. Basically, the question is: on what lines should the next population census be conducted? For this purpose the argument is divided into three main parts. The first deals with sampling versus a full count, the second inquires into the most suitable type of supplementary data that could be used in a future census, and the third suggests remedies for some of the limitations that came to the surface when the first census operation was completed.

Part I: Sampling versus Full Count

The 1955/56 population census was conducted on a sampling basis in rural areas[2] and as a full count in urban areas. In all, the count included 68 towns, a number of which were no more than large villages. This last point is very important, because a considerable proportion of the rural population in some provinces lived in large villages, covered by sampling methods, although bigger than some of the towns enumerated separately and fully.

Some of the arguments that were advanced for adopting sampling in rural areas and a full count in urban areas follow. First, there is a tendency towards homogeneity in the characteristics of the populations of rural areas, and in these circumstances sampling is adequate, while a full count in urban areas is necessary because of the heterogeneity of the characteristics of urban populations. The fallacy in this argument lies in the fact that not all rural areas in the Sudan can claim this homogeneity. Some of these areas have been subjected to economic development through heavy investment in irrigation schemes. With a monetized economy superseding a subsistence economy, the repercussions on the characteristics of the population are considerable. For example, the occupational structure becomes more complex; instead of the population having a few occupations as is the case in the subsistence sector, the need for varied goods and services broadens the range of occupations. Further, variations in occupations carry with them variations in other characteristics, e.g. fertility, mortality and literacy. For sampling to be adequate in these circumstances, the size of the sample needs to be very much larger than that employed in Sudan. This, together with the high cost per person enumerated by sampling, as compared with the cost when a full count is adopted, makes it clear that there was little advantage in adopting sampling methods in the developed rural areas.[3]

Second, sampling was advocated for rural areas in such a vast country as Sudan in view of transport limitations. While transport presented real difficulties in areas thinly populated with nomadic or semi-nomadic tribes, it was no great problem in the more thickly populated rural areas mentioned above where distances between villages are not considerable. A scarcity of field personnel was also advanced as a reason for sampling being preferable to a full count in rural areas. This however ignores the fact that supervisors and enumerators were recruited in great part from schoolmasters, of whom the *per capita* ratio is in fact highest in the more developed rural areas. There are certain other factors related to development that favour a full count census in the more developed areas.

When the census frame was being constructed, it was discovered that the administrative *omodia/sheikhship* structure was more complicated than had been anticipated in the areas under discussion. The *omodia* was chosen as the first-stage sampling unit and the *sheikhship* as the second-stage sampling unit. In most of these areas we were confronted with overlapping sheikhships. The following example illustrates this

Table 1

Popularity of Enumeration Techniques

Province		Number of persons enumerated under technique: (000)								
Code	Name	Total	1	2	3	4.1	4.2	4.3	4.4	4.5
(1)	(2)	(3)	(4)	(5)	(6)	(7)	(8)	(9)	(10)	(11)
1	Bahr el Ghazal	70·9	—	70·9	—	—	—	—	—	—
2	Blue Nile	199·8	—	3·9	12·2	4·8	2·9	—	—	166·0
3	Darfur	112·1	—	0·3	11·9	12·9	8·4	9·2	0·6	69·2
4	Equatoria	50·1	—	27·7	—	—	—	—	—	22·4
5	Kassala	70·6	—	—	39·5	5·2	—	15·8	—	11·2
6	Khartoum	30·4	—	—	3·0	5·9	—	0·5	—	21·0
7	Kordofan	141·7	—	35·9	13·7	5·9	4·4	5·3	—	76·6
8	Northern	87·5	—	2·0	6·4	4·6	3·4	1·9	2·[illegible]	66·6
9	Upper Nile	98·7	4·8	75·2	—	—	7·2	—	—	11·6

PERCENTAGES

Province		Percentage of persons enumerated under technique:								
Code	Name	Total	1	2	3	4.1	4.2	4.3	4.4	4.5
(1)	(2)	(3)	(4)	(5)	(6)	(7)	(8)	(9)	(10)	(11)
1	Bahr el Ghazal	100·0	—	100·0	—	—	—	—	—	—
2	Blue Nile	100·0	—	2·0	6·1	7·4	1·5	—	—	83·1
3	Darfur	100·0	—	0·3	10·3	11·5	7·5	8·2	0·5	61·7
4	Equatoria	100·0	—	55·3	—	—	—	—	—	44·7
5	Kassala	100·0	—	—	54·4	7·3	—	22·4	—	15·9
6	Khartoum	100·0	—	—	9·9	19·5	—	1·6	—	69·0
7	Kordofan	100·0	—	25·3	9·7	4·1	3·1	3·7	—	54·0
8	Northern	100·0	—	2·2	7·3	5·2	3·9	2·2	3·0	76·0
9	Upper Nile	100·0	4·8	76·2	—	—	7·2	—	—	11·8

Technique 1. Well-defined village.
2. Scattered *tukls*.
3. Nomadic.
4.1. Compound, village-nomadic.
4.2. Compound, village-scattered *tukls*.
4.3. Compound, scattered *tukls*-nomadic.
4.4. Compound, village-nomadic scattered *tukls*.
4.5. Compound, well-defined-large-village.

Source: First Population of Sudan 1955/56, Methods Report, Vol. II.

situation: The followers of sheikhs (headmen) Z and Y may live in villages A, B and C; those of sheikh X in villages C and D; and those of W in villages D and E. When sheikhships overlapped in this manner it was impossible to obtain from the lists of sheikhships and taxpayers in an *omodia* (chieftainship), the number of taxpayers in any one village. Overlapping was quite different from the straightforward case of followers of two sheikhs living in the same village. When the followers of a given number of sheikhs lived in the same village and there was no overlapping, it was not difficult to obtain the number of taxpayers in the village.

It is believed that the breakup of the old sheikh/followers system, by which the

Table 2

Type of Supplementary Data Used

TOTAL NUMBERS OF NAMES ON LISTS

Province		Type of supplementary data used[1]						
		AT, HT	DCT DT, TL Tax L	ER	HH	LER	PT	Total
Sudan	(000)	76·6	506·3[2]	276·7	186·4	47·5	393·7	1,487·2
	%	5·2	34·0[2]	18·6	12·5	3·2	26·5	100·0
Bahr el Ghazal	(000)	—	121·5	15·7	—	—	54·1	191·3
	%	—	63·5	8·2	—	—	28·3	100·0
Blue Nile	(000)	—	—	121·9	82·4	47·5	50·7	302·5
		—	—	40·3	27·2	15·7	16·8	100·0
Darfur	(000)	—	126·7	—	—	—	50·8	177·5
	%	—	71·4	—	—	—	28·6	100·0
Equatoria	(000)	—	93·3	—	—	—	41·6	134·9
	%	—	69·2	—	—	—	30·8	100·0
Kassala	(000)	7·4	—	26·9	56·9	—	36·1	127·3
	%	5·9	—	21·1	44·7	—	28·3	100·0
Khartoum	(000)	—	—	—	36·4	—	—	36·4
	%	—	—	—	100·0	—	—	100·0
Kordofan	(000)	69·2	—	—	—	—	160·4	229·6
	%	30·1	—	—	—	—	69·9	100·0
Northern	(000)	—	—	112·2	—	—	—	112·2
	%	—	—	100·0	—	—	—	100·0
Upper Nile	(000)	—	164·8	—	10·7	—	—	175·5
	%	—	93·9	—	6·1	—	—	100·0

1. *Abbreviations Used*

AT = Animal tax lists.
DCT = District combined tax lists.
DT = District tax lists.
ER = Parliamentary Electoral rolls.
HH = Lists of Heads of Households.
LER = Local Government electoral rolls.
PT = Poll tax lists.
TL = Tribute lists.
Tax L = Tax lists unspecified.

2. This figure covers a number of different types of tax lists used, the most important of which is tribute lists with 25·5 per cent. This type of tax lists follows poll tax lists with 26·5 per cent.

followers of one sheikh lived together, was a direct result of economic development. The position now is that followers of different sheikhs from different tribes live side by side, in one and the same village. In the circumstances a new enumeration technique called 'large-village-compound-technique', not envisaged until after the pilot census was conducted, had to be devised to take account of overlapping sheikhships. Some light may be thrown on the proportion of the population living in large-sized villages to the total population by Table 1 which shows the number of persons enumerated in the sample under each enumeration technique. As can be seen in the table, 83 per cent of the sampled rural population in Blue Nile Province was enumerated using the 'large-village-compound-technique'. The Blue Nile Province is followed by Northern Province with 76 per cent and Khartoum with 69 per cent.

Another limitation to the use of sampling in the Blue Nile and Khartoum Provinces was the absence of suitable supplementary data[4] in the form of tax lists or electoral rolls, either because of low correlation with population size or some other defect such as being out of date or subject to double counting, or to the exclusion of some specified classes of people. Further, because followers of different sheikhs within one village were not clearly demarcated, it was not possible to use tax lists, as those tax lists were available by sheikhship. For this reason, supplementary data taking the village as the unit had to be provided. In such circumstances the collection of names of heads of households had to be resorted to.

The argument used is this. As an economy develops and as the subsistence sector gives way to a monetized economy, such an institution as the poll tax begins to die. Poll tax lists formed an excellent source of supplementary data, as they were highly correlated with population size and had to be kept up to date for the purpose of tax collection. In developed areas, the need for them has disappeared and, in the absence of other suitable lists, the census-takers had to resort to another device, namely the collection of the names of heads of households. An alternative would have been a full count, especially in view of the fact that the collection of names was an extra operation which was quite expensive and put more pressure on the available personnel. This task was similar in its magnitude to the census operation proper. It had to be started six months before the census was scheduled to begin. The same kinds of persons were engaged as enumerators and supervisors for this task as those later employed for completing the census questionnaire. They were also given an intensive training course. On average, the fieldwork took between two to three months. The data was then processed at the census headquarters before it could serve as supplementary data. A glance at the following table will show that this procedure was mainly resorted to in the Blue Nile, Khartoum and Kassala Provinces.

Taking the total number of heads of households collected in the whole of the Sudan as 100, we find that the Blue Nile Province was responsible for 44·2 per cent followed by Kassala with 30·5 per cent and Khartoum with 19·5 per cent. No data is available from the *Methods Report*, Volume II, on the extra field cost incurred as a result of the operation of collecting names of heads of households. Some data is however available on part of the field costs in the shape of numbers of 'collection of names days' as well as the daily pay per collection enumerator. These are shown below.

The figures in column (4) of the above table show part of the extra cost incurred in the field in the collection of names of heads of households. To this should be added the cost of salaries of census officers and supervisors and the important item of transport. This does not include headquarters costs in processing the data, for stationery, personnel etc. However, it may be safe to assume that the collection of names of heads of households increased the cost of the census in the areas subjected to this procedure by at least 20 per cent. How much would the total field cost have been if a full count had been used in the Blue Nile Province instead of a sampling

Table 3

Field Costs in Collections of Names

Province	Number of enumerator-days spent on collections of names	Daily pay per enumerator £(S)	Col. (2) × Col. (3) £(S)	Total field costs £(S)
(1)	(2)	(3)	(4)	(5)
Blue Nile	2,190	0·447	979	18,478
Kassala	1,040	0·460	478	14,730
Khartoum	232	0·600	139	7,810

Source: Column (2) from column 5 of Appendix 4.10 of the *Methods Report*, Vol. II, p. 102.
Column (3) from column 7 of Appendix 4.11 of the *Methods Report*, Vol. II, p. 110.
Column (5) from column 10 of Appendix 4.11, *op. cit.*, p. 111.

census? A rough calculation, using the average field cost per enumerated person in Wad Medani town, which was fully enumerated and which lies in the Blue Nile Province, shows that the total cost would have been £(S)24,840.[5] As can be seen from column (5) of the above table, the total field cost in the Blue Nile Province, using sampling, was £(S)18,478. This means that a full count census would have cost roughly 34 per cent more than a sampling census. On balance, in view of the superiority of a full count census over a sampling census, the extra expenditure entailed by a full count would be justifiable.

Part II: The Question of Supplementary Data

In the attempt to cut down the sample size to a suitable minimum, resort was made to supplementary data, characterized by a high correlation to population size. We shall now attempt to answer the question: what is the best type of supplementary data available for a future population census in the light of the experience gained from the 1955–56 population census?

Table 2 above shows by province the types of supplementary data used. Poll tax lists were the most common, especially in the three Southern Provinces and in certain parts of the north. However, there are doubts as to whether these lists will be available in future, owing to opposition to them and a desire for replacement of poll tax by other forms of taxation. Most of the tax lists available in the north suffer from a duplication of names owing to a variety of available employments. A person may be both a taxpayer for land cultivated and a taxpayer for animals in the same area or in another area. On this account, the collection of names of heads of households was resorted to in a number of areas in northern Sudan, but not in the Southern Provinces and some parts of the north where poll-tax lists were both available and suitable and where the collection of names of heads of households was complicated.

Thus, it might be suggested that the most suitable form of supplementary data to be used in a future census are the lists of heads of households. These proved to be most suitable as supplementary data in the areas where this procedure was adopted. There is no question of duplication or unsystematic coverage or other defects which affect ordinary tax-lists. The revision of tax lists, which was conducted at various stages before the enumeration by the census officers, during the enumeration by the visiting officials from the Department of Statistics, and before analysis by members of the analysis section, can be dispensed with. This, however, could only be achieved at a cost, as the procedure for collecting the names of heads of households proved to be expensive in the few areas where it was conducted. However, if the procedure is adopted throughout the country, some economies might be made especially as it would be the only type of supplementary data being employed.

However it is doubtful in view of the magnitude of the task of collecting the names of heads of households for the whole country whether this is in fact feasible. The collection of names of heads of households must be done as near as possible to the date of enumeration, and preferably not more than six months before. Assuming that the enumeration would spread over a period of 12 months, as in the case of the 1955–56 census, that would mean that both operations (i.e. the collection of names of heads of households and the enumeration proper) would have to be rushed through in a period of 18 months. This would increase the burden of the field personnel. A census officer cannot effectively supervise the collection of names of heads of households in one census group of his census area and conduct the enumeration proper in another. It is doubtful whether enough personnel would be available to act simultaneously as both the collectors of names and enumerators proper. Further, in the census office, it is doubtful whether the processes of packing and unpacking, dispatching and receiving the collection of names and material, as well as the enumeration proper, could be handled at the same time. Finally, it is doubtful whether the collection of names of heads of households could be conducted successfully in the scattered 'tukls' areas or where people are nomadic; there has to date been no experience of this procedure in such circumstances.

Taking all these points into account, it might be argued that the most suitable form of supplementary data for use in a future census are the electoral rolls. If properly revised, they would serve the purpose equally well as the lists of heads of households. But electoral rolls are not always available by sheikhship or headmanship; and sometimes they are available for units larger and sometimes smaller than the sheikhship. As for the south, there is as yet no direct representation; therefore, supplementary data in the form of electoral rolls are not available. Perhaps, a solution might be to adopt local government electoral rolls as supplementary data.

Part I of this study has shown that a full count is preferable to a sampling census in the so-called developed rural areas of the country. Part II has shown that in view of the lack of suitable supplementary data, especially in the more developed areas, a sampling census would be quite costly if resort were made on a large scale to the collection of names of heads of households. The question may now be asked: what form should the next census take in rural areas? The answer seems to be the following. Where the 'large-village-compound technique' was used in the six northern provinces, a full count could be used, leaving sampling to look after the three Southern Provinces and the nomadic and semi-nomadic areas in the six Northern Provinces. The full count could cover about 50 per cent of the rural population of Sudan. This may set the upper limit. Problems arising from a shortage of transport and field personnel might make it difficult to cover all areas by a full count, especially in Darfur, Kordofan and Kassala Provinces. A less ambitious target would therefore be to confine a full count to the majority of the rural population of the Blue Nile, Khartoum and Northern Provinces.

Part III: Tabular Matter

MODE OF LIFE

In a country like the Sudan, which is experiencing considerable economic and social change, classification by mode of life assumes great importance. First, comparison of the results of two censuses with respect to such characteristics throws a great deal of light on the extent of economic change in the period between the two censuses. Second, the mode of life of the people affects their fertility and mortality. Thus, for the purpose of the 1955–56 census tabulations, the mode of life was a common denominator. For example, tabulations by mode of life and fertility would indicate the extent of any fertility differential between nomadic and settled populations or between rural and urban populations. Other characteristics can be examined similarly. It is therefore necessary that the method used to determine the mode of life, should accurately reflect the real position.

There were four categories of mode of life: urban large, urban small, rural sedentary and rural nomadic. While there are no obvious defects in the *Final Report* figures for urban large or urban small, except those which might arise as a result of different definitions (that is, what area should be considered as urban large or urban small), the division between rural sedentary and rural nomadic does not represent a true picture, even if we can find agreement on the definition of 'nomad'.

The 1955–56 *Final Report* shows that the nomadic population amounted to 18·8 per cent[6] of the total population of the six Northern Provinces. This figure grossly underestimated the nomadic population. The reason for this is that the enumeration technique was used at the analysis stage to determine the mode of life of the population of the area in question. This might appear to be a reasonable line of action. However, a good part of the nomadic population was enumerated at the time of the year when they were settled in their headquarters (*dars*). A 'settled' enumeration technique was therefore used, and so at the analysis stage they were considered as settled. In other words, only that part of the population that was enumerated under the nomadic enumeration technique was considered as nomadic. Other nomads, who were enumerated at the time of the year when they could easily be reached, either congregated around wells or temporarily settled in scattered huts in their fields during the cultivation season, were enumerated by non-nomadic techniques and were not considered as nomadic.[7]

In an attempt to re-estimate the nomadic population of the six Northern Provinces,[8] the writer calculated that between 30 and 36 per cent of the population of these Provinces was nomadic, compared with the figure of 18·8 per cent published in the census *Final Report*. The implications of this discrepancy on, for example, the extent of the difference between 'nomadic' and 'settled' fertility can be seen in the following. The number of children under five years per 1,000 females of child-bearing age for rural sedentary is shown as 951 compared with 752 for rural nomadic.[9] The inclusion of nomadic women with low fertility amongst 'settled' women, has had the effect of depressing the average for the 'settled' women. In other words, the procedure adopted during the analysis stage, has led to an under-estimation of the difference between nomadic and settled fertility. Similar distortions occur in other tables. The right procedure would have been the determination of mode of life from the information available about each census area, group, *omodia* or *sheikhship*; and each schedule should have been coded accordingly.[10]

OCCUPATION AND SOCIO-ECONOMIC GROUP

Similar anomalies appeared in connection with tables by occupation and socio-economic group. Two questions were asked during the census about occupation, one about the main occupation and another about subsidiary occupation. On this point the *Supplement to Interim Reports*[11] states:

> 'No rigid definition could be laid down on what constituted a primary occupation and what a secondary. Various definitions of primary occupation suggested themselves, such as occupation from which a person derived the largest income, or the occupation on which he spent most time. But none was practicable . . . The only practicable course—and the one adopted—was to record a person's primary occupation, in the event of his having several occupations, as the one he considered most important.'

There is however no guarantee that this was adopted in practice, either because it was difficult for the respondent to decide which occupation was more important, or because the enumerator interpreted the 'more important occupation' as the occupation in which one was occupied for the greater part of the year or that in which the respondent was actually occupied at the time of the interview. There is evidence that the last definition was used. This is apparently the case with the Messeriya Humur tribe, which is known to be primarily a nomadic[12] cattle-owning tribe. This tribe was enumerated between 7 and 25 August,[13] possibly the time when they are on their land cultivating. The table by occupation gives the following data for males over puberty in this tribe's census area.

Table 4

Main occupation for Males over Puberty, C.A. 772

	Total	%
Gainfully Employed	25,407	100
Farmers	17,385	68·4
Nomadic animal owners	3,543	14·0
Shepherds	2,512	9·9
Others	1,967	7·7

Source: Table 5.14, Main Occupation, Census Areas, *1955/56 First Population Census of Sudan: Final Report*, Vol. II, Khartoum, 1960, pp. 348–50.

The above table indicates that the Messeriya Humur are mostly farmers, although they are known to be predominantly nomadic cattle owners or shepherds. The anomaly has further repercussions on all tables by socio-economic group, against which many other characteristics are cross-classified, i.e. fertility, mortality, marital status, age and sex composition, etc. No questions were asked about the socio-economic group. It was determined in the population census office during the analysis, usually by reference to the occupation of the head of household. All the members of the household were, as a rule, placed in the same socio-economic group as the head of household.[14] In this way not only are figures by socio-economic group misleading, in that some nomadic animal owners or shepherds were included under 'cultivators',[15] but also cross tabulations by socio-economic group and other characteristics, say, fertility, mortality, etc., must be equally defective.

LANGUAGE SPOKEN AT HOME

The figures given in the census reports for language spoken at home must be used with great care. The information was obtained from the household head by asking him what was the language spoken within the confines of the home by members of his household. Included in the household in a substantial number of cases, especially in the urban areas, were servants. Often these were of different ethnic and linguistic groups than the head of household. Nonetheless the servant would be classed as speaking the language of the master. This matter is of greater significance than might appear at first glance. Both Smirnov and McLoughlin have been seriously misled in their discussion of linguistic acculturation by accepting the figures quoted in the census reports at their face value.[16]

A final point may now be added in connection with tabulations. In the circumstances of Africa, more data is needed, as mentioned at the beginning of this paper, on marital conditions. For example, information on such aspects as polygamy for males and frequency of marriage for both sexes should be found very useful in throwing light on differential fertility. This latter aspect seems to be neglected, and it is suggested that an extra one or two questions would not overload the questionnaire unduly.

Footnotes

1. The writer is grateful to Professor I. Cunnison, Head of the Department of Social Anthropology, University of Khartoum, who read the text and gave very valuable advice.
2. In each census area the aim was to take samples of a size sufficient to limit the sampling error of the estimated total population of the census area to within fiducial limits of 10 per cent (at the 0·05 probability level), i.e. to a size sufficient to keep the standard error within 5 per cent. The sampling fractions used at the various stages were those which would give the required degree of accuracy at minimum cost.
3. The writer has in mind the Blue Nile Province, most of which is inhabited by people who are dependent on the Gezira Scheme. The same applies with equal force to the greater part of Khartoum province, which is the centre of commerce, industry and trade and where the rural settled areas around the Three Towns (Khartoum, Khartoum North and Omdurman) have always been the main suppliers of the urban population with its food requirements. The Northern Province is similar but for different reasons. The inhabited part of this province is overpopulated in that the population is very much concentrated in villages in a narrow strip along the Nile. The Province, in the meantime, is more technically advanced than other Provinces, from relatively high degree of skills amongst its labour force as well as education amongst the population generally.

The case presented above for a full count census applies with more force to the 1970 census, because since 1955/56 the area under irrigation has more than trebled, as a result of the Managil Extension and Khasm el Girba settlement project. Further, more land is being put under permanent irrigation from the Roseires Dam.

4. It was not practicable to attempt to estimate the population of each census area by taking a sample and multiplying the average number of persons per village (or per *sheikhship*) by the number of villages (or *sheikhships*) in the census area. With such a method, to obtain any reasonable degree of accuracy, it would have been necessary to include nearly all villages (or *sheikhships*) in the sample. In order to reduce the size of the sample, the use of supplementary data which was highly correlated with the population size was introduced. Such data existed in the form of animal tax lists in the case of nomads, and poll-tax lists in the case of people who lived in the less-developed areas of the south and west of the Sudan.
5. Cost per person enumerated in Wad Medani town (Column 14 of Appendix 4.11, *Methods Report*, Volume II, p. 111) was £(S)·012. Total population of the Province was 2,070,000, i.e. £(S)·012 × 2,070,000 = £(S)24,840.
6. *First Population Census of Sudan 1955/56, Final Report*, Volume 1, Table 1.5, p. 5. The three Southern Provinces have been excluded from the calculation because of the difficulty of arriving at a good working definition for nomadism in these Provinces.
7. For a full account of the enumeration techniques used see the writer's *Population Census of Sudan 1955/56, A Methods Report*, Department of Statistics, Republic of Sudan, Khartoum 1960.
8. 'A Re-estimation of Sudan's Nomadic Population' accepted for publication in Sudan Notes and Records, Vol. XLVII, 1966.
9. Table 2.9 'Measures of fertility by mode of living', *Final Report*, Vol. I, p. 41.
10. For further suggestions regarding reclassification of modes of life see *Methods Report*, *op. cit.*, chapter 9.
11. *First Population Census of Sudan 1955/56, Supplement to Interim Reports*, Khartoum, July 1956.
12. This information was kindly passed to the writer by Professor I. Cunnison, Head of the Department of Social Anthropology and an authority on the Humur.
13. *Methods Report*, Vol. II, Appendix 4, 3, p. 50.
14. Introduction to all three volumes of the *Final Report*.
15. There were the following socio-economic groups: Nomadic Animal Owners, Sedentary Animal Owners, Cultivators, Unskilled in Rural Areas, Unskilled in Urban Areas, Skilled in Rural Areas, Skilled in Urban Areas, Managerial and Professional.
16. S. R. SMIRNOV, 'Voyage en République Soudanaise', *Des Africanistes Russes parlent de l'Afrique*, Paris, 1960, p. 244, and F. M. MCLOUGHLIN, *Language-Switching as an Index of Socialization in the Republic of the Sudan*, USA, 1964. See also F. REHFISCH, 'A Study of Some Southern Migrants in Omdurman', *Sudan Notes and Records*, Vol. XLIII, 1962.

13 The 1970 census programme for the African region: a comment

B. Gil

International Labour Organization, Geneva

The United Nations Statistical Office has produced a draft of the revised *Principles and Recommendations* for the 1970 round of World Population Censuses. The Regional Commissions of the United Nations, including the Economic Commission for Africa (ECA), were asked to make comments on the draft recommendations of the UN. (see Annex to this chapter).

About two years ago, the ECA produced a very valuable document that relates to the history of African censuses in the decade 1956–64. In this document the failures and defects of past censuses have been pointed out. Recently (21–26 June 1965) a working group of census experts at the ECA produced its comments on the draft *recommendations* of the UN. This document deals mainly with concepts and definitions and with the census questionnaire contents for Africa. As a demographer, I would be the last one to deny the importance of such a discussion, though I must stress that some of the conclusions reached seem somewhat inappropriate for Africa (e.g. the question on citizenship or ethnic group has been given a first priority order while such important information as place of birth has been placed in the second priority list).

However, my main comment is that such documents as that of the working group are only a small part, perhaps only a beginning, of what one might call a census programme for Africa. The shortcomings of the past censuses in Africa consist not so much in the inadequacy of concepts, definitions and questionnaire contents, as in the field of the application of the concepts and more generally in the field of the implementation of the UN *recommendations.*

To give an idea of what I mean by a more realistic and complete census programme for Africa, I list the following essential requirements:

1. Compilation of an inventory of the human technical resources of each country in Africa that intends to take a census around 1970; examination of their availability for census purposes on the one hand and an estimate of census requirements on the other hand.
2. Estimation of the intellectual and technical potentialities i.e. persons who could be trained to become census experts and qualified census staff.
3. Inventory of the existing material resources and estimation of census requirements in the field of finance, transport, statistical and printing equipment and other census-type services.
4. Preparation and co-ordination of a time-table of censuses in Africa in order to space them out according to local and foreign assistance possibilities.
5. Preparation of instructions, manuals and other documents based on African standards and experiences in the fields of map preparation, testing, evaluation and processing procedures.
6. Training of African census experts, which is one of the most important prerequisites for the success of the 1970 censuses. Africa will require 150 to 170

experts (three to five experts per country in the fields of statistics, demography, geography, machine processing, etc.). Neither UN technical assistance nor bilateral agreements are in a position to supply such a large number of experts. Hence the training of African qualified staff is the only solution. The training of such a large number of African experts has to be spread over a number of years.

Finally, to grasp fully the importance of such a programme one should be made aware that, according to my estimates, Africa is going to spend between 15 and 20 million pounds sterling (present price level) on the 1970 censuses. The programme I have in mind, to ensure that these census investments are fruitful and not wasted, might cost about a quarter of a million pounds, i.e. about one-eightieth of the total expected expenditures on censuses in Africa around 1970.

Annex

The following text (E/CN.14/CAS.4/12), originally presented to the Fourth Conference of African Statisticians, Addis Ababa, 8–17 November 1965, is included here because of its relevance.

The formulation of the African programme for the 1970 censuses of population and housing

United Nations Economic and Social Council Economic Commission for Africa

Introduction

The general objectives of the 1970 World Population and Housing Census Programmes have been stated in the United Nations document *Progress Report on the 1970 World Population and Housing Census Programmes* (E/CN.3/337). The 1970 World Programmes consist of a number of related international, regional and national activities designed to assist countries in the conduct of population and housing censuses in the period 1965–74.

An important element of United Nations participation in the Programme has been the preparation of the documents *Principles and Recommendations for a Population Census: Draft Recommendations for 1970 Censuses* (E/CN.3/330) and *Principles and Recommendations for a Housing Census: Draft Recommendations for the 1970 Censuses* (E/CN.3/332). These principles and recommendations reflect the experiences of a large number of countries, representing all regions, in the 1960 round of censuses, and are intended to provide a broad framework which can be modified on a regional basis to meet local requirements.

The Formulation of the African Programme

Progress to date was summarized in the ECA document *The 1970 Population and Housing Census Programmes in the African Region* (E/CN.14/CAS.4/CPH/10) which also outlines possible future lines of action by which the countries of the African region may develop the regional adaptation of the worldwide programme. The course proposed is parallel to that being followed in Europe, Latin America and Asia and the Far East and includes regional meetings at which detailed consideration may be given to the principles and recommendations for the planning and conduct of population and housing censuses, the topics to be investigated, the definition and specification of these topics, the tabulations to be made and the dissemination of the results. A suggested time-table was given in the document E/CN.14/CAS.4/CPH/10, arranged in a way which would fit in with the timing of the worldwide programme.

The Working Group on Censuses of Population and Housing

In order to prepare concrete proposals which could be put before the Fourth Conference of African Statisticians, a meeting was convened by the Economic Commission in co-operation with the United Nations Statistical Offices and the Bureau of Technical Assistance Operations. This Working Group on Censuses of Population and Housing met in Addis Ababa from 21 to 29 June 1965 and was attended by participants from eight member and two associate member states, and representatives of ILO and the North African Demographic Training and Research

Centre. The Report of the Working Group is presented to the Conference as document E/CN.14/CAS.4/CPH/11.

It will be seen from the report that the Working Group covered a very wide field in relation to censuses of population and housing but was not able, in the time at its disposal, to give attention to the question of tabulations to be recommended for the African programme. It is therefore proposed that the Working Group should be convened for a second session (subject to the availability of funds), early in 1966.

Some Notes on Recommendations of the Working Group

GENERAL

The Working Group was in broad agreement with the United Nations *Principles and Recommendations* both for population and housing. It was felt that these were, with some exceptions, applicable in African conditions and could be used as a framework for the collection of data which would meet national needs without sacrificing international comparability.

PROVISIONAL LISTS OF TOPICS TO BE INVESTIGATED IN AFRICAN CENSUSES

The Working Group after lengthy discussions endorsed:

(a) a Provisional List of Topics for inclusion in the 1970 Round of African Population Censuses (para. 49 of the *Report*), and

(b) a Provisional List of Topics for inclusion in Housing Census or Survey in the 1970 Programmes (para. 96 of the *Report*).

The Provisional List of Topics for a *population census* consisted of three sections headed: Basic Priority I, Basic Priority II and Priority III. As it was strongly asserted that Priority I and Priority II were of equal status, it is suggested that the Conference might endorse the following minor change in presentation of the Provisional List:

1. *Basic Topics*
   (a) For inclusion in a complete census.
   (b) For inclusion in sample surveys where inclusion in complete censuses is not considered feasible.
2. *Further Desirable Topics*

The Provisional List of topics for a *housing census or survey* consisted of 22 items, the first 17 of which were recommended as a minimum programme for a housing inquiry to be integrated in a population census; the complete list would be suitable for a more intensive survey of African housing to be carried out, in most instances on a sample basis. The items appearing in the Provisional List were said to be present in the order of importance assigned to them. However the following points must be taken into consideration:

(a) It was felt that the discussion on housing had not been as satisfactory to the Group as it would have wished, because of lack of continuity of experience at national levels and also because of shortage of time.

(b) The Group did not reach agreement on the definition of a housing unit for application in African inquiries.

(c) The Group recommended that the question of the definition of a housing unit and the specification of the types of housing unit be given fuller discussion at the next session of the Working Group.

(d) The Group also recommended that the question of the priorities of the topics listed in paragraph 96 be taken up again at the next session.

Conclusion

The attention of the Conference is drawn to the importance of the suggestions made by the Working Group. The Conference, as the body to which the Working Group reports, may wish to express its views on the general findings of the Group as summarized in the *Report*, and may wish also to consider the points raised in the preceding paragraph, especially the latter part. It is a matter of urgency that the Working Group at its second session have the benefit of the comments of the Conference and the timing is such that this is the only available occasion. These comments could then be incorporated in the text of the Draft African Programme for the 1970 censuses and would facilitate the eventual adoption by the Fifth Conference of the final version of the Programme.

14 Measuring current population changes

D. F. Heisel

Institute for Development Studies
University College, Nairobi, Kenya

Introduction

Accurate and up-to-date information on the composition and patterns of change of population is a primary requisite of intelligent decision-making in a modern nation state. Fundamental to all else, it is necessary to know population size, rate of growth, and the component patterns of fertility and mortality. This is particularly true for states with developing economies whose resources must be husbanded with meticulous care. Planning for growth obviously requires the best possible knowledge of the characteristics and prospects of the population being planned for.

The most commonly used apparatus for producing such information is the census-registry system: a periodic enumeration of the population concurrent with the recording of births and deaths as they occur. Information obtained in this manner lends itself to use in the occurrence/exposure rate concept basic to demographic analysis. Registered events are the occurrences, while person-years of exposure are estimated from the enumerated populations. However, a fully effective census-registry system is not found in any African nation today. A variety of only partial approximations to the ideal system are found, such that the data which are produced require special scrutiny and analysis before they can be made useful. The conclusions which they provide must be taken with substantial margins of probable error. Furthermore, the prospects of establishing effective national census-registry systems in the reasonably near future must be considered poor. If nothing else, the costs are likely to be prohibitive in these developing societies where there is so much to be done with so little capital.

The following comments will suggest a line of development which might usefully be considered in the light of the needs for information and the shortage of usable and reliable data. First, the nature of existing sources of data and the more important difficulties they present will be briefly described. Then, a cursory review will be given of some of the methods developed to extract maximum information from these data. Finally, since the products of the use of these methods do not fully meet the needs for information, one additional set of procedures, the use of frequent enumeration with or without continuous registration in sample areas, will be introduced. Specific instances of the use of such procedures will be described and some general remarks on their possible relevance in Africa will be made. Attention will be limited throughout to procedures appropriate to a whole national population.

Existing Procedures

Existing sources of demographic data in Africa are restricted to censuses, surveys and special inquiries. There are no national systems of registration of vital events, at the levels of completeness, sufficient to provide useful demographic information. Complete registration is found in some smaller geographic areas and for special segments of some populations, but nowhere in Africa on a universal national scale. The difficulties of establishing a complete registration system appear to be the most intractable of all those hindering the improvement of the supply of demographic data.

In the absence of registration, enumeration or cross-sectional survey procedures provide most of the useful information about population. In his review of sources, van de Walle indicates that demographic data gathered by means of such procedures is currently available for just over four-fifths of tropical Africa's population.[1] In most cases, sample surveys were employed in place of complete enumerations. In general, this investment in the quality as opposed to the quantity of individual records seems to have been fully justified.

There has been considerable variation from one inquiry to another in the amount of detail recorded. Censuses and surveys have ranged from highly elaborate multi-purpose investigations using sophisticated schedules down to what are little more than head counts. What is of particular importance here is the gathering of cross-sectional data which can be used to fill the gap left by the absence of current registration of vital events. The goal is still to obtain occurrence/exposure rates. Attempts have been made to obtain records of births and deaths by means of questions during the surveys, thereby producing information comparable to what could be available if the events were recorded as they occurred. For example, women over age 15 years may be asked to report children born during some recent time period (usually a year), children ever borne, or both. Deaths to children ever borne and deaths in a household during a recent time period can provide information on mortality. (The different time periods—preceding year, lifetime, or other—can be used to increase accuracy through methods to be discussed below.) Additional specification may be available through detailed recording of mother's age and marital status, sex and birth order of children, sex and age of the deceased, and so forth. In particular, the utility of information on fertility and mortality is obviously much enhanced if detailed information on age is also available.

Experience gained over recent years has shown that the census-survey system can indeed produce useful demographic information in the absence of an effective census-registry system. However, experience has also shown that there are persistent and difficult patterns of error in the data. These difficulties would, of course, plague us if other data-producing systems were used as well.

Specific reference is made here to patterns of error commonly found in Africa; comparable problems will be found to some degree in almost any other publication. The following are among the most serious:

1. The complete omission of some individuals who should be included. This becomes especially serious when some particular subgroup is enumerated with unequal completeness or when there is varying completeness between successive censuses or surveys.
2. Failure to report all vital events especially, but not solely, when long periods of recall are involved. For example, older women exhibit a consistent tendency to under-report the number of children they have ever borne and especially the number who have died during their lifetime. In general, it appears that the longer the period of recall, the higher the likelihood of omission.
3. Erroneous dating of vital events when they are reported. A birth or death which in fact occurred more than 12 months earlier may be reported as having occurred in the previous year. Conversely, a more recent vital event may be ascribed an earlier date. This pattern of error is more serious when a population shows a systematic tendency either to update or to predate. Moreover, the tendency to systematically misdate may be correlated to other characteristics such as age, level of education, and so on.
4. Age misstatement. Reports on age distribution for children up to ten years old give a marked number of children aged exactly five or ten years; clearly, accurate knowledge of age is not common. In addition, there are marked patterns of avoid-

ance of certain broader age categories. For example, African age distributions show shortages, most noticeable for females, of persons reported in their teens or early twenties. There is often a corresponding inflation of the adult years. Finally, there may be a tendency for all ages to be reported incorrectly.

Given census-survey data laced with such errors, methodologists have developed an impressive array of analytical techniques to extract as much reliable information as possible. Used along with the demographer's traditional tools, these techniques have greatly furthered analysis of African data. They have been ably surveyed elsewhere[2] and so will be only briefly noted here. Three of the most important contributions have been the development and application of:

(a) Methods for converting reports of lifetime experience of vital events into current rates (and vice versa);
(b) Model life tables; and
(c) Stable and quasi-stable population theory.

(a) *Conversion of Reports.* Where the fertility experience of women of given age groups has been recorded for two time-periods, lifetime and (usually) previous year, it is most useful for analytic purposes to be able to compare the two values directly. This can be done if it is recognized that, in the absence of sustained trends, the two kinds of reports measure the same fertility pattern in different ways. Techniques worked out by Brass convert measures based on one period of report into the corresponding measures on the other. A powerful method is available to evaluate fertility patterns with reasonable accuracy or to locate and measure errors of reporting.

In the case of mortality, attention must be given primarily to the possibilities of extracting information from retrospective reports by mothers of various ages, concerning children ever borne who have died. A procedure, also developed by Brass, provides a means of converting such reports of proportions of dead children into life table mortality rates.[3]

(b) *Model Life Tables.* The mortality rates obtained from women's reports can provide no more than an estimate of mortality conditions affecting a population. Since it is largely the experience of children that is considered, survivorship can be estimated only for the earlier years. However, the use of model life tables gives much broader relevance.

It is an empirical observation of great importance that the age pattern of human mortality for each sex is quite regular. Thus, it has been possible to construct mathematical functions such that, if mortality for one age is given, that for all other ages is determined with considerable accuracy. For example, if infant mortality can be satisfactorily estimated, a complete life table is available.[4]

(c) *Stable or quasi-stable Population Theory.* In addition to the separate analysis of fertility and mortality, as the techniques just described facilitate, it is most useful if they can be considered in their mutual relationship. This can be done by means of stable or quasi-stable population theory.[5]

The central idea is that a specific proportional age distribution will result from unchanging schedules of fertility and mortality in a closed population. Along with this stable age distribution, a variety of other parameters of the stable population are thus determined.

Further, it has more recently been found that the requirement of unchanging mortality is not strictly essential. If the mortality schedule alters in a regular fashion (for example, if the change can be described as a movement from one level of mortality to another, for a given set of model life tables), the resulting age distribution, which is called 'quasi-stable', very closely resembles the completely stable case. Where the assumptions of quasi-stability are reasonable, analysis can proceed by constructing the implied age distributions and determining other parameters. These can then be used directly to describe the population or, more commonly, made the basis of critical analysis through comparison with empirically observed values.

The application of these methods and others to census-survey data has given considerable effectiveness to African demography. However, it has not by any means answered all of the questions one might wish to ask and the answers produced often fall short of the desired level of accuracy. From the point of view of both demographic scholarship and the application of demographic information to policy problems, we are left with uncomfortable margins of possible error and lack of detail.

Again, at times there is interest in precisely those kinds of information which the data and methods just described are least well-suited to produce. The methods often proceed most effectively on the assumption that fertility is and has been essentially constant or that mortality is varying in some regular and relatively simple fashion. However, it may be of importance to make the validity of this assumption a matter of empirical investigation. This might be especially the case where policies are established with the understanding that they will have a significant impact upon fertility or mortality.

For another example, the rate of population growth is an item of great importance to the economic and social planner. A single census-survey or even a succession of enumerations is very limited in its ability to provide this information on a reasonably up-to-date basis, especially where vital processes are changing quickly.

In general, one would hope to see African demography grow most rapidly by a continuing development of both field procedures and methods of analysis. As a probably useful supplement to procedures now widely employed, we may consider the use of intensive enumeration in sample areas, possibly accompanied by continuous registration.

Intensive Field Procedures

Experiments on the improvement of demographic data by use of intensive field procedures have been carried out in a number of countries, using somewhat varying approaches. Broadly speaking, they all show two characteristics. First, in no case is there an attempt to cover the total population of the nation. Either purposively selected or probability samples are used. Second, recording procedures are especially adapted to coping with patterns of error such as those described above. These procedures are distinguished from the techniques already discussed in that they place emphasis on field operations rather than on subsequent analysis leading to the estimation of error. The emphasis on fieldwork takes the form of more intensive contact with the respondents.

Some of the more useful possibilities can be brought out by consideration of specific cases.[6] The following comments do not attempt a complete description of any of the experiments. Selected aspects are discussed in order to suggest the range of possibilities.

EXPERIMENTS USING FREQUENT ENUMERATION AND CONTINUOUS REGISTRATION

Pakistan.[7] One of the most ambitious operations of this type is the so-called 'Population Growth Estimation' experiment, begun in Pakistan in 1962. A probability sample was used comprising 24 regions with about 5,000 persons in each. There are 12 regions in East Pakistan and 12 in West Pakistan.

In most of the regions, there is both registration of vital events and frequent enumeration. Registration is carried out by a full-time paid worker who actively moves through his region seeking out births and deaths. Complete enumerations are made once each year and then are updated quarterly. Annual fresh enumerations are carried out without reference to the previous year's lists. Comparison of the successive year's lists with matching of individuals could presumably be made but has not been attempted. At each quarterly visit, respondents are asked to report vital events that occurred in the preceding year. Thus, each vital event should be recorded five times—four times in enumeration and once by the registrar.

Enumeration procedures are independent of the activities of the registrars, and vice versa. Personnel, administration and records of the two systems are kept completely separate in the fieldwork phase. Therefore the model for estimating births, deaths and the extent of registration developed by Chandrasekar and Deming seems to be applicable.[8] The analysis then necessitates the matching of all vital events recorded by registration with those reported in enumeration. Where there is a failure to match, rechecks are made in the field to resolve the discrepancy. This stage of the procedure has proven to be time-consuming, arduous, and not entirely satisfactory.

In general, however, the Population Growth Estimation experiment shows an impressive capability to detect and record vital events accurately, in a situation where large-scale errors should be expected. It has offered a fruitful try-out for a variety of techniques that might be adapted to other conditions. Indeed, India and Thailand are beginning similar experiments, but with smaller sample units.

Turkey.[9] Another major experiment in intensive field operations has recently begun in Turkey. A notable feature of this case is the sample design which takes into account the high level of regional heterogeneity in the country. Turkey has been divided into five regions and three main cities. Samples (consisting of rural villages and urban blocks) will be drawn separately in each segment and successive segments are being taken into the field operations between 1965 and 1968.

Procedures in the Turkish experiment are somewhat simpler than those employed in Pakistan. Enumerations with reporting of vital events are made on an annual basis. Intensive registration will be carried out in only one-fifth of the villages or blocks. Comparisons of enumeration data with that produced by the registry will not include matching on an event-by-event basis but will be done in terms of gross numbers. However, a programme of intensive re-enumeration of a sample of recently enumerated households will be used to improve reliability. Results are not yet available to permit empirical evaluation of this experiment.

EXPERIMENTS USING FREQUENT ENUMERATION WITH OVERLAPPING RECALL PERIODS

India.[10] Through use of the National Sample Survey, a series of experiments to estimate vital events has been made. These experiments have used frequent enumerations without attempting to register events upon occurrence. The mode of questioning resembled that used in the quarterly enumeration phase of PGE. Upon enumeration, the respondents were asked to report vital events that had occurred during a preceding time period. The time period was made sufficiently long so that it overlapped earlier enumeration. Therefore vital events accurately reported should be recorded more than once, with the specific number of times dependent upon the length of the time period and the frequency of enumeration.

Emphasis in the analysis of these data was given to the problem of omission of vital events in reporting. Two findings are especially noteworthy. First, it has been possible to estimate the magnitude of 'recall lapse', that is, the progressively greater omission of events as the time between the event and its reporting increases. R. K. Som carefully analysed reports for the previous year by number of months before reporting. He showed that, if the correct death rate with no recall lapse is taken to be 100, the index for the twelfth previous month dropped to 67 in Indian data for 1953–54 and to 90 for Upper Volta for 1960–61. Moreover, a regular function of declining index values by month could be reasonably fitted to the data.

Similar results were obtained when the total recall period was altered to two years (respondents were asked to report vital events 'last year' and 'the year before last') and the enumerations were made annually. Levels of the omission were, as could be expected even greater for the longer time span.

A second noteworthy finding was that it is useful to employ a longer time span of reporting, divided into segments. It was found that then the segments closer in time to the actual date of reporting show less omission than if those segments alone were used. For example, the respondent is asked to report births last year and births the year before last. He will then apparently report births during the preceding 12 months with fewer omissions than if he was merely asked to report births in the previous year alone.

Morocco.[11] Another experiment using overlapping recall periods was carried out in Morocco. A random sample of some 64,000 persons was used in the period 1961–63. In this case, analytic emphasis was placed on the importance of misdating of events which were in fact reported.

Field procedures consisted of three 'rounds' of contacts with respondents. The first and second rounds were carried out completely independently. Reports of vital events during overlapping periods were requested on the first two rounds and the discrepancies were checked and reconciled on round three. It was found that for 85 per cent of the reported births and 59 per cent of the reported deaths there was complete agreement between the first two rounds. In the remaining cases various rules were applied to resolve conflicting reports. Although frequent, on the average, the errors of dating tended to cancel out.

These results from India and Morocco suggest an important general point: Even without an accompanying programme of continuous registration, intensive enumeration with questions designed to make use fully of the field procedures, can substantially raise levels of reliability of reports.

EXPERIMENTS USING FREQUENT ENUMERATION ALONE

Guanabara–Cauquenes.[12] These experiments were designed to determine the extent to which demographic data could be obtained, using the simplest possible intensive enumeration field procedures. The basic method starts with the enumeration of a sample of households. Then, on subsequent contacts with members of the sample, vital events which have occurred since the previous visit are recorded. Neither continuous registration nor overlapping recall periods are built into the procedures. (In fact, an overlapping recall period was used in Guanabara on the terminal visit. However, this device does not seem to have been considered an intrinsic part of the design and is apparently not going to be used in the forthcoming Cauquenes programme.) Visits are approximately quarterly.

The Guanabara study (on an urban population) has been completed; in Cauquenes a replication on a largely rural population is under way. Random samples of 12,000 and 20,000, respectively, were used. The results appear to have been reasonably satisfactory in Guanabara. Birth and death rates (with important assistance from the overlapping recall data of the final round) as well as other demographic characteristics, accord well with evidence from other sources.

However, the lack of more extensive internal checks provides no direct measures of accuracy beyond plausibility of appearance. On the other hand, it must be recognized that the simplicity of the method achieves lower costs and very quick results.

Senegal.[13] Procedures similar to those used in Guanabara and Cauquenes have been experimented with during recent years, in Senegal. Here, however, revisits are made annually. In addition, random sampling methods were not employed. Two homogeneous political districts, comprising together some 50,000 people, were purposively selected for the study.

Independent field operations which might be used as mutual checks of reliability were not attempted. On subsequent visits, previously made records were in the hands of the field staff. An advantage was the speed of reporting—results were published and distributed three months after the end of field operations. However, reliability remains problematic.

It is worth noting that simple and flexible procedures of the Guanabara–Cauquenes or Senegal type have the further advantage of providing a most useful frame for special studies. In Guanabara, an investigation of school-leavers was made on one round; in Senegal, extra attention was given to women who had not borne a child during the two years' duration of the study.

General Comments

The preceding discussion has shown something of the range of possibilities for using intensive field procedures. The rather considerable variation itself suggests that no single optimum set of techniques can be established *a priori*. There will have to be adaptation and innovation in response to the conditions found in any given situation. However, a few final generalizations seem worth making.

First, these procedures will necessarily require sampling methods—and specifically representative samples—if the results are to be fully useful. This will demand careful attention but it is not essentially a different problem from that already faced in the sampling done for the single-contact demographic surveys now widely in use in Africa.

In one particular detail, however, a difficulty does seem to be more serious. These methods almost always involve area sampling at some stage, along with the continuing contact with individuals. Therefore, the handling of migration, especially that out of the sample areas, requires greater care. In several of the experiments—Guanabara stands out—this problem has been approached with considerable sophistication. However, further attention would undoubtedly be rewarding.

Second, it must be recognized that these procedures may seem expensive in comparison to the small amounts that have sometimes been given to the gathering of demographic data in Africa. However, the costs of carrying out such research must be weighed against the costs of not having the information. In addition, in some cases the expenses may not be particularly high. Some requirements may be met by sharing (e.g. data-processing equipment) and some by loan (e.g. advisory personnel from international agencies, foundations, and so on). As a case in point, it has been estimated that for the Guanabara–Cauquenes experience, US $5,000 per year should suffice for samples of 12,000 to 20,000 persons. In general, however, costs will depend on the complexity of the procedures used in the specific local context.

Last, it is obvious that in the array of procedures, we have not yet discovered any single best one. It remains to be determined how the balance between precision and simplicity can most effectively be struck. On the one hand, it is essential to avoid piling check upon doublecheck until the procedures sink under the weight of their own elaboration. On the other, there is no gain if simplicity is obtained at the cost of reliability.

It is in this area of innovation and adaptation that the greatest development is possible. The effectiveness of these procedures can be substantially increased. For example, experiments in matching and comparison using only sub-samples might be further explored. Greater exploitation, within the framework of intensive field operations, could be given to the methods developed to analyse census-survey data. In general, continuing experimentation and application should be expected to make a substantial contribution to African demography.

Footnotes

1. E. VAN DE WALLE, *Availability of Demographic Data by Regions in Tropical Africa*, Chapter 2.
2. WILLIAM BRASS, 'Methods of obtaining basic demographic measures where census and vital statistics registration systems are lacking or defective', paper presented at the United Nations World Population Conference, Belgrade, 1965.
3. Detailed references on the sources and application of these methods can be found in the paper by Brass cited above.
4. Widespread use of model life-tables began with the set published by the United Nations in 1955, *Age and Sex Patterns of Mortality*, St/SOA/Series A, No. 22, United Nations, New York, 1955. More recent developments are described in BRASS, *op. cit.*, and COALE, 'Estimates of Demographic Measures through the Quasi-Stable Age Distribution', in *Emerging techniques of Population Research*, Proceedings of the 1962 Annual Conference of the Milbank Memorial Fund, New York, 1962.
5. See, for example, BOURGEOIS-PICHAT, 'Utilisation de la notion de population stable pour mesurer la mortalité et la fecondité des populations des pays sous-developpées', *Bulletin of the International Statistical Institute*, 36 (2), 1958; COALE, *op. cit.*; *The Future Growth of World Population*, St/SOA/ Series A, No. 28, United Nations, New York, 1958.
6. A very useful review of these experiments in greater detail than is possible here can be found in W. P. MAULDIN, 'Estimating Rates of Population Growth', paper presented at the International Conference on Family Planning Programmes, Geneva, 1965.
7. N. AHMED and K. KROTKI, 'Simultaneous Estimations of Population Growth', *The Pakistan Development Review*, Vol. III, No. 1, Spring 1963; K. KROTKI and N. AHMED, 'Vital Rates in East and West Pakistan—Tentative Results from the P.G.E. Experiment', *The Pakistan Development Review*, Vol. IV, No. 4, Winter 1964.
8. C. CHANDRASEKAR and W. E. DEMING, 'On a Method of Estimating Birth and Death Rates and the Extent of Registration', *Journal of the American Statistical Association*, Vol. 44, No. 245, March 1949.
9. N. FISEK, Y. HOPERKAN, and J. RUMFORD, *The Role of the Turkish Demographic Survey in the Family Planning and Rural Health Programmes*, Ministry of Health and Social Welfare, Republic of Turkey, Ankara, 1965.
10. R. K. SOM, 'On Recall Lapse in Demographic Studies', *International Population Conference, Wien, 1959*; INDIA STATISTICAL INSTITUTE, 'The Use of the National Sample Survey in the Estimation of Current Birth and Death Rates in India', *International Population Conference*, New York, 1961.
11. G. SABAGH and C. SCOTT, 'An Evaluation of the Use of Retrospective Questionnaires for Obtaining Vital Data: The Experience of the Moroccan Multi-Purpose Sample Survey of 1961–1963', paper presented at the United Nations World Population Conference, Belgrade, 1965.
12. *Guanabara Demographic Pilot Survey*, ST/SOA/Series A/35, United Nations, New York, 1964; C. ARRETX, C. and J. L. SOMOZA, 'Survey Methods, Based on Periodically Repeated Interviews, aimed at Determining Demographic Rates', *Demography*, Vol. 2, 1965.
13. P. CANTRELLE, 'Repeated Demographic Observation in a Rural Area in Senegal', *World Population Conference*, Belgrade, 1965.

15 Vital rate surveys in tropical Africa: some new data relevant to sample design

Christopher Scott

Regional Statistical Adviser, Economic Commission for Africa

Introduction

In recent years many countries in Africa have undertaken demographic surveys on a sampling basis, one of the main purposes of such surveys being the estimation of vital rates. The sample design adopted for these surveys has been essentially the same in all cases: a single-stage cluster sample involving a complete enumeration of the sampled area units. The latter have generally been villages or census enumeration areas, sometimes grouped or split before sampling to yield units of roughly constant population, typically 300. Usually the units have been stratified by geographical or ethnic characteristics, then sampled with constant probability.

This very simple sample design has many advantages. In particular, the use of cluster sampling, or complete enumeration within primary units, presents the following advantages:

(a) There is no need for a special house-listing operation, which would be necessary to provide a household sampling frame if two-stage sampling were used.

(b) There is no need to worry about the exact definition of 'household', the enumerator's instructions being simply to cover everyone in the selected localities.

(c) Double counting of the same death reported by more than one household is more easily eliminated.

(d) In the case of a multi-round (follow-up) survey, the problem of sampling households which arrive between rounds is more easily handled.

Despite these advantages, there is inevitably some loss in sampling efficiency in using a cluster design when a positive correlation exists between cluster members. The question therefore arises of the magnitude of this loss, of the increase in sample size necessary to compensate for it, and of the optimum size of cluster when the loss is set off against the saving in fieldwork costs resulting from a cluster-sample design.

These are classical problems of sampling treated in every textbook.[1] Their solution depends essentially on the computation of the ***intra-class correlation***, δ, for the population and variable in question, a statistic which measures the ratio of the between-cluster variance to the total variance, or in other words, the extent to which the variable under study is itself clustered. For example, if deaths tended to be substantially more frequent in some villages than others instead of being distributed randomly among villages, then the variance of the death rate between villages would be higher, so that δ would be greater, the loss in sampling efficiency due to cluster sampling would be larger, the number of clusters necessary to achieve a given sampling error would be greater, and the optimum cluster size allowing for costs (assuming δ constant) would be smaller.

Instead of a cluster design (complete enumeration within selected area units), it

Table 1

Effects of Clustering for 23 Rural Strata in Cameroon

Survey	STRATUM			Birth rate per 1,000	Death rate per 1,000	No. of clusters in sample	Mean population per cluster $= N$	Births		Deaths	
	Geographical and ethnic description	Est'd. popln.	Area sq. km.					Intra-class correlation $= \delta$	Proportionate variance increase due to clustering $= \delta N$	Intra-class correlation $= \delta$	Proportionate variance increase due to clustering $= \delta N$
(1)	(2)	(3)	(4)	(5)	(6)	(7)	(8)	(9)	(10)	(11)	(12)
North	Fishing, rice	48,000		44·9	20·9	8	391	+0·0012	+0·46	+0·0008	+0·32
	Cattle. Moslems	29,000		35·0	14·2	7	340	−0·0008	−0·28	+0·0043	+1·47
	Mountain terraces	168,000		62·2	40·0	15	325	+0·0025	+0·80	+0·0022	+0·70
	Mountains, no terracing	75,000		40·1	37·0	14	310	+0·0022	+0·67	+0·0012	+0·37
	Plains. Cotton. Pagans	232,000	38,700[1] (all North strata)	42·6	24·9	20	346	+0·0026	+0·90	−0·0005	−0·17
	Plains. No cotton. Pagans	104,000		43·9	27·8	12	330	+0·0054	+1·77	+0·0027	+0·90
	Cotton. Moslems	153,000		27·6	20·1	28	348	+0·0047	+1·63	+0·0063	+2·20
	No cotton. Moslems	105,000		29·3	26·1	16	321	+0·0031	+1·00	+0·0012	+0·40
	Mountains. Kapsikis	22,000		67·0	52·2	7	289	−0·0011	−0·33	+0·0081	+2·34
Centre and East	Savannah. Bafia. Yambassa	58,000	4,000	38·7	20·9	10	347	−0·0002	−0·07	+0·0003	+0·10
	Savannah. Baya	42,000	29,300	44·9	24·7	7	291	+0·0003	+0·10	+0·0032	+0·92
	Cocoa. Kozime I	32,000	55,600	35·0	20·4	6	280	+0·0009	+0·25	+0·0051	+1·43
	Coffee. Maka	48,000	6,200	29·9	21·6	8	312	−0·0013	−0·40	+0·0018	+0·56
	Coffee. Kaka, Pol, Badoum, Kozime II	73,000	18,500	48·6	20·8	12	280	−0·0013	−0·35	+0·0007	+0·20
	Cocoa. Betis	162,000	25,300	27·5	22·1	16	333	+0·0013	+0·43	+0·0022	+0·73
	Cocoa. Eton	137,000	3,000	42·4	18·5	11	354	+0·0001	+0·05	−0·0002	−0·08
	Cocoa. Bane, Ewondo	140,000	6,400	32·7	14·4	12	324	−0·0008	−0·25	+0·0012	+0·39
	Cocoa. Boulous	166,000	35,600	36·2	14·1	14	320	+0·0026	+0·83	+0·0031	+0·98

Table 1 (*continued*)

Survey	STRATUM			Birth rate per 1,000	Death rate per 1,000	No. of clusters in sample	Mean population per cluster $=N$	Births		Deaths	
	Geographical and ethnic description	Est'd. popln.	Area sq. km.					Intra-class correlation $=\delta$	Proportionate variance increase due to clustering $=\delta N$	Intra-class correlation $=\delta$	Proportionate variance increase due to clustering $=\delta N$
(1)	(2)	(3)	(4)	(5)	(6)	(7)	(8)	(9)	(10)	(11)	(12)
Coast	Bassa tribe	86,000	10,500	42·1	18·7	8	314	−0·0013	−0·42	+0·0020	+0·62
	Others	75,000	13,400	32·3	29·5	10	316	+0·0004	+0·12	−0·0004	−0·12
West	North. Savannah	527,000	16,800	51·2	29·5	33[2]	928	+0·0013	+1·25	+0·0017	+1·56
	Centre. Forest	258,000	22,800	53·0	34·6	34	379	+0·0043	+1·63	+0·0101	+3·81
	South. Plantations[3]	49,000	2,100	48·0	22·2	6	410	+0·0042	+1·74	−0·0005	−0·19

Notes: 1. Strata interpenetrate and it is not possible to give their areas individually.
2. Includes 5 abnormally small clusters (mean pop. 72) which have been excluded in computing columns 8–12.
3. The region is characterized by plantations, but the plantation population was sampled by a different method and is excluded here.

General Note: All data for columns 5–6 and 9–12 are based on approximations—see Annex.

would be possible to introduce a second stage of sampling within area units. For example, a household listing might be carried out within selected units, and a sample of households selected. Essentially the same questions may be asked about such a sample design, namely what is the magnitude of the loss in sampling efficiency in comparison with a simple random sample, the increase in sample size necessary to compensate for this, and the optimum sample size at the second stage (i.e. the optimum number of households to select in each selected area unit) when account is taken of costs. These questions are answered by almost exactly the same analyses as those relevant to the case of a cluster design and the two problems will not be distinguished in this paper except where necessary.

Results from Surveys in Cameroon

No analyses appear to have been published giving values of δ observed in African demographic surveys, and it is the purpose of the present note to supply such data.

The results are taken from four regional demographic surveys conducted in Cameroon, as follows:

Northern Region (fieldwork January–June 1960)
Centre and East (March–November 1962)
Coastal Region (January–March 1964)
West Cameroon (January 1964–February 1965).

Data are published by permission of the Directorate of General Statistics, Mechanography and Economic Accounts of the Cameroon Federal Republic, which conducted the surveys and performed the necessary computations. The material covers a fairly wide variety of types of populations, although limited to a single country. Table 1 gives the results. Their use is discussed below. The method of computation employed is described in the Annex to this chapter.

Using the Results for the Planning of Surveys

The data of Table 1 are presented here in the hope that they may be of value in the planning of similar demographic surveys in tropical Africa. This involves generalizing from the experience of Cameroon to other places and other times. Obviously, this is hazardous: however, the 23 strata for which data are reported in Table 1 have little in common and cover a wide variety of non-nomadic rural populations; it would be reasonable to suppose that few such populations in other tropical African countries fall outside the limits of those reported in the table. Urban strata have been excluded because the available material is limited and the sampling method in Cameroon has often been somewhat different.

Values of the intra-class correlation δ may be considerably influenced by the fineness of stratification, efficient stratification meaning a lower value of δ. One cannot reasonably expect to estimate this efficiency in numerical terms in advance of the survey; however, it may be indicated to some extent by the total population and area of each stratum, as well as by the degree of precision in the verbal description of the stratum. These are shown for each stratum in Table 1, together with the estimated birth and death rates. A statistician wishing to plan a survey in another tropical African country might compare his own proposed strata with those of Table 1, attempt to find strata in the table very roughly comparable in fineness of definition and (probably less important) in vital rates, and assume that his δ will be of roughly the magnitude found for such strata in the table. Though this is not a very scientific procedure it is probably the best available, and certainly better than ignoring the problem.[2]

Such an advance estimate of δ is of value for two purposes: fixing the optimum cluster size and determining the total sample size.

OPTIMUM CLUSTER SIZE

For a given total sample of persons, an increase in cluster size has two effects: first, increase in sampling error; second, saving in cost.

Calculation of optimal cluster size involves determining a mathematical function for each of these effects, and then computing the cluster size which gives the minimum sampling error for a given cost, or minimum cost for a given sampling error (the two problems have the same solution).

We assume from now on that all clusters are of approximately equal size. In practice they may vary considerably without appreciably vitiating the arguments below.

The sampling error variance for cluster or two-stage sampling is approximately proportional to

$$\frac{1}{mn}[1+\delta(n-1)] \qquad \ldots\ldots(1)$$

where m is the number of primary units (PUs) in the sample and n the number of secondary units (SUs, usually persons, or households—in this paper we shall work in terms of persons from now on) selected for the sample in each sampled PU. If there is complete enumeration within PUs—cluster sampling—then n is the cluster size.

As regards costs, it is probably fair to say that for most surveys in Africa the sample size has been limited more by the size of the field force that can be effectively controlled than by total cost.[3] Most African surveys also have to operate against a time limit of some kind, e.g. the funds must be spent within a given year, or the work must be completed before the statistician's contract expires, or in time for the data to be used in preparing the next national plan.

If these conclusions are accepted then the limiting factor is the available number of *enumerator-days*, and the 'cost' should take account only of this.[4] Now it is reasonable to suppose that the number of enumerator-days used is influenced by the sample size in two ways:

(i) Each cluster, or PU, takes up some enumerator time irrespective of the number of persons interviewed within it (time for travel to the PU, for interviewing the local authorities, finding accommodation, etc.). This time may be termed T_1 enumerator-days.

(ii) Each ultimate unit (i.e. each person interviewed) takes up a certain amount of the enumerator's time, say T_2 enumerator-days.

The value of T_1 varies mainly according to whether the enumerators work singly i.e. one per PU, or as a team, say four or five per PU. If singly, T_1 may be about two or three enumerator-days. If as a team, the number of days is the same but the number of enumerator-days is larger since all the team is affected together, so that T_1 then becomes, say, from 8 to 15.

T_2 also varies widely. In theory one would expect to cover at least 30 individuals per day ($T_2=1/30$), but in practice this level is seldom achieved and figures as low as 10 per day ($T_2=1/10$) may be common.

The total available enumerator-days being constant, we have:

$$T_1m+T_2mn = \text{constant}$$

or, dividing by T_2 and writing $T=T_1/T_2$

$$Tm+mn = \text{constant} \qquad \ldots\ldots(2)$$

We may call T the 'cost-ratio' between first- and second-stage fieldwork. We have seen that where enumerators work singly, the cost ratio may vary from about 20 to

90, while where they work in teams of four or five, it may vary from about 80 to 450.[5]

Minimizing the expression (1) subject to (2) leads to:

$$n_{\text{opt.}} = \sqrt{\left[\frac{1-\delta}{\delta}\,T\right]}$$

$$= \sqrt{T/\delta} \text{ approx.} \qquad \ldots\ldots(3)$$

Some typical values of n_{opt} are shown in Table 2.

Table 2

Optimum size (number of persons) of second stage sample per primary unit

	Cost-ratio between first and second stages = T	Intra-class correlation = δ				
		0·001	0·002	0·003	0·004	0·005
	(1)	(2)	(3)	(4)	(5)	(6)
Enumerators working singly	25	158	112	91	79	71
	50	224	158	129	112	100
	75	274	194	158	137	122
Enumerators working in teams	100	316	224	183	158	141
	200	448	316	258	224	200
	300	549	388	316	274	240
	400	633	448	365	316	283

In Cameroon, a typical value of δ was 0·002. (The unweighted average in Table 1 is 0·0013 for births and 0·0025 for deaths.) T was estimated very approximately at 150. It therefore appears that the cluster size generally adopted (somewhat over 300) was quite close to the optimum.

It can be easily shown that the optimum is very flat, in the sense that the value of n can deviate quite far from the optimum without much effect on the 'cost'. For example, if we take $\delta = 0{\cdot}002$ and $T = 200$, the value of n_{opt} is 316. If, however, the cluster size is fixed at half the optimum—say 150 instead of 316, the 'cost' is only 14 per cent higher than the minimum.

When applying equation (3), it should be recalled that in the case of complete enumeration within PUs, n means the cluster size, while in the case of two-stage sampling it means the number of SUs selected per PU. (Note that if the SUs are households, T_2 has to be estimated in terms of households.) In the former case, any variation in n implies a variation in the size of PUs and this must be expected to affect δ. Thus, our assumption that δ is constant is unrealistic for cluster sampling.

We may allow for the variation of δ if we know the equation relating δ to n. This is difficult to determine from available data: where n has been allowed to vary between different strata or different surveys, the concomitant variation observed in δ is likely to be due to other factors differentiating these fields of study. If the data could be broken down into smaller geographical areas within PUs, such as hamlets, the problem might be solved, and it would be useful to provide for this in any future survey.

Common sense suggests that δ should decrease with increasing n, but less rapidly than n increases. A possible model would be

$$\delta = A/\sqrt{n} \qquad \ldots\ldots(4)$$

Minimizing (1) subject to (2) and (4) leads to the following equation for optimal n:

$$n^2+(1-T)\,n+3T = 2\,\frac{T}{A}\sqrt{n} \qquad \ldots\ldots(5)$$

This leads generally to somewhat larger values of n_{opt} than those shown in Table 2, except in the column $\delta=0{\cdot}001$ where the new n_{opt} are somewhat smaller. However, since there are large margins of error in all the parameters and since the optimum is very broad, the practical implications of this adjustment are slight.

Very roughly, then, we may say that a cluster size of a few hundred, assuming team enumeration, or between 100 and 200 assuming individual enumeration, is likely to give a sample not far from optimal efficiency for most vital rate surveys in tropical Africa.

TOTAL SAMPLE SIZE

The decision on sample size will depend on the precision required of the survey.

If the vital rate per 1,000 is R and the acceptable sampling standard error is σ_R, then the total sample size required on the assumption of random distribution of vital events would be

$$\frac{1{,}000R}{\sigma_R^2}\ \text{people} \qquad \ldots\ldots(6)$$

In fact, however, the events are not randomly distributed, and δ measures the extent to which they are clustered. Columns 10 and 12 of Table 1 show the factor by which the sample size, calculated from formula (6), must be increased to attain the same precision in view of the clustering. For example, where this factor is shown as 0·5, the sample size calculated from (6) must be increased by 50 per cent.[6]

It will be seen that δN varies considerably, averaging about 0·5 for births and 0·9 for deaths. The decision for any particular survey should depend on a careful comparison of the proposed survey strata with those of Table 1, but if this fails an argument along the following lines might be admissible:

(i) Since birth and death rates usually have to be compared, and differenced to get a natural growth rate, they should both have about the same absolute precision per 1,000 population.

(ii) If this is assumed, application of formula (6) will now give a considerably larger required sample for the birth rate than the death rate (about twice as large).

(iii) We might now apply formula (6) for the birth rate and double the result. This amounts to assuming $\delta N=1$ for births, which is fairly conservative, since few strata in Table 1 reach this level. For deaths, this gives a sample about four times as large as that given by (6), and therefore corresponds to a δN of 3. Again this is conservative, since few strata reach this level for deaths.

(iv) If the stratification is very rough it might be desirable to triple rather than double the result of formula (6).

Thus, in the absence of more detailed evidence a sample of about $100{,}000/\sigma_B^2$ persons would appear to be reasonable, where σ_B is the acceptable sampling error per 1,000 for the birth rate. If the available stratification is very coarse, the figure of 100,000 might be increased to 150,000.

Note that these conclusions relate to each region for which it is desired to estimate vital rates. They also relate to a single year: if variation in time is to be considered, using a survey spread over a period of years for the purpose of estimating a time-average, one would need to know the intra-class correlation corresponding to the effect of time-clustering, i.e. the amount of variation between years. There appears to be no available evidence on this for African populations.

Annex

The use which it is proposed to make of the data in Table 1 requires only very rough accuracy in the data. Moreover, values of δ derived from the Cameroon surveys, even if computed by the most efficient method, would have very large sampling error. For these reasons, it appears justifiable to use a number of simplifying approximations in computing the data. These are described below.

1. The vital rates in the table are *unweighted* averages of the rates for the PUs in the strata concerned. This assumes that all PUs in a stratum have the same population numbers. (The mean cluster size, shown in column 8, is however the true mean.)

2. The correct value of δ is:

$$\delta = \frac{N}{N-1}\left(\frac{V_b}{V} - \frac{1}{N}\right)$$

where V_b is the between-cluster variance and V the total variance. We have ignored the multiplier $N/(N-1)$. The formula again assumes that the clusters of PUs have constant population N.

3. We have estimated V_b from the formula

$$V_b = \frac{1}{m-1}\sum_{i=1}^{m}(R_i - R)^2$$

where $\bar{R}$ is the unweighted average of the rates. Again this assumes equal sized clusters.

4. We have estimated V from the Poisson assumption, thus:

$$V = 1{,}000\bar{R}$$

This assumes that the frequency of vital events is rare, or more exactly, if p is the ratio of the number of events to the population, we ignore p^2 in comparison with p.

The only conceivable source of serious error from this series of approximations is that resulting from the assumption of equal sized clusters. If it is allowed that the clusters vary in size, then the vital rates become ratio estimates and we have to consider the possible correlation between the vital rate and the cluster size. To get an idea of the importance of this error we selected two strata:

(i) The first stratum of the Centre and East survey, births. This stratum was selected simply as the first that came to hand. It is reasonably typical as regards variation in cluster size.

(ii) The tenth stratum of the Centre and East survey, deaths. This was selected as the 'worst' case, where the cluster size was particularly variable and appeared to be associated with the vital rate. It has since been eliminated from the study, as an urban stratum, and does not appear in Table 1.

For each of these strata we computed the variance V_b in two ways:

$$V_b = \frac{1}{m-1}\sum_i (R_i - \bar{R})^2$$

$$V_b = 10^6 \frac{m^2}{m-1}\left[\frac{\sum y}{\sum x}\right]^2 \left[\frac{1}{\bar{x}^2}\sum(x-\bar{x})^2 + \frac{1}{\bar{y}^2}\sum(y-\bar{y})^2 - \frac{2}{\bar{x}\bar{y}}\sum(x-\bar{x})(y-\bar{y})\right]$$

where y = number of events, x = population.

The first formula is that used in computing δ for Table 1. The second is the correct formula, taking account of the variable cluster size and the fact that the vital rate is a ratio estimate.

For the first stratum, the approximate method gave a result 9 per cent too low; for the second, 18 per cent too low. This confirms that the error due to the approximations is negligible in relation to sampling error and the use to which it is expected to put the data.

One further approximation should be noted. In the Cameroon surveys, when the selected PU had more than twice the desired population a systematic sample of one house in h was selected within it, h being an integer chosen so as to give a sample of approximately the desired magnitude in the PU. This second stage sample was now regarded as the selected PU, and the 'cluster size' is the population of the selected houses, although in reality it is not a cluster in the sense of an exhaustive sample. This was comparatively rare and has been entirely ignored in the present analysis. It does not affect the estimate of δ for the PU, though 'δN' should read 'δn' for such PUs.

Footnotes

1. See for example: HANSEN, HURWITZ and MADOW, *Sample Survey Methods and Theory*, Wiley, New York and London, 1953.
2. The values of δ shown in the table are subject to large sampling errors. Any negative value is almost certainly due to sampling fluctuations and should be assumed to represent some small positive value.
3. In support of this statement, we may consider what decision would be made if one had the possibility of modifying the sample design to yield a lower overall cost but with a larger number of enumerators (this might be achieved, for example, by using larger and fewer clusters, thus economizing on vehicle costs). In most African surveys such a solution would be rejected because of the impossibility of controlling the larger field force.
4. Evaluation in terms of the number of supervisor-days or field-organizer-days would not alter the analysis, assuming the relative numbers of personnel at these levels are fixed.
5. This variation is very large. If account had to be taken of total costs, rather than field time, the range of variation would be considerably wider, mainly because of the very wide variation in transport costs and the difficulty of allocating these between primary and secondary sampling stages.
6. For the case of cluster sampling, $N = n$, but for two-stage sampling N is the total population within any one PU (assumed the same for all PUs) and n is the population selected in each PU. The table can be used for both cases.

16 The use of existing data

W. I. Brass

London School of Hygiene and Tropical Medicine, United Kingdom

The materials for the estimation of fertility, mortality and growth rates in African countries are limited and defective; it is clearly important, therefore, that they should be used as effectively as possible. I have recently written much on such problems both in general terms[1] and with specific attention to Africa.[2] The present paper necessarily deals with much the same principles and applications but from a different approach.

My aim is to consider the kinds of data, suitable for estimating basic demographic measures, that exist in Africa and to suggest the appropriate methods of analysis. It will not be possible to do more than indicate how the techniques are applied; my main purpose is to assess the strengths and weaknesses of the different methods which have been used or proposed. Emphasis will be on points which have not been examined thoroughly elsewhere, with only brief reference to procedures expounded previously in more detail, even if this detracts from the balance of the paper.

The existing data considered are obtained from censuses or inquiries that apply to the whole or a substantial part of the population of a country, either by the inclusion of all persons or from a properly representative sample. Most of the discussion is equally relevant to demographic surveys of small communities but the particular characteristics of such projects will not be examined. Statistics of vital events from registration, periodic surveys and follow-up studies in Africa are, at present, too incomplete or limited in extent to be of much direct help in the estimation of basic rates for countries or large regions. It is worth noting that the term 'existing' is taken here to denote information which could be obtained from the observations and which has not necessarily been published. Unfortunately, reports of African censuses and inquiries have too frequently been deficient in the detailed tabulation of results; sometimes adjusted or graduated distributions have been presented without the original observations. One reason for this has been obvious distortions in the latter, but sophisticated analysis to discover and allow for errors requires the raw data.

The process of detecting and adjusting errors depends on a combination of comparative checks, demographic models and reasonable assumptions. Techniques for checking and the structure of models are parts of the general body of demographic knowledge which can be called upon for the study of all populations. The interpretation of the results obtained by application of the knowledge and establishment of satisfactory assumptions for the making of adjustments can only be effectively based on a close familiarity with the methods of data collection and insight into the characteristics of the population. Routine procedures may give very misleading answers if applied in circumstances only slightly different from those for which they were designed.

Apart from numbers, the most fundamental demographic information obtained from a census is the population distribution by sex and age. In recent years there have been major developments in the theory of the relations of fertility, mortality and growth rates with age distributions, and allied advances in the practice of estimating measures of the former from the shapes of the latter. Lotka showed more than

40 years ago that, if age specific fertilities and mortalities remain constant in a population not affected by migration, then birth, death and natural increase rates tend to limits which can be calculated. In addition the age distribution approaches a fixed, stable form, which is easily computed from the life table and the limit rate of natural increase. In the past decade it has been shown that, even if there is a systematic but moderate trend in mortality, the age distribution will still conform closely to the stable form calculated from the current life table and natural increase. This result and the associated implications are usually called 'quasi-stable population theory'.

For many African populations the assumptions that fertility has remained nearly constant for a long time and there has been no dramatic fall in mortality are reasonable. Often male age distributions have been affected by temporary or permanent migration, but the corresponding statistics for females have been affected to a much smaller extent; temporary movements of young women to employment are less common, and when they migrate their children often go with them, which reduces the distortion of the age distribution. Quasi-stable population theory can, therefore, be usefully applied to much of the African age data.

In order to make effective studies of this kind, some knowledge of mortality patterns is necessary. Direct information is so scanty that heavy reliance must be placed on models constructed from the experience of populations with accurate vital statistics. The pioneer system is the United Nations model life tables in which (separately for males and females) there is one unit of the set at each mortality level. The system is now being extended and made more flexible but there has been little study of the practical uses of the new developments. Meanwhile, there have been other approaches to the construction of model life tables, the most notable being that of Coale and Demeny. The principles of construction are similar to those of the United Nations but four 'Regional' sets of tables, each showing distinctive patterns, have been produced. An important advantage is that the characteristic measures of the tables—birth and death rates, expectations of life, proportions in each age group, etc. —and of the corresponding stable populations, with different rates of natural increase, have been calculated in detail. Applications are thus greatly facilitated. I have developed a rather different but flexible procedure by which model life tables are generated from mathematical relations with standard mortality schedules.

If an age distribution were quasi-stable and reported *very accurately*, it would be possible to separate the components of fertility, mortality and natural increase with fair certainty. The births would be obtained from the level of the age distribution curve at age zero. In practice it is necessary to estimate the level from the numbers in the early age intervals, e.g. at under one or under five years, by extrapolating the curve backwards. This is the basis for the well-known 'reverse-survival' technique which has often been used for Asian populations. However, numbers at under one and under five years are particularly badly reported because of omissions and age errors. Frequently, to avoid the difficulty the projection backwards has been from the numbers in the 5–9 years group. To make the extrapolation it is necessary to utilize estimates of the rate of increase in births and of the mortality at early ages. I do not believe the procedure has much value in Africa because

(a) age errors are too large;
(b) early mortality patterns vary very greatly in different sets of model life tables and there is evidence that they may be even more extreme in developing countries;
(c) in most populations, estimates of the rate of increase are too doubtful.

In all life tables, death rates in the years around ten are low. In this region, therefore, the rate of natural increase has the dominant effect on the change in numbers with age. In theory this fact can be used in conjunction with model life tables to give a good estimate of the growth rate and hence, as a residual, of mortality. Suggestions have been made that the procedure should be used in studies of populations where data are limited. The estimates, however, are very sensitive to age errors and birth fluctuations; in my view, data for African populations cannot be analysed by these means with hope of anything but accidental success.

If different rates of natural increase are applied to the life tables in a system, ranges of stable populations are obtained. The theoretical age distribution which best fits the observations can be selected on some criterion and the measures of fertility, mortality and growth of the stable population taken as estimates for the real one. This type of approach has frequently been adopted in Africa and elsewhere. The method is valuable but its difficulties and limitations have not always been understood or the results properly interpreted.

We will assume first that there is good evidence that the mortality pattern in the population is in accord with some set of model life tables. Even with this restriction, it is possible to find a range of stable populations with different levels of mortality and natural increase which yet give age distributions in good agreement with each other and the observations. The small variations among the models are completely masked by errors and fluctuations in the age data. The point is illustrated in Table 1.

Table 1

Percentages, Based on United Nations Model Life Tables, for two Stable Female Populations, Compared with Observed Values for the Fouta Djallon Region of Guinea, 1954–55

United Nations model level	Exact age in years					Rates per 1,000		
	5	15	25	35	45	Births	Deaths	Natural increase
30	15·9	40·8	60·2	74·6	85·0	44	27	17
55	16·4	42·0	61·1	75·0	84·8	42	17	25
Fouta Djallon	17·5	39·8	58·9	74·9	86·2	—	—	—

It will be noted, however, that birth rates do not differ much in the two theoretical stable populations. In fact, it is in general true that the broad shape of the age distribution is largely determined by fertility, which fixes the height on the curve of the zero point at birth relative to the number of women in the reproductive period. A stable age distribution which fits the observations well will, therefore, give a fair estimate of the birth rate but cannot separate out the mortality and natural increase components with any pretence of accuracy.

The situation is much worse if the information about the mortality pattern, particularly at early ages, is weak. The use of different sets of model life tables will give acceptable stable age distributions with an even wider range of mortality and growth measures; the estimates of birth rates will also vary appreciably. There is good evidence, which cannot be summarized here, that in many West African populations mortality at 1–4 years is very high relative to the level at under one year; the situation in East Africa is less clear. The north region model life tables of the Coale–Demeny system incorporate such a pattern, although not with such extreme features as have been claimed for African mortality, and will often be the best for applications of quasi-stable population theory.

The more distorted the age distribution the more difficult it is to establish sound criteria for selecting the most appropriate stable population. Fitting by statistical methods such as least squares is not necessarily satisfactory since the assumption is that the age errors are divided fairly equally between positives and negatives over the range; the distortion may indeed be mainly in one direction. There appear to be certain consistencies in the age distribution distortions of African population data but these are neither certain nor universal. An illustration is given in Table 2 which shows observed and fitted stable populations for two sets of observations. The distribution for Kenya was fitted by least squares[3] but that for the first agricultural sector of the Ivory Coast by the use of independent estimates of mortality and natural increase.

Table 2

Percentages under Given Ages in Observed and Fitted Female Age Distributions

Exact age in years	Kenya (1962)		Ivory Coast (1957–58)[1]	
	Observed	Fitted	Observed	Fitted
5	17·8	18·5	24·1	19·5
15	44·8	45·8	45·6	47·5
25	63·6	65·2	64·6	67·3
35	79·2	78·7	81·5	80·8
45	88·3	87·8	90·4	89·8

1. First agricultural sector.

In both populations the observed proportions under 15 years are a little less than the stable values; in the Ivory Coast, however, a far higher number were reported as under five years compared with the fitted distribution but in Kenya rather fewer. Even modest errors in the observed percentages under early ages (e.g. five years) have a considerable effect on the estimated birth rates; it is better, therefore, to use a method of fitting which gives reasonable agreement between theoretical and observed distributions at later years. It is not possible to state any general objective criterion, but I have found, in practice, that a fitted stable population with a slightly higher percentage under 15 years than observed gives the most satisfactory results for data on females. Under-estimation of ages of young adult males seems to be more common.

As indicated already, it is not possible to obtain satisfactory measures of death and natural increase rates by these means. If an independent estimate of the growth rate has been obtained from two successive censuses (of equal completeness or suitably adjusted), the choice of stable populations is restricted to those with this characteristic. Although the difficulties of choosing the best mortality pattern and method of fitting still apply, estimates of birth rates and the incidence of deaths between the censuses is obtained. It should be recognized however that the discovery of a satisfactory stable population does not confirm the accuracy of the growth rate since good agreement could have been achieved even if the estimate was very erroneous. There are direct methods for constructing life tables from the numbers surviving from one census to the next but an accuracy of age recording which has nowhere been attained in tropical Africa is required.

In many censuses and sample inquiries in Africa, questions have been asked about births and deaths. The data collected have been of two broad types. The first consists of reports of births and deaths in a short preceding period, usually a year. Generally, the births are classified by age of mother at the time of the survey and the deceased by age at death. The second type of information is on the total numbers of children ever born to each mother and how many of these have died. Again the data are normally divided by age of mother; occasionally some classification of ages of children at death is also attempted. Both these types of statistics are subject to serious errors and various analysis techniques for overcoming the effects have been developed.

If the births and deaths in the preceding year were recorded accurately, current rates would be obtained immediately; given satisfactory age reporting, a life table and fertility and reproductive measures could also be calculated. In fact, experience has shown that the reports of vital events in African surveys have been undependable. Overstatement and understatements of numbers have both been common and the errors for births and deaths have not always been in the same direction; the extent to which the misreporting of deaths varies with the age of the deceased is also far from clear. In Indian surveys of a similar kind it has been shown that omissions of events increase as the date of occurrence recedes into the past. Corrections have been derived by fitting curves to the number of births or deaths reported for each month of the preceding 12 or 24; the level of the curve at the point zero gives an adjusted value for the true number of events per month. Recently the procedure has been applied by R. K. Som to some African data, which also suggest that omissions were greater for more distant events. However, in the application of the technique it is assumed that the time scale is correct. No allowance is made for possible overstatement of numbers due to the inclusion of events which happened outside the period, a feature which has certainly occurred in African inquiries. It is not clear how the method should be used with such data but further exploration is certainly justified.

Kuczynski pointed out a long time ago that the mean number of children ever born to women past the reproductive ages gave a direct measure of completed fertility. The main disadvantages of this index are:

(a) it refers to fertility of the past rather than the current level; and
(b) the older women are the most likely to omit births in retrospective statements.

Omissions of births by the older women have, in fact, been substantial in nearly all African inquiries although the precise reasons are not known. Forgetting of children who died young, failure to report family members who have moved away and the inability to count where numbers are large, are all possibilities. In the early 1950s Myburgh and the writer developed rather different techniques for the estimation of mean completed family sizes by taking into account the total children born to the younger women. The effects of omissions are thus reduced and the fertility experience is closer to the current levels. There is still scope for the application of these methods when age information is lacking or is very inadequate.

More refined procedures are possible when the statistics are by age group of women. Investigation usually shows that the increase, with age in mean children ever born per woman, is too slight in the later years of the reproductive period to be reasonable, giving clear evidence of progressive omissions; often the means fall at ages beyond reproduction. If a distribution of specific fertility rates is postulated (taken either from the experience of a similar population or a model system), the corresponding mean children ever born to women in each age group can be derived. [I have published several ways of doing this.] The level of the specific fertility rates can then be adjusted by a constant factor to give agreement of the calculated and observed mean children ever born for the younger women, e.g. at ages up to 30 years. The calculated mean family size at the end of reproduction is an estimate corrected for omissions by the older women and, to some extent, fertility changes. The main short-coming of this method is the lack of consistency in specific fertility distributions in different populations; the choice of an inappropriate pattern may lead to a substantial error. It has been suggested that the rate of increase of omissions of children with age can be calculated from the trend, at years beyond reproduction, of reported mean children ever born. Adjustments are then derived on the assumption that the same rate applies at younger ages. In my view the method is unsound because it relies too heavily on the weakest section of the data and on a very doubtful assumption. It gives silly results when applied to the statistics for many African populations.

The limitations of the information on children ever born are reflected in the reports of the number who have died. If the chances of omission were independent of whether the child was still alive or not, the proportion dying would not be affected. In nearly all African data, however, the percentage of children reported by the older mothers as having died, changes too slowly with age to be consistent with any acceptable mortality pattern. In general, the plausible suggestion that nearly all the living children are reported by the mothers, and that the omissions are solely of those who have died, is not in accord with the data. There is, therefore, no sound basis for the determination of a correction. The percentages of children dead for the younger women, however, usually have no obvious anomalies.

If the ages of children at death have been reported, e.g. under one, 1–4 years, etc., it would appear that probabilities of dying could be calculated immediately by relating the deaths to the corresponding births. However, a bias exists, unless an allowance is made for the children still alive in these age groups who have not experienced the full force of mortality; the effect can be appreciable for young mothers. In addition, the statements of ages of children at death are subject to all the difficulties of establishing periods of time accurately: these difficulties have contributed greatly to the distorted results for the living and for errors in the number of events reported in the preceding year. To overcome these problems, I have developed a simple method of translating percentages of children dead, by age group of mother, into the probabilities of dying, in standard intervals from birth. The percentages are multiplied by a factor, read from a table, depending on rough measures of the characteristics of the specific fertility distribution. Thus the percentages of children dead to mothers aged 15–19, 20–24, 25–29 and 30–34 years give the probabilities of dying by age 1, 2, 3 and 5 years respectively and so on. These estimates are very insensitive to errors in ages and the characteristics of the fertility distribution but make no allowance for omissions. The technique has been applied to data for many African populations, and in nearly all cases has given child mortality levels considerably higher than the incidences calculated from records of deaths in a preceding period.

If an acceptable measure of child death rates has been arrived at, by the application of these techniques or other means, a life table with the same level of mortality can be chosen from a model set. Estimates of death rates at later years are thus obtained. It must be realized that the results are very approximate and uncertain unless there is strong evidence that the set of model life tables has the right mortality pattern. For example, the different regional sets of the Coale–Demeny system lead to very varied estimates, particularly if only infant mortality under one year is known. I believe that errors could be even larger than indicated by the variations among these regional life tables, because they do not fully allow for the more extreme relations between adult and childhood mortality that may occur when death rates are falling rapidly.

More powerful techniques of analysis can be applied when data have been collected both of vital events in the year preceding the inquiry and of children ever born. Thus the method described above for correcting the mean children ever born per woman, in age groups by reference to a standard fertility distribution, can be used, but with the specific rates calculated from births in the preceding year. The necessary assumption is the relatively weak one that errors in reports of the births do not depend appreciably on the age of mother. Although it is in theory possible for the estimates to be distorted by particular forms of age misreporting, the method has given satisfactory results with data from many African populations.

Exactly the same procedures can be applied to the relation between specific rates of first births in a year and the proportion of women in each age group who have become mothers; when fertility is stable the latter measures should be equal to the cumulation of the former rates, from the start of reproduction to the appropriate age. In my view this check on the level of recording of the current first births can be particularly valuable, because it depends only on a simple statement of whether a woman has become a mother or not. In practice only information for the younger women is needed, since few have their first child after the age of 30, with consequent reductions in the effects of progressive omissions or fertility trends. The statistics required for the application could easily have been extracted from the data collected in a number of African inquiries, but little has been published.

Similar checks can be made on the level of mortality, for the mortality rate estimated from the percentages of children ever born who are reported as dead, can be compared with the corresponding measure calculated from deaths in the preceding year. Again, a correction factor can be obtained which adjusts the child deaths in the year to give agreement with the retrospective estimates. The assumption that the correction factor can be applied to the current deaths reported at later ages is, however, not a plausible one, since the chances of omission may easily vary with age and status in the community. No very satisfactory solution can be suggested. Perhaps the best is to seek for a suitable model life table, in conformity with the estimated child mortality, and with adult death rates somewhere between those calculated when the correction factor is and is not applied, respectively.

If fertility and mortality are estimated by these methods, the corresponding stable population age distributions can be calculated. Comparisons with the reported ages then provide a powerful independent check of the validity of the estimates. It will be clear from the comments in the earlier part of the paper that the check is of fertility and child mortality and not of the adult death rates or of the natural increase. Clairin has advocated the inclusion of a question about deaths of parents in African demographic surveys; this was done in the 1963–64 inquiry in Chad and the data have just become available. The proportions of fathers' and mothers' deaths to age of respondents supply some information about adult mortality, although the establishment of the relationship between these statistics and conventional life table measures raises difficulties. I have been examining the problem and hope to produce some results soon. If this new approach can provide a satisfactory check of the accuracy of the recording of adult deaths in the previous year, the most notable limitation in the attempt to collect vital statistics by censuses or surveys will be removed.

Footnotes

1. 'Methods of obtaining basic demographic measures where census and vital statistics registration are lacking or defective', a paper presented for Meeting B.6 of the UN World Population Conference, Belgrade, September 1965—an extensive review of the subject for all areas of the world.
2. 'Uses of census or survey data for the estimation of vital rates', presented at the UN Economic Commission for Africa seminar on vital statistics, Addis Ababa, December 1964—describes a particular set of techniques in some detail.
3. By J. G. C. Blacker.

17 Estimates of fertility and mortality in tropical Africa

Ansley J. Coale

Office of Population Research, Princeton University, USA

From 1961 to 1964 the Office of Population Research at Princeton University conducted an extensive study of fertility and mortality in tropical Africa. One purpose of this research was to construct estimates of birth rates, of total fertility, of infant and child mortality, and of crude death rates for provinces or other geographical subunits below the national level. In this paper I shall give a brief summary of these estimates.

Since none of the nations or territories of tropical Africa maintains a complete register of births and deaths, the estimates constructed at Princeton were necessarily derived from censuses or demographic surveys. Some 24 censuses or surveys were available to us, presenting data collected since 1950 that includes information from which it is possible to estimate indices of fertility. As Map 1 (a map of the average density of provinces or districts) shows, there are at least some population data based on statistical surveys for almost every country or territory of tropical Africa. The only prominent exceptions are Ethiopia, the Somali Republic and French Somaliland. However, as Map 2 (a map indicating estimates of total fertility by province) shows, many of the censuses or surveys do not provide information from which, we felt, approximate estimates of fertility could be derived.

The methods of estimation employed were of two principal sorts:

1. Methods based on the age composition of a population, supplemented by indications of the rate of natural increase or of the approximate level of mortality.
2. Methods based on retrospective reports of demographic experience, including the number of children ever born to each woman and the number of these surviving, and reports of births and deaths occurring in a recent period, usually the year before the census or survey.

The most secure estimates are for populations where the two general methods provided figures that were in close agreement. The mutual confirmation of an estimated level of fertility derived from the reported age composition of a population and from the completely independent source of reported births during the last year supplemented by reported average number of children ever born, is strongly reassuring. In nearly every instance where both forms of data were available for analysis the estimates were closely consistent. This agreement also indirectly increases the confidence of the user in estimates based on only one method of estimation, when the data needed for the other method do not exist.

Estimation based on the age composition of a population was accomplished by selecting from a tabulation of some 5,000 model stable populations one that matched the recorded population in the general features of its age composition (such as the proportion under age 15 and under age 35), and in some additional characteristic, such as the intercensal rate of increase or the level of child mortality shown by the proportion of children ever born who have survived.[1]

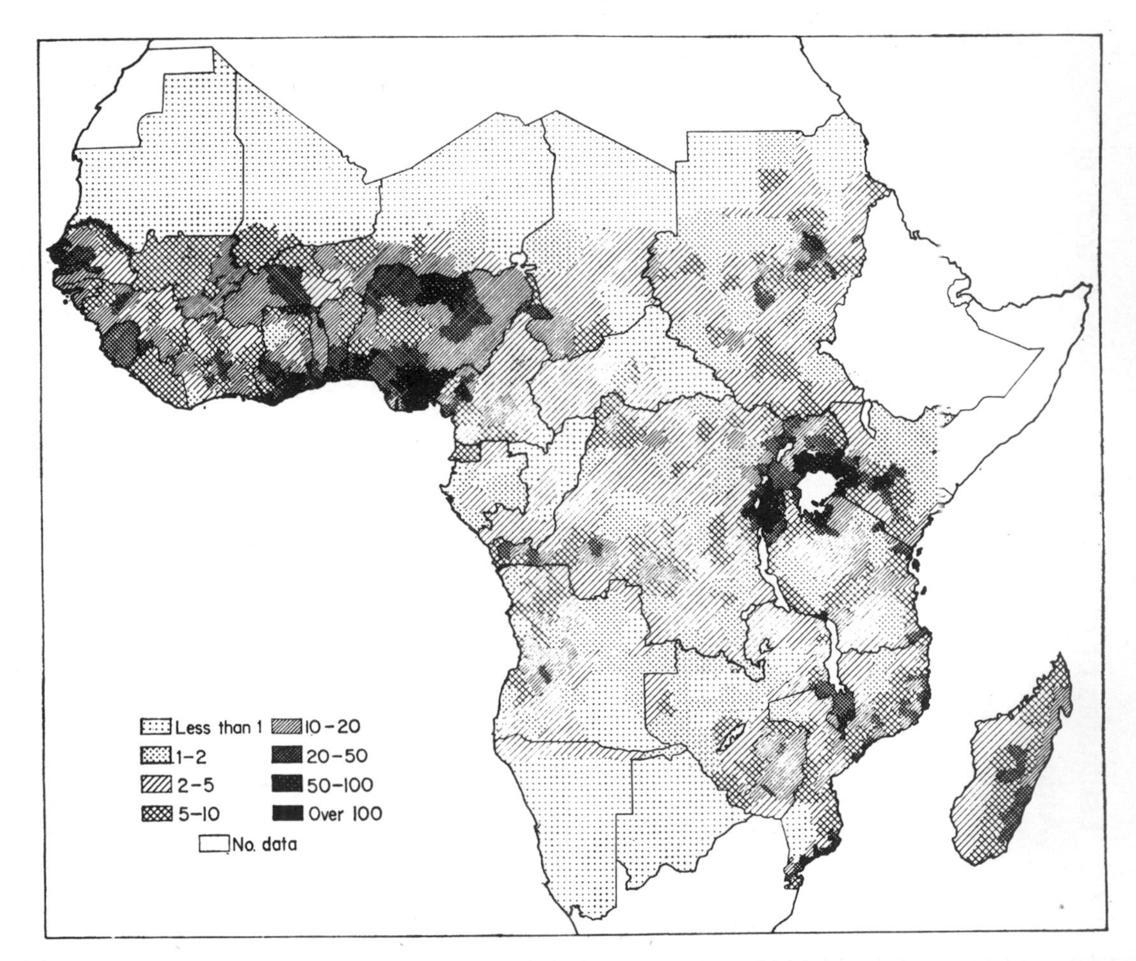

Map 4 Tropical Africa: settlement density of indigenous population exclusive of towns of 20,000 or more inhabitants.

(Persons per square mile)

Source: A. J. Coale, ch. 17; data as shown on Table 1.

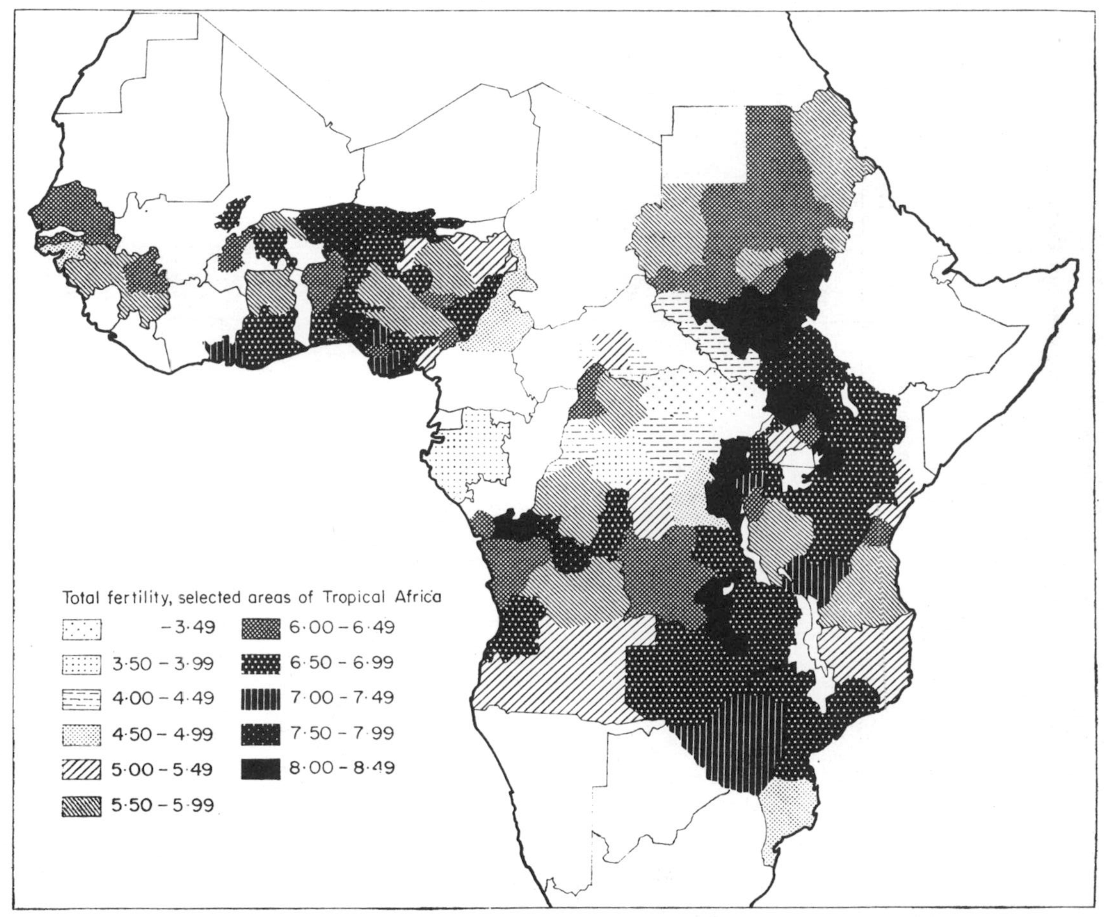

Map 5 Tropical Africa: total fertility

Source: A. J. Coale, ch. 17; data as shown on Table 1.

Table 1

Estimates of Fertility and Mortality in Selected Populations of Tropical Africa

Area	Year of census or survey	Births per thousand population	Deaths per thousand population	Total fertility	Proportion of children surviving to age 2 (l_2)	Infant deaths per thousand live births $(_1q_0)$
West Africa						
Dahomey	1961	49	33	6·4	0·719	0·221
North		47	32	6·1	0·752	0·194
South		50	33	6·6	0·705	0·232
Ghana*	1960	50		6·5		
North		44	—	5·6	—	—
South		50	—	6·6	—	—
Guinea	1954–55	46	38	5·8	0·688	0·246
Forest		45	43	5·7	0·647	0·281
Fouta Djallon		47	35	5·9	0·711	0·228
Maritime		44	33	5·6	0·698	0·238
Upper Guinea		49	44	6·1	0·694	0·241
Ivory Coast						
1st Agricultural Sector	1957–58	55	32	7·3	0·751	0·195
Mali						
Mopti	1956–58	50	40	6·9	0·574	0·344
Niger*	1960	58	29	7·7	0·731	0·211
Stratum 1		34	—	4·2	—	—
Strata 2 through 6		59	—	7·9	—	—
Nigeria*	1952–53					
Eastern Region	1953					
Bamenda		49	—	6·3	—	—
Cameroons		41	—	5·3	—	—
Calabar		57	—	7·5	—	—
Ogoja		50	—	6·5	—	—
Onitsha		51	—	6·7	—	—
Owerri		55	—	7·3	—	—
Rivers		54	—	7·1	—	—
Northern Region	1952					
Adamawa		50	—	6·5	—	—
Bauchi		46	—	5·9	—	—
Benue		46	—	5·9	—	—
Bornu		43	—	5·5	—	—
Ilorin		50	—	6·5	—	—
Kabba		46	—	6·9	—	—
Kano		46	—	5·9	—	—
Katsina		43	—	5·5	—	—
Niger		44	—	5·7	—	—
Plateau		49	—	6·3	—	—
Sokoto		50	—	6·5	—	—
Zaria		50	—	6·5	—	—
Western Region	1952					
Abeokuta		50	—	6·5	—	—
Benin		55	—	7·3	—	—
Colony		44	—	5·7	—	—
Delta		49	—	6·3	—	—
Ibadan		66	—	9·1	—	—
Ijebu		47	—	6·1	—	—
Ondo		57	—	7·5	—	—
Oyo		58	—	7·7	—	—
Portuguese Guinea	1950	37	31	4·8	0·731	0·211

* Estimates based on data not subjected to detailed critical analysis.

Table 1 (*continued*)

Area	Year of census or survey	Births per thousand population	Deaths per thousand population	Total fer-tility	Proportion of children surviving to age 2 (l_2)	Infant deaths per thousand live births ($_1q_0$)
West Africa (*cont.*)						
Senegal†	1960–61	49	—	6·3	—	—
Senegal Valley	1957	46	27	6·3	0·717	0·223
Upper Volta	1960–61	49	36	6·5	0·660	0·270
Mossi People		50	39	6·7	0·629	0·296
Peul People		42	23	5·8	0·750	0·195
Western People		46	31	6·1	0·695	0·241
Central Africa						
Angola	1940 and 1950	45	38	5·8	0·656†	0·273†
Benguela		53	46	6·8	0·654†	0·275†
Bie		39	41	5·0	0·710†	0·228†
Huila		42	31	5·4	0·787†	0·166†
Luanda		50	42	6·4	0·591†	0·329†
Malange		44	41	5·6	0·652†	0·276†
Central African Republic						
Central Oubangui	1959	35	33	4·4	0·730	0·212
Banda People		32	35	4·1	0·718	0·222
Mandjia People		40	31	5·3	0·733	0·210
River People		33	29	4·2	0·766	0·183
Congo (Kinshasa)	1955–57	45	26	5·9	0·792	0·163
Equateur		39	23	5·0	0·801	0·155
Katanga		52	22	8·2	0·841	0·124
Kasai		45	30	5·9	0·744	0·201
Kivu		53	30	7·1	0·774	0·177
Leopoldville		49	25	6·7	0·800	0·156
Orientale		32	24	4·0	0·833	0·131
Cameroon						
North	1960	38	31	4·9	0·705	0·232
Hill Pagans		45	38	5·8	0·673	0·259
Moslems		27	28	3·5	0·754	0·193
Plain Pagans		42	32	5·3	0·688	0·246
Gabon†	1960–61	26	—	3·5	—	—
Southern Rhodesia†	1962	49	—	7·1	—	—
Zambia†	1963	49	—	6·9	—	—
East Africa						
Burundi	1952–57	46	22	6·4	0·796	0·156
Kenya†	1962	48	18	6·8	0·831	0·132
Central		46	13	6·6	0·878	0·098
Coast		40	20	5·4	0·807	0·151
Eastern		47	15	6·8	0·860	0·111
Nyanza		55	26	7·9	0·754	0·193
Rift Valley		45	12	6·5	0·889	0·089
Western		55	23	8·1	0·782	0·170
Mozambique		42	31	5·4	0·730	0·212
Central		52	38	6·7	0·679	0·254
North		39	32	5·0	0·786	0·167
South		36	30	4·6	0·743	0·201
Rwanda	1952–57	50	23	7·0	0·796	0·156
Sudan	1955–56	49	21	7·3	—	—
Arabs		47	—	6·1	—	—
Beja People		44	—	5·7	—	—

† 1940 data.

Table 1 (*continued*)

Area	Year of census or survey	Births per thousand population	Deaths per thousand population	Total fer-tility	Proportion of children surviving to age 2 (l_2)	Infant deaths per thousand live births $({}_1q_0)$
East Africa (*cont.*)						
Sudan (*cont.*)						
Central Southerners		58	—	8·3	—	—
Eastern Southerners		60	—	7·9	—	—
Nuba People		44	—	5·7	—	—
Nubiyin People		47	—	6·1	—	—
Western Southerners		33	—	4·1	—	—
Westerners		46	—	5·9	—	—
Tanzania†	1957	46	26	6·4	0·754	0·193
Central		47	25	6·6	—	—
Eastern		43	27	5·7	—	—
Lake		48	31	6·9	—	—
Northern		48	17	6·9	—	—
Southern		42	23	5·5	—	—
Southern Highlands		52	25	7·4	—	—
Tanga		45	23	6·2	—	—
Western		44	27	5·9	—	—
Uganda	1959	48	25	6·7	0·780	0·172
Buganda		41	23	5·4	0·795	0·160
Eastern		46	27	6·1	0·758	0·189
Northern		57	27	8·4	0·777	0·174
Western		53	25	7·7	0·794	0·161

The retrospective information on births during the preceding year was adjusted to be consistent with the average number of children reported as ever born to them by women in their twenties. This adjustment was necessary because of a widespread tendency, discovered by William Brass, for respondents to report births that had occurred in a period in some populations longer and in others shorter than the one year stipulated in the census or survey.

Childhood mortality was estimated by analysing the proportion of children reported as surviving among those ever born by women in successively higher age groups. William Brass had devised an elegant technique for using such information to estimate the proportion of infants dying before their first birthday, second birthday, third birthday, fifth birthday, etc., on the basis of information drawn from the demographic surveys or censuses.

Because it is the purpose of this paper to summarize results rather than techniques I shall not attempt to give more than this sketchy indication of the nature of the methods employed.

In discussing the estimated levels of fertility and mortality presented in Map 5 and Table 1, I must emphasize that the results are of very uneven quality. In general the methods of estimation are more reliable in determining the approximate level of the birth rate than of the death rate. In fact the most we can claim for estimated mortality is that the figures given for the proportion surviving to age two, in Table 1, can be accepted as a rather firm indication of the upper limit of survival to age two in the three to five years preceding the date of the census or survey. If there is a tendency for women to omit a higher proportion of dead children than surviving children, in reporting those ever born (and this possibility seems quite plausible, especially in Africa), childhood mortality would tend always to be somewhat higher than indicated by these figures. Estimates of adult mortality and of the overall death rate are the least trustworthy of the figures we present. It was necessary to assume that the typical relationship between childhood and adult mortality rates found in other areas with good statistics prevailed in tropical Africa, or to make rough adjustments to figures (usually internally inconsistent) on deaths in the pre-survey year, or to estimate the crude death rate by subtracting an often untrustworthy estimate of the rate of natural increase from a merely approximate figure for the birth rate.

In any event, estimates of mortality, even when of acceptable quality, can be considered as characteristic only of the period to which the data are pertinent—usually the four- or five-year interval preceding the census or survey. This reservation must be clearly in mind when comparing mortality levels in different areas. The past two decades constitute a period of extremely rapid declines in mortality in many of the less developed countries of the world, as low cost but effective techniques of medicine and public health have been exported to these areas from the industrialized countries, often with the assistance of the World Health Organization or UNICEF. Some of the areas of tropical Africa have no doubt shared in this rapid change in mortality rate, which in other parts of the world has reached or exceeded changes in expectation of life at birth of one year each calendar year. Thus the difference between the estimated death rate of 26 per 1,000 in Tanzania and of 18 per 1,000 in Kenya is of dubious validity because of the differences in the basis of estimation; but even if the difference in mortality is accepted as valid, a large part could be caused by the five-year interval between the censuses from which the data were taken.

Although fertility is more amenable than mortality to estimation from survey or census data, and is less subject to recent fluctuation in most African populations, variations in the extent and quality of available information cause variations in the probable accuracy of fertility estimates. The most trustworthy estimates are those for the Congo, where in 29 districts there was very strong agreement between birth rates derived on the one hand from the age distribution, and on the other from survey responses on births during the preceding year, after adjustment for the evident omission in some districts of children who had died. Moreover, birth rates derived from registered births also correlated very highly with the other estimates of fertility; as did (in a negative sense) the proportion childless among women in the central ages of childbearing. The figures on birth rates and total fertility in Dahomey, Guinea, Ivory Coast, Mali, the Senegal Valley, Upper Volta, the Central African Republic, North Cameroon and Uganda are also of relatively high quality, as indicated by the general agreement between the age distribution and estimates based on retrospective data. Although the recency of the 1962 census of Kenya and the lack to date of published material on the sample survey that accompanied the census have prevented the detailed critical scrutiny and analysis that would be desirable, there is enough internal consistency in the retrospective data and the age distribution to provide substantial confidence in the levels of estimated fertility. The estimates for Tanzania are less reliable, being derived from age distributions that had been subjected to smoothing. The least reliable estimates are for Nigeria, the Portuguese territories, Ghana, Senegal, Gabon, Southern Rhodesia, Zambia and the Sudan.

In general the reader can trust the relative levels of fertility within the sub-units of a nation or territory more than relative figures derived from two different data systems. On the other hand the geographic pattern of fertility differences revealed in Map 4 bolsters our belief that estimates of fertility derived from different data systems are for the most part approximately consistent. The source of this reassurance is a notable tendency for unusually high and low fertility to extend across international boundaries, notwithstanding the difference in form of the data systems, and often in methods of estimation in the two countries.

The most striking feature of the birth rates and total fertility figures given in Table 1 is the very large range, with birth rates varying from about 30 to 60 per

1,000 and total fertility (the number of children that would be born during the lifetime of each woman experiencing the given fertility rates) ranging from about 3·5 to over 8. A ridge of high fertility in East Africa extends from the south-eastern Sudan down through parts of Uganda and Kenya, through Rwanda and Burundi and parts of Tanzania, and through the southern and eastern provinces of the Congo into Zambia, Southern Rhodesia and the southern province of Mozambique. The provinces in this strip show a total fertility of 6·5 or higher. Somewhat lower fertility is found along the East African coast from the coastal province of Kenya to the northern part of Mozambique. The lowest fertility in tropical Africa is in a region extending, apparently, from the west coast in Gabon through north-central and north-western provinces of the Congo into the south-western region of the Sudan. Unfortunately, we were not able to construct acceptable estimates for the Congo (Brazzaville), for the southern part of Cameroon or for any but a small portion of the Central African Republic to confirm the continuity of this low fertility strip, but it is noteworthy that low fertility persists into the northern part of Cameroon. The high fertility ridge mentioned earlier appears to have a spur extending to the west coast of Africa through the southern provinces of the Congo and the northern provinces of Angola. Another strip of exceptionally high fertility is found along the coast in West Africa, from coastal Nigeria to the Ivory Coast, with a branch extending up through the western part of Nigeria into parts of Niger and Upper Volta.

As mentioned earlier, estimates of mortality in tropical Africa are less well founded and more dependent on the date of the census or survey than fertility estimates. The crude death rate probably ranges from no more than 15 per 1,000 in some provinces to more than 40 per 1,000, infant mortality rates from less than 100 per 1,000 to over 300, and expectation of life at birth from less than 30 years to over 45. A fair generalization is that mortality in tropical Africa is among the highest in the world, although some provinces have already secured the advantages available in modern health techniques.

The variations in fertility recorded in Table 1 and Map 5 should not be allowed to convey a false impression that the average fertility of tropical Africa is anything other than very high. The birth rate for all of the populations analysed combined is about 49 per 1,000 and total fertility for tropical Africa is probably about 61–62 children. Only Latin America from Mexico to Peru and Brazil has fertility approximately this high. These extremely high fertility rates are combined with mortality that also is among the highest in the world. The recent experience of other developing areas suggests that tropical Africa is in the early phase of rapidly accelerating population growth. In some areas, for example, Kenya and the Sudan, the rate of natural increase has apparently already reached about 3 per cent per annum. In other words, tropical Africa is now beginning to encounter the whole range of new problems that other developing countries know very well—the barriers to social and economic progress that come with extremely rapid population increase.

Footnote

1. The model stable populations appear in ANSLEY J. COALE and PAUL DEMENY, *Regional Model Life Tables and Stable Populations*, Princeton, Princeton University Press, 1966.

18 Some demographic indicators for Africa

R. K. Som

Demographic Section, Economic Commission for Africa, Addis Ababa, Ethiopia

The general demographic situation in the African countries was reviewed in the article 'Recent demographic levels and trends in Africa', published in the *Economic Bulletin for Africa, 1965*: the position in the eastern sub-region was presented in the document 'The Demographic situation in Eastern Africa' (E/CN.14/LU/ECOP/2), prepared for the sub-regional meeting on Economic Co-operation in East Africa, held in Lusaka in October 1965. In this article, some demographic indicators for the African countries are presented relating to a more recent period.

Demographic research in Africa until recently was handicapped by lack of up-to-date and reliable data. The position is, however, improving and is expected to improve considerably with the African programme for the 1970 round of censuses of population and housing.[1] Today, only Ethiopia and Somalia, constituting together an estimated 8 per cent of the total population in Africa, have not yet conducted nation-wide population inquiries. Population censuses or demographic inquiries have been undertaken at least once for all the other areas: those conducted during 1964 are listed in Annex Table 1.

For the purpose of this article, the continent of Africa is divided into five sub-regions: North, West, Central, East, and South. The allocation of the countries into sub-regions is generally on the lines of the distribution of the countries by sub-regions adopted by the Economic Commission for Africa, excepting for the southern sub-region.

Total Population and Density

TOTAL POPULATION

With about one-fourth of the total land surface of the world, Africa, in mid-1964, contained 303 million persons which is about 9 per cent of the total population of the world.

The populations of the individual countries within each sub-region in Africa in 1960 are shown in Table 1, arranged in decreasing order of magnitude. The extreme unevenness of the distribution of population among the different countries is also apparent from the summary, Table 2. The two lower quintiles consist of 22 areas, each with population less than 1·6 million: together these contribute only 11 million or 3·7 per cent of the total population of Africa. On the other hand, the highest quintile of 12 countries with population of 7·3 million and over contribute together 212 million or 69·9 per cent of the total population of Africa. The three most populous countries are Nigeria with 56 million (18·6 per cent of the total population of Africa), the United Arab Republic (Egyptian region) with 29 million (9·5 per cent) and Ethiopia with 22 million persons (7·3 per cent). The other six countries with population above 10 million are the Republic of South Africa, the Democratic Republic of Congo, Sudan, Morocco, Algeria, and the United Republic of Tanzania.

Table 1

Areas and Mid-1964 Estimates of Population and Density

Sub-region and country	Area sq. km. (000)	Population		Density of population per sq. km.
		Mid-1964 estimate (000)	Percentage distribution	
AFRICA TOTAL	*30,161*	*302,832*	*100·0*	*10*
North Africa	*8,485*	*72,395*	*23·9*	*9*
UAR (Egypt)	1,000	28,900 *	9·5	29
Sudan [1]	2,506	13,180	4·3	5
Morocco	445	12,959	4·3	29
Algeria	2,382	10,975†	3·6	5
Tunisia	125	4,565	1·5	37
Libya [2]	1,760	1,559 *	0·51	1
Spanish Possessions in North Africa:	268	257	0·08	1
Spanish North Africa [3]	0·03	157	0·05	5,167
Spanish Sahara [4]	266	48	0·01	0
Ifni	1·5	52	0·02	34
West Africa	*6,104*	*96,110*	*31·7*	*16*
Nigeria	924	56,400	18·6	61
Ghana	239	7,537 *	2·5	32
Upper Volta	274	4,750	1·6	17
Mali	1,202	4,485†	1·5	4
Ivory Coast	322	3,750	1·2	12
Guinea	246	3,420	1·1	14
Senegal	196	3,400	1·1	17
Niger	1,267	3,250	1·1	3
Dahomey	113	2,300† [5]	0·8	20
Sierra Leone	72	2,200 *	0·7	31
Togo	57	1,603 *	0·5	28
Liberia	111	1,041	0·3	9
Mauritania	1,031	900 [5]	0·3	1
Portuguese Guinea	36	525	0·2	15
Gambia	10	324	0·1	32
Cape Verde Island	4	220†	0·07	55
St. Helena, including dependencies	0·4	+5	0·002	13
Central Africa	*5,360*	*26,627*	*8·8*	*5*
Congo, Democratic Rep. of	2,345	15,300	5·0	7
Cameroon	475	5,103†	1·7	11
Chad	1,284	3,300 * [6]	1·1	2
Central African Rep.	617	1,320	0·4	2

Source: United Nations, *Demographic Yearbook, 1964, Statistical Yearbook, 1964 and Statistical Papers,* Series A, Vol. XVIII No. 1, *Population and Vital Statistics Report* (data available 1 January 1966).

* Provisional.
† United Nations estimate.
1. *De jure* population.
2. Excluding alien armed forces stationed in the area. The mid-1964 estimate relates to the figure obtained during the census conducted on 31 July 1964.
3. Comprising Alhucemas, Ceuta, Chafarias, Melilla and Peñón de Vélez de la Gomera.
4. Comprising the Northern Region (former Saguia el Hamra) and the Southern Region (former Río de Oro).
5. African population only.
6. Estimate for African population based on results of sample survey.

Table 1 (*continued*)

Sub-region and country	Area sq. km. (000)	Population		Density of population per sq. km.
		Mid-1964 estimate (000)	Percentage distribution	
Central Africa (*cont.*)				
Congo (Brazzaville)	342	826	0·3	2
Gabon	267	459	0·2	2
Equatorial Guinea[7]	28	263	0·09	9
Sao Tomé and Principé	1·0	56	0·02	56
East Africa	*5,125*	*72,005*	*23·8*	*14*
Ethiopia	1,184	22,200	7·3	19
United Rep. of Tanzania:	940	10,325†	3·4	11
Tanganyika	937	9,990	3·3	11
Zanzibar	3	335	1·1	112
Kenya	583	9,104	3·0	16
Uganda	236	7,367	2·4	31
Madagascar	596	6,180	2·0	10
Malawi	119	3,900†	1·3	33
Zambia	746	3,600	1·2	5
Rwanda	26	3,018[5]	1·0	116
Burundi	28	2,500†	1·0	89
Somalia	638	2,350†	0·8	4
Mauritius, with dependencies	2·1	742†	0·2	353
Reunion	2·5	382	0·1	153
Comoro Islands	2·2	210	0·06	96
French Somaliland	22	81	0·03	4
Seychelles	0·4	46	0·02	115
South Africa	*5,087*	*35,695*	*11·8*	7
South Africa, Rep. of[8]	1,221	17,474	5·8	14
Mozambique	783	6,872	2·3	9
Angola	1,247	5,084	1·7	4
Rhodesia	389	4,140	1·4	11
Lesotho	30	733	0·2	24
South West Africa[9]	824	564	0·2	1
Botswana	575	543[10]	0·2	1
Swaziland	17	285	0·09	17

7. Formerly known as Spanish Equatorial Region, comprising Territories of Fernando Póo (which includes Annobon) and Rio Muni (which includes Corisco and Elobeys).
8. Excluding data for Walvis Bay, which is an integral part of South Africa but is administered as if it were part of South West Africa (population* 12,568 in 1960).
9. Including data for Walvis Bay which is an integral part of South Africa but is administered as if it were part of South West Africa (population* 12,568 in 1960).
10. *De jure* population: includes an estimate of 14,150 for nomad population.

Note: In this, as in other tables, the components may not always add up to the total shown, because of separate rounding off.

Table 2

Distribution of African Countries According to Total Population

Population (million)	Number of countries	Total population	
		Number (million)	Percentage distribution
Less than 0·4	11	2·1	0·7
0·4–<1·6	11	9·2	3·0
1·6–<3·6	10	27·4	9·1
3·6–<7·3	11	52·4	17·3
7·3 and above	12	211·7	69·9
Total	55	302·8	100·0

DENSITY OF POPULATION

There were, in 1964, about ten persons per square kilometre of total area of Africa as compared to the world average of 23. This is the level of Northern and Latin America and of the USSR, and higher only than that in Oceania (Table 3).

However, there are great variations in the density of population between the different sub-regions, between individual countries, and between different localities within each country. The data for the African countries and sub-regions, shown in Table 1, show that of the African sub-regions, the highest density is recorded in the West (16) and the East (14), and the lowest in the Central (5) and the South (7). However, even the highest density of population in Western Africa is exceeded by all the sub-regions of Europe and Asia, except for South-west Asia, which has a density of 14, and by Middle America, the Caribbean, and Polynesia and Micronesia, among the other regions of the world.[2]

Among the individual countries in Africa, excluding the small islands and possessions, the density ranges from one or less in Libya, Mauritania, South West Africa, and Bechuanaland (Botswana), to 89 in Burundi and 116 in Rwanda. The distribution of the countries according to density of population is also shown in the summary, Table 4.

Of the ten countries with density of 36 and above, only four have any substantial population, viz., Burundi (2·5 million), Rwanda (3·0 million), Tunisia (4·6 million) and Nigeria (56·4 million).

It is clear that except for a few areas (for example, most of the Nile river area, some areas in the equatorial highlands, parts of Western Africa, and the small islands), there does not seem to be much pressure of population on land in Africa as measured by the density of population in relation to the total land area.

As Africa is still mainly agricultural, two more useful measures of the pressure of population on land are the densities of the total population and of the rural population per square kilometre of arable land. For Africa, this density was 114, as compared with the world average of 212 in 1960 (Table 5). This is higher than those in Oceania, USSR and Northern America, but half that in Latin America (206) and one-third that in Asia (377). Defining the rural population as those living in places of less than 20,000 persons, the density of rural population per square kilometre of arable land was 99 in Africa, as compared with the world average of 160. This is again higher than the figures for Oceania, USSR and Northern America, but much lower than those in Latin America (140) and Asia (313).

Table 3

Population, Rate of Increase, Birth and Death Rates, Area and Density for the World-Regions

Major divisions and regions	Estimate of mid-year population (millions)						Rate of population increase per cent[1]		Birth rate per 1,000	Death rate per 1,000	Area sq. km. (000)[2]	Density[3]
	1930	1940	1950	1958	1960	1963	1958–63	1960–63	1958–63	1958–63	1963	1963
WORLD TOTAL	2,070	2,295	2,517	2,895	2,990	3,160	1·8	1·9	34	16	135,756[4]	23
Africa	164	191	222	262	273	294	2·3	2·5	46	23	30,216	10
America[5]	242	274	329	395	411	439	2·2	2·2	32	12	42,050	10
Northern[5]	134	144	166	192	199	208	1·6	1·6	24	9	21,515	10
Latin	108	130	163	203	212	231	2·7	2·8	40	14	20,535	11
Asia[7]	1,120	1,244	1,381	1,598	1,651	1,748	1·8	1·9	38	20	27,621	63
East[6]	591	634	684	772	793	828	1·4	1·4	33	19	11,725	71
Southern[7]	529	610	697	826	858	920	2·2	2·4	42	20	15,896	58
Europe[8]	355	380	392	418	425	437	0·9	0·9	19	10	4,929	89
Oceania[5]	10·0	11·1	12·7	15·1	15·7	16·8	2·1[9]	2·2[9]	27	11	8,532	2
USSR	179	195	180	207	214	225	1·6	1·6	24	7	22,402	10

Source: United Nations Demographic Yearbook, 1964

1. Average annual rate per cent of population increase.
2. Comprising land area and inland waters, but excluding uninhabited polar regions and some uninhabited islands.
3. Population per square kilometre of area.
4. Including French Southern and Antarctic territories.
5. Hawaii, a state of the United States of America, is included in Northern America, not in Oceania.
6. Excluding the USSR, shown separately below.
7. Excluding the USSR, but including both the Asian and European portion of Turkey.
8. Excluding the USSR, and the European portion of Turkey included in Southern Asia.
9. Rate reflects combined effect of natural increase and migration.

Table 4

Distribution of African Countries in Density Groups

Density (Population per sq. km. of area)	Number of countries	Percentage of total population of Africa
1–3	10	4·3
4–10	12	22·9
11–18	12	20·6
19–35	11	29·7
36 and above	10	22·5
Total	55	100·0

Table 5

Estimated Density of Population, 1960

Region	Persons per sq. km. of		Rural population[1] per sq. km. of arable land
	Total area	Arable land	
WORLD TOTAL	22	212	160
Africa	9	114	99
America	10	125	76
Northern	9	88	48
Latin	10	206	140
Asia	60	377	313
Southern	54	272	—
East	68	645	—
Europe	86	278	167
Oceania	2	56	26
USSR	10	97	61

Source: Economic Commission for Africa, 'Recent demographic levels and trends in Africa', *Economic Bulletin for Africa, 1965; United Nations, Population Commission, Report of the Thirteenth Session, 1965* (E/CN.9/202).

(1) Places with population less than 20,000.

Fertility and Mortality

Registration of vital events is either non-existent or defective over most parts of Africa, and although attempts are being made to achieve complete civil registration,[3] substitute measures have to be relied upon for quite some time to come. Sample surveys are now being increasingly used to provide directly the basic vital rates, either by the method of retrospective inquiries, or by repeated observations. However, caution must be exercised to eliminate different types of errors and biases in the collected data, whether obtained on a sample or on a complete enumeration basis. The reliability of the estimates obtained from limited data by the use of analytical methods, e.g. 'reverse-survival' estimates, depends on the robustness of the assumptions involved. Mortality estimates, especially relating to infants, are also much less satisfactory than are the fertility estimates.

In this article, only those fertility and mortality measures have been discussed which can be taken to be fairly reliable, and relating to the general population. Civil

Table 6

Measures of Fertility and Mortality

Sub-region and country	Year	Type of data	Fertility measures			Type of data	Mortality measures		Rate of natural increase per cent	Expectation of life at birth	
			Crude birth rate (CBR) per cent	General fertility rate per cent	Gross reproduction rate		Crude death rate (CDR) per cent	Infant mortality rate (IMR) per cent		Date	Years
North Africa											
UAR (Egypt)	1950–55	C(1)	45[1]	182[2]	2·8[1]	D	21[3,4]	178[4,5]	—	1960	52·6
Sudan	1955–56	B	45–54[6]	202–242[7]	3·0–3·5[6]	B	20–25[6]	186[6]	2·5–3[6]	1955	40[6]
Morocco	1962	B	46[4]	223[7]	3·4[4]	B	19[4]	149[4]	2·7[4]	1960	49·6[8]
Algeria:											
Moslems[9]	1944–49	C(2)	45[1]	188[4]	3·0[1]	D	—	—	—	1948	35[10]
Tunisia	1961	A	43[4]	192[4]	3·1[4]	D	26[11]	—	—	—	—
Libya	1944–49	C(2)	43[1]	186[2]	3·0[1]	—	—	—	—	—	—
Spanish North											
Africa: Ceuta	1963	A	21[8]	86[7]	—	A	7·5	62	1·4	—	—
Melilla	1961	A	19[8]	81[7]	—	A	7·4	41	1·2	—	—
West Africa											
Nigeria[12]	1952–53	D	53–57[1]	—	3·6–3·8[1]	—	—	—	—	—	—
Ghana	1960	B	47–52[13] 4·2	203–224[7]	3·0[1,14]	B	24[13]	156[13]	2·3–2·8[13]	1960	38·7[15]
Upper Volta[16]	1960–61	B	53[17] 5·2	212[17]	2·9[18]	B	35[17]	182[18]	1·8[17]	1960–61	32[18]
Mali[18]	1960	B	61 5·1	240	3·8	B	30	123	3·1	1957	26
Ivory Coast[18,19]	1957–58	B	55[19]	220	3·2	B	35	138[4,20]	2·0	1956–58	35
Guinea[18,21]	1954–55	B	62 5·3	223	3·5	B	40	216	2·2	1954–55	27
Senegal[18]	1960–61	B	43[22]	174	2·6	B	17	93	2·66	1957	37[23]
Niger[18,24]	1959–60	B	52 4·1	232	3·5	B	27	200	2·5	1959–60	37
Dahomey[18,25]	1961	B	54 4·5	227	3·3	B	26	111	2·8	1961	37[26]
Togo[18]	1961	B	55 5·7	228	3·5	B	29	127	2·6	1961	35
Mauritania	1961–62	B	47[13,27]	—	—	B	25[13,27]	—	—	—	—
Portuguese Guinea	1940–45	C(2)	47[1]	—	2·4[1]	—	—	—	—	—	—
Gambia	1962–63	D	39[8]	—	2·5[26]	D	21[8]	—	1·77[8]	1962–63	43[26]
Cape Verde Islands	1962	A	42[8] 4·2	147[7]	—	A	12	95[28]	3·0[8]	—	—

Table 6 (*continued*)

Sub-region and country	Year	Type of data	Fertility measures: Crude birth rate (CBR) per 1,000	General fertility rate per 1,000	Gross Reproduction rate	Type of data	Mortality measures: Crude death rate (CDR) per 1,000	Infant mortality rate (IMR) per 1,000	Rate of natural increase per cent	Expectation of life at birth: Date	Years
Central Africa											
Congo, Democratic Republic of[29,30]	1955–57	B	43[8]	156[2]	2·4[1]	B	20[8]	104[8]	2·3[8]	1950–52	39[8]
Cameroon[18,31]	1962	B	37	132	3·2	B	18	76	1·9	1962	46
Chad[18]	1964	B	46	148	2·4	B	31	165	1·5	1964	30
Central African Republic[18]	1959–60	B	48	157	2·5	B	26	190	2·2	1959–60	34
Congo (Braz.)[18]	1960–61	B	41	149	2·5	B	24	180	1·6	1960–61	37
Gabon[18]	1960–61	B	35	116	2·1	B	30	229	0·6	1960–61	32
Sao Tomé and Principe	1963	A	51[13]	260[7]	—	A	18·4[13]	140[13,32]	3·34	—	—
East Africa											
Tanganyika[30,33]	1957	D	46	175	2·8	D	24–25	190	2·1–2·2	1957	37·5
Zanzibar: Pemba[33]	1958	D	45	—	1·9	D	23	171	—	1958	42·8
Zanzibar[33]	1958	D	32	—	2·4	D	21	157	—	1958	40·3
Kenya[30,33]	1948[34]	D	50[4]	—	3·2	D	20	—	3·0	1948	45[26]
Uganda[4,35]	1958–59	B	42	187	2·6[36]	B	20	160	2·2	1958–59	44[26]
Madagascar	1950–55	C(2)	45[4]	163[4]	2·4[4]	B	19[37]	—	—	—	—
Zambia[4,30]	1950	B	57[38]	181	3·5	D	19	259	3·2	1963	40[39]
Rwanda[30,41]	1957	B	52·0[1]	220[1]	3·3[1]	B	13·7	137[40]	3·83	—	—
Burundi[30,42]	1957	B	46·6[1]	173[26]	2·6[1]	B	17·4	121[40]	2·92	—	—
Mauritius ex. dep.	1964	A	38·1	179[7]	2·8[43]	A	8·6	56·7	2·95	1962	60[1,28]
Reunion	1964	A	43·3	189[7]	3·1[43]	A	9·9	74·2	3·34	1951–55	50
South Africa											
South Africa, Rep. of: Bantu	1950–55	C(1)	46[1]	198[2]	3·0[1]	—	—	—	—	—	—
Mozambique	1949–50	C(2)	47[1]	166[4]	2·6[1]	D	—	—	—	1940	45[30]
Angola	1940–45	C(2)	49[1]	178[4]	2·7[1]	D	—	—	—	1940	35[30]
Rhodesia[30,44]	1953–55	B	48[4]	207[4]	3·1[4]	D	14[4]	122[4]	3·0[4]	1953–55	48·5
Lesotho	1955–56	B	40[1]	—	2·4[1]	D	23[4]	181[4]	1·7[4]	1955–56	41[45]
Botswana	1936–41	C(2)	41[1]	175[1]	2·7[1]	—	—	—	—	—	—

registration systems have been considered the source of data only in Tunisia (for births only), and the small off-shore islands. Reliable civil registration statistics for limited segments of the population, as in the Republic of South Africa, have not been considered.

FERTILITY

The three measures of fertility considered are: (Crude) Birth Rate, General Fertility Rate, and the Gross Reproduction Rate. The Birth Rate is computed per 1,000 population and the Fertility Rate per 1,000 female population aged 15–49 years. The Gross Reproduction Rate is defined as the number of daughters that would be born to a generation of women having, at each age in the potential child-bearing period of their lives, the age-specific female birth rates observed for a given population at a given time, on the assumption that none of the women die before reaching the limit of their potentially fertile years.

The birth rates listed in Table 6 generally range from 35 to 59, excluding the small areas of Ceuta, Melilla and Zanzibar with low rates, and Mali and Guinea with rates of 61–62. The modal group is 45–49. Birth rates between 55 and 59 are recorded in Nigeria, Ivory Coast, Togo and Zambia. All these high birth rates of 55 and above except one are for countries in West Africa. It appears that, excepting for this sub-region, the other sub-regions have generally the same levels of fertility. This is also confirmed by the general fertility rates and the gross reproduction rates. The sub-regions are also generally homogeneous in regard to birth rates although there are some countries which do not conform to the average pattern within a sub-region.

The fertility rates range from 116 in Gabon to 240 in Mali, and the gross reproduction rates from 2·1 in Gabon to 3·8 in Mali, excluding the small, off-shore islands which have in general low rates.

For Africa as a whole, the average birth rate is estimated at 46 per 1,000 and the gross reproduction rate at 3·1 around 1960. Africa had the highest birth rate amongst the world regions; the rates in the other regions range from 24 in Northern America and the USSR to 43 in South Asia, the world average being 34 per 1,000 (Table 3).

MORTALITY

The three measures of mortality considered are: (Crude) Death Rate, Infant Mortality Rate, and the Expectation of life at birth. The Death Rate is computed per 1,000 population and the Infant Mortality Rate per 1,000 live births. Expectation of life is the average number of years of life remaining at birth.

The death rates listed in Table 6 range from 14 in Rwanda and Rhodesia to 35 in Ivory Coast and 40 in Guinea, excluding the small unrepresentative areas with low rates. Out of the 38 rates shown in the table, 28 lie between the limits of 15–34 per 1,000; the modal group is 20–25 per 1,000.

The infant mortality rate is considered an important indicator of the level of living and the health standard of a country. Excluding the low rates in small unrepresentative areas, of the 33 rates shown in Table 6, 24 lie between 100 and 225 per 1,000. The rates beyond these limits are for Cameroon (76), Senegal (93) with rates below 100, and for Gabon (229) and Zambia (259). However, for the reasons stated earlier, the low mortality rates have to be treated with caution.

The expectations of life at birth, shown in Table 6, vary from 26–27 in Mali and Guinea to 50 or more in the UAR (Egypt), Morocco, Réunion and Mauritius.

For Africa as a whole, the average death rate is estimated at 23 per 1,000 and the life expectancy at birth 41 around 1960. As with the birth rate, the death rate in Africa is estimated to be highest amongst the world regions. The rates for the other regions range from 7 in the USSR to 20 in South Asia, the world average being 16 (Table 3).

Type Codes:

A. Complete registration statistics.
B. Sample Survey data.
C(1). 'Reverse-Survival' estimates, relatively reliable data.
C(2). 'Reverse-Survival' estimates, data of low or uncertain reliability.
D. Other estimates.

1. *Population Bulletin of the United Nations, No. 7–1963* (ST/SOA/SER.N/7).
2. Estimated by the United Nations Population Division.
3. For 1956, revised rate adjusted for under-registration of 23 per cent, estimated from localities having Health Bureaux.
4. *Economic Bulletin for Africa*, Vol. V, January 1965; Chapter B.I, 'Recent Demographic levels and trends in Africa'.
5. For 1959.
6. *United Nations, Population Studies No. 37* (ST/SOA/Series A/37) 'Population Growth and Manpower in the Sudan'.
7. Estimated by the Economic Commission for Africa.
8. *United Nations, Demographic Year Book*, 1964.
9. Estimates for 1954, prepared by Mohammed Kerkoub at the North African Demographic Centre, Cairo ('Estimations des paramètres démographiques de la population musulmane de l'Algérie et projections démographiques') are: CBR 51, GFR 238, GRR 3.4, CDR 21, $^{0}e_{0}$ 41 for males and 46 for females.
10. Corresponding to average of United Nations mortality levels corresponding to 1,000 m_x values obtained from mortality data.
11. Estimated rate for 1959, basis unknown.
12. Excluding data for the province of Sardauna (the former British Northern Cameroons).
13. United Nations, *Population and Vital Statistics Report* (data available as of 1 January 1966 (ST/STAT/SERA/75).
14. Relating to 1950–55.
15. Corresponding to the official projected population used for development plan.
16. Adjusted estimates, computed at the Princeton office for Population Research, are 49 for births, 36 for deaths and 270 for infant mortality (all per 1,000): ANSLEY J. COALE 'Estimates of fertility and mortality in Tropical Africa', *First African Population Conference*, Ibadan, 1966.
17. Adjusted rates on analysis by recall period, made at the Economic Commission for Africa, on basis of data supplied by INSEE, Paris; the unadjusted rates were 50% for births, 32% for deaths, 1·8% for natural increase and 200% for general fertility rate.
18. Institut National de la Statistique et des études Economiques, *Enquête démographique récente réalisée en Afrique noire d'expression française et à Madagascar: Tableau d'ensemble*, Avril, 1965.
19. In the same paper as in note 16, adjusted estimates for 1957–58 are: birth rate 55, death rate 32 and infant mortality rate 195.
20. For 1956.
21. In the same paper as in note 16, estimates for 1954–55 are: birth rate 46, death rate 38 and infant mortality rate 246.
22. In the same paper as for note 16, estimate for 1960–61 is 46.
23. For Bassee Vallee (population estimated 270,000), based on results of 1957–58 Sample Survey of 77 rural villages and five urban centres.
24. In the same paper as in note 16, estimates for 1960 are: birth rate 58, death rate 29, and infant mortality rate 211.
25. In the same paper as in note 16, estimates for 1961 are: birth rate 49, death rate 33 and infant mortality rate 221.
26. Estimate made at the Economic Commission for Africa on double interpolation in a graph prepared from Table 21 of the United Nations, *The Future Growth of World Population, 1958* (St/SOA/SER.A/28) based on stable population model.
27. Estimate for 27 urban centres, based on births during 12 months period preceding urban census.
28. For 1959.
29. In the same paper as in note 16, estimates for the same period are: birth rate 45, death rate 26 and infant mortality rate 163.
30. For African population only.
31. For Eastern and Central divisions of East Cameroon (the former French Cameroons).
32. For 1958.
33. J. G. C. BLACKER, 'The Demography of East Africa', in *The Natural Resources of East Africa*, E. W. Russell, ed., Nairobi, English Press, 1962.
34. In the same paper as in note 16, estimates for 1962 are: birth rate: 48, death rate 18 and infant mortality rate 132.

35. In the same paper as in note 16, estimates for 1959 are: birth rate 48, death rate 25 and infant mortality rate 172.
36. 1959 census report.
37. For 1957–61.
38. In the same paper as in note 16, the birth rate for 1963 is estimated to be 49 per 1,000.
39. Based on analysis of census results.
40. For 1952.
41. In the same paper as in note 16, estimates for 1952–57 are: birth rate 50, death rate 23 and infant mortality rate 156.
42. In the same paper as in note 16, estimate for 1952–57 are: birth rate 46, death rate 22 and infant mortality rate 156.
43. For 1960.
44. Based on 1953–55 Sample Survey.
45. Estimate based on Sample Survey.

Rate of Growth of Population

The rate of natural increase of population, which is obtained from the difference between the birth and death rates, is given in Table 6 for the African countries. The rate so derived is subject to the same limitations as are the components, as there is no certainty that the errors in the components would cancel out while taking the difference. On the other hand, the rate of growth of population, computed from population censuses or sample surveys conducted at two points of time, has also the limitation of varying degrees of accuracy and coverage: the most common limitation is perhaps the under-enumeration in the previous census or sample survey or in the official estimates, leading to an implausibly high rate of growth. However, even if accurate data were available, the rate of growth of population, computed as above, would differ from the rate of natural increase, as the migration across national borders is an important factor in many African countries.

Of the 32 rates of natural increase listed in Table 6, 28 lie in the range 1·5–3·5 per cent, and 16 in the range 2·1–3·0 per cent. For Africa as a whole, the rate of natural increase of population can be taken at 2·3 per cent around 1960.

Estimates of population in the different world regions have been computed by the United Nations. From these, the rates of growth for the periods 1958–63 are shown in Table 3. For 1958–63, the average annual per cent rate of population increase in Africa, 2·3 per cent, was lower only than that in Latin America with 2·7 per cent. For 1960–63, the rate of growth of population in Africa is estimated at 2·5 per cent per year, lower again only than that of Latin America, which had 2·8 per cent. However, the population estimates made by the United Nations indicate that in about two decades Africa may have the highest rate of population growth of the world regions.[4]

Concluding Remarks

Next to Latin America, Africa has the highest rate of growth of population. However, in contrast to densely populated developing regions at a relatively advanced stage of development, most of Africa is sparsely populated and still at an early stage of development. There is also the prospect of further acceleration of the rate of growth of population in the near future.

It is clear that possibly sooner than can now be anticipated the African countries will have to make population trends the subject of a deliberate and comprehensive policy in their planning for economic and social development, and not merely an item to be taken into account in their planning: some other countries of the world are now taking this view.[5] The recent resolution of the United Nations Economic and Social Council enables the United Nations now to provide advisory services and training on action programmes in the field of population at the request of Governments desiring assistance in this field.[6]

Annex Table 1

Coverage of Censuses and Sample Surveys Conducted in 1964[1]

Country	Coverage	Date(s)	Type	Population enumerated
Botswana	Total population	Jan.–June 1964	C	d.f. and d.j.
Cameroon	Indigenous Population West Cameroon Region (former UN Trust Territory of S Cameroon)	1964	S	d.f. and d.j.
Dahomey	Total population Town of Cotonou	April 1964	C	d.f. and d.j.
Ivory Coast	Total Population (Remainder, except Katiola; the area SW of Sassandra river and Bouna in NW)	June 1963–June 1964	S	d.f. and d.j.
Libya	Total population	31 July 1964	C	d.j.
Madagascar	Total population Secondary towns (5,000+ inhabitants)	1962–64	C	d.f. and d.j.
Chad	Regional	Dec. 1963–July 1964	S	d.f. and d.j.
Mauritania	*National	*1964	S	d.f. and d.j.
Niger	Nomads	*1964	S	d.f.

Source: United Nations Economic Commission for Africa, *Methods and Problems of African Population Censuses and Surveys, 1955–1964* (E/CN.14/CAS.3/3/Rev.1); INSEE, *Enquête démographique récente réalisée en Afrique noire d'expression française et à Madagascar: Tableau d'Ensemble*, Paris, 1965.

Note: Asterisks mark the operations for which documentation is inadequate for complete analysis: C = Census; S = Sample Survey; d.f. = *de facto*; d.j. = *de jure*.

1. A Demographic Sample Survey was conducted in Burundi in March–August 1965.

Footnotes

1. The African programme is at present being evolved. See the *Report of the Working Group on Censuses of Population and Housing, Addis Ababa*, and *Report of the Second Working Group on Censuses of Population and Housing, Addis Ababa*, 23 February–4 March 1966 (E/CN.14/CAS.5/CPH/8).
2. United Nations, *Demographic Yearbook 1964*, Table 2.
3. See the *Report of the African Seminar on Vital Statistics*, Addis Ababa, December 1964 (E/CN.14/CAS.4/VS/14), reprinted as *Final Report of the African Seminar on Vital Statistics, Addis Ababa, Ethiopia, 1964*, Statistical Papers, Series M, No. 41, United Nations, New York, 1965.
4. United Nations, *Provisional Report on World Population Prospects as Assessed in 1963*, New York, 1964 (St/SOA/SER.R/7), Table 5.6.
5. United Nations Population Commission, *Draft Report to the Economic and Social Council on the Thirteenth Session of the Commission* (E/CN.9/L.78).
6. United Nations Economic and Social Council, *Resolution Adopted by the Economic and Social Council, 1084* (XXXIX), *Work Programmes and priorities in population fields* (E/RES/1084 (XXXIX)), 30 July 1965.

19 The assessment of infant and child mortality from the data available in Africa

Remy Clairin
Paris, France

Introduction

This paper deals with the mortality of children under five years of age. Whenever the term 'child mortality' is used, it refers to the deaths of children aged one to four and does not include the deaths under one year, which constitute 'infant mortality'.

The infant mortality rate is a basic demographic index because there is a strong negative correlation between this and the health status of a population. Experience has shown in some cases that, through rather inexpensive medical action, it is possible to lower this rate materially, which is practically tantamount to a rise of the birth and fertility rates of the population concerned.

Unfortunately, the collection of reliable data in this field raises very serious difficulties. Some underrecording of infant deaths, in some cases on a very large scale, is to be expected. Both the crude birth and death rates are then underestimated, although the observed rate of natural increase remains unchanged. This paper aims at presenting some attempts to check the crude data available from mainly the Republics of Upper Volta and Chad.

INFANT AND CHILD MORTALITY IN AFRICA

A striking characteristic of most, if not all, mortality patterns in African countries is that 4q1, the probability of death between the first and the fifth birthday, is extremely high and usually of the same order of magnitude as 1q0, the infant mortality rate. This is shown by the following figures for five countries or areas:

	Upper Volta	Chad	Northern Cameroon	Western Cameroon	Dahomey
1q0	0·182	0·160	0·197	0·139	0·111
4q1	0·218	0·127	0·173	0·147	0·194

This behaviour deviates considerably from the standard life-tables of the United Nations, as shown below (in rounded figures).

	Table 22	Table 25	Table 27
1q0	0·150	0·180	0·200
4q1	0·075	0·099	0·118

The 'Regional Life Tables', worked out by Coale and Demeny of Princeton University, aim precisely at accounting for the differences in mortality patterns found in various regions (independently of the level). The following table shows some interpolated values of 4q1, for three levels of infant mortality and from the eight sets of tables (four regions and two sexes):

1q0	4q1							
	EAST		WEST		NORTH		SOUTH	
	Males	Females	Males	Females	Males	Females	Males	Females
0·150	0·057	0·072	0·080	0·097	0·114	0·131	0·112	0·133
0·180	0·074	0·090	0·100	0·120	0·141	0·160	0·150	0·171
0·200	0·084	0·103	0·114	0·135	0·158	0·180	0·175	0·214

If only the mortality under five years is taken into consideration, the best agreement with the data observed in Africa is found in the North and South regional models for females.

The explanation of the high level of child mortality seems to lie mainly in the weaning. It would be highly desirable to get some precise data on the approximate weaning age. There is no doubt that the average age differs widely from one group to the other. All that can be safely said is that it lies somewhere between one year and two and a half years.

Infant Mortality

SOURCES OF INFORMATION

In most surveys or inquiries in francophone Africa, information on births and deaths of children has been derived from two main sources:

1. For each household, the births by sex and the deaths by sex and age were recorded for the 12 months preceding the day of enumeration.
2. For each woman past the age of puberty (usually fixed at 14 or 15 years), the enumerator recorded:
   (a) the live births occurring during the past 12 months, stating whether the children were surviving or not (usually the month of birth and, if relevant, the month of death were also jotted down); and
   (b) the total number of children ever born to the woman by sex, and the number of children surviving among these.

A serious weakness of all these data is that the facts are not observed directly but are based on what people can remember. When reference is made to the 12 months' period preceding the day of the survey, another serious difficulty arises in the delimitation of that period, and thus 'fringe effects' are likely to occur. Supplementary information is supplied by the collection of data on the age distribution of the population (including in many cases, a distribution by months of age of the children under one year).

'TOTAL' AND 'APPARENT' INFANT MORTALITY

For a generation, the infant mortality rate is defined as the proportion of the children of that generation who die before reaching their first birthday. The recording of all those deaths implies the observation of two consecutive 12 month periods. In practice, a good approximation of that rate can be estimated by the ratio of infant deaths having occurred during a certain period to the number of births during the same period. Some of the infant deaths are those of children born before the beginning of the period. Both series are derived from the answers of the heads of households.

In order to avoid the overlapping of two generations, one can consider only the children born and dead during the 12 months' period. The ratio of their number to the number of live births is referred to in this paper as the 'apparent' infant mortality rate. It can be measured from two sources:

(a) the statements by the women of the children born to them during the past 12 months and their survival;

(b) the recording of the births having occurred in the household during the same period and the number of children enumerated under one year of age. The 'apparent' infant mortality is obtained by the difference between the two numbers, and therefore it is liable to very large fluctuations.

MAIN SOURCES OF ERRORS

1. *For all questions concerning events occurring during the past twelve months.*

This has already been mentioned. The fringe effect is often especially important for the last month, for which figures may be strongly under- or overestimated. In order to evaluate that effect, it is of the greatest interest to have a distribution of the events by month.

2. *As regards the statements of births and deaths by the heads of households:*

(a) Omission of births and deaths of children whose life was very short.

(b) Inclusion in the one year age-group of children born before the beginning of the 12 months' period and who died during that period before reaching their first birthday, thus bringing down the observed total infant mortality rate closer to the 'apparent' rate and raising the 1q1 ratio.

3. *As regards the statement by women:*

(a) *Current fertility.* A technique of interview has been worked out which, in theory, should exclude any error (if the 12 months' period has been correctly observed). The following questions should be asked, in this order:

(i) Did the woman deliver a child during the past 12 months?
(ii) (If the answer to (i) is 'yes') Is the child alive?
(iii) (If the answer to (ii) is 'no') Did the child cry after being born?

So there are four possible combinations of answers:

	Question (i)	*Question (ii)*	*Question (iii)*
Nothing	No	—	—
A still birth (no recording)	Yes	No	No
A live birth (child not surviving)	Yes	No	Yes
A live birth (child surviving)	Yes	Yes	—

In fact, it is impossible to make sure that, in all cases the questions were asked in the proper way, and there is a risk of omitting the children who died very shortly after their birth or of recording stillbirths as live births. In most cases no information was gathered concerning the births to women who died during the 12 months' period. Their number is not negligible. In Cameroon the above information was sought from the relatives of those women.

(b) *Total fertility.* In this case, no elaborate questioning or checking is possible and errors in the numbers of children ever born and those who died are much more likely to happen especially in the case of older women.

Data on Infant Mortality in Upper Volta and Chad

(crude data from records of observations)

	Upper Volta	Chad
TOTAL POPULATION	4,377,700	2,524,370
(a) **From statements by heads of households**		
Births during the year:		
Males	107,779	57,280
Females	106,217	55,080
Total	213,996	112,360
Crude birth rate (per 1,000)	49·6	44·2
Deaths under one year		
Males	19,758	10,020
Females	19,247	7,950
Total	39,005	17,970
(b) **From statements by women**		
Children born during the year		
Boys	105,436	56,480
Girls	105,958	54,380
Total	211,394	110,860
Surviving at time of survey		
Boys	92,598	49,100
Girls	92,437	48,030
Total	185,035	97,130
Deceased		
Boys	12,838	7,380
Girls	13,521	6,350
Total	26,359	13,730
(c) **Persons enumerated under one year of age**		
Males	91,423	49,050
Females	89,568	48,440
Total	180,991	97,530
Sex ratio at birth (number of boys for 100 girls)[1]		
From the household recording	101·5	104·0
From the questioning of women	99·5	103·9
Sex ratio of survivors		
From the questioning of women	100·2	102·2
From the age distribution	102·1	101·3
Crude infant mortality rates calculated from statements by heads of households (per 1,000)[2]		
Boys	183·3	174·9
Girls	181·2	144·3
Both sexes	182·3	159·9

1. The data for Chad are consistent, while those for Upper Volta are not.
2. In Chad it is obvious that there has been a large misreporting of the sex of the deceased persons. This is confirmed by the general pattern of the observed mortality (the overall crude death rate is 37 per 1,000 for males and 26 per 1,000 for females).

DATA OBTAINED FROM THE INTERVIEWS OF WOMEN

The number of births during the past 12 months reported by the women is equal to 98·8 per cent of the births recorded in the households in Upper Volta and to 98·7 per cent in Chad. The actual differences are respectively 2,602 and 1,500 births. Most, if not all that difference can be explained by the omission of children born to women who died during the past 12 months. If we apply to those women the observed current fertility rates (for a period of six months), we arrive at 1,300 births in Upper Volta and 900 in Chad. These estimates must form a lower limit for they are based on the assumption that there is no correlation between child-bearing and death.

However, the returns on causes of deaths show that approximately 1,650 puerperal deaths of women were recorded in Upper Volta and 900 in Chad. Unfortunately, no distinction was made between the deliveries of live children on one hand and still births and miscarriages on the other. This cause accounts for 11 per cent in Upper Volta and 7 per cent in Chad of all deaths occurring to women aged 15–49. If we assume, (a) that all women who died from child-bearing gave birth to a live child, and (b) that the fertility of women who died from any other cause was identical to that of the surviving women, we can set an upper limit for the estimation of the number of children born to the deceased woman. For Upper Volta it would be 2,800 children, compared with the lower limit of 1,300 children mentioned above. It does not seem unreasonable to take the average of those figures, that is to say 2,050. For Chad the corresponding number would be 1,300.

How about the survival of those children? It can be safely said that, at least in the rural areas of those countries, the chances of survival of those children were practically nil. Thus, almost all of them can be classified as 'born and deceased during the past 12 months'.

'Apparent' infant mortality. Accordingly the figures obtained from the statements by women would be as follows (for both sexes):

Born during the past 12 months	Upper Volta	Chad
Surviving	185,040	97,130
Deceased	28,410	15,030
Total	213,450	112,130

The 'apparent' infant mortality rates are as follows (for 1,000 births):

		Upper Volta	Chad
Without adjustment			
Males		121·8	130·7
Females		127·6	116·8
	Both sexes	124·7	123·8
After adjustment:	Both sexes	133·1	134·0

In Chad the difference between the rates by sex is much lower in the case of 'apparent' infant mortality than for total infant mortality.

Ratio of 'apparent' infant mortality to total infant mortality

	Upper Volta	Chad
Crude apparent mortality	68·4%	77·4%
Adjusted apparent mortality	73·0%	83·8%

The ratio observed in Upper Volta seems to be much more plausible than that observed in Chad.

Number enumerated under one year of age. In Chad, the number of persons enumerated under one year is almost exactly equal to the number of survivors among the children born during the past 12 months. In Upper Volta, the former is smaller by about 1·6 per cent (3,000 persons). An adjustment from the detailed data on infant mortality suggests that this is to be attributed essentially to an underestimation of the number of children of 11 months' age. It is the fringe effect again. Such a small difference is sufficient to alter materially the assessment of 'apparent' infant mortality by this method. The 'apparent' rate so computed would be 154·2 per 1,000 instead of 133·1 per 1,000.

The ratio of the 'apparent' rate to total infant mortality would jump to 84·6 per cent and be very close to that found in Chad, where both methods give the same figure.

Infant Mortality by Month of Age—Fitting by Bourgeois-Pichat's Equation

If P_n is the probability of death from birth to age n (in days), it has been ascertained in a number of cases that P_n can be expressed, except in the very first stages of life (but in any case after the completion of the first month of age) by the following function, stated by Bourgeois-Pichat:

$$P_n = a+b \log^3 (n+1)$$

'ENDOGENOUS' AND 'EXOGENOUS' INFANT MORTALITY

Among the deaths of infants, a distinction can be made between:

(a) deaths due to congenital malformations, or the circumstances of the delivery (premature or abnormal): these are analogous to stillbirths (they are hereafter referred to as 'endogenous' deaths); and

(b) deaths due to other causes—such as accidents, infection or the influence of environment (they are hereafter referred to as 'exogenous' deaths).

The 'exogenous' infant mortality does not differ much from the mortality at later ages, considering the physical weakness of young children.

The parameter measures the 'endogenous' mortality.

The quantity, $b \log^3 (n+1)$ [or bT_n, with $T_n = \log^3 (n+1)$] measures the 'exogenous' infant mortality up to age n.

In view of the extreme scarcity of information available on African countries, it is difficult to give any order of magnitude for the parameters a and b. Tentatively one can say that values between 0·005 and 0·008 seem plausible for b. As for a, the uncertainty is much larger. Values ranging from 0·0200 to 0·1200 or even more cannot be excluded *a priori.*

Infant Mortality for Various Parameters of Bourgeois-Pichat's Equation 'Exogenous Mortality' to Certain Ages

Age	$\log^3(n+1)$ *or* (T_n)	Parameter b		
		0·006	0·007	0·008
1 month	3·356	0·0203	0·0235	0·0268
2 months	5·747	0·0345	0·0402	0·0460
3 months	7·587	0·0455	0·0531	0·0607
4 months	9·091	0·0545	0·0636	0·0727
5 months	10·424	0·0625	0·0730	0·0834
6 months	11·599	0·0696	0·0812	0·0928
7 months	12·653	0·0759	0·0886	0·1012
8 months	13·616	0·0817	0·0953	0·1089
9 months	14·508	0·0870	0·1016	0·1161
10 months	15·337	0·0920	0·1074	0·1227
11 months	16·114	0·0967	0·1128	0·1289
12 months	16·846	0·1011	0·1179	0·1348

For selected values of parameters, *a* and *b*, the corresponding values of the infant mortality rate would be:

Infant Mortality Rate

a	*b*		
	0·006	0·007	0·008
0·0200	0·1211	0·1379	0·1548
0·0400	0·1411	0·1579	0·1748
0·0600	0·1611	0·1779	0·1948
0·0800	0·1811	0·1979	0·2148
0·1000	0·2011	0·2179	0·2348
0·1200	0·2211	0·2379	0·2548

EFFECTS OF OMISSIONS

What is the repercussion on the observed rates and on the value of Bourgeois-Pichat's parameters, of the omission of a fraction of the 'endogenous' deaths (and of the corresponding births) if the other infant deaths are recorded correctly?

If B is the actual number of births, the number of deaths up to age n (after the first month) is given by $D=B[a+bT_n]$

If a proportion, k, of the 'endogenous' deaths is unrecorded, the observed number of deaths is:

$$D' = B[a(1-k)+bT_n]$$

But the observed number of births is equal to:

$$B' = B(1-ak)$$

The observed rates become:

$$\frac{D'}{B'} = P'_n \frac{a(1-k)+bT_n}{1-ak} = a'+b'T_n$$

The cumulative distribution of infant deaths can still be fitted to a straight line, according to Bourgeois-Pichat's law, but the parameter b is slightly overestimated.

Example

Birth rate = 45 per 1,000

$$a = 0{\cdot}0800$$
$$b = 0{\cdot}0070$$

Infant mortality rate:

$$\begin{aligned} \text{'endogenous'} &= 0{\cdot}0800 \\ \text{'exogenous'} &= 0{\cdot}1179 \\ \hline \text{Total} &= 0{\cdot}1979 \end{aligned}$$

If a is underestimated by 50 per cent (which is not absurd)

$$B' = B \times 0{\cdot}96$$

The observed birth rate is 43·2 per 1,000

$$a' = \frac{0{\cdot}08 \times 0{\cdot}5}{0{\cdot}96} = 0{\cdot}0417$$

$$b' = \frac{0{\cdot}007}{0{\cdot}96} = 0{\cdot}0073$$

Observed infant mortality rate:

$$\begin{aligned} \text{'endogenous'} &= 0{\cdot}0417 \\ \text{'exogenous'} &= 0{\cdot}1228 \\ \hline \text{Total} &= 0{\cdot}1645 \end{aligned}$$

The applying of Bourgeois-Pichat's formula cannot detect errors in 'endogenous' mortality.

Nor can it detect omissions of 'exogenous' deaths, distributed in the same proportion at all ages (which practically almost never occurs).

But this formula can be very useful to correct errors (under- or overstatement or distortion of ages at death) which occur in different proportion at the different ages, especially omissions increasing according to the age of the deceased children. This is very likely to happen for the deaths of children born before the beginning of the 12 months' period.

'APPARENT' INFANT MORTALITY RATES

Assuming that the birth rate is constant and that the births are evenly distributed over the year (no seasonal effect), it is possible to estimate the number of survivors enumerated under one year of age, for a given number of births. Over one month of age, the arithmetic mean of the numbers of survivors at the beginning and the end of the month can be taken (for one birth per month).

$$P_n = \frac{S_n + S_{n+1}}{2}$$

(where P_n is population aged n months, and S_n survivors at n months)

For the first month, lacking any precise information, the following formula was used:

$$P_0 = 0{\cdot}2S_0+0{\cdot}8S_1$$

For one birth per month, we arrive at the following figures:

Population at age

Less than one month	$1-0{\cdot}8a-2{\cdot}685b$
1 month	$1-a-4{\cdot}552b$
2 months	$1-a-6{\cdot}667b$
3 months	$1-a-8{\cdot}339b$
4 months	$1-a-9{\cdot}757b$
5 months	$1-a-11{\cdot}012b$
6 months	$1-a-12{\cdot}126b$
7 months	$1-a-13{\cdot}134b$
8 months	$1-a-14{\cdot}062b$
9 months	$1-a-14{\cdot}923b$
10 months	$1-a-15{\cdot}725b$
11 months	$1-a-16{\cdot}480b$
Total	$12-11{\cdot}8a-129{\cdot}462b$

For one birth per year the total proportion of survivors enumerated under one year of age would be:

$$1-0{\cdot}983a-10{\cdot}788b$$

$0{\cdot}983a+10{\cdot}788b$ indicates the proportion of children born during the year and deceased before the time of the enumeration, consequently it measures the 'apparent' infant mortality rate.

Ratio of the 'Apparent' Infant Mortality Rate to the Total Infant Mortality Rate
(according to parameters a and b)

a	b=0·006			b=0·007			b=0·007		
	Infant mortality rate A	'Ap-parent' rate B	B/A per cent	Infant mortality rate A	'Ap-parent' rate B	B/A per cent	Infant mortality rate A	'Ap-parent' rate B	B/A per cent
0·0200	0·1211	0·0844	69·7	0·1379	0·0952	69·0	0·1548	0·1060	68·5
0·0400	0·1411	0·1041	73·8	0·1579	0·1148	72·7	0·1748	0·1256	71·9
0·0600	0·1611	0·1237	76·8	0·1779	0·1345	75·6	0·1948	0·1426	73·2
0·0800	0·1811	0·1434	79·2	0·1979	0·1542	77·9	0·2148	0·1622	75·5
0·1000	0·2011	0·1630	81·1	0·2179	0·1738	79·8	0·2348	0·1846	78·6
0·1200	0·2211	0·1827	82·6	0·2379	0·1935	81·3	0·2548	0·2043	80·2

The ratio decreases slightly when b becomes higher, but it is mainly sensitive to variations of a.

Application of Bourgeois-Pichat's Formula to the Upper Volta Data: Upper Volta (1960–61)

Age in months	Percentage of all infant deaths occurring at that age	Cumulative percentages	Observed infant mortality rates	Adjusted rates $P_n = 0{\cdot}06 + 0{\cdot}0077\,T_n$
0	46·3	46·3	0·0844	0·0858
1	10·4	56·7	0·1034	0·1043
2	8·2	64·9	0·1183	0·1184
3	8·5	73·4	0·1338	0·1300
4	4·6	78·0	0·1422	0·1403
5	4·4	82·4	0·1502	0·1493
6	5·2	87·6	0·1597	0·1574
7	2·7	90·3	0·1646	0·1648
8	2·5	92·8	0·1692	0·1717
9	2·8	95·6	0·1746	0·1781
10	2·5	98·1	0·1788	0·1841
11	1·9	100·0	0·1823	0·1897

The graph suggests that a straight line of equation $0{\cdot}06 + 0{\cdot}0077 \log^3 (n+1)$ could be fitted. The agreement would be satisfactory except for the last four months. The fitted figures appear in the last column. The deviation observed at the end of the distribution may reasonably be attributed to the inclusion in the one year age group of children born before the beginning of the twelve months' period. This is supported by the rather sharp decline in the last month.

If we assume that the 'endogenous' deaths have been correctly recorded, the infant mortality rate would be as follows:

'endogenous' = 0·0600
'exogenous' = 0·1297

Total = 0·1897

The 'apparent' infant mortality rate would be 0·1367 (72·1 per cent of the total rate), which does not differ widely from the observed one (0·1331).

Application of Bourgeois-Pichat's Formula to Chad Data

Age in months	Percentage of all infant deaths occurring at the age	Cumulative percentages	Observed infant mortality rates	Adjusted rates ($P_n = 0{\cdot}039 + 0{\cdot}007\,T_n$)
0	38·6	38·6	0·0617	0·0625
1	11·8	50·4	0·0806	0·0792
2	7·3	57·7	0·0923	0·0922
3	6·3	64·0	0·1023	0·1026
4	6·1	70·1	0·1121	0·1120
5	4·1	74·2	0·1186	0·1202
6	4·1	78·3	0·1252	0·1276
7	3·6	81·9	0·1310	0·1343
8	4·2	86·1	0·1377	0·1406
9	2·6	88·7	0·1418	0·1464
10	4·1	92·8	0·1484	0·1518
11	7·2	100·0	0·1599	0·1569

As in the case of Upper Volta, the equation of the straight line $P_n = 0{\cdot}039\,a + 0{\cdot}007 \log^3 (n+1)$ was estimated from the graph. It is to be noted that while the fitted rate is higher than the observed one in Upper Volta, it is the contrary here. The 'fringe effect' in the last month is in the opposite direction. (The number of deaths happening during the 11th month seems to have been almost doubled.)

We arrive at the following figures for the infant mortality rate:

'endogenous' = 0·0390
'exogenous' = 0·1179

Total = 0·1569

The theoretical 'apparent' mortality rate would then be 0·1139 (i.e. 72·6 per cent of the total rate) compared with the observed figure of 0·1340.

Since the infant mortality rate was assessed from statements by heads of households while the 'apparent' rate was obtained from the questioning of women, the difference between the above figures might suggest some deaths were omitted by the heads of household. This might explain the considerable and not quite plausible difference found between the 'endogenous' mortalities of these countries, which is surprising since both populations live on the same latitudes and have attained approximately the same level of development.

Mortality in the 1–4 Age Group

The following table shows the detailed figures obtained in Upper Volta and Chad.

Age in completed years	UPPER VOLTA				CHAD			
	Number enumerated	Number of deaths	Death rates	Probability of death	Number enumerated	Number of deaths	Death rates	Probability of death
1	108,053	11,068	0·1024	0·0974	47,170	3,030	0·0642	0·0622
2	150,274	10,803	0·0719	0·0694	114,310	3,640	0·0318	0·0313
3	173,434	7,951	0·0458	0·0448	116,940	2,710	0·0232	0·0229
4	148,199	3,702	0·0250	0·0247	113,100	1,870	0·0165	0·0164
1–4	579,960	33,525	0·0578	0·2175	391,520	11,250	0·0287	0·1269
5–9	664,434	9,970	0·0150	0·0723	451,110	4,770	0·0106	0·0516

DISTORTIONS OF AGE DISTRIBUTION

Assuming that the probabilities of death were correctly observed and a rate of natural increase of 1·5 per cent, the estimated number of persons for each age group would be as follows (in thousands):

Age	UPPER VOLTA		CHAD	
	Observed	Estimated	Observed	Estimated
1	108	163	47	89
2	105	147	114	84
3	173	136	116	80
4	148	130	113	78
Total 1–4	580	576	392	332
5–9	664	592	451	360

In Upper Volta, the total number of persons in the age group 1–4 seems to have been recorded with relativé accuracy, while an overstatement is obvious in the age group 5–9 which compensates partially the deficit observed around the age of 15, especially for females. In Chad the numbers in both age groups have been largely overestimated.

The question arises whether the distortions of the ages of deceased persons and of survivors follow the same pattern. No answer can be given at this stage. In any case the rise of the mortality after one year of age (with a maximum lying somewhere between the complete ages one and three) is quite obvious.

EXTRAPOLATION OF BOURGEOIS-PICHAT'S FORMULA AFTER ONE YEAR

We find the following figures for Upper Volta, as compared with the observed rates:

Extrapolation				Observed			
190	0·1897			190	0·1823		
290	0·2408	1q1	0·0631	290	0·2619	1q1	0·0974
390	0·2762	1q2	0·0466	390	0·3131	1q2	0·0693
490	0·3040	1q3	0·0384	490	0·3439	1q3	0·0448
590	0·3271	1q4	0·0332	590	0·3600	1q4	0·0246
		4q1	0·1696			4q1	0·2173

By applying to the whole year the probability of death in the last six months, we come to the figure of 0·0742 and here too the existence of a maximum in age one is evident.

Extrapolation of probability of death

From 6 months—to less than 1 year	0·0742
1 year	0·0974
2 years	0·0694
3 years	0·0448

Comparison with Estimations from Child Survivorship Ratios (Brass Technique)

The method worked out by Brass applies to women up to the age of 65, but experience has shown that, at least in Africa, the figures for women over 55 are not reliable. The following table shows the results for Upper Volta and Chad.

Age group of women	UPPER VOLTA					
	Probabilities of death from birth			Probabilities of death by age or age group		
	q	Observed	Adjusted	q	Observed	Adjusted
15–19	1q0	0·182	0·243	1q0	0·182	0·243
20–24	2q0	0·262	0·333	1q1	0·097	0·119
25–29	3q0	0·313	0·393	1q2	0·069	0·090
30–34	5q0	0·360	0·417	2q3	0·068	0·040
				4q1	0·218	0·230
35–39	10q0	0·406	0·452	5q5	0·072	0·060
40–44	15q0	0·425	0·469	5q10	0·031	0·031
45–49	20q0	0·446	0·490	5q20	0·050	0·063

Age group of women	CHAD					
	Probabilities of death from birth			Probabilities of death by age or age group		
	q	Observed	Adjusted	q	Observed	Adjusted
15–19	1q0	0·160	0·185	1q0	0·160	0·185
20–24	2q0	0·212	0·255	1q1	0·062	0·085
25–29	3q0	0·237	0·296	1q2	0·031	0·056
30–34	5q0	0·267	0·324	2q3	0·039	0·040
				4q1	0·127	0·171
35–39	10q0	0·304	0·360	5q5	0·052	0·053
40–44	15q0	0·342	0·376	5q10	0·054	0·026
45–49	20q0	0·409	0·410	5q15	0·103	0·053
50–54	25q0	0·454	0·431	5q20	0·075	0·037

As regards Upper Volta, the table shows a very close agreement between the observed and the fitted figures except under one year (i.e. for the infant mortality rate).

Life Table for 1,000 Survivors at Age 1 (Upper Volta)

Survivor at age	Observed	Adjusted
1 year	1,000	1,000
2 years	903	881
3 years	840	802
5 years	782	770
10 years	726	724
15 years	703	701
20 years	677	674
25 years	643	631

The assumption that the fitted infant mortality rate is correct would lead to the following consequences:

(i) the observed birth rate should be multiplied by 1·0704, thus bringing it to the value of 53·1 per 1,000 instead of 49·6 per 1,000;

(ii) if all the omitted deaths belonged to the 'endogenous' mortality, the under-estimation of the 'endogenous' deaths would be 54 per cent;

(iii) the parameters of Bourgeois-Pichat's formula would be:

$$P_n = 1{\cdot}1218 + 0{\cdot}0072 \log^3 (n+1)$$

instead of:

$$P'n = 0{\cdot}0600 + 0{\cdot}0077 \log^3 (n+1).$$

The fitted 'apparent' infant mortality rate would be 0·1974. The basic question that could be raised is whether the data on total fertility should be more reliable than the data on current fertility. As far as the recording of the live births and the deaths pertaining to the 'apparent' infant mortality is concerned, it could be expected that the technique of interview outlined above would provide relatively accurate results, if properly applied. On the other hand, the retrospective questions, on births and deaths which occurred years ago, are more likely to lead to errors, especially in respect of children whose life was very short.

The fitted figures might suggest that there was a tendency among women to overestimate the number of their short-lived children (if only for reasons of prestige). This might be partially due to the inclusion of stillbirths in the number of children ever born. The only conceivable way to obviate, as far as possible, that source of errors would be to question each woman about her historical record (marriages, dissolutions, pregnancies and their outcomes) from the time of puberty onwards. It should be done in the most thorough way and be carefully cross-checked with any other information at hand. It is not an easy procedure and is bound to take much time. But that technique is being used in two demographic surveys currently being carried out in two parts of Cameroon. As regards Chad, the comparison between the two series of figures shows much more irregularity, which can be explained by the considerable distortions of the observed age distribution.

COMPARISONS WITH OTHER RESULTS

In the table below, the figures between ages one and four for Upper Volta and Chad are compared with the data (observed and fitted by Brass's technique) for three other areas where demographic sample surveys have been carried out lately, but where detailed data by year of age are not (or not yet) available.

	UPPER VOLTA		CHAD		DAHOMEY		NORTHERN CAMEROON		WESTERN CAMEROON	
	Observed	Fitted	Observed	Fitted	Observed	Fitted	Observed	Fitted	Observed	Fitted
$_1q_0$	0·182	0·243	0·160	0·185	0·111	0·170	0·197	0·226	0·139	0·137
$_4q_1$	0·218	0·230	0·127	0·171	0·194	0·216	0·173	0·195	0·147	0·180
$_5q_5$	0·072	0·060	0·052	0·053	0·069	0·038	0·055	0·069	0·060	0·065
$_5q_{10}$	0·031	0·031	0·054	0·026	0·126	0·089	0·106	0·031	0·057	0·039

The figures for Western Cameroon are peculiar in that an almost perfect agreement is found between the observed and fitted rates under one year, while the fitted rate for age group 1–4 is higher than the observed one by about 20 per cent. These are only provisional data and the results of that survey, which seem to be of high quality, are being analysed.

Conclusion

It is essential for demographic analysis and projection to obtain precise and accurate information on infant mortality and child mortality up to five years. Until now the African data on that subject have been rather unreliable or inconsistent with each other. Therefore new techniques must be evolved, or procedures which have been used only in isolated cases and have given satisfactory results, should be generalized. It would be particularly interesting to determine the common characteristics (if any) of infant and child mortality in Africa. One or several patterns could thus be described which could be used to improve crude data or to complete partial information.

The following recommendations could be made:

(a) We should insist very strongly on the recording of as much information as possible on all children who died before reaching the age of five. The age at death should be noted in days under one week, in weeks under one month and in months for all children *deceased under the age of three*. The causes of death should be recorded as precisely as possible. In particular, for all children aged one or two, it is essential to know whether the death happened before or after weaning.

(b) The questioning of women on their reproductive histories should be conducted with the utmost care. The questionnaire being used in certain parts of Cameroon has already been mentioned in that connection.

(c) The best way to obtain accurate data on this subject is the survey by continuous observation of a population (follow-up). Such inquiries, which are often very burdensome to carry out, are still very rare. One of their main advantages is that they throw some light on the fluctuations of mortality from one year to the next.

It must be kept in mind that, while an isolated inquiry gives information on the level and pattern of mortality for a given year (or more exactly for a period of 12 months plus the duration of the survey), the data on child survival take into consideration the mortality during a number of years (variable according to the age of women). It is conceivable that those data, properly analysed, could be used to investigate the existence of long period trends (normally declines in infant mortality).

20 Infertility in tropical Africa

A. Romaniuk
Faculty of Social Sciences, University of Ottawa, Canada

Many of the earlier writings on African demography were devoted to problems of infertility and depopulation in tropical Africa; in contrast, the present tendency is rather to emphasize problems connected with high fertility. Discussions among African demographers now revolve around topics such as family planning, a subject that holds a prominent place in the literature concerning countries that face a population pressure.

There has indeed been a drastic reappraisal of the demographic situation of tropical Africa. This has come as a result of surveys conducted in recent years which have revealed quite rapid population growth consequent upon both lower mortality and especially higher fertility than had generally been expected. While justly rectifying some older erroneous views of African demography, this new look should not obscure a fact of the utmost social, demographic and medical importance, namely, that an important minority of the population is subject to infertility. The purpose of this paper is to draw attention to the existence of this phenomenon, to show its scope, and, as far as available data will permit, to examine the underlying causes.

Since this paper is concerned with infertility as a demographic problem (and not with the definition of infertility in a medical sense), there is a need to define a 'normal' fertility standard by which the degree of infertility can be measured. There are reasons for believing that a birth rate of 50 to 60 per 1,000 is *typical* for African populations. Such rates have been revealed by many surveys, and actually should be expected to occur in a population:

(a) not resorting to birth control to any significant extent:
(b) practising universal and early female marriages; and
(c) subjected to a low expectation of life at birth.

The latter condition is of importance in assessing the possibility of a high birth rate, for normally the lower the expectation of life, the higher the birth rate for a given age schedule of fertility rates. Where these conditions of high fertility prevail and in addition, the population does not practise prolonged abstinence during the lactation period, although this occurs in Africa more frequently than it is usually believed, one might well expect from such a population a birth rate of 60 per 1,000.

In the light of available statistics, it appears that the proportion of women of over 45 years of age who are childless amounts to about 5 per cent in populations with birth rates of 50 to 60 per 1,000. This percentage corresponds to what might be termed 'natural sterility'.

Statistical Evidence on Infertility

In spite of progress in recent years in gathering demographic data on populations of tropical Africa, the limitations and shortcomings of this material are still too considerable to permit a full statistical treatment of infertility for the whole of Africa. In certain countries no census has yet been taken; in others, the data have been published only for wide regions, thus possibly concealing sub-regions of low fertility. Nor are the available figures on fertility levels directly comparable, either because of differential errors involved in basic data or because of the variety of types of measurement that are used from country to country. Nevertheless, the available data suffice to give some idea about the degree of infertility suffered by the populations of certain areas and the geographical distribution of this phenomenon throughout the continent.

Thus, in the Congo (Kinshasa), while the national average birth rate is 45 per 1,000, the range of regional variations is as wide as 20 (Bas Uele) and 60 per 1,000 (North and South Kivu). In contrast, sterility, in terms of the proportion of women of over 45 years of age who never conceived a child, varies from 5 per cent (Kivu) to 50 per cent (Bas Uele), the national average being 20 per cent. A vast zone of conspicuous infertility emerges in Central Congo, along the Congo River and its confluents, coinciding largely with the natural habitat of the Mongo, a large ethnic group of about a million people. Another area where infertility is of even more marked incidence is the north-western part of the Congo along the Uele River, and is inhabited by approximately one million Azande and Mangbetu. In view of the prevailing low fertility rate, insufficient to overweigh the mortality rate, depopulation is a real threat that is being faced in this area. About half of the Congo's population is troubled with the problem of infertility to some degree; 22 per cent of the population has a birth rate of less than 35 per 1,000, 7 per cent a rate of less than 25 per 1,000.

To a less extent, the neighbouring Sudan is facing a similar problem. The two southern districts, Zande West and Zande East, inhabited mainly by people of the same ethnic stock (Zande) as those living in the Uele areas of the Congo, present a sharp contrast to the other provinces, many of which exhibit an unusually high fertility level, even by African standards.[1]

The same is true in the Central African Republic, where, according to a survey conducted in 1959, the birth rate drops from 55 or more in M'Boum, Sara, Baya, Mandjia, etc., to 20 per 1,000 in Nzakara. The latter are people ethnically akin to the previously mentioned Zande of the Congo and the Sudan who are likewise subject to a high degree of sterility.

On the Atlantic Coast, the whole of Gabon appears to be deeply affected by infertility; its birth rate is only 36 per 1,000 according to the demographic survey carried out in 1960–61.

A survey undertaken in 1960 in northern Cameroon reveals among Moslems a birth rate of 29 per 1,000 and childlessness of about 35 per cent among women 25 to 45 years of age.[1a] Previously, E. Ardener[2] had produced evidence of conspicuous infertility among the Bakwari of the former British Cameroon.

Regional variations in fertility in East Africa can be determined mainly in terms of the proportion of children in the population. Examining the number of children under 16 years of age in the population, the 1957 census results showed Tanganyika to be outstanding with three main zones of relatively low fertility. The first consists of the coastal districts of rural Tanga (35·7) and Pangani[3] (31·0), facing Pemba and Zanzibar Islands; the second is in the vicinity of Lake Victoria, with a low point in Bukoba (35·9); and the third is in the neighbourhood of Lake Tanganyika centred on the Kigoma district (38·6). Closer to the centre, the Tabora district shows also a relatively low proportion of children (35·5). Tanganyika as a whole has a ratio of 44·3. This latter proportion corresponds to a birth rate of about 47 per 1,000, in a stable population characterized by an expectation of life at birth equal to 35 years.[4] With the same assumption of expectation of life, the birth rate would be 29 for the Pangani district and 35 per 1,000 for the Bukoba district. The 1948 census had revealed that 17 per cent of Tanganyikan women over 45 years of age were childless.

In Uganda, the two provinces situated in the neighbourhood of Lake Victoria, Eastern Province and especially Buganda, have lower fertility rates than Northern and Western Provinces. The 1959 census shows the proportion of children under 16 years of age as 38·2 per cent for Buganda and 49·4 per cent for the two latter provinces. The corresponding stable population birth rates are 38 and 56 per 1,000, for an expectation of life at birth equal to 35 years. The 1948 census reveals that the proportion of childless women over 45 years of age is 18 per cent for all Uganda and 24 per cent for Buganda province. A survey of a sample of Buganda women disclosed that 31·6 per cent of women over 45 years of age, 'all of whom reported some marital experience',[5] were childless.

For Kenya, the 1948 census showed the lowest proportion of children in Kericho (32·2), situated in the neighbourhood of Lake Victoria, and in the coastal districts of Malindi (37·7) and Lamu (36·7). Kenya's national average is 46·6.

J. G. C. Blacker[6] reports a birth rate of 32 per 1,000 for the Afro-Arabs of Zanzibar Island and 21 per 1,000 for Zanzibar Town, and doubts whether the latter rate is adequate to ensure population replacement. It is of interest to note that the Asian minority living on this island exhibits a birth rate of 40 per 1,000, and this in spite of the fact that Asians show a pattern of more delayed marriage than do Afro-Arabs. The cause of this low fertility becomes manifest when one realizes that 25·1 per cent of women over 46 years of age on Zanzibar Island and 37·7 in Zanzibar Town, are childless.

The earlier reports on infertility among various populations of Madagascar are confirmed by the 1961 census results which disclose a low ratio of children under 15 to total population for a number of districts such as: Vohipeno (31·9 per cent), Desalamp (32·9), Marovoay (33·5), Mttstnjo (32·9), Soalala (32·2), Nosst-De (31·5), Ankazoabo (29·7) and Miandrivazo (32·8).

West Africa emerges with a more homogeneous pattern of high fertility, though several cases of relatively low fertility have been reported. The Peul, a semi-nomadic group whose natural habitat overlaps several states (Senegal, Upper Volta, etc.), are reported by various sources to be less prolific than the other ethnic groups whose territory they share. In Upper Volta, for example, according to figures reported by R. Clairin,[7] the birth rate observed among the Peul is 43, against an average of 50 per 1,000 for the whole of Upper Volta. Another case is that of the Bobo (Upper Volta), where childlessness prevails at a rate of 25 per cent among women over 25 years of age.

CONCLUSION

From this necessarily incomplete account three outstanding points seem to emerge. First, infertility is a phenomenon widely spread in tropical Africa and particularly in its central areas. Second, there appears to be some relationship between geographical position, either exposure to outside contact or location such as closeness to the Congo or Uele Rivers or to Lake Victoria, and infertility. Lesser zones appear in some coastal districts. However, not until a detailed map of fertility for tropical Africa as a whole is constructed will it be possible to acquire a full understanding of the mechanism by which the agents of infertility have spread over the continent. Third (a point probably even more important for further research on the social background of infertility) the boundaries of definite zones of infertility coincide often with the natural habitat of specific ethnic groups. It follows from this that a fertility map, to be really meaningful, must be based, as far as possible, on the tribe or ethnic group as a unit.

The Causes of Infertility

It is not intended to recount the various theories which have been proposed over the years to explain infertility. Many of them are hardly worth refutation, although they were for years in the limelight of literature on African demography. Rather, empirical evidence accumulated during recent years will be employed to examine the most prominent factors of fertility in order to single out those which are likely to affect infertility in Africa, and thus to formulate an hypothesis serving further research in this field.

MARRIAGE FACTORS

The most significant features of African marriage patterns likely to exert an influence on fertility are:

(a) the universal and early marriage of females;
(b) the prevalence of polygyny; and
(c) high conjugal mobility.

In terms of age at marriage and the proportion of married women, there are no significant and systematic differences between low and high fertility populations.[8] The most commonly observed average age at first marriage is approximately 16 years for females. This must be regarded as favourable to high fertility. Marriage at a somewhat more mature age, observed so far in only a few instances, occurs among highly fertile populations, examples of which are Burundi (22 years)[8] and Bakongo (19 years). There appears to exist a more pronounced tendency toward precocious marriages among populations suffering from high sterility. This might be ascribable partly to the desire amongst men to marry girls who have not yet been contaminated. Whether the premature exposure to sexual intercourse increases or reduces the fertility of those populations is difficult to determine.

The effect on fertility of polygyny, in which, according to region, 20 to 50 per cent of married women are involved, is still a controversial matter. Many people have considered, and still consider, polygyny to be one of the main factors contributing to low fertility in Central Africa. This is an exaggerated, if not erroneous, view. It is true that available statistics indicate that wives in polygynous households are less fertile than are those in monogamous ones. This may be due, in part, to fewer coital performances per polygynous woman, to the older average age of polygynous husbands, and to a selective process conducive to a higher proportion of sterile women in polygynous households. However, when appropriate adjustment is made for the latter factor, the gap between monogamous and polygynous fertility rates is considerably reduced. Moreover, the depressing effect that the generally lower polygynous fertility exerts upon the overall fertility level may be largely offset by the effect that polygyny is likely to exercise on female nuptiality, i.e. earlier marriage and easier remarriage of widows and divorced women. Granted even that polygyny may play a more active role in the dissemination of venereal diseases, this fact does not suffice to make polygyny a major factor of infertility. Nor is there any significant correlation between the prevalence of polygyny and the birth rate by region.

Conjugal mobility is generally high in Africa, because of the frequent occurrence of both widowhood and divorce. This may impair fertility in two ways:

(a) by the loss of opportunity to conceive, consequent upon diminished sexual activity;
(b) by the dissemination of venereal disease through frequent change of spouses.

The effect of the former is probably offset partly by the high rate of remarriage and the prevalence of illegitimate births. The instability of marriages is likely to be more common among populations with high sterility, as among Africans barrenness is a major motive to divorce. The effect of the latter on fertility may be counterbalanced by gains in fecundity due to remarriage, to the extent that sterility can be considered as a married couple's problem.

It can be concluded that no major variability observed in the regional birth rates in Africa can in any way be attributed to matrimonial factors.

PRACTICES OF ABORTION AND CONTRACEPTION

Induced abortion was considered by some earlier demographers to be one of the main devices by which control of population growth had been achieved in primitive societies. Many still believe that low fertility in Africa is ascribable to either:

(a) induced abortions and resulting complications; or
(b) post-coital infusions used as prophylactic devices.

As for the first point, the real issue is not whether abortion is known to Africans but how extensive and efficient is its practice. The writer has accumulated in the Congo evidence that various tribes are acquainted with the use of abortion as well as with some contraceptive methods, and that they actually do resort to them, but only occasionally. Abortion may be employed to prevent the birth of a child conceived in adultery or by an unmarried girl where a strong ban on illegitimacy exists. A married woman may attempt abortion in response to maltreatment inflicted upon her by her husband or his family. Coitus interruptus, and even condoms among more sophisticated people, are reported to be used in order to avoid conception during the lactation period.

It also has been reported, for example, that Mongo girls, in order to escape maternity, which they are said not to appreciate when still young, resort to abortion or contraception. Such attitudes can indeed develop under specific conditions of social disorganization, as in urban centres among the so-called 'free women'. But, a comparison of the high illegitimate birth rate among the Mongo girls with the legitimate birth rate suggests that there is nothing general about the alleged attitudes. Africans are known to place high valuation upon children and great pressure for high fertility comes from the kinsfolk, while sterility is considered a disgrace.

No objective studies have ever been made to assess the efficiency of the abortion methods in use. However, one can presume that among a large variety of the devices reported to be used, many are magical; others may prove efficient, or even dangerous, entailing complications, such as temporary or permanent sterility, in individual cases. Complications resulting from abortion have been observed and described in various medical works.

Post-coital infusions as a prophylactic device are reported to have been observed among many populations exhibiting high sterility. It is believed that many conceptions have been prevented in this way. In one area in the Congo a special educational campaign against this particular contraceptive practice has been undertaken, apparently with some success, for the number of births seems to have increased since then.[9]

A population exposed to venereal disease may resort to the use of some types of infusions, either to prevent contamination or to alleviate the post-coital discomfort that women suffering from the disease may feel. Such practices may reduce the number of conceptions, especially in the case of subfecund women.

But these practices can hardly have any marked effect on fertility, unless they are used systematically. It is highly unlikely that this is the case since most women have neither the appropriate equipment for infusions nor the self-discipline to implement them properly and systematically.

DISEASES AND MALNUTRITION

In Africa, sanitation and diet are deficient in many respects. Malaria, leprosy in humid regions, inadequate sex hygiene, malnutrition, and the universal intestinal worms, are but a few characteristics of what may be generally termed 'tropical insalubrity'.

These deficiencies can be expected to exercise an adverse effect upon the reproductive process by impeding conception, through the delay of puberty, premature menopause, temporary sterility, and by impairing the normal development of the foetus. Therefore, it should not be surprising to find among African populations a somewhat higher incidence of miscarriages, stillbirths and maternity accidents. The few studies made on this account seem to substantiate this, but they do not yield sufficient evidence to suggest that these biological factors bear any substantial responsibility for infertility.

On the whole, those studies that have attempted to examine the relationship between fertility and particular biological factors have been found to be deceptive in their results. Thus, statistics do not clearly substantiate a rise in fertility in countries (Ceylon, Cyprus, Venezuela) where a nation-wide control of malaria has been successfully carried out.[10] It should not be concluded from this failure that paludism is completely irrelevant to fertility. What is more likely is the fact that the malarial effect is not significant enough to be discernible through statistical series which are subject to various contradictory influences.

The attempts to clarify the eventual incidence of leprosy on fertility are not very conclusive either, though Dr Radna[11] has found among the Mabudu (Congo) more sterile women who are leprous than sterile women who are not leprous. However, it might be noted that leprosy normally develops mostly at ages when the procreative capacities of women are beginning to decline.

Theories relating infertility in Central Africa to dietary conditions and to psycho-biological factors are legion. At one time, a commonly accepted theory was that particular tribes in Central Africa were experiencing some kind of a radical degeneration. It was also argued that contact with Europeans was likely to create such emotional conditions (psychological trauma) that reproduction was inhibited.[12] Changes in old dietary habits and the introduction of new food may, it was also said, prove harmful for the endocrinal and sexual functions. In particular, the paste made of manioc, which is now the basic dietary element in Central Africa, has been said to have a toxic effect on the sexual cells, as a result of its high acidity. The contribution that these theories make to the knowledge of the effects of biological factors on sterility are nugatory and are mentioned here only as a matter of information.

VENEREAL DISEASE

The purpose of this section is to examine the available statistical and clinical evidence supporting the hypothesis according to which venereal disease is a major cause of infertility in tropical Africa. The data used here refer mainly to the Congo.

Statistical Evidence

There are in the Congo two sources providing data on venereal diseases:

(a) hospitals and dispensaries, which are supposed to keep records on persons having been treated for a venereal disease;
(b) medical surveys, where the inhabitants were examined at their homes for particular diseases, including syphilis and gonorrhea.

Before independence (1960), nearly half the Congolese population were checked yearly in this way.

According to medical reports for 1956, there were 67,000 cases of syphilis and 175,000 cases of gonorrhea in a population of about 12,500,000 inhabitants. These figures stand no comparison whatsoever with the great extent of sterility observed in this country. Even in such districts as Equateur and Tshuapa, where sterility affects 35 to 45 per cent of all women, the medical survey shows a percentage of venereal infections amounting to respectively 5 and 7 per cent only, for the entire population subjected to medical survey (see Table 1). When calculated against adults of procreative age (15 to 45), to whom the check for venereal diseases was generally restricted, the percentage rises to approximately 16. It is true, some of the women who are recorded as sterile may have recovered in the meantime from a previous infection which caused sterility. On the other hand, not all infected persons necessarily become sterile.

Table 1

Indices on Fertility, Sterility and Venereal Diseases for the Province of Equateur[14]

District	Birth rate per 1,000	Sterility per 100 women 25–45 years of age	Syphilis(S)[1]	Gonorrhea(G)[1]	(S)+(G)
Equateur	33	39	29·4	38·3	67·7
Tshuapa	29	41	24·7	27·2	51·9
Mongala	43	25	7·5	24·9	32·4
Ubangi	46	18	4·3	15·7	20·0
Gemena (Territory)	56	7	3·1	4·3	7·4

1. Per 1,000 persons examined for all diseases, during the 1957 medical survey.

Underreporting of venereal disease is a common feature of morbidity statistics all over the world. There is more than one reason to expect the underreporting to be strong in a country like the Congo. Thus, hospital records evidently concern only persons who have been treated for infection. While city residents are by now generally aware of the danger of infection and normally seek treatment, this is not yet the case with village people; these, as a medical officer pointed out, seldom go to a doctor for acute gonorrhea, and eventually do so only much later when complications arise. On the other hand, considering the conditions under which medical surveys are conducted, the check is superficial and is confined mostly to adult persons; not all adult women are checked for these infections. The detection of chronic cases is rather difficult, even under the best technical conditions.

While inadequate as a measure of the absolute level of venereal disease, the medical survey data proves useful in revealing relative regional variations, for it might be assumed that underreporting is fairly even across the country. The most reliable set of data is the one concerning the new cases of syphilis revealed by the medical survey. It is probably easier to diagnose syphilis in its early stages than in its later ones, when it may often be confused with yaws, a non-venereal disease occurring frequently in tropical Africa. The data on syphilis are reported by province and for the two provinces with high sterility incidence, Equateur and Orientale, by districts.[13] This makes a total of 13 territorial units, including the Kwango, an area placed under the supervision of a special medical agency (FOREAMI).

The index of newly discovered cases of syphilis related to the birth rate yields a negative correlation coefficient of −0·82 for these 13 territorial units. This indicates a strong causal relationship between infertility and syphilis.

Though a certain association between the incidence of syphilis and that of gonorrhea is to be expected, it is not necessarily a close one. Moreover, syphilis is apparently less important than gonorrhea as a cause of sterility in the Congo. Therefore, additional useful evidence about the relationship between the gonorrhea and syphilis, on the one hand, and the birth and sterility rate on the other hand, is provided by Table 1 for the districts of Equateur Province. The medical data for this province are available in more detail and are probably more reliable than for any other province in the Congo. The contrast is particularly striking, both in terms of fertility and in terms of venereal incidences, between the low sterility territory of Gemena and the high sterility districts of Equateur and Tshuapa.

A significant correlation between, on the one hand, fertility rates and, on the other, the frequency of strictures (a late manifestation of gonorrhea) and gonorrhea, has been found by H. B. Griffith[15] in the districts of Uganda. The calculated correlation coefficient amounts respectively to $-0{\cdot}59$ and $-0{\cdot}64$. These findings, combined with some qualitative observations, 'strongly suggest', as the author puts it, 'that Uganda fertility is largely determined by gonorrhea.'[15]

Clinical Evidence

A more direct way of determining the cause of sterility would be an adequate clinical examination of a sample of sterile women. Little has been done so far in this respect, but one study of particular interest is the one conducted by Dr Allard,[16] in Befale Territory (Congo), an area of high sterility. There 578 childless women in reproductive ages, or about one third of the estimated number of sterile women in the Befale Territory, have been subjected to a complete clinical and gynaecological examination (vaginal smear, tubal insufflation, radioscopy, biopsy of womb, etc.).

The results revealed a large number of anomalies, many of which are generally regarded as classical complications of syphilis and especially of gonorrhea. For 348 women out of 578, various lesions in the area of genital organs became apparent under direct clinical examination. Further examination in depth disclosed different pathological conditions of the uterus and of tractus obstruction (182 cases), vaginal stricture (26) and inflammation of the genital tract (188). The examination of menstrual cycles disclosed 206 cases of irregular cycle, 396 of dysmenorrhea, 185 of hypermenorrhea, etc. As the survey had been primarily undertaken with the object of treating women for sterility, long-term or hopeless cases were excluded from the sample. (Sixty-three pregnancies are known to have occurred after treatment.) But the results that were obtained are sufficiently indicative of the frequency and variety of troubles occurring among the childless women examined.

Gonococcus is suspected to be the main cause of these troubles. Indeed the infection from gonococcus is believed to be frequent in the area of Befale. Thus, a check of adult men undertaken in the area revealed that 60 per cent of the men were infected (1955).

A similar study conducted by Dr Welche[17] in other areas of high sterility in the Congo, Kibombo and Kasongo, revealed various sequelae of genital diseases. About 75 per cent of individuals had been or were still contaminated, according to Dr Welche's estimates for these areas.

Although various complications traceable to gonorrhea have been revealed by clinical examination, the microscopic disclosure of Neisseria Gonorrhea is comparatively rare. Dr Allard, mentioned above, reports that the culture performed proved to be positive only in a quarter of 70 female cases. The difficulties of cultural demonstration of gonococci are stressed in many recent medical reports.[18] The possibilities of some not yet known types of genital diseases, or of the transmutation of the old species, should also be taken into consideration. Dr Welche, quoted above, observed that among some populations fertility is not conspicuously low while the venereal incidence seems to be high. This led him to raise the question of a differential sensitivity to gonorrhea. As to its origin, he queried the possibility of its being either a bacteriological problem, perhaps associated with some gonococcal mutation, or a histological phenomenon in the sensitivity of the membranes.[19]

SEXUAL PROMISCUITY

Whereas an infectious venereal disease may be transmitted from an outside source as a result of mere coincidence, the rapidity and extent of the spread of the infection is conditioned by the sexual behaviour of a community. The empirical basis for the hypothesis, according to which the cause of conspicuous infertility in Africa lies in venereal diseases, would be strengthened were there to be found a significant association between birth rates and some index of the degree of sexual mobility.

One way of providing some measurement of the degree of sexual freedom among unmarried females, is to compute the ratio of illegitimate fertility to legitimate fertility. In order to construct an index of illegitimacy (mainly among girls), the ratio of cumulated illegitimate to cumulated legitimate fertility rates up to 25 years of age has been used for the Congo. There are only few divorcees and widows under 25 years of age. For simplicity, the ratio of the general rates of illegitimate to legitimate fertility (15–44) has been used for the provinces. The main variability in the ratio of illegitimate to legitimate rates stems mainly from the differential sexual behaviour of girls in particular African populations. For girls, indeed, a quasi-complete sexual freedom among certain populations contrasts with the most severe repression of sexual intercourse among others. For divorcees and widows (except during the mourning period), sexual tolerance is quite common.

Table 2

Correlation Coefficients between Birth Rate and Index of Illegitimacy

The Congo* (24 districts)	−0·36
The Congo* (with the exception of the strongly deviating district of Luapula Moero)	−0·49
Léopoldville Province† (22 territorial units)	−0·80
Equateur Province† (26 territorial units)	−0·22
Oriental Province† (26 territorial units)	−0·62

* Ratio of cumulated illegitimate to cumulated legitimate fertility rates up to age 25 years.
† Ratio of the general rates of illegitimate to legitimate fertility (15–44 years).

Though some coefficients are low, on the whole they indicate a tendency associating the level of birth rate in a community with the degree of sexual freedom among girls.

The quantitative measurement of the sexual behaviour of married persons is a more delicate question. Nevertheless, some kind of approximation of marital tensions and conflicts can be provided by the court records of sentences for conjugal offences. In Africa, adultery is at the origin of many judicial affairs classified as 'conjugal offences'. The Congo is the only country for which relevant data could be obtained. As the efficiency of the judicial organization varies largely between districts, as well as probably the degree of under-registration of judicial cases in general, there is no sense in constructing an index of 'conjugal behaviour' on the basis of the ratio of the total number of recorded conjugal offences to the total population. It has been considered as more appropriate to calculate such an index by totalling all recorded conjugal offences against the total of recorded offences of all classes. The resulting proportion of 'conjugal offences', related to the birth rate yields a correlation coefficient of −0·78 for the whole of the Congo with its 24 districts, and −0·80 for the Province of Equateur for which data on 'conjugal sentences' are available by territory (26 units).

Table 3

Summary of Main Empirical Findings for the Congo, Translated into Correlation Coefficients

Birth rates and sterility rates (24 districts)	−0·89
Birth rates and newly observed syphilis index (13 areas)	−0·82
Birth rates and illegitimacy index (see definition above)	−0·36
Birth rates and illegitimacy index (without Luapala Moero)	−0·49
Birth rates and proportion of sentences for conjugal offences (see text for definition)	−0·78

The above findings are open to criticism on various points. Thus, it can be implied that there might be a portion of auto-correlation in the index of 'conjugal offences' related to the birth rate, since sterile couples are likely to resort more frequently to courts, for instance, for divorce. The divorce cases, however, form only a part of all affairs classified under the heading of 'conjugal offences'. It should also be noted in this connection that there is no correlation between the proportion of divorces and the birth rate by region for the Congo. Another objection may be addressed to the use for the purpose of correlation of the ratio of the illegitimate fertility rate to the legitimate rate versus the birth rate by region. Thus it could be implied that, where fertility is low, the rate of legitimate fertility will be relatively low as compared to the rate of illegitimate fertility, the former being depressed by the secondary sterility occurring at later ages. This would imply a certain amount of auto-correlation. But here again the significance of the argument should not be exaggerated. Indeed, it should be pointed out that this ratio for the Congo has been computed for females under the age of 25, eliminating to a large extent the possible effect of secondary sterility. Moreover, the factor that to a large extent determines the infertility level is the primary sterility and not the secondary one. According to certain estimates made by Welche, quoted in this paper, the former contributes 75 per cent of sterility against 25 per cent for the latter.

Notwithstanding these limitations, the evidence points definitely to the existence of a sequence of events one would logically expect to occur. The birth rate is low because of the high incidence of sterility; the latter is caused by venereal disease, the incidence of which varies with the degree of sexual promiscuity.

CONCLUSION

First, the sterility which has been observed in areas of low fertility is physiological and not voluntary. This view is strongly supported by the study of various cultural and biological factors related to fertility. Second, there are indications that the physiological sterility observed in low fertility areas is caused by venereal disease. Third, the empirical data are not yet sufficient to reveal *specifically* the kind of venereal infection to which the sterility observed can be ascribed, though the prevalence of gonorrhea is borne out by various medical testimonies. Further medical research is needed to determine exactly the nature of the venereal diseases involved. The medical nature of infertility in tropical Africa, and its social and demographic implications, require further research on an interdisciplinary basis.

Footnotes

1. KROTKI, K., *Estimating Vital Rates from Peculiar and Inadequate Age Distribution* (Sudanese Experience), Dissertation Abstracts, Univ. Microfilms, Ann Arbour.

1a. Last minute data received from Mr J. M. Callies indicate that infertility in the Cameroon is more serious than it was generally supposed.

2. ARDNER, E., *Divorce and Fertility, an African Study*, Oxford University Press.

3. See D. E. ROBERTS and R. E. S. TANNER, 'A Demographic Study in an Area of Low Fertility in North-East Tanganyika', *Population Studies*, Vol. XIII, No. 1, July 1959, pp. 61–80.

4. COALE-DEMENY, *Stable Population Model North* has been used for estimating the birth rate. An expectation of life of 35 to 45 years has been used by J. G. C. Blacker for his projection of population of Tanganyika.

5. RICHARDS, A. T. and REINING, P., 'Report of Fertility Surveys in Buganda and Buhaya', 1952, in F. LORIMER (ed.), *Culture and Human Fertility*, UNESCO, 1954, p. 403.

6. BLACKER, J. G. C., 'Population Growth and Differential Fertility in Zanzibar Protectorate', *Population Studies*, Vol. XV, No. 3, 1962.

7. CLAIRIN, R., Personal communication.

8. VAN DE WALLE, E., *Marriage in African Censuses and Inquiries* (unpublished), Princeton.

9. LODEWYCKX, CH., *La dénatalité Nkundo. Expérience Bunianga*, Cepsi No. 13, Elisabethville.

10. PAMPANA, E. J., 'Effect of Malaria Control on Birth and Death Rates', *World Population Conference* Rome, 1954.

11. DE RADNA, *L'état démographique de quelques populations des environs de Paca* (incomplete reference).

12. SHWERS, G. A., 'Les facteurs de la dénatalité au Congo Belge', *Recueil de Travaux de Sciences médicales au Congo Belge*, No. 3, Jan. 1945.
13. *Rapport Annuel de la Direction Générale des Services médicaux, Congo Belge, 1957*.
14. Medical data for Equateur Province (unpublished).
15. GRIFFITH, H. B., 'Gonorrhea and Fertility in Uganda', *The Eugenics Review*, July 1963.
16. ALLARD, R., 'Contribution gynécologique a l'étude de la stérilité chez les Mongo de Befale', *Ann. Soc. Belge Méd. Trop.*, 31, XIII, 1955, pp. 629–31.
17. VELGHE, A., 'Résumé de l'étude de la situation démographique des populations en territoires de Kibombo et de Kasongo. Des causes médicales de la dénatalité à Kibombo et de la dénatalité à Kasongo', *Rapport FBEI*, 1952.
18. See *Bulletin of the World Health Organization*, Vol. 24, No. 3 (Gonorrhea Treatment Problems), and No. 262 (WHO Expert Committee on Gonococcal Infections, 1963).
19. VELGHE, A., *ibid.*, p. 175.

The author is indebted to his colleague, Rev. T. L. Beauchamp, and to Mr T. Schevciw for their comments on the draft of this paper. The study published here has been supported by a grant received from the Canada Council.

21 The seasonality of vital events in selected cities of Ghana: an analysis of registration data relating to the period, 1956–1960

Jerzy Holzer
Institute of Statistics, University of Ghana, Ghana

Introduction[1]

This paper deals with the analysis of monthly data of births and deaths from selected cities of Ghana for the period 1956–60. The examples used in discussing main problems are Accra and Kumasi.[2] The vital data have been collected in registers by registrars in the areas in which the compulsory registration has been implemented.

Compulsory registration of births and deaths was introduced in 36 towns of Ghana by *Births, Deaths and Burials Ordinances* enacted during the period 1912–47. In the remainder of the period under consideration, compulsory registration was extended to one other township, Tema. Prior to 1912, death registration had been implemented in Accra as a result of the *Deaths and Burials Registration Ordinances* of 1888.

The 37 towns and townships, in which compulsory registration was enforced, had a population of 1,070,000 in 1960, i.e. 16 per cent of the total for Ghana.[3] However, it is necessary to stress that the population within the areas is not representative of the population of Ghana as a whole. A further problem is that the data are incomplete even in those areas where registration is compulsory. However, it is probable that the registered births represent more than 70–80 per cent of the total births in particular towns.

It is difficult to compute directly the level of under-registration, but an estimate can be made. These calculations are presented in Table 1, which shows the registered number of births of the period 1958–60 and the enumerated number of children aged 0 (under one year) at the 1960 census. Table 1 includes only those towns in which compulsory registration of vital events had been implemented and where the total number of enumerated children below one year of age was more than 1,000 at the 1960 census.

It is necessary to stress that some of the births registered in a given calendar year may have occurred in a previous calendar year, while those occurring during the year under consideration may not have been registered until a subsequent year. But these differences do not affect to any great extent the calculations presented in Table 1. Similarly, the enumeration in urban areas of infants born outside urban areas will have but a slight effect on the results.

An estimate was made of the number of children born during the previous 12 months. The census population was multiplied by a reverse survival ratio calculated on the assumption that the Accra and Kumasi infant mortality rate was 100 per 1,000 live-births and that the infant mortality rate of the remaining cities was 150. For any particular town, completeness of registration is thus measured by dividing registered births in 1960 by the births estimated to have occurred during the 12 months prior to the 1960 census.

For all seven cities, under-registration is at the level of 22 per cent, assuming that the census enumeration of children aged 0 was accurate and that the chosen infant mortality rates were correct. The percentages of under-registration differ from town

Table 1

Registered and Estimated Births in Selected Ghanaian Cities, about 1960

Cities	Births registered during the year			Census 1960. Children below one year	Estimated number of children born during 12 months prior to the 1960 census	$\frac{R_B}{E_B} \times 100$
	1958	1959	1960			$(7)=\frac{(4)}{(6)}\times 100$
1	2	3	4	5	6	7
Accra	10,635	11,503	11,491	12,934	14,200	81
Cape Coast	1,288	1,491	1,543	1,476	1,700	91
Koforidua	1,112	1,180	1,093	1,350	1,600	68
Kumasi	5,231	5,612	5,780	7,607	8,400	69
Sekondi	1,077	1,244	1,302	1,158	1,300	100
Takoradi	1,504	1,820	1,794	1,613	1,900	94
Winneba	807	834	769	1,015	1,200	81
Total	—	23,684	23,772	—	30,300	78

Table 2

Crude Vital Rates in 1960 According to Census and Registration Data

Cities	Crude birth rates according to		Total death rates[3]	Infant death rates according to	
	Census data[1]	Registration data[2]		Census data[4]	Registration data[5]
	per 1,000 persons			per 1,000 live-births	
Accra	42	34	12	78	96
Cape Coast	41	37	15	59	65
Koforidua	46	31	14	61	90
Kumasi	47	32	13	63	92
Sekondi	38	38	11	48	48
Takoradi	46	44	11	72	76
Winneba	47	30	27	168	263

1. Estimated number of children born during the 12 months prior to the 1960 census per 1,000 of the population then enumerated.
2. Registered number of births in 1960 per 1,000 of the population enumerated at the 1960 census.
3. Registered number of deaths in 1960 per 1,000 of the population enumerated at the 1960 census.

Registered number of infant deaths in 1960:

4. Divided by the number of children estimated to have been born in the 12 months prior to the 1960 census;
5. Per 1,000 registered live-births (1960).

to town. The lowest, 68 per cent, is in Koforidua, and the highest, 100 per cent in Sekondi. The high percentage for Sekondi might have resulted from incorrect reporting of the normal place of residence of mothers of infants born at the Sekondi Hospital. However, the birth rates estimated from census data are lower than expected and thus a probable explanation for this discrepancy is that census enumeration of age 0 was defective.

There are no methods by which to measure the completeness of death registration. Using the available census and registration data, it is possible, however, to compute two types of crude birth and death rates. The results of this computation have been presented in Table 2. The explanation of the method used is given below the table.

Inspection of the death rates shown in Table 2 suggests that death registration is less complete than birth registration. For example, an infant death rate of 48 per 1,000 live-births for Sekondi is obviously far too low.

It is necessary to stress that the birth and death rates presented in this table are not accurate. Moreover, as yet, there are insufficient data to calculate correct vital rates.

Hypothesis

It is hypothesised that the under-registration of vital events is spread randomly throughout the calendar year; i.e. that any fluctuations during any calendar year in the numbers of births and deaths occurring in any city do not result from seasonal differentials in the completeness of vital registration. This can be asserted with some degree of confidence because:

(a) the universe from which the registered births and deaths, and thus any unregistered births and deaths, have been drawn is large;

(b) the proportionately low level of under-registration of births;

(c) the absence of any reason for accepting the view that information such as sex and month of occurrence of a birth or death is incorrectly reported during registration.

We intend to testify the hypothesis relating to the randomness of the basic data by taking into consideration the seasonality of births and deaths according to sex. If the distribution of births and deaths for each sex is similar it is fair to assume that they were drawn randomly from their respective universes.

Source of Data and Method Used to Collect Data

The birth and death registration process occurs as follows:

> One line in the register contains the information about one event (birth or death). Events are noted by order of reporting rather than by order of occurrence.

Thus, one can find events which had happened at different periods registered within the span of one day on the same page.

The register of births includes the following information: name in full, sex, mother's maiden name, mother's nationality, date of birth, and date of registration. Unfortunately there are no data on the mother's age.

The register of deaths includes the following information on the deceased: name in full, age, sex, nationality and tribe, address in full, occupation, religion, place of residence at time of death, period of continuous residence in the registration area, cause of death, duration of illness, date of registration, place of burial.

When studying the seasonality of births and deaths, one must choose events according to month and year of birth or death instead of month or year of registration. Because of certain practical considerations, the information could not be placed on punch-cards, and thus it has been possible to correlate only two variables, i.e. sex of

Table 3

Live-Births Occurring in 1956 by Year of Registration

Year of registration	Month of birth												Total	Percentages
	Jan.	Feb.	Mar.	Apr.	May	June	July	Aug.	Sep.	Oct.	Nov.	Dec.		
ACCRA														
1958–60	1	1	2	2	—	1	3	2	—	2	—	1	15	0·1
1957	2	2	1	6	4	6	9	9	16	26	37	70	188	2·1
1956	741	700	708	729	789	765	780	778	719	797	741	675	8,920	97·8
Total	744	703	711	735	793	772	792	789	735	825	778	746	9,123	100·0
KUMASI														
1958–60	5	6	5	2	8	4	3	5	4	1	1	—	44	1·1
1957	4	7	5	8	7	14	18	22	29	53	96	337	600	15·2
1956	248	236	294	277	310	289	309	319	346	333	290	60	3,311	83·7
Total	257	249	304	287	325	307	330	346	379	387	387	397	3,955	100·0

the newly-born child or deceased and the month of occurrence of these vital events.

The frequency distribution of births and stillbirths was made according to sex and calendar months. Deaths were divided into two groups, i.e. of infants aged less than one year, and of persons aged one year and over. The frequency distributions of both groups of deaths were tabulated according to the sex of deceased persons and the calendar month of death.

The period of observation covers five years from 1956 to 1960. For both sexes more than 98 per cent of births were registered either within the calendar year of occurrence or in that following the year during which the birth had occurred. Table 3 shows, as an example, the distribution of births in 1956 in Accra and Kumasi according to month of occurrence of births and date of registration.

Method Used to Calculate Seasonal Indices

The basic data are the vital events falling within the period 1956–60, i.e. they cover 60 separate months. All months were assumed to span exactly 30 days. Thus, months such as December or February which were of a different length were multiplied by the appropriate coefficient so that they carried a weight of one, which is the weight of a 30-day month such as November.[4] The adjusted basic data are referred to here as x_i.

The first step in the analysis of a time series is to isolate the trend. The method of least squares was used to find the equation of an appropriate trend line. The equation of the straight line is written:

$$y_i = a+b.t_i \qquad \ldots\ldots(1)$$

where

$$a = \frac{\sum x_i}{n} \qquad \ldots\ldots(2)$$

$$b = \frac{\sum x_i.t}{t\sum^2} \qquad \ldots\ldots(3)$$

and

$$\sum t_i = 0 \qquad \ldots\ldots(4)$$

Therefore, *a* expresses the average monthly number of occurrences of a given type of vital event during the period 1956–60; and *b* represents the average monthly increase or decrease in the number of these occurrences during the same period.

The next step was to determine the relationship (termed here $\bar{x}_i'$) between the adjusted monthly data (x_i) and the monthly trend value, for which purpose the following formula was employed:

$$x_i' = \frac{x_i}{y = a+b.t_i} \qquad \ldots\ldots(5$$

The percentages show monthly fluctuations.

The ratio between the adjusted monthly data and the smoothed (trend) values varies considerably from year to year, as a result of different random and non-random factors. Therefore, we had to find the arithmetic mean ($\bar{x}_i$) of the ratios for any particular month during this quinquennium in order to eliminate these fluctuations and thus to isolate the purely seasonal component.

Finally, we have to find the index (S_i) for any particular month. This is done by adjusting $\bar{x}_i$ for biases introduced during the computation process.

Thus,

$$S_i = \frac{\bar{x}_i.100}{\frac{1}{12}\sum_{i=1}^{12}\bar{x}_i} = \frac{\bar{x}_i.1{,}200}{\sum_{i=1}^{12}\bar{x}_i} \qquad \ldots\ldots(6)$$

Discussion of the Seasonality of Births

The basic data for each month are those of the month of occurrence, not of the month of registration. The data for the various cities will not be combined, as some differences can be expected in seasonal fluctuations of vital events in Accra and Kumasi. Here it is assumed that the Accra indices represent the seasonality of cities of coastal areas and Kumasi's indices represent the seasonality of cities of inland areas.

The differences in temperature, rainfall and number of rainy days are shown in Table 4.

Table 4

Temperature, Rainfall and Number of Rainy Days

Month	Temperature[1]		Rainfall[2]		Number of rainy days	
	Accra	Kumasi	Accra	Kumasi	Accra	Kumasi
January	81·0	77·1	0·59	0·67	2	2
February	81·7	79·7	1·33	2·31	2	5
March	82·2	80·5	2·27	5·38	5	10
April	82·1	80·1	3·40	5·65	6	10
May	80·7	79·4	5·46	7·15	10	13
June	78·3	77·6	7·10	9·21	13	17
July	76·1	75·5	1·80	4·96	7	13
August	75·6	74·3	0·58	2·92	5	11
September	77·3	76·3	1·40	6·95	7	17
October	78·7	77·7	2·63	7·94	8	28
November	80·3	78·4	1·38	3·86	4	11
December	81·2	77·7	0·88	1·21	2	3

1. Average in degrees Fahrenheit.
2. Monthly mean in indices.

Source: E. BOATENG, *A Geography of Ghana*, Cambridge University Press, Cambridge, 1960, pp. 29 and 34.

It is possible to distinguish the following seasonal rainfall régime of Accra and Kumasi.[5]

	Accra	Kumasi
Rainy season	March–June and September–November	March–June and September–November
Maxima	May, June October	June October
Dry season	December–February	December–February
Maximum	January	January

The highest number of births occurs in Accra during the period April–July and May is the peak month. The births of the period April–July are conceived, it might be noted, during the end of the rainy-season.

The data for May, to take an example, can be explained as follows. If there were only seasonal variations, the number of births in May would be 66 per cent higher than the number which would be expected if changes in the number of births had resulted purely from the trend of growth.

In Kumasi the season with the highest number of births is one month earlier (March–May), April being the peak month. If there were only seasonal fluctuations, the number of births in April would be 94 per cent higher than the number that would be expected from the trend of growth. The period with the highest number of births is much shorter in Kumasi than in Accra. Moreover, Kumasi's maximum is much sharper than that of Accra, and in addition Kumasi has a secondary maximum in October which is much lower than that recorded for April.

The following table summarizes seasonal fluctuations in births for Accra and Kumasi.

	Accra	Kumasi
Maxima	March–July	March–May and September–November
Month with highest number of births	May	April and October
Minima	August–February	January–August and December–February
Month with lowest number of births	December	June and January

It is necessary to stress that there are only slight sex differentials in the seasonality of births. In Accra the highest number of births occurred in April for males and in May for females. But in Kumasi, April is the month with the highest number of births, regardless of sex. Moreover, the secondary maximum of births, occurring in September, is more important for females than for males in both Accra and Kumasi. The range of values is almost the same for both cities and this is true for both sexes.

The values of the upper and lower extremes of the indices of seasonal births are presented in the following table.

Town	Male and female	Male	Female
Accra	$93 < S_i < 107$	$90 < S_i < 109$	$93 < S_i < 111$
Kumasi	$95 < S_i < 109$	$94 < S_i < 109$	$92 < S_i < 111$

Discussion of Seasonality of Total Deaths

In Accra, mortality is higher in the first half of the year than in the second half. The greatest mortality occurs in Accra during the period January–July, while April is the month with the highest number of deaths.

Assuming that there were only seasonal fluctuations, the total number of deaths would be 13 per cent higher in April than would be expected if changes in the number of deaths had resulted purely from the trend of growth. Monthly differences in the level of mortality are not significant during the first half of the year, except in January, when mortality is markedly low.

In Kumasi high mortality occurs during the first quarter of the year only. The greatest number of deaths is in January, the mid-point of the dry season. Assuming seasonal fluctuations only, the total number of deaths is 23 per cent higher than would be expected from the trend of growth. In Kumasi, in the latter half of the year, higher levels are reached in three separate months, May, October and December, but these levels are lower than expected from the trend of growth.

The values of the upper and lower extremes of the seasonal deaths' indices are presented in the following table:

	Accra	Kumasi
Maxima	January–July	December–May
Month with highest number of deaths	April	January
Minima	August–December	June–November
Month with lowest number of deaths	October	August

The monthly numbers of registered deaths are relatively lower than the numbers of births. The number of deaths for each sex fluctuates around the level of 100 per month. In spite of this, there is a similar distribution of deaths by sex for both Accra and Kumasi which confirms the hypothesis, stated earlier, about the random character of the data.

The extreme values of the seasonal indices of total deaths extend over a wider range than do the extremes for births. However, differences between the ranges are not very significant. The extreme values of the seasonal indices for total deaths are presented in the following table.

Town	Male and female	Male	Female
Accra	$80 < S_i < 112$	$76 < S_i < 116$	$75 < S_i < 119$
Kumasi	$86 < S_i < 123$	$83 < S_i < 121$	$88 < S_i < 125$

Discussion of the Seasonality of Infant Deaths

The distribution of the indices of seasonality of the deaths of infants (i.e. children aged less than one year) differs from that of total deaths, but the months for which the extreme values occur are the same. Moreover, the seasonality of infant mortality seems to follow different patterns in Accra and Kumasi. It is difficult to make a categorical statement because of the low numbers of registered infant deaths. The number of infant deaths registered each month varies in Accra from 16 to 66 for each sex, and in Kumasi from 4 to 28.

In Accra, high infant mortality occurs during the period January–June while the highest number of infant deaths occurs in April. Now, May is the month with the highest number of births. Moreover, mortality reaches the highest level during early infancy. Obviously, therefore, there is a close correlation between the period of high births and the period of high infant mortality. If there were only seasonal fluctuations, the number of infant deaths in April would be 32 per cent higher than the number which would be expected from the trend of growth. The lowest number of infant deaths occurs in October, which is also the period with the lowest number of births in any one year.

Infant mortality does not display such clear patterns in Kumasi, and the Kumasi seasonal indices differ significantly from those of Accra. However, numbers are so small that further discussion would be of limited value. The pattern of seasonality of infant deaths in Accra can be summarized as follows.

Maximum	January–June
Month with highest number of infant deaths	April
Minimum	July–December
Month with lowest number of infant deaths	October

Sex patterns of seasonality of infant deaths do not vary significantly in Accra. This observation further supports the hypothesis that inaccuracies are randomly distributed.

The table below shows the extreme values for the seasonal indices of infant deaths.

Town	Male and female	Male	Female
Accra	$11 < S_i < 132$	$62 < S_i < 135$	$75 < S_i < 127$
Kumasi	$79 < S_i < 115$	$77 < S_i < 129$	$59 < S_i < 133$

Conclusions

A close analysis of the data enables us to reject the hypothesis that registration, *per se*, has been determined by non-random factors. However, the number of infant deaths occurring in Kumasi was so small that in this one case it has proved impossible to reject the hypothesis with any degree of confidence.

During the year there are two periods with high numbers of births. The highest number occurs in April, May and June while a secondary, but lower, maximum is reached in September, October and November.

The pattern of seasonality of deaths in Kumasi differs significantly from that of Accra. The highest level of mortality occurs during January–July in Accra but in December–May in Kumasi.[6]

There is a close correlation between the period of high infant mortality and a high number of births. Thus high infant mortality occurs in Accra during the period January–June.

Accepting the hypothesis that the mode of collection of data was random, one can estimate a sex-ratio for births and deaths (except for deaths in Kumasi).

For Accra the estimated sex-ratio of births is 102·5 and that for Kumasi is 103·5. By contrast the sex-ratio of births estimated from 1960 census data is 100·7 for Accra and that for Kumasi 103·6. Thus, the sex-ratio obtained for Accra may throw further light on deficient age-reporting during the 1960 census.

For Accra the estimated sex-ratio of death is 121·8, for infant deaths in Accra the estimated sex ratio is 113·1.

Footnotes

1. The paper presents preliminary results of the research in the field of demography which has been conducted in the Institute of Statistics, University of Ghana. The full results of the investigation was published by the Institute of Statistics in 1966.

The author would like to acknowledge the interest and help he received, in the collection of basic data from the Registrar-General's Office in Accra. He is indebted to Dr D. I. Pool for his valuable comments. Acknowledgements are also due to the Institute's Research Assistant, Mr A. A. Amartey, who was responsible for the collection and compilation of data and for necessary computations.

2. The paper presents preliminary results of the investigation, therefore some numbers may be changed.
3. *1961 Statistical Yearbook*, Central Bureau of Statistics, Accra, p. 19.
4. The adjustment has important consequences for the computation of the seasonality of vital events. The method used here is the same as that used by the author to find seasonality of vital events in Poland. *Podstawy analizy demograficznej* (The Fundamentals of Demographic Analysis), PWE, Warszawa, 1963, pp. 51–54, 210–16, 277–84.
5. Prof. E. A. Boateng states 'The only significant division of the year here (in Ghana) is into rainy seasons and dry seasons. It is pointless to use the terms winter, spring, summer and autumn in connection with the climate of Ghana,' *A Geography of Ghana*, Cambridge University Press, 1960, p. 37.
6. It is worth pointing out that the seasonal fluctuations of births and deaths are pronounced in Ghana just as in Poland. However, Dr Karol J. Krotki stated for Pakistan . . . 'that births have more pronounced seasonal movements than deaths' ('Seasonality of Vital Events in East and West Pakistan', reprinted from *Indian Population Bulletin*, p. 9).

22 Estimating fertility levels in Ghana

Dov Friedlander
Hebrew University, Jerusalem

Introduction

During 1961 an experimental registration of vital statistics in three small towns in Ghana was undertaken. The experimental registrations were carried out for a period of six months and were followed by sample surveys designed to collect both demographic and sociological data. (For various reasons two additional towns were surveyed where no vital registration had been carried out, one of which was the important town, Sekondi-Takoradi.)

This paper deals with the relative effectiveness of different methods of estimating fertility in Ghana. Fertility estimates have been obtained by five different methods of which four are *direct* methods using the data collected in the registrations and surveys. The fifth is an *indirect* method based on stable population theory. For this, the age distribution of the Ghanaian population as recorded in the 1960 census was utilized.

The experimental vital registrations were carried out by local Health Officers, while the survey interviewing was done by students of the University of Ghana. The main characteristics of the places covered are given in Table 1. The towns surveyed were chosen from different regions of southern Ghana, but they were not selected as being representative of these regions.

Table 1

The Main Characteristics of the Communities Covered by the Study

Town	Location or tribal area	Total population at the 1960 census	Number of persons selected in original sample survey	Number of persons actually interviewed	Percentage response	Whether vital statistics registration carried out
Anomabo	Coastal Fante	5,423	3,618	2,555	71	Yes
Tsito	Volta-Ewe	2,800	2,800	2,355	84	No
Mpraeso[1]	Kwahu-Akan	6,918	3,459	2,346	68	Yes
Larteh	Akwapim Ridge	6,381	3,190	2,602	82	Yes
Sekondi-Takoradi	Coastal Urban	123,313	17,274	9,359	54	No

1. Including Atibie

Fertility Estimates by Direct Methods[1]

THE QUESTIONNAIRES

The vital registration questionnaires contained only a very small number of questions. The main reason for this was to enable the registrars to achieve as full a coverage as possible rather than to attempt to collect detailed and elaborate information on each case. In the surveys, two different questionnaires were employed. The first was a household form on which was recorded information about the house, all members of the household and about all births and deaths that had occurred in the household during the previous 12 months. The second was a form to be completed in respect of each female aged 14 and above, on which details were recorded about marital and child-bearing history. From these two questionnaires it was possible to obtain several sets of data on the fertility of the communities studied.

FERTILITY LEVELS AND COMPARISON OF METHODS (DIRECT METHODS)

Fertility estimates can be obtained from this study in several ways:

(a) From vital registration records. (These included, among other details, the age of the mother.)

(b) From the surveys:

(i) On the Household Form each head was asked to give details about all the births that had occurred in the household during the previous 12 months. (These included the ages of the mothers.)

(ii) On the Female Form each woman was asked whether or not she had given birth to a child in the previous 12 months.

(iii) The last set of estimates is also derived from the Female Form. Each woman was asked to list all the children she had ever borne, stating ages of the living children, ages at death and year of death of deceased children. By subtracting 'present' age of children (alive or dead) from the age of their mothers, a new variable was obtained—age of mother at time of birth of each of her children.

The crude birth rates calculated from these data are shown in Table 2. These cannot be used to compare fertility levels *between* communities, since the latter differ substantially in their age and sex structure.

Table 2

Comparison of Crude Birth Rates as Obtained from Different Kinds of Estimates

	Crude birth rates[1] obtained from			
Place	Vital registration records	Survey: Births in households in 'last 12 months'	Survey: whether or not women had a confinement 'in last 12 months'	Survey: recording women's child bearing history
Anomabo	46	56	59	52
Tsito	X	46	52	43
Mpraeso	56	54	50	53
Larteh	41	40	36	36
All rural towns	48	49	50	46
Sekondi-Takoradi	X	48	52	51

1. Strictly speaking, the different types of rates shown here do not refer precisely to the same period. In particular those of column 5 are based on the fertility experienced by women in the quinquennium previous to the survey.
X No registration.

The purpose here is to show the general fertility level and to demonstrate the extent of agreement in the various birth rates. This agreement appears to be quite reasonable, except with Anomabo. Indeed, the combined rates for all four rural towns are in very close agreement, as are those for Sekondi-Takoradi. Roughly speaking, the crude birth rate is just under 50 per 1,000 population for the above towns, which seems very high even by Afro-Asian standards.

It was hoped that the 'registration' fertility rates, the data for which were collected under supervision, by fairly reliable registrars, would provide the best estimates in the sense that under-registration would be kept to a minimum. On the other hand, it was expected that the survey results would be subject to varying degrees of under-estimation due to such factors as memory failure on the part of respondents, and the reluctance of mothers to report deceased children, to mention only the most obvious. In fact, as the results show, there is no definite pattern of difference between the four different types of rates.

Age specific fertility rates calculated from the four different sets of data, for all rural towns and for Sekondi-Takoradi are shown in Table 3. As in the case of the crude birth rates of Table 2, there is no systematic pattern of difference between the rates of the various sources. It had been hoped, when planning this study, to get from the different sets of age specific fertility rates some indication as to which of the methods used would be more efficient under particular circumstances, but the results do not give such indications. This is compensated for by the consistency in the age specific fertility rates between the various methods of data collection. In fact, the only age group where large discrepancies exist is in the 45–49 years' group.

Table 3

Comparison of Age Specific Fertility Rates as Obtained from Different Kinds of Estimates

Age of mother	ALL RURAL TOWNS				SEKONDI-TAKORADI		
	Age specific fertility rates obtained from:				Age specific fertility rates obtained from:		
	Vital registration records	Survey: births in households in 'last 12 months'	Survey: whether or not women had a confinement in 'last 12 months'	Survey: recording women's child-bearing history	Survey: Births in households in 'last 12 months'	Survey: whether or not women had a confinement in 'last 12 months'	Survey: recording women's child-bearing history
15–19	164	168	155	160	86	87	109
20–24	350	311	322	329	317	324	384
25–29	298	313	283	249	248	262	274
30–34	230	245	240	227	272	238	249
35–39	179	203	195	184	165	143	162
40–44	92	112	127	117	107	115	86
45–49	33	40	93	40	39	89	48
GRR	3·3	3·4	3·4	3·2	3·0	3·1	3·1

In conclusion, as far as can be judged from our experience, it cannot be claimed that any particular method used to collect fertility gave better results in any sense.

The registration data were certainly the most expensive to obtain and required rather elaborate arrangements. If we had wished to go beyond the establishment of fertility differentials, as we did with some of the survey data, it would have been necessary to carry out the registration for a much longer period in order to secure an adequate number of cases. Thus it seems that only the experience in organization, and the educational value of introducing temporarily an experimental registration system in a developing country, may justify the efforts involved in such an undertaking. But if the aim is to have a single study on fertility levels and differentials, one could probably obtain equally good results, involving lower costs, by a survey.

As far as the different fertility questions of the survey are concerned, there is, according to our experience, very little to choose between the three. However, we feel that the fertility data derived from women's child-bearing history may serve a useful purpose. These data may make possible an examination of fertility trends in the previous 30–40 years (if such examination is at all relevant in high fertility communities), provided the data are reasonably accurate. Perhaps even more important, it is possible, from such data, to estimate child mortality rates.

On the other hand there is no doubt that the gathering of details about all the children born to a woman, whether alive or dead at the time of interview, particularly for older women (where there might be ten or more such children), is not easy. This task requires reliable and intelligent interviewers, more time per interview, and more willingness to co-operate on the part of the respondents. It seems to us that, in cases where individual women are being interviewed, it would be advisable both to record details about the child-bearing history of each woman and in addition to ask her specifically whether or not she has had a confinement in the previous 12 months.

Estimating the Fertility Level for Ghana by an Indirect Method

A fifth estimate of the fertility level in Ghana was obtained by application of Stable Population Theory. It is based on the fact that the age structure of a stable population is, in practice, affected mainly by its fertility level and only slightly by its mortality. Thus, a hypothetical stable age distribution was estimated such that it was 'as close as possible' to the Ghanaian age structure as recorded in the 1960 census, assuming an appropriate mortality level. From this a crude birth rate of 45 per 1,000 was obtained, which is fairly close both to the estimates shown in Table 2 and to the estimate given in the UN Demographic Yearbook 1963.[2]

Footnotes

1. From the registration and surveys. This section of the paper is based on part of an unpublished manuscript by D. FRIEDLANDER and R. T. SMITH, *The Demographic Characteristics of a few Ghanaian Communities*.

2. For technical reasons, the details of this technique cannot appear in the present volume. A manuscript describing the technical details can be obtained by application to the author.

23 Some aspects of fertility studies in Ghana

S. K. Gaisie

Sociology Department, University of Ghana, Ghana

Sources of Data and Fertility Indices

A survey of original and largely unverifiable material, from the past 73 years, namely population census[1] and vital statistics, shows the value and validity of the data at the disposal of the student of Ghanaian demography. Both the decennial census returns and the vital statistics[2] collected so far are so defective that one has little confidence in their innate reliability when all the possible adjustments and refinements have been made. A full appraisal of the census returns and vital statistics is beyond the scope of this paper and the reader may refer to the following: R. R. KUCZYNSKI (1948), S. K. GAISIE (1964), *Ghana Census*, Vol. V (1965).

The birth statistics which have been collected from the registration areas are too defective to be of any good use. The 1931 Chief Census Officer stated in his report: 'Registration of Births and Deaths is in force in 30 populous centres. Figures obtained from them however cannot be considered as strictly accurate, or applicable to the country generally. Pregnant women tend to return to their native village for childbirth in order to obtain the assistance of their mother, family, native doctor, ancestors and the tribal deity' (Cardinall, 1931). In 1938 it was reported that 'the high [crude birth] rates recorded for Mampong (98·3) and Somanya (103·4) call for comments. Both these places are situated on busy trade routes, and a large percentage of the total numbers of births registered in each were births voluntarily registered from the surrounding rural areas.' (*Report of Principal Registrar*, 1938, p. 3.)

Apart from the fact that the vital registration system is incomplete and that people are not used to the system, the registration officials rarely enforce the legal provisions relating to registration. In his 1925/26 report the Principal Registrar stated: '. . . in the case of birth rates in particular, little reliance can be placed on statistics received from several areas where the legal provisions relating to birth registration are very inadequately enforced.' (*Report on Births and Deaths, 1925/26.*) With regard to the nature and the quality of the existing birth statistics in Ghana, Kuczynski had this to say (1948):

> 'In view of the uncertainty of the population figures and the peculiar, urban character of the registration areas it is very difficult rightly to appraise the returns. It should be noted, however, that while the official birth-rate fluctuated in 1931–38 between 31·5 and 34·7 it rose to 36·2 in 1939 and to 38·1 in 1940. This seems to indicate that registration improved considerably in those two years. But in 1941–43 the numbers of births registered were again considerably lower than in 1940. As there is no reason to assume that birth registration was complete in 1940, many births may have remained unregistered prior to 1939 and in 1941–43.'

In view of the deficiency and unreliability of the available data on fertility, it might appear, at first sight, that the difficulty of measuring the fertility of populations of developing countries would arise mainly from the inadequacy of birth registration or census returns. This, however, is not the real source of difficulty; it is perfectly possible to study the fertility of a population with no system of birth registration by means of special inquiries or surveys, while the fertility of a population not covered by censuses may be studied on the basis of well-kept civil registers. As a result of non-existent or incomplete registration systems in the developing countries, most of the fertility studies are based on census or special surveys. This method of research can be adapted to the study of trends; a type of analysis most suitable for statistically underdeveloped countries where for the time being long-term trends are of greater importance than short-term trends. It is not surprising, therefore, that all the fertility studies conducted so far are based on special surveys or census.

With regard to the type of data we are dealing with, a great deal of care must be exercised in the selection of the indices to be employed in the evaluation of the fertility data which have been collected by means of sampling techniques. In order to measure the rate at which populations are reproducing themselves, demographers rely for most part on two basic indices, namely the birth rate and the fertility ratio. In the light of available information on fertility, there is little to be gained by an attempt to use any other conventional indices to gauge the fertility of the populations of developing countries. Methods and demographic models are therefore being employed in the analysis of data on vital events in developing countries. Some of these have been generally discussed by Brass (1965).

In its simplest and crudest form the birth rate is merely the ratio between the number of births that have occurred in a particular year and the number of persons in the population. Several requirements must be met before the birth rate can be used with any degree of confidence. Complete and accurate birth registration is one of these, and this is not available in Ghana.

Thus, our field of choice is limited in the sense that the types of demographic measures to be employed are dictated by the type of data available for analysis. It is quite possible to employ certain conventional measures in a modified form, but the extent of modification and the suitability of such measures may be determined by the nature and the quality of the data at the disposal of the research worker. The mean number of children per woman, completed family size and child–woman ratio are the commonly used indices for the measurement of fertility in developing countries.

Despite the fact that the relevant data required for the computation of crude birth rate are not available, some estimates have been prepared by means of indirect methods. The application of Puerto Rican age specific fertility rates (1947–51) to Ghanaian women aged 15–49 in the 1948 fertility sample survey yielded a crude birth rate of 49 per 1,000 (Gaisie, 1962). This figure is very close to the one (i.e. 52 per 1,000) which was computed by the United Nations for the period 1945–49. (The UN estimate was based on 1948 census results—UN *Demographic Year Book, 1963*.) The crude birth rates of 51 and 50 for 1950–54 and 1955–59 respectively were the results obtained by the application of 'reverse-survival' method to 10 per cent sample tabulation of the 1960 population census results (UN 1963). A crude birth rate of the order of more than 40 per 1,000 persons is indicative of high fertility. In 1931 a questionnaire was circulated to all medical officers and they were asked to obtain the following information from each of a hundred 'old women', i.e. those who had passed their menopause:

(a) The number of still-born;
(b) The number born alive;
(c) The number who died before walking;
(d) The number who died before puberty.

The survey provided information on the fertility of women who had passed their menopause, but it failed to give information on current fertility (i.e. fertility of women in the child-bearing ages). Secondly, the sample cannot be regarded as representative of the whole country because the 'old women' were taken haphazardly and barren women were excluded (Cardinall, 1931).

In 1948 a fertility sample survey of women aged 15 years and over was conducted as part of that year's census-taking. The information sought covered age in years, number of children ever born, and number of children alive at the time of the census. It was suggested by the Census Commissioner that very little information was obtained from younger women, especially if unmarried and without children. Such omissions tended to underestimate the mean number of children for the younger women. The figures for the older women were not regarded, however, as more reliable and free from errors (Gold Coast Census 1948). In the 1931 survey the average number of children per woman was computed to be 5·8 (for the country), as compared with 6·5 for the 1948 survey. Fortes recorded 6·6 for Agogo (Lorimer, 1954) and a survey in Koforidua yielded 6·8 children per woman (Kuczynski, 1948). Average number of children per woman were computed to be 6·15 and 5·60 for rural and urban populations respectively (Gaisie, 1964).

The average number of children between 6 and 7 years, per woman living through the child-bearing period, provides the most reliable index of the general level of fertility among women in Ghana during recent decades. Figures in this vicinity have been computed for other areas in Ghana (see Table 1).

Table 1

Children ever born per Woman at Specified Ages: Samples of Ghana Population

Ages of women	15–19	20–24	25–29	30–34	35–39	40–44	45–49	50+
Sample (Rural) [1]	0·61	1·61	2·57	3·57	4·69	5·59	5·88	6·15
Ghana (Total) [2]	0·59	1·59	2·60	3·70	4·68	5·36	6·14	6·56
Ashanti [2]	0·54	1·53	2·83	3·89	5·00	5·69	6·61	7·37
Colony [2]	0·55	1·61	2·56	3·65	4·52	5·38	5·95	6·52
Northern Territories [2]	0·71	1·62	2·55	3·69	4·77	5·21	6·25	6·05
Agogo [3]	0·50	1·58	2·36	3·58	4·75	5·46	6·22*	
Accra [4]	1·13	1·85	2·60	3·41	3·92	4·85	5·36*	
Sekondi-Takoradi [5]	0·58	1·65	2·70	3·61	4·35	5·05	5·41	5·60

1. Data for Anomabo, Mpraeso, Larteh and Tsito (Gaisie, 1964).
2. *The Gold Coast Census of Population, 1948, Report and Tables*, Tables 30, 31, p. 396.
3. Data from Fortes 'A Demographic Field Study' etc. quoted in Lorimer, p. 76.
4. 'Unpublished data for Accra provided by Statistics Department, Government of the Gold Coast; returns for 1,162 women aged 15 years and over', quoted in Lorimer, p. 76.
5. Gaisie, 1964.

* Figures for age group 45–59.

It is clear from Table 2 that Ghana's fertility is high (if we assume that the figures obtained from the sampling studies are representative of the whole country). In Table 2 the figures for Ghana are compared with those for high fertility countries. The fertility of Ghana is seen to be as high as that of India, Brazil and Puerto Rico, and higher than that of some West and East African countries. Instances of fertility even higher than the estimates for Ghana have been reported. For example, in Taiwan the total fertility rate in Yunlin Hsien for women aged 45–49 in 1952 was 7·2 (Gaisie, 1964). A rate of 9·6 for married women has been recorded for American Hutterites. The observed fertility in Ghana may be regarded as the result of some factors favouring high fertility, and others operating in the reverse direction.

In view of the limits set by the available data, the child–woman ratio is another possible direct index which we can use to gauge the fertility of Ghana. This index measures fertility of a more recent time than the completed family size, which represents the average fertility prevailing over the last fifty or sixty years. The fertility ratio, moreover, measures what might be called 'effective fertility', not the number of births as such, but that figure reduced by the substantial mortality during infancy.

Table 2

Mean Numbers of Children Born to Cohorts of Completed Child-Bearing: Various Countries

Country	Year	Ages	Children per woman
Puerto Rico [1]	1946	45+	6·6
	1948	49–53	5·7
Brazil [2]	1940	50+	6·2
India (Travancore-Cochin) [3]	1951	50+	6·6
(Banaras Tehsi) [3]	1956 [1]	45–49	6·6
(Poona) [3]	1951	50+	6·4
Ghana (Census)	1948 [4]	50+	6·56
(Sample)	1961	50+	6·00
Guinea (Fouta Djallon)	1955 [5]	50+	5·50
West Cameroon (Bakweri)	1958 [6]	50+	4·51
Zanzibar	1958 [7]	46+	2·93
Pemba	1958 [7]	46+	3·7
Tanganyika	1948	45+	4·4
Buhaya Sample	1952	45+	3·7
Uganda	1948	45+	4·8
Buganda Sample	1952	45+	3·0

1. Roberts and Stefani (1949)
2. Hatt (1952)
3. Chandrasekaran (1954)
4. Lorimer (1958)
5. Rele (1962)
6. Andener (1962)
7. Blacker (1962)

It is well known that under-enumeration is particularly large in the youngest age groups, not only because infants and children are passed over altogether, but their ages are often misreported. The error, however, is less for the first five years than for the first twelve months alone. In this study, the fertility ratio is defined as the proportion of children under five years to 1,000 women aged 15–44. The ratios computed from Smith and Friedlander sample data and the 1960 census returns are set out in Table 3. (See Gaisie, 1964.) With the exception of Tsito and Sekondi-Takoradi the census ratios tend to be higher than the ratios computed from the sample data. Most of the differences between the census and the sample ratios may be due to a greater under-enumeration of children under five years in the sample survey than in the census. The proportion of women in the age group 15–44 in both the sample and the census for every village or town are almost equal and any difference will have insignificant effect on the ratios.

Table 3

Ghana: Fertility Ratios: Proportion of Children Under 5 Years to 1,000 Women Aged 15–44 Years

Source	Anomabo	Mpraeso	Larteh	Tsito	Sekondi-Takoradi	Ghana
Sample	790	781	745	844	798	—
Census	922	957	861	809	789	906

In Table 4 the ratios in Table 3 are compared with those computed for other countries and Ghana stands out as one of the countries with the highest 'effective fertility'. Both the census and the sample ratios put Ghana into the category of countries with high fertility. We have, however, to be cautious in carrying the interpretation too far, since some of the differences between figures may be attributed to under-enumeration and differential infantile and early childhood mortality. Secondly, in view of the time lapse between figures, Ghana's high ratios may to some degree be a reflection of improvements in infant and childhood mortality.

Table 4
Fertility Ratios for Various Countries

Country	Year	Fertility ratio
Ghana[1] (Census)	1960	906
(Sample)	1961	795
Swaziland[2]	1956	944
Tanganyika[2]	1948	979
Nigeria[2]	1953	1,118
Cameroon (West Cameroon)[2]	1953	1,064
Puerto Rico[2]	1940	725
Zanzibar and Pemba[2]	1958	564
	1950[3]	606
Jamaica[2]	1953	556
South Africa[4]	1936	710
India[5]	1930	775
Japan[6]	1930	574
France[6]	1936	319
USA[6]	1940	293
Uganda[2]	1948	874
Yao[6] (Malawi)	1946	738

1. 1960 Census returns and Friedlander and Smith survey.
2. UN, 1959.
3. Combs and Davis, 1951.
4. Badenhorst, 1952.
5. Davis, 1951.
6. Mitchell, 1949.

For the purpose of eliminating some of the errors presumed to have been caused by misreporting of ages and under-enumeration of children under five years, we considered the ratio of the number of children under 15 to the number of women between the ages of 15 and 44 years. The results (see Table 5, Gaisie, 1964) present almost the same fertility pattern as reflected in Tables 3 and 4. Ghana's ratios come very close to those computed for high fertility developing countries by the United Nations (UN, 1960).

Table 5
Ghana: Fertility Ratios: Proportion of Children Under 15 per 1,000 Women aged 15–44 Years

Source	Anomabo	Mpraeso	Larteh	Tsito	Sekondi-Takoradi	Ghana
Sample	1,898	2,060	2,456	2,169	1,961	—
Census	2,080	2,178	2,340	2,104	—	2,004

Estimated Gross and Net Reproduction Rates

Despite the limitations set by the data available in developing countries, demographers and other social scientists (sociologists and social anthropologists) have devised a variety of simple methods for estimating gross and net reproduction rates. The Gulwicks (*Sociological Review*, 1938–39), Fortes (*Sociological Review*, 1943), and Schapera (1943) used the average numbers of live-born females to women past child-bearing as an estimate of G. R. R. Blanc and other French social scientists working in the former French overseas territories in Africa used the same method with a slight modification (Blanc 1959). Blanc, for instance, averaged the mean number of children corresponding to the age-groups straddling the ages of menopause, i.e. 45–49 and 50–54, and divided the result by two (assuming the sex-ratio to be one) to obtain what he termed as GRR.

There are, however, some serious objections to the use of these figures as a measure of the prevailing gross reproduction rate. First, they do not account for those women who did not survive the child-bearing period. If it is only the fecund who die before menopause, then we are dealing with a sample which is unrepresentative because the less fecund women are automatically selected. The opposite may be true, of course, but whatever be the case the estimates would be based on an unrepresentative sample of women. Such estimates also refer to a remote period (about 50 or more years) and they fail to reflect the current fertility levels.

An attempt has been made to use certain demographic models to overcome some of the deficiencies mentioned above. The 'reverse survival' method and the stable population concept were employed in formulating the models (Gaisie, 1964). The estimates of GRR and NRR are set out in Tables 6 and 8. The estimated GRR for Ghana as a whole (using the 1960 census results) are 3·33 (estimate based on girls aged 0–4 and women aged 20–39) and 3·26 (estimate based on girls aged 5–9 and women aged 25–45). Using quite a different method and data obtained by asking women in rural towns (Anomabo, Tsito, Mpraeso and Larteh) 'whether or not they had given birth during the last 12 months', Friedlander[3] computed the GRRs of the rural towns to be between 3·2 and 3·4 and for Sekondi-Takoradi between 3·0 and 3·1.

Table 6

Estimated Gross Reproduction Rate

Source	Anomabo	Mpraeso	Larteh	Tsito	Sekondi/ Takoradi	Ghana
Sample	3·3	2·9	3·0	3·3	2·8	—
Census	3·4	3·4	3·3	3·3	3·1	3·3

Table 7

Estimated Gross Reproduction Rates for various Countries

Country	Year	GRR
Ceylon[1]	1949	2·6
India (Cochin)[2]	1936–37	2·6
Guinea (West Africa)[3]	1955	3·5
Puerto Rico[4]	1945	2·7
Malawi (Yao)[5]	1948	3·2
Ruanda-Urundi[3]	1957	2·6
West Cameroon (Bakweri)[6]	1957–58	2·0
Ghana (Census)	1960	3·3
Ghana (Sample)	1961	3·0
Japan[7]	1949–51	1·8
England and Wales[8]	1950–54	1·1
USA[8]	1950–54	1·6
France[8]	1950–54	1·3

1. Huyck (1954).
2. Ghosh Varma (1940).
3. Blanc (1959).
4. Combs Jr. and Davis (1951).
5. Mitchell (1949).
6. Ardener (1962).
7. Barclay (1958).
8. UN (1958).

Table 8

Estimated Net Reproduction Rates

Source	Anomabo	Mpraeso	Larteh	Tsito	Sekondi-Takoradi	Ghana
Sample	2·1	2·0	2·1	2·3	1·96	
Census	2·1	2·4	2·3	2·3	2·2	2·3

Fortes recorded estimated GRR of 3·1 and 3·2 for the Tallensi, in northern Ghana and the Ashanti respectively (Fortes, Lorimer, 1954). A gross reproduction rate of 3, about 36 per cent higher than that prevailing in England and Wales (Table 7) over 100 years ago, gives a clear indication of high fertility.

The results are presented in Table 8. Our analysis shows that a Ghanaian woman living through the child-bearing period replaces herself with about two daughters. Such a rate means a doubling of the population in a generation.

Trends in Fertility

The available data make any analysis of fertility change difficult, but an attempt has been made to exploit the data for information, if any, on fertility trends in Ghana.

Women at different ages at the date of a survey are passing or have passed through the reproductive period during different calendar periods. A comparison, therefore, of fertility ratios of women of different ages reflects, however imperfectly, the historical course of fertility. Quite apart from the errors elsewhere discussed (Gaisie, 1964) in such an analysis, this comparison may be regarded as a comparison in fertility of greatly overlapping calendar periods of time, with the cohort of ages 40–44 representing the period just having ended, and with older cohorts representing progressively earlier periods. The average number of children per woman for the various cohorts are presented in Table 9. The first four columns relate to mean number of children ever born per woman, while the last column sets forth similar data compiled for married women only. Table 9 does not suggest any strong evidence of either rising or falling trends. What suggestions of movements are there appear to point towards increase in fertility over time, but this may be largely due to sampling errors. Even if

Table 9

Mean Number of Children Born to Cohorts of Completed Child-Bearing

Cohort	All women				Fertile women only
	(1)	(2)	(3)	(4)	(5)
40–44	5·77	5·59	5·36	5·46	6·31
45–49	5·11	5·88	6·14	6·22	6·63
50–54	5·59		6·36		6·09
55–59	5·91	6·15	6·83	6·09	5·77
60–64	5·98		6·54		6·42
65+	6·36		6·67		6·80

Sources: (1) and (2) Gaisie, 1964.
(3) 1948 Census Report, Table 31, p. 396.
(4) Lorimer, 1958.

the differences are partly real they are certainly not important differences, at least in terms of the evidence of a secular movement in fertility of a magnitude of that frequently observed elsewhere. The estimated GRRs based on different cohorts of girls and women do not give any indication of changes in fertility over the decade preceding the 1960 census.

Conclusion

The fertility of Ghanaian women can be regarded as fairly high from the various tests possible with rather imprecise data. The results obtained by the use of different indices point to the same conclusion.

Between six and seven live births is the commonest average number produced by women who complete the reproductive span. Child–woman ratio of over 700 and a gross reproduction rate of the order of three place Ghana among the group of Afro-Asian and Latin American countries characterized by high fertility.

The social and cultural conditions which favour high fertility have been discussed elsewhere (Gaisie, 1964). Children are greatly valued, and the social and political institutions make it not only possible but desirable and praiseworthy for a woman to bear children all through her procreative years. The institutional factors operating through some intervening variables such as low age at marriage and absence of permanent celibacy are largely responsible for the observed high fertility levels. Modern changes have not as yet altered the traditional social structure to such an extent as to initiate a decline in fertility. As children are highly valued, not only by the parents but also by the members of their lineage, where influence in the local activities depends to some extent on their numbers, no radical change in reproductive habits is likely to occur as long as the corporate organization of lineage remains so important in Ghanaian rural social life. Although some educated people talk about the advantages of a small family, very few of them actually use contraceptives within marriage. The analysis of urban–rural differentials does not give any clue as to the possible decline in fertility as initiated in the towns (Gaisie, 1964). In the first place, the urban–rural differential is masked by such a plethora of factors that no definite conclusion can be drawn, and the differential, assuming it exists, is too small to be certainly indicative of any decline in fertility. There has apparently been no diffusion effect and while urbanization in itself may be expected to have some influence in decreasing total fertility, this is not likely to be large without other concomitant changes.

While there is evidence to suggest that death rate is declining, the birth rate, in the light of available evidence, has, if anything, risen. The widening gap between these rates is one of the problems now confronting developing countries with regard to economic developments.

References

ARDENER, E. *Divorce and Fertility*, Oxford University Press, London.

BADENHORST, L. T. 'Population Growth and Differential Fertility in the Union of South Africa', *Population Studies*, Vol. XI, No. 2, 1962.

BARCLAY, G. *Techniques of Population Analysis*, New York, 1958.

BLACKER, J. G. C. 'Population Growth and Differential Fertility in Zanzibar Protectorate', *Population Studies*, Vol. XV, No. 3, 1962.

BLANC, R. *Handbook of Research in Underdeveloped Countries* (English version), London, 1959.

BRASS, W. *Methods of Obtaining Basic Demographic Measures where Census and Vital Statistics Registration Systems are Lacking or Defective*, United Nations World Population Conference, Belgrade, 1965.

CARDINALL, A. W. *The Gold Coast, 1931*.

CHANDRASEKARAR, C. 'Fertility Trends in India', *Proceedings of the World Population Conference, 1954*, Papers, Vol. 1, New York, 1956.

COMBS, J. W. and DAVIS, K. 'The Pattern of Puerto Rican Fertility', *Population Studies*, Vol. V, No. 2, 1951.

DAVIS, K. *The Population of India and Pakistan*, Princeton, 1951.

GULWICK, A. T. and GULWICK, G. M. 'A Study in Indian Fertility', *Eugenics Review 3*, 1948.

FORTES, M. 'Fertility of Agogo Women', Lorimore, F., *Culture and Human Fertility*, UNESCO, 1954. 'A Note on Fertility among the Tallensi of the Gold Coast', *Sociological Review, 35* (4–5) July–October, 1943.

GAISIE, S. K. *An Analysis of Fertility Levels and Differentials in Contemporary Ghana*, 1964 (M.A. thesis held by the London School of Economics). *Gold Coast Census*, 1948. *Ghana Census*, Vol. V, 1965.

HATT, P. K. *Background to Human Fertility in Puerto Rico. A Sociological Survey*, Princeton University, 1952.

HUYCK, E. 'Differential Fertility in Ceylon', *Population Bulletin of the United Nations*, No. 4, December, 1954.

KUCZYNSKI, R. R. *Demographic Survey of the British Colonial Empire*, Vol. 1, 1948.

LORIMER, F. *Culture and Human Fertility*, UNESCO, Paris, 1954.

MITCHELL, J. C. 'An Estimate of Fertility in some Yao Hamlets in Liwonde District of Southern Nyasaland', *Africa, XIX*, 4, 1949.

RELE, J. R. 'Some Aspects of Family and Fertility in India', *Population Studies*, Vol. XV, No. 3, 1963. *Report of the Principal Registrar*, Ghana, 1938. *Report on Births and Deaths*, Ghana, 1952/26.

ROBERTS, L. J. and STEFANI, R. L. *Patterns of Living in Puerto Rican Families*, Rio Piedras, University of Puerto Rico, 1949.

SCHAPERA, I. *Migrant Labour and Tribal Life*, London, Oxford University Press, 1943.

SMITH, R. T. and FRIEDLANDER, D. Unpublished Data. (See Gaisie, S. K., M.A. thesis held by LSE above.)

UNITED NATIONS. *Demographic Year Book*, 1950, 1958, 1963.

Footnotes

1. With the exception, of course, of the 1960 census results.
2. Registration system covers about 12 per cent of the Ghanaian population.
3. Friedlander, unpublished data (see Gaisie, 1964).

24 Exploratory analysis of data concerning Indians and Pakistanis in Africa

J. M. Boute
Kinshasa, Congo

This paper deals with the analysis of existing data, mostly census data, of populations that originated in the subcontinent of India and Pakistan and which are now in Africa.[1] We shall limit our attention to the eastern half of the Continent where non-African ethnic groups were of sufficient size to warrant the presentation of separate statistical series.

The raw data obtained for Asian groups in East African countries are tabulated in a different manner from that used in the other countries considered: Indians, Pakistanis and Goans are given separately in most statistical series of Kenya, Tanzania[2] and Uganda, whereas elsewhere all Indo-Pakistanis are included under one heading with descendants of other Asian peoples. The latter in fact never exceed a tiny percentage of the total.

Table 1

Total Number of Indo-Pakistanis at most Recent Census, Selected African Countries

Country	Census year	Indo-Pakistanis
Mozambique	1955	15,235
Tanzania[1]	1957	76,536
Zanzibar and Pemba	1958	18,334
Uganda	1959	71,933
South Africa	1960	477,414
Malawi	1961	10,630
Rhodesia	1961	7,260
Zambia	1961	7,790
Kenya	1962	176,613

Source: Census Reports.
1. Then Tanganyika, see Footnote 2.

The Asian populations of Africa have everywhere increased through migration. However, in some places, such as South Africa, the effect of such movements is no longer of any practical demographic significance. Elsewhere, the significance of migration cannot be overlooked. Granted that the relative importance of net migration has diminished with regard to the general population increase, the cumulative effect of previous migrations must still be taken into account. For present purposes, this means that even though some information is available regarding the Asian populations of the countries of the former Federation of Central Africa and of Mozambique, we cannot isolate the effect of various migrations in such a way as to permit the application of existing analytical techniques, for example, quasi-stable population analysis or the methods proposed by W. Brass. New data are thus required for these countries before anything can be asserted about the vital rates of Indo-Pakistanis living there.

It can be shown for Tanzania and Uganda that, whatever the annual age pattern of past migration, it did not result in a foreign-born age structure which would disturb the stability of the total Indo-Pakistani age distribution. For East Africa and South Africa, data on age distributions is supplemented by other data, such as official life tables, series of children ever born to women by age and proportions of subsequent deaths among these children.

The results obtained by the use of quasi-stable population analysis and Brass's various techniques leads to the following:

Table 2

Estimates of Indo-Pakistani Vital Rates[1]

Country	Census year	Crude birth rate	Crude death rate	Rate of growth
South Africa	1946	48	16	32
	1951	48	12	36
	1960	39	9	30
Tanzania	1957	39	10	29
Uganda	1959	40	10	30

1. Per 1,000.

The most interesting feature of our analysis is the fertility trend between 1945 and the late fifties. J. G. C. Blacker has indicated a decline in the fertility of Asian females of Tanzania between 1948 and 1957.[3] The same trend is found to exist in Uganda and South Africa throughout this period.[4]

There is no evidence that this decline is due to the significant use of contraceptives or to a greater infertility of ever-married women. The better sex-ratio of those of marriageable age would even imply a more regular sexual life. One finds, however, a common feature in the three countries, namely declining proportions of married women, especially among young adults. This latter decline implies postponement of marriage.

That changing proportions of single women may adequately account for declining fertility can be shown in the following way. Using acceptable age specific fertility rates for the last census year, one adjusts series of mean parity of women in each five-year age group by modifying the age specific fertility rate; this is done by means of the appropriate correcting factor based on the proportion of ever-married women in the age group. The correcting factor consists of a ratio of the proportion ever married of a certain age at an earlier period to the proportion of ever married of the same age at the last period considered.[5] Adjusted series of this kind were computed for Tanzania and for Uganda at two census periods ten years apart: the expected percentage of decline convincingly matches the intercensal observed one, as shown in Table 3.

To date, there are no convenient data which would permit us to determine what extra-demographic factors played the most decisive rôle in bringing about marriage at a later age. Indians and Pakistanis are mostly city dwellers; they are mainly employed in such sectors as commerce, finance and the civil service; their income is high by African as well as by subcontinental standards.

The factor most likely to bear on marriage postponement seems to be education. The sex-ratio of enrolled pupils at the secondary school level is steadily improving among Asians. However, how this factor determines later age at marriage remains uncertain, since, even after leaving school, girls can still get married at a compara-

Table 3

Tanganyika and Uganda: Observed and Expected Decline in Number of Children ever born to Indo-Pakistani Women by five-year Age Groups

Country	Age of women	Percentage decline in mean parity	
		Observed	Expected
Tanzania 1948–57	15–19	40·0	41·0
	20–24	25·3	23·9
	25–29	20·3	16·0
	30–34	15·8	9·8
	35–39	11·8	11·7
	40–44	10·1	8·0
Uganda 1948–59	15–19	59·5	62·5
	20–24	20·3	26·1
	25–29	11·9	13·9
	30–34	5·9	7·6
	35–39	7·5	4·2
	40–44	7·7	0·8

tively young age. Few women attend establishments of higher education. Education, it seems, continues to influence age at marriage even after school leaving.

More data, relating fertility to social, economic, and cultural factors, will be needed before we can assert which factor is really at work. If marriage postponement is not accompanied by other factors, the declining trend in fertility might soon harden into a constant level after only a slight reduction of the gap between natality and mortality.

Footnotes

1. These pages summarize some of the results published in a recent study: BOUTE, J., *La démographie de la branche indo-pakistanaise d'Afrique*, Nauwelaerts, Louvain-Paris, 1965.
2. Only continental Tanzania is considered in this paper. Data from the 1958 census of Zanzibar and Pemba cannot be aggregated with those of the 1957 Tanganyika census.
3. BLACKER, J. E. C., 'Fertility Trends of the Asian Population of Tanganyika', *Population Studies*, 13(1), July 1959, pp. 46–60.
4. The main evidence for East Africa is taken from intercensal change in the series of children ever born to women at various ages, whereas for South Africa, it is taken from the markedly changed age distribution between 1951 and 1960 at younger ages. This decline has a bearing on the use of the methods leading to the estimates of Table 2. The results shown should be considered as slightly over-estimated.
5. For further explanation, see BOUTE, J., *op. cit.*, pp. 205–09.

25 Migration in tropical Africa

R. Mansell Prothero
Department of Geography, University of Liverpool, UK

Introduction

Overall in the field of population studies there has been a relative neglect of migration. Though this statement applies in varying degrees to different parts of the world it is particularly relevant to population studies in tropical Africa. Here there is a general paucity of sound demographic data to serve as a basis for population studies (Lorimer, 1961; Smith and Blacker, 1963). Much remains to be done to obtain reasonable data on birth and death rates, but there is an even greater dearth of reliable quantitative data on migration, the remaining variable in population change. In general terms it is known that mobility in a variety of forms characterizes sections of African population and that some are more prone to movement than are others.

There has not yet been an attempt to review and to systematize, if this is indeed possible, the data on migration available from censuses conducted in tropical Africa since 1945. The first round of post-war censuses produced data of limited value for the study of migration, and in some censuses where relevant data were collected, they were then not tabulated and published. In spite of these limitations, a review study of migration, if undertaken, would provide a useful overall appreciation of the nature and characteristics of migration as revealed by standard censuses.

While rightly stressing the importance of census data, it is a fact that there is a tendency for the demographic view of migration to be somewhat restricted, particularly in the circumstances of population mobility which have existed in tropical Africa in the past and which are to be found in many areas at the present day (Prothero, 1964). Measures of migration that may be obtained from decennial, or even quinquennial, censuses, and from official returns for immigration and emigration, reveal only a part of the total mobility that occurs. Several important categories of population movement may be missed out altogether in census data relating to migration, others may be recorded only inadequately, and it may be impossible to distinguish in the data one form of mobility from another. A broad view of the various types of population mobility in tropical Africa, though it may be of a qualitative nature only, is an essential preliminary to devising means of obtaining quantitative assessments.

Types of Population Mobility

Various types of population mobility may be distinguished on the basis of characteristics of continuity and change:

(a) movements that took place in the past, but which have now ceased to exist;
(b) movements that have continued from the past into the present day; and
(c) movements that have developed in recent times, mainly during the present century.

Within each of these categories it is possible to note changing human circumstances which have resulted in mobility, and also ways in which human circumstances themselves have been changed as a result of population movements.

PAST MOVEMENTS

In the past, movements of population were responsible for the diffusion of ideas, techniques and material equipment. The study of these has been advanced considerably in recent years through the interdisciplinary co-operation of historians, social anthropologists, geographers, linguists, serologists, botanists and workers in other fields. These movements are of lesser importance in this discussion, though they can be of relevance in present-day population studies. Legacies of past movements, resulting from warfare, slaving, devastation with consequent depopulation, are to be noted in patterns of the distribution of population in some parts of tropical Africa today and may thus be of contemporary significance. Sparse population and associated problems of development in central Tanzania and in parts of West Africa are due, at least in part, to depopulation in the past (Gillman, 1936).

CONTINUING MOVEMENTS

There are two major types of population movements that have continued from the past into the present day. The first is associated with *pastoralists*, whose movements vary greatly in their characteristics, though all are conditioned essentially by the need to find pasture and water for stock where these are scarce. Variations during the year in the availability of these commodities necessitate seasonal movements, which may be cyclic and/or transhumant in character, such as are practised by the Fulani in West Africa and the Somali in north-east Africa (Dupire, 1962; Hopen, 1958; Lewis, 1961; Stenning, 1959). Besides these annual movements there may also occur what is described as 'long-term migratory drift' extending over many centuries, such as has led to the diffusion of the Fulani throughout the northern parts of West Africa (Stenning, 1959) and the Somali in the Horn of Africa (Lewis, 1961).

The volume, pattern and timing of the seasonal movements of pastoralists may be known in general terms, but specific detailed information is available only from case studies of particular groups in limited areas (see previous references cited). Census data on migration are likely to reveal nothing regarding these movements, and pastoralists are notorious for the problems that they present to census authorities who attempt to include them in a relatively accurate enumeration. It is not without significance that Somalia, with the highest proportion of nomadic pastoralists in its population of any country in Africa, is now one of the very few countries in the continent that has yet to conduct a first census of the population. There is the further basic problem presented to census organizers of distinguishing meaningfully between nomadic and sedentary populations. For example, in the first census of the Sudan in 1955/56 the proportions of 14 and 78 per cent for these two groups in the total population of the whole country were undoubtedly misleading (Krotki 1958). The former figure was certainly an underestimate of those elements in the population mobile for the whole or part of any year.

The second group of traditional movements continuing to the present day is that of *pilgrims*, particularly from the Muslim areas of tropical Africa in a generally north-easterly direction via the Republic of the Sudan towards Mecca and Medina in Saudi Arabia. The main flow seems to be from the northern parts of West Africa, along routes which have been followed for many centuries (Riad, 1960), but numbers are increasing with increased conversion to Islam and with improvements in communications (Mather, 1956; Prothero, 1965). It is possible to do little more than make qualitative statements, since data on the numbers of pilgrims and on the detailed pattern and timing of their movements are very sparse. Even in the Republic of the Sudan, which is the African focus for pilgrims, there is little available information, though the effects and implications of pilgrim movements for the country are considerable. Some data could be collected on pilgrims who use modern and regular means of transport, e.g. who travel by air charter from West Africa; but there are numbers unknown who travel overland, often making their outward and homeward journeys in stages that extend over many years.

Here again census data are likely to reveal very little. In the first Sudan census in 1955 some 200,000 West Africans were counted (about 3 per cent of the total population), and the actual number was probably greater since some undoubtedly registered as Sudanese, though their legal claim to nationality would probably not be upheld (Davies, 1964). But any such figure for West Africans would not represent accurately the number of pilgrims en route through the Sudan. Some of the people in this group have been settled in the country for many years and may include people who were born in the Sudan but still maintain their West African links.

RECENT MOVEMENTS

The advent of widespread colonial administration in tropical Africa in the late 19th century and early in the present century brought to an end some long-established types of population movement associated with conditions of political and social instability. At the same time, in the conditions of peace and security with which they were replaced, new forms of population mobility developed.

Downhill movements of people have taken place, and still continue, from remote and relatively inaccessible highland areas, which offered protection in the past (Froelich, 1952; Gleave, 1963, 1965; Mercier, 1952). These movements have resulted in important local redistributions of population and have often initiated the development of various social and economic problems.

Movements associated with rural–urban migration are a more important feature of the mobility that has developed during the colonial era. They are associated with economic developments in tropical Africa and with the related phenomena of urban growth (Mercier, 1963; UNESCO, 1956). Africa has become increasingly drawn into the mainstream of world economy in the spheres of agricultural and mineral production and, more recently, in industrial development. Major areas of production are still limited in size, but in them have developed demands for labour which often cannot be met by the immediate local supply (Green and Fair, 1962; Mitchell, 1961). Much, but by no means all, of the economic development has been concentrated in towns and at ever-increasing rates people have been moving from rural areas to rapidly expanding urban centres. Although the overall proportion of urban population in the total population of tropical Africa remains low (around 10 per cent), the figure is subject to considerable regional fluctuations (up to a maximum of over 50 per cent in the Western Region of Nigeria; Steel, 1961).

It has been shown that both centrifugal and centripetal forces operate in rural–urban migration (Mitchell, 1959). Conditions in rural areas may encourage, or may even force, people to seek opportunities to gain a livelihood away from traditional agricultural pursuits. At the same time towns offer, or at least seem to offer, to the countryman advantages and amenities that are not available in rural areas. Factors in rural and urban areas which influence migration may be further classified into two major categories. The first group comprises economic factors (e.g. rural poverty manifested in relatively low living standards, often due to population pressure and land hunger), and the second, social and psychological factors (e.g. the desire to break away from the constraints of traditional social organization and obligations in the rural areas, and to exchange these for the greater social freedom of the towns). The economic factors have been shown to be the more important (Mitchell, 1959), but there has been a tendency in recent years to underrate the part that the latter may play. Their rôle may be subtle but none the less significant.

Several types of rural–urban migration may be recognized, primarily differing from one another in the length of absence of the migrants from their home areas (Panofsky, 1963). Seasonal movements of labourers, mainly men, take place from rural areas during months of the year when there is little agricultural activity, and when there are demands for labour in urban areas or in more economically advanced areas of agricultural development (Prothero, 1957, 1959, 1962). The latter are important in providing opportunities for employment, and attention has been drawn recently to the neglect of what is termed 'rural–rural' migration (Barbour, 1965). There are also instances of urban–rural migration, where people from towns go to work in surrounding rural areas during periods of maximum agricultural activity. Western Nigeria provides an example of this type of movement; here, relationships between town and country are very close and many towns have developed from what were originally rural settlements (Mabogunje, 1962; Mitchel, 1961). In addition cocoa, the main cash crop, has marked seasonal labour requirements and provides a satisfactory economic return for those engaged in the various activities associated with harvesting and handling it.

In seasonal migration, absences from home areas are usually for periods of up to six months, and distances travelled to and from work may amount to hundreds of miles. West Africa, south of the Sahara, from Senegal to Cameroon, is probably characterized by greater seasonal migration than is found elsewhere in tropical Africa. From inland countries like Mali, Upper Volta and Niger, and from the northern parts of Ivory Coast, Ghana and Nigeria, male migrants move generally in a southward direction during the long dry season, which may last from October until April. Their home areas are poorly endowed and underdeveloped and they seek employment in more precociously developed rural and urban areas. These include areas of export cash crop cultivation, the major commercial and administrative centres, and seaports (Rouch, 1957). After working in these for from two to five months, migrants then return home to cultivate their farms with the onset of the next wet season.

For the most part these migrations are spontaneous and uncontrolled; organizations for recruiting workers do not operate and workers have no formal contracts with their employees. Minimal, and usually no, records exist which might provide data of even the numbers employed. Normal censuses do not provide any data on these annual movements in terms of their pattern and timing. Some indication of the volume of migrants would be given in a *de facto* census if this were taken at the time of year when the migrants were away from their home areas and provided that data were collected on birthplace; but seasonal migrants could be clearly distinguished from others only if there were also data on duration of residence. Bearing in mind that seasonal migrants are numbered not in tens but in hundreds or thousands, a *de facto* enumeration taken at a time when they were away from home would produce serious under-assessment of population in the major source areas of migrants. Such under-assessment could produce difficulties in analyses based on census returns of the demographic situations in these areas.

Compared with seasonal migration, short-term migration also mainly involves men seeking work in towns, at mines and in agriculture, but for periods of up to two years' duration. These men may be either on contract for a specified time or may be 'target' workers who set out to earn a specific sum of money. Wives and children remain in the rural areas and migrants return there at the end of a period of work, though it is usual for them to spend several such periods away from home during their working lives.

East, Central Africa and South-central Africa (Uganda, Kenya, Tanzania, Ruanda, Burundi, Congo-Leopoldville, Zambia, Malawi, Rhodesia, Angola and Mozambique) are characterized by these short-term migrations, rather than by seasonal movements as in West Africa (Mitchell, 1961; Southall, 1961). The latter do occur, as in the movements of migrant labourers from the East African mainland to the islands of Zanzibar and Pemba for the clove harvest (Prothero, 1965). Where labourers are seeking work for longer periods, there is usually a greater measure of organization for migrant labour, though in some areas still only a minority of migrants are dealt with by recruiting organizations (e.g. with the labour force for the sisal plantations in Tanzania: Hurst, 1959). Control of migrants has been stricter in South-central Africa than elsewhere, particularly from the main source areas in Mozambique, Malawi, Zambia and Angola to the mining and industrial complexes of the Transvaal in South Africa (Houghton, 1958; Mitchel, 1961). This control has been exercised through the operations of recruiting organizations (particularly the Witwatersrand Native Labour Association), with workers entering into contracts with their employees, and with travel arrangements being made for them to and from places of work (Witwatersrand, 1959). Recently the attitudes of some of the independent African countries towards political developments in South Africa and Rhodesia, the next most important employer of migrant labour, have had some effect in reducing migrant movements.

The influence of political change may also be seen in Congo (Kinshasa), where a high degree of stabilization of labour had been achieved under Belgian administration. Political and economic instability since independence has had its effects upon this situation. Unemployment has increased in the towns and a new element in population mobility has developed with the movements of refugees both within and out of the country.

Where migrant workers are recruited or may otherwise enter into some formal agreement with their employers, some data on them is available. Migrant labour to the Republic of South Africa is without doubt the best documented in the whole of Africa. Elsewhere, the extent to which workers may avoid recruiting organizations, where these exist, seriously affects the completeness and accuracy of records. The lack of any time pattern in short-term movements makes it likely that much less data on such migrations will be available from official censuses than for seasonal migrations, unless specific questions are asked regarding migrant labour in the census. In Lesotho, where migrant labour to South Africa makes a major contribution to the country's economy, the census of 1956 enumerated the *de facto* population and also the absentee population by Principal and Ward Chiefs' Areas. These were then combined to give the *de jure* population for the country (Basutoland, 1956).

The two final categories of movements in rural–urban migration concern those who have left the rural areas and settled permanently in the towns. Definitive movements of this nature may be the result of an immediate and final decision to migrate, but in many instances they come after several periods of urban employment as either seasonal or short-term migrants. Men who settle permanently tend to be either accompanied by their wives and families from the start or they are joined by them after they have become established in the towns.

Having made the break with the rural areas does not mean that people entirely lose their migrant characteristics. There is evidence of considerable movement within towns, associated with the need to search for employment and accommodation. When these are found there may still be a need to commute from one to the other. Daily movements between residential areas on peri-urban fringes and commercial and industrial areas located elsewhere are becoming increasingly characteristic of the large towns in tropical Africa and present many problems, for example where transport services are inadequately developed.

Measures of definitive movements to towns may be obtained from place of birth and duration of residence data in official censuses. There are as yet virtually no measures of the daily movements of peoples in towns and little information on the social and economic problems that are associated with them.

This section on contemporary population movements in tropical Africa would be incomplete without reference to several minor categories of mobility, which may nevertheless be of importance in the limited situations in which they occur. Such movements are associated with small-scale trading activities, sometimes over long distances, or with other traditional activities such as farming and fishing, which may be over long or short distances and are usually seasonal in character. Finally, there are the quite recently developed movements of refugees to which reference has been made. These have occurred within the present decade not only in Congo (Kinshasa) but also from the Sudan and from Rwanda, concentrating particularly upon Uganda, and to a less extent in countries in West Africa. No accurate counts of these refugees are available but those in individual countries in East Africa are numbered in tens of thousands.

This review is intended to draw attention to the considerable variety of migration which occurs in tropical Africa. This is certainly not fully appreciated and standard collections of population data in censuses do not usually take account of many of these movements. The section that follows outlines in further detail some of the measures of migration which may be obtained from recent censuses and makes reference to other means that have been employed to accumulate quantitative data on migration.

Measurement of Migration

In the absence of an overall review of the data relevant to migration in post-war censuses in tropical Africa, the references made here are selective and not comprehensive. They are primarily to post-war censuses in British and former British territories with which the writer has first hand experience, drawing also on considerable assistance from colleagues.[1] Similarly, the references to ways of studying migration, other than by census, are also made from experience. Though selected, these examples are generally representative for much of tropical Africa.

POST-WAR CENSUSES

The first round of censuses in the late 1940s and the early 1950s in general asked few, if any, questions directly relevant to migration. Data on place of birth and on duration of residence were either completely lacking or were available only in the most general terms. The 1948 census in the Gold Coast asked if people were born where they were enumerated or, if not, whether they were born in the South, Ashanti, the Northern Territories, Togoland or Other British Foreign Country. The data obtained provided indications of trends though not of amounts of migration, and only with reference to the major administrative units into which the country was divided. Nevertheless, they were considerably more revealing than any of the data from the 1952/53 census of Nigeria, which included no questions on place of birth. The only data from this census which could be used to indicate anything on migration were sex ratios, and the accuracy of these may well have been affected in some areas, for example in the Muslim parts of Nigeria, through under-enumeration of women (Prothero, 1956).

Using data from the East African censuses of 1948 (Uganda and Kenya) and 1948 and 1957 (Tanganyika), a simple but effective method was devised to indicate the comparative tendency of members of the different tribal groups to migrate away from the tribal home area (Southall, 1961). The total number of each tribe enumerated in the home district was subtracted from the total number of the tribe recorded in the census, and this was then expressed as a percentage and termed the 'emigration rate'. Differences in rates brought out very clearly the tendency of some tribes to provide more migrants than others, and in many instances explanations can be advanced for these varying characteristics. Applying this index to data for the male and female populations brought out some further interesting contrasts both within and between tribes. It was possible to calculate the index because the East African censuses enumerated for all major tribal groups in all enumeration areas. Such detailed ethnic enumeration was lacking in the Nigerian census of 1952/53, where in the Northern Region, for example, only three major tribes (Hausa, Fulani and Ibo) were enumerated (Prothero, 1962). Apart from these, the selection of tribes to be enumerated was left to the discretion of the authorities in individual provinces, resulting in a lack of uniformity, a measure of confusion and only very fragmentary data for other than the major tribes. With these data it would be impossible to calculate emigration rates by the method employed in East Africa.

The same means of determining tribal migration might be employed with the tribal data from the Uganda census of 1959 and the Kenya census of 1962. In each of these censuses the major tribes were enumerated in each of the enumeration areas and the data have been published down to county level for Uganda and to district level for Kenya. Besides indicating the tendency of the different tribes within each country to migrate, the tribal census data for Uganda and Kenya also include information on non-Ugandan and non-Kenyan African populations. In the former, some tribes from outside the country, which are represented in considerable numbers, were recorded separately, e.g. Banyarwanda (378,656) and Rundi (138,749), and so also were the Kikuyu though their total (914) in Uganda is very small (Uganda, 1960). In addition others from the then Ruanda-Urundi and from Kenya, who were not of these tribes, were recorded in an 'unspecified category', one for each of these countries, and this was done also for people from the Sudan and Tanzania. Egypt, Ethiopia, Somalia, the Comoro Islands and Madagascar were grouped together in a category 'Non-Africans' (*sic*), and those from other African countries not already specified were classified as 'Other Africans'. In Kenya the classification for non-Kenyan population was much less elaborate, and they were recorded as from Tanzania, Uganda, the Sudan, Ethiopia, Rhodesia and Nyasaland, Ruanda-Urundi and Other African Countries respectively (Kenya, 1962).

The censuses of the present decade have shown a general advance in the quantity and quality of data obtained in them. This applies to the data suitable for indicating the migratory characteristics of population, though these data are by no means ideal. They continue to be generalized and make any detailed quantitative assessment impossible.

In the Ghana census of 1960 the classification place of birth data was similar to but slightly more detailed than that used in 1948. The categories and the percentage of population assigned to each of them are given in the following table.

Table 1

1960 Ghana Census: Place of Birth

Place of birth	Percentage of total population
1. Born in locality in which enumerated	58
2. Born in another locality, but in the same region	22
3. Born in another region	12
4. Born abroad	8

Categories 2 and 3, which distinguished between intra- and extra-regional migration inside Ghana, inevitably produced some arbitrary results, since distinction cannot be made between migration involving a change of residence of several hundred miles within a region, and migration entailing movement over a very short distance but crossing a regional boundary.

Population movement and growth in Ghana, based on the 1960 data, have been studied by Engmann (1965) and by Hunter (1965), both of whom draw attention to the deficiencies of the data, but nevertheless make assessments of the patterns of movement and growth. Over two-fifths of the population enumerated away from place of birth indicates a high degree of mobility, but the limitations of data preclude any study of either seasonal migration or of regional characteristics of migration. Hunter's analysis showed that place of birth data was of limited value as an index for population growth, for though there was a positive linear regression between immigration (i.e. persons born outside the locality in which enumerated) and population growth, the coefficient of correlation was low ($r=0{\cdot}498$). There was better correlation ($r=0{\cdot}789$) between immigration and sex ratio, the latter based on the 15–44 years age group. Sex-ratio and growth showed a positive linear regression and a fairly strong coefficient of correlation ($r=0{\cdot}686$) and Hunter concluded that '. . . the sex-ratio may to this extent be regarded as an indication of trends in population growth and migration.' The overall patterns of migration revealed in Ghana are of movement to the urban centres, widespread emigration from the northern savanna areas and the Volta Region, and immigration to the forest areas, particularly to the developing areas of cocoa cultivation in western Ashanti and Brong-Ahafo. In addition there are foreign-born migrants who accounted for 8 per cent of the total population.

In the 1963 census of the African population in Zambia birthplace data were recorded for two broad categories—in Northern Rhodesia and elsewhere. There was no further break-down by district or otherwise in the first category, but in the second there was a break-down to country of birth (Southern Rhodesia, Malawi, Angola, Mozambique, Tanzania, Congo and Other Countries). However, these details have been published only for the whole of Northern Rhodesia. Further information has been published showing the allocation of indigenous and non-indigenous (by country) population between three categories of land in Zambia—African Rural Areas, Crown Land Farming Areas and Urban Areas. The non-indigenous population was divided between these three as 60, 8 and 32 per cent respectively. Figures for persons born inside and outside (unspecified) Zambia are given in greater detail for provinces and districts and allocated to the three areas mentioned above.

For provinces only, numbers are given by sex in two main age groups (viz. born before 1942, born 1942 and after), according to main countries of birth. For example, the population of Barotseland is shown by sex and age according to the place of birth in Zambia, Angola or Other Countries. Data such as these give some indication of patterns of immigration into Zambia, but there is no indication of migration within the country. These movements are in fact the largest. Kay, who has analysed the data of the 1963 census, has stated that the sex ratios can be used to throw light on movements within the country, but he speaks of this as being 'circumstantial evidence' (Kay, 1966). Data for labour migration within Zambia were to be found in 'Labour and Population Statistics', published in the *Annual Report of the Ministry of African Affairs* up to and including 1962. They recorded the numbers of taxable males as follows: living at home; employed but home on leave; at work locally within Province; outside Province but within Territory (i.e. Zambia); outside Territory in (Southern) Rhodesia, Malawi, South Africa, Tanzania, Congo and Elsewhere.

These data were collected by villages, but were not made available at this level; they were given by Chiefs' Areas in District Reports and by Districts in Provincial Reports, but none of these was published. They were published only for Provinces and the Territory in the *Annual Report*. Where they could be consulted at Chiefs' Area and District level, they permitted plotting the migration of manpower within and outside Zambia. No information was available on the movement of women and children.

In these examples from some of the post-war censuses conducted in tropical Africa the limitations of the available migration data are clearly apparent. If data are available at all, they are general and not detailed or specific in character, both as to the origin and the destinations of those involved in migration. Quantitative measures of the amount of migration are very difficult to obtain and it is usually only the general trends in migration that can be distinguished. Furthermore, where it is possible to determine the migration of population by analysis of place of birth data, it is still not possible to indicate the length of time that migrants have been away from their places of birth, because of the absence of any data on duration of residence. Even if census schedules were to include questions on this characteristic, there would still be problems involved in memory lapses in dating length of residence, and the fact that for various reasons migrants might be reluctant to give accurate answers to these questions.

Other Measures of Migration

Apart from the data derived from standard censuses, measures of migration have been obtained in tropical Africa in the period since 1945 by other means. In two instances in particular, arrangements were made to record the numbers of migrants and certain of their characteristics. The first of these surveys was undertaken in north-western Nigeria in 1952/53, and the second was an interterritorial study in West Africa made with particular reference to Ivory Coast and Ghana, and the countries adjacent to them. In each case an organization was established specifically for the survey and checkpoints were established at places along routes travelled by migrants.

The survey in Nigeria was undertaken in Sokoto Province by the Federal Department of Statistics during the dry season 1952/53, following the general census taken in July 1952 of the population of the Northern Region of Nigeria. The Government Statistician had proposed a survey throughout the Region, and the Sokoto Survey was intended at the time to be pilot in character, with the hope that similar surveys would be carried out elsewhere following the initial experience gained. In fact no other surveys of this kind have been undertaken in Nigeria, though there were no inhibiting experiences in the Sokoto survey. Within the limits of resources then available the survey was able to collect migration data such as had never been known previously, and with which there is nothing comparable from any other part of the country.

The survey was designed to enumerate the seasonal movements of people within and out of the province and lasted from mid-October 1952, until the beginning of March 1953, thus spanning nearly the whole of the dry season. Two main groups of migrants were included, though the information collected did not permit of clear differentiation between them. One of these is made up of the *masu cin rani* (lit. 'men who eat away the dry season'), who move, often with their families, distances of between 20 and 40 miles. Some of these are seeking employment, as weavers, potters or thatchers; others go to farm where there is water available for small-scale irrigation, and to fish. The other group, the one that figured largely in the survey, is made up of the *yan tuma da gora* (lit. 'young men who jump with a gourd'), who travel long distances outside of the Province to find work in other parts of Northern Nigeria, in other regions of the country, and in Ghana.

Migrants were counted at 16 checkpoints established at strategic places along known migrant routes. Little initiative was required by migrants if they wished to avoid these check points. They could be by-passed without difficulty, and there must have been migrants who took this avoiding action, in mistaken fear of the reasons for making the survey. At the same time there was no means of preventing double, or even treble, counting of migrants in the north and then subsequently in the centre and south of the Province. Probably there was some cancelling of errors due to avoidance and multiple counting. 259,000 migrants were counted, of whom 67,000 were estimated to have been double-counted. However, since avoidance took place and since not all routes were covered, it was estimated that the total number of migrants was not less than a quarter of a million.

Data were collected on the origins and destinations of migrants, on their reasons for migration, on their occupations at places of work, and on the number of times that they had migrated. Each of these groups of data were subdivided into what inevitably had to be very broad categories, to accord with the limited competence of the enumerators in the survey and with the ability of migrants to answer their questions. For example, migrants were asked if they were migrating for the first, second, third or the fourth or more times, but no attempt was made to find out if some had been undertaking seasonal migrations over a much longer period, to determine to some extent whether or not migration on its present scale had reached these proportions only in recent years. No information was collected on the means of travel used by the migrants and the routes by which they travelled.

In spite of these limitations the survey provided most useful data which, if not accurate in detail, yet provided much new information and quantitative indications which were not available previously. The Federal Department of Statistics presented these data in tabulated form with only the minimum of comment (*Federal Statistics*, 1954). They were subsequently analysed and discussed in the light of further investigations undertaken in Sokoto Province (Prothero, 1957 and 1959).

During the 1952/53 survey there was no liaison with the authorities in the then French territories (Niger and Dahomey) adjacent to Sokoto Province. This was most unfortunate since some of the migrants recorded came from these territories and others were proceeding to them. Migrant labour in tropical Africa in general takes little note of international boundaries and studies therefore should have inter-territorial co-ordination and co-operation. Moves towards these were made at a meeting of the Human Sciences Committee of the Commission for Technical Co-operation in Africa south of the Sahara (CCTA) in Bukuvu in 1955, when a West African Migrations Study Committee was set up.

This committee, responsible for initiating the study of migrant movements in Ivory Coast and Ghana and adjacent territories, was directed by Dr Jean Rouch of the Musée de l'Homme, Paris. The study included a number of related projects and has been the most elaborate undertaken in West Africa, or indeed in any part of tropical Africa. It involved a team of research workers together with field staff; an interesting feature was that those employed in interviewing migrants were drawn where possible from the ethnic groups contributing the majority of the migrants. Ivory Coast and Ghana, major foci of migrant labour in West Africa, were the main bases for the various studies undertaken, with less direct attention being given to Mali, Upper Volta, Niger and Togo, which are major source areas of migrants.

The studies were undertaken in 1958 and 1959, beginning in Ivory Coast and subsequently extending to Ghana. They were aimed at obtaining statistical data on migrant movements that would be suitable for analysis and comparable for all places in which they were collected. Standard questionnaires were therefore designed for use in Ivory Coast and in Ghana and sample groups of migrants were questioned over 12-month periods at various checkpoints within and on the borders of the countries. General questionnaires were used to obtain demographic and ethnic data, and then specific questionnaires were used to build up a more detailed picture of the migrations. The latter recorded the activities of migrants, their reasons for choosing particular areas for work and details of their journeys.

In Ivory Coast it was possible to concentrate all activities for the collection of data at Bouaké, an important centre of communications on which almost all migrants moving either northward or southward are obliged to converge. Data were collected at the railway station and at the bus and lorry park, supplemented by sociological inquiries concerned with Bouaké as a centre of attraction and transit for migrants. Selecting centres for the collection of data in Ghana was more complicated because though Kumasi in Ashanti is the most important migrant centre in the country, it does not have the exclusive function of Bouaké in this respect. A sociological investigation, comparable with that at Bouaké, was undertaken there. Migrants travelling on north–south routes in Ghana must cross the Volta river, and checkpoints were set up at the main ferries at Yeji and Bamboi and subsidiary inquiries were made at Otisu and Bouipe.[2] Movements of migrants into Ghana from the east, from Togo and Dahomey, were recorded at the frontier posts of Aflao, Noepé, Batoumé, Kpadafe, Klouto and Bado.

The statistical data from the various surveys were processed in Ivory Coast and, together with a number of working papers, were considered at a symposium in Niamey in February 1961. Discussion there ranged over the methodology of the surveys, the demographic and ethnic data that were collected, and the rôle of migrants in the countries from which they originate and in those to which they go to find work. Attention was drawn to the problems of organizing surveys of migrant labour, of the need for efficiency and for studies in depth to avoid superficiality. Surveys of this kind need to be undertaken by teams of specialists representing the various social sciences (such as demography, sociology, ethnology, statistics, economics, geography and medicine) involved in studying the nature of migrations and their implications. The terms of reference are so wide that the individual can deal competently only with limited aspects.

Apart from some very general progress reports and papers of individual research workers, there has been no major publication of the results of the CCTA migration survey, and no further work has been undertaken in West Africa (Piault, 1961; Rouch, 1959). The failure to publish the full results of such a major pioneering piece of work is most regrettable. The light that they would throw upon features so little examined and understood would be of the utmost value, not only for the countries involved in the study, but also for others from the useful comparisons that might be made. Equally important would be the information on the methodology of the surveys and their evaluation, from the point of view of comparable studies that one hopes will be undertaken one day in other parts of tropical Africa.

The Ivory Coast/Ghana project was the first major attempt at an international study of migration in tropical Africa and since so much migration crosses international boundaries this approach is essential if the best possible results are to be attained. In tropical Africa it is impossible to expect any clear and meaningful distinction between internal and international migration as they are usually understood. The official data for the latter refer only to immigration and emigration through ports, airports and frontier posts and cover only a minority of those who pass into and out of countries. The comparatively recent demarcation of international boundaries in tropical Africa, and their many inconsistencies and anomalies in relation to traditional human distributions, have militated against any great concern for them, particularly by people living adjacent to them who rarely observe the formalities normally associated with crossing from one country to another. Along many sections of international boundaries in Africa there are no frontier posts anyhow, and where they are located they may be avoided without difficulty if there is any incentive to do so. With the assumption of independence by African states existing boundaries have been accepted, though they were much criticized during the colonial era. On the whole they have become more significant, and it remains to be seen whether independent states will attempt greater control over movements of population that cross international boundaries than did the colonial administrations, and, furthermore, whether they will be successful in this.

Prospects and possibilities

Prospects in the immediate future for improvements in data, and information on migration in tropical Africa do not appear to be particularly encouraging. General improvements may be expected in what may be obtained from standard censuses, but the limitations that have been indicated in these will remain.

There is certainly scope for further analysis and co-ordination of existing data, not only for positive gain but also to further clarify and emphasize limitations. Comparability of census data between different countries has still to be achieved, but it may be hoped that the present activities of the Statistics Division of the UN Economic Commission for Africa, in helping to plan for the 1970 round of censuses, will contribute towards this. The possibilities of including questions on the census schedules on duration of residence as well as on place of birth should be considered, in order to provide some means at least of distinguishing between short-term and seasonal migrants and those who have been settled for a long time in the places at which they are enumerated.

Migration studies of the types organized in Nigeria and in Ivory Coast/Ghana should be promoted, especially of an interterritorial character. But no such studies appear to be contemplated according to a member of the UN Economic Commission for Africa to whom a question was put at the UN World Population Conference in September 1955. It is unfortunate that not even proposals for such studies are being put forward.

In a survey undertaken by the writer in 1960, for the Division of Malaria Eradication of the World Health Organization, of population movements in Africa in relation to malaria eradication, the dearth of basic information and data was all too apparent (Prothero, 1961). These basic data relate to the volume, pattern and timing of migrations. In a number of instances where limited studies of migration have been carried out, mainly by sociologists and social anthropologists, there has been little attention given to these aspects and rather more esoteric features of migration have been investigated. More may be known of the effects of migration on marital stability and on other social problems than on how many people migrate, where they originate and to where they go, the routes by which they travel and the times at which they travel. For the effects of migration on disease transmission and eradication it is such basic facts that are required and they are also needed for other aspects of social and economic development. But for the most part they are not available, and the mobility of population may therefore act as a deterrent to progress because accurate allowance cannot be made for it in planning for various developments. In tropical Africa in the future more needs to be known about all types of migration in its many different aspects. International co-ordination and co-operation are essential. Though achievements to date are limited, enough is known to make possible the successful planning of future investigation, so that migration may no longer be the 'Cinderella' of population studies in tropical Africa.

Footnotes

1. Particularly by Dr J. M. Hunter, University of Durham, formerly of the University of Ghana, and Dr G. Kay, University of Hull, formerly of the Rhodes-Livingstone Institute, Lusaka, to whom acknowledgement is made for their help.
2. For earlier studies of migrant labour movements across the Volta ferries see R. B. Davison, *Migrant Labour in the Gold Coast*, Department of Economics, University College of the Gold Coast, Accra, 1954.

References

BARBOUR, K. M., 'Rural–rural migrations in Africa: a geographical introduction', *Cahiers de l'Institut de Science Economique Appliquée*, 1965, pp. 47–68.

BASUTOLAND, *Census of Basutoland*, 1956.
DAVIES, H. R. J., 'The West African in the economic geography of the Sudan', *Geography*, 49, 1964, pp. 222–35.
DUPIRE, M., *Peuples nomades*, 1962.
ENGMANN, E. V. T., 'Population movements in Ghana: a study of internal migration and its implications for the planner', *Bulletin Ghana Geographical Association*, 10, 1965, pp. 41–65.
FEDERAL STATISTICS, *Report on labour migration, Sokoto Province*, Department of Statistics, Lagos, 1954.
FROELICH, J. G., 'Densité de la population et méthodes de culture chez les Kabré du Nord Togo', *Comptes rendus du Congrés International de Géographie, Lisbonne, 1949*, Tome 4, Section 5, 1952, pp. 168–80.
GILLMAN, C., 'A population map of Tanganyika Territory', *Geographical Review*, 26, 1936, pp. 353–75.
GLEAVE, M. B., 'Hill settlements and their abandonment in western Yorubaland', *Africa*, 33, 1963, pp. 343–52.
———, 'The changing frontiers of settlement in the uplands of Northern Nigeria', *Nigerian Geographical Journal*, 8, 1963, pp. 127–41.
GREEN, L. P. and FAIR, T. J. D., *Development in Africa*, Johannesburg, 1962.
HOPEN, C. E., *The pastoral Fulbe family in Gwandu*, 1958.
HOUGHTON, D. H., 'Migrant labour', in SMITH, P. (ed.) *Africa in transition*, 1958.
HURST, H. R. G., 'A survey of the development of facilities for migrant labour in Tanganyika during the period 1926–1959', *Bulletin Inter-African Labour Institute*, 4, 1959, pp. 50–91.
KAY, G., Personal communication, 1966.
KENYA, *Population Census 1962, Volume II: Population of census areas by tribe and sex*, Directorate of Economic Planning, Ministry of Finance and Economic Planning, 1962.
KROTKI, K. J., *First population census of Sudan 1955/56: 21 facts about the Sudanese*, Khartoum, 1958.
LEWIS, I. M., *A pastoral democracy*, 1961.
LORIMER, F., *Demographic information on tropical Africa*, 1961.
MABOGUNJE, A. L., *Yoruba towns*, Ibadan, 1962.
MATHER, D. B., 'Migration in the Sudan', in STEEL, R. W. and FISHER, C. A. (ed.), *Geographical essays on British tropical lands*, 1956.
MERCIER, P., 'Densités de la population dans le moyen Dahomey', *Comptes rendues du Congrés International de Géographie, Lisbonne, 1949*, Tome 4, Section 5, 1952, pp. 181–91.
———, 'Urban explosion in developing countries', *UNESCO Courier*, 1963, pp. 50–55.
MITCHEL, N. C., 'Yoruba towns', in BARBOUR, K. M. and PROTHERO, R. M. (ed.), *Essays on African population*, 1961.
MITCHELL, J. C., 'The causes of labour migration', *Bulletin, Inter-African Labour Institute*, 6, 1959, pp. 12–46.
———, 'Wage labour and African population movements in Central Africa', in PROTHERO and BARBOUR, *op. cit.*, 1961.
PANOFSKY, H., 'Migratory labour in Africa' (Bibliographical article), *Journal of Modern African Studies*, 1, 1963, pp. 521–29.
PIAULT, M. P., 'Migrations des travailleurs en Afrique de l'Ouest', *Bulletin, Inter-African Labour Institute*, 8, 1961, pp. 111–30.
PROTHERO, R. M., 'The population census of Northern Nigeria, 1952: problems and results', *Population Studies*, 10, 1956, pp. 166–83.
———, 'Migratory labour from north-western Nigeria', *Africa*, 37, 1957, pp. 251–61.
———, *Migrant labour from Sokoto Province, Northern Nigeria*, Kaduna, 1959.
———, 'Population movements and problems of malaria eradication in Africa', *Bulletin, World Health Organization*, 24, 1961, pp. 405–25.
———, 'African ethnographic maps with a new example from Northern Nigeria', *Africa*, 32, 1962, pp. 61–64.
———, 'Migrant labour in West Africa', *Journal of Local Administration Overseas*, 1, 1962, pp. 149–55.
———, 'Continuity and change in African population mobility', in STEEL, R. W. and PROTHERO, R. M. (ed.), *Geographers and the tropics: Liverpool essays*, 1964.
———, *Migrants and malaria*, 1965.
RIAD, M., 'The Juk n: an example of African migrations in the sixteenth century', *Bulletin Institut Français d'Afrique Noire*, Ser. B. 22, 1960, pp. 476–85.
ROUCH, J., 'Migrations au Ghana', *Journal Societé des Africanistes*, 26, 1957, pp. 33–96.
———, 'The study of migrations in West Africa', *Africa*, 29, 1959, pp. 417–19.
SMITH, T. E. and BLACKER, J. G. C., *Population characteristics of the Commonwealth countries of tropical Africa*, University of London, Institute of Commonwealth Studies, *Commonwealth Papers*, 9, 1963.

SOUTHALL, A. W., 'Population movements in East Africa', in BARBOUR and PROTHERO, *op. cit.*, 1961.

STEEL, R. W., 'The towns of tropical Africa', in BARBOUR and PROTHERO, *op. cit.*, 1961.

STENNING, D. J., *Savannah nomads*, 1959.

UGANDA, *General African Census 1959, Volume II, Part 1: Tribal Analysis for Protectorate, Provinces, Districts and Counties*, East African Statistical Department, 1960.

UNESCO, *Social implications of industrialisation and urbanisation in Africa south of the Sahara*, 1956.

WITWATERSRAND, 'Organization of migrant labour in the South African mining industry by the Witwatersrand Native Labour Association', *Bulletin, Inter-African Labour Institute*, 4, 1959, pp. 40–49.

26 Some aspects of population movements in Kenya

S. H. Ominde

Department of Geography, University College, Nairobi, Kenya

Introduction

Although concern in Kenya over population pressure upon land is of long standing, two new aspects of the population question have emerged in the post-colonial era. On the one hand, there is the point of view that regards human numbers as a resource element in development: on the other hand, there is the equally powerful view that considers increasing human numbers a liability. In East Africa, concern with the study of population has concentrated largely on the total numbers, the rate of increase and the related problem of growth. This is partly a reflection of the serious limitation of data and the absence of reliable bases for interpretation. The data available have permitted the geographical analysis of the distribution of total numbers and a superficial impression of man–land relationships. Other social scientists have with incomplete data attempted to answer questions concerning the demographic pattern and growth of the population.[1,2]

Among geographers, contributions to population research have been limited largely to distribution maps. These studies, though valuable because of the overall picture presented, have given undue weight to less dynamic features of population than those which are of direct importance to the social and economic planners.

This paper deals with the geographical mobility of population, an aspect that has received little attention. The neglect of this area of research has been forced upon the scholars by the lack of adequate data, aggravated by the instability of administrative boundaries. This study utilizes the administrative boundaries prior to the reorganization that followed the Regional Boundary Commission's recommendations in 1962.[3] It is primarily concerned with the Kenya-born section of the African population and is essentially a study of internal movements of population. The rural–urban movement has been examined elsewhere.[4] This paper will largely examine the interprovincial movements which are mainly from the more to the less developed parts of rural Kenya.

Mobility of Population in Kenya

In an attempt to assess the volume of migrant population we may first turn to the following pattern of external sources of births as recorded for the six census areas in 1962.[5]

This summary of incoming population brings out the contrast between, on the one hand, the Rift Valley, Nairobi Extra-Provincial district, the Coast and Central Province and, on the other hand, Nyanza and Southern Province. The Rift Valley accounted for over 43 per cent of the total and the Nairobi Extra-Provincial district for about 26 per cent of the total. But a closer analysis will subsequently show that the Central Province associates more closely with the second group of Provinces. The main receiving areas outlined above must be considered as forming a different category from Nyanza Province and the Southern Province which had only 4·61 per cent and 2·09 per cent of the total respectively.

Table 1

Kenya: Persons Born outside Province of Enumeration, 1962

Census Area	Persons	Percentage
Nairobi Extra-Provincial district	155,588	25·73
Central Province	67,629	11·18
Coast Province	77,626	12·84
Nyanza Province	27,900	4·61
Rift Valley Province	263,333	43·55
Southern Province	12,624	2·09
TOTAL	604,700	100·00

Source: 1962 census.

Of the total 604,700 interprovincial migrants, the contribution of Kenyan sources by census areas are shown in Table 2.

Table 2

Kenya: Birthplace of Interprovincial Migrants, 1962

Census Area	Persons	Percentage
Nairobi Extra-Provincial district	8,901	1·47
Central Province	215,356	35·61
Coast Province	5,741	0·95
Nyanza Province	211,482	34·97
Rift Valley Province	41,887	6·93
Southern Province	106,502	17·61
Northern Province	14,831	2·45
TOTAL	604,700	99·99

Source: 1962 census.

A clearer picture of the striking imbalance of population and a measure of the direction of flow may be seen from the following comparisons.

Table 3

Kenya: Interprovincial Immigration and Emigration since Birth, 1962

Census Area	Total immigrants	Total emigrants	Gain(+) Loss(−)
Nairobi Extra-Provincial district	155,588	8,901	146,687(+)
Central Province	67,629	215,356	147,727(−)
Coast Province	77,626	5,741	71,885(+)
Nyanza Province	27,900	211,482	183,582(−)
Rift Valley Province	263,333	41,887	221,446(+)
Southern Province	12,624	106,502	93,878(−)

Source: 1962 census.

The balance of inward and outward moving populations showed three areas that had gained population. The Rift Valley had a large net gain of 221,446 persons from outside the Province, Nairobi Extra-Provincial district 146,687 and the Coast Province a net gain of 71,885 persons. Three provinces which showed a loss were Nyanza Province (183,582), Central (147,727) and Southern (93,878).

The Rift Valley Province emerged as the most important destination of the migrant element of Kenya's population, attracting about 44 per cent of the total. This is also important in the elucidation of some of the factors underlying the general shifts of population in the country. Migrant sources were dominated by Central Province with 48·24 per cent of the total and Nyanza with 43·58 per cent. The remainder were contributed by the neighbouring provinces and the Nairobi Extra-Provincial district.

Out of the total movement of 155,588 persons into the Nairobi Extra-Provincial area, an analysis of source area showed that the Central Province with 42·64 per cent predominated. The second most important source was Nyanza Province in the Lake Victoria basin. This Province contributed 31·31 per cent. The Rift Valley, Coast and the Northern Provinces were insignificant as sources of Nairobi Extra-Provincial migrant population.

Causes of Population Movements

It is not possible, within the limits of this paper and in the present state of research on population mobility, to deal exhaustively with the causes and effects of such movements. In this section the fundamental geographical features of the movement will be stressed and an attempt made to focus attention on the possible implications of the movements.

The first feature that emerges is the correspondence between the sources of population and the denser population regions of the country. There is a large flow of population from the region near Lake Victoria with North Nyanza, Central Nyanza and Kisii districts as the main feeder areas. Another important source is the eastern Highlands of Kenya, especially the dense population cluster around Mount Kenya, Aberdares, including the Kikuyu districts of Kiambu, Fort Hall, Nyeri, Embu and Meru. Some of the highest known rural densities, comparable to the great population centres of south-east and southern Asia, have been recorded in this area. East of the Rift Highlands, the residual hills of Machakos and Kitui, with their poor economies in relation to population, are further sources of the Republic's migrant population.

The association of the main supplying regions and the principal population centres suggests the pressure of population on land resources as a factor inducing people to move out, not only from rural to urban areas, but also from one part of rural Kenya to another. The problem of man–land ratios is complex and is not the subject of this paper. However, it is certainly a factor in those areas where densities of well over 500 persons per square mile have been reached in predominantly African rural areas. Certainly it will be noted that the dominant ethnic elements in the migrant population come from areas of high population density, where the rural economy is predominantly subsistence.

But, if the uneven distribution of population has been one of the decisive factors influencing the volume and direction of movement, the past economic policy of the country must be recognized as providing the initial impetus for this important movement. There was a marked contrast between the former 'White Highland' area and the districts that were predominantly African and in which a different land policy and type of agriculture were pursued. It is for this reason that the Rift Valley has been the main goal of the migrant population. The demand for labour in the modern farms that developed in the north, west and east Rift Highland districts explained the large flow of migrants to these districts. The urbanization associated with this economic revolution tended to intensify the attraction of those areas in which towns were located.

The importance of the Nairobi Extra-Provincial district and the dominance of Nakuru district in the Rift Valley Province are indications of the importance of pre-Independence economic policies and consequent urbanization. These policies have resulted in a widening gap between the rural centres of population and the main areas of economic growth, differences that are reflected in the following per capita income of the Provinces relatively gaining population and those from which there has been substantial emigration.

Table 4

Kenya: Per Capita Income [Monetary only], 1962

Area	£ sterling
Nairobi Extra-Provincial district	252·55
Rift Valley Province	22·58
Coast Province	38·78
Central Province	12·15
Nyanza Province	5·94
Southern Province	5·41

Source: Economics and Statistical Division, Ministry of Finance and Economic Planning.

However, these are merely generalized figures, that mask the disparities in the condition of the rural population. Much of the wealth in Nairobi, for instance, is in the hands of non-Africans. No allowance is made in these figures for differences within the main emigrant areas of the Central, Nyanza and Southern Provinces.

Effects of Population Mobility

Population mobility is a vital field of interest to social and economic planners. The students of population geography are particularly interested in the selective impact of the movements on the rural population, and in the qualitative aspects of the moving population and its bearings on such problems as urbanization.

EMIGRATION RATES

On the basis of the 1962 census, emigration rates, expressed as a percentage, reveal considerable differences between the main ethnic elements in the Provinces. The figures given below are derived by subtracting the home district total from the national total and the resulting figure is expressed as a percentage of all those of the ethnic group.

Throughout the country, migration rates for the principal ethnic groups are much higher for the male section of the population than for the females. Within each Province, certain groups have been more affected by this movement. Emigration was least among the nomadic pastoralists and more in evidence among the cultivators.

THE AGE–SEX CHARACTERISTICS OF THE RURAL AND URBAN POPULATION

The implications of the population migrations in the whole country are most clearly reflected in age–sex pyramids. Analysis of these pyramids brings out first the distinctive contrast between the main supplying and receiving rural areas of Kenya.

From the main source districts (represented by Central and North Nyanza, Machakos and Fort Hall) migration causes a deficiency in the male population between the ages 19 and 44. The age–sex pyramid for Central Nyanza is typical of

Table 5

Kenya: Emigration Rates of the Principal Ethnic Groups by Provinces

Group	(Percentages)		
	Total	Males	Females
Central Province			
Kikuyu	40·0	42·3	37·8
Tharaka	15·9	16·6	15·3
Embu	6·6	9·1	5·1
Mbere	3·4	5·5	1·6
Meru	1·9	3·0	0·8
Nyanza Province			
Luhya	17·6	21·7	14·3
Luo	14·0	16·8	11·2
Iteso	13·3	14·6	12·1
Kuria	8·1	11·7	4·6
Kisii	4·9	6·6	3·3
Southern Province			
Kamba	12·4	15·6	9·3
Masai	9·3	10·7	8·0
Rift Valley Province			
Nandi	37·2	38·0	36·3
Pokot	30·4	32·8	28·1
Sabaot	19·4	19·7	19·2
Kipsigis	16·5	17·6	15·4
Elgeyo	9·8	10·3	9·2
Tugen	5·9	7·5	4·3
Marakwet	2·8	3·8	1·8
Northern Province			
Somali/Galla	3·6	3·7	3·5
Samburu	3·4	4·3	2·6
Coast Province			
Pokomo/Riverine	33·0	35·0	31·0
Swahili/Shirazi	21·4	21·4	21·4
Bajun	19·8	20·9	18·7
Taita	14·3	18·3	10·7
Mijikenda	11·2	13·0	9·3

those districts from which large scale movements have taken place. But this is not characteristic of other districts such as Gusii South and Elgon Nyanza which have been affected by outward movements to a less extent. In the Central Province, Kiambu is one of the main source districts but the population pyramid does not show the deficiency indicated in the Fort Hall district. This is probably due to the effect of movement into Nairobi environs and possibly the plantation farming activity that attracts substantial migration into the district.

The districts that formerly formed part of the 'White Highlands', or in which modern large-scale non-African farming predominated, show a marked excess of population between ages 19 and 44. This is the typical population pattern of most of the Rift Valley farming districts such as Nakuru, Naivasha, Uasin Gishu and Trans-Nzoia. The pattern is also found in the Kericho district in which the development of tea plantations has created a large demand for labour.

The excess of population between ages 19 and 44, although a feature of receiving rural areas, is more striking in the urban areas which have been a migration goal of increasing importance. Both are characterized by a high rate of masculinity.

Conclusion

Population mobility is but one aspect of the differences that exist in the basic resources of Kenya. But this paper concludes that it is the selective development of these resources and particularly the economic policies of an earlier colonial period that are reflected in the volume and direction of flow of the population.

Social and economic planning must take into account the established flow of population from the main population regions of the Lake Basin, the Eastern Rift Highlands and the residual hills east of the highlands. In terms of volume, the total population involved appears to be small. But it has been shown that migration, though most intense in certain parts of the country, is nationwide, and the impact is greater on certain ethnic groups than on others.

Footnotes

1. J. E. GOLDTHORPE, 'The African Population of East Africa: A summary of its Past and Present Trends', *East African Royal Commission Report*, 1953–55, Appendix VII, pp. 462–73.
2. J. G. C. BLACKER, 'Population Growth and Urbanisation', *Report of the United Nations Mission to Kenya on Housing*, 1965, Appendix A, pp. 59–64.
3. GOVERNMENT OF KENYA, *Report of the Regional Boundaries Commission*, Cmnd. 1899, HMSO, Appendix XVI, Map 7.
4. S. H. OMINDE, 'Population Movements to the Main Urban Areas of Kenya', *Cahiers d'Etudes Africaines*, Vol. V, No. 20, 1965, pp. 593–617.
5. MINISTRY OF ECONOMIC PLANNING AND DEVELOPMENT, Economics and Statistics Division, *Birth Place*, Kenya Population Census, 1962 (10 per cent Sample Census).

27 Population distribution in Sierra Leone

John I. Clarke
Geography Department, University of Durham, UK

The first national census of Sierra Leone was held on 1 April 1963. Publication of the three volumes of the final report of the census, planned for the last quarter of 1965, has occurred too late for use in the preparation of this paper, for which only the advance reports and other limited data were available.

Previous Censuses and Estimates

Previous censuses held in the former Colony and Protectorate of Sierra Leone have been critically analysed by Kuczynski.[1] They were much more useful and reliable for the tiny Colony, occupying some 256 square miles mostly on the Sierra Leone Peninsula, than for the much larger Protectorate, which measured 27,669 square miles. In the Colony, irregular censuses were held from 1802 until 1860 and decennial censuses from 1871 until 1931, but they had different degrees of comprehensiveness. In contrast, so-called censuses were held decennially in the Protectorate from 1901 to 1931, but they were little more than reasoned guesses or estimates. Even the report of the 1948 census of the Colony and Protectorate of Sierra Leone, which gave a total of 1,860,000 persons, was merely 'a flimsy document consisting of a single sheet of paper folded down the middle'.[2] Subsequent estimates were largely based on the number of taxpayers per district multiplied by an assumed number of persons per taxpayer, which varied from 3·4 to 7·0 according to the district. From these calculations it was estimated at the time of the census that the total population of Sierra Leone was about 2,500,000.

The 1963 Census

At the 1963 census 2,180,355 persons were enumerated. Inevitably, the census total was received with some disappointment and criticism. There were fears that the census total would reduce the country's international prestige and prejudice her chances to attract foreign financial aid. Yet there are more than 20 political units in Africa with smaller populations, and ten of them are independent: Central African Republic, Congo (Brazzaville), Dahomey, Gabon, Gambia, Liberia, Libya, Mauritania, Somalia and Togo. Moreover, the main reason for a small population is that Sierra Leone is small in area (27,925 square miles)—it will fit into Africa no less than 414 times. Indeed by African standards her 1963 population density of 78 per square mile is high and is exceeded by only five other African states: Rwanda (263 per square mile), Burundi (250), Nigeria (156), Tunisia (93) and Gambia (79).

Some politicians inferred population decline from comparison of the census total with previous estimates. Some felt that the total should have been nearer 4 or 5 million, and made accusations of under-counting, although the post-enumeration survey indicated that persons missed in the census equalled only 3½ per cent of those enumerated,[3] implying a real total of about 2¼ million.

Differing views arose from the study of the disparities between previous estimates and census figures of the various districts and Provinces of Sierra Leone (Table 1). These disparities were greatest in Southern Province, where former estimates had been high; but they had been low in Western Area (i.e. most of the former Colony). Comparison of the census method with former estimates does not show the census

Table 1

Sierra Leone: Population Data by Province and District

District	1956 estimate[1]	1960 estimate[2]	1963 census	Popn. density per sq. ml. 1963	Popn. per representative[3] 1963	Females per 1,000 males	Males 15–54 per cent of total popn.
Bo	250,000	400,000	209,754	104	23,306	963	29·4
Bonthe	100,000	88,626	80,139	57	16,028	1,056	24·8
Moyamba	213,634	226,889	167,425	63	33,485	1,062	23·6
Pujehun	129,523	129,267	84,869	54	21,217	1,124	23·5
Southern Province	693,157	844,782	542,187	71	23,573	1,031	26·0
Kailahun	224,364	142,179	150,236	97	37,599	1,145	22·0
Kenema	195,076	296,064	227,428	97	32,490	851	34·3
Kono	125,788	151,977	167,915	78	33,583	847	33·5
Eastern Province	545,228	590,220	545,579	90	34,099	922	30·7
Bombali	181,041	201,355	198,776	64	39,755	1,173	19·3
Kambia	122,800	123,782	137,806	115	34,451	1,083	21·7
Koinadugu	124,000	118,840	129,061	28	43,020	1,073	21·6
Port Loko	208,369	257,096	247,463	112	41,244	1,050	22·6
Tonkolili	164,220	202,405	184,460	68	36,892	1,120	21·4
Northern Province	800,430	903,478	897,566	65	39,025	1,099	21·3
Freetown	70,000	100,000	127,917	23,600	21,319	902	30·9
Rural areas	60,000	60,000	67,106	267	11,814	888	29·3
Western Area	130,000	160,000	195,023	762	16,252	897	30·4
SIERRA LEONE	2,168,815	2,498,480	2,180,355	78	29,464	1,017	25·6

1. D. T. JACK, *Economic Survey of Sierra Leone*, Freetown, 1958.
2. *Provinces Handbook*, 1961.
3. Includes 62 elected members and 12 Paramount Chiefs.

to have a high degree of accuracy. It is questionable whether the administrative census method used in anglophone territories of West Africa should be retained or discarded in favour of the sampling inquiry techniques used in francophone countries.[4] Certainly, the latter technique provides more valuable data on population movement. The limited questionnaire for the Sierra Leone census did not include questions on fertility, mortality or marital status.

Publication of the provisional census results also confirmed unease regarding the uneven population size of the 62 electoral constituencies, which range from less than 3,000 inhabitants to nearly 80,000. There are nine constituencies with less than 15,000 inhabitants, and seven with more than 55,000, the average being about 33,500. Apart from the unusually small constituencies of the Western Rural Area, there is no clear regional pattern of constituency sizes save a tendency for larger populations in northern districts than in southern districts (Table 1). Inevitably, there have been calls upon the Government to effect a more equitable parliamentary representation.

Another delicate matter raised by the census is the comparative numbers of the two principal tribes, the Mende and the Temne. According to the census, the former, who provide the majority of the present Government, slightly exceed the Temne, but together they account for 60·7 per cent of the total population (Table 2).

In contrast, the once dominant Creole community now number only 41,783 or 1·9 per cent of the total.

Table 2

Sierra Leone: Tribal Composition, 1963

Tribe	Number	Per cent
Mende	672,831	30·9
Temne	648,931	29·8
Limba	183,496	8·4
Kono	104,573	4·8
Koranko	80,732	3·7
Sherbro	74,674	3·4
Susu	67,288	3·1
Fula	66,824	3·1
Loko	64,459	2·9
Madingo	51,024	2·3
Kissi	48,954	2·3
Creole	41,783	1·9
Yalunka	15,005	0·7
Krim	8,733	0·4
Gallinas/Vai	7,986	0·4
Gola	4,854	0·2
Kru	4,793	0·2
No tribe/Others	33,415	1·5

Despite these various misgivings, the Sierra Leone Government decided to accept the census results, though the late Prime Minister Sir Milton Margai announced his intention of holding another census two years later.

Population Distribution and Density

Publication of the census will be by administrative divisions and by locality. The administrative divisions are:

(a) Eastern, Northern and Southern Provinces, containing 12 districts and 146 chiefdoms; and

(b) Western Area, including Freetown and six rural areas of the Western Rural Area.

Localities are defined as cities, towns and villages.

Although some 2,900 enumeration area maps were prepared for the census, the quality of base maps was inadequate. The old 1 : 62,500 coverage was often inaccurate and the new 1 : 50,000 coverage (based on air photographs) was at an early stage. Moreover, there was insufficient time and money for preparation of a large number of enumeration area maps from air photographs. Another difficulty is that no accurate maps of chiefdom boundaries are available, and chiefdom areas represent only crude estimates. Analysis of population distribution and density on the basis of chiefdom data can therefore give no more than a generalized picture. More detailed geographical analysis of the population distribution of Sierra Leone awaits the preparation of a population map at 1 : 500,000 from enumeration area maps and data, using the system recommended by the IGU Commission on a World Population Map.[5] Despite these deficiencies, it is possible for the first time to attain a reasonable general picture of population distribution within the country.

Sierra Leone's compact territory has neither desert voids nor great concentrations of population. Nevertheless, population densities of chiefdoms range from less than

20 to nearly 250 per square mile, and analysis of the frequency distribution of population densities (Table 3) shows that over half of the population live on one-quarter of the area, and over three-quarters on one-half of the area. The level of population concentration is much lower than in most developed countries, but it is growing, especially in recent decades, through migration, which is a response to the changing pattern of economic activities.

Table 3

Sierra Leone: Population Concentration, 1963

Density class per sq. ml.	Area		Population	
	Percentage	Cumulative percentage	Percentage	Cumulative percentage
150 and over	7·40		25·67	
100–149·9	14·54	21·94	23·06	48·73
75–99·9	16·18	38·12	18·05	66·78
50–74·9	24·21	62·33	19·15	85·93
25–49·9	22·15	84·48	10·67	96·60
Less than 25	15·52	100·00	3·40	100·00

The traditional pattern of population distribution reflected mainly the influence of relief and rainfall, slavery and tribal warfare, vegetation and farming practices. These and other influences are still discernible in the settlement map, and account for many of the regional disparities in population density. The 20th century has brought four major new influences upon the population pattern: modern communications, urbanization, export agriculture and mining. At present these influences are localized in a few areas, and this tends to intensify the unevenness of population distribution.

The general population map of Sierra Leone reveals two rather amorphous zones of population concentration within the north-western and south-eastern quarters of the country. The north-western quarter, which includes the Freetown agglomeration and Makeni, has swamp rice-farming, fishing, iron-ore mining (at Marampa) and some market gardening. In contrast, the south-eastern quarter is important for diamond mining, and for the production of cocoa, coffee, piassava, palm-oil and kernels, as well as some forestry. These are the developing zones, with the main urban centres and hospitals, and with the only rail, air and good road links. They are attractive to migrants, not only from other parts of Sierra Leone—as we see in the maps of tribal distributions,[6] from the 1963 census—but also from other West African countries, Europe, the Lebanon and India. Swindell's analysis of the origins of the labour force at Marampa iron-ore mine[7] and of diamond-mining workers[8] emphasizes the considerable mobility of population.

Elsewhere, population densities are lower. In the far north and the north-east, sparse populations are associated with mountainous terrain, Guinea savanna, cattle farming and poor communications, as well as a dearth of towns and of medical facilities. Sparse populations also occur along the hilly and forested Liberian border zone and along the southern coasts, where there has been less development of swamp rice-farming than in the north-west. The old ports of Sulima and Bonthe are dead and dying respectively, and the area has suffered decline. Fortunately, recent developments of rutile and bauxite mining in the south may bring some revival.

In sum, economic influences of the 20th century have greatly modified the population map of Sierra Leone by encouraging migration. But it would be wrong to ascribe a close correlation between population density and migration, either in regions of departure or arrival.

Centrality

The general distribution of population in Sierra Leone and the compact circular shape of the country encourages the study of centrality or central tendency of the population.[9] A remarkable fact that emerges is that the geographic centre, the mean centre of population and the median centre (or point of minimum aggregate travel) all lie within 18 miles of each other in Bonkolenken chiefdom along the southern-fringe of Northern Province and on the margins of Mende and Temne country. The two centres of population lie within 10 miles of each other to the south of Magburaka and to the west of the geographic centre, having been 'pulled' westwards by the population of Freetown. This central tendency of population distribution, which of course takes no account of communications, is worthy of serious consideration for the provision of social services, at present unequally distributed in relation to population.[10]

Urbanization

Although population density is high for this part of West Africa, Sierra Leone is still overwhelmingly rural. More than three-quarters of the population live in localities with less than 1,000 inhabitants (Table 4) and more than four-fifths in localities with less than 2,000. There is no official definition of urban status in Sierra Leone, but if we accept the arbitrary size limit of 5,000 inhabitants, then 18 localities and 13·0 per cent of the total population may be classed as urban (cf. 23·1 per cent of Ghana's population in 1960). As an indication of the increased urbanization of recent decades, it may be noted that in 1927 (at the time of the first major topographic survey of Sierra Leone) only two localities, Freetown and Bonthe, had more than 5,000 inhabitants.

Table 4

Sierra Leone: Population in Localities by Size-class, 1963

Size of locality	Number	Population	Percentage
30,000 and over	1	127,917	5·9
15,000–29,999	1	26,613	1·2
10,000–14,999	5	62,531	2·9
5,000– 9,999	11	66,236	3·0
2,500– 4,999	30	102,627	4·7
1,000– 2,499	108	157,829	7·2
Below 1,000		1,636,602	75·1
		2,180,355	100·0

The 5,000 population threshold of urban status is useful but far from ideal. After functional analysis of towns in Sierra Leone, Harvey[11] considers a threshold of 1,000 inhabitants along with two central place functions as more appropriate, in which case 80 localities would be termed urban and the total urban population would be 414,572 or 19·0 per cent of the total.

Freetown exhibits such primacy that its population (127,917) is more than the combined populations of the 11 next largest towns. With its inner and outer suburbs of Murray Town, Kissy, Wilberforce, Lumley, Aberdeen, Goderich and Wellington, the Freetown agglomeration contains 162,571 persons or 7·5 per cent of the total population. This level of hegemony is not unusual in Africa, where some new capitals have experienced mercurial growth. It is exceeded, for example, by Dakar and Monrovia. Freetown has doubled in size only since the Second World War; more rapid development has been hindered by its restricted hinterland and the smallness of the country. Nevertheless, a rising proportion of the secondary and tertiary sectors of the population is concentrated in the capital and its supremacy is assured. Present growth results not only from migration; mortality is lower than elsewhere, partly owing to the fact that Western Area, with one-eleventh of the total population, has more than one-third of the hospital beds in the country.

In the Provinces, urbanization is incipient and localized, the traditional settlement pattern being of large villages with daughter settlements. Urbanization has largely resulted from:

(a) the establishment of administrative centres;
(b) the evolution of commercial agriculture;
(c) the creation of the railway (1895–1916) and the more recent road network; and
(d) the development of mining (iron ore, diamonds, gold, chrome, bauxite and rutile) since 1930.

Mining, especially of diamonds, has exerted a powerful influence on the pattern of small urban centres, but this influence may be temporary as neither diamond nor iron-ore mining is expected to outlive this century.

The present pattern of towns therefore conforms closely with the pattern of population distribution. In the future, urbanization in the provinces will be greatly influenced by Government planning. New roads and plantations could substantially modify the present pattern.

Distribution by Age and Sex[12]

Age data are probably the most unreliable of all aspects enumerated at the census. Age and sex distributions reveal most of the biases characteristic of African demographic data,[13] notably:

(a) underreporting of the age-group 10–14, especially of females;
(b) underreporting of young and mid-adult men giving low ratios of males to females, though an appreciable national influence here is the temporary, periodic emigration of Sierra Leonean males for education and work;
(c) preferential reporting of women in the central reproductive age-groups; and
(d) overreporting in the age-group 65 and over.

The resulting age-pyramid is irregular and unbalanced (Table 5), though in general terms it cannot be very inaccurate. From the census we find that 36·7 per cent are under 15 years, 54·3 per cent under 25 years and 71·7 per cent under 35 years. The overall sex-ratio is 983 males per 1,000 females.

Analysis of the age and sex data of the 1963 census is impeded by the absence of vital statistics and of reliable earlier census data, save in the case of the Western Area. There in 1962 the crude birth rate was 41·4 per 1,000 and the death rate 18·6 per 1,000, giving a natural increase rate of 22·8 per 1,000. But these figures are certainly not accurate or typical of Sierra Leone as a whole, for in the provinces mortality is undoubtedly much higher. Nevertheless, there is no reason to suppose important regional variations in differential fertility and mortality or in bias of data. Regional patterns of age and sex composition are therefore likely to be mostly reflective of migrations.

Most migrants, African and expatriate, are males, who form substantial majorities in areas and towns experiencing inward migration (Table 1). The census revealed that the diamond-mining area of eastern Sierra Leone had a total excess of 46,309

Table 5

Sierra Leone: Age and Sex-structure, 1963

Age-groups	Numbers	Percentages	Females per 1,000 males
Under 5	377,335	17·3	1,014
5–9	280,619	12·9	920
10–14	142,420	6·5	874
15–19	194,378	8·9	1,346
20–24	190,784	8·7	1,526
25–29	207,753	9·5	1,221
30–34	172,183	7·9	1,106
35–39	136,384	6·3	882
40–44	114,758	5·3	822
45–49	85,531	3·9	714
50–54	69,957	3·2	736
55–59	41,760	1·9	729
60–64	55,954	2·6	857
65 and over	110,509	5·1	868
TOTAL	2,180,355	100·0	1,017

males in April 1963 (a month when mining is in full swing). This excess was spread over 19 chiefdoms, in five of which sex-ratios were less than 700 females per 1,000 males. The male preponderance was even greater in the towns of the diamond-mining area, and in several there were less than 500 females per 1,000 males. A large excess of 10,543 males in Western Area was mainly located in the Freetown agglomeration which offers opportunities for employment and education. Three other areas have much less significant male surpluses: Kaffu Bullom and Loko Masama chiefdoms of Port Loko district, where rice farming, fishing and the port of Pepel are key factors; the northern border area, where Fula cattle-herders from Guinea are numerous; and Sherbro Urban District Council in the south. Elsewhere females outnumber males, especially in the Temne and Limba areas of north-central Sierra Leone, the source area of so many migrants. Even the iron-ore mine at Marampa has little effect—largely because it is long-established and workers' families have settled down.

Analysis of the numbers of males aged 15–54 as proportions of total populations of administrative units emphasizes the marked contrast between:

(a) an extensive area in south-eastern Sierra Leone with high proportions in this age-group; and
(b) a fairly compact belt in north-central Sierra Leone with low numbers aged 15–54.

The former area includes not only the diamond districts, but also new rice-farming areas as well as part of the cocoa and coffee areas. The rice-farming areas of the north-west also have an above-average proportion of men aged 15–54. Extreme values are 49·8 per cent in Wando chiefdom (Kenema district) and 17·8 per cent in Gbanti Kamaranka (Bombali district), the median value being 22·9.

It has been suggested that the present pattern of population distribution is not merely a product of recent migrations, but also reflects physical and traditional influences. It is not surprising, therefore, that the coefficient of correlation between sex ratios and population densities is only 0·502, certainly not as high as in Ghana.[14] Nevertheless, all the signs indicate increasing mobility of population.

Footnotes

1. KUCZYNSKI, R. R., *A Demographic Survey of the British Colonial Empire*, Vol. 1, British West Africa, London, 1948, pp. 19–307.
2. BANTON, M., *West African City, A Study of Tribal Life in Freetown*, London, 1957, p. 78.
3. BENJAMIN, E., 'The Sierra Leone Census, 1963', *The Bulletin. The Journal of the Sierra Leone Geographical Association*, No. 9, 1965, pp. 63–71.
4. KAYSER, B., 'La démographie de l'Afrique Occidentale et Centrale', *Les Cahiers d'Outre-Mer*, Vol. 18, 1965, pp. 73–85.
5. In preparation by Mrs F. Bangura, Department of Geography, Fourah Bay College, the University of Sierra Leone.
6. HARVEY, M. E., 'Ethnic Groups' in *Sierra Leone in Maps* ed. by CLARKE, J. I., London, 1966.
7. SWINDELL, K., 'Origins of Marampa Labour Force', *ibid.*
8. SWINDELL, K., 'Diamond Mining in Sierra Leone', *Tijdschrift voor Economische en Sociale Geografie*, Vol. 57, 1966, pp. 96–104.
9. CLARKE, J. I., *Population Geography*, London, 1965, pp. 33–36.
10. CLARKE, J. I., 'Educational Establishments' and 'Medical Establishments' in *Sierra Leone in Maps*, *op. cit.*
11. HARVEY, M. E., Personal communication.
12. CLARKE, J. I., 'Sex-Ratios in Sierra Leone', *The Bulletin. The Journal of the Sierra Leone Geographical Association*, No. 9, 1965, pp. 72–77.
13. LORIMER, F., BRASS, W., and VAN DE WALLE, E., 'Demography', Chapter 10 in *The African World*. LYSTAD, R. A. (ed.), London, 1965, p. 286.
14. HUNTER, J. M., 'Regional patterns of population growth in Ghana 1948–60', *Essays in Geography for Austin Miller*, WHITTON, J. B. and WOOD, P. D. (eds.), Reading, 1965, pp. 272–90.

28 Population growth and distribution in the Upper Region of Ghana

T. E. Hilton

Geography Department, University of Ghana, Ghana

Introduction

The Upper Region of Ghana comprises seven Local Authority areas lying along the northern frontier (11° N) with a total area of 10,548 square miles. Only in the south-west is there any great discrepancy between tribal group boundaries and those of Local Authority areas. A majority of the 'indigenous' population speak languages and dialects of the Lobi, Mole-Dagbani and Grusi groups. In each division there are non-Ghanaian minority elements; of these, the numerically more important are Gurma, Mande and Songhai speakers, especially in Kusasi.

International boundaries cut across tribal and clan divisions, there being no difference in the physical environment on either side. The population and economic problems of the area so divided are similar on the two sides of the boundary, save that on the Ghanaian side they are often more acute because of greater population densities. In some inhabited portions of Frafra, for instance, densities exceed 450–500 per square mile. In a restricted zone of Upper Volta along the frontier immediately to the north density reaches 192–320 per square mile, but in general lower densities prevail until 12° N is reached.[1] The generalization about relatively high population densities in Ghana applies in less degree to much of Lawra and Wala facing south-western Upper Volta across the Black Volta, while in only very limited areas of adjoining northern Togo do densities even approach the 200 per square mile calculated for eastern Kusasi.[2]

The following generalized features of economic life and environment bear upon settlement and population movement.

Economic Life

The family, living in its own compound, remains largely a separate self-supporting economic unit. As often in areas where an aboriginal society has been subjected to the rule of warrior invaders, land was regarded as belonging to an earth-god, here Wuni whose intermediary is the *tindana* (loosely rendered 'earth-priest', cf. Mossi *tengsoba*, etc.). To acquire land it was usual to approach the chief; he, if satisfied, would refer to the *tindana*, who alone, in traditional usage, can convey land, and to whom the interest reverts if the line fails. This system is being slowly undermined under modern conditions. The *tindana* determines planting times and other features of agricultural practice, and to this day agriculture in northern Ghana remains more a custom than a business.

The whole area has been farmed over, though parts of it not for many years. It comprises mainly granites and greenstones surrounding Voltaian sandstones. There is a striking difference between the often dense population of the former and the sparse population of the latter.[3] Secondary savanna-woodland predominates in uninhabited riverine and more sparsely peopled watershed areas, park savanna of densely peopled areas is derived from this by removal of shrubs and trees of little economic importance, whilst more useful varieties, e.g. shea, baobab, bombax (used for canoes), and perhaps most useful, duwan, are generally preserved.

Only the Black Volta is perennial. Water shortages and soil erosion become increasingly serious. Well-sinking programmes increase supplies temporarily but worsen future prospects and dams constructed in Land Planning and some other areas supply their immediate neighbourhood most of the year. Piped supplies operate only in a few larger centres.

The north has neither minerals nor cocoa. Economic life remains bound up with subsistence agriculture. In the Upper Region, in 1960, 91·5 per cent of men returned as employed were engaged in agriculture (96·1 per cent in Builsa) as were 77·8 per cent of employed women[4]; most others devoted some time to it. The percentage of employed women in agriculture exceeds 85 in Lawra and Frafra, where the male/female ratio is lowest.

From Wa northwards, in increasingly closely settled and intensively farmed country, Lobi and Dagarti agriculture contrast sharply.[5] Among the matrilineal Lobis, who live in scattered compounds and who pay bride price in cattle, stock rearing is important, and they tend their own animals. Heavily manured compound farms, averaging 3·25 acres and occupying 57 per cent of cultivated land, are most important. The patrilineal Dagartis, living in nucleated settlements, pay bride price in cowries: their cattle are less important and are tended by Fulanis with attendant disadvantages. Compound farms are unimportant; bush farms with fallows allowing considerable regrowth of secondary bush, averaging 13·9 acres, accounted for 67 per cent of cultivated land. The crop economy resembles that of North Mamprusi, described below, with yams grown by Lobis on favoured spots, and by Dagartis on newly broken ground.

There is much deserted land in eastern Wa and southern and eastern Tumu, along the notoriously unhealthy Kulpawn and Sissili rivers. Elsewhere in Tumu, large nucleated villages are surrounded by grassland with scattered shrubs, once cultivated but now worked out, beyond which is thick savanna-woodland from which yam-grain farms have been carved.

In North Mamprusi, owing to pressure of population, dispersed settlement with permanent cultivation is the rule. Compound farms are cropped almost continuously with the aid of household waste and animal droppings and subsidiary bush farms have in course of time fragmented and been built upon by overflow from the original compounds. Land shortage and concomitant problems are most acute in Frafra; here crude calculation gives 1·91 acres of land per person in inhabited areas. Sample surveys by Lynn[6] in the 1930s show compound farms occupying 60 per cent of the cultivated area. Their mean size was 4·28 acres, his and other estimates giving 0·4–0·8 acres supplying each person. After another 30 years of substantially the same process, checked only a little by the efforts of Agriculture Officers and others, more land has gone out of cultivation, due to erosion (and probably exhaustion) and retreat from the rivers.

Grains predominate. Cereals, mainly millet, with some guinea corn (sorghum), occupy over 90 per cent of the cultivated area in Frafra: imports are necessary in lean years when conditions approaching famine may appear. Important pulses sown along with grain are cowpeas and pigeon peas; increasing cultivation of sweet potatoes, vegetables and peppers is diversifying diet; rice and tobacco are cash crops grown in some bottom lands.

Livestock are still kept mainly for uneconomic purposes; only richer chiefs have large herds. Animal population, as well as human population, presses on the land. Fowls are available for food and sold for cash. Mixed farming is making some headway, more so in Kusasi, and six Land Planning Schemes operate where problems are most acute.[7]

Population

THE PROBLEM

The population of northern Ghana (the present Northern and Upper Regions) is less than that which the area might be expected to support. It has become concentrated in certain restricted areas, leaving large tracts virtually uninhabited. Though lack of water is often responsible, many well-watered areas, now practically or completely deserted, have supported considerable populations during the past century. In Table 1 a preliminary contrast is brought out between the Regions of Ghana. In the Upper Region maximal densities are attained side-by-side with areas of complete depopulation and others where this seems imminent.

Table 1

Ghana: Population Growth by Regions, 1948–60

Region	Area in sq. mls.	1948		1960		Average annual per cent increase
		Population	Density[1]	Population	Density[1]	
Western	13,051	860,911	66·0 (26)	1,377,547	105·6 (41)	5·01
Accra Capital district	995	221,614	222·7 (87)	491,817	494·3 (193)	10·16[2]
Eastern	7,698	667,342	86·7 (34)	1,094,196	142·1 (56)	5·33
Volta	7,943	495,957	62·4 (24)	777,285	97·9 (38)	4·73
Ashanti	9,417	579,472	61·5 (24)	1,109,133	117·8 (46)	7·84
Brong-Ahafo	15,273	246,769	16·2 (6)	587,920	38·5 (15)	11·52
Northern[3]	27,175	381,088	14·0 (5)	531,573	19·5 (8)	3·25
Upper	10,548	658,195	62·4 (24)	757,344	72·0 (28)	1·28
GHANA	92,100	4,111,348[4]	44·6 (17)	6,726,815	73·0 (28)	5·30

1. Figures in parentheses give approximate densities per square kilometre.
2. 6·23 per cent, if Accra Municipality is excluded.
3. Excluding throughout Yeji and Prang, included in 1960 with Brong-Ahafo.
4. African population; does not include 6,770 non-Africans and 332 persons 'not accounted for'.

Many causes have contributed to depopulation. Though slave raids ceased 70 years ago, their effects were lasting since areas whence people were driven were invaded by game, bringing a large increase in tsetse infestation and hindering reoccupation. After about 1907, pacification and increased commerce facilitated the spread of sleeping sickness away from the Volta; by 1938 Lawra, Tumu and Wa were the south-east corner of a huge epidemic that depopulated the entire vicinity of the Black Volta and the lower reaches of its major tributaries. By 1951 the Department of Tsetse Control had reduced trypanosomiasis in Lawra-Tumu by 99 per cent, and in Wala, more liable to renewed infection from immigrant Lobis, by 85 per cent. Control measures were followed by increased settlement.[8]

Endemicity of onchocerciasis (river blindness) follows the distribution of granite and is not confined to the larger rivers: breeding of the vector, simulium damnosum, starts as soon as a stream begins to trickle, and larvae and pupae are found under every small cascade. Onchocerciasis causes blindness, closely related to depopulation: the problem is not static, it is progressive, nor is the disease a killing one—its victims are mostly men in the prime of life who are comparatively disabled but who may live on for many years. Its elimination would add not to the population to be supported but to the working efficiency of that population. The most sinister area for blindness in Ghana is the Sissili Valley. The north experiences the other diseases found in that part of Africa, especially cerebro-spinal meningitis, which is promoted by the minimally ventilated Lobi houses.

In areas of concentrated pressure on the land, primitive farming methods and annual grass burning have led to widespread soil exhaustion, followed by soil erosion, probably the most important factor in causing further concentration of population. The spread of waterborne diseases has quickened the movement towards the watersheds while the virtual elimination of rinderpest has greatly increased the number of animals competing with man for use of the land. If numbers sink below a certain level the process probably becomes irreversible. Malnutrition appears more as an effect than a cause until the vicious circle, loss of energy, less land farmed, less food (even less energy) has been once completed. The problem has long been most serious in Frafra.

DISTRIBUTION AND DENSITY

In considering the statistics presented here it must be remembered that each census can fairly claim to have been more accurate than its predecessor. Some aspects of the demographic pattern were first included in the 1960 census; thus a fully valid comparison between them and previous conditions is impossible.

In Ghana as elsewhere the war years were in many ways years of stagnation; in addition to the more obvious consequences of the state of conflict, the country was cut off from surrounding territories which had long supplied it with immigrants and labour. Nevertheless, over the 1931–48 period we see taking shape the pattern of population development which was to intensify itself after 1948, with the largest numerical increases in earlier-developed southern Ghana, but the greatest proportional increases in the old Ashanti, where large areas previously neglected or little developed were and still are being opened up.

In both the 1931–48 and 1948–60 periods, northern Ghana showed the least percentage increase; from 1948 to 1960 the Upper Region's population increased by 15·5 per cent as compared with 75·7 per cent for the rest of Ghana. Of 69 Local Authorities in Ghana at the time of the 1960 census four only showed a decline in the 1948–60 period, and two of these were in the Upper Region (Table 2): Frafra's decrease (8·2 per cent) shared by all its rural subdivisions, was second only to that of Tongu, in the south-eastern coastal plains.

In the following section certain aspects of population change illustrating the above argument are noted.

Wala and Lawra. On the Black Volta watershed and slopes west of 2° 25′ W in Wala, and in western Lawra to within a few miles of the northern frontier, population is much denser than is usual in the Guinea savanna-woodland zone of Ghana. Settlement approaches the Black Volta closely, with only a narrow uninhabited riverine strip north of the Kamba confluence. In over 1,000 square miles of Wala, densities average 90 per square mile, although Lawra has over 200 per square mile. Concentration is greatest in the Lawra–Jirapa–Boo and Nandom–Lambussie–Tuopari areas, where serious soil exhaustion and erosion are seen.

In eastern Wa the effect of improved communications in maintaining population, and that of factors operating in riverine areas to decrease or eliminate it can be seen.

Table 2

Ghana: Population Growth in the present Upper Region, 1931–60

Adminis-trative Division	Area in sq. mls.	1931		1948			1960		
		Population	Density[1]	Population	Density[1]	Average per cent annual increase	Population	Density[1]	Average per cent annual increase
Wala	3,362	72,323	21·5 (8)	85,479	25·4 (10)	1·07	130,973	38·9 (16)	4·44
Lawra	1,085	63,844	58·8 (23)	88,436	81·5 (32)	2·27	114,193	105·2 (41)	2·43
Tumu	2,687	29,281	11·1 (4)	31,092	11·6 (5)	0·36	43,540	16·9 (7)	3·87
Builsa	857	49,080	57·3 (22)	51,215	59·8 (23)	0·26	50,922	59·4 (23)	−0·05
Kassena-Nankanni	634	71,790	113·2 (44)	91,051	143·6 (56)	1·58	93,397	147·3 (58)	0·21
Frafra	735	132,479	180·2 (70)	163,474	222·4 (87)	1·38	150,028	204·1 (80)	−0·67
Kusasi	1,188	151,715	127·7 (50)	147,448	124·1 (48)	−0·17	174,291	146·7 (57)	1·52
Upper Region	10,548	570,512	54·1 (21)	658,195	62·4 (24)	0·90	757,344	72·0 (28)	1·28
Northern Ghana[2]	37,723	860,925	22·8 (9)	1,039,283	27·5 (11)	1·22	1,288,917	34·2 (13)	2·00

1. Figures in parentheses give approximate densities per square kilometre.
2. Excluding throughout Yeji and Prang, included in 1960 in Brong-Ahafo.

Densities never exceed 25 per square mile. Population is found chiefly on or near two routes. A 1951 reconnaissance found wide areas badly eroded or so exhausted as to need a long period of recovery, and numerous villages deserted since the raids of Babatu and Samory (i.e. before 1895). Any scheme, it was decided, would have to be postponed entirely pending prophylactic measures against onchocerciasis.

The Kamba valley, depopulated by trypanosomiasis, was, after clearing, the theatre of a resettlement scheme inaugurated in 1940. This met with very limited success, because the settlers chosen often refused to help themselves; later spontaneous immigration, however, was more effective.

Wa, an administrative centre, is the only large town. An important general and kola trading centre, with many new government installations, it increased from 5,156 to 14,342 between 1948 and 1960.

Low densities east of 2° 25′ W are of long standing and many small units have disappeared since 1921. After 1948 increase on and near the Wa–Bulenga road kept pace with that of the rest of Wala but was less than this in the large settlements east of Fian. Improved communications also seem to have halted the drain of population from the lonely Funsi–Kundungu area beyond the Kulpawn where, although there are food surpluses, tsetse and simulium are common.

Most important in Wala's increase is Lobi immigration, considerable before 1948 and much accelerated since that date. It shows itself in the filling up, in mainly small or moderate sized units, of vacant land fairly near to the Black Volta, especially between Wechiau and the main road south of Wa. There is much movement back and forth across the Black Volta, contact with parent settlements being maintained, and this has spread infection.

Tumu. Tumu has experienced, in aggravated form, all the agencies of depopulation. Save perhaps between Tumu and Wallembelle and in parts along the northern frontier west of Gollu, settlements are small islands fighting against the surrounding bush. Parts were laid waste by Babatu in the 1890s. Simulium infestation is intense along the Kulpawn; the Sissili–Kanyanbia district is the most unpleasant for simulium and the area of Ghana most afflicted with blindness. Deaths from cerebrospinal meningitis have occurred continually; entire villages have disappeared due to trypanosomiasis.

In villages south of Tumu, the old wide spacing of the compounds, formerly tiny autonomous republics planted out of bowshot of one another, is maintained, along with cattle kraals of temporary Fulani huts. Further north the need for defence against external foes has apparently overridden mutual distrust, and compounds are close.

There was notable increase and influx into the southern portion as around Wallembelle. This slowed down after 1948, while villages further north, especially those on motor roads, gained appreciably. Settlers avoid the riverine areas. South and west of Wallembelle, densities fall abruptly. Over 400 square miles, mainly along the Kulpawn, is uninhabited, and much of the 650 square miles of minimum densities in the Sissili–Kanyanbia area is virtually so. Here life is a never-ending struggle against the bush, disease, and wild animals and the divisions fronting upon the Sissili have long suffered depopulation.[9] A dozen small settlements disappeared between 1921 and 1948, others followed after that date. Conditions are worst in the north-east; the Kassenas seem unable to deal with elephants, roan antelope and monkeys that ravage the crops, and slow starvation results. Even in their roadside villages, Pina, Kunchoggo and Basisan, they cannot keep the bush at bay.

Tumu produces a food surplus and the population is increasing. Yet tsetse has never been wholly eradicated, and in many parts simulium swarms. In most areas, population densities are dangerously low. Retreat to the watersheds increases the danger of soil exhaustion; clearing, resulting in increased run-off, encourages simulium infestation.

Builsa and Kassena-Nankanni. Builsa and Kassena-Nankanni suffered badly from slave raids. Both overpopulation and underpopulation are seen as factors influencing decline. Inhabited sections form islands in deserted bush and peripheral densities are generally low. In the Sissili valley conditions resemble those in eastern Tumu. Three small settlements mapped in western Kaiyoro have almost disappeared. Nakom has lost population steadily since the 1920s; a few compounds and a chief's house are visible from the road, with ruins nearby and in the bush approaching the river. Its 47 square mile area has a density of 21 per square mile. Topsoil has virtually ceased to exist, granite outcrops dot the area, and small rocky streams drain to the Sissili. Such was the state of manpower when Waddy visited the area in 1950 that the blind were led out to work in the fields. Of 204 men examined, aged 30–50, 39 were blind.[10] Attempts to induce people to move to a healthier place failed.

Kanjarga alone of the sections bordering the Sissili gained after 1948. Density in Bechawnsi has dropped to 5·4 per square mile. Its subdivision, Vare, superficially attractively sited in a well-watered valley, had 175 people in 1921 and only 32 in 1960. In Doninga's riverine section of Wupiensa, less than half the compounds counted in 1948 survive. Gbedemblisi, the southernmost subdivision, had a density of 13 per square mile.

People avoid the Asabelika (save near the main road and opposite Kolugu) and the Atankwidi south of 10° 15′ N. On the spur between the Asabelika and Bulpegi, Jakwanstambia and Korogadoni are dying out and between the two main rivers Kologu and Naga contain much deserted land. Density in Naga falls to 24 per square mile, and Kologu's outlying section Akundaw, a mile from the Atankwidi, now has one inhabited compound.

The highest densities occur in a belt north-east from Sandema, which itself had 202 persons per square mile and a substantial intercensal increase of 50 per cent. Over 200 square miles of north-eastern Kassena-Nankanni, density was 274. Close settlement approaches the Atankwidi, but it is not considerable. Soil exhaustion and erosion are common, and the Dedoro–Tankara watershed, most seriously affected, has been declared a Land Planning Area.

Navrongo is of long-standing administrative importance. It has an important market, is a kola trading centre and as early as 1936 many lorries engaged in the salt, fish and cattle trade to Ouagadougou called there. 'Navrongo Central' has over 5,000 people, but the central nucleus is much smaller and less urban in appearance than Bolgatanga.

Frafra.[11] Endemic onchocerciasis or uninhabited country follows the rivers which border Frafra; in these and other riverine areas conditions favouring tsetse are found. The Red Volta especially cuts an uninhabited swathe through the north's most densely peopled part. Main settlements stand 3 to 4 miles back from the river, and the bush encroaches further.

Bolgatanga's growth dates from the opening of Pwalugu ferry in 1937. It then became the 'road-head' for the kola trade and the junction of three trade routes into French territory via Navrongo, Bongo and Bawku. Traders from Ashanti, Dagomba and Nigeria came to settle, and its market grew. Outside Bolgatanga, settlement is completely dispersed; in places like Bongo and Tongo, a mission house, Local Authority Office or market give some appearance of a nucleus.

In two areas densities exceed 512 per square mile, one on the Kulubiliga–Kuldaga watershed, into which already overcrowded area population moved from riverine districts, the other around Bolgatanga and Zuarungu. Otherwise densities are highest on the west, reaching 420 per square mile in western Bongo, facing the overcrowded

Table 3

Ghana: Estimated Uninhabited and Inhabited areas and Densities on Inhabited Portions of Frafra, 1948 and 1960

Division	Uninhabited (1960) (sq. mls.)	Inhabited (1960) (sq. mls.)	Density of inhabited portion[1]	
			1948	1960
Bolga[2]	33	111	422·1 (165)	421·1 (165)
Bongo	28	150	380·1 (148)	347·8 (135)
Nangodi	12	41	423·9 (166)	326·0 (127)
Sekoti	11	20	258·7 (101)	211·3 (83)
Talense	204	125	296·4 (115)	268·1 (105)
Frafra	288	447	365·5 (142)	335·6 (131)

1. Figures in parentheses give approximate densities in persons per square kilometre.
2. Densities for rural Bolga, i.e. not including Bolga town, work out at 392·8 (150) for 1948 and 374·8 (146) for 1960.

area of Kassena-Nankanni. Sections around Sambrungo continued their pre-1948 increase, partly due to immigration but elsewhere in Bolga, with few exceptions, rural populations declined.

In eastern Bongo a four-mile-wide uninhabited strip fringes the Red Volta, and retreat continues. The District Commissioner remarked of Akulmasa (1947):

> 'Twenty years ago this area was as densely populated as any, but the people are gradually dying out. . . . Now there are only three compounds left on the original site, and a new settlement is growing up a mile or two to the west. The headman moved his own compound last year . . . the visible difference in his health since he moved is considerable.'

The Beo–Adaboya area on the watershed behind is remarkable even in Frafra for erosion and exhaustion, yet it averaged 300 persons per square mile.

Talense fronts on all three main rivers, and the Kuldaga and Kulubiliga cross it. It has the greatest amount of uninhabited land in Frafra. Depopulation has been most considerable and widespread in eastern Talense along the Red Volta watershed and the Kulubiliga. Kumbude is disappearing. A separate subdivision of 399 people in 1931, in 1960 it was the southernmost section of Datoko with only 130, in spite of receiving the population of Dagari moving back from the river. Further decreases seem inevitable in this beleaguered area, where densities (68 per square mile) are already much lower than in any inhabited part of Frafra.

Decline and retreat are long standing. In mainly uninhabited terrain further south Bapela and Baynola, separate subdivisions in 1931, have ceased to exist as such. Only four small communities, Biungu, Nungu and Old and New Tula, survive, in spite of flies and isolation, because of fishing in the White Volta and dearth of land elsewhere. Biungu was a separate subdivision in 1921 (population 551) and 1931 (population 363). The four communities combined had 154 inhabitants in 1960.

Over western Talense, declines were not so evident. Densities in the southern portion averaged 254 per square mile rising to 414 approaching Bolgatanga.

Table 4

Ghana: Comparative Population Statistics, Agolle and Toende Subdivisions of Kusasi, 1931–60

Division	Area in sq. mls.		1931		1948			1960		
	Total	Un-inhabited[1]	Population	Density[2] (inhabited portion)	Population	Density[2] (inhabited portion)	Average annual per cent increase	Population	Density[2] (inhabited portion)	Average annual per cent increase
Agolle	763	113	100,750	155·0 (61)	106,045	163·1 (64)	0·31	131,050	201·6 (79)	1·97
Toende	425	144	50,965	181·4 (71)	41,403	147·3 (58)	−1·10	43,241	153·9 (60)	0·37
Kusasi	1,188	257	151,715	162·9 (64)	147,448	158·4 (62)	−0·17	174,291	187·2 (73)	1·52

1. Probably somewhat increased by 1960.
2. Figures in parentheses are per square kilometre.

Kusasi. In Kusasi the population pattern resembles that in Frafra: clearly defined uninhabited strips, 257 square miles in all, border the main rivers, from which population still retreats.

Immigration caused much increase in the then recently acquired strip of Togoland, particularly between 1921 and 1931, shown in 1931 by an excess of males over females, quite exceptional in northern Ghana. This slowed down between 1931 and 1948.

Bawku is the last of a series of towns on the north-eastern trade route which became prominent with the kola trade; unlike some it has not died with its passing; growth (3,752 in 1931, 12,719 in 1960) has resulted from improved transport and communications. Motor vehicles first reached Bawku in 1926; by 1937, with Bolgatanga, it was replacing Tamale as a principal centre for the livestock trade and lorries from Gao and Niamey are seen. Over a quarter of its 1960 population came from outside Ghana.

THE TIDE OF MIGRATION

Emigration is northern Ghana's traditional answer to the population problem and will probably long continue to be so. It has intensified but has partly changed in character. Well before 1931 there was immigration into northern frontier districts from lands further north, attributed by Cardinall[12] to the economic impulse forcing people southwards from the Sudan zone, mainly due to increasing desiccation of the Saharan fringe. One may regard migration from northern Ghana as an extended aspect of this.

Formerly, most migrants returned home for planting; married men rarely took their wives and families, but would send for them on finding a steady job. The present tendency is towards longer term migration, although most northerners still intend to return home eventually.

Table 5

Northern Ghana: Males per 100 Females in Population of Working Age

Local Authority	1931			1948			1960		
	15–45	46 and over	Total	16–44	45 and over	Total	15–44	45 and over	Total
Wala	88	100	90	87	105	90	75	140	86
Lawra	84	100	86	73	88	75	61	121	72
Tumu	75	59	72	83	100	86	72	121	80
Builsa	82	70	86	74	91	80	61	150	82
Kassena-Nankanni	97	63	89				66	130	79
Frafra	92	56	88	84	79	83	59	130	73
Kusasi	97	71	92	96	101	98	75	163	90
Upper Region	91	72	88	84	91	85	67	139	81
NORTHERN GHANA	95	81	92	89	95	90	75	149	88

Note: The excess of females over males in the younger age group was 12,414 in 1931, 26,307 in 1948 and 65,017 in 1960: the numbers of males so counted at the three censuses were 136,707, 134,826 and 133,708 respectively.

Not only have census dates varied, but censuses were taken before seasonal migrants would normally be expected home and age returns are generally their least satisfactory feature. Statistical criteria preclude exact comparisons, but the significance of the figures above is plain. In 1960, in Ghana as a whole, males aged 15–44, from whom the bulk of the migrants are drawn, comprised 19·8 per cent of the population: the same group made up only 17·5 per cent of the population of the Upper Region.

The increase in volume and tempo of migration shown in Table 6 reflects both deteriorating conditions in the Upper Region and increasing demand for labour in the south with its accelerated economic development.

Table 6

Ghana: Numbers belonging to main Upper Region Tribes counted outside Northern Ghana, 1948 and 1960

Tribe	Males (1960)		Females (1960)		Both sexes (1948)
	Number	Percentage	Number	Percentage	
Dagarti	24,860	24·1	10,570	10·7	11,725
Lobi	3,330	16·8	1,970	11·1	2,516
Walba	5,560	23·0	4,320	18·7	3,153
Sissala	5,080	17·4	2,930	9·7	1,784
Builsa	5,580	17·7	2,630	8·5	1,345
Kasena	430	2·5	170	0·9	651
Nankanni and Gurense	30	0·1	20	0·1	162
Frafra	21,780	30·5	9,320	13·9	8,453 (Frafra, Talense, Namnam)
Talense	360	2·3	140	0·8	
Namnam	10	0·1	0	0·0	
Kusasi	11,390	18·0	5,190	8·9	1,971
Total	78,410	19·1	37,260	9·3	31,760

Notes: 1. Lobis and Dagartis overlap into western Gonja, a few also may have come direct from Haute-Volta or the Ivory Coast.
2. 1948 figures probably show some understatement due to uncertainties of nomenclature.

Table 7

Northern Ghana: Numbers and Percentages of the Population born in Other African Countries, 1960

Local Authority	Males		Females	
	Number	Percentage	Number	Percentage
Wala	7,102	11·0	6,491	9·8
Lawra	2,748	5·2	3,074	5·0
Tumu	1,218	5·8	1,447	6·4
Builsa	176	0·7	103	0·4
Kassena-Nankanni	701	1·6	2,385	4·8
Frafra	927	1·3	1,721	2·1
Kusasi	6,420	7·3	6,386	7·3
Upper Region	19,292	5·3	21,607	5·5

It was formerly considered that the annual exodus of a large number of adult males did not have any unfortunate effects on social and economic life. Since the main southerly migration took place after the harvest, and the main northerly one before the planting season, agricultural production did not suffer, and, in fact, the absence of a large number of adult males in the dry season when food was short was undoubtedly beneficial.

This view now needs some reconsideration. Longer term migration results in reduced numbers available to cultivate the land, and has other sociological effects. The 1960 figures show an increase in the expectation of life, and suggest that men now tend to live longer than women, probably because most of them will have spent at least part of their lives in the more favourable environment of the south, whereas far fewer women, especially in the older age groups, will have done so.

Table 7 shows that population loss from northern Ghana is partly made up by migrants moving into Ghana from further afield.

Conclusion

In the Upper Region, as in the rest of Ghana, the 1948–60 period was characterized by the accentuation and acceleration of demographic trends that had begun to appear before 1948. One-ninth of the area of the country, it now supports one-ninth of the country's population.

The situation seems least serious in Wala. No excessively high densities have appeared. In inhabited portions there is an estimated average of 13·67 acres of land per person, but much of this land in eastern Wala is of very poor quality. Lawra has 5·52 acres per person by the same token, but there is serious overcrowding in the Nandom, Jirapa and Lawra areas where, in parts of all these districts, topsoil has virtually disappeared.

After 1948, Tumu's proportionate increase in population was much greater than before, yet deterioration and decline continued in its worst hit area. The plight of the Kassenas in the Sissili area of north-eastern Tumu and western Kassena-Nankanni could hardly be worse. People of this tribe rarely emigrate, and in this area they are dying out.

In old Mamprusi we see successive stages of the retreat from the two rivers, increased occupation of the watersheds with subsequent increased erosion and finally total unfitness of the land for human occupation. South Mamprusi has never developed the high densities seen further north. Near the north–south course of the White Volta in this area the process seems obvious but less advanced. Large settlements remain comparatively near the river, which here flows over sandstone terrain. During the 1931–60 period population decreased by a quarter, and between 1931 and 1948 every settlement for which a comparison could be made decreased. Some larger settlements appeared to recover after 1948, while small ones mapped and recorded at the earlier date have disappeared.

In Kusasi and Frafra continuous strips of uninhabited terrain have developed along main streams, while sections marginal to these continue to decline or disappear. The process has gone further in Frafra; significantly in 1960 there were eight times as many Kusasis outside northern Ghana as in 1948, the largest percentage increase recorded. In Kassena-Nankanni and Builsa what may be a penultimate stage has been reached, with isolated populated areas on the watershed, surrounded by uninhabited land. Tumu to the west may exemplify the last stage, when the exhausted land is no longer able to support any standard of living for its dense population, and the bush comes in once more. Twenty-five years ago Lynn pointed out that evidence available suggested that, once land has become completely exhausted, it takes many decades to recover.

Density maps constructed by the writer confirm not only retreat from the rivers and continuing depopulation of riverine sections, but also, in North Mamprusi, declining densities on some watershed lands to which the population retreated, and which can no longer support them. Yet in spite of these decreases there were in North Mamprusi 63,000 more mouths to feed in 1960 than there were in 1931; increased expectation of life gives an increase in the sector of the population no longer able to undertake hard work.

Frafra may indeed have reached the point of no return, with recovery impossible in the foreseeable future. It has been realized for two decades that the maintenance of an agricultural population of the present density, with an adequate standard of living, is impracticable: it may be that the area must pass through a depopulation stage before recovery may be considered feasible. There is little hope that riverine areas, now deserted, will become of much use in absorbing surplus population.

Resettlement schemes have made little progress while the position continues to deteriorate. The most ambitious, the Frafra Resettlement Scheme, was launched in 1953, after calculations showed that 80,000 people (12–13,000 compound families) would have to be moved in order to guarantee optimum land use. By the end of 1958 398 families had actually gone to Damongo. Those settlers still remaining are now the concern of the Agricultural Extension Services. Even development of the infrastructure can aggravate the fundamental problem. An area 50 yards wide and 47 miles long (Bolgatanga-Bawku) required for a new road will take away 855 acres of cultivatable land; gravel pits, road camps and miscellaneous installations all contribute to eat steadily into the area's one scanty resource.

I have stressed the importance of soil exhaustion and erosion in this paper. Its continuance, inevitable in the areas of dense population where old traditional agricultural methods prevail, means that each generation faces a worse problem than the previous one.

Footnotes

1. *Cartes Ethno-Démographiques de l'Afrique Occidentale*, Feuilles 3 and 4 Nord, IFAN Dakar, 1963.
2. *Ibid.*, Feuilles No. 5, IFAN Dakar, 1954.
3. T. E. HILTON, *Ghana Population Atlas*, Nelson, 1960, p. 28.
4. *1960 Population Census of Ghana*, Vol. IV, Accra, 1964.
5. J. H. HINDS, *Agricultural Survey of the Lawra-Wa Area*, Report to Department of Agriculture, Accra, 1951.

   H. P. WHITE, 'Provisional Agricultural Regions of Ghana', *Journal of Tropical Geography*, Singapore, Vol. XI, April 1958, pp. 90–98.
6. C. W. LYNN, 'Agriculture in North Mamprusi: A review of a decade's progress', *Farm and Forest*, Vol. III, No. 2, June 1942.

   J. C. MUIR and T. L. WILLIAMS, 'Agriculture in Navrongo and Zuarungu', *Department of Agriculture Year Book*, Accra, 1930.

   J. BRIAN WILLS (ed.), *Agriculture and Land Use in Ghana*, OUP, 1962, esp. chs. 8, 15, 20, 23 and 24, describes present-day agriculture.
7. T. E. HILTON, 'Land Planning and Resettlement in Northern Ghana', *Geography*, Vol. XIV, No. 4, November 1959, pp. 227–40.
8. H. LABOURET, *Les tribus du rameau Lobi*, Institut d'Ethnologie, Paris, 1931.

   H. LABOURET, *Nouvelles notes sur les tribus du rameau Lobi*, IFAN, Dakar, 1958.
9. J. GUINNESS, *A Report on the Origins and Journeys of the People of Tumu*, unpublished manuscript, 1932.
10. B. B. WADDY, *Onchocerciasis and blindness in the Northern Territories*, unpublished manuscript Kintampo, 1951.
11. T. E. HILTON, *Le peuplement de Frafra, district du Nord-Ghana*, IFAN, Dakar, 1965.
12. A. W. CARDINALL, *The Gold Coast, 1931*, Accra, 1931, p. 152.

29 Some factors of population distribution in the Middle Belt of Nigeria: the examples of northern Ilorin and Kabba Provinces

S. A. Agboola

Department of Geography, University of Ife, Nigeria

Introduction

The 'Middle Belt' is now well known as a problem region in Nigeria. Extensive empty spaces, low population densities, the relative insignificance of export crops, dependence on food crop production, environmental difficulties that hinder economic development, and considerable political instability, are some of the better known characteristics of the Belt. Of all the ills of the region, however, population perhaps poses the most fundamental problem, for, as Trewartha has noted, it is the point of reference from which all other elements are observed.[1]

This paper examines briefly the patterns of population distribution in a part of the Middle Belt and the well-established view that it is a relatively empty part of Nigeria. An attempt is also made to test the validity of some of the factors usually regarded as explaining the pattern of population distribution in the area. Northern Ilorin and Kabba, lying within the Belt, have been chosen as a testing ground.

Population Distribution

The patterns of population distribution in the region clearly divide it into three areas:

(a) The relatively densely populated areas mainly in central and northern Ilorin Division located within the Belt, but with extensions into the Shonga, Ogudu, and Lafiagi areas of Lafiagi-Pategi Division.

(b) The virtually empty areas in southern Lafiagi-Pategi Division, eastern Igbomina district, northern Yagba districts, and extensive parts of Bunu, Aworo, and Kakanda districts of Kwara Division.

(c) The areas carrying moderate population concentrations over limited areas in central Yagba and riverine parts of Lafiagi-Pategi Division, Kupa and Kakanda districts of Kwara Division.

(a) Ilorin, the largest urban centre of the study area, is situated to the extreme south of the Belt, but it is centrally placed within the fairly densely populated Ilorin Division. This dense concentration extends southwards outside the Belt, where areas with population densities of above 400 persons per square mile are more extensive than inside the Belt. The population distribution in this part of the Middle Belt has some outstanding characteristics.

First, the whole area is very closely settled. Unlike other parts of the Belt, virtually unoccupied areas are limited in extent and are confined to the peripheries of the Division.

Secondly, population densities over extensive areas are not only above the 40 persons per square mile Middle Belt average, but densities of between 200 and 400 to the square mile are attained over considerable areas. Around district headquarters like Oloru, Lanwa, Ejidongari, Share, Paiye, Jebba and Shonga, densities are usually above 400 to the square mile.

Thirdly, apart from the fact that areas carrying population densities of over 400 are more extensive south of Ilorin, population distribution in Ilorin Division, both inside and outside the Middle Belt area, show considerable uniformity. This is unlike other parts of the study area where population distribution is markedly different in areas inside and south of the Belt. The population distribution in the area is predominantly rural. In fact, outside Ilorin, there are no other settlements with populations above the 5,000 mark. Small agricultural settlements, which give the Division some of the highest settlement densities in the area, are the predominating feature. The areas with densities above 400 are confined to Ilorin and the district administrative headquarters, while areas of small farm settlements carry densities varying from 200 to 400.

(b) The distribution of the virtually empty areas shows some interesting patterns. In the first place, they tend to coincide with the boundaries separating one tribe from the other. This is the case between the Igbomina district of Ilorin Province, the Yagba districts to the east, and the Nupe districts to the north-east. In this extensive empty space, the Igbominas tend to cling to areas towards Ilorin to the west, Ajase, and Omu-Aran to the south, while the Nupes of the Lafiagi-Pategi Division tend to concentrate in settlements along the Niger. The same thing is true of the empty area between Lafiagi-Pategi Division to the north and the Yagba districts to the south. The second noticeable pattern concerns a triangular area to the east of the study area. This vast area coincides with the extremely hilly eastern part of the Middle Belt. Most of the forest reserves in the study area are located in these extensive empty tracts of country. Population distribution there is extremely limited in extent, and confined to areas around Akutupa, at the foot of the Akutupa ridge, and the Agbaja plateau to the north of Lokoja.

(c) The areas of moderate population concentrations over limited areas are to be found mainly along the River Niger and its floodplain. The only other areas are central east and west Yagba districts. Two main concentrations are found along the Niger. The more important one is in Shonga and Lafiagi districts where settlements are located on the Niger floodplain. The second one stretches from Pategi to Eggan where settlements are closer to the Niger. In the first concentration, areas with densities of 50–200 and 200–400 are quite common, while in the second most areas exhibit densities of less than 50.

Two questions arise. First, to what extent is the population distribution in northern Ilorin and Kabba typical of the Middle Belt of Nigeria, and second, how far does the present study support former generalizations about population distribution in the Belt?

Doubts may be raised as to the validity of including Ilorin Division with its fairly dense rural population in the Middle Belt, usually regarded as sparsely populated. A close examination of population distribution in the Middle Belt shows that sparseness of population distribution does not apply to its entire area. The fairly dense rural population concentration in Ilorin Division is repeated in similar concentrations in Plateau and Adamawa Provinces. The moderate population concentrations of the riverine parts of Lafiagi-Pategi Division have their counterparts in the rice-producing Bida Division, and adjoining parts of Niger and Benue Provinces. Also, the empty spaces of Bunu, Awori and Kakanda districts in the study area correspond to the extensive empty parts of Borgu and Kontagora Divisions. Population distribution in northern Ilorin and Kabba Provinces can therefore be said to be typical of that of the Middle Belt in many respects.

Buchanan and Pugh, who appear to be the originators of the Middle Belt concept in the geography of Nigeria, observed that very low population densities are typical of most parts of the Belt, unlike other parts of Northern Nigeria except Bornu Province.[2] The point must be made that the authors had at their disposal only population estimates based on the 1931 census, which was itself not very reliable. Also, they had at their disposal only Divisional population densities that showed large parts of the Middle Belt with very low population densities. But even with other population figures available at present, and with the use of mapping techniques which bring out local variations in population distribution, this generalization is still valid but with some reservations. The general pattern is subject to considerable local variations. Not only are there extensive areas of fairly high density, but there are others that on a Divisional basis could be described as carrying low population densities, which in fact carry fairly high densities in some places. But what seems to put the population distribution of the Belt into bold relief, more than any other feature, is the fairly extensive empty areas. The Belt can be considered as having within it more of such areas than any other part of Nigeria. For instance, in northern Ilorin and Kabba, as much as 60 per cent of the area is virtually uninhabited, even though 20 per cent of this is in forest reserves. An additional 27 per cent carries population densities below the Middle Belt average of 40. The Buchanan–Pugh generalization is valid to the extent that even at present there are extensive empty areas in the Middle Belt, but the sparse population distribution is by no means applicable to the whole area, as limited areas of fairly dense population exist. Such areas may remind us that parts of the Middle Belt have carried dense population in the past; but one wonders whether, under present circumstances in Nigeria, it can sustain dense concentrations over extensive areas.

Some Factors of Population Distribution in the Middle Belt

Two of the approaches to an understanding of the Middle Belt population problem are important. The first is the historical approach, which seeks to explain the present sparseness of population distribution in the Belt in terms of the serious devastation of extensive areas in the Jihad operations of the 19th century. Under the circumstances, the serious population problem of the Middle Belt could be solved either through a high rate of natural increase of the population or through the attraction of immigrants from other parts of Nigeria. The increase there, however, appears to be no higher than in other parts of Nigeria, and is unlikely to change in any appreciable way the sparse population distribution covering large areas. The capacity of the Belt to attract immigrants from elsewhere is also thought to be low. Thus a biogeographic approach is necessary to achieve an understanding of the population of the Belt. This approach sees the biogeographic complex as a negative force which stands in the way of any appreciable immigration of people into the Middle Belt. While the present pattern of population distribution is explicable in terms of its past history, the biogeographic complex plays an important part in the perpetuation of the pattern.

The Historical Approach

There is a considerable body of evidence that large-scale depopulation in the past of parts of the Middle Belt is largely responsible for its present pattern of population distribution. This contention will be examined here for northern Ilorin and Kabba Divisions, an area in the southern Middle Belt. The two main population characteristics of northern Ilorin and Kabba that require explanation are the fairly dense concentrations in northern Ilorin, standing in bold contrast to the very low densities in surrounding areas.

The main parts of the area where the historical approach is relevant are the northern parts of the Yagba districts, southern Lafiagi-Pategi Division, and parts of Oke-Ode district, all areas with very low rural population densities.

Oral evidence and the written accounts of travellers who went through the area in the 19th century have facilitated a comparative study of its population in the past and at present. In the Yagba district for instance, there are many examples of settlements thought to have been much larger in the past. In the cases of Ejiba in West Yagba district, and Ilafin in East Yagba district, oral evidence is confirmed by the presence of ruins, many now overgrown with weeds. At Ilafin, the ruins of the former town wall, said to mark the former limit of the built-up area of the village, are now almost one-quarter of a mile from its present outer limits. Although available oral evidence is inadequate and inconclusive, the suggestion can tentatively be made that considerable depopulation took place, at least in parts of the Yagba district, in the fairly recent past.

The accounts of travellers who passed through the Yagba area in the last century are more helpful. At the time of May's visit in 1858, he saw an area of open, picturesque country, with hills, green knolls, perpetual cultivation and constant clusters of huts.[3] But he reported later that there were frequent attacks from Ilorin, Nupe, and Ibadan, which created an atmosphere of 'doubt, fear, and suspicion, forced neglect of agriculture, stoppage of trade and communication . . .' and general depopulation. Similarly, in southern Nupe country (i.e. southern Lafiagi-Pategi Division), Vandeleur saw a countryside which had been completely depopulated by the 'continuous raids, with the few remaining unfortunate natives living in constant dread of being captured and sent into the depths of the western Sudan.'[4] Wallace also referred to a stretch between Kabba and Eggan, an area coinciding with much of northern Kabba Division and southern Lafiagi-Pategi Division, as being formerly 'a densely-populated country' though it did not contain as many as 200 people at the time of his visit.[5] There is also the case of Oke-Ode district which was attacked from two directions at the same time; from the south by the Ibadan army and from the west by the Jama'a, the Ilorin-based Muslim army, which carried the Jihad into the Yoruba country.[6] The above evidences, leaves one in no doubt, that considerable depopulation in the area was caused by incessant warfare in the 19th century.

Some of the areas mentioned above, which bore the brunt of this period of insecurity and destruction of life coincide with virtually uninhabited and sparsely-populated areas of northern Ilorin and Kabba today.

Standing as an oasis of stability and power, in contrast to the instability and great confusion in surrounding areas, is the Ilorin emirate. Especially during the second half of the 19th century, with the Jama'a, the army of the Jihad, based on its soil, Ilorin not only successfully defied old Oyo, the headquarters of the Oyo Empire, but eventually caused its downfall and subsequent evacuation in 1839.[7] The military strength of Ilorin, at a time when other Yoruba towns were falling, was favourable not only to stabilization of the existing population, but also to the attraction of refugees from the troubled areas around. Freedom from the Oyo Empire meant freedom from involvement in the many internal wars that seriously depopulated the north-western part of Yorubaland after the evacuation of Old Oyo. Ilorin's population during this period increased rather than decreased with slaves from elsewhere and Hausa and Fulani immigrants, many army personnel, considerably swelling its population.

These developments around Ilorin in the 19th century may have contributed to the present size of Ilorin town, but they do not explain the fairly high rural densities in the surrounding districts. Two main factors appear to have been responsible for this. These are the system of land ownership in Ilorin Division towards the end of the last century, and the reorganization of the administrative machinery, initiated by Lord Lugard in the early years of this century.

During the closing years of the 19th century, during a calm following the turbulent years of warfare, the Fulani Emir of Ilorin parcelled his whole area into fiefholds, given to chiefs, cadet branches of the ruling houses, powerful slaves, and occasionally to Yoruba chiefs who had accepted the Fulani conquest. But one of the conditions attached to the granting of the fiefholds was that all fiefholders must live at Ilorin, so ensuring that they did not become too powerful for the Emir to control. This created a class of absentee landlords living at Ilorin but with farming communities established on their land. For instance, in the Afon district, Burnett observed, 'men, having acquired their lands from the Emir in the early years of the Fulani invasion, brought out their friends, followers and slaves, and settled them on their lands returning themselves to Ilorin, leaving a representative on the land.'[8] Such a situation must have encouraged the drifting of urban population into the surrounding districts. The initial settlers would have been joined by others from troubled areas, once life on the farm settlements was known to be peaceful and reasonably secure.

Another trend that lent impetus to the migration of people into the countryside was the re-organization of the administrative machinery initiated by Lord Lugard. District heads were appointed for the first time by the British administration, which took over control from the Fulani early in the present century. Many of the chiefs so appointed, like the Fulani-appointed fiefholders before them, lived in Ilorin town. One result of this administrative arrangement, according to Hermon-Hodge, was 'the movement of considerable bodies of people, the followers of the chiefs so appointed, and formerly idlers in Ilorin town, out to the sparsely populated countryside, to the benefit and increase of agriculture.'[9]

The Biogeographic Complex

The thesis in this case is that the biogeographic environment is not favourable to many aspects of development which would have attracted immigrants from outside the Middle Belt. The main components of the biogeographic environment considered include soils, vegetation and climate, with special reference to their effects on plant and animal life.

Soil survey work in Northern Nigeria has not yet reached the stage of completeness and intense coverage that would make it possible to establish the relationship between soil and the agricultural economy of the Middle Belt. But soil surveys carried out on the Ilorin Experimental Farm site, in the Riverine Area School of Agriculture, Kabba, and the Osara Experimental Farm have thrown some light on the soil characteristics.[10] What is common to the three areas is the widespread occurrence of iron-pan formation in the subsoil. The survey of the Ilorin farm revealed a vesicular iron-pan surface underlying shallow red loams, the iron-pan soils coming near the top soil on the higher and middle slopes. In the Kabba area the thickness of the iron-pan layer is as much as 4 feet. Similarly, the survey at Osara has shown a large proportion of iron-pan soils, which, together with skeletal soils, cover the greater part of the area.

Though available evidence gives prominence to the widespread occurrence of iron-pan soils, the present knowledge of soils in the Middle Belt does not allow valid generalizations to be drawn. First, the three areas of which the soils have been surveyed, are of limited extent, and are not necessarily representative of the whole area. Second, iron-pan soils, since they still have a few inches of overlying top soil, probably satisfy the needs of traditional agriculture, with its emphasis on foodcrop production, the mainstay of the Belt's economy. One exception, however, which can be validly made, is the Agbaja plateau, where ironstone is exposed on the surface over considerable areas, while in others the top soil is so thin as to have adverse effects on crop yields.[11] But the iron-pan soils, though not necessarily limiting foodcrop production, might cause serious difficulties in mechanized agriculture, and thereby impede development. The Mokwa experience has underlined this danger very clearly.[12] Yet some soils in the area although of limited extent have considerable potentialities. The soils of the Niger and Benue floodplains may yet prove the backbone of the

Middle Belt's agricultural development. Already the capacity of the Niger floodplain for supporting sugar-cane and rice farms has been proved beyond doubt, and the Kainji dam should enhance the irrigation possibilities of these floodplains and adjacent river valleys.

THE TRYPANOSOMIASIS PROBLEM

The main vegetational problem of the Middle Belt is trypanosomiasis and its effects on cattle rearing. The only tsetse-free part of northern Nigeria is in the extreme north, covering much of Sokoto, Katsina, Kano and Bornu Provinces. It has been suggested that the sub-humid climate of the northern plains with its wide range of temperature and low humidity is unfavourable to the fly. The more humid conditions, the taller grasses and woodland vegetation along the river valleys of the Middle Belt are thought to offer a more favourable habitat.[13] This contrast between the Sudan zone and the Guinea savannah Middle Belt explains the concentration of Nigeria's cattle population in the former area and its little importance in the latter. Experiments carried out at Ilorin during the 1930s showed that *zebu* cattle, which have higher economic value than the *muturu* cattle, cannot thrive under Middle Belt conditions. Even the *muturu* and *ndama* breeds of cattle, although capable of resisting trypanosomiasis, can do so only if not subject to much work.[14] Apart from the tsetse menace, the grasses of the Belt, especially during the rains, are too luxuriant and coarse to be suitable for cattle feed.

CLIMATE AND THE PROBLEM OF INTRODUCING EXPORT CROPS

One of the dominant factors inhibiting economic development in the study area is its failure to grow export crops. Of particular interest in this regard is the failure of repeated attempts at introducing the Allen variety of cotton into many parts of the area. The early years of this century, up till 1925, saw the Ilorin area as an important exporter of cotton lint. This was the period when the local varieties, especially *Gossypium acrifolium*, were acceptable but an early attempt was made to replace local short-stapled types with the longer-stapled Allen variety. While this did well in the Sudan zone of Northern Nigeria, trials in the Ilorin area gave very disappointing results. Experiments carried out in the area from 1910 to the 1930s, showed that rainfall and pests are important factors accounting for the failure of the crop in this area. Rainfall in August and after October were observed to have adverse effects on cotton fields. A definite relationship was also observed between rainfall and cotton stainer attack between November and February.[15] Similar problems have been encountered in attempts to introduce export crops like cocoa, oil palm and groundnuts into the Middle Belt.

Conclusion

The problem of the Middle Belt is lack of human resources to develop its economic potentialities, however limited these may be. Although extensive areas are either virtually empty or carry low population densities, fairly dense concentrations in restricted parts have proved the capacity of much of the belt for sustaining higher population densities. The developments taking place along the Rivers Niger and Benue, and other important rivers of the area, may yet attract immigrants from other parts of Nigeria. The inflow of people, especially from overcrowded parts of Nigeria, appears to offer the main possibility of effecting changes in the present pattern of population distribution in the Belt.

Footnotes

1. G. T. TREWARTHA, 'A case for population geography', *Annals*, Association of American Geographers, Vol. XLIII, p. 83.

2. K. M. BUCHANAN and J. C. PUGH, *Land and People in Nigeria*, London, 1955, pp. 61–62.
3. D. J. DAY, 'Journey in the Yoruba and Nupe countries in 1858', *Journal of the Royal Geographical Society*, 1860, pp. 212–33.
4. S. VANDELEUR, 'Nupe and Ilorin', *Geographical Journal*, Vol. 10, 1897, pp. 349–74.
5. Nigeria: *Colonial Office Annual Report*, No. 409, 1902, p. 21.
6. H. B. HERMON-HODGE, *Gazeteer of Ilorin Province*, London, 1929, p. 64.
7. W. BASCOM, 'Urbanism as a Traditional African Pattern', *Sociological Review*, Vol. 7, No. 1, 1959 p. 36.
8. HERMON-HODGE, *op. cit.*, p. 168.
9. *Ibid.*, p. 164.
10. G. M. HIGGINS and P. R. TOMLINSON, 'Soils of the Western Climatic Middle Belt', paper presented to 4th meeting of CROACUS, Samaru/Mokwa, 3–11 November 1961.
11. An agricultural survey of the Agbaja Plateau by the Geography Department, University of Ife, revealed this.
12. K. D. S. BALDWIN, *The Niger Agricultural Project, An experiment in African Development.*
13. BUCHANAN and PUGH, *op. cit.*, p. 61.
14. D. H. BROWN, 'Ilorin Stock Farm', *Farm and Forest*, Vol. IV, 1943, pp. 3–7.
15. T. G. MASON and G. H. JONES, 'A first survey of factors inhibiting the development of the cotton crop in Nigeria', *Third Annual Bulletin*, Agricultural Department, Lagos, 1924, p. 24. Also F. D. GOLDING. 'A statistical survey of the infestation of *Dysdercus spp.* on cotton in Nigeria', *Fourth Annual Bulletin*, Agricultural Department, Lagos, 1925.

30 Population distribution, settlement and soils in Kano Province, Northern Nigeria 1931–62

M. J. Mortimore

Department of Geography, Ahmadu Bello University, Zaria, Nigeria

Kano Province is of interest to the student of demographic problems since it contains one of the densest concentrations of population on the African continent, nearly two million people living at densities in excess of 300 persons per square mile, in what has appropriately been termed the Kano close-settled zone. Furthermore, the pattern of growth and distribution of this population is presently undergoing important changes, linked with the transition from the traditional agricultural economy, which existed before the construction of the railway from Lagos to Kano in 1912 (Nguru, 1930), to an increasingly commercialized peasant agriculture in which the production of groundnuts is growing in importance. This transition is being accomplished against the background of an accelerating natural increase which has brought the population of the central districts of the close-settled zone near to, if not past, the maximum which they can support from agricultural resources, even at the minimum standard of living acceptable today. It is the purpose of this study to examine these changes in distribution so far as the availability of data permits. The census of 1952 and the preliminary returns of the census of 1962, made available by the Greater Kano Planning Authority, are sufficiently accurate for this purpose, and Kano Province is fortunate in possessing large-scale maps of most of its 41 constituent districts, which permit the analysis of population distribution on a larger scale than in most other provinces of Northern Nigeria.

Kano Province, which includes, in addition to Kano Emirate, the Emirates of Kazaure, Gumel and Hadejia, extends over an area of 16,360 square miles and contained in 1962 a population of 4,329,307 at an average density of 260 per square mile. Despite this high overall density, marked contrasts occur within the Province, from less than 25 per square mile in parts of Tudun Wada district in the extreme south to over 700 in Ungogo and Kumbotso, the 'home districts' adjacent to Kano itself (Map 6). Unoccupied areas are virtually absent with the exception of, first, the flood-plains associated with several large rivers flowing north-eastwards into the Chad Basin, where the frequent occurrence of flooding discourages agriculture and obliges the siting of villages at a distance, and second, a large part of Tudun Wada district in the south, where the Provincial boundary crosses the demographic 'watershed' from the Kano close-settled zone to include a fragment of the densely populated cotton- and tobacco-growing belt along the Zaria–Jos road in Zaria Province.

It has been pointed out by earlier writers that the density of population decreases outwards from Kano through concentric zones of similar density,[1] from over 500 per square mile in the innermost zone to 150 per square mile at distances of 30 or 40 miles from Kano. However, simple numerical analysis of Map 6 shows that the density gradient, if followed outwards from Kano, steepens noticeably at a density of about 360 per square mile; this figure may therefore be conveniently adopted as a minimum density in defining the extent of the close-settled zone. This has been done in Map 7. It can be seen that the shape of the zone is not circular but approximately elliptical, orientated from north-west to south-east, and Kazaure is also the centre of a small densely populated zone.

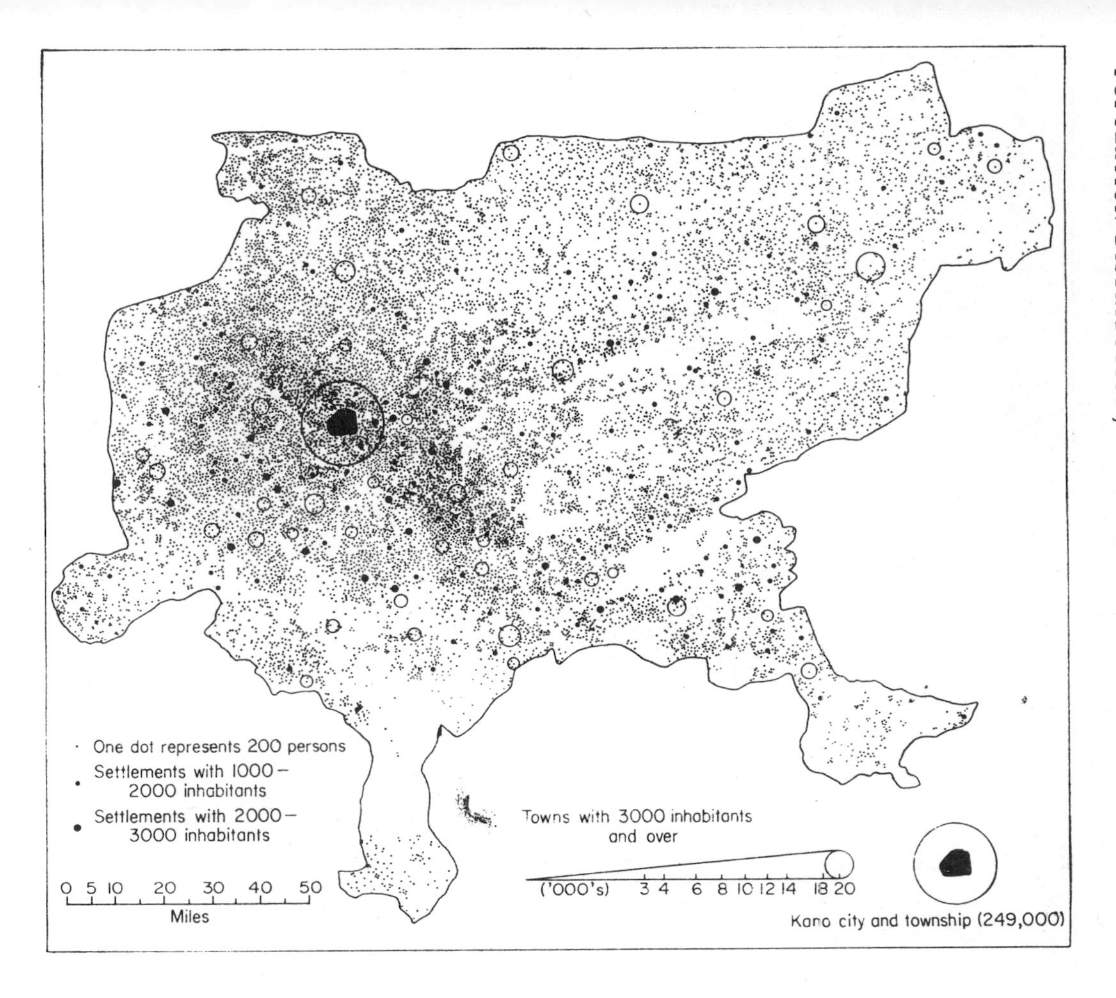

Map 6 Kano Province: population distribution.

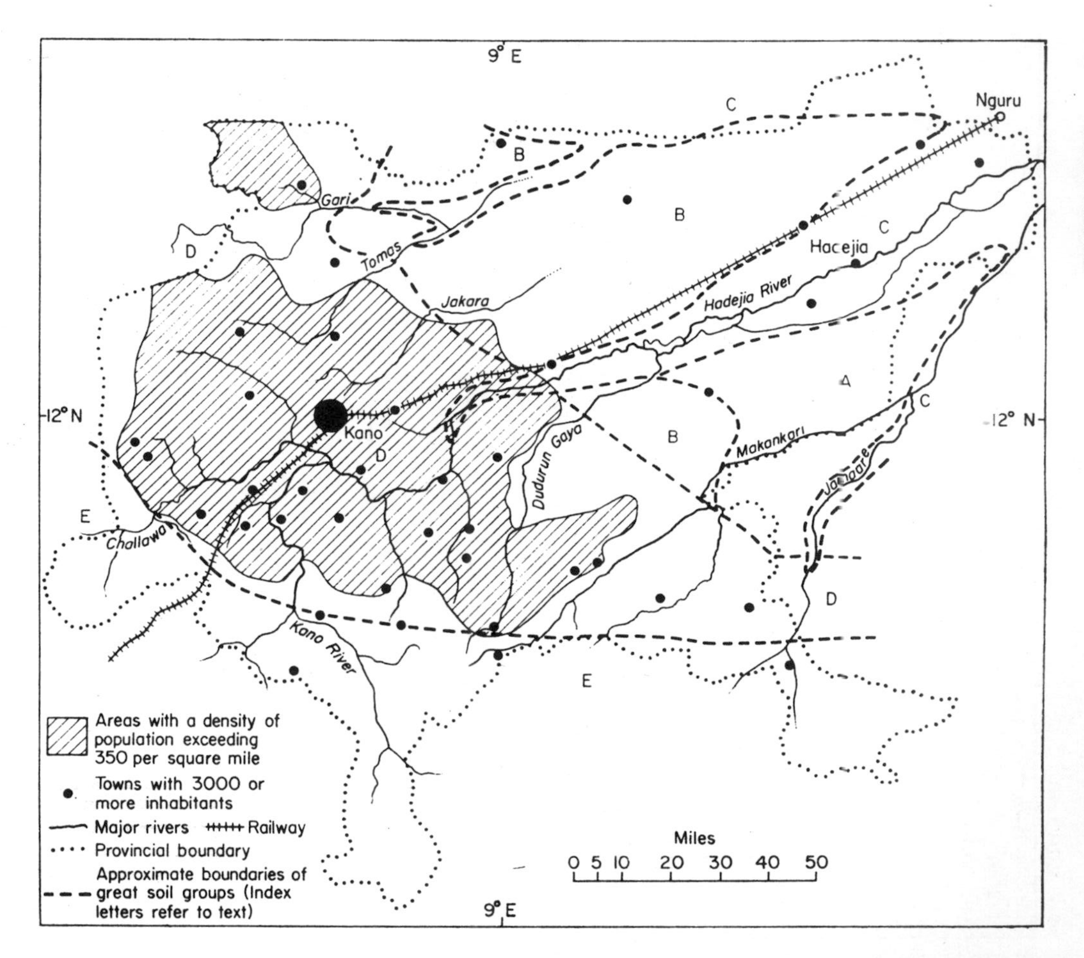

Map 7 Kano Province: close-settled zone and approximate boundaries of great soil groups.

Soils and Land Use

The boundaries of the great soil groups have recently been revised for this part of Nigeria,[2] which lies astride five pedological zones of fundamental importance from an agricultural point of view (Map 7). The central dunefield, which is of Pleistocene origin, has given rise to weakly developed soils on loose sediments whose parent material was derived from the sedimentary Chad deposits which underlie the dunes (A). They possess a large proportion of sand, little or no organic matter, a very weak profile development and a high infiltration rate (Table 1). In the Azare area of Bauchi Province these soils have been described as the Gadau Association by Pullan,[3] inherently poor in minerals and of low fertility. Also developed on former sand dunes overlying sedimentary rocks of the Chad series, but possessing a better profile development, and less freely drained, the soils of the outer dunefield (B) extend over large areas in the north-east of the Province and also occur on the southern periphery of the first group. They are classified as brown and reddish-brown soils of arid and semi-arid regions, and near Hadejia they have been described as the Birniwa Association by Pullan.[4] They have developed on long parallel seif dunes aligned from north-east to south-west and include wash soils developed on the lower slopes.

Table 1

Kano Province: some Properties of the Main Soil Groups[1]

Great soil group[3]	Parent material	Percentage clay and silt	Percentage carbon	Infiltration rate	CS : FS[2] ratio
(A) Weakly developed soils on loose sediments	Dune sands (Chad deposits)	10·9	0·14	6·5	1 : 4·6
(B) Brown and reddish-brown soils of arid and semi-arid regions	Dune sands (Chad deposits)	10·9	0·16	2·7	1 : 3·2
(D) Group B with lithosols on ferruginous crusts	Dune sands (Basement Complex)	14·6	0·23	2·3	1 : 5·1
(E) Ferruginous tropical soils	Drift and weathered Basement Complex	32·1	0·54	0·2	1 : 11·9

1. Top 24 inches of the profile.
2. CS : FS—Coarse sand : fine sand ratio.
3. Terminology for the great soil groups from VAN D'HOORE'S *Explanatory Monograph for the 1 : 5,000,000 Soil Map of Africa*, CCTA, Lagos.

In the interdunal hollows occur soils of the Galadi Association which are characterized by seasonal waterlogging. Within the dunefields, belts of hydromorphic and halomorphic soils of varying width (C), orientated from south-west to north-east, are associated with former alluvial plains and with the present reduced drainage system, of which the largest component is the Hadejia River. Included here are Pullan's Garun Gabbas, Hadejia, Hago and Maranda Associations of the Hadejia area, some of which have sand dunes situated upon them, reducing their actual surface area. They are generally fine sand or clay, and are subject to seasonal waterlogging, though not always infertile. Also included are the soils of the Maigatari alluvial complex in the extreme north, remnants of a formerly extensive drainage system, generally sandy in texture and often relatively fertile. Whereas the dunefield soils owe their character to the existence of arid conditions during Pleistocene times, when rainfall was probably not more than 6 inches per annum (compared with 25–35 at present), these hydromorphic soils are developed on material transported by rivers during a much wetter period pre-dating the formation of the dunes.

The fourth group (D) consists of brown and reddish-brown soils of arid and semi-arid regions, with lithosols on ferruginous crusts. Like groups (A) and (B), they have developed upon wind-transported dune sands, but derived this time from underlying rocks of the granitic Basement Complex. They possess a larger proportion of silt or clay but also lack a well-developed profile, and suffer from a poverty of organic matter. However, being situated over granitic rocks they are inherently richer in minerals, and it has been suggested that deep-rooted farm trees play a vital rôle in tapping this supply and re-distributing minerals, especially phosphates, at the surface where they can benefit growing crops.[5] Finally, represented in the south and east of the Province only, are ferruginous tropical soils of the Zaria type (E), derived from drift and weathered material overlying acid granitic rocks and much richer in organic content than any of the other groups; they also have a much larger proportion of clay and silt. Table 1 summarizes the chief characteristics of groups (A), (B), (D) and (E).

It will at once be apparent that the Kano close-settled zone occurs almost entirely within the limits of the fourth group (D), and the same is true of the smaller zone surrounding Kazaure. The Katsina close-settled zone is also located on soils of this group; indeed it may be misleading to regard Kano and Katsina as separate concentrations of population since they are joined by a belt of high density bounded on both sides by important soil boundaries. A clue towards the understanding of this relationship can be obtained by observing the uses to which the great soil groups are put at the present day.

In Bauchi and Bornu Provinces the weakly developed soils of the central dunefield have been largely ignored by agriculture and permanent settlement, although in Kano they seem to support a higher density of population. The outer dunefield soils (B) are however better developed and support abundant crops of groundnuts, although grain crops, especially guinea corn, do not do so well as on soils of the arid brown group (D) which are heavier, richer, and form the basis for the intensive cultivation which is practised throughout the close-settled zone. It is readily apparent to the observer that on the arid brown soils a much larger proportion of the cultivated area is given to guinea corn, the most demanding of the three main crops, which is also planted at much greater densities on these soils than on the dunefield soils, thereby giving higher yields per acre. Higgins has found that the purchases of groundnuts per 100 square miles are at a similar level on both soil groups (Table 2).[2]

Table 2

Groundnut Purchases at Marketing Board Buying Stations, 1962/63–1964/65

	Soil group (B)	Soil group (D)
Average annual purchases (tons)	164,698	333,430
Total purchases per 100 sq. mls. (tons)	1,373	1,482

Land use, however, is generally much less intensive on the dunefield soils than on the arid brown soils, where 80 per cent of the total area is commonly under cultivation in any one year. The greater importance of groundnuts in the economy of the dunefield soils is clear, even though production for home use, which is normally a very small proportion of output, is presumably higher on the arid brown soils owing to the greater density of population.

The hydromorphic soils, which vary in character and fertility, are limited in their agricultural potential by seasonal waterlogging. The ferruginous soils (E) support in Zaria and Katsina good crops of guinea corn, millet and groundnuts, as well as several crops which cannot normally be grown successfully in Kano, such as cotton, tobacco and yams. The transition from the arid brown to the ferruginous soils groups coincides with the change from Sudan to northern Guinea Savanna vegetation and with a considerable increase in annual rainfall; this is a boundary of great importance in Northern Nigeria.

The economy of Kano Emirate before 1912 was based upon the cultivation of the grain crops, guinea corn and millet, which grow well on the arid brown soils although guinea corn does better on the heavier, redder soils while millet prefers the sandier. Taxation, an old feature of Hausa local administration, normally took the form of payments in grain. The importance in former times of the subsidiary crops, cassava (grown in separate fields) and groundnuts (often intercropped with guinea corn and millet) was probably less than at present; the significance of cowpeas then is uncertain. Given such a crop complex, a basic orientation towards subsistence production, and the proximity of an urban market for surplus grain, the preference shown by past generations of farmers for the arid brown soils *vis-à-vis* the dunefield soils can be understood. The concentration within this area of settlements containing more than 3,000 inhabitants in 1962 (Map 7) emphasizes this preference, since these are all old-established walled towns from which the Hausa and later the Fulani aristocracies controlled the tributary agricultural areas.

This is not to claim a crude control of population distribution by soil character alone. The present high densities in the close-settled zone are to some extent the result of inertia, in that the need for security, which was formerly met under the umbrella of the most powerful of the Hausa emirates, no longer militates against the dispersal of population to outlying areas. But dispersal requires decisions by many to move, and meanwhile natural increase is daily raising population densities higher. Possibly the political factor may help to explain why the Kano Hausa did not expand southwards in larger numbers on to the inherently richer ferruginous soils; but it may be questioned whether these soils, with more clay and less well-drained, were generally suitable for intensive agriculture of the type characteristic of Kano.

The commercial significance of Kano itself, centre of road and rail communications and of cash-crop buying activities, is now greater than ever as an attractive force for migrants; the population of Kano City and Township increased by 91 per cent between 1952 and 1962. Furthermore, a symbiotic relationship has developed between the city and its environs, which is a major contributory factor in the maintenance of high population densities in the close-settled zone. At the core of this relationship is the exchange of firewood, which is obtained by felling the abundant farm trees, and manure, produced from household refuse and an enormous sheep and goat population within the City, which provides a significant proportion of the large fertilizer input required by these intensively-cultivated soils. In addition, there is a large rural weaving industry in the environs of Kano which is based on the City markets and supplements income from agriculture. These and other aspects of rural–urban relations between Kano and its environs have been examined elsewhere.[6]

Changing Patterns of Population Distribution

Introducing the time perspective, in the distribution of population added by natural increase or net immigration between 1952 and 1962, the close-settled zone is not

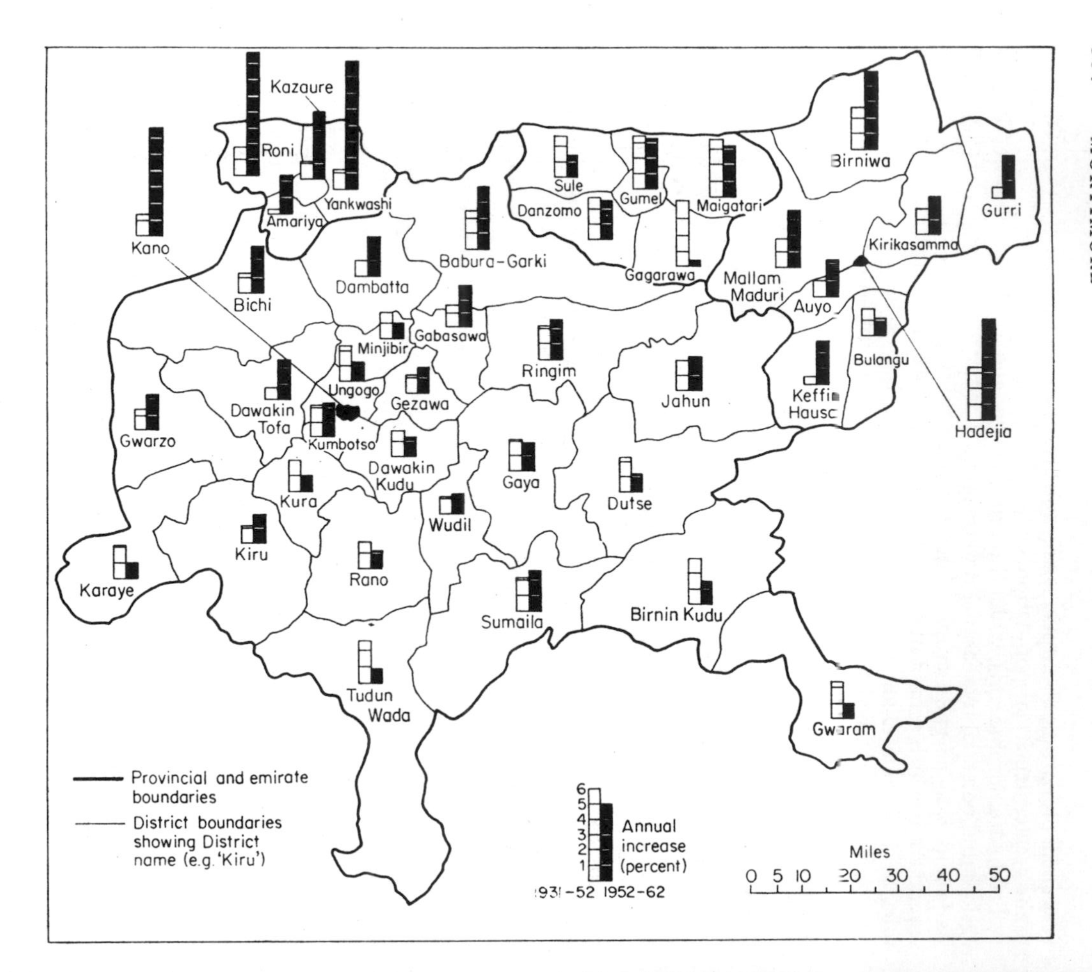

Map 8 Kano Province: percentage increase in population between 1931–52 and 1952–62 in each district.

prominent (except for Dawakin Tofa district, west of Kano), and apart from Kazaure Emirate (in the north-west) the additional population is fairly evenly distributed. This implies that the smaller populations of the north-eastern districts are currently growing at a faster rate than the much larger ones closer to Kano, a fact confirmed by Map 8 which shows the annual increase (per cent) in each district. The fastest-growing towns are all situated outside the arid brown soils, with the exception of Kano itself, while many of the old towns within the limits of these soils have seen no increase or actual decline.

While the dunefield soils are not ideally suited to the needs of a grain-growing economy they lend themselves well enough to groundnut cultivation, and the abundant opportunities for the sale of this crop together with a growing shortage of land in the central districts have favoured the expansion of agriculture on these soils, especially since there is no longer any security risk involved in settling in sparsely populated areas. An annual increase in population of over 2 to 2½ per cent, which appears to be the probable rate of natural increase in Kano Province, implies migration, either from the central districts or from areas farther north, in Niger Republic. Information on this point is lacking, although no evidence was found of significant emigration from three villages about five miles north of Kano in Ungogo district.[7] Further evidence of the development of a market-orientated agricultural economy on the dunefield soils is to be seen in the rapid growth, already referred to, of urban centres and in the location of several of the largest of these along the railway from Kano to Nguru (Map 7).

These trends may be examined in longer perspective by taking into account the results of the census of 1931, although this was probably less accurate than that of 1952 (Map 8). The fastest growth (over 2 per cent per annum) between 1931 and 1952 took place in the three central districts, Ungogo, Kumbotso and Kura, and in an outer zone, both north and south, which was separated from the central districts by an intermediate zone of slower increase (less than 2 per cent per annum). The outer zone included Gumel Emirate, but most of Hadejia and all of Kazaure Emirates experienced an annual increase of less than 2 per cent. In this pattern of approximately concentric zones, the rapid growth of population in the central districts should be viewed in the light of Kano's importance as a market for the products of rural industries, which assume great importance in the rural economy there, as well as the fact that agriculture reaches a maximum intensity aided partly by supplies of manure from the city itself. A less acute shortage of land must have contributed to the higher rates of growth prevalent on the periphery of the close-settled zone, while the intermediate zone, benefiting from neither of these advantages, suffered an economic disincentive to population increase.

This zonal pattern has been changed since 1952 (or probably earlier) by the limitation of the highest rates of increase (more than 2·5 per cent per annum) to the northern parts of the Province. On the soils of the dunefield this has taken place under the stimulus of a growing market-orientated agriculture and a relatively abundant supply of land. The increased rates of growth north and west of Kano are harder to understand, since this area already possessed a high density in 1952. The pressure on land resources in these arid brown soil districts must be approaching the maximum possible with existing agricultural techniques. The southern districts, on the other hand, have ceased to grow rapidly, with the exception of Sumaila. Information suggests that the current of immigrant farmers in search of new land has been much reduced as such land has come into increasingly short supply, even on the ferruginous soils of the southern periphery of the Province. Indeed, the low rates of increase (less than 1 per cent per annum) in Karaye, Tudun Wada and Gwaram suggest net emigration. This may also be taking place in districts which are increasing currently at less than 2 per cent per annum.

Conclusion

An attempt has been made to show that present-day population distribution patterns in Kano Province can be related to the distribution of the great soil groups, because these groups vary in their utility to an agricultural population. The relative economic potential of different soils, and therefore their capacity to support population, may change as the nature of the agricultural economy itself changes under the impact of new conditions, and especially with the shift from subsistence towards commercial production. The separate rôles of historical inertia and of economic change in bringing about the present-day distribution of population can then be isolated.

It is clear that the present demographic situation in Kano Province is a complicated one. Considerable rural–urban migration is taking place, not only to the overwhelmingly large centre of Kano City and Township (whose population in 1962 was 249,000), but also to certain favoured local centres, especially railway towns (such as Mallam Maduri and Ringim) and centres of local administration and markets (such as Hadejia, Kura, and new Rano). There is reported to be considerable migration within the Province, of farmers from the overcrowded districts in search of new land; this movement extends outside the Province, and Kano Hausa are to be found farming in many parts of Northern Nigeria. Within districts migration is taking place between rural areas and from rural areas to the towns. In the Province as a whole the centres of most rapid growth have shifted from the arid brown soils of the south and west to the dunefield soils of the north and east. The numerical significance of all these movements and trends is unfortunately not capable of precise evaluation at present.

Footnotes

1. BUCHANAN, K. M., and PUGH, J. C., *Land and People in Nigeria*, 1955, p. 62; GROVE, A. T. 'Population densities and agriculture in Northern Nigeria', in BARBOUR, K. M., and PROTHERO, R. M., *Essays on African Population*, 1961, pp. 115–36; PROTHERO, R. M., *Northern Nigeria 1:1,000,000 Population Distribution and Density Maps*, compiled from the 1952 census of Nigeria; MCDONNELL, G., 'The dynamics of geographic change: the case of Kano', *Annals of the Association of American Geographers*, Vol. 54, 1964, pp. 355–71.
2. The author is indebted to Mr G. M. Higgins and Mr K. Klinkenberg, of the Soil Survey Section, Institute for Agricultural Research, Ahmadu Bello University, for allowing him to benefit from work still in progress on the distribution of the great soil groups in Northern Nigeria and their relationship to agricultural production (the subject of a forthcoming publication).
3. PULLAN, R. A., *A Report on the Reconnaissance Soil Survey of the Azare (Bauchi) area*, Bulletin no. 19, Soil Survey Section, Regional Research Station, Ministry of Agriculture, Samaru, 1962.
4. PULLAN, R. A., *A Report on the Reconnaissance Soil Survey of the Nguru-Hadejia-Gumel area*, Bulletin no. 18, Soil Survey Section, 1962.
5. VINE, H., 'The soil resources for increased production', *Farm and Forest*, Vol. 9, 1948, pp. 21–27.
6. MORTIMORE, M. J., and WILSON, J., *Land and People in the Kano close-settled zone*, Ahmadu Bello University Department of Geography, Occasional Paper No. 1, 1965, pp. 91–101.
7. MORTIMORE, M. J., and WILSON, J. *op. cit.*, pp. 25–38.

31 Some reflection upon the nutritional problems of dense farm populations in parts of Nigeria *

I. S. Dema

Department of Chemical Pathology,
University of Ibadan, Nigeria

Population Densities and Settlement Patterns

Southern Nigeria constitutes the most densely peopled part of Africa outside the Nile Valley and the rich mining districts of Southern Rhodesia. The people of the Yoruba Region of the west, who exhibit settlement densities of about 300 persons per square mile, tend to concentrate into large clusters. This is indicative of fairly advanced central administrative and commercial organization. The North is relatively sparsely peopled (50–130 persons per square mile), but the populations are located around the seats of powerful native rulers. In contrast, the denser populations of 700–800 persons per square mile in the Ibo areas of Eastern Nigeria, where there are less powerful traditional authorities, tend to live in widely scattered settlements so as to maintain sufficient farmlands for their subsistence.

FOOD AND NUTRITION PROBLEMS OF THE POPULATION

Although it is not intended to repeat here the gloomy Malthusian fears that population is about to outstrip resources, a theory based on the assumption that agricultural production and land resources are inelastic, it is still important not to ignore the observation that most farming districts in Nigeria are over-crowded and will therefore be facing some food supply problems.

The nutritional health of the people is generally poor as evidenced by the following observations[1]:

(i) low birth weights;
(ii) poor lactation performance;
(iii) retarded physical and psychological development in early childhood;
(iv) protein-calorie deficiency diseases in children;
(v) high mortality rates for infants and young children;
(vi) emaciation and loss of strength in working adults, particularly during the season of greatest agricultural activity, i.e. tilling and sowing, which comes at a time when food stocks are low.

Although the populations are largely agricultural these health problems testify that food supplies are not keeping pace with the rapid growth in human numbers. This report, therefore, is an examination of the farming and food problems of these dense populations so as to suggest possible improvements in their agricultural and economic development. The review is based on recent studies of health and diet in relation to agricultural systems in the following Nigerian communities[2]:

1. the Cocoa Belt of Ibadan-Ilesha, Western Nigeria;
2. the savanna farmlands of Oyo-Ibarapa, Western Nigeria;
3. the millet economy of Pankshin, Northern Nigeria;
4. the gullied farmlands of Maku (Awgu) in the northern part of Eastern Nigeria;

5. the Cross River Rice Area in the region of Idembia (Abakaliki), Eastern Nigeria; and
6. the area of dense oil palm canopy over sandy soils as in Urualla (Orlu) and Adiasim (Abak) in Eastern Nigeria.

Demographic Structure: Farm Labour and Food Supply

The Nigerian farming community is made up of about 48 per cent active workers aged 15–65 years, 49 per cent young persons under 15 years of age, and about 3 per cent elderly people aged over 65 years. The corresponding figures for an industrial community, such as the United Kingdom, are 32 dependents to 68 active workers, thus emphasizing the considerably greater burden which the Nigerian farming family bears in having to provide subsistence for its relatively large number of dependents.

The above situation is further worsened by the drift from the villages into the towns to follow non-agricultural trades of young active workers (aged 15–21) who yet continue to be dependent, at least for some time, on the proceeds from their families' farms. With more and more children going to school, those at work on the family farm form a declining proportion of the total population that is being fed.

LAND AND FOOD SUPPLY

Information is still being collected on the total amounts of land available per person in these communities. All the areas studied follow some food cropping sequences, with a fallow period at the end. The fallow system is becoming disorganized, because of increased demands on the available land for cash cropping, as in the free cash cocoa areas, or due to loss of farmlands through gully erosion, as in parts of Eastern Nigeria. From the actual measurements of cultivated fields it has been possible to calculate the figures shown in Table 1 relating to the amount of cropped land per person.

Compared with the most crowded European farming countries, Holland and Belgium,[3] where the average cultivated acreage per person is about 0·5, most of the Nigerian farming communities studied are very densely populated; the most crowded farmlands being in Eastern Nigeria with only 0·12 to 0·15 cultivated acreage per person. Even in the less peopled parts of the country, the fragmented and remote nature of the holdings make it difficult for the farmer to crop extensively unaided by machines or co-operative effort.

MIGRATION TO ALLEVIATE POVERTY AND STARVATION

The farmers in the densely populated districts contrive to make themselves self-sufficient in foods by practising very intensive mixed cropping. However, in order to augment the meagre incomes from their small farms, some of the adult males in these crowded parts of Eastern Nigeria migrate seasonally to work on hired farms, or even as farm labourers, in the timber and tree crop areas further south, and in Mid-Western and Western Nigeria, sending home various remittances. Taking one example, human population counts conducted during the study of Maku (Awgu) in 1963 showed that the adult male to female ratio rose from 68 per cent in April to 86 per cent in August of the same year. The explanation is that men who intend to move out on temporary labour migration hurry through the more laborious farm work of clearing and tilling the land early in the rains so that they can get away by April. The farms are looked after by the women and children while their menfolk are away. The men then begin to return home around August to participate in lifting the yam, a traditional crop harvested with religious celebrations.

This seasonal labour migration from the densely peopled Ibo areas of Eastern

Table 1

Cultivated Land and Food Supply

Farm Community	FOOD PRODUCTION Cultivated areas per person		FOOD CONSUMPTION As percentage of requirement	
	Total crop acreage	Food crop acreage	Calorie intake	Protein intake
WEST				
Ilesha				
Abebeyun, 1960–61	1·59	0·83	98	79
Igun ,, ,,	1·95	0·39	87	78
Ijana ,, ,,	1·87	0·73	87	72
Oke Ila ,, ,,	0·56	0·39	79	43
Oyo				
Ilora, August 1965	0·40	0·31	79	43
Ibarapa				
Igbo Ora, August 1964	0·37	0·31	82	53
Ibadan				
Akufo, November 1961	0·99	0·53	88	65
Osegere, August 1963	0·56	0·27	80	64
NORTH				
Pankshin				
Vodni, November 1961				
Moslems	0·93 }	0·93 }	147	135
Non-Moslems			125	105
EAST				
Awgu				
Maku, 1962–63	0·12	0·12	74	60
Abakiliki				
Idembia, 1962–63	0·13	0·13	73	52
Orlu				
Urualla, 1962–63	0·14	0·14	83	67
Abak				
Adiasim, 1962–63	0·15	0·15	76	62

Nigeria has also been noted by other workers in Okigwi[4] and Awka districts.[5] Many of the young men are even forced to emigrate to work on the Spanish plantations in Fernando Po.

DEPENDENCE FOR FOOD CONSUMPTION ON FARMED LAND

An examination of the people's dietary sources has shown that they depend largely on what grows on their farms, as this is considered to cost them nothing in cash. Because of transport difficulties and rigid preferences for local foods, generally starchy staples, the calorie and protein intakes tend to increase with the size of cultivated land as shown in Table 1. Some kinds of livestock are kept, but animal protein figures very little in the diet. The only important exception to this dependence on the farm is in the permanent tree crop areas, e.g. the Ilesha cocoa belt, where considerable tracts of land carrying this crop are no longer available for raising foods. It would be expected at first sight that incomes from cash crops would be used to provide more food, but in fact they are expended in payments for imports urgently needed for economic development and also to satisfy other needs besides food, for example clothing, building, education and medical care.

INFLUENCE OF CROPPING AND FOOD INTAKES UPON PHYSICAL DEVELOPMENT

The physical development of children from these respective communities has been compared with the growth of children of well-to-do Nigerians. By matching the physique data with the corresponding figures on food intakes and food crop acreages, it is found that, in general, the larger the food crop area the better the chances of adequate subsistence and the closer the physique of the children approaches that of the children of well-to-do Nigerian parents.

To sum up, an examination of sizes of family farms, dietary intakes and the resulting physical development of children in Nigerian rural communities has shown that these are interrelated through the food crop acreage per person. Thus populations better placed in regard to the amount of land under food crops seem to have better diets and more robust physical development. They are also more settled and less tempted to migrate in order to avoid poverty and starvation.

SUGGESTIONS FOR THE DEVELOPMENT OF AGRICULTURALLY CROWDED AREAS

Small farms, however well worked, as in Maku (Awgu), are under severe pressure. They predominate in the least fertile parts of the country, namely, the gullied tracts and acid sands of Eastern Nigeria. The farmers grow mainly root crops that cannot be sold at high profits. Trade in the agricultural products needed in the growing industries of the country should be stepped up so that farming is more profitable. Side by side with the above, agricultural extension services should be intensified in the following ways:

(a) a drive against animal and crop diseases and pests which tend to reduce the quantity and quality of farm produce;

(b) better storage and processing of farm produce;

(c) more balanced cultivation of cash crops and staple foods of high nutritional quality;

(d) improvements in soil fertility through fertilizer applications;

(e) extension of cultivatable lands through irrigation of dry areas, reclamation of swamps and eroded valleys;

(f) diversification into animal husbandry, including fish farming, to make more efficient use of available labour and crop residues and to provide additional cash incomes and dietary protein.

WHAT TO DO WITH THE SURPLUS RURAL POPULATION

(a) *Land Resettlement Schemes.* It has often been suggested that the population should be moved from crowded pockets to sparsely populated zones; this of course, presupposes the availability of fertile lands in the new area. Apart from uncertainties about crop yields, no authority in the country thinks of setting up innumerable farm settlements, in view of the heavy capital outlay.[6] A few farm settlements alone cannot, however, solve the food and economic problems of the surplus rural populations.

(b) *Establishment of Industries.* Finally, there is an urgent need to find subsidiary occupations for the surplus farming population so as to increase incomes from non-farm sources and thus help to arrest the waves of migration. In this regard, rural industries, such as woodwork, pottery, weaving and basket work, all of which could be based on locally available raw materials, would provide subsidiary occupations for farmers during the slack period between sowing and harvesting the main crop. Such alternative occupations would also reduce the temptation to sell the bulk of the food from the family farm. Apart from making use of some of the farm produce, economic developments in the urban centres would help to attract unprogressive farmers into industry and leave behind a relatively small but efficient agricultural population to produce more food.

The country needs a bold plan of industrialization, side by side with agricultural improvements, in order to raise living standards in the densely populated rural districts.

Footnotes

* Gratitude is due to the Rockefeller Foundation for generous grants to support a project directed first by Professor W. R. F. Collis (former Director of Institute of Child Health, University of Ibadan), and later by the author, in the study of health in relation to diets and agricultural factors in Nigerian communities. Indebtedness to UNICEF/FAO/WHO is also acknowledged in their sponsoring the field training courses now being held annually in Ibadan in food science and applied nutrition, from which contributory material for this report has been obtained in respect of Osegere, Igbo Ora and Ilora in Western Nigeria.

1. DEMA, I. S. *Nutrition in relation to agricultural production*, Ch. 2, Medical evidence of malnutrition in Nigeria 1965 (Publication in press sponsored by FAO/WHO/UNICEF), FAO, Rome.

2. COLLIS, W. R. F., DEMA, I. and OMOLOLU, A. 'On the ecology of Child Health and Nutrition in Nigerian Villages', *Trop. Geog. Med.* 14, 1962, pp. 140 and 201.

COLLIS, W. R. F., DEMA, I. and LESI, F. E. A. 'Transverse survey of health and nutrition, Pankshin, Northern Nigeria', *West African Medical Journal*, 11, 1962, p. 131.

DEMA, I., 'Cropping systems and dietetic survey', in GILLES, H. M.: *Akufo; an environmental study of a Nigerian village community*, 1964, Ch. 3, p. 13.

DEMA, I. S., 'Nutritional assessment of peasant farming', *Proceedings of the Agricultural Society of Nigeria*, 1963, p. 13.

UNICEF Fellows

Osegere Survey, University of Ibadan, 1963.

Igbo Ora Survey, University of Ibadan, 1964.

Ilora Survey, University of Ibadan, 1965.

3. YATES, P. L., *Food, land and manpower in Europe*, Macmillan, London, 1960, p. 142.

4. GREEN, M. M., *Ibo village affairs*, Sidgwick & Jackson, London, 1947.

5. GROVE, A. T., 'Soil erosion and population problems in South-eastern Nigeria', *Geog. J.* 117 (3), 1951, p. 291.

6. BALDWIN, K. D. S., *The Niger agricultural project*, Blackwell, Oxford, 1957.

32 Some cultural factors in the critical density of population in tropical Africa

G. J. Afolabi Ojo

Department of Geography, University of Ife, Nigeria

The Concept of Critical Density of Population and Its Significance

The concept, the *critical density of population* (CDP), was recently defined by William Allan as 'the human carrying capacity of an area in relation to a given land use system, expressed in terms of population per square mile; it is the maximum population density which a system is capable of supporting permanently in that environment without damage to the land.'[1] It is the level of density of population 'beyond which degeneration leading to ultimate collapse is bound to set in.'[2] Max Gluckman, in his foreword to Allan's book, *The African Husbandman*, describes the CDP in a similar vein as 'a point beyond which the land would begin to deteriorate.'[3] Throughout this book, which is concerned with the clarification, illustration and application of the concept of the CDP in relation to a variety of land use systems and areas in Africa south of the Sahara, other similar examples of such definitions may be found.

It is enough to add here that the CDP is the marginal point of population density at which unrewarding or uneconomical diminishing returns set in, either when the population is increasing or when the quality of the land is diminishing or when any of the variants composing the CDP is being markedly and adversely affected. The CDP is a function of the population (its distribution, quality and rate of change), the methods and systems of land use, the tools employed, the crops grown, and also of the edaphic, climatic and other physical conditions of the area. It is dependent on a combination of these factors rather than on any one of them individually, although at any particular time one of the factors may be dominant.

In actual practice, population density is often related to the type of dominant economy prevailing in an area, since an economy is the epitome of the physical and cultural conditions of its area. Each of the major types of economy in tropical Africa has different land requirements, varying from hunting and gathering, which are least land-demanding, to agriculture which is most land-demanding. Tropical agriculture is, therefore, a reliable indicator of both the population density and its relation to the CDP at any particular time. For instance, in tropical agriculture as soon as bush fallow farming is eliminated as a continuous feature from the land-use pattern, then the critical density of population is attained and permanent cultivation supervenes.[4]

There is probably no aspect of population that has more significant and practical implications for man in the process of his utilization of the earth's resources than that of the CDP. Neither the total number of inhabitants nor their density as such fully relates man to the essential resources available in a particular environment. Even when the concept of density is stretched taut, it does not conjure up much more than the idea of so many people per square mile or that of so many acres per head of population. It may be granted that the terms 'underpopulation' and 'overpopulation' imply respectively inadequate and overadequate numbers of inhabitants in an area. But these terms, essentially relative, are not specifically defined, and so have introduced much vagueness and many generalizations into ideas concerning population pressure. One example may suffice to illustrate this point. In 1958, when T. H. Davey wrote on 'Population Pressure: Cause and Cure', he claimed that, 'As yet Africa is not much concerned by population pressure since it is, broadly speaking, underpopulated and can sustain a very considerable expansion in numbers. In Nigeria, however, population pressure has developed in particular agricultural areas which have densities as high as 1,300 per square mile. Moreover, the censuses of 1931 and 1952/53 have revealed an increase of inhabitants from 20 to 31 million, an expansion of 58 per cent in 20 years. Considering the relative infertility of much of this country, it is clear that this is a problem which is likely to be of considerable importance in the not very distant future.'[5] The argument is based on four facts: first, that the area is underpopulated except for some areas with high densities of population; second, that the expansion rate is high; third, that much of the country is relatively infertile, and last that population pressure is an imminent danger. The thesis of the present study is in agreement with all these points, as will become clear later. But the question arises whether the first three could lead to the conclusion of the fourth, that population pressure is imminent. It is doubtful.

On the whole, most of our prognostications concerning the relation between resources and population are deficient for one or more of the following reasons. There appears to be no readily available yardstick for measuring the population of an area other than taking note of the total number of people in the area; the estimate of high densities of population in some areas is based on the simple idea of numbers of people per square mile. Further, the significance of the high rate of population growth depends on the starting level from which that growth begins and the upper level beyond which it cannot afford to go; invariably, no account is taken of these extremes. Finally, the issue of the infertility or otherwise of the soil depends on a large number of factors, among which the use to which the land is put and the method employed are most important, so that a long-standing judgement on fertility or infertility is tenuous indeed. Any assessment of the level of pressure reached by such considerations is bound to contain many vague generalizations and may include a number of inaccuracies and improbabilities.

No claim is made for the elimination of these weaknesses in the concept of CDP, which, since it also depends on several variables difficult to evaluate, is bound to be, to some extent, a victim of similar deficiencies. For example, it has been pointed out elsewhere that in the estimation of CDP of traditional land use systems in Africa south of the Sahara the most puzzling and intractable of all the problems involved is the assessment of the cultivatable percentage of land.[6] Nevertheless, this much can be claimed for CDP; it takes account of as many as possible of all the variable factors governing man's numerical strength and his use of the resources of the land; it is much more specific than the ideas of overpopulation and pressure; it tends, if all other things remain equal, to spotlight the danger point in the relationship between man and land. In other words, it is at the point of the CDP that the practical and worthwhile implications of the inevitable interaction between man and the resources of the land are appreciated. How seriously one should take warnings of impending population pressure and explosion in a particular area will depend on how far the present population density is from the calculated CDP.

At a time when many people are concerned with improving the fortunes of tropical Africa, the problem of population pressure upon resources is among the most fundamental and urgent which require attention and action.[7] It is therefore necessary to consider the problem using better defined concepts, such as that of the CDP. This is done hereafter by treating, among other things, the following questions. First, on what side of the CDP are some selected countries, regions and districts of tropical Africa? Second, what factors, especially cultural ones, are responsible for allocating them to the side of the CDP on which they are found? And last, could the present population densities sustain the changes desired and anticipated to bring tropical Africa squarely within the 20th century and, if neither over-ambitious nor unrealistic, to enable the region to catch up with the more advanced countries of the world?

Some Estimates of Critical Density of Population

Stamp once estimated the optimum population that the most densely populated parts of Eastern Nigeria would be able to support to be about 134 persons per square mile.[8] This figure could be taken as the estimated CDP for that time, that is prior to 1938. Two similar calculations made by Grove may be cited. He estimated that the land occupied by the Bemba of Zambia was incapable of supporting more than ten persons per square mile at the level of their system of shifting cultivation.[9] And, for the central districts of the Kano Region the critical figure of population density has been estimated at about 150 to 200, the variation reflecting soil conditions.[10] More recently, Allan worked out similar figures for some scattered areas south of the Sahara. The following table shows those for a few agricultural districts that are precisely delimited.[11]

Table 1

Africa: Estimates of Critical Densities of Population

District	Area in sq. mls.	Estimated CDP
Petauko (northern Zambia)	1,054	19·5
Fort Jameson (northern Zambia)	956	25
Serenje Plateau of the Lala (northern Zambia, across Congo–Zambezi watershed)	1,000	6·5
Ilamba (southern side of Congo–Zambezi watershed)	379	24

The above figures of the CDP, like all other figures of population, have no particular claims to precision. The population figures on which they are based are understandably riddled with a lot of deficiencies resulting in appreciable margins of error. Prothero has already shown that the estimated margin of error of 5 per cent in the case of the 1952–53 Nigerian census really meant over 1,500,000 people.[12]

An estimate of the percentages of cultivable and habitable areas is yet to be made for many parts of tropical Africa. This is not an easy task even in parts of the world with an established practice of land use surveys.

Factors lowering the Critical Density of Population

Southern Nigeria is an area with enough variation to typify very broadly most of the other regions within tropical Africa in the consideration of factors affecting the CDP. In this region, as in any other in tropical Africa, the CDP levels of the different unit areas are constantly changing, irrespective of the level of the pressure of population. This situation of flux is related to the fact that the cultural elements leading to these changes are themselves characterized by change.

In the history of the occupation of southern Nigeria, all parts had population densities below the CDP level until recently. Now, there is, everywhere, a defined upward trend bringing the population densities closer and closer to the CDP in areas where it has not actually been reached or surpassed. Among cultural factors responsible for this trend, the following deserve some consideration.

LAND TENURE

There are everywhere new concepts and practices of land tenure and holding, since the idea of family or community landholding is fast giving way to concepts of individual possession, or at least of single family possession. The former practices of loose ownership were tailored to the requirements of the subsistence economies of the traditional days. Later, however, the establishment of a cash-crop economy, especially where based on perennial crops like cocoa, rubber or oil palm, has further underscored the necessity for a more rigorously defined ownership. There is, therefore, a tendency for larger quantities of land to be held in fewer hands and pressure is bound to increase significantly when the present have-nots begin to press their claims for land.

TRADITIONAL METHODS OF LAND USE

The traditional methods of land use to some extent led to a situation where the population which the land could sustain was not high. Whether by shifting cultivation or rotational bush fallow, the fertility of the soil, accumulated through many years of careful tending on the part of nature, is exposed and thereby endangered. Most of the methods of land use involved the following processes: removal of the forest cover, ring-barking of trees that defied felling, bush-burning and the turning over of the fertile layer of the soil, which at best is skin-deep. These processes led to erosion, laterization, and the virtual breakdown of the soil, especially in areas where the period of fallow was decreasing as a result of increasing population pressure. Eventually, failing concrete efforts to renew the soil, the loss sustained through its use reduces its carrying capacity. As pointed out by R. K. Udo, the clearance of forests and continuous use of ground without replenishing, account in large measure for the present infertile acid soils in parts of Eastern Nigeria, which paradoxically now has a heavy population density.[13] It is rather the method of use of the land, than the advancing Sahara or the desiccation of northern tropical Africa, that accounts for 'degeneration into an inhospitable wilderness.'[14]

MODERN METHODS OF LAND USE

Strenuous efforts are being made to introduce and practise mechanized agriculture in many parts of tropical Africa.[15] So far it does not appear that certain aspects of modern methods of agriculture are an improvement on the traditional in relieving pressure on the land. More acres per head are needed for farming under modern methods, and plantation agriculture, which is bound to assume an increasingly important position, requires extensive land by its very nature thus involving government participation, through which the use of vast expanses of land is made feasible. Again, the application of machinery to farming in scattered pockets entails not only further opening of the forest with its attendant problems but also that with machine power, the requirements of land per person will rise tremendously although modern mechanized farming guarantees increased output. The rate at which forest is being destroyed through modern farming has not yet been accurately estimated; however, it is certainly more than that under shifting cultivation, which was some time ago estimated to be 1,000 square miles a year in Nigeria.[16]

CASH CROPS

As pointed out previously, the absorption of certain perennial tree-crops into the existing agricultural pattern necessitated the acquisition of more acres of land per farm. This is so particularly in respect to perennial cash crops such as cocoa, kolanut, rubber and oil palm trees. Present circumstances dictate that every farmer who wants to be prosperous should grow cash crops. Consequently, there has been a noticeable shift to the latter, which has been responsible for lowering the CDP in areas where cash crops have come to stay because they have displaced food crops from first place, and land requirements have risen correspondingly.

IMPROVED HEALTH

So far, only the cultural factors affecting the land itself have been considered. But there are also factors that affect man, the user of the land, such that the balance between man and land at any particular time is subject to alterations reflecting changes in the number of inhabitants and their skills.

Over nearly all of tropical Africa, modern methods of medical science are making more healthy and effective hands available for work on the land. A few years ago, Davey illustrated the effect of ill-health on productivity and land requirements in saying that 'sickness in adults is an even greater drain on economic resources than premature death because the sick individual remains a consumer but incapable of production.'[17] The contention here is that the intensity of sickness has waned so that a steadily diminishing number of sick people is to be found, especially in the labour-supplying age-group between 17 and 55 years. This is already having its impact on the land which is being more effectively used in increasingly larger quantities per person.

RAPID POPULATION GROWTH

In respect to Central Africa, J. C. Mitchell judges that 'the probabilities are that the birth rate is not likely to change for some years to come while the death rate, due to improved medical facilities and a decline in the prejudice against using them, will decrease.'[18] This evaluation is equally applicable to other parts of tropical Africa that are also beginning to improve living conditions. Rapid population growth would seem to be inevitable. Throughout tropical Africa there is nothing that ranks as high as children in the estimation of the inhabitants. Even with the rising proportion of literate and highly educated southern Nigerians, the family is nearly as large as it was in the days of extensive polygamy. Nor does the practice of monogamy necessarily mean fewer children. Family planning seems to be widely known among the élite in tropical Africa, but not in terms of setting limits on the number of children in each family.

IMPROVING SKILLS

This part of the world is witnessing an appreciable rise in literacy, especially through the mass education of children of school age. Although fewer and fewer of the educated youths want to go back to the land, this is likely to be only a temporary feature, because the ever-rising rate of unemployment among school-leavers means that some will have to return to the land in order to live. When this time comes, there will be a more conscious effort than before to own and cultivate larger units. Furthermore, there will be a more enlightened attitude toward the use of machinery and modern methods of agriculture and acquisition of modern skills will become relatively easy. Thus, more pressure will be exerted on the land, and the CDP will be approached at a faster rate than before.

Factors Raising the CDP

SCIENTIFIC FARMING

Factors that bring the CDP closer to the present level of population pressure are not the only ones at work. Some aspects of modern methods of cultivation have resulted in a higher output per acre and per person than in the traditional system. Modern plant breeding and genetics, and the application of fertilizers, enabling crops to thrive in areas formerly regarded as marginal, have resulted in a smaller number of people being able to produce for an increasingly larger number of non-producers. The effect is to decrease the land requirement per person of the total population, thereby making the CDP higher than would have otherwise been the case.

Another aspect of improved farming is the increasing use of livestock as the menace of trypanosomiasis is being successfully countered along many fronts. New breeds and varieties of livestock have been introduced to areas formerly considered doubtful or marginal and are being moved gradually into areas formerly known to be unsuitable for livestock rearing. Thus, the prospects of mixed farming are becoming brighter. Agricultural output, both in quantity and quality, can probably be improved so that more and more will be got from each acre under cultivation.

DIVERSIFIED ECONOMIES AND OCCUPATIONS

Formerly, nearly everyone was employed in farming or was dependent on subsidiary farming activities for a living, so that almost all directly exerted pressure on the land. Tropical Africa has now entered a more advanced phase, of diversified economy and occupational pattern, with a decreasing proportion of the people dependent on agriculture for a living. In this way the CDP tends towards a higher level. It should be noted, however, that the provision of modern amenities, such as pipe-borne water, has resulted in some saving of labour formerly expended in domestic services. The labour thus saved has been diverted to the main job on hand so partially compensating for the reduction in the actual number of hands engaged on the farm.

DRIFT TO THE TOWNS

There is a marked drift to towns because of their more diversified employment opportunities, especially in secondary industry and the Services. This tends to decrease the actual number of people left behind in the rural areas to be directly dependent on land for agricultural purposes. The ports, the regional and provincial administrative centres, the commercial centres, the manufacturing and industrial towns, all attract population from the rural areas. It could be argued that this further widens the gap between the prevailing pressure of population and the CDP in rural areas since there is a decreasing number of people left behind to manage the land. In this case some land may revert to bush with one of two consequences: if quickly covered by vegetation, it may be protected from erosion and thus have its fertility naturally restored through fallowing; on the other hand, if the land is not overgrown fast, erosion may set in, with further depletion of fertility.

The drift to towns is predominantly a one-way traffic but its effects on the CDP are essentially two-way. In the rural areas it tends to keep the CDP higher. In the urban areas, congestion and cut-throat competition ensue. The normal level of the CDP is soon reached and bypassed, and the area of urban land per capita becomes so small as to be negligible. The continuous movement into the towns aggravates the situation so that many towns of tropical Africa 'now have more inhabitants than they can support or regularly employ'.[19]

MIGRATION

Migration is a cultural and economic phenomenon capable of having tremendous impact on man–land relationships. In recent times, tropical Africa has witnessed unprecedented movements of peoples, as in the case of 'Kikuyu families working by the month or squatting permanently on European farms all over the eastern part of the White Highlands;'[20] or, as in the former Federation of Central Africa, where legal action was necessary as a control, between Northern and Southern Rhodesia on the one hand and among the three territories on the other;[21] or again as with migrants from parts of Eastern Nigeria, mainly to the plantations in the Cameroon Republic, Fernando Po and other neighbouring Spanish Islands.[22] The problem of 'parallel societies' is enacted in other parts of tropical Africa where peoples of different cultures, more particularly the European and the indigenous, are brought together. As pointed out by Prothero with regard to migrations in Sokoto Province, the loss sustained in an emigrating labour force may be compensated for by migrants on their return, bringing in much more money than they could accumulate within the Province.[23]

WEAKENING SOCIAL TIES

Migration, whether involving the individual or families, leads to the weakening of social ties, bonds and obligations. Through migration, gaps are created within the family structure both at home, whence the adventurous persons have departed at their most productive ages, and in the 'new-found-settlements', where newcomers have no family structure into which to enter and fit. The effects of such movements, which may be for long periods between home-town and labour-centre, on the type and quantity of the traditional labour force in the rural areas are best seen in the example of the breakdown of traditional group farming, the details of which are given elsewhere.[24] In sum, migrations, the drift to towns, 'free' primary education, the ever-decreasing ability of obas and chiefs to organize free labour, the breakdown of practices based on social structure and relationships, the gradual disuse, even in the rural areas, of subscription clubs and societies—all these evidence weakening social ties tending to reduce the number of virtually free hands which a farmer can muster for his work. In some other respects these changes have beneficial effects.

Land that was in former times out of bounds for agricultural or other productive purposes has now been released for use as a result of the changing attitudes of the people. In almost every part of tropical Africa some portions of land were set apart as shrines or groves for religious purposes. Other plots were allotted for ancestral cults and worship as in the case of the *egungun* (masqueraders) of Yorubaland. Some animals that had special regard among the people (vultures, monkeys and bats in southern Nigeria) had their forest habitats left undisturbed. The forest reserved for the corpses of those killed by lightning or smallpox and of women who died while still pregnant or as a result of unsuccessful labour, was, in most towns, quite extensive. In some parts of Yorubaland, forests were also set aside for the corpses of debtors. In all these cases, the land was uncultivated, the forests were untouched, their resources unexploited and tabooed. Such forest lands have been opened up and used for sundry purposes now that their traditional uses have been discarded as a result of the changing attitudes and beliefs of the people.[25] The release of such land for productive uses has increased the land available in each area, and has consequently worked in favour of a higher CDP level.

Conclusion

Although accurate and comprehensive figures of the CDP are not yet known, the overall trend in tropical Africa, except in a few areas, is that the population density is gradually approaching a critical level. Already there are some areas where there is a precarious and threatening balance between the land resources and the inhabitants. With further improvements in the practice of agriculture and industry, however, it is possible that less and less acreage of land will be required for satisfying human needs, so that an increase in population density may not necessarily escalate population pressure towards the CDP level.

None the less, the general position in tropical Africa is that there is still enough land to allow for much desired expansion and development towards the economic levels of advanced countries. There is still great need for a clear understanding of differentials in climatic and soil conditions on the one hand and in changing cultural factors on the other, such that the resources of the land may be used to the best advantage, coupled with a re-distribution of the population.

The problem of population in tropical Africa is not to find the *least* number of people for the effective occupation of the area but to estimate the greatest number of people that an area can profitably support. Hence estimation of the CDP of local areas and microregions in Africa is urgent if the land is to be most widely used.

Footnotes

1. ALLAN, W., *The African Husbandman*, Oliver and Boyd, 1965, p. 89.
2. *Ibid.*, p. 76.
3. *Ibid.*, p. 5.
4. GROVE, A. T., 'Population Densities and Agriculture in Northern Nigeria', in *Essays in African Population*, K. M. BARBOUR and R. M. PROTHERO (eds.), London, 1961, p. 125.
5. DAVEY, T. H., *Disease and Population Pressure in the Tropics*, Ibadan, 1958, p. 13.
6. ALLAN, W., *op. cit.*, p. 24.
7. STEEL, R. W., 'The Population of Ashanti: A Geographical Analysis', *Geographical Journal*, Vol. CXII, January 1949, p. 64.
8. STAMP, C. D., 'Land Utilization and Soil Erosion in Nigeria', *Geographical Review*, Vol. 28, 1938 pp. 32–45.
9. GROVE, A. T., *op. cit.*, p. 115.
10. *Ibid.*, p. 125.
11. ALLAN, W., *op. cit.*, Chapter VIII.
12. PROTHERO, R. M., 'Post-war West African Censuses', in *Essays on African Population, op. cit.*, p. 13.
13. UDO, R. K., 'Patterns of Population Distribution and Settlement in Eastern Nigeria', *Nigerian Geographical Journal*, Vol. VI, December 1963, No. 2, p. 82.
14. BRYNMOR JONES, 'Desiccation and the West African Colonies', *Geographical Journal*, Vol. XVI, May 1938, p. 402.
15. For an account of such efforts in a typical area, see OJO, G. J. A., 'Trends Towards Mechanized Agriculture in Yorubaland', *Nigerian Geographical Journal*, Vol. 6, No. 2, December 1963, pp. 116–29.
16. BRYNMOR JONES, *op. cit.*, p. 413.
17. DAVEY, T. H., *op. cit.*, p. 4.
18. MITCHELL, J. C., 'Wage Labour and African Population Movements in Central Africa', in *Essays on African Population, op. cit.*, p. 240.
19. STEEL, R. W., 'The Towns of Tropical Africa' in *Essays on African Population, op. cit.*, p. 266.
20. SOUTHALL, A. W., 'Population Movements in East Africa', in *Essays on African Population, op. cit.*, p. 171.
21. MITCHELL, J. C., *op. cit.*, pp. 203–05.
22. UDO, R. K., 'Sixty Years of Plantation Agriculture in Southern Nigeria: 1902–1962', *Economic Geography*, Vol. 41, No. 4, October 1965.
23. PROTHERO, R. M., 'Population Patterns and Migrations in Sokoto Province, Northern Nigeria', in *Natural Resources, Food and Population in Inter-Tropical Africa*, London, 1956.
24. OJO, G. J. A., 'The Changing Patterns of Traditional Group Farming in Ekiti, North Eastern Yoruba Country', *Nigerian Geographical Journal*, Vol. 6, No. 1, June 1963, pp. 31–38.
25. For further details refer to Chapters 6, 7 and 8 of OJO, G. J. A., *Yoruba Culture, A Geographical Analysis*, University of London Press, 1966.

33 African rural-urban migrants in the main migrant areas of the Lagos Federal Territory

C. N. Ejiogu

Department of Demography, Australian National University, Canberra, Australia

Introduction

The population of the Lagos Federal Territory has apparently grown from 99,690 in 1921, to 126,108 in 1931, 230,256 in 1950, and 665,246 in 1963. The accuracy of particularly two of these counts is very much doubted. The 1921 census was a mere estimate, and that of 1931 was affected by the world economic depression, among other factors, and its accuracy has been questioned. But the 1950 census of Lagos claimed only a 5 per cent error of coverage, while the 1963 results must yet stand the test of demographic analysis. However, the trends presented in Table 1 show evidence of rapid population increases mainly caused by the heavy influx of people from other parts of Nigeria and beyond.

Table 1

Lagos: Growth of Districts, 1921–63

	Total	Lagos Island	Ikoyi and Victoria	Mainland Districts
1921				
Population	99,690	77,561	2,231	15,823
1931				
Population	126,108	90,192	5,241	26,539
Intercensal increase per cent	26·5	16·3	134·9	67·7
Average intercensal growth rate per annum	2·3	1·5	8·9	7·6
1950				
Population	230,256	135,612	15,058	79,586
Intercensal increase per cent	82·6	50·4	187·3	199·9
Average intercensal growth rate per annum	3·2	2·2	5·7	5·9
1963				
Population	665,246	253,857	96,038	315,351
Intercensal increase per cent	188·9	87·2	537·8	296·2
Average intercensal growth rate per annum	8·5	4·9	15·3	11·2

Sources: 1950 census of Lagos, p. 26.
1963 census preliminary figures.

Increased natural growth was also a product of the migration into Lagos of young adults of reproductive age whose fertility was high, and of the fall in infant mortality in recent years.[1] The masculinity of the population, especially of the districts studied in the survey described here, remained high, being 130 males per 100 females in 1950. The diversity of its African ethnic groups, 98 per cent of the Lagos population in the same year, is also typical of a migrant population. No other city in Nigeria is characterized by such a variety of the tribes of the country as is the Territory of Lagos.

The distribution in districts by number of inhabitants shows a shift in population location from the congested Island to the Mainland suburbs and Ikoyi, where housing schemes have been concentrated in recent years. Slum clearance in Lagos Island in 1956 also caused the movement of an estimated 20,000 residents, most of whom were permanently rehoused on the Mainland. Thus, over 60 per cent of the population of the Territory now live in the Mainland districts and Ikoyi where this investigation was carried out.

A random sample of 605 dwelling houses was drawn from the Mainland and Ikoyi sections of a complete housing list for the Federal Territory and one household was randomly selected within each house in order to keep the survey within manageable size. Before the subsequent analysis, interviews were to be weighed in proportion to the number of households per house. Interviewers recruited from the Department of Statistics and the Census Office, Lagos, were employed. The survey was carried out between June and October 1964.

The information sought included the demographic characteristics of the household members and socio-economic factors relating to migration. Five hundred and ninety-six households, containing 3,339 persons, were successfully interviewed. In this paper only some of the demographic characteristics of the sampled population will be discussed.

Composition of Households[2]

Five in every six householders in the sample were born outside Lagos (505/596) and more than 80 per cent of the households in every location had migrant heads. In spite of this, about 49 per cent of the population studied were born in Lagos, the majority being children under 15 years of age (41 per cent of the sample were under 15). The majority of the householders studied were migrant adult males, three-quarters of whom were married and had been resident in Lagos with their wives for more than ten years.

The household size varied from an average of five persons in Yaba and Ikoyi to six in Suru Lere and Ebute Metta, the oldest residential area on the Mainland, to seven in LEDB (Lagos Executive Development Board) Housing Estates, built for families displaced in the slum clearance on the Island and low income workers.[3] As shown in

Table 2

Lagos: Distribution of Household Types by Location*

	Single person	Conjugal couple	Nuclear family	Extended family	Composite household	Group household	Total
Suru Lere	19 (12·3)	1 (0·6)	56 (36·4)	56 (36·4)	22 (14·3)	—	154
LEDB Estates	—	2 (1·7)	62 (53·0)	35 (29·9)	17 (14·3)	1 (0·9)	117
Ebute Metta	7 (3·6)	6 (3·1)	92 (47·7)	58 (30·1)	27 (14·0)	3 (1·5)	193
Yaba	10 (8·8)	2 (1·7)	41 (36·0)	37 (32·0)	20 (17·5)	4 (3·5)	114
Ikoyi	1 (5·6)	—	6 (33·3)	3 (16·8)	8 (44·4)	—	18
All Locations	37 (6·5)	11 (1·9)	257 (43·1)	189 (31·4)	94 (15·8)	8 (1·3)	596

Figures in brackets are percentages of total for each location.
* The analysis at this stage excludes some locations in the survey area and the weighted results.

Table 2, an average of 43·1 per cent of the households were nuclear families,[4] thus stressing the effects of urban housing conditions on family size and structure in these Lagos suburbs. However, if only two types are considered, namely nuclear and extended,[5] the majority of households in these districts, for various cultural and economic reasons, remained extended.

The high percentage (44·4) of composite households (i.e. households with members not all related to the head of household) in Ikoyi, a high income residential suburb, was due to the number of domestic servants in the households in the location. The demand for domestic servants is high in Lagos, particularly among middle- and upper-class households. Most of the servants are paid, but, among most African families, it is less expensive and more convenient for them to live as members of the family sharing in the same feeding and lodging arrangements. Seven out of the eight group families (i.e. households in which none of the members are related) live in Ebute Metta and Yaba. These were mainly students who shared rooms in these suburbs, particularly in Yaba where most educational institutions are located.

Migration and Regional and Ethnic Groups

The migrant groups studied were mainly Nigerians from the four Regions of the Federation, with only 2·4 per cent from the West African states of Dahomey, Togo, Ghana and Sierra Leone. Immigration from these countries is not on any significant scale, as the city does not offer much economic attraction to them.

The Yoruba from the contiguous Western Region of Nigeria were the dominant groups forming 50·4 per cent of the migrant population studied. The Ibo of the Eastern and Mid-Western Regions made up 24·1 per cent of all migrants. Others included the Edo-speaking group of the Mid-Western Region, who formed 9·7 per cent of all migrants, the Ibibio and Efik from the east (9·4 per cent), and the Hausa of Northern Nigeria (2·1 per cent). The dominant position of the Yoruba in their proportion of the total population is shown in Table 3. But the higher number of Yorubas born in Lagos, compared with the Lagos-born of other groups, slightly reduced the number of migrant Yorubas.

Table 3

Lagos: Main Ethnic Groups in the Total, Migrant and Lagos-born Population

Ethnic Group	Total	Migrant	Lagos-born
Yoruba	1,986 (59·5)	856 (50·4)	1,130 (68·8)
Ibo	688 (20·6)	409 (24·1)	279 (17·0)
Edo and Urhobo	296 (8·9)	164 (9·7)	132 (8·0)
Ibibio and Efik	228 (6·8)	159 (9·4)	69 (4·2)
Hausa	40 (1·2)	36 (2·1)	4 (0·2)
Other Nigerian	43 (1·3)	32 (1·9)	11 (0·7)
Non-Nigerian Africans	58 (1·7)	41 (2·4)	17 (1·0)
All Groups	3,339 (100·0)	1,697 (100·0)	1,642 (100·0)

Figures in brackets are percentages.

There seems to have been a general increase in the volume of immigration in the years prior to and after independence in 1960, a period of rapid economic development in Lagos. The volume was greatest for the Western Region but the rate of increase in the same period was highest for the Eastern and Northern Regions and outside Nigeria (Table 4). This must be seen as the combined effect of recent in-movement from the regions and the rate of out-migration, which varies from one region to another, as also of mortality. Perhaps coincidentally, the regions (Eastern,

Northern and part of Mid-Western) which recorded the highest rate of recent migration also have the greatest tendency for return migration of their workers from Lagos, particularly at old age or retirement.[6] [However, with rising living standards and improved communications, Lagos is attracting migrants from further afield.]

Table 4

Lagos: Birth Region of Migrants by Period of Migration

PERIOD OF MIGRATION	REGION OF BIRTH					
	All Regions	Western Region	Mid-West Region	Eastern Region	Northern Region	Outside Nigeria
All periods	1,697 (100·0)	754 (100·0)	229 (100·0)	515 (100·0)	136 (100·0)	63 (100·0)
1955–64	1,048 (61·8)	413 (54·8)	134 (58·5)	362 (70·2)	99 (72·8)	40 (63·5)
1945–54	379 (22·3)	176 (23·3)	58 (25·3)	109 (21·2)	23 (16·9)	13 (20·6)
1935–44	172 (10·1)	95 (12·6)	25 (10·9)	39 (7·6)	7 (5·1)	6 (9·5)
Pre-1935	98 (5·8)	70 (9·3)	12 (5·2)	5 (1·0)	7 (5·1)	4 (6·4)

Migration and Sex and Age

The age and sex structure of the population was that typical of immigrant areas. In addition to the large number of children under 15 years (a sign of a rapidly growing population), 71·9 per cent of the adult population were under 35 years of age, with males in the majority. The sex ratio of 117 males per 100 females is relatively high when compared with Lagos as a whole, the country in general and other places shown in Table 5. As might be expected, the number of males moving into the area in search of jobs is increasing. Nevertheless, the table shows a steady fall in the sex ratio, partly due to greater migration of females and children and partly as a result of growth by natural increase owing to greater permanency in resident migrant families.

Table 5

Comparison of Sex Ratios (males per 100 females) in the Survey Area, Lagos Territory, Accra, Nigeria and Ghana

	1931 census	1950 census	1952/53 census	1961 housing inquiry	1964 sample survey
Nigeria	108·0	n.a.	95·7	n.a.	—
Lagos	125·7	118·5	115·4	108·0	—
Survey Area	n.a.	130·0	n.a.	116·5	117·6

	1948	1960
Ghana	102·2	102·2
Accra	111·6	113·6

Sources: *1931 Census of Nigeria*, p. 9.
1950 Census of Lagos, p. 29.
1952/53 Census of Nigeria, p. 5.
Report on Lagos Housing Enquiry, June 1961, p. 5.
1948 Census of the Gold Coast, p. 45.
1960 Census of Ghana, pp. 8–9.

The details of age and sex composition, as set out in Table 6, reveal certain characteristics of migration patterns in the area studied. First, the normal sex ratios below the age of ten years relate to children who were almost entirely born in Lagos. Children of this age rarely migrate alone; they were brought by families, as likely to bring daughters as sons, or were born after the families reached Lagos.

Table 6

Lagos: Sex Ratios of the Sample Population by Age

	Males	Females	Sex ratios
Total population			
All ages	1,805	1,534	117·6
0–4	228	248	91·9
5–9	263	270	97·4
10–14	243	207	117·4
15–24	479	320	149·4
25–34	287	275	104·4
35–44	175	136	124·6
45–54	92	40	230·0
55 and over	38	38	100·0
Lagos-born			
All ages	834	807	103·3
0–4	210	221	95·0
5–9	210	215	97·7
10–14	143	119	120·2
15–24	164	122	134·4
25–34	49	66	74·2
35–44	35	35	100·0
45–54	15	15	100·0
55 and over	9	14	64·2
Migrants			
All ages	970	727	133·4
0–4	18	27	66·7
5–9	53	55	96·4
10–14	100	88	113·6
15–24	315	198	159·1
25–34	238	209	113·9
35–44	150	91	164·8
45–54	67	35	191·4
55 and over	29	24	120·8

The sex imbalance is perceptible at ages 10–14, rising further at 15–19 years of age and reaches the first peak at ages 20–24, the age interval of maximum in-migration of single males.

Masculinity is lowest at 25–34 years of age, which is when most adult males marry and/or are joined by their wives. It will be shown in the next section that 95·3 per cent of the married females are in this age bracket, this being more the case for migrants than for Lagos-born females.

The second peak of sex ratio occurs between 40–54 years of age and could be explained partly by low survivorship, with widows returning to their native homes. The widowers in most cases remarry younger women than themselves and remain in paid employment. Mis-statement of age at advanced ages most likely affects the female population most since househeads, mainly males, gave the ages of their wives and other members of their households. But this pattern of return migration of older adult females, which was also observed in the 1950 census,[7] is very common among non-working migrant wives. It may take the form of occasional visits to the home-centre for trade, farming, or during periods of childbirth, perhaps for two years or more, or final return at old age or widowhood.

Migration and Marriage

In the survey, married condition was regarded as a state which involved some permanent relationship between opposite sexes, carrying with it social and economic responsibilities, whether contracted through indigenous rites or Western marriage ordinances. In order to distinguish between temporary unions and effective marriage, the interviewers inquired from the couple the type of marriage performed.

Four-fifths of the effective marriages in the areas were monogamous with 45 per cent of them registered, the majority with Christian Church blessing. The rest were said to have been performed according to customary laws, thus showing the influence of the cultural and traditional system on marriage patterns in this premier city.

Polygynous marriages accounted for nearly 14 per cent of marital conditions within households, and the number of such wives resident in Lagos at the time of the survey ranged from two to five. Some household heads had wives living away from Lagos.

More than half the adults were married with 89 per cent of the wives (503/565) living with their husbands. Most of those living away from their husbands were wives of new immigrants. This high proportion of wives living with their husbands points to the effectiveness of the married life of the migrants.

There were significant differences in the marriage patterns of adult males and females in relation to age and in the marital conditions of migrant and non-migrant males and females of the same age, as seen in Table 7. There were also differentials by region of birth, but the ethnic groups did not show statistically significant differences. The latter result draws attention to the greater influence in the city of such other factors as migration, sex and age on marriage rather than ethnic differentials.

Generally females married much earlier than males. While only 3 per cent of the males, 15–24 years of age, were married, no less than 35 per cent of the females of the same age were married. The male/female marital differential remained marked at ages 25–34 in which almost all females were married compared with only 58 per cent of males. The difference disappeared at ages 35–44 years as indicated in Table 7. But, whereas about half of the unmarried males in this age interval were divorced or widowed, almost three-quarters of the unmarried females were widowed, and all the unmarried women aged 45 years and over within households were widowed, compared to three-quarters of unmarried males of the same age who were divorced and/or widowed.

The incidence of widowhood in both sexes at these ages reveals relatively high mortality in the general population. Most widowers remarried but the widows who had passed reproductive age were too old to remarry. The presence of a large number of widows in Lagos featured prominently in the findings of the social survey conducted by Peter Marris of the London Institute of Community Studies in 1958/59, particularly in Lagos Island and Suru Lere Rehousing Estates.[8] While some migrant widows remained in Lagos, a substantial number of them left for their native homes, particularly those who were less equipped for urban employment.

The marital status of the migrants and Lagos-born adult males and females showed striking differences. While half of the migrant males aged 15 years and over were married, only 30·9 per cent of the Lagos-born males of the same age were married.

Table 7

Lagos: Marital Status by Sex and Age 15 years and over

	Male		Female	
	Married	Single	Married	Single
Total population *All ages* (15+)	488 (45·0)	597 (55·0)	538 (67·7)	257 (32·3)
15–24	13 (2·7)	466 (97·3)	111 (34·7)	209 (65·3)
25–34	166 (57·8)	121 (42·2)	262 (95·3)	13 (4·7)
35–44	183 (96·8)	6 (3·2)	115 (94·3)	7 (5·7)*
45 and over	126 (96·9)	4 (3·1)	50 (64·1)	28 (35·9)*
Lagos-born *All ages* (15+)	84 (30·9)	188 (69·1)	132 (52·4)	120 (47·6)
15–24	3 (1·8)	161 (98·2)	23 (18·8)	99 (81·2)
25–34	24 (49·0)	25 (51·0)	59 (89·4)	7 (10·6)
35–44	34 (97·1)	1 (2·9)	32 (91·4)	3 (8·6)*
45 and over	23 (95·8)	1 (4·2)	18 (62·1)	11 (37·9)*
Migrants *All ages* (15+)	404 (49·7)	409 (50·3)	406 (74·8)	137 (25·2)
15–24	10 (3·2)	305 (96·8)	88 (44·4)	110 (55·5)
25–34	142 (59·7)	96 (40·3)	203 (97·1)	6 (2·4)
35–44	149 (96·7)	5 (3·3)	83 (95·4)	4 (4·6)
45 and over	103 (97·2)	3 (2·8)	32 (65·3)	17 (34·7)*

Note: *. Mainly widows and divorcees.

The female differentials were even more marked as shown in Table 7. The age–sex distribution of the two populations showed that the migrants on the whole married much earlier and most female migrants came to Lagos married or potentially married. This significant difference in the marital conditions of the migrant and non-migrant adult males and females shows that marriage in Nigeria may well be viewed differently in the city than in more rural areas where more than 70 per cent of the migrants were born. Other factors, such as education, must also have affected the marriage pattern of the males and females of each group.

Migration and Education

There were observable differences between the educational attainments of the migrants and Lagos-born aged 15 years and over, when it could be assumed that basic education has been completed. Table 8 shows a wide disparity in the education levels reached by male and female migrants. Higher educational attainment was a necessary condition for male preparation for urban jobs, while most female migrants came as wives or potential wives who did not consider their educational qualifications as carefully as persons seeking employment. It is pertinent, at this point, to realize that 48 per cent of the females 25 years of age and over, a majority of whom were married, had no education. And, in fact, almost seven-tenths of the females in employment were salesworkers, mainly petty-traders, while the non-employed housewives formed nearly half of all married women.

The gap at all levels between the education of males and females was narrower for the Lagos-born than for migrants owing to greater educational opportunities and

Table 8

Lagos: Education by Sex and Age, 15 years of age and over

		None	Primary	Secondary	Professional	University
Total population						
15–24	M	24 (5·0)	227 (47·4)	203 (42·4)	20 (4·2)	5 (1·0)
	F	56 (17·5)	183 (57·2)	74 (23·1)	6 (1·9)	1 (0·3)
25–34	M	26 (9·1)	97 (33·8)	112 (39·0)	29 (10·1)	23 (8·0)
	F	124 (45·1)	94 (34·2)	41 (14·9)	14 (5·1)	2 (0·7)
35–44	M	26 (13·8)	67 (35·4)	64 (33·9)	14 (7·4)	18 (9·5)
	F	56 (45·9)	39 (32·0)	21 (17·2)	5 (4·1)	1 (0·8)
45 and over	M	32 (24·6)	48 (36·9)	38 (29·2)	7 (5·4)	5 (3·9)
	F	34 (43·6)	32 (41·0)	7 (9·0)	5 (6·4)	—
Lagos-born						
15–24	M	2 (1·2)	65 (39·6)	90 (54·9)	5 (3·1)	2 (1·2)
	F	11 (9·0)	74 (60·7)	34 (27·9)	2 (1·6)	1 (0·8)
25–34	M	6 (12·2)	17 (34·7)	15 (30·6)	4 (8·2)	7 (14·3)
	F	18 (27·3)	33 (50·0)	12 (18·2)	3 (4·5)	—
35–44	M	2 (5·7)	12 (34·3)	14 (40·0)	2 (5·7)	5 (14·3)
	F	12 (34·3)	17 (48·6)	6 (17·1)	—	—
45 and over	M	2 (8·3)	7 (29·2)	14 (58·3)	1 (4·2)	—
	F	7 (24·1)	13 (44·9)	7 (24·1)	2 (16·9)	—
Migrants						
15–24	M	22 (7·0)	162 (51·4)	113 (35·9)	15 (4·8)	3 (0·9)
	F	45 (22·7)	109 (55·1)	40 (20·2)	4 (2·0)	—
25–34	M	20 (8·4)	80 (33·6)	97 (40·8)	25 (10·5)	16 (6·7)
	F	106 (50·7)	61 (29·2)	29 (13·9)	11 (5·3)	2 (0·9)
35–44	M	24 (15·6)	55 (35·7)	50 (32·5)	12 (7·8)	13 (8·4)
	F	44 (50·6)	22 (25·3)	15 (17·2)	5 (5·7)	1 (1·2)
45 and over	M	30 (28·3)	41 (38·7)	24 (22·6)	6 (5·7)	5 (4·7)
	F	27 (55·1)	19 (38·8)	—	3 (6·1)	—

Note: Numbers in brackets are percentages.

other facilities open to Lagos girls from an early age. This and a broader outlook towards girls' education are probably factors that induce city-born females to postpone marriage longer than their migrant counterparts.

Migration and Occupation by Age and Sex

The two demographic factors which shaped the occupational structure of the population were the age and sex distributions. Non-demographic factors were the greater opportunities for school attendance created by free primary education in Lagos, variations in the economic pursuits of males and females, the predominance of a non-agricultural economy, and the effect of return migration on the older adult labour force.

The large number of children under 15 years caused a high child-dependency ratio of 55·4 per cent. The low aged-dependency ratio of only 1·6 per cent could be attributed to the return movement of the aged migrant population. Those of labour force age formed only 53 per cent of the total population. However, the economic activity rates presented in Table 9 shows that more than 90 per cent of children between 5–14 years were attending school and about 45 per cent of young persons 15–19 years of age were still in school.

The significant difference in the rate of participation in economic activities between males and females points to certain limitations in working opportunities for females. Lower educational attainment of females limit opportunities for their

Table 9

Occupational Structure of the Population by Sex and Age 5 years+

	Economically active		School attendance		Housewives only	Retired (Males)	No occupation	
	Males	Females	Male	Female			Males	Females
All ages (5+)	834 (52·9)	443 (34·5)	649 (41·2)	518 (40·4)	258 (20·1)	16 (1·0)	78 (4·9)	66 (5·1)
5–14	16 (3·2)	31 (6·5)	462 (91·3)	418 (87·6)			28 (5·5)	28 (5·9)
15–24	277 (57·8)	151 (47·2)	172 (35·9)	97 (30·3)	62 (19·4)		30 (5·3)	10 (3·1)
25–34	260 (90·6)	147 (53·5)	15 (5·2)	3 (1·1)	118 (42·9)		12 (4·2)	7 (2·5)
35–44	170 (97·1)	76 (55·9)			55 (40·4)		5 (2·9)	5 (3·7)
45–54	91 (98·9)	24 (60·0)			15 (37·5)		1 (1·1)	1 (2·5)
55 and over	20 (52·6)	15 (39·5)			8 (21·0)	16 (42·1)	2 (5·3)	15 (39·5)
All ages (15+)	818 (76·4)	412 (51·0)	187 (17·5)	100 (12·4)	258 (31·9)	16 (1·5)	50 (4·7)	38 (4·7)

employment; the attitude of some employers and husbands towards wives' employment, and above all the reproductive rôle of women are among the factors militating against sex equality in wage employment. This may be reflected in the comparatively low percentage of economically active females in the 15–24 age bracket, the increasing percentages at later ages up to 54 being associated with the fact that over half of the married women combined home-keeping with employment as salesworkers, teachers, nurses, dressmakers or in service occupations.

The retired formed only 1 per cent of the non-gainfully employed since most of the migrants returned home on retirement. In effect, about 4·7 per cent of adult males and females within households had no occupation, and did not regard this as their expected condition. This might represent the extent of unemployment in the city.

A general feature of the economically active was the very small number (0·3 per cent) in agriculture or fishing. Almost 25 per cent of the employed were clerks of various types, a little over one-fifth were salesworkers, mainly petty-traders and small businessmen, and nearly the same percentage were craftsmen or production workers. Professionals, technicians and related workers made up almost 15 per cent of the economically active but unskilled labourers and service-workers formed only 14 per cent, since most of them live in the low-rent suburbs of the Lagos periphery, outside the Federal Territory. About 5 per cent were in the managerial, administrative and executive categories.

As would be expected, more migrants than Lagos-born were in the labour force because of the large number of children under 15 years amongst the latter group. Moreover, more migrant children under 15 years (3 : 1) were in employment. Thus, migration has been the main source of labour supply in Lagos. On the other hand, 64 per cent of the Lagos-born wives were in paid employment compared with 47 per cent of migrant wives, this, among other factors, being a result of the differentials in their educational attainments.

Conclusions

The survey has emphasized the effect of migration and the subsequent natural increase of migrants on urban growth.

The size of household in the survey area varied with type of residential location, ranging from five in the high income residences of Ikoyi and Yaba to seven in the low income housing estates of Suru Lere and the old residential areas of Ebute Metta. Two-fifths of all members were children under 15 years of age.

The high proportion of married migrant male householders living with their wives in Lagos and the increasing permanence of residence have made family life an established pattern.

Recent migration of families with children has raised the number of children in the immigrant population. Abnormalities in the age–sex structure reflect the pattern of migration into and out of Lagos. Ages of maximum migration (in and out) were marked by high masculinity, while the lowest sex ratios occurred at ages when many married women were involved in migration as with wives accompanying their husbands.

There has been, however, a considerable decline in the male–female sex ratio as more wives join their husbands and more unmarried females from the regions, particularly the Western Region, seek jobs in Lagos. There is now a marked trend towards sex equalization in these predominantly migrant areas. This might show that Lagos has reached a stage of urbanization when relative decline in mortality, as in fact is the case,[9] is being outstripped by uncontrolled fertility,[10] the latter boosted because opportunities for female migration are growing. Although migrant males probably have relatively high educational attainments compared with the average of emigrant areas, the educational standards of the males of the host community were higher in terms of secondary education.

Footnotes

1. *Annual Report of the Federal Medical Services*, Lagos, 1959, p. 31.
2. A household consists of a group of people who live together sharing in common feeding and sleeping arrangements. 'Household' for this study is largely interchangeable with 'family'.
3. Low income workers are those whose annual income does not exceed £330.
4. A nuclear family consists of father, mother and children.
5. Extended family comprises the father, mother, children and other relatives.
6. *Population Census of Lagos*, 1950, p. 10.
7. *Ibid.*, p. 9.
8. MARRIS, P., *Family and Social Change in an African City*, London, 1961, p. 144.
9. *Annual Report of the Federal Medical Services*, Lagos, 1959, p. 31.
   Ibid., 1961, unpublished.

The official Crude Birth Rate for Lagos has risen from 62·9 in 1960 to 80·1 per 1,000 in 1961. 'The birth figures were inflated by the registration of births from outside Lagos by parents who use the Lagos address of relatives so that their children might qualify for the Lagos free primary education scheme on attaining school age,' *Ibid.*, 1961 unpublished.

10. Child–woman ratios (per 1,000 women 15–49 years of age):

Lagos	1950 census	448·6
Survey Areas	1950 census	474·7
Survey Areas	1964 sample survey	637·2

Marital fertility ratio (per 1,000 women 15–44 years of age, 1964, 15–49 years of age):

Lagos	1950 census	612·9
Survey Areas	1950 census	600·6
Survey Areas	1964 sample survey	924·3

Source: 1950 Census of Lagos, pp. 38, 54.

PART II

THE SITUATION WITH REGARD TO POPULATION GROWTH AND ECONOMIC DEVELOPMENT[1]

Introduction

J. C. Caldwell

Department of Demography, Australian National University
Canberra, Australia

Part I of *The Population of Tropical Africa* assembles the research reports on demographic trends in tropical Africa. The essence of these findings is that fertility rates in most countries are very high, death rates are still high by world standards but are falling, perhaps rapidly, and natural increase in most cases is already at a level double that experienced by industrializing Europe in the 19th century. Tropical African birth rates are much higher than in the contemporary West; in many developing countries death rates can be reduced three or four times as fast as they were in Europe (Kirk and Nortman, ch. 35); and in a nation such as Ghana, the experience of urbanization in the last three decades has been equivalent to that of the United States, England or Sweden over a century (Addo, *v.* app. CP34).

Such population phenomena and demographic findings sway governmental policy, whether or not social scientists proceed beyond merely recording their findings. Thus, political decisions may well alter the phenomena, and are therefore legitimate subjects for study in the population field. Most tropical African governments are undertaking some social and economic planning, and all hold that rises in individual living standards are desirable. However, just as the first Plans are being implemented or formulated, they are 'beginning to encounter the whole range of new problems that other developing countries know very well—the barriers to social and economic progress that come with extremely rapid population increase' (Coale, ch. 17).

The slow conquest of disease and the increasing probability that life can be sustained to old age with small risk of its being capriciously and suddenly ended during childhood or maturity is widely recognized among the people of tropical Africa as the single greatest advance of recent times. Economic development cannot be simply equated with rise in national income per head. Any real measure of development should take into account the spread of peace and order, the provision of better education and health, the improvement of the distribution of income and the increase in leisure. 'Mortality and fertility decline are parts of economic progress' (van de Walle, ch. 36).

Policy debate will inevitably centre on governmental intervention to facilitate the curbing of high fertility, for there is already consensus on such intervention to reduce mortality. Too little work has in fact been done in interrelations of economic and demographic change in developing countries, as was shown by the failure at the Ibadan Conference to locate, among the 150 million inhabitants of tropical Africa, one person who was working full time on the question. Even so, certain propositions put to the Conference do seem to receive substantial support from experience elsewhere in developing countries. Rapid population growth 'poses grave problems for those countries struggling to improve the quality and well-being, as opposed to the mere numbers, of their citizenry' (Kirk and Nortman, ch. 35). We can no longer say that 'no decline in fertility can occur without a significant rise in income', because such declines will probably be 'brought about, not by economic development itself, but by voluntary choice on the part of the state' to provide family planning facilities and presumably to urge their use or at least to publicize their existence (van de Walle, ch. 36). An example of this is the interest of the Kenyan Government in the relation of population and economic questions and their consultation with experts on these matters.

The problems of what constitutes dense population or a high rate of population growth are very complex, as the debate on long-term carrying capacities in Part I reveals. Population increase and an advance of the farming frontier into the fallow may cause no apparent damage in five years but might conceivably cause immense damage in the course of 50 years. Already in some places, e.g. Zambia, the marginal productivity of subsistence agriculture is very low, thus warranting the use of the term 'overpopulation' (van de Walle, ch. 36). But the effect of demographic change on the rural population is far from simple. The mortality decline which has produced what may prove to be embarrassing growth in population, has also inevitably been accompanied by a reduction in morbidity. Ojo argues that considerable compensation has been received in the better health of the work force (Ojo, ch. 32), which is beginning to overcome such conditions as 'guinea-worm infection [which] may prejudice a year's crop if the farmers are laid up during the harvest season by ulcers and abscesses' (Lucas, ch. 38). Another complexity is provided by the pattern of seasonal migration, which means that population usually domiciled in one area may earn part of its income elsewhere, usually in the modern sector of the economy. Thus, population in a given area might not always be so dense as would appear.

Both subsistence and cash agriculture in tropical Africa are plagued by various problems, some of them related to population growth. According to van de Walle, subsistence agriculture is in the greater danger, because it is invading the fallow without raising its technological level, and so, in Kimble's terminology,[2] it is failing to evolve into self-perpetuating agriculture. The problems of cash agriculture are best described as arising from a global situation where 'the number of coffee drinkers is growing less rapidly than the number of coffee growers' (van de Walle, ch. 36).

There is difficulty in determining whether the supply of labour is outstripping the demand and, if so, by how much. For what in the town or elsewhere in the modern sector of the economy is unemployment is in the subsistence sector the much less measureable amount of underemployment. As shown in Part I, there is unemployment in many African towns. New industries, often established with imported plant, are frequently as economical in the use of labour as is the case in developed economies. In these circumstances the direct creation of new jobs in the modern sector of the economy can be expensive.

High rates of population growth, and more specifically, high fertility levels, produce problems other than those connected with investment and employment. One is that of an age structure where children predominate, thus causing both consumption and education costs to be relatively high compared with the labour output of adults. It is this 'broad-based' population structure, together with the actual rate of population increase, that has made education in tropical Africa expensive in terms of both capital and skilled labour long before universal schooling is attained. In Nigeria education is now second only to agriculture as a source of employment (Yesufu, ch. 8). 'In developing countries, there is in effect a race between population growth and educational development, each new infant coming into the world being a potential addition to the ranks of the illiterate. In some developing countries the absolute number of illiterates and under-educated persons is increasing, even though their proportion to total population is decreasing' (Smith, ch. 34).

Population Policies

The reduction of morbidity and mortality, to a very considerable extent through direct governmental action and expenditure, is the stated aim of every administration in tropical Africa. Many governments report the allocation of approximately one-tenth of the budget to these purposes. A recent survey of the policies of African governments shows that, 'most point to the expenditure of a large proportion of the budget on health, the extension of health services especially in rural areas, mass campaigns against specified diseases, and the securing of assistance from such international organizations as WHO and UNICEF' (Caldwell, ch. 37). As in the case of Nigeria, it is now politically required of any régime that the health work continue (Lucas, ch. 38).

But, although in tropical Africa there is no similar unanimity with regard to government intervention to lower high fertility or to reduce rates of natural increase, there is some interest in such intervention, and there will presumably be more. Van de Walle comments that 'The question of fertility decline . . . perhaps cannot be evaded much longer' (ch. 36). The Ghana *Seven Year Development Plan* speaks of 'the demographic situation which lays this heavy burden of savings on the population,' commenting subsequently that, 'until the birth rate is reduced the population will continue to grow and the number of young will remain proportionately large'[3] (Caldwell, ch. 37). Admittedly this change is not expected quickly, for 'the success that we have had in bringing down the death rate in one generation will not be matched by a similar success in bringing down the birth rate' (*ibid.*).

In 1965 Ghana established a committee to report on the population question. In the same year Kenya invited a mission of experts to the country to report on the effects of rapid population growth and to suggest means of curbing it. In early 1966 most of the mission's recommendations were accepted, thus making Kenya the first country in mainland tropical Africa to adopt an interventionist population policy and to use central government resources in an attempt to reduce the birth rate.

In a 1964–65 survey of population policies in Africa, a distinction has been drawn between ex-French and ex-British colonies in tropical Africa (Caldwell ch. 37). In the former, French laws and administrative practices have ensured that there has been very little knowledge of contraception, legalized sterilization or legalized abortion. In the latter, there has long been some importing and retailing of contraceptives and some history of sterilization and induced abortion on a very limited scale with rather stringent safeguards. Two points might be noted. In the ex-French countries, the pro-natalist legislation, although still retained, is usually regarded as a colonial heritage subject to re-examination in the light of changing circumstances, as has in fact occurred north of the Sahara in Tunisia (Brown and Daly, ch. 43). In the ex-British countries, there is a legal framework that could, interpreted slightly differently, allow a rapid expansion in the provision of either sterilization or abortion facilities, should such courses of action ever be thought desirable. For some time, municipal or health department funds or facilities have been used to assist family planning organizations in parts of Kenya, Rhodesia and Nigeria, and, to a less extent, in some other countries.

Governmental policies are also changing with regard to international migration, with administrative action sometimes ahead of legislative reformulation. In large units of the old French or British African empires, movement from one territory to another created neither administrative nor financial problems. This is not the case in the newly independent states, for the home electorate demands that its employment rights be protected against foreign competition, and the remittance of earnings by migrants across borders can help create balance of payments difficulties.

This is not the whole story, however; as Smith shows quoting Borrie's argument,[4] the 'migratory flow amongst neighbouring regions or nations with extremely high population growth rates is likely to remain an essential outlet for surplus labour, for in many areas investment levels cannot quickly be stepped up to a point where they can cope with their own increases in population of working age' (Smith, ch. 34). Nevertheless, Sierra Leone, Botswana and Mauritius are already discouraging permanent immigration on population or employment grounds. The policy survey shows that no country in tropical Africa desires any longer to encourage unrestricted immigration, although most seek selected immigrants, especially those with skills (Caldwell, ch. 37). Some countries have already evicted various foreign nationals, especially those occupying a large proportion of specific employment. Sierra Leone has removed foreigners from the diamond fields; Niger has dismissed citizens of Dahomey from her public service; Ivory Coast has expelled some foreign immigrants and Ghana has made it more difficult to cross her borders.

In connection with internal migration policy, debate continues on the desirability of relieving population pressure by government-organized resettlement schemes to move population from densely to sparsely settled areas, especially to areas only recently cleared of disease. Such schemes have occasionally had an expensive, and not very successful, history in some other parts of the world, notably Indonesia. In tropical Africa their most vigorous proponents are francophone countries, although some other countries, Tanzania for instance, also have plans. In Nigeria resettlement schemes have not been favoured on the grounds of high cost (Dema, ch. 31), and it is doubtful whether they could cope with rapid population growth in East Africa (Saxton, Serwadda, Saxton, ch. 42).

To a very considerable extent, population policies in tropical Africa, especially with regard to fertility control, will be influenced by what happens elsewhere. The extent to which the new, post Second World War, nations influence each other in development planning, is, in terms of any previous experience, astonishing. A summary of trends outside Africa draws attention to governmental intervention, or large-scale intervention with governmental encouragement, in the provision of family planning services, especially in India, Pakistan, Korea, (Taiwan) Republic of China, (Mainland) China, Ceylon, Malaysia, Hong Kong, Singapore, Turkey and Chile (Kirk and Nortman, ch. 35). Such services are voluntary, are regarded as part of the health and welfare programmes, have involved relatively minor expenditure to date, and are supported by prior survey investigations, which show that in almost all parts of the developing world most people favour the provision of these services.

The position in non-tropical Africa is the one most likely to influence tropical Africa. In the United Arab Republic government support has encouraged the establishment of family planning clinics, currently being set up at a rate exceeding one per week (El Shafei, *v.* app. OS 3). In Tunisia a national population policy has evolved since Independence in 1956, through such stages as the emancipation of women, abolition of polygamy, the limitation of welfare support to the first four children, the removal of restrictions on the import, sale and use of contraceptives, and the legalization of abortions for women with five or more living children, to the implementation of a family planning action programme in June 1964, with the assistance of The Ford Foundation and The Population Council (Brown and Daly, ch. 43). Morocco and Algeria have recently been showing a great deal of interest in the Tunisian programme (Kirk and Nortman, ch. 35).

Possibilities of Family Planning in Tropical Africa

The practice of family limitation is but one aspect of profound social change, especially as it affects family relations and attitudes. Economic change, the spread of communications, formal education, urbanization and political revolution have all brought immense transformation to tropical Africa since the beginning of the century. What effect have such changes had on married life and the structure of the family?

In urban areas at least, basic changes in relationships and practices within the family are certainly occurring. This has been demonstrated among the urban, socio-economic élite in Ghana,[5] and Ohadike's work in Lagos suggests that ramifications of change extend far down the social scale, at least in the towns (Ohadike, ch. 39). Female ages at marriage are rising, while the age-gap between spouses is narrowing, and attitudes are changing in this regard in the same direction. Such changes are most far-reaching in the case of the educated. The practice and approval of polygamy declines with education, adherence to Christianity, socio-economic position and relative youth. Unstable marriage may well be declining and is certainly least in evidence in the Christian community. Pool has been investigating three specific hypotheses in Ghana: that marriages are postponed in urban areas; that a greater incidence of temporary liaisons in urban areas reduces exposure to conception; and that there is a greater interest in and awareness of family planning in urban areas. He believes that the nature and timing of demographic transition in Africa may differ at least as much from the patterns of Asia and Latin America as did these from the experience of the West.

All these movements are more likely to facilitate consultation between spouses on family planning and presumably its practice as well. But consultation is not yet the usual thing, and the practice of family planning is carried on by only a small minority. Morsa's survey[6] in Tunisia reveals a pattern beginning to be familiar in many parts of the developing world (Brown and Daly, ch. 43): most adults would favour access to methods of family planning but very few claim to know any method. In Lagos, for example, only a third of married women know a method to limit family size, and only a twelfth have ever practised any method (Ohadike, ch. 39). In most cases the method was total or periodic abstinence.

The analysis by the Saxtons and Serwadda of patients at the Kampala Family Planning Clinic in Uganda indicates that early family planners in tropical African society are women likely to be married to wage earners (clerks, typists, teachers, public servants, cashiers, accountants or doctors) working in the still small modern sector of the economy. These women are not likely to have completed primary schooling, inasmuch as only 30 per cent spoke English, a usual achievement of primary school graduates. 'From these data, we conclude that the husband is playing a prominent rôle in the decision for the woman to start family planning' (Saxton, Serwadda, Saxton, ch. 42). The Lagos University Medical School team finds that the majority of women practising family planning have at least some secondary education, while their husbands are on an average still better educated (Daramola *et al.*, ch. 41). In view of the relatively few tropical Africans who have yet had the opportunity to attend secondary school, it is not surprising that 'the education level of either the respondent, the husband or both, is positively correlated with the use of family planning methods. In our sample, the more educated the community, the more frequently do residents apply knowledge of family planning' (*ibid.*).

'Throughout tropical Africa there is nothing that ranks as high as children in the estimation of the inhabitants' (Ojo, ch. 32). While this is true, it should be pointed out that modifications are appearing. It has been shown that in Ghana, wherever urban ways of life or a cash economy or even the provision of schooling have flowed into the country, a substantial proportion of the population feels that very large families are undesirable because of the difficulty of supporting them.[7] Ohadike finds in Lagos that half his respondents see disadvantages in what they term 'large families' (Ohadike, ch. 39). Nevertheless, only one respondent in ten wants fewer than five children, and the average ideal is 6·7. The ideal size of the completed family falls with the amount of education of either wife or husband, youthfulness, higher occupation, better residential area, amount of rent paid, monogamy and adherence to Christianity. There is, of course, considerable interrelation amongst these categories, in which, it should be noted, the proportion of persons is increasing in all tropical African countries, so that ideal family size is likely to fall, thus generating an increased demand for means to limit procreation.

Other points might be noted from the findings of the Lagos University Medical

School group (Daramola, ch. 41). First, among the respondents, many of whom come from the better-off residential areas of Lagos, urgency to maximize family size is not so great as in the past for mortality had reportedly claimed only a quarter of the children born. Second, the desire for sons may not influence family size in Africa as in parts of Asia, for according to a majority of the respondents sons and daughters are equally important. Third, three-quarters of Lagos respondents and half of those in the North approved in principle of contraception (Daramola, ch. 41). (This was not the case with regard to the practice of abortion; here the approval rate fell to 20 per cent and 37 per cent respectively. Nevertheless, some practice of illegal abortion is quite widespread (Caldwell and Romaniuk chs. 37, 20).)

The increasing recognition of population pressures, especially within the family structure, and the expressed desire to limit families noted in some surveys should not obscure the fact that contraception has to date been practised by only a very small number of tropical Africans, without apparently any appreciable effect on national birth rates anywhere. However, in anglophone Africa family planning clinics have been established in nearly every country during the last decade (Caldwell, ch. 37). In most of these countries the number is still small, and there has been a decided tendency to concentrate in the capital. Often government or local government personnel have played key rôles in the founding of the clinics. From about 1964 a quickening of activity has been observed, partly arising from greater interest in population questions of people in official positions and partly from the availability of contraceptives more suited to mass use in Africa. Attendance at Kampala clinics doubled every six months in 1964 and 1965 (Saxton, Serwadda, Saxton, ch. 42). According to results of the Lagos Medical School team survey (ch. 41), information about family planning clinics most frequently comes from friends. Friends are followed in importance as informants by Health Centres in Lagos and by radio in Northern Nigeria. Neither newspapers nor television were of any real importance at the time of the surveys, but in Lagos this position may have changed rather rapidly by late 1965.

Beyond Africa's shores, family planning clinics are multiplying in Mauritius, and the Government is financially supporting both the orthodox Family Planning Association and the Action Familiale, which employs the licit Catholic method of contraception, periodic abstinence or rhythm. It is possible that contraception has already had some effect on the birth rate, for it fell between 1957 and 1964 from 42·6 per 1,000 to 38·1, a decline that was equalled by the parallel decline in the death rate, thus leaving the rate of natural increase at its previous level of 3·0 per cent.

Until recently most family planning clinics in tropical Africa concentrated on female methods of contraception and restricted their contacts largely to the wives.[8] Many of those in charge now feel this to have been a major error, having discovered, as was found in a series of interviews carried out in rural Uganda, that women often regard decisions on family size as matters to be decided by 'God, Providence and their husbands' (Saxton, Serwadda, Saxton, ch. 42). In 1964 and 1965 oral contraceptives and IUDs were increasingly distributed by tropical African clinics. The Saxtons and Serwadda believe the IUDs responsible for the 'revolution' in attendance at the Kampala clinic (*ibid.*), and most doctors working in the family planning field in tropical Africa feel that IUDs create the first real possibility for successful penetration of rural areas by clinics.

Whether during the next decade family planning methods will be used on a sufficient scale to make a significant decrease in tropical African birth rates almost certainly depends largely on governmental policies and even on governmental intervention. It seems likely that sufficient social, educational and economic change has occurred to allow a reduction in birth rates, if governments provide family planning facilities and publicity, but that insufficient change has occurred to produce spontaneous reductions in fertility without governmental encouragement.

The survey of governmental policy shows that few anglophone countries regard increased population as a particularly desirable aim in itself (Caldwell, ch. 37). In 1965 Tanzania, Zambia, Sierra Leone and Botswana certainly leaned this way, but only Tanzania and Malawi desired a higher birth rate and did not envisage that governmental decisions in the population field would eventually become a part of social and economic planning. In 1965 most tropical Africans were living in countries ruled by governments that will probably at some date be prepared either to accept foreign assistance for family planning schemes or to allow private associations to accept such assistance. The examination of governmental policies is of particular importance for tropical Africa, because of the key rôle played by central administration in other sectors of the population field. The centralized nature of colonial administration, the way in which power was transferred at Independence and the emphasis on social and economic planning have all increased the importance of government and its policy. Most of the reduction in mortality has arisen not from the treatment of patients by private doctors but from the actions of health and public works departments and the establishment of government hospitals and clinics. In fact, if large-scale family planning does come, it is difficult to imagine that there will not be a demand for services to be provided through government supported health clinics and for supplies to be either free or subsidized along the same lines adopted for medicines.

One other point might be noted. It is likely that a small reduction in birth rates will occur as a result of later female marriage, though this may be submerged by other factors operating to raise the birth rate. Governmental policies such as those that provide secondary and tertiary education cannot but raise marriage ages for at least some females from rural societies where marriage used to occur at or shortly after puberty. If Ohadike's findings (ch. 39) in Lagos are general, as seems likely, female age at marriage should rise with increased education and urban living, trends that are already discernible in every country in the region.

Demographic Training

Demographic training and research will have to be closely interrelated in tropical Africa, for so much research is needed that in the long run only local personnel can meet the demand. The demand has already risen steeply, and is related to questions of development (Jupp, ch. 45), leading to the conclusion that demographic studies must be extended so as to 'provide planning authorities with data they require to reach decisions based on rational choice' (Iro, ch. 46). As an example of this interrelation between academic and governmental interests, geography departments of African universities often assist governmental authorities with studies of migration, urbanization or town development (*v.* app. Tetteh, SR 2; Eze, SR 5; Mortimore, SR 6; Ominde, SR 8). And it is now becoming more common for places such as the University of Ghana and the Centre for Population Studies of the University of Ibadan (*v.* app. Aryee, SR 1 and Okonjo, SR 13) to undertake work on the validity of censuses or on rates of demographic change.

To date, the need for research results has meant that population studies have had to be carried out by universities or university departments that provide little training in the field of demography (Caldwell, ch. 44). In the University of Ibadan, for instance, population research has been undertaken in such diverse departments as Sociology, Economics, Geography, Agriculture and the Faculty of Medicine (Okonjo, SR 4). Indeed, the scarcity of African population data and research work has meant that any university department undertaking even a few population lectures is virtually forced to do some local research of its own in the field (Ominde, SR 8).

Such research needs—in other social science fields as well as demography—have led African universities to experiment with special research units, which apparently will increasingly be used for training graduate students. The Institute of African

Studies and the Institute of Statistics at the University of Ghana and the Nigerian Institute for Social and Economic Research at the University of Ibadan all now employ demographers (Aryee, SR 1 and Okonjo, SR 4).

A significant development has been the establishment of the Centre for Population Studies at the University of Ibadan (Okonjo, SR 13). It is hoped the Centre will play an important rôle in the development and utilization of population statistics in Nigeria by serving as a non-governmental consultant in census and other operations. The staff will carry out studies on the methodology used in past censuses, as a guide to future ones, and will undertake analyses and produce monographs on all future censuses. The possible range of activities of such centres can be considerable, as is indicated by the descriptions of 34 planned, continuing or completed projects at the Ibadan Centre (Okonjo, SR 13). The Ibarapa Community Health Project of the University of Ibadan resembles the research unit, in that it is a joint enterprise of various Faculties and Departments and is used for higher level training and research purposes as well as for acquainting medical undergraduates with rural problems (Okonjo, SR 4 and *v.* app. Barber, *et al.*, CP. 20). An interdisciplinary demographic unit is now being formed at the University of Ghana to analyse the 1960 Census of Ghana.

These research units have been able to obtain substantial foreign financial assistance, especially from American foundations, but in addition, as shown above 'Such research has had, and will continue to have, a good chance of governmental support, because the findings are often in demand for planning purposes' (Caldwell, ch. 44).

The continuation of this research, as well as much governmental demographic and statistical work, depends on the expansion of appropriate training in African universities. Not only is there a growing tendency to depend on the universities for the training of middle-level personnel in these fields, but the universities in Africa as a whole will have to train almost 300 higher level personnel within the next five years if middle-level personnel are to be satisfactorily placed (Jupp, ch. 45). The alternative is a considerable rise in the rate of importation of non-African demographers, something which many believe not to be possible on the necessary scale (Gil, ch. 13).

In the University of Ghana, a demography programme has been built up around the needs of the 1960 census with the financial support of the Population Council (*v.* app. Aryee, SR 1). Although the study of demography was originally confined to the Sociology Department, teaching and research have subsequently spread to the Economics Department and to the two special institutes mentioned above. The only other extensive teaching in demography is to be found at the University of Khartoum, where two courses are offered, but, courses or lectures on demography are given rather widely within such departments as Sociology, Geography or Economics (Caldwell ch. 37).

The basic problem is to secure enough foreign demographers for enough time to found a self-sustaining course, until demographers of local origin return to the university and settle into permanent academic positions. So far this has occurred only at the University of Ghana, and even there staffing problems still exist (Aryee, SR 1). At Makerere University, the 'Department of Sociology . . . feels a sense of urgency about teaching demography, particularly at undergraduate level, [but] as yet has not been able to teach demography proper', because of failure to recruit staff or to ensure some external financial and staffing arrangement that could overcome this problem (Desai, SR 7).

The African universities are key institutions in the new independent states. In many fields, demography included, they are not only training institutions, but reservoirs of valuable and rare skills that governments will long have to draw upon. The accompanying map shows that all independent, anglophone countries, except tiny Gambia, have at least one university being established, and, in fact, that there is one

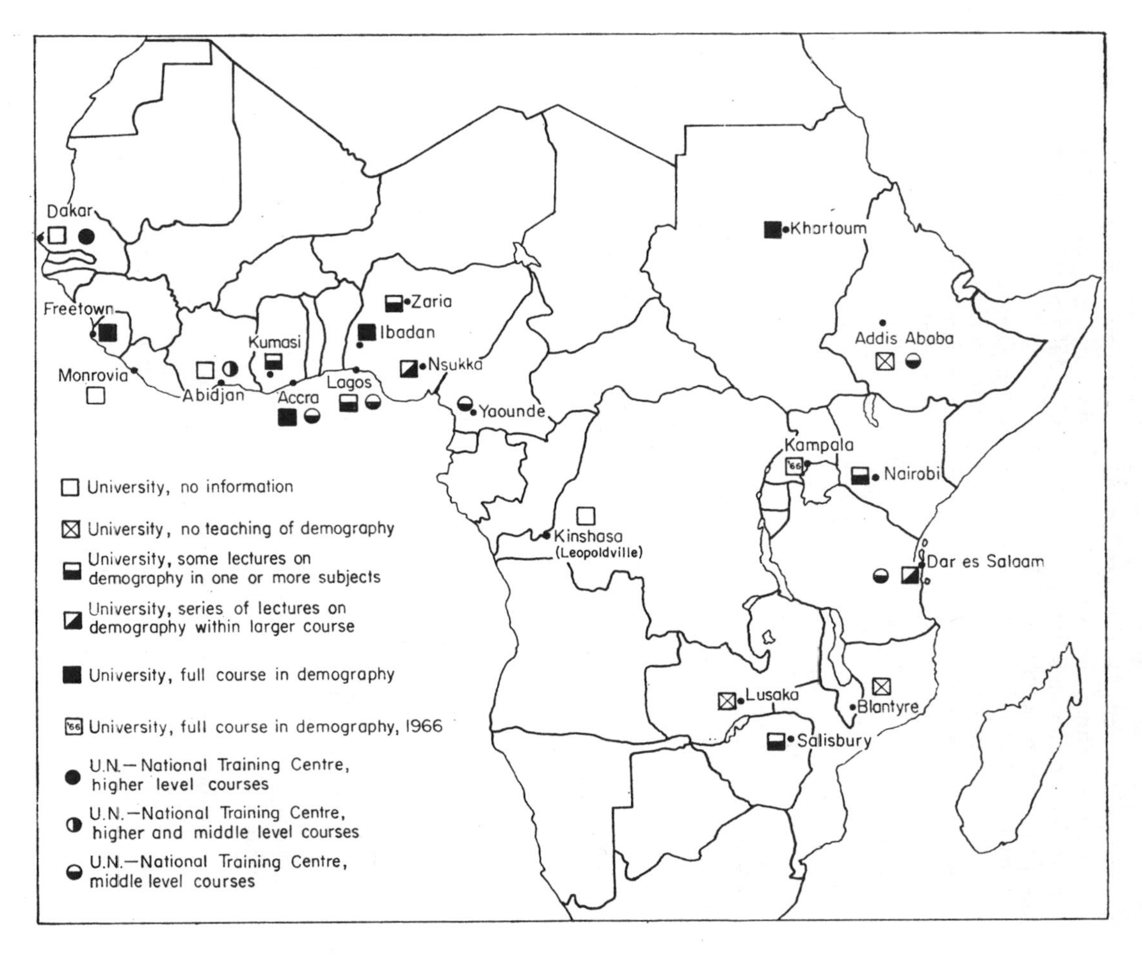

Map 9 Tropical Africa: Universities and United Nations—National Centres showing reported demographic instruction

Source: J. C. Caldwell, ch. 44. K. M. Jupp, ch. 45.

in each capital, well placed to proffer assistance to governments. The universities charged with technical know-how and with independence of approach may well be the best location for interdisciplinary units to bring out census monographs with the co-operation of the census offices.

'Demographic training in Africa outside the universities began in an organized way in the early 1960s when many newly-independent states realized that information on the size, structure, and rate of growth of their populations was seriously deficient' (Jupp, ch. 45). A shortage of statisticians and demographers, suddenly realized and aggravated because of the needs of the newly independent régimes and the taking of the 1960 censuses, was partly met by assistance from the United Nations, which signed agreements with individual governments for the establishment of special training centres with shared responsibilities and costs. The emphasis was first on middle-level training, but this was later supplemented by increasing concern for higher-level training. By the end of 1965, output of trainees was still rising, with the result that, during the first half of the 1960s, a fifth of all higher-level and a quarter of the middle-level statisticians trained in Africa had been produced by these non-university centres. The most pronounced shortage is still that of middle-level trainees.

A very high-level centre, such as the North African Demographic Centre in Cairo, can combine intensive training at an advanced level with research projects 'of immediate interest and utility to the governments of all countries of the region' (El Shafei, SR 10 and Jupp, ch. 45). Such regional centres may well flourish. The smaller centres will probably ultimately be combined with universities or other tertiary educational institutions.

In most cases United Nations technical aid is designed to meet the crises caused by sudden national growing pains and is almost never expected to become permanent. The crises of the early 1960s in the training of African demographers and statisticians arose at a time when some African countries had not yet established universities and when the others had universities that had not developed to the point or in a direction where they could easily introduce or expand such training. But the long-term trends are clear. Eventually, but possibly not before the 1970 census round, responsibility for all centres, except such major institutions as those at Cairo or Dakar, will probably pass from international to national organizations.

International Co-operation and Technical Aid

In the field of demography, far more than is the case with most university studies, co-operation of all types, both internal and international, is imperative. The large-scale gathering of data can be satisfactorily undertaken only by governments, and here international advice and assistance are often important. One of the oldest forms of co-operation, and still one of the most certain, is that provided by overseas university education, particularly post-graduate education and training at such universities as the London School of Economics and Political Science and the Office of Population Research at Princeton (Glass, OS 4; Coale, SR 12). A related form of international co-operation is the granting of scholarships such as those offered by the Population Council and the Economic Commission of the Council of Europe (Kirk OS 6; Clairin SR 11). Such scholarships frequently provide the only means for taking advantage of external university training.

The forms of international aid that will be dispensed within Africa are largely of the type indicated either by the history of demography teaching and research programmes or by the visit of the population mission to Kenya in 1965. Trained foreign personnel and often the funds to support them are going to be necessary for new projects in the population field, until the projects themselves and planned ancillary training yield skilled local citizens capable of taking over. This interim period, in the case of the demography programme at the University of Ghana, was five to six years in length, and it is not likely to be appreciably shorter elsewhere.

Interrelations

The apparently diverse topics in this volume are much more intimately connected in the African scene than might at first be apparent. Nearly all the new tropical African nations believe strongly in social and economic planning irrespective of their dominant political faiths. In the sense of social planning, most assume that they must have some population policy and must be interventionist in some population matters.

It is in this context that one must view the growing demand for demographic information. Until recently, African countries have had no very clear idea about the magnitude of their population phenomena. This is partly because there was no reasonably comprehensive data of the christening, wedding or burial type that could be used to estimate birth, marriage, death or even total population levels, and partly because population change was beginning to take place so rapidly that any estimates quickly became outdated. Most African governments are now very keen to acquire accurate and up-to-date demographic information on their peoples and have sought technical aid quite widely for this purpose. (See Part I for available data on population in tropical Africa.)

At the same time, it is generally recognized that technical assistance has had two major shortcomings. First, there is no guarantee that such assistance can be found when it is most needed (and, in any case, it can never be found on such a scale or so cheaply that governments can seek all the information required). Second, it is regarded as a transient phenomenon, and does not build up a corps of persons identified with the country, in the eyes of the government and citizens, and who are reasonably certain to work out their full careers in the same kind of job.

The answer lies in demographic training overseas, and ultimately in locally based training. In the long run most projects are jeopardized if they do not undertake or make arrangements for training, preferably from the outset of the project, that will eventually produce persons with the same type and levels of skill that had originally to be imported.

With the upsurge in planning and the determination of the new governments to promote economic development and social change, it is inevitable that those giving technical aid in the population field will examine the implications of very high birth rates and rising rates of natural increase and even suggest forms of governmental intervention that will yield faster rises in living standards. Similarly, training courses will be expected to design or recommend research projects that will investigate such questions. These issues do not necessarily confront university or government demographers in countries with lower rates of population growth, less awareness of being relatively very poor in a global context, and, related to the last, a greater inclination to adopt laissez-faire policies in the field of social change. It is not expected that demography programmes in tropical Africa will lose their academic objectivity, but it will be impossible for them to remain outside population policy debates, even if their main rôle is to shape research so as to provide reliable information for such debates.

Much of the discussion during the coming decade will inevitably centre on birth rates, family size and the possibility of inducing changes in the existing pattern. Public policy in these matters will be regarded as a subject for university concern, and research workers will be under the same kind of pressure to assist governmental committees in demography as they have long been in public health.

Nevertheless, it is to be hoped that the unavoidable concern of the immediate future with the fertility aspect of demographic studies will not blind those working in the field to the fact that longer-term academic and national interests demand as balanced as possible an investigation into *all* aspects of African demography.

Footnotes

1. This survey is based primarily upon the papers presented to the First African Population Conference, University of Ibadan, Nigeria, 3–7 January 1966, and on the discussion arising from them at the Conference. Where reference is made to oral statements, discussion leaders' remarks or general discussion, a reference number, given in brackets, refers to the Appendix at the end of this volume.
2. H. T. KIMBLE, *Tropical Africa*, New York, 1962, Vol. 1, p. 28.
3. Ghana, *Seven-Year Development Plan, 1963–64 to 1969–70*, Office of the Planning Commission, Accra, 1964, p. 8.
4. W. D. BORRIE, 'International Migration as related to Economic and Demographic Problems of Developing Countries: Moderator's Report', paper delivered at the United Nations World Population Conference, Belgrade, August–September 1965.
5. J. C. CALDWELL, 'Family Formation and Limitation in Ghana: A Study of the Residents of Economically Superior Urban Areas', *Family Planning and Population Programs, A Review of World Developments*, Chicago, 1966; ——'Demographic Prospects' in WALTER BIRMINGHAM, I. NEUSTADT and E. N. OMABOE (eds.), *A Study of Contemporary Ghana*, Vol. II, *Some Aspects of the Social Structure of Ghana*, London, 1966; ——, 'Fertility Differentials as evidence of Incipient Fertility Decline in a Developing Country: the case of Ghana', *Population Studies*, xxi, No. 1, July 1967; ——, *Population Growth and Family Change in Africa: the Ghanaian Urban Elite*, Australian National University Press, Canberra, 1968.
6. JEAN MORSA, 'The Tunisia Survey: A Preliminary Analysis', *Family Planning and Population Programs, op. cit.*
7. J. C. CALDWELL, 'Fertility Attitudes in Three Economically Contrasting Rural Regions of Ghana', *Economic Development and Cultural Exchange*, xv, No. 2, January 1967, pp. 217–238.
8. J. C. CALDWELL, 'Africa', *Family Planning and Population Programs, op. cit.*

34 Africa and the World Population Conference

T. E. Smith
Institute of Commonwealth Studies, London, UK

According to provisional figures, 55 of the 821 participants attending the World Population Conference at Belgrade from 30 August to 10 September 1965 came from African countries. Figures for other continents were 230 from America, 146 from Asia, 319 from Europe and 10 from Oceania, while 61 participants came from the United Nations and the specialized agencies. In terms of a ratio of participants to population among the major developing regions, Africa did better than Asia but not as well as Latin America. A total of 24 African countries sent participants or observers, Ghana topping the list with nine, the United Arab Republic coming second with six and Nigeria third with five.

A number of papers contributed to the Conference were devoted *in toto* or in large part to some aspect or other of African demography, and a provisional list of these papers is to be found in the Annex to this chapter. Some of the long 'background' papers also contain much useful information for the student of African population, but, as these papers are of a basically non-regional character, they are not listed in the Annex. A number of these background papers, usually in a much revised form, can be expected to appear ultimately as part of the second edition of the United Nations volume, *The Determinants and Consequences of Population Trends*.

Reliability of African Basic Demographic Data

A theme that appeared in many of the written and verbal Conference contributions relating to tropical Africa was, not very surprisingly, the lack of reliable basic demographic data. This was particularly stressed by those who wrote about the making of population projections. Adams and Menon (paper 425) pointed out that, given the existing state of basic statistics, 'projection work thus far carried out for countries of tropical Africa, has had to rely very heavily on various types of demographic models'. Van de Walle (paper 25), in making projections, used estimates of fertility and mortality which 'are not representative of most areas in tropical Africa, and constitute slender evidence of general tendencies. The attempted projection is largely a statistical exercise in which trends and hypotheses, valid for selected areas, are extrapolated to entire regions.'[1] Romaniuk (paper 244) noted, as other writers have on various occasions, that information on fertility for tropical Africa is better than that on mortality and added that there is a tendency for the projection-makers to assume an annual rise in expectation of life at birth of six months per year over the next 20 years, without in fact having produced an 'analysis of underlying factors' which would justify such an assumption. The evidence contained in these three World Population Conference papers alone all pointed to the need to look to the future at the African Population Conference and to discuss the work which lies ahead in the collection and analysis of African demographic data, and not to spend too much time on the discussion of past work.

The session that was perhaps most relevant from an African point of view of all among the World Population Conference sessions, was that on methods of obtaining basic demographic measures where data are lacking or defective (B.6). At this meeting time was devoted to the discussion both of non-traditional methods of obtaining data and of methods of handling defective data. One of the papers (207) submitted for this meeting described recent work on birth and death statistics in Senegal, where the same group of people is visited annually to obtain retrospective details of births and deaths which occurred during the previous 12 months; Cantrelle, the author, expressed the view that repeated annual visits to the same people produce better results than a single retrospective inquiry. Also of interest in the African context was the description given by Jain (paper 195) of the Indian programme for improving birth and death registrations. This programme aims at the complete registration of births and deaths in a randomly selected sample of towns and villages, with independently conducted periodic surveys to ascertain the size of the population and to obtain a second record of the births and deaths. The two sets of results are to be matched and discrepancies will be investigated. From the sample results, it is hoped to construct reliable estimates of state and national vital rates. Both these methods involve repeated interviews with the same group of people, and, at the session, the Moderator (Brass) warned of the possibility that continuous contact through surveys, propaganda, advice, etc., might destroy the representativeness of the units sampled; there is clearly a real prospect of such a possibility in a longitudinal survey of death rates.

During the discussion on methods of handling defective data, it became clear that work done, in Asia and particularly in India, on recall lapse in retrospective inquiries had a relevance for the correction of data in similar inquiries in Africa. This is a field pioneered by Som (formerly of the Indian Statistical Institute and now of ECA) and other Indian colleagues, and his paper (262) with the title, 'Response biases in demographic enquiries', was one of those invited for meeting B.6. Whilst the development of techniques for the correction of recall lapse and other types of bias is obviously important, it is even more vital to design surveys in such a way as to minimize errors of bias and response, and this, it was suggested at the meeting, was a matter to which too little attention had so far been given.

Fertility and Family Planning in Africa

Africa south of the Sahara received very little mention in the four sessions on fertility and family planning. The paper by Henin (280) considered the possible effects of economic change on fertility patterns and levels by comparing the fertility experience of groups of people settled in the Gezira Scheme in the Sudan with that of other nomadic groups. The former were found to have higher fertility with higher marriage rates and lower age at marriage. A paper by Wuelker (42) estimated the crude birth rate in Togo at 55 from data taken from the most recent census; the author considered that there was little likelihood of an early change in Togolese attitudes to childbearing.

As regards Africa north of the Sahara, there were three papers on fertility in the United Arab Republic, one of which (219) was of particular interest in the African context in so far as it showed that the inverse relationships between fertility and education and between fertility and occupational status, so characteristic in the fertility decline of the developed countries, are to be found in the urban areas but not in the rural areas. In the rural areas it is in fact the professional and administrative classes who appear to have the highest fertility. There were two useful papers (299 and 249) evaluating the progress of family planning in the UAR and Tunisia respectively.

Mortality

In the sessions on mortality Africa was again largely ignored, not very surprisingly in view of the paucity of basic data. Dealing with infant and early childhood mortality, Gwendolyn Johnson's paper (418) stated that, 'Sample surveys undertaken during the 1950s in a number of countries of Africa south of the Sahara provided estimates of levels of infant mortality: among ten countries the range was from 130 infant deaths per 1,000 live births in Ruanda-Urundi (1952) to 293 in Mali (1955–57). Two countries with higher rates in addition to Mali were Nyasaland and Northern Rhodesia with 242 and 292 respectively. . . . The validity of some of these data are questionable, but the figures are likely to understate rather than to exaggerate the levels of infant mortality.'

In African conditions total mortality over the first three or the first five years of life is in fact likely to be a more useful measure than infant mortality *per se*. Stolnitz' paper (442) entitled 'Recent mortality declines in Latin America, Asia and Africa' is of very limited use to the student of African demography, and the same comment can be made of the background paper on 'Factors affecting health and mortality' (461).

Migration in Africa

Africa came more into the picture in the sessions on international migration and internal migration. Tropical Africa is one of the few regions in which international migration of non-Europeans is currently of numerical importance; it is more akin to migration between one European country and another than to European intercontinental migration in so far as it tends to be of a temporary nature with a heavy preponderance of males among the migrants. Contributed papers on migration, international and internal, included an interesting sociological essay by Southall (paper 395) in which there was an admission that, in East Africa, 'The demographic effects of labour migration are as yet impossible to state with any refinement. . . . The only overall indication of the scale of labour migration is the crude one of employment figures'; a paper by Gil (368) on immigration into Ghana, which was able to argue from a census figure of 522,000 foreign-born Africans in that country in 1960 and from the occupational distribution of those foreign-born, that the immigrant flow did not seem to be economically indispensable—indeed Gil indicated that plans for economic development, by effectively using the native Ghanaian population, would decrease the demand for unskilled immigrant labour; a paper by Myburgh (19) on the effect of foreign investment on migration in English-speaking Central Africa; and a general paper on rural–urban migration in Sub-Saharan Africa from Prothero (97).

In discussing the economic aspects of international migration at the relevant session, the Moderator (Borrie) suggested that the 'migratory flow amongst neighbouring regions or nations with extremely high population growth rates is likely to remain an essential outlet for surplus labour, for in many areas investment levels cannot quickly be stepped up to a point where they can cope with their own increases in population of working age. In Africa, with its many new nations with relatively small populations, efficient use of manpower will require movement across national boundaries. . . .' It remains to be seen to what extent political factors and nationalist sentiment will hinder the flow of migrants across national boundaries in the future, but it is surely true that the present level of migration must be large enough to justify money and effort spent on obtaining improved quantitative information on international migration within the continent. The possibility that remittances may make an important contribution to national income in some African countries also justifies close investigation, and it may be noted here that one of the contributed papers to the World Population Conference (Gil's) referred to the fact that remittances of foreign nationals working in Ghana were limited to 50 per cent of their gross monetary incomes following the depletion of that country's foreign exchange reserves.

The discussion on internal migration was largely focussed on rural–urban migration and was supplemented by a session on demographic aspects of urban development and housing. In Africa, as in other developing regions, it is the more educated among the rural people who leave the villages for the towns, and, as in the case of international migration, the migrants are highly concentrated in the younger ages. In most developing countries, including many African countries, the cities are often unable to absorb the migrants at the pace at which they arrive, whilst the rural areas, from which the more talented and better educated young people have migrated, increasingly become economically stagnant and socially unattractive. At the Conference, descriptions were given by participants from Cameroon and Pakistan of efforts that are being made to create new rural values compatible with development and to make the rural areas generally more attractive. Knowledge of the factors affecting rural–urban migration in tropical Africa is particularly deficient, and in this context the recent survey on migration undertaken in Ghana may provide useful lessons for other African countries.

Demographic Aspects of Development

The demographic aspects of various types of social and economic development were an important part of the World Population Conference programme. In the relevant sessions, discussion, in so far as it concerned the developing areas, tended to look at the picture as a whole and not at any particular region. The following notes, which are necessarily highly selective, may be of interest to those with a special concern for African demography:

LABOUR SUPPLY AND EMPLOYMENT

One topic discussed was whether women should be encouraged to participate in non-familial economic activity in developing countries where there is already a good deal of unemployment and underemployment. On the one hand a greater proportion of women in paid employment might help in the reduction of birth rates and in improving the supply of skills; on the other hand it would seemingly aggravate employment problems in the short run. A Swedish participant said that her government was so confident of the benefits of increased female participation in the labour force in any circumstances, that that country had focussed part of its technical assistance programme to Africa on vocational training for women.

In discussing the shortage of skilled workers in developing countries for the implementation of economic development plans, it was suggested that, though there was an urgent need for increasing the proportion of highly qualified specialists and skilled workers through technical training, skilled manpower could only be used effectively at home within a suitable economic and social framework. Considerable concern was expressed regarding the number of doctors, teachers and technicians from developing countries who go abroad for training and subsequently take up permanent employment in one of the industrially advanced countries. The opinion was expressed that this problem could not be solved until it had been made more attractive for skilled manpower to stay in the developing countries or to return to them after training.

EDUCATION

In developing countries, there is in effect a race between population growth and educational development, each new infant coming into the world being a potential addition to the ranks of the illiterate. In some developing countries the absolute number of illiterates and under-educated persons is increasing, even though their proportion to total population is decreasing. In general the distribution of population and the degree of urbanization are related to educational development.

The relationship between educational development and population growth is reciprocal. An increase in educational levels has long been known to have an effect on the rates of fertility, mortality and internal migration. The point in the educational process at which the relationship with fertility begins to operate varies from the mere attainment of literacy in some areas to a minimum of high-school education in others, but it is found that the educational attainment of females is more significant than that of males in this respect. In towns and cities the effect of education on fertility is more pronounced than in rural areas.

URBAN DEVELOPMENT AND HOUSING

In many developing countries, including some number of those in tropical Africa, one or two very large and rapidly growing cities contain a high proportion of the total urban population, and the smaller towns tend to stagnate or to grow relatively slowly, though there are exceptions to this rule. On the periphery of many of the largest cities are to be found two geographically separated and vastly different types of settlement, on the one hand new housing developments for the relatively wealthy and on the other shanty towns in which urban administrative rules do not apply or are not enforced and large numbers of poor people are accommodated in housing of a very low standard.

For the developing regions generally it has recently been estimated that an over-all housing programme of eight to ten dwellings per 1,000 population would be needed annually to provide both for population increase and for the gradual replacement of the existing stock of housing. On the basis of the most recent figures, only four countries in the world, all European, are known to attain an annual housing output of this level—Sweden, Switzerland, West Germany and the USSR.

ECONOMIC GROWTH

In the opening address to the World Population Conference, reference was made to the fact that the results of the Development Decade had, until then, been disappointing. Rapid population growth had apparently been an important impediment to development. A number of contributed papers and oral statements describing the experience of countries of North Africa and Asia indicated that high natural rates of population growth had tended to reduce the rates of savings, investment and economic growth and to create problems of employment.

The economists present at the World Population Conference tended, however, to regard the rate of population growth, although of importance, as not the *most* important variable in determining economic growth. For this reason economists were perhaps less pessimistic than demographers when discussing the problems of the less-developed countries.

Footnote

1. It should be noted that, quite apart from methodology, van de Walle's projections are not comparable with those contained in UN, *Provisional Report on World Population Prospects as Assessed in 1963*, because he excludes certain tropical African countries from his projections and accepts a different 1960 base population, particularly for Nigeria.

Annex

Provisional list of World Population Conference papers dealing in whole or in large part with Africa

NUMBER	AUTHOR	TITLE OF PAPER
19	C. A. L. MYBURGH	Migration in relationship to the economic development of Rhodesia, Zambia and Malawi.
25	E. VAN DE WALLE	Future growth of population and changes in population composition: Tropical Africa.
42	DR G. WUELKER	Effects of Social and Family Patterns on the Population increase in Togo (West Africa).

NUMBER	AUTHOR	TITLE OF PAPER
56	G. SABAGH and C. SCOTT	An Evaluation of the use of retrospective questionnaires for obtaining vital data: The experience of the Moroccan multipurpose sample survey of 1961–63.
68	DR G. VUKOVICH	The UAR project for measuring vital rates in rural areas.
70	R. BLANC	Les perspectives de population: problèmes pratiques d'établissement dans les pays en voie de développement.
79	A. E. SARHAN	Mortality trends in the United Arab Republic.
80	C. J. MARTIN	Demographic aspects of capital formation in economies with large subsistence sectors (Africa).
97	DR R. M. PROTHERO	Characteristics of rural–urban migration and the effects of their movements upon the composition of population in rural and urban areas in sub-Saharan Africa.
108	F. N. AGBLEMAGNON	Aspects démographiques de la croissance économique: le cas du Togo.
109	A. L. N'DIAYE	Les difficultés de la croissance rapide de la population dans un pays sous-peuplé. Un exemple: Le Sénégal.
120	J. G. C. BLACKER	Use of sample surveys to obtain data of age structure of the population where respondents in a regular census enumeration cannot give accurate data. Some Kenya experiments.
121	M. S. KHODARY	International co-operation in the setting up of the North African Demographic Centre.
155	M. SEKLANI	Le coût de la croissance démographique d'après le plan de développement de la Tunisie (1962–71).
175	J. C. CALDWELL	Demographic training and research in tropical African universities which employ English as the medium of instruction.
190	B. V. ANDRIANOV	Urbanization in Africa and its influence on the ethnic processes.
193	A. ASSOULINE	Evolution naturelle de la population et développement économique au Maroc.
201	DR ABDEL-KHALIK and MR ZIKRY	Fertility differentials of the UAR women.
207	P. CANTRELLE	Observation démographique répétée en milieu rural au Senegal: méthode et premiers résultats.
219	M. A. EL-BADRY and H. RIZK	Regional fertility differences between socio-economic groups in the UAR.
237	J. L. SADIE	The demographic factors involved in the provision of educational facilities in the Transkei.
241	Y. MIURA	A comparative analysis of operational definitions of the economically active population in African and Asian statistics.
244	A. ROMANIUK	Projection basis for populations of Tropical Africa.
249	DR G. BROWN and DR A. DALY	Evaluation du programme de planning familial de Tunisie.
262	R. K. SOM	Response biases in demographic enquiries.
280	R. A. HENIN	Some aspects of the effects of economic development on fertility in the Sudan.
289	J. D. DURAND	World population estimates, 1750–2000.
299	PROF. H. M. HUSEIN	Evaluation of progress in fertility control in UAR.
336	S. SAIDI	Aspects démographiques de la main-d'oeuvre et de l'emploi.
350	A. BERRADA	Fécondité en fonction de la profession du chef de foyer et de l'âge de la mère.
360	A. A. IGUN	Demographic approach to the problems of social and economic development in Africa.
364	E. N. OMABOE	The population pressure and the development of new areas.
368	B. GIL	Immigration into Ghana and its contribution in skill.
375	B. EL-TAWIL and R. TABBARAH	Population and labor force growth in selected African countries.
382	O. DIA	La croissance urbaine du Cap-Vert, Dakar.
395	A. SOUTHALL	The demographic and social effects of migration on the population of East Africa.
418	G. Z. JOHNSON	Public health activities as factors in levels and trends of mortality and morbidity in developing countries.
425	E. ADAMS and P. S. MENON	Types of data and studies needed to improve the basis for population projections in Tropical Africa.
445	K. M. BARBOUR	Problems of evaluating and locating census data as preliminary stages in the analysis of internal migration.
469	DR U. A. THEIN	Some aspects of urban explosions in developing countries.

35 Population policies: the world scene

Dudley Kirk and Dorothy Nortman
The Population Council, New York

Population policy is here used in the sense of governmental action designed to modify existing population trends in the interest of national objectives and of national welfare. Broadly speaking, every state has a 'population policy', namely, to promote the physical well-being and to prolong the life of its citizens. In historical perspective, modern states have been spectacularly successful in this objective. Happily, great further progress is in sight, especially in those countries that still have relatively high death rates.

It is this very success that has given rise to a new kind of population policy and the one that is the particular subject of this paper—population policy designed to check runaway population growth. This new type of population policy is little more than ten years old. A generation ago, in the 1930s, the most conspicuous population policies were the nationalistic and pronatalist policies of Germany, Italy, Japan, and the Soviet Union. In other industrial countries there was also concern about the continuing decline in the birth rate, though this was not expressed in such specific and blatant pronatalist policies as in the countries mentioned. Unfortunately, even in the more democratic countries repressive measures against birth control were sometimes applied with the justification of maintaining or increasing the birth rate though more commonly this happened in the name of religious doctrine and morality. While the situation was very different in colonial areas, population growth was also often consciously promoted through such measures as land reclamation and settlement, improved transport, elementary public health programmes, etc.

Today the climate of opinion has changed radically. In the industrial countries, concern about relatively low birth rates has subsided with their stabilization at a level ensuring continued population growth. In the developing countries, the rising rates of population increase have led to fears that these will outdistance economic growth. There is concern that economic progress will be dissipated in supporting more people with little or no improvement in individual well-being. All too often this is the reality in the developing countries today.

This situation has come about because of the acceleration of rates of population growth referred to by publicists as the 'population explosion'. With the modern medical armamentarium against disease, it is possible for developing countries to bring down death rates three or four times as rapidly as they fell from similar levels in 19th-century Europe. Almost everywhere, both in industrial and in developing countries, we see continuing progress in the reduction of deaths and in raising the average expectation of life.

In the earlier and slower pace of the 'demographic revolution' in Europe, reduction of death rates was followed by declines in the birth rates so that the resultant rates of population growth were relatively modest. This has not yet occurred in most of the developing countries. Pre-modern, high birth rates are perpetuated; combined with falling death rates these produce accelerating rates of population growth. As a consequence, human history has never previously seen such massive population growth as is now occurring in much of the underdeveloped world. In and of itself this is not bad; it reflects great achievements in our endless struggle to postpone death and promote human well-being. But it poses grave problems for those countries struggling to improve the quality and well-being, as opposed to the mere numbers of their citizenry.

A review of present and emerging population policies logically begins with Asia, partly because this is numerically the chief home of mankind and partly because this is the region where the new national population policies first appeared. Asia has 55 per cent of the world's population and in that continent there has been the greatest awareness of population pressure and of mounting population growth as a handicap to economic progress.

India and Pakistan

These two countries of the Asian subcontinent have led the world in the adoption of national family planning programmes. With some 500 million people, India is the second largest country in the world and was the first to declare a national programme. In the words of the first Director of Family Planning, Lt Col. B. L. Raina, 'After independence it became obvious that family planning was not only necessary on the basis of humanitarian concern for individuals, but was also of the most fundamental importance to the plans for over-all economic development of India.'[1]

A modest allocation of funds for family planning was included in the First Five-Year Plan (1951–56) but the programme was not implemented on a large scale before the Second Plan (1956–61). The increase in tempo of activity is suggested by the following information on expenditures and authorizations:

FIVE-YEAR PLAN	RUPEES (millions)
First (1951–56)	1·5
Second (1956–61)	21·6
Third (1961–66)	261·0
Fourth (1966–71)	950·0 (allocated)

Thus far the establishment of family planning clinics has been the main channel for providing contraceptive supplies and services to the people. Several thousand such clinics have been established, often as a part of regular health centres. This has been supplemented by sterilization 'camps', in which this simple but definitive method of family planning was offered to men who desired it. The voluntary response has been surprisingly large; since 1963 there have been over 100,000 male and female sterilizations per year, and the total is approaching one million. But even this is small in relation to the total problem. In the matter of supplies, chemical contraceptives and condoms are now manufactured in India and the manufacture of plastic intra-uterine devices has been inaugurated. These are being distributed through both private and public channels.

While provision of services and supplies is the heart of the family planning programme, effective education, publicity, record keeping, research and evaluation are integral aspects. Each of these factors receives attention in India's family planning programme. To provide leadership in research, training and evaluation, a Central Family Planning Institute is being organized. All 16 States now have Family Planning Officers, usually at the level of Assistant or Deputy Director of Health Services. Training in demography, bio-medical research and communication is given in the medical schools, the universities and the Demographic Training and Research Centre in Bombay. The need to improve the collection of vital statistics and to develop more sensitive indicators of fertility trends is considered urgent. Finally, the programme hopes to get down to the local level, to use village midwives and indigenous doctors as well as more specialized personnel to advocate and provide family planning services. It is also expected that other social reforms such as later age at marriage will be pursued to help establish the small family norm.

While the achievements of the Indian family planning programme have been important they have been small in relation to the task and the objective. The objective of the programme is to achieve as rapidly as possible a decline in the annual birth rate from 42 per 1,000, as currently estimated from national sample surveys, to a birth rate of 25. It is doubtful if the programme has yet had an appreciable effect on the national birth rate, though the means of measuring changes in the rate are too defective to detect year-to-year trends. The lack of measurable reductions in the birth rate is not surprising in view of the enormity of the problem. Eighty per cent of India's huge population is scattered over 500,000 villages, in which 400 dialects are spoken. Age-old traditions of family life, often desperate conditions of poverty, widespread ignorance and illiteracy, and many less obvious obstacles contribute to the vast inertia that must be overcome to launch a successful programme.

Despite difficulties, the programme is gaining momentum and a great increase of activity is planned for the Fourth Five-Year Plan (1966–71). Under the Plan, the first year's goal is to insert one million IUDs, with 20 million planned for the five-year period. The 'camp' technique, which proved successful for sterilization procedures, is contemplated for IUD service and training. The Five-Year Plan also anticipates five million vasectomies and ten million effective users of traditional contraceptives. If these goals materialize, the yearly number of births prevented is expected to be nine million by 1975. The emphasis on newer methods of contraception may well accelerate the progress of the programme.

The urgency of the population problem in India is suggested by the current crisis in food. At the end of 1965 the Indian Government reported that it would need 10 to 14 million tons of imported food grains to meet the famine caused by the worst drought of the century. Because of the severe drought, India's crop is estimated to have been 80 million tons in 1965 compared with 88 million in 1964. The famine has been a catastrophe, but the food crisis is chronic. For several years now the US has been sending 20 per cent of its total wheat crop to India, providing 7 per cent of that nation's food grain consumption.

Pakistan's efforts to implement a national family planning programme have encountered many of the problems noted in India. Expenditures on family planning (chiefly for the establishment of clinical service) have averaged only about one cent per person each year. But, as in India, the problems have been even more those of organization and administration than of lack of funds.

In July 1965, Pakistan adopted a plan for upgrading and reorganizing the Family Planning Directorate with a five-year budget of 300 million rupees. The new Plan as implemented would raise annual per capita expenses on family planning to 12 cents. A major innovation is to be the insertion of intra-uterine devices (IUDs) by midwives under general medical supervision. The local midwives will receive incentive payments for referrals and insertions, presumably to compensate them for loss of income in the prevention of births. No less than 50,000 village midwives are to be recruited and given a five-week training course by 1970.

The target is to make family planning available to everyone. In drawing up the present plan, weaknesses revealed in the programme under the Second Five-Year Plan (1960–65) were carefully studied. That plan reached 100 per cent of its target in the establishment of clinics but only 31 per cent in patients attending the clinics, 42 per cent of the personnel projected for training, and 17 and 15 per cent respectively in the distribution of condoms and foam tablets. Failure to reach goals was attributed, among other reasons, to the clinic orientation of the programme, emphasis on the urban population, who constitute only 13 per cent of the total, and the addition of family planning to existing health and medical services already concerned with other responsibilities.

Korea and Taiwan

These two Far Eastern countries are outstanding in the success of their family planning programmes. The two programmes are described in greater detail in S. M. Keeny, 'Korea and Taiwan: Two National Programmes', in *Studies in Family Planning*, No. 6, Population Council, New York, March 1965. An official Family Planning Policy was approved by the Government of Korea in 1961. A month later the Health Ministry removed the ban on the importation and home production of contraceptive supplies and soon thereafter a family planning organization was established in the Ministry of Health.

The target of the Family Planning Programme is to reduce the annual rate of natural increase in Korea from an estimated 3 per cent in 1963 to 2·5 per cent in 1966 and to 1·82 per cent in 1971. According to the Health Ministry, this goal requires the prevention of about 1·5 million births in the ten-year period. The Economic Planning Board estimates that by 1980 implementation of the population policy will result in a growth rate of 1·16 per cent per annum compared with 3·15 per cent under a laissez-faire situation and will produce a per capita income 36 per cent above the level that would otherwise prevail.

The Korean Government is pursuing its family planning with vigour. The present level of expenditures on family planning, at 6·8 cents per capita in the last budget, is at this time the highest in the world. Korea has trained and equipped some 2,200 full-time workers in the field, or an average of one for each 2,500 women in the childbearing ages. The new plastic intra-uterine devices figure largely in the Korean programme and the monthly rate of insertions has reached about five per 1,000 women in the childbearing ages. On an annual basis, this is something of the order of 15 per cent of the 'target' women, i.e. those of reproductive age not presently pregnant, lactating, sterile, already practising contraception effectively or desiring more children.

Unfortunately, the official vital statistics of Korea are far from complete and there is no sure way of determining the present effect of the family planning programme on the birth rate. Nevertheless, the impact of the programme is surely being felt, as has been confirmed by experimental projects which have achieved success in reducing fertility.

The family planning programme in Taiwan is not an implementation of an official family planning programme. Nevertheless, a nation-wide network of family planning services has been established through the Provincial Health Ministry. This larger programme was associated with an extensive report, compiled under the leadership of the Health Commissioner, presenting population projections if family planning were *not* undertaken. The cost of educating the children and providing other services if there were no family planning, in part motivated the Economic Planning Board to authorize funds for a ten-year omnibus health programme, including family planning services.

The feasibility of a national programme was demonstrated by the results of a mass action research project in family planning in the city and district of Taichung. This study has become rather a classic in family planning research and is commonly regarded as evidence of what can be achieved with a carefully designed programme. This action experiment is described by Bernard Berelson and Ronald Freedman in 'A Study in Fertility Control', *Scientific American*, 210 (5), pp. 3–11, May 1964. The wide and rapid acceptance of the IUD in Taichung led to its adoption as the principal method used in the nation-wide programme.

The principal feature of the family planning in Taiwan is the goal of inserting 600,000 IUDs within five years. This would give loops to about one-third of the married women of childbearing age, including those who marry in the period. The initial target of 100,000 insertions for 1965 was in effect achieved.

An outstanding feature of the Taiwan programme is the excellent statistical evaluation. Performance against targets can be compared at the level of the individual worker, and there is detailed evaluation of the programme in relation to different areas, the acceptability of different contraceptive methods, the age and other characteristics of women accepting the IUD, etc. Especially important are a series of small experiments designed to achieve greater efficiency and to try out new ideas. For example, the practicability of offering coupons good for free IUD insertions for only a short time, the distribution of supplies by mail, and different methods of diffusing information and of stimulating motivation have been tested.

As compared with India and Pakistan, Korea and Taiwan are small countries. In addition, they are relatively advanced, particularly Taiwan, as measured by such indices as literacy and education. Nevertheless, the rapid development of family planning programmes in these countries from pilot projects into successful national action programmes is of great importance. In neither country has the programme been in effect on a sufficient scale or for a long enough time to say just how successful it has been. But one thing is clear: the programmes are moving rapidly and are a success. The experience of these countries almost certainly will demonstrate that with effective organization and training, and with the use of the latest contraceptives, government efforts can indeed reduce fertility.

In other east and south-east Asian countries, for the moment excluding Mainland China, there are as yet no formal national population policies. However, in several areas, notably Hong Kong, Singapore, Malaysia and Ceylon, the governments do subsidize private family planning associations. In Singapore and in Hong Kong, the family planning associations are among the most successful private agencies in this field in the world. The widespread services provided by the association in Singapore may well have been a factor in the rapid fall of the crude birth rate from 45·4 per 1,000 in 1952 to 34·5 per 1,000 in 1962. The birth rate in Hong Kong, which was 32 per 1,000 in 1962, is also relatively low for Asia, but this is at least in major part attributable to distortions of the age structure of the population associated with the influx of refugees from Mainland China.

In Malaysia the birth rate is also falling, especially among the population of Chinese background. The Malaysian government is reported to be considering the establishment of a formal programme of population control.

In Ceylon the government has received technical assistance from the Swedish Government in pilot projects implementing family planning in two communities. The results have been encouraging, and a national programme is being planned.

In Thailand a major action experiment has been conducted under the sponsorship of the National Research Council and others are under consideration. The first, in the rural district Pho-tharam, has been in operation little more than a year but the results already suggest a ready acceptance of contraceptive services in Thailand if they are provided by the government.

Mainland China

The position of Communist China with reference to population control and family planning has been the subject of much speculation. In 1956 and 1957 Premier Chou En-lai and President Mao Tze-tung were quoted as making statements favourable to the adoption of family planning, and subsequently it was reported that a birth control campaign had been initiated and services provided in government health centres.

However, in 1958, the political winds shifted and the birth control campaign was brought to a halt. While little mention appeared in the press about birth control, abortion and sterilization, there is nevertheless evidence that contraceptive devices were not banned and continued to be generally available in the cities and that abortion and sterilizations were not made illegal. In 1962 there was a resumption of the birth control campaign and in January of that year the State Council revised import duties to permit contraceptive supplies to enter China duty-free. At the end of the year the *Peoples Daily* began to print advertisements to promote the sale of publications in which birth control was advocated. At the same time the government began to advocate later age at marriage.

Mainland China does not appear to have a formal population policy, but it is quite clear that family planning information and materials are supplied as a part of the public health services. Japanese doctors who visited China in March and April 1964 and in July 1965 report that family planning is promoted as a part of the maternal and child health programme and that all methods of contraception, including sterilization and induced abortion, are available. Oral contraceptives are used as well as various forms of the IUD, which has become quite a popular method.

The official attitude was presumably stated by Premier Chou En-lai during his African tour of 1964. In Conakry, Guinea, he was interviewed by Edgar Snow at considerable length on this and other matters. Premier Chou is quoted as follows:

> '. . . We do believe in planned parenthood, but it is not easy to introduce all at once in China and it is more difficult to achieve in rural areas, where most of our people live, than in the cities.
>
> 'The first thing is to encourage late marriages . . .
>
> 'Since the Second World War Japan has achieved a remarkable decline to [a population growth rate of] about 1 per cent. We have sent people to Japan to study means and results there. Our present target is to reduce population growth to below 2 per cent; for the future we aim at an even lower rate.
>
> 'However, I do not believe it will be possible to equal the Japanese rate as early as 1970—for some of the reasons mentioned. For example, with improved living conditions over the past two years, our rate of increase again rose to 2·5 per cent. Therefore our emphasis on planned parenthood is entirely positive; planned parenthood, where there is increased production of goods and services, is conducive to raising the people's standard of living. That is why we have been very carefully studying it during the past few years.'[2]

The annual rate of increase of 2·5 per cent would mean some 17 million additional population each year.

Middle East and North Africa

Three governments of this region have initiated programmes at various levels: Turkey has announced a national population policy; Tunisia is preparing to undertake a national family planning campaign early this year; and the government of the United Arab Republic has established some birth control services.

In Turkey, a new law providing the legal framework for financing and implementing a nation-wide family planning programme was signed by the President in April 1965. Responsibility for the programme rests with the Ministry of Health but explicit in the law is the co-ordination of this ministry with others, Rural Affairs, Agriculture, Education, and so on. The goal is to achieve widespread contraceptive practice among the five million married women of reproductive age. The goal is a 10 per cent decline in fertility in each five year period during the next 15 years.

Operationally the programme will utilize the existing facilities of the Health Ministry, but full time family planning personnel will be added. The 700 gynaecologists in the country will be supplemented with 200 medical graduates, who, after a three month training course, will be the nucleus of a mobile family planning team to take the programme to the people. The IUD will be offered free, and orals, foams, condoms and rhythm at cost. Although supplies are now imported, local manufacture is contemplated.

Turkey has advantages for a successful family planning programme in that it is homogeneous in nationality and language, which suggests a rapid cultural diffusion once family planning practice begins to take hold. In a national survey conducted in 1964, women were found to support the idea of family planning by a majority of 3 to 1. Moreover, 70 per cent of the men and 79 per cent of the women answered affirmatively the question, 'Should the government have a programme to give information to those people who want to keep from having too many children?' Popular support for the programme seems to be assured.[3]

To give the programme depth, education and publicity are to be directed at the non-married as well as the married. On the high school level, the Ministry of Education plans to emphasize human reproduction in biology courses and population trends in the social studies curriculum. Two educational programmes are envisaged for the armed forces, one for married military personnel, the other for all enlisted men just prior to their release. The objective of this educational campaign is not merely for the personal edification of the soldiers, but for the rippling effect upon the population at large as the conscripted men return to civilian life.

The Tunisian family planning programme is discussed in another paper (ch. 43). An experimental programme designed to develop a practical family planning service was initiated in 1964. Clinical trials with the IUD were established in three hospitals in the city of Tunis and in three family planning clinics established in maternal and child health centres. The success of this programme has led to plans for a national campaign with a goal of 120,000 women using the IUD within a two-year period. A unique feature of the Tunisian programme is the use of the Destourian Socialist Party workers as a major source of information and publicity.

It is likely that the establishment of the family planning programme in Tunisia will have some repercussions beyond its borders. Algeria and Morocco, for example, have indicated much interest in the Tunisian programme.

In the UAR the government's interest in family planning goes back at least a decade, to when the National Population Commission, formed in 1953, opened four planned parenthood clinics. The Government has continued to have an active interest in population matters and there have been important expressions of this concern by leaders of the government. Thus in the May 1962 draft of the National Charter, President Nasser declared:

> 'Population increase constitutes the most dangerous obstacle that faces the Egyptian people in their drive towards raising the standard of production in their country in an effective and efficient way . . . Attempts at family planning deserve the most sincere efforts supported by modern scientific methods.'[4]

However, some frustration has been encountered in the meagre public response to the services introduced by the government, and a substantial governmental programme has not existed until very recently. The government has requested foreign assistance in obtaining 50,000 IUDs and the moulds to manufacture IUDs within the country. There is a resurgence of interest in governmental and private circles, and it is believed that new contraceptives, especially the oral pills and the IUD, may make a full-scale government programme more feasible and acceptable.

Africa South of the Sahara

No formal population policies or national family planning programmes yet exist in Africa below the Sahara. Nevertheless, Dr Caldwell's paper (ch. 37) finds considerably greater official readiness for such programmes than had been suspected. African countries firmly believe in economic and health planning by government. It is quite possible that they entertain fewer doubts about government guidance in development than do the new nations of any other continent. There is a growing awareness that the reduction of infant mortality and of other deaths produces rapid population growth, so rapid as to threaten the achievement of economic goals. There is a growing realization of the key importance of population growth, as opposed to population density, as a factor affecting the dynamics of economic development.[5]

Latin America

This region has the most rapid rate of population growth of any major part of the world. Until quite recently this has not been a cause of much public concern, partly because of the predominant Catholic religion and partly because these countries have a traditional image of themselves as underpopulated with a large area capable of new settlement.

Two developments seem to be bringing an important change in the attitudes of governments in the region. The first of these is a realization that in Latin America, as in many other parts of the world, population growth is eating up a large share, in some cases all, of the economic growth being achieved. A second factor has been the growing consciousness of the problem of abortion. Abortion is becoming increasingly common, the problem has become of major concern to the medical profession and their reaction has been an important stimulus toward more liberal attitudes on contraception. A co-ordinated fertility survey in eight Latin American capitals, co-ordinated by the United Nations Demographic Centre for Latin America in Santiago, has revealed favourable attitudes towards family planning in a large segment of the populations concerned.

Until recently it was thought unlikely that governments of the region would adopt national population policies because of the opposition of the Church. However, it seems quite likely that in a number of countries family planning may be instituted as a regular public health service. This has already occurred in Chile, is to be instituted in Honduras, and is under serious consideration in Colombia.

Conclusions

As recently as ten years ago, there was only one country in the world with a national population policy, namely India. Now several important countries have national population policies and national family planning programmes. A substantial number of others seem to be moving in this direction.

In this matter of population policies, leadership has been taken by the countries of the underdeveloped world and particularly Asia. No European country has adopted a policy of restricting population growth, though be it said, there has not been the same occasion. Throughout almost all of Europe, including the European part of the Soviet Union, the birth rate is now relatively low and the rate of population growth modest. Nevertheless, several European countries, particularly Catholic countries, have maintained restrictive legislation against the distribution and prescription of contraceptives. In this respect, the new countries often have fewer inhibitions and generally more consideration for the voluntary choice of couples in these matters.

What are the characteristics of the national family planning programmes so far?

1. They have been wholly voluntary. There are no sanctions for or against the use of family planning except for certain economic incentives to take advantage of free service.

2. The family planning programmes have universally been considered as a matter for administration by the Ministries of Health. Family planning is apparently generally regarded as a matter of health and welfare.

3. Up to now, the economic investments in family planning programmes have been relatively small, and this is in part responsible for their modest effects. Even with the gathering momentum of programmes in the Asian countries, the economic costs of such programmes are a minor part of the development budgets. Family plan-

ning is, of course, in no case considered as an alternative to maximum efforts for economic development.

4. The family planning programmes have not encountered much overt opposition. The governments have usually been more conservative than the people. Surveys of the knowledge, attitudes, and practices of general populations in the underdeveloped areas almost universally show a majority favourable to family planning. In every country there is a large reservoir of potential users of government family planning services.

5. The implementation of family planning programmes has been found to be greatly facilitated by the new contraceptives, especially the oral pills and the IUDs. These have the tremendous advantage of being dissociated from sexual intercourse and are therefore much more practical for most peoples.

6. Some of the programmes are beginning to show real successes, notably those of the governments of Korea and Taiwan, and the efforts of the private family planning associations in Singapore and Hong Kong.

Population trends and especially birth rates can no longer be regarded as a 'given' factor not subject to change. It is apparent that the great majority of the world's families would like to control their size given the appropriate information, the services, and methods suitable to their ways and conditions of life. There is increasing evidence that the 'population dilemma' of the modern world is at least partly amenable to solution by government action in providing voluntary family planning services.

Footnotes

1. LT COL. B. L. RAINA, *Family Planning Programme Report for 1962–1963*, New Delhi, 1963 (mimeo), p. 3.
2. *New York Times*, 3 February 1964.
3. This national survey on population will serve as a valuable reference point on many aspects of knowledge, attitudes and practices relating to family planning preceding the institution of a national programme, cf. 'Turkey: National Survey on Population', in *Studies in Family Planning*, No. 5. Population Council, December 1964.
4. United Arab Republic Information Department, 1962.
The Charter, draft presented by President Gamal Abdel Nasser on 21 May 1962, p. 53.
5. Since this paper was written Kenya has undertaken a plan to introduce family planning through its public health services.

36 The relationship between population change and economic development in tropical Africa

Etienne van de Walle
Princeton University, U.S.A.

The Influence of Economic Development on Population Change

By economic development we mean, for practical purposes, rise in national income per head. Unfortunately, this classical definition neglects a number of factors that are inherent in economic progress such as peace and order, better education and health, better distribution of income, and increased leisure. Investments in hospital facilities or campaigns to eradicate malaria compete in the national budget with investments in power plants or agricultural extension. The latter may result in higher income, while the former cannot figure in national accounting. In a meaningful way, components of population change—mortality and fertility decline—are parts of economic progress. One should remember that these factors are important, but the problem is easier to state when restricted to the effects of a rise in income per head on population change, i.e. on the following variables: fertility, mortality and migration.

It is not certain that a meaningful relationship any longer exists between economic change and mortality change. Economic development in the West probably has influenced mortality. Today, mortality decline in developing countries depends more on allocation of a small fraction of national income to strategic outlays (vaccinations, residual insecticides, etc.) than on the rise of national income and can be out of proportion to economic development.

In the present state of our knowledge, we cannot say either that fertility will be affected when income per head reaches a critical point, or that no decline in fertility can occur without a significant rise in income. In the past, it was customary to deny any early prospect of fertility decline in Africa. This opinion was grounded on African values, which favour large families. Experience taught that it takes a long time to alter such values in any significant portion of a population. Today one can be less certain because of two developments.

1. 'Social engineering' in the field of fertility has ceased to be a Utopian concept as demonstrated in Korea and Taiwan where vigorous campaigns appear to have initiated fertility decline. The advent of a cheap and effective contraceptive (the loop) and tested techniques of diffusion now give powerful instruments to governments to lower fertility.

2. The interest demonstrated recently by a tropical African government in information concerning such a decline, and increasing realization in the continent of the macro-economic disadvantages of rapid demographic growth.

Even so, any fertility decline would be slow and would make little difference to our reasoning. Furthermore, as with mortality decline, it would be brought about, not by economic development itself, but by voluntary choice on the part of the state.

As for migration, it is affected in major ways by economic development. Development is inseparable from large-scale movements from areas of lesser to areas of higher economic opportunity (e.g. rural–urban movements).

The Effect of Population Growth on Economic Development

Three aspects of the effect of population growth must be distinguished: the age distribution of a population, its growth rate, and its size.[1] The discussion will be restricted to the effects of demographic growth *per se*, without distinguishing the specific influence of changing mortality or fertility. The latter has much the greater effect on age distribution. Much literature has been devoted to the economic implications of the age distribution,[2] and most of it is summed up in the burden of dependency argument. The ratio of dependents (young children and old people) to the labour force is a precise notion, easy to measure by using standard demographic data (e.g. the ratio of persons aged zero to 14 years and 65 years and over to persons aged 15 to 64 years); that measurement is influenced in unambiguous ways by changes in vital rates. It is affected mostly by fertility changes, although these are unlikely in the near future in tropical Africa. The unfavourable effect of mortality decline on the dependency burden is compensated by a qualitative improvement of the labour force by better health and a larger proportion of younger workers. Finally, the whole concept may be of doubtful relevance when there exists considerable unemployment or underemployment, and when ages of entry into and exit from the labour force are not precisely defined.

The rest of this paper is devoted to two effects of population growth: its action on saving and investment and on increase of agricultural density.

The first question is considered often in terms of a rule of thumb which is popular among planners because of its simplicity: a population with a rate of increase of 1 per cent per year will use up in investment 4 per cent of the gross national income just to stand still and make no progress.[3] For instance, if the population of Western Africa grows by 2·3 per cent annually between 1965 and 1980, an annual investment of 9·2 per cent of national income will be necessary to accommodate the increase, and only the investment in excess of this rate will contribute to an improvement of the standard of living. The corresponding 'demographic investments' are 6·8 and 10·8 of gross national income respectively in Central and Eastern Africa, for growth rates estimated at 1·7 and 2·7 per cent.[4] Since it has been estimated that saving represents 6 per cent of GNP in Africa, the computation highlights the efforts required, as well as the need of foreign investment.

The model ends up in a prescription which can do no harm: invest as much as possible, and try to obtain from aid and foreign interests what cannot come from domestic sources. The underlying reasoning, however, is fallacious. The rule of thumb seems magical, and it is not always clear why there is a necessary relationship between investment and national income.

Assuming that the aggregates used in the following discussion are precisely measurable, and that GNP for a given year is 100, the latter is produced by a certain amount of capital, and may be considered as a rate of return on that capital. In fact, the French speak of a 'national rate of interest', but it is more conventional to use the reciprocal, i.e. the ratio of capital to output. Assuming that the national capital is four times the GNP (or, in our example, is equal to 400), it equips a labour force of given size—which size does not matter here—at a certain level of productivity. Now if this labour force grows by a certain percentage,[5] so goes the argument, the national capital will have to grow by the same percentage to maintain productivity. If capital growth is financed by saving out of current GNP, growth of 1 per cent of the labour force calls for an equal growth of the national capital, from 400 to 404 in our example, these four points being allocated from the GNP.

This reasoning assumes that additions to the capital stock are in the same relation to new output as aggregate capital to total output, and that productivity remains constant. These simplications are not necessary to the use of capital-output ratios. In general, it is implied that marginal capital-output ratios are used. The figure is not always 4 to 1, and estimates have tended to come down in recent times. A single ratio for the whole economy has little meaning, and planners try to distinguish by sectors. This preoccupation has given rise to strategies of development advocating investment by priority in sectors where capital-output ratios are low. This complicates the model considerably.[6]

Even the simple model has one great advantage: it constitutes an effort to integrate population growth into theories of development and economic planning. As such, it is commendable since this factor is often left out of the reasoning. The didactic value of the model must be distinguished from its practical usefulness. The orders of magnitude may be wrong, but it points to one very important fact; the process of population growth is costly in terms of saving and investment.

Some Methodological Problems

We have assumed that capital and output were measurable quantities. This assumption cannot be accepted without discussion in regard to some African economies, where 90 per cent of the population depend on subsistence agriculture. The term 'subsistence' implies that no saving is possible, since real income fails to rise much above the minimum required to subsist. Actual usage of the word is rather loose. C. J. Martin makes it a synonym of self-sufficiency.[7] If the etymology is accepted, and the word is used in the way Malthus used it, then demographic growth in the subsistence sector offers a paradox. We shall use the word as a synonym of 'traditional', assuming that little saving takes place in that sector.

A. T. Grove compared several stages of agricultural density in Northern Nigeria. He opposed high densities in northern Katsina which have given rise to land impoverishment and emigration to even higher densities in the environs of Kano City where the yields of intensive farming allow better living conditions.[8] Periodic fallow has been eliminated in the latter case; irrigation and mixed farming are practised; manure and household refuse from the city are used as fertilizers. What has taken place must be considered as capital investment, not of a spectacular kind, but of numerous small accretionary capital inputs that cannot be computed in national accounts. The following definition has the problems of underdeveloped countries in mind, 'By capital is meant the accumulated stock of resources which contributes to a larger flow of goods and services through time, or which serves as a reserve sustaining a higher level of consumption at a time of more urgent demand or need than would otherwise be possible.'[9] The same authors state, about direct investment in agriculture: 'In the conventional estimates of capital resources and of capital formation in underdeveloped countries the results of the expenditure of time, effort and money in the creation, extension, improvement and upkeep of agricultural holdings are often disregarded.'[10] It would go against vested practice to include household refuse and manure as capital goods, but they improve the land in a permanent way.

Since most inputs in subsistence agriculture are not monetized, the problem of computing capital investment is in practice insoluble. Similarly, as Phyllis Deans said when speaking about putting a price tag on subsistence output, 'The figure for subsistence output can never be more than a token figure.'[11] Since both numerator and denominator are token figures, a capital–output ratio for the subsistence sector is meaningless.

The Dual Economy

The most elegant way out of this quandary is proposed by W. A. Lewis.[12] Whatever happens in the subsistence sector, he suggests, will not lead to development. Saving and investment that matter occur only in the capitalist sector, meaning the sector using 'reproducible capital': machines, roads, dams, cement and metal, capital that is self-cumulative, producing more capital goods. (This is no indictment of agriculture as opposed to industry, since agriculture may be capitalistic.) Capital–output ratios are meaningful tools in this context.

Population growth in the capitalist sector obeys rules different from those applying to the economy as a whole, and is the result mostly of migration in the labour force. It is strictly regulated by economic factors as in classical theory. The entry of labour is determined by the opening up of jobs at the going rate of wages, and it cannot have any deleterious effect on the capitalist sector. As with many other features of the model, this is not very realistic; the capitalist sector will react to shanty towns by investing in housing, to urban poverty by importing food, and so on. In fact, the flight from the countryside into the city can become a serious drag on the modern sector, because the city is the place where the underemployment of the subsistence sector will crystallize into unemployment.

The subsistence sector is characterized by an unlimited supply of labour. This means that labour is so under-utilized that subsistence production will not be hurt if a large quantity of labour is removed. We do not say that labour has a zero marginal productivity, meaning that increases in the labour force would not contribute anything to the total product; we do not even say that marginal productivity is declining as output rises, or is below average productivity. It is sufficient that it be very low. The seasonality of African agriculture implies long periods during which manpower lies idle and can be diverted to the capitalist sector. Barber argues that the division of labour between the sexes in Central Africa allows males to leave indigenous agriculture for extended periods without harm to productivity.[13] Watson estimates that at any given time 50 per cent of the males can be absent from the Mambwe village without effect on total production.[14]

It is interesting to note that the stage of an economy where marginal productivity is below average productivity has received a special name: overpopulation. The word has been used often as a synonym for high density, i.e. ratio of people to land area, without specifying what people (commanding what technology) and what land; Very densely populated lands often have unusually high fertility. Density is a deceptive concept, as illustrated by comparing the Nile valley with the Sahara desert. The latter may be overpopulated with one person per square mile, since a second person would not significantly increase the product. However, with adequate capital, it may be possible to exploit oil wells in the desert, which will permit a much higher density.

The main relevance of the dualist model to the problem of the effect of population growth on the African economy is that natural increase, considered as an independent variable, occurs mostly in the subsistence sector, while entrance into the modern sector is regulated by the growth of the latter. Thus, increasing densities are a major feature of the subsistence sector and, when decreasing returns are initiated, they raise the problem which has obsessed economists ever since Malthus. But, as Coale observes, the main problem is that density increases not with respect to land, but with respect to capital that is not supplied in sufficient amount to the subsistence sector.[15]

Some investment takes place. The very fact that the rural population of tropical Africa often is growing rapidly without recognizable deterioration of standards of living is an indication thereof. So far, it has usually been possible to accommodate more people by tilling more land or by rationalizing agriculture with well-known tribal methods such as manuring. The conditions of a frontier economy, where capital provided by the growing population has been sufficient to preserve the level of living—sometimes a very low level indeed—have been widely realized for two reasons. First, a margin has been afforded by lands lying fallow. Second, there has been a considerable increase of productivity in the contemporary period, due to the introduction and rapid spread of new crops.[16] These factors have not created a surplus, and the indigenous economy has been more concerned with survival than with growth.

The Possibility of Rural Evolution

The approach of developing the capitalist sector and of letting the subsistence sector take care of itself has given rise to the southern African pattern of development. When a country is endowed with rich ore deposits, foreign capital is available in large supply, and there exists an international market for the product. The unlimited supply of labour can be kept in the subsistence sector by various means, and development takes place in the capitalist sector. Population appears only as denominator in the misleading concept of national income per head.

The main cause for concern is that, despite the apparent wide availability of land, the agricultural system may not be capable of incorporating fast population growth without incurring permanent damage. This is the gist of Gourou's argument.[17] The slash-and-burn system, he maintains, is well adapted to tropical conditions characterized by poor and unstable soils, but is static and cannot adapt itself to the dynamics of population increments. It reacts by shortening the fallow period instead of by intensifying agriculture. This sets in motion a series of irreversible processes such as soil erosion, laterization, dislocation of the soil structure and destruction of the plant cover, and leads to permanent impairment of fertility. Despite the example of many successful transitions to self-perpetuating agriculture,[18] the bulk of the African population still relies on shifting cultivation, and the danger cannot be overlooked. For a given level of technology, the optimum densities may be fairly low, as exemplified in the *chitemene* agriculture practised by the Bemba of Zambia, where the optimum density has been evaluated around eight persons per square mile.[19] It could even be said that the lower the densities, the less intensive the cultivation and as a consequence, in case of fast population growth, the larger the dangers of impoverished soil, overstocking and erosion. This constitutes a paradox only if one considers high density as an index of overpopulation rather than as the result of more efficient land use.

The Bemba might improve their agriculture at least to the technical level reached by neighbouring tribes, and appear to have done so under exceptional circumstances.[20] However, the obstacles to evolution are not physical or technical, but social, psychological and institutional. African tenure systems usually are characterized by communal ownership of the land. This feature ensures to everyone free access to land as part of one's political rights. Population increases are accommodated automatically, in contrast with other legal situations where they lead to heavy rents in favour of landlords and to the emergence of a landless class. Communal ownership leads to the subdivision of land and to a dangerous reduction of the fallow period, without compensating efforts to increase productivity. The traditional system 'may, by its failure to provide adequate incentive to the individual to put effort or money into the land, militate against its conservation and improvement. It may, owing to the limitations to the form of security which it provides, delay the introduction of permanent cash crops, and, generally, of better farming methods. It may make it impossible for the farmer to raise loans on the security of his land for purposes designed to increase its productivity.'[21]

Population pressure has been alleviated by temporary migration, an attempt to use the unlimited supply of labour without really leaving the subsistence sector. It has afforded a breathing spell for subsistence agriculture to avoid evolution, and appears to have affected productivity in perverse ways. A. Richards wrote after revisiting Bembaland in 1957 that 'the standards of efficiency in gardening seemed to me to have gone down with so many young men away'.[22]

The danger of population pressure on the land is not restricted to those regions of

Africa that have a thriving industrial or mining sector, or to those where large migratory movements take place. The need to rationalize African agriculture is felt everywhere on the continent. It is interesting to note that evolution toward individual tenure has often occurred, if at all, not as a reaction to population pressure, but to the extension of cash crops giving monetary value to the land and its product. Among the Nyakyusa of Tanzania, the increasing scarcity of land is 'probably the most significant feature of modern life.'[23] 'The younger Nyakyusa men find increasing difficulty in obtaining arable land now that there are no longer vacant areas to be taken up and the older men are no longer prepared to cede their land rights in favour of the younger generations, as they traditionally did. . . .'[24] This is the result, not so much of population increase as of the success of coffee and paddy rice cultivation, and the young men migrate in search of other opportunities. Thus, population growth is not the only factor accounting for the shortage of land. The State has an important rôle to play to further rural evolution and to complement the efforts of tribal organization.[25]

Monetary Investments in the Subsistence Sector

This brings us back to another implication of rapid population growth on the land. It appears that capital is not missing so much quantitatively as qualitatively. There is great need of certain types of capital investment in strategic places: rural extension, scientific research, education and training, marketing, etc. Any improvements of the living standards of the majority hinges on such investments, and they will not be forthcoming by the very fact of growth, in contrast with investments required to maintain consumption standards at the subsistence level. The problem is not essentially demographic, but some of the costs of population growth will affect the national budget. Education is the foremost example. The increase of the education bill is more than proportional to the increase in population. New investments in school buildings, teacher training, etc. to meet a given target (such as universal education within thirty years) will have to be given higher priority if population should double in the meantime, than if it were stationary.

The rural sector requires monetary capital to preserve its productivity and to increase its level of living. Most governments today are committed to improving the latter. The reason is partly a relative judgment of the purposes of economic development, but it makes good economic sense to encourage development simultaneously in both sectors. In the end, the capitalist sector will benefit by having a prosperous rural partner, and the latter has several functions to play besides being a source of cheap labour for industrialization: it must be a source of food, a source of capital and foreign exchange, and a market for industrial production. The arguments have been discussed elsewhere[26]; we shall mention some of their demographic aspects.

It might be asserted that a large population is an asset in fulfilling these functions. Martin has argued that growing industry in East Africa requires abundant labour which cannot be provided easily by a sparse population.[27] Certainly, without increase in productivity, production might be affected in the short run by the removal of labour. 'In view of the potential that exists for increasing agricultural output per man, it is to be expected that labour-supply problems in manufacturing and other growing industries will not be serious, provided that intelligent and vigorous efforts are made to enhance farm productivity.'[28] Historically, the shortage of unskilled labour must be attributed to the primitive character of the rural economy and to the unusually large labour requirements of the mining industry. But the demand for migrant labour from traditionally large employers has tended to decrease. Unemployment is now a feature of African cities. This is due in part to the slackening of foreign investment in recent years. New industries incorporate all the labour-saving devices of Western technology. For instance, mining in West Africa is capital-intensive, and the number of jobs created directly for local employment is often of the order of one for $100,000 to $250,000 invested; there is some indirect creation of employment. The overall figure of $4,000 per head is often quoted as that needed to transfer rural population to non-rural jobs.[29] An ECA report estimates that in Africa (excluding South Africa) 'over the last two decades industrial employment has increased roughly by about one million persons. But during this period nearly 25 million persons of working age were added to the labour force. Thus, although the pace of industrial expansion in Africa has been rapid, it has so far had only a limited influence on raising the level of income per head, transforming the economic structure or providing new employment.'[30]

The magnitude of the task of providing new employment outside of agriculture is staggering even in Africa where the resource endowment is favourable. Growth will continue to be absorbed on the land, but 'it is a reasonable, almost an essential objective that within a generation most countries should plan to provide non-agricultural employment for the whole of their additions to the labour force.'[31]

Large segments of African population have depended for their relations with the modern sector, e.g. for tax money, clothing, and school fees, on the growing of commercial crops. Their future prospects are sometimes mediocre. In demographic language, one could say that the number of coffee drinkers is growing less rapidly than the number of coffee growers. Stabilization of prices can be effective only if production is curtailed. If an international agreement attributes a quota in the market to one particular country, the income per head will depend, not on the amount of coffee sold, a fixed quantity, but on the number of growers.

All the arguments advanced thus far, in connection with the rôle of agriculture, appear to involve fast population growth as a handicap rather than as an asset. However, the possibility of economies of scale is often considered to be an argument in favour of growth, since the latter is the process of optimizing one's size. It is claimed that substantial advantages would result from higher densities than are prevalent now.[32] There may be advantages in a denser population even in the subsistence sector, in so far as social overhead will be more economical to provide, but economies of scale in the strict sense are practically restricted to the industrial sector. The main advantage expected is that a larger population will provide a larger market for industrial goods.

The extent to which this factor upsets disadvantages inherent to growth is easy to overestimate. Technical economies in many industries are exhausted with firms of rather limited size. This is true for types of goods for which there exists a large African market despite low incomes: blankets, soap, wooden furniture, etc. Furthermore, one should think of a market as of a multi-dimensional notion, of which number of people and density constitute only the two-dimensional upper layer, but where depth is constituted by the importance of income per head.[33] Modern industry cannot depend on large numbers of impoverished peasants with unlimited prospects for natural increase.

Conclusion

The aim of this paper has been to explore the implications of present population growth for the economic development of tropical Africa. By 1980, we must expect in tropical Africa[34] a population of about 240 million, compared to the present total of 150 million. The males aged 15 to 64 years, or the potential labour force, will increase from 44 to 80 million during the same period. Undoubtedly most of the increase will remain in the rural sector, and require considerable investment in agriculture. The question of fertility decline, deliberately left out of the discussion, perhaps cannot be evaded for much longer.

Footnotes

1. A. J. COALE and E. M. HOOVER, *Population Growth and Economic Development in Low-Income Countries*, Princeton University Press, 1958, pp. 18 ff.
2. It is reviewed in P. DEMENY, 'Demographic Aspects of Saving, Investment, Employment and Productivity', *UN World Population Conference, Belgrade 1965*, WPC 460, pp. 11 ff.
3. Sometimes the rate of 3 per cent, or another figure, is used.
4. These estimates are taken from E. VAN DE WALLE, 'Future Growth of Population and Changes in Population Composition: Tropical Africa', *UN World Population Conference, Belgrade 1965*, WPC 25.
5. In the long run, population growth and labour force growth are identical. Since capital investment is a long-term process, we neglect short-term differences due to changes in fertility, mortality or migration.
6. DEMENY, *op. cit.*, pp. 39 ff.
7. C. J. MARTIN, 'Demographic Aspects of Capital Formation in Economies with Large Subsistence Sectors (Africa)', *UN World Population Conference, Belgrade 1965*, WPC 80, p. 1.
8. A. T. GROVE, 'Population Densities and Agriculture in Northern Nigeria', in K. M. BARBOUR and R. M. PROTHERO (eds.), *Essays on African Population*, London, 1961, pp. 115 ff.
9. P. T. BAUER and B. J. YAMEY, *The Economics of Under-Developed Countries*, Cambridge Economic Handbooks, 1957, p. 24. The discussion, pp. 24–31, is illuminating. See also: UN Capital Formation Statistics: *Problems and Methods with special reference to under-developed countries*, E/CN3/227, 1957.
10. *Op. cit.*, p. 29.
11. PHYLLIS DEANE, *Colonial Social Accounting*, Cambridge University Press, 1953, p. 226.
12. W. A. LEWIS, 'Economic Development with Unlimited Supplies of Labour', *The Manchester School*, May 1954.
13. W. BARBER, *The Economy of British Central Africa*, Oxford University Press, London, 1961.
14. W. WATSON, *Tribal Cohesion in a Money Economy*, Manchester University Press, 1958.
15. A. J. COALE, 'Population and Economic Development' in P. M. HAUSER (ed.), *The Population Dilemma*, The American Assembly, Prentice Hall, 1963, p. 58.
16. If manioc from South America was introduced by slavers needing a convenient supply of food for the sea passage, then, paradoxically, the slave trade may have contributed more to the population of Africa than to its depopulation!
17. P. GOUROU, *The Tropical World*, London, 1953 (translation).
18. The expression is used by H. T. KIMBLE, *Tropical Africa*, Vol. I, Doubleday, 1962, p. 28. He quotes as pre-European examples, the hills of Northern Togo, the Ruanda-Urundi plateau and the slopes of Kilimanjaro and Meru.
19. The Bemba have been described by A. I. RICHARDS, *Land, Labour and Diet in Northern Rhodesia*, London, 1939.
20. RICHARDS (*op. cit.*, pp. 327–28) tells of a Bemba village adopting the Bisa system of self-perpetuating agriculture because they had 'used up all the trees.' Watson contrasts the more sophisticated shifting cultivation of the Mambwe with Bemba agriculture (*op. cit.*, pp. 20 ff.). G. KAY describes the adaptations made by some Bemba subgroups in reaction to the shortage of *chitemene* land: 'Agricultural Change in the Luitikula Basin Development Area', *Human Problems in British Central Africa*, June 1962, pp. 21 ff.
21. Conclusions of the 1956 Arusha Conference, quoted in FAO, *Africa Survey*, Rome, 1962, p. 62.
22. Quoted by G. KAY, *loc. cit.*, p. 32.
23. P. H. GULLIVER, *Land Tenure and Social Change among the Nyakyusa*, East African Studies No. 11, EAISR, Kampala, 1958, p. 2.
24. *Op. cit.*, p. 36.
25. See H. A. OLUWASANMI, 'Land Tenure and Agricultural Improvement in Tropical Africa', *Journal of Farm Economics*, August 1957, pp. 731 ff.
26. B. F. JOHNSTON and J. W. MELLOR, 'The Role of Agriculture in Economic Development', *The American Economic Review*, September 1961, pp. 566 ff.
27. C. J. MARTIN, 'The Relationship of the Labour Force in East Africa to Economic Development', *Proceedings of the International Population Conference*, New York, 1961, Vol. II, pp. 485 ff.
28. JOHNSTON and MELLOR, *op. cit.*, p. 576.
29. L. TABAH, 'Comparison des évaluations des besoins en capitaux des pays en voie de développement', *World Population Conference, Belgrade 1965*, WPC 292, p. 4.
30. UN, *Industrial Growth in Africa*, ECA, New York, 1963, p. 9.
31. COALE, *op. cit.*, p. 67.
32. For instance, *Economic Bulletin for Africa*, Vol. II, June 1962, Chapters II and V, *passim*.
33. For those who can visualize a fourth dimension, the income elasticity of demand for industrial product should be mentioned.
34. Tropical Africa is defined here as the Continent minus countries verging on the Mediterranean and Red Seas, the Republic of South Africa, the High Commission Territories and South West Africa. The estimates are taken from VAN DE WALLE, *op. cit.*

37 Population policy: a survey of Commonwealth Africa

J. C. Caldwell

Department of Demography, Australian National University, Canberra, Australia

Commonwealth Africa

In mid-1963, Commonwealth Africa was estimated to contain over 104 million inhabitants of whom all but a million in Lesotho (Basutoland) and Swaziland lived within the tropics. The Commonwealth countries accounted for over a third of the population of the continent and about nine-tenths of that of the countries invited to the African Population Conference in Ibadan.[1] The exceptions are the Sudan and Liberia, which nevertheless share some of the legal and other traditions described below, and which are much closer in terms of legal tradition to the Commonwealth countries than they are to those where French, Portuguese or Spanish are the administrative languages. In order of population size, the Commonwealth countries are Nigeria, with about half the total population, Tanzania, Kenya, Ghana, Uganda, Rhodesia, Malawi, Zambia, Sierra Leone, Lesotho, Botswana, Gambia and Swaziland. Rhodesia and Swaziland are included here as Commonwealth countries because of Britain's membership.

Taking for the moment only one aspect of population policy, it might be noted that all countries which were British colonies were at that time at least implicitly in the same legal and administrative position with regard to birth control as was the population of Britain. Most Commonwealth governments assume this position to have continued. Abortion on medical grounds and sterilization with safeguards have been permitted, but the laws have been stringent enough to ensure that comparatively few operations were performed. However, the legal framework is sufficiently elastic to permit a radical change in that regard if administrative attitudes were to alter markedly. At the time of independence, the import, or theoretically manufacture, of contraceptives, together with their sale or distribution, was legal.

> 'A British colonial class bought contraceptives openly at pharmacies and sought advice on the subject from their doctors. The question of family planning clinics had often been raised, unofficially but within the British community, before independence. Neither the British administration as such nor the British establishment were much given to claiming the benefits of greater population or the need for settling sparsely populated areas.'[2]

This position is quite different from that which prevailed in colonial times in, for instance, most adjacent countries of French administration. The majority of these countries:

> 'retain French laws prohibiting or greatly restricting the import, manufacture or sale of contraceptives and the performance by doctors of operations to induce abortion or sterilization. Such laws have been much more effective in achieving their stated end in the simpler economies and small urban societies of Africa than they were in the more complex situation found in France itself. In most ex-French, sub-Saharan countries there is very little use of modern contraceptives by the African population, and very little talk of establishing family planning clinics. In many of

them, the governments are very conscious of what they regard as underpopulation. However, most administrations do regard the legal restrictions on contraception as largely of French heritage, which, in common with much other of French heritage, might some day be re-examined to see if they are in the best national interest.'[3]

Most governments have to adopt policies or at least assume attitudes about some aspects of population phenomena. The writer planned a long-term, comparative study of population policies in tropical Africa. One part of this study was an attempt in early 1965 to obtain statements on the policies of African governments. The initial approach was made in each case through the Head of State, and this was subsequently supplemented by communications with cabinet ministers and the permanent heads of departments. The replies to such inquiries take time and consideration. Therefore, it is pleasing to be able to report that all independent members of the Commonwealth except two have replied, and, of the two, the statement of Ghana has been delayed only because of the effort that has been put into determining the replies. At the time of writing, word was still awaited from Uganda and Swaziland. Much of the following analysis has been derived from these replies. The case of Mauritius will be examined at the same time because of its comparative proximity to tropical Africa. It might be noted that, although three-quarters of the replies came from the office of the head of government, the remainder were given to such ministries as that of Health to answer. In some cases certain policies may be carried out by Departments of Health with neither opposition nor stated approval from the Cabinet.

Population Planning

It was inquired whether each government believed that its country would benefit from a much larger population. Four (Tanzania, Zambia, Sierra Leone, and Botswana), representing 18 per cent of the population of the surveyed area, replied 'Yes', and seven, representing 82 per cent of the population, 'No'.

Three further questions were then asked: whether the government believed in economic planning, whether it believed that some kind of population planning should be an integral part of economic planning, and whether it believed that population growth could be so rapid as to hinder attempts to raise living standards.

All Commonwealth countries affirmed their belief in economic planning. This belief in such planning from the outset has been one of the most significant features of the emergence of new states in Africa and Asia over the last 20 years. Agreement about the probable need for some type of population planning, by which a reduction of the rate of natural growth was usually meant, was universal except in parts of East Africa. Tanzania and Malawi regarded it as unnecessary at this stage of their development. It might be noted that such a near consensus could not have been achieved on this point in Asia so soon after independence, although it can now. All countries believing in some population planning agreed that population growth could be excessive and hence economically harmful. Those disagreeing restricted themselves to the observation that this was not at present felt to be the position in their countries.

Ghana is not yet represented in this survey. But, it might at this stage be appropriate to quote from its current Development Plan to illustrate some of the thinking that has gone on there on the subject of population growth.

> 'A young and growing population like Ghana's means that every bread-winner has to provide for a proportionately larger number of dependents than he would in a country with a stagnant or relatively older population. The burden of savings required of the Ghanaians now working must consequently be greater than it would otherwise be. In addition, the present low levels of productivity and incomes make it harder for Ghana to save than it is for a wealthier community to save.
>
> This makes it necessary for the Government and people constantly to remind and rededicate themselves to the task of economic development. For it must be empha-

sised that the demographic situation, which lays this heavy burden of savings on the population, is not likely to show any significant changes in the short-run. The success that we have had in bringing down the death rate in one generation will not be matched by a similar success in bringing down the birth rate. Until the birth rate is reduced the population will continue to grow and the numbers of the dependent young will remain proportionately large. A growing population presents an opportunity as much as a problem. As there are more mouths to feed so also are there eventually more hands for work. A sustained stream of productive investment at an adequate rate is required to turn this opportunity into reality.'[4]

Migration Policy

In most countries, the oldest type of population policy has been that relating to the regulation of migration. Such regulation has had to be considered more in recent years, because many of what are now international borders were little more than internal boundaries in the extensive British and French empires. Furthermore, independent governments are much more likely to feel a prior responsibility for securing employment for their own nationals than is a colonial government.

The present position is that no government wishes actively to encourage unrestricted or unselective immigration. However, the majority do wish to attract, for at least limited periods, individuals with various technical skills or those who are trained teachers or in some cases persons with capital to invest. Gambia wishes to continue attracting seasonal labour for farming and fishing. Only a few countries, Sierra Leone, Mauritius and Botswana, discourage permanent immigration because of population or employment problems, but a greater number are not enthusiastic about the immigration of specific non-African groups, especially for certain types of employment such as retailing.

Only Mauritius is as yet so worried about land or employment problems that it could be said to encourage permanent emigration, and even in this case no financial assistance is given to date. However, Gambia clearly places no obstacles in the path of Gambians wishing to settle elsewhere. Few Commonwealth countries do much to discourage emigration, although some obviously have misgivings especially when skilled persons are involved.

The Control of Morbidity and Mortality

Until comparatively recently in the world's history, governments did not usually view the reduction of disease and the lowering of death rates as a major part of their responsibilities. These times have gone almost everywhere in the world. Every government in Commonwealth Africa regards health as a major concern and all unqualifiedly feel that the most rapid reduction possible of death rates is a desirable aim. Most point to the expenditure of a large proportion of the budget on health, the extension of health services especially into rural areas, mass campaigns against specified diseases, and the securing of assistance from such international organizations as WHO and UNICEF.

In all countries, death rates are believed to be falling, in some quite steeply, but in none on the mainland are statistics sufficiently good to be able to plot the exact path of mortality. However, in Mauritius, where the crude death rate had already sunk to 12·8 per 1,000 by 1957, it was down to 8·6 in 1964.

In most countries population growth rates are apparently already quite high, in some very high, and it is this continued decline in mortality that, together with high birth rates, has produced an acceleration in natural increase.

The Question of the Birth Rate

When asked whether the governments regarded the present high level of birth rates as satisfactory, only four replies were 'Yes' and one (Malawi) qualified the answer immediately with the statement that it was hoped that the birth rate would not rise any further. Three (Tanzania, Zambia, Sierra Leone) would in fact like a higher birth rate, but are not certain about what the present level is. Tanzania and Sierra Leone share hopes that the more intensive settlement of some areas will assist economic development.

Three governments (Mauritius, Rhodesia, Nigeria) now desire lower levels of fertility, all having adopted such viewpoints within comparatively recent times, while a fourth government (Kenya) appears to be moving towards a similar position. (Note: later in 1966 Kenya adopted a national family planning programme, thus making it the first sub-Saharan country to do so.) About two-thirds of the population of Commonwealth Africa live within these four territories. In Mauritius, the government has diagnosed 'overpopulation' as one of its chief socio-economic problems and, following a pilot scheme which began as early as 1963, is now subsidizing voluntary family planning schemes. It might be noted that in Mauritius, perhaps alone of the countries examined in this paper, the birth rate has already begun to decline. Between 1957 and 1964 it fell from 42·6 per 1,000 to 38·1, but, because of an equal drop in the death rate, natural increase remained at 3·0 per cent per annum.

CONTRACEPTION

In all Commonwealth countries, unlike some non-Commonwealth countries such as for instance Somalia, the practice of contraception is legal. In all Commonwealth countries, with one possible exception, the public advocacy of contraception is legal. In some, the mass media have not yet been used in this way, and in one or two it has to date 'not been officially encouraged'. But some publicity, such as that featured in the press and radio of Lagos, has been quite striking.

In all Commonwealth countries, unlike large areas of Francophone Africa, the import of contraceptives is legal, although it is possible that such materials would have to compete with other desired goods for import licences. Similarly, their manufacture is legal, although it does not appear that this is as yet taking place anywhere. In some countries import duty is charged. The level in Rhodesia, for instance, is at present 15 per cent. In all Commonwealth countries the sale of contraceptives is legal. In most, but apparently not all, medical prescriptions are required for the purchase of oral contraceptives. Similarly, free or subsidized distribution through family planning associations, private or government hospitals or other outlets is legal in all countries. The use of dispensaries in government hospitals as an outlet for contraceptives is in fact on the increase.

STERILIZATION AND ABORTION

In all Commonwealth countries operations to induce sterility are legal. Operations on females are far more common than are those on males. In some countries a medical reason must be given, but in others social grounds are sufficient. In some countries only the consent of the patient is needed, while in others the spouse's permission must also be obtained. In most countries the decision can be made by a single doctor, but in Botswana agreement must be sought from a panel of doctors. Invariably, the operation must be performed by a medically qualified person.

In spite of some conflict in the replies to the question on abortion, it does appear that the legal position of abortion in all Commonwealth countries is still the same as in Britain. A decision must be made by more than one doctor that the termination of a pregnancy is necessary to protect either the life or health of the woman concerned. There is little evidence that these conditions are being relaxed or more broadly interpreted in any African Commonwealth countries, and legal abortions are not very common. In all countries there is some illegal abortion, but official knowledge of the subject is slight, and estimates of the level of illegal abortion vary widely. All that can be said is that it is not at present on such a scale as to be regarded as a major demographic phenomenon. Some illegal abortions are performed by qualified doctors, but undoubtedly the greater number in villages by women using traditional methods. A survey in the economically better-off suburbs of Ghana's major towns showed that between a third and a half of respondents thought that abortion was quite common in Ghana.[5] This is supported by government statements condemning the practice and threatening to increase the penalties for infringement of the law.

Population Control

FAMILY PLANNING SERVICES

Although family planning services are by no means commonplace as yet in most of Commonwealth Africa, such services already have something of a history stretching back in some cases almost a decade.

> 'The first successful attempts to found family planning movements or to establish clinics occurred in Rhodesia in 1955, Uganda in 1956, Kenya in 1957, Mauritius in 1957, Nigeria in 1958 and Sierra Leone in 1959.
>
> However, a perceptible quickening of activity occurred around 1964. In that year the Family Planning Council of Nigeria was formed and began to recruit a full-time organizer and other staff for an expanded clinic programme. The Kenya and Uganda movements began to expand and the Mauritius Government decided to co-operate in the encouragement of the setting-up of clinics. The use of IUCDs (intra-uterine contraceptive devices) was begun by many clinics.
>
> By mid-1965 the position appeared to be this. . . . In Rhodesia there were several clinics in the capital, Salisbury, and others were found in major towns. Kenya had twenty-one clinics, of which fourteen were in the capital, Nairobi. Uganda had three clinics in the capital, Kampala, but these were supplemented by four African home visitors. In Nigeria there were four clinics in the capital, Lagos, and one in the second town of the country, Ibadan. In Sierra Leone there was still only one clinic, attached to the Freetown Maternity Hospital, but midwives from upcountry were trained in contraceptive methods during special courses. In Liberia . . . a Family Planning Association was based on the Monrovia Maternity Hospital and the Director of Nursing provided both advice and contraceptive materials. . . . In Zambia two family planning clinics were being assisted by the Rhodesian Family Planning Association. It should also be remarked that some of the Protestant missions in tropical Africa have shown an increased interest in providing information about family planning or allowing the establishment of clinics in conjunction with missions or mission hospitals. Beyond the continental coast, family planning clinics are now being opened in numbers in Mauritius, where the Government has begun subsidizing two family planning organizations, and the first one was established on the Seychelles during the year.
>
> Except . . . in Mauritius, the clinics still cater particularly for urban population, often with by far the most provision for the inhabitants of the capital.'[6]

In Ghana, information about family planning has in the past been provided in two or three centres as part of a larger programme of activities by voluntary associations, and there did seem to be a possibility that the main hospital in the capital, Accra, might become a source of such information.

Thus, in most African Commonwealth countries there are some family planning clinics. Many receive assistance and encouragement from persons employed in government health services and sometimes the use of facilities. In a couple of the small territories assistance is given directly through the government health system, but this has not yet occurred in the larger, independent countries. However, in four or five countries (Nigeria, Mauritius, Rhodesia, Botswana, and apparently to some extent Kenya) some governmental assistance is being given to private or semi-private clinic systems, although it should be noted that in Lagos the administering agency can largely be identified with the city administration. In Mauritius the Government is supplying a substantial subsidy not only to a traditional-type family planning association, but also to the Action Familiale which specializes in licit Catholic methods.

It might be noted that the governmental provision of medical facilities, treatment and to a less extent medical supplies is widely assumed in independent African countries, especially in the case of rural population. If a greater demand for family planning services becomes established, it is likely that there will be pressure for the services to be provided through government hospital clinics and rural health services and for the contraceptive supplies to be made available either free or subsidized to a considerable extent.

THE QUESTION OF ASSISTANCE IN POPULATION CONTROL

In much of Africa such services as those connected with health receive a considerable amount of external technical and other assistance. It seemed possible that in some parts of tropical Africa family planning schemes might expand in the way that has occurred in parts of Asia and North Africa, and thus it appeared logical to inquire about the sources of aid for either governmental or private programmes which appeared to be acceptable in various countries.

Of the eleven Commonwealth countries or territories included in the survey, six replied that they would not be opposed to governmental schemes receiving help from an international agency (presumably WHO) for the provision of family planning services, and five gave answers ranging from the statement that the government had as yet given no thought to the matter to the observation that the government did not at present intend to introduce family planning. In no case did any country state that it was fundamentally opposed to the idea of such aid. The same pattern of answers emerged in the case of assistance to private family planning schemes, with the exception of one territory where it was felt that the government would probably be opposed.

Answers followed the same pattern when a question was asked about assistance from a foreign government for a governmental scheme, although in one case the qualification was added that it depended on which government. Rather surprisingly, the answers were also much the same when the possibility of assistance from a foreign government for a private scheme was raised. When asked about aid for private schemes, in five countries this would be unlikely to be opposed, in five the question was not thought to be relevant at the time when it was asked, and in one there would probably be opposition.

In the case of assistance from an external private organization, such as a Foundation, once again six would probably not be opposed, one probably would, and five did not consider it relevant at the time.

In general terms, the survey findings and other information can be summarized as follows. At the beginning of 1965, about two-thirds of the people of Commonwealth Africa lived in countries where the governments would probably be prepared to receive themselves or allow private organizations to receive some form of external assistance for extending family planning services (i.e. Nigeria, Mauritius, Rhodesia, Sierra Leone, Gambia and Botswana). Another sixth lived in countries where the position was far from clear, and where the governments may well have been in transition to the outlook of those described above (i.e. Kenya and Zambia—possibly Uganda would also be found here). A further sixth were to be found in countries which do not particularly favour the expansion of family planning at this time (i.e. Tanzania, Malawi and Lesotho—perhaps Ghana would be found here).

EXPERIENCE WITH POPULATION CONTROL IN COMMONWEALTH AFRICA

In another paper an attempt was made to document the history and evaluate the success of several family planning schemes in this area.[7] No attempt will be made to repeat that exercise here, but some of the findings will be quoted. The first is that in no country in the area has the use of family planning facilities yet been extensive enough to cause any appreciable change in the birth rate or the volume of natural increase. The second is that in some countries the foundation has already been laid for an extension of services which might have an appreciable effect. The following is a summary of some of the experience of existing family planning schemes.

> 'The bottlenecks to more rapid expansion in order of stated importance were defined as lack of finance, shortage of trained personnel, insufficient publicity and unsureness of governmental support. Also listed were the logistics of supplying remote and rural areas, rural illiteracy, the suspicion of those holding more traditional attitudes and some Catholic opposition. On the latter point, however, it might be pointed out that a survey among economically better-off urban families in Ghana showed little significant association between willingness to use family planning clinics and the religion of either husband or wife.[8] Furthermore, in Mauritius, the Catholic Church is accepting government aid for an organization encouraging family limitation by approved methods.
>
> When asked what they would do differently if they were to start their family planning movements over again, the most common answer received from those who had worked to establish these movements was that they would try much harder to secure governmental support at every stage in the project. In addition they stated that they would make attempts at an earlier stage to overcome each of the bottlenecks listed above.'[9]

Conclusion

The terminology used in the discussion of population policy can easily give rise to emotional reactions. It might be appropriate, therefore, at this point in this attempt to summarize past and possible future governmental policies and actions to point out what has been meant by the term, 'population control'. As used here it has simply meant any governmental action which might affect in any way population size or growth rates. Thus migration and health policies both fall under this heading. So does the provision of family planning facilities for those who wish to make use of them. It is difficult to imagine any direction in such matters, except possibly in the refusal to allow the provision of such facilities, in the way in which governments must dictate with regard to certain other social and economic matters.

In the majority of African Commonwealth countries there is little of the belief in 'underpopulation' that is a feature of some other parts of the continent. Part of the reason is simply that this group of countries is not sparsely settled. In 1963 they contained over a third of the continent's population on about a seventh of its area, and with an average population density of over 60 persons per square mile were approximately level with the average for the whole world.

Many governments in the area are giving some thoughts to questions of migration regulation. Some are worried about such financial matters as the effect upon foreign exchange holdings of the remittance of earnings by migrants. Others hope to encourage at least the temporary immigration of those with skills and to discourage the permanent emigration of trained persons.

In all countries there is a determination to continue to spend considerable sums on health programmes designed to reduce sickness and to lower the death rates. There is no similar consensus about birth rates, although the majority of governments are apprehensive about present high fertility levels and hope that some decline will occur. In all countries contraceptives are legally sold, and in most the provision of family planning facilities is not discouraged. In fact there has been within the last two years a marked increase in governmental willingness to assist with the provision of these facilities. Nor would the majority of governments resent external aid assisting the spread of family planning services.

The majority of governments are becoming increasingly apprehensive of certain aspects of rapid population growth, namely the implications for investment and the economically inefficient age structure of such populations, and many development plans are likely to echo the words already quoted from the Ghana Plan.

Footnotes

1. I.e. those, apart from the Republic of South Africa, where university education is in English.
2. J. C. CALDWELL, 'Africa', *Family Planning and Population Programs: A Review of World Developments* (The Proceedings of the International Conference on Family Planning Programs, August, 1965), Chicago, 1966, p. 166.
3. *Ibid.*, p. 167.
4. Ghana, *Seven-Year Development Plan. 1963/64 to 1969/70*, Office of the Planning Commission, Accra, 1964, p. 8.
5. J. C. CALDWELL, 'Family Formation and Limitation in Ghana: A Study of the Residents of Economically Superior Urban Areas', *Family Planning and Population Programmes*, *op. cit.*, p. 611.
6. J. C. CALDWELL, 'Africa', *op. cit.*, pp. 169–170. In this paper a more detailed analysis of the provisions of family planning facilities has been made than is possible here.
7. *Ibid.*, pp. 163–181.
8. J. C. CALDWELL, 'Family Formation and Limitation in Ghana', *op. cit.*, p. 609; ——, *Population Growth and Family Change in Africa: the Ghanaian Urban Elite*, Australian National University Press, Canberra, 1968.
9. J. C. CALDWELL, 'Africa', *op. cit.*, p. 178.

38 Public health priorities and population pressure in developing countries

Adetokunbo O. Lucas

Department of Preventive and Social Medicine, University of Ibadan, Nigeria

'The rapid increase in the population of many developing nations has been attributed largely to the successful application of modern public health measures. The dramatic reduction in death rates has led to a rapid and continuing growth of population. There is increasing concern about the "population explosion"; it is feared that it will slow down the pace of economic development and put great strains on the limited resources of these nations, making it impossible for the people to take full advantage of development in education, industry and technology.'[1] This concern has stimulated considerable interest in the problem of population control; the main approach has been through the study of fertility and methods of controlling it. The broad aim is to check the rapid growth of the population by a lowering of the birth rates. Population control by means of a high death rate is not acceptable ethically or politically. It follows, therefore, that the efforts to reduce disease and death must continue unabated. The purpose of this paper is to discuss public health work against the background of the population problem and to examine the considerations by which health planners decide their order of priorities.

What Should be Tackled First?

In developing countries, the public health authorities are faced by many challenging problems which demand urgent action. They have to deal with a large amount of disease in the community, high morbidity and mortality rates, usually with totally inadequate resources. It is therefore always necessary to decide which problems can be tackled first, what proportion of available resources must be devoted to different needs, and what emphasis must be laid at each stage on the different services to the community. Not infrequently, orderly development is interrupted by the outbreak of widespread epidemics and natural disasters.

WOMEN AND CHILDREN FIRST

Although no strict rules can be laid down for all developing countries, there are certain basic patterns of morbidity and mortality that suggest possible approaches to the problem. In most of these countries the characteristic picture is of high mortality rates amongst children. In some parts of West Africa, about half of the children born die before their fifth birthday. The mortality rate in this age group is '40 times higher than the comparable rates among children of the same age in affluent countries.'[2] Another common feature is the high frequency of maternal morbidity and mortality. It is therefore logical to regard the services for children and pregnant women as among the priorities in these communities. With good child health services, it is hoped that, not only would death rates fall, but that the children who survive would grow into healthy and fit adults. Furthermore, children under 14 years of age constitute about 50 per cent of the population in many of these countries and this is further justification for giving special attention to this group.[3] The cultural view of the Western world 'Women and children first', must not be exaggerated to mean 'women and children alone'. However, arguments that favour the policy of giving high priority to the health of children and pregnant women are unassailable. What needs to be determined is the balance between the needs of this group and those of the rest of the community. In order to appreciate this problem one could examine the extreme case in which all the health resources were devoted to the care of pregnant women and children. The expected result in this hypothetical case would be a rapid decline in the child death rate and an improvement in the health of pregnant women. The population would increase mostly because more children survived. There would be little or no immediate effect on the health of the most economically productive group, adult males and of women outside the childbearing age group. The initial effect would be to increase the number of consumers without increasing the number or the ability of the producers within the community. This trend would aggravate the effects of population growth by increasing the proportion of dependents in the community. This effect would be particularly undesirable in areas where food shortage is a constant threat, and unless some means can be found to increase supplies, the advantages gained from controlling certain childhood diseases might be wiped out if they were to be succeeded by malnutrition and famine. With increasing relative shortage of other resources, such as housing, schooling and employment, it might prove difficult to sustain the initial gain that accompanied the introduction of health measures. It follows, therefore, that the development of health resources should be on the basis of a balanced programme; it should be balanced externally with development in other fields—economic, industrial and agricultural—and also balanced internally, providing services to meet the needs of all sections of the community.

The Practical Implications

Although it is unlikely that any government would set up the type of service that is described above, certain major projects could have this net effect. It would seem desirable that the expected benefit from each major project should be examined in terms of its effects on different sections of the population. An interesting example is the problem of malaria in the tropical rain-forest belt. In these areas, malaria is holoendemic, the characteristic picture being of severe morbidity and high mortality in childhood, with a high degree of immunity in the adult indigenous population excepting pregnant women. An interesting study was carried out by Schofield and his colleagues in such an area in New Guinea.[4] They compared two districts, in only one of which they had achieved the control of malaria. They observed that the control of malaria had benefited children of all ages, that there was significant but sub-optimal improvement in the indices which they measured in women, but that there was little effect on adult men. They concluded that the economic capacity of the community had not been improved by malaria control. Because of the high mortality in childhood and in pregnancy, it is highly desirable to control malaria in such an area. In order to produce a lasting improvement in the welfare of that community it is necessary to produce a comparable advance in the economic capacity of the community.

THE HEALTH OF THE ECONOMICALLY PRODUCTIVE GROUP

The toll of disease in the adult population may not be in such dramatic form as among children. Apart from such epidemic diseases as smallpox, meningococcal meningitis and cholera, the usual pattern is of high prevalence of endemic diseases, which produce chronic disability, high sickness absence rates from work, and low productive efficiency. The health needs of the adult community cannot, therefore, be assessed accurately in terms of deaths or severe acute illnesses. The evaluation must be made from a study of morbidity as well as mortality data. The former should include the occurrence of clinical illness which the patient is aware of, as well as subclinical disease which may not be so clearly apparent. In tropical Africa, there is a high frequency of various parasitic infections, some of which are perhaps more dramatic than deadly. The occurrence of severe disability from these infections is also well known.[5] For example, heavy hookworm infection is associated with severe anaemia; guinea worm infection may prejudice a year's crop if the farmers are laid up during the harvest season by leg ulcers and abscesses; pulmonary tuberculosis is recognized as a prominent cause of disability in many developing countries.

Often it is optimistically stated that with general development all these problems would disappear. This is true of some of these infections which would become less prominent with increasing economic advancement. On the other hand others become aggravated, at least initially, by such modernization. Thus, for example, increasing urbanization has accentuated the problem of overcrowding in many African cities. The introduction of irrigation schemes and the building of dams have increased the risk of schistosomal infections in some parts of the world. It is particularly important when the occurrence of disease itself prejudices economic and industrial advancement. Large industrial companies and government projects usually include the provision of medical services for their workers, but in many developing nations these cover only a small proportion of the adult working population. The farmers, the self-employed and those who are working for small companies usually do not have access to such services.

Conclusion

Public health policies in developing countries should aim at the improvement of the health of the whole community. The priorities should be selected largely but not exclusively by reference to groups at special risk (children and pregnant women). The aim should be both to reduce the mortality rate in the high risk group and to diminish morbidity in the economically active group. Such a balanced policy would ensure that some of the strain that is produced by population growth is offset by the increased economic capacity of the adult population.

Footnotes

1. J. M. STYCOS, 'The outlook for World Population', *Science*, Vol. 146, 1964, pp. 1435–40.
2. Editorial, 'Pre-school Protection Programme', *Journal of Tropical Paediatrics and African Child Health*, Vol. 9, 1964, pp. 65–66.
3. CICELY D. WILLIAMS, 'Maternal and Child Health Services in Developing Countries', *Lancet*, 1964, No. 1, p. 345.
4. F. D. SCHOFIELD, A. D. PARKINSON, and A. KELLY, 'Changes in Haemoglobin Values and Hepatosplenomegaly produced by Control of holoendemic Malaria', *British Medical Journal*, 1964, No. 1, pp. 587–91.
5. H. M. GILLES, *Akufo: An Environmental study of a Nigerian Village Community*, Ibadan University Press, 1964.

39 A demographic note on marriage, family and family growth in Lagos, Nigeria

P. O. Ohadike

Department of Geography, University of Ibadan, Nigeria

The following is a summary of certain demographic information related to family formation in Lagos, Nigeria. The facts presented were gathered by a small random sample survey of currently married African women of all sections and classes domiciled within the municipal area. The survey was undertaken between March and August 1964. A sampling fraction of 1 in 32 houses was employed, and 596 women were interviewed, 44·3 per cent of whom were from Lagos Island, 14·9 per cent from Ebute-Metta (East and West), 9·1 per cent from Yaba, 21·0 per cent from Suru-Lere and Idi-Oro, 4·0 per cent from Ikoyi and 6·7 per cent from Apapa and surrounding districts. The survey questionnaire, administered by 15 trained interviewers of the Federal Office of Statistics, Lagos, sought rather extensive information on the interrelations between levels of fertility and socio-economic background characteristics, and attempted an assessment of variations in attitudes towards family size and family planning. However, the focus of this paper will be confined to some aspects of marriage, family, fertility patterns and differentials.

Summary Description of the Characteristics of the Sample

The age structure of the women interviewed showed that 65·3 per cent were aged 15–34 years, another 21·1 per cent between 35 and 44 years, and only 13·6 per cent over 45 years of age. They came from all the Regions of Nigeria, and only 1·2 per cent were from places outside the country, principally from the nearby West African territories of Ghana and Dahomey. Most respondents and their husbands were either Christians or Moslems, 16·5 per cent being Catholics, 43·7 per cent Protestants and 37·2 per cent Moslems. Adherents of traditional religions made up the remaining 2·6 per cent of the sample.

The traditional indifference to the education of girls in most Nigerian tribes is reflected in the imbalance between the educational level reached by respondents and their husbands. A little less than half (47·5 per cent) of wives, as against 20 per cent of husbands, had never been to school. Among the wives, the largest percentage of the educated (62·6 per cent) had primary education, 24·3 per cent had secondary education, 7·7 per cent had attended Modern schools, and only 4·5 per cent had received University and/or professional training. Of the educated husbands, 9·4 per cent claimed to have had University and/or professional education, 45·1 per cent reached the secondary school level, 42·3 per cent to the primary level, and only 0·4 per cent attained the Modern school level. Surprisingly, only 1 per cent of educated wives and 2·7 per cent of educated husbands claimed to have received Arabic education, in spite of the significantly large Moslem representation in the sample. The education of both wives and husbands was significantly correlated with age as well as religious membership.

Over half the wives (51·3 per cent) claimed they were housewives and had no other jobs. Of the presently occupied wives, 62·8 per cent were self-employed traders, almost half of whom were polygynously married, 14·1 per cent were professional workers (mainly teachers and nurses), 10·7 per cent were office clerks, typists, cashiers and saleswomen, and 8·3 per cent were craftswomen mainly in dressmaking and weaving trades. Husbands were occupationally more heterogeneously distributed than wives. Only 4 per cent of the husbands were recorded as jobless, and of the 24 husbands in this category, 15 proved to be retired old men. Of all employed husbands, 10·3 per cent and 8·7 per cent were respectively in professional and administrative jobs, 29·1 per cent were clerical workers of some sort, 22·9 per cent were artisans and craftsmen, and 13·5 per cent were traders and small businessmen. Farmers and fishermen were the least represented, forming only 2·6 per cent, whereas 4·7 per cent and 8·0 per cent were transport/communication workers and persons in the labouring and services group respectively. A significant association between type of work and age on the one hand and education on the other was observed. In general, where a particular type of job required some technical skill and/or educational training, the bulk of the wives and husbands engaged in them were drawn from the younger generation.

There existed a marked relationship between socio-economic status, living conditions and educational attainment. The state of housing suggested severe overcrowding. Over half of the households lived in one room, and the *per capita* rate of accommodation ranged from over two rooms per household in the better-off districts of Ikoyi and Apapa to just a little over one room in Lagos Island, which suffers most from this congestion. The average for the whole sample was 3·7 persons per room. The better educated had more living space and indeed more salubrious surroundings. Monthly rent ranged remarkably from £1 5*s* to £5 per room, while the overall average per room was approximately £3 3*s*.

Factors and Differences in Marriage

In this section, type of marriage and age at marriage will be examined against the background of their incidence among different socio-economic groups. The marriage records of respondents showed that over six-sevenths (86·4 per cent) were enjoying their first marriages, and very few of those with more than one marriage had possessed more than one other husband previously. The rate for single, monogamous marriages for wives is quite high, and if comparisons are not spurious, it is higher than any published one in West Africa known to the writer. However, it should be noted that J. C. Caldwell's most recent study of economically superior urban areas in Ghana maintained that 'about three-quarters of recorded marriages were first marriages'.[1] Studies in Ghana and the Cameroons, where larger proportions of rural population were involved, show rates far lower than the above.[2] In the sample, over three-quarters of respondents with more than one marriage indicated that their former unions ended by either divorce or separation, while the rest (22·2 per cent) claimed widowhood. The occurrence of unions subsequent to the first was highest for wives of Moslem and traditional faith and least for Catholics.

POLYGYNY

The noticeable incidence of polygyny, in such a non-agricultural urban setting as Lagos, illustrates the fact that for many people it is an expression of a way of life with deeply embedded religious and cultural obligation. There is no evidence in the sample to suggest the absence of polygyny among any particular social group. But there is ample indication that the institution, if it is not already doing so, will in the near future decline, particularly in the urban areas. One source of evidence is the differential incidence of marriage types within social groups showing the decline of the practice with continuing social change. Social status, measured by the quality of residence, education, and occupation, were negatively correlated with the occurrence of polygyny. The most potent single factor making for change had been education, which, considering the amount of progress in this direction, makes one suspect a

Table 1

Lagos: Incidence of Polygyny by Social and Economic Classes

Characteristics	Type of marriage	
	Monogamy	Polygyny
ALL RESPONDENTS (wives)	68·6	31·4
Residence		
High	83·8	16·2
Middle	63·9	36·1
Low	67·3	32·7
Age of Wife		
15–24	82·1	17·9
25–34	72·5	27·5
35–44	61·9	38·1
45+	43·2	56·8
Age of Husband		
15–24	92·3	7·7
25–34	87·3	12·7
35–44	65·0	35·0
45+	49·7	50·3
Education of Wife		
University and Professional	100·0	—
Secondary School	92·1	7·9
Primary and Others	72·6	27·4
None	57·5	42·4
Education of Husband		
University and Professional	95·6	4·4
Secondary School	71·6	28·4
Primary and Others	62·7	37·3
None	63·9	36·1
Occupation of Husband		
Professional and Administrative	82·6	17·4
Clerical and Allied	75·4	24·6
Traders and Small	37·7	62·3
Businessmen	37·7	62·3
Artisans and Craftsmen	65·2	34·8
Unskilled	68·9	31·1
No Occupation	79·2	20·8
Religion of Wife		
Catholics	82·7	17·3
Protestants	76·7	23·3
Moslems	52·8	47·2
Traditional	62·5	37·5
Total Years Married		
0–9	83·6	16·4
10–19	64·4	35·6
20+	54·1	45·9

Note: Figures are percentages of total marriages in each category.

further decline. As would be expected from their religion, Moslem and traditional worshippers exhibited a higher rate of polygynous marriages, though some 17·3 per cent of Catholics and 23·3 per cent of Protestants were also polygynously married. A positive association was noted between age and total number of years married on the one hand and polygyny on the other; the older and the longer married respondents were more involved.

Nevertheless, in view of attitudes expressed towards polygyny, one should not be too certain of the trend suggested above. There were still many women, even among those married to monogamists, who did not disapprove of polygyny. In this survey, about a third of the women interviewed approved of polygyny, the degree of approval varying positively with age and negatively with education. More Moslems and traditional believers favoured it, but, significantly enough, some 17·3 per cent Catholics and 24·1 Protestants were also in favour. The commonest reason given by 57·1 per cent of these women, was the provision of social, domestic and economic assistance in the household, while another 20·7 per cent spoke of making the family large or ensuring that the husband had children by some means, in the case of the barrenness of the first wife. Only 3 per cent maintained that the system alleviates prostitution by increasing the chance for women to get married. Another 11·6 per cent stated that custom and religion approved of it. Thus, although over two-thirds of women were against polygyny, and evidence of its decline existed, there will probably continue to be a sizeable minority support for the institution. It could be seen that reasons for favouring polygyny have their roots in tradition, which dies hard. Christianity has only whittled down its incidence but has failed to ban it altogether.

AGE AT MARRIAGE

The significance of the biological fact of reproductive age is linked with the equally important social fact of age at marriage. Fecundity is believed to be at its highest immediately after physical maturity; deferring child-birth is associated with a mounting impairment of physiological efficiency.[3] The average menarchial age for Nigerian girls is about 14 years, and, in one study by Tanner and his associates, the range within which 95 per cent experienced menarche was 11·2 to 17·0 years.[4] If getting married were exclusively a physiological function, one would expect the mean age at marriage to gravitate around the mean for maturity. But this is rarely the case, as marriage is also a function of various other social factors. In fact, in accordance with previous expert opinion, age at marriage, contrary to popular uninformed assessment, is fairly high in Lagos.[5] In this study the average age at first marriage was 19·8 years for wives and had been, at that time, 28·1 years for husbands. Thus, husbands married much later, but the rather striking discrepancy in the mean age difference quoted could be explained by the presence of polygynous marriages and probably the fact that, owing to the higher expectation of living standards and the difficulty of accumulating enough money to meet marriage and wedding expenses,[6] the age at marriage must have been on the increase for men, but probably not to a comparable degree for women. Beside the fact that husbands were more educated than wives, and needed greater economic security to be able to provide for the family, there was the added factor of customarily later male entrance into marriage.

However, available indications point to a narrowing of the gap in age between spouses at marriage. It has been indicated above that polygyny is on the decline, and with this will probably come a decrease in spousal age difference. As women become increasingly educated, a similar trend may follow. For instance, the spousal age difference at marriage by education of wife as revealed in this study, showed a negative association ranging from an average of 5·3 years for University and professionally educated wives, to 8·7 years for those with no schooling. But, perhaps the clearest indication from the point of view of this survey, as illustrated in Table 2, was that, generally, women interviewed, of all social levels, thought that the ideal age for marriage should be higher than their actual age at marriage. This of course presumes that the already high male age at marriage does not increase much higher than observed. The overall average ideal age was 21·4 years as against the wives' actual age of 19·8 years. When choosing an ideal age for marriage, many women, particularly the educated, thought that females should reach their majority in age and be socially, educationally and economically equipped for married life.

Both actual and ideal age at marriage, as can be seen from Table 2, showed a considerable variation between social and economic groups. Age at marriage may have declined. In 1921 the Rev. Samuel Johnson maintained that Yoruba men 'were seldom married before the age of thirty and the young women not before twenty.'[7] This is plainly no longer the case. A 50-year-old respondent from Ijebu, interviewed in central Lagos, blamed modern civilization for the decline in marriage age. It is

Table 2

Lagos: Distribution of Mean Age at Marriage by Socio-economic Characteristics

Socio-economic characteristics	Age at marriage			
	Actual		Ideal	
	Number of respondents	Mean	Number of respondents	Mean
TOTAL (Wives)	590	19·8	589	21·4
(Husbands)	587	28·1	—	—
Wife's Present Age [Years]				
15–24	145	17·1	141	19·3
25–34	241	20·2	241	21·8
35–44	124	20·9	126	22·3
45+	80	21·6	81	22·4
Education of Wife				
University and Professional	14	25·2	14	24·5
Secondary School	76	22·4	76	22·9
Primary and Others	222	18·9	221	21·3
None	278	19·5	278	20·8
Residence before Marriage				
Non-City	251	18·9	254	20·7
City	339	20·4	335	21·9
Wife's Religion				
Catholics	103	19·4	104	20·4
Protestants	255	20·1	254	21·9
Moslems	216	19·6	215	21·3
Traditional	16	18·9	16	20·8
Wife's Occupation				
None	301	19·0	302	20·9
White Collar	73	23·1	73	23·3
Traders	181	19·6	179	21·3
Crafts and Others	35	20·8	35	22·2

possible that a trend for younger marriages is underway. Women between 15 and 24 years of age had a mean age at first marriage of 17·1 years. While this might be expected, it was more significant that the average for subsequent age groups increased progressively until it reached 21·6 years for those 45 years and over. Women resident in the city for most of the five years before marriage married later than non-city women. Among educated groups, the relationship was positive, higher educational attainment being accompanied by higher average age at marriage. Traditional worshippers had the lowest average of 18·9 years followed closely by Moslems and Catholics. Protestants shared the highest average of 20·1 years. Occupational variations reflected significantly the differences in educational attainment, showing that white collar workers had the highest average of 23·1 years and wives not working the lowest of 19·0 years. Craftswomen and traders had an average of 20·8 and 19·6 years respectively. As can be seen from Table 2, the mean differences in ideal age at marriage exhibited a similar pattern as that outlined for the actual ages at marriage, though generally the averages were higher and hence, if present attitudes could influence future actions, it might be expected that average age at marriage would increase.

The Family

ATTITUDES

For psychological, social or economic reasons, considerable numbers of children are wanted and are cherished by most Nigerians. The official crude birth rate in Lagos rose from 32·9 in 1940 to 60·2 in 1960.[8] The explanation may be partly better health, but it would appear that this apparent vast increase must be explained largely in terms of better statistics. A crude birth rate of the latter magnitude, if it persists, suggests completed family size of over seven children judging from the experiences of populations with comparable crude rates.

Although a considerable number of respondents (48·0 per cent) declared categorically that the possession of many children is not advantageous, citing the economic as well as diverse social drawbacks involved, it transpired that very few of the respondents shared the small family ideal. Only 10·1 per cent thought that three to four children were ideal for a family, a substantial 39·2 per cent chose five to six children, while another 45·3 per cent chose more than six children. Some 4·4 per cent retorted that Providence alone could determine the ideal. Thus, as can be seen from Table 3, the average ideal number of children for all respondents was 6·7 children.

But, high as the overall average may be, stratification of respondents into groups of similar social and economic characteristics revealed the existence of interesting variations, which inevitably emphasize more the overriding influence of age and particularly education as associated determinants of status categories and therefore of accompanying group attitudes in rapidly changing societies. What might be regarded as a small family-ideal of four or five children, was expressed only by wives who had, or whose husbands had, University and/or professional education. Those wives with secondary education had an average ideal of 5·4 children; those with primary school education and those who went to Modern school had 6·4 and those with no schooling 7·5 children. A similar negative association was shown in terms of husband's education. The youngest wives had the lowest average ideal of about six children, and this increased with age, until those 45 years and over desired an average of 7·2. Classification by occupation, type of residence, accommodation and monthly living expenses showed that the better-off sections had the lowest average ideal size. In religious terms, Catholics and Protestants were significantly alike with averages of 6·5 and 6·4 respectively. They were, however, lower than either Moslems with 7·3, or traditional worshippers with 6·8. Polygynously married wives, who incidentally were less educated and included a smaller proportion of Christians, gave a higher average ideal size than their monogamously married counterparts.

Table 3

Lagos: Mean Ideal Number of Children by Socio-economic Characteristics

Characteristics	Number of wives	Average ideal
TOTAL WIVES	564	6·7
Ages of Wives		
15–24	142	6·3
25–34	228	6·5
35–44	118	7·2
45+	76	7·2
Education of Wives		
University and Professional	14	4·2
Secondary	72	5·4
Primary and Others	215	6·4
None	263	7·5
Education of Husbands		
University and Professional	44	4·8
Secondary	205	6·2
Primary and Others	206	7·0
None	109	7·8
Wife's Occupation		
White Collar	72	5·2
Traders	164	7·1
Artisans	26	6·5
Unskilled	9	6·6
No Occupation	293	6·9
Occupation of Husband		
White Collar	263	6·1
Traders	75	7·2
Artisans	146	7·1
Unskilled	58	7·4
No Occupation	22	7·1
Rooms Occupied		
1 room	208	7·1
2 rooms	146	6·5
3 rooms and over	110	5·9
Type of Marriage		
Monogamous	393	6·4
Polygynous	171	7·3
Quality of Residence		
(a) High Class	79	5·6
(b) Middle Class	147	6·2
(c) Lower Class	338	7·2
Religion of Wives		
Catholics	102	6·5
Protestants	247	6·4
Moslems	200	7·3
Traditional	15	6·8
Monthly Living Expenses		
0–199 Shillings	246	7·1
200–399 Shillings	199	6·7
400+ Shillings	119	6·1

The presence of this almost universal high ideal family size is accompanied by an equally general lack of interest of wives in determining family size. Only a little more than one quarter (27·5 per cent) admitted ever discussing this with their husbands, and here again the influence of age and education is paramount. The younger and the more educated, the higher the proportion who ever discussed the subject. One-fifth of those who never discussed it thought it was unnecessary or unimportant; another one-sixth maintained that custom and tradition proscribed such discussion; religious prohibitions were given by another fifth, and just over one-tenth (13·7 per cent) had never thought of it, while another tenth feared their husbands would not welcome such discussions. There were, however, some 8·3 per cent of the younger wives who felt that it was not yet time for such discussions because they were recently married or had not had enough children.

ACTUAL FERTILITY PATTERN AND DIFFERENCES

In communities practising little contraception, fertility differences such as are found in highly developed societies are seldom easily discernible. Probably this is because observed differences are associated mainly with the effects of what might be regarded as intractable determinants of natality. Deliberately planned determinants that have proved effective, particularly in places of recent fertility decline, are, to say the least, hardly ever used within wedlock. Nearly two-thirds of respondents interviewed denied knowledge of any contraceptive method, and only 9·2 per cent admitted that they ever used any method, this being less than a quarter of the third who knew any method. The single commonest known method was periodical abstinence or avoidance. Thus, in terms of usage and effectiveness of method, the respondents of this survey were largely non-practisers of contraception.

The average number of children ever born alive to respondents was exactly 4·0 and the average number of those still alive was 3·2. Including reported conceptions that did not reach their term, the average number of pregnancies was 4·3 per woman. Of the 596 women, only 29 had never been pregnant, and of 46, including the never pregnant, who had no living children, six were in that condition because all those they had borne were dead. Evidence of infertility for these presently married wives is hard to establish considering that 84·2 per cent of childless wives had been married for less than four years and some 96·5 per cent of those reporting no pregnancy ever were still in the reproductive age group. If we regard women who were 45 years of age and over as no longer capable of reproduction, then the completed fertility for this group averaged 6·8 children ever born and 5·3 children still alive. This yielded a survival rate of 77·9 per cent, which is considerably higher than that of 66·7 per cent indicated for the same age group in the 1950 census of Lagos.[9] As would be expected, age was very significantly and positively correlated with fertility. Wives between 15 and 34 years of age had an average of nearly three live-births as against six for those 35 years and over. In general, some salient differences in the number of children ever borne were evident among wives of varying demographic and socio-economic characteristics. In the analyses that follow, absolute differences as well as differences within age groups using weighted averages will be discussed with specific references to Table 4.

(a) *Age at Marriage, Maternal Age and Fertility*. Within maternal age groups, there were some slight but notable differences in fertility by age at marriage. Wives in the 15–34 years of age bracket who were married between 10 and 19 years of age, were on the average 24·0 per cent more fertile than those of the same age who were married at 20 or more years. Similarly, those who were 35 years or more, who were married between 10–19 years of age, had a fertility level 5 per cent higher than their counterparts who married when they were 20 or more years. It thus seems that to-

Table 4

Lagos: Mean Number of Children Ever Born by Age of Wives and by Social and Economic Characteristics

Characteristics	Present age of wives						
	15–34		35+		Total		
	Number of wives	Mean births	Number of wives	Mean births	Number of wives	Mean births	Adjusted mean
TOTAL WIVES	389	2·8	207	6·1	596	4·0	—
Age at Marriage							
10–19	216	3·1	72	6·3	288	3·9	4·2
20+	173	2·5	135	6·0	308	4·0	3·7
Total Years Married*							
0–9	255	2·1	1	1·5	256	2·1	1·9
10–19	103	4·6	57	5·2	160	4·8	4·8
20+	1	5·5	97	6·8	98	6·8	5·9
Type of Marriage							
Monogamous	296	2·7	113	6·1	409	3·6	3·9
Polygynous	93	3·3	94	6·1	187	4·7	4·2
Residence							
High	51	2·9	29	5·8	80	3·9	3·9
Middle	104	2·6	54	6·7	158	4·0	4·0
Lower	234	2·9	24	5·9	358	4·0	3·9
Rent Paid							
79 Shillings	158	2·8	83	6·1	241	3·9	3·9
80–159 Shillings	118	2·8	44	6·1	162	3·7	3·9
160+ Shillings	72	2·7	21	6·2	93	3·5	3·9
None	41	3·4	59	6·0	100	4·9	4·3
Rooms Occupied							
1 room	228	2·6	100	5·7	328	3·6	3·7
2 rooms	102	3·1	51	6·6	153	4·3	4·3
3 rooms+	59	3·1	56	6·3	115	4·6	4·2
Monthly Expenses							
199 Shillings	173	2·7	81	5·3	254	3·5	3·6
200–399 Shillings	142	3·0	70	6·8	212	4·2	4·3
400+ Shillings	74	3·0	55	6·3	129	4·4	4·1
Wife's Education							
Secondary and Over	69	1·8	21	6·4	90	3·3	3·4
Primary and Others	169	2·7	54	6·2	223	3·5	3·9
None	151	3·3	132	6·0	283	4·5	4·2
Husband's Education							
Secondary and Over	183	2·6	77	6·1	260	3·6	3·8
Primary and Others	145	3·0	72	6·2	217	4·0	4·1
None	61	3·3	58	5·9	119	4·6	4·2

* Excludes three women who refused to answer and another 79 who had been married more than once and actual duration of marriage could not be assessed.

Table 4 (*continued*)

Characteristics	Present age of wives						
	15–34		35+		Total		
	Number of wives	Mean births	Number of wives	Mean births	Number of wives	Mean births	Adjusted mean
Wife's Occupation							
White Collar	55	2·1	18	6·5	73	3·2	3·6
Traders	97	3·4	85	6·1	182	4·7	4·3
Craftswomen	17	2·7	9	6·2	26	3·9	3·9
Unskilled	1	—	8	6·0	9	5·3	1·8
None	219	2·8	87	5·9	306	3·7	3·9
Husband's Occupation							
White Collar	202	2·6	74	6·0	276	3·5	3·8
Artisans	109	2·9	49	6·0	158	3·9	4·0
Traders	38	3·5	39	6·3	77	4·9	4·5
Unskilled	33	3·1	28	5·7	61	4·3	4·0
None	7	3·5	17	6·8	24	5·8	4·6
Wife's Religion							
Catholic	75	2·8	29	5·9	104	3·6	3·9
Protestants	172	2·7	86	6·1	258	3·9	3·9
Moslems	135	2·9	83	6·1	218	4·1	4·0
Traditional	7	4·1	9	5·5	16	4·6	4·6

wards the end of their reproductive life the initial range of difference between marriage cohorts narrows down.

(b) *Marriage Duration, Maternal Age and Fertility.* Differences in the level of fertility by duration of marriage and by age of wives were evident, and the high and marked relationship both within age groups and for all wives was direct. For the most part, the level of fertility increased with longer duration of marriage from 2·1 children ever born for those married for periods less than nine years, through 4·8 for those married for 10 to 19 years and finally to 6·8 for those whose marriage had lasted for 20 years or more. Weighting did not alter the trend indicated, except that it reduced the fertility of those married for nine years and less to 1·9, and that of those 20 years and over to 5·9.

(c) *Type of Marriage, Maternal Age and Fertility.* There were some observed differences in fertility between women married to monogamists and those married to polygynists. The association, though statistically significant, was only slight and perhaps too much should not be made of it. As a matter of fact, those wives married to polygynists had slightly more children, but this, rather than any other reason, was probably a function rather of the type of marriage than of the age structure and the social circumstances of the respondents in each marriage category.

As can be seen from Table 4, the average for wives who were 35 years or more, was, for both types of marriage, 6·1 children ever born. What might be regarded as a significant difference between wives of the two marriage types, who were less than 35 years old, was associated with the fact that there were more polygynously married wives in the upper limits of the age group, by virtue of which they had more children ever born than their monogamously married compeers who were concentrated nearer to the lower limit. Thus, whereas 45·2 per cent of polygynously married wives below 35 years of age were 30 years or more, only 24·7 per cent of those married to monogamists were of the same age. The effect of this structural age difference came out clearly in weighting the average for each marriage group, thus assuming that they had a similar age structure. This reduced the excess of 1·1 children ever borne by polygynously married wives over those married to monogamists to just 0·3. Considering the greater incidence of illiteracy among wives of polygynists, complemented by the less youthfulness of their age structure, there appears to be little justification for ascribing observed differences to the type of marriage.

(d) *Living Conditions, Maternal Age and Fertility.* Items such as residence, defined by the apparent quality of houses, number of rooms occupied, rent paid and monthly living expenses of respondents were singly cross-classified by maternal age with fertility. Among residential groups, there existed very little overall differences in fertility, and the statistical association between the two variables was not significant. Occupants of higher class residences were only slightly less fertile, in fact 2·6 per cent less, than either middle or lower class occupants. However, weighting by age put the middle class 2·6 per cent above the other two classes. Among rent-paying groups, discounting the effect of maternal age, some slight significant differences in fertility emerged, showing a negative relationship ranging from 3·9 children ever born for the lowest rent-paying group to 3·5 for the highest group. It seemed that the difference by rental status was more impressive. The average fertility for the non-rent-paying group was 25·6 per cent higher than that for the group with the highest fertility among the rent-paying groups (subdivided by rent paid). Even when the averages were weighted, the influence of maternal age, which caused the disappearance of differences within rent-paying categories, was least felt by those who lived rent-free. Their average was still 10·3 per cent higher than the average of any of those with rent-paying status. Families not paying rent were usually drawn from people who had lived in Lagos for generations or who were living in the houses of relatives. The significant relationship of fertility to number of rooms occupied was positive. The average of 4·6 children ever born to those who lived in three rooms or more was 27·7 per cent higher than that to those living in one room, and just 7·0 per cent more than that to those in two rooms. When the averages were weighted by maternal age, the difference between occupants of two rooms and those of three rooms and over virtually disappeared and left those in one room still with the lowest fertility. It may, of course, be the large size of some families that force them to rent more than one room. Like the relationship of fertility to number of rooms, that to monthly living expenses was also positive. Of the three expenditure groups, the fertility average of 4·4 children ever born to those who spent 400 shillings or more was highest. Standardization by maternal age put the fertility of the middle group, spending between 200 and 399 shillings, above those whose expenditure was immediately above or below.

(e) *Education, Maternal Age and Fertility.* Maternal age and marriage duration apart, the one single social trait associated clearly with fertility differences was education—obviously a factor that impedes early marriage. The relationship observed was linear and negative by education both of wives and of husbands. Wives who received education up to secondary school and above were the least fertile, and so were those whose husbands attended secondary school or higher institutions. Wives who had only primary or Modern school education and those who never went to school were respectively 6·1 per cent and 36·4 per cent more fertile than those with secondary education and above. Those without any education were also 28·6 per cent more fertile than those with primary or Modern school training. The weighted averages still showed comparable differences. This time, the excess fertility of those with primary or Modern school education over those with secondary and above rose to 14·7 per cent, that of those without education over the same group declined to 23·5 per cent, and that of those who never went to school over those with primary or Modern school came down to 7·7 per cent. When wives were classified according to their husband's education, those whose husbands were educated to secondary school and above had the least number of children ever born, and in general the pattern of differences was very similar to that observed above in the classification by the education of wives. Those whose husbands had primary education, and those whose husbands never went to school, were respectively 11·1 per cent and 27·8 per cent more fertile than those whose husbands had been to secondary schools or higher institutions. These differences, though reduced in magnitude, persisted after weighting by age.

(f) *Occupation, Maternal Age and Fertility.* Any discussion of occupational differences in fertility in developing societies should take into account, as in this survey, the effect of age and education as factors associated with occupational placement. It would seem that differences among occupational classes represented, partially at least, a carry-over of educational as well as maternal age differences. Although the pattern of relationship between occupation and fertility is not as clearly delineated as in the case of education and age, the indication is that couples in occupations requiring some educational training tended to be less fertile. Thus, when wives were distinguished by their own occupations, white-collar workers had the lowest average of 3·2 children ever born, artisans and craftswomen had 3·9, traders 4·7, unskilled workers 5·3, and unemployed wives, many of whom were still very young, had 3·7. Some of these differences were, however, to a considerable extent due to disparities in maternal age. When this was controlled, the average for wives in white-collar occupations increased to 3·6, but was still the lowest level. There was no change in the fertility of artisans and craftswomen, and that of traders dropped from 4·7 to 4·3 children ever born, still higher than levels for either white-collar or artisans and craftswomen.

Also, wives who were matched on the basis of their husband's occupation showed considerable variations in fertility. Women married to white-collar workers had the lowest average of 3·5 children ever born; wives of artisans had 3·9, traders 4·9, unskilled workers 4·3 and unemployed husbands 5·8. As in the case of classification on the basis of occupation of wives, standardization of maternal age narrowed down to observed variations in fertility. The mean for white-collar workers went up to 3·8 but that was still the lowest registered level for any occupational class. Artisans and unskilled workers reached identical levels of 4·0, while traders and unemployed husbands, with respectively 4·5 and 4·6 average ever born, were highest.

(g) *Religious Affiliation, Maternal Age and Fertility.* There appeared to be some appreciable variations in fertility by religious class. Moslem and traditional worshippers, with an average of 4·2 children ever born, appeared to be some 10·5 per cent more fertile than Christians with an average of 3·8. In fact, Moslem wives alone were 7·9 per cent higher than Christian wives. Catholics were slightly lower than Protestants and far lower than Moslems. But whatever the differences, the degree of association between fertility and religious affiliation was not statistically significant, and the differences appeared to be smoothed out when averages were standardized by maternal age. Not only is Moslem fertility higher than that of any other religious group, but in both ideal and expected fertility, and in opinion regarding size of family, their score was the highest. Their average ideal family size of 7·3 children was at least 14·1 per cent higher than the ideal for Christians, and their average expected number of children was similarly 12·1 per cent higher. The probable influential factors associated with these differences, setting aside religious attitudes and observances, were age and education. Data from this survey indicated a close relationship between education and religious affiliation on the one hand, and on the other hand between education and youthfulness. In the first instance, Christians were more educated than Moslems and traditional worshippers, and in the second place the better educated were the younger wives. These facts might partially account for the higher actual and ideal fertility of the Moslems.

Summary

1. To the extent that more than one marriage experienced for presently married wives is a measure of marital instability, Moslems and traditional believers had the highest rate, as did the least educated women.

2. The practice of polygyny, though common to all social groups, including Christians, remains mainly the prerogative of the older generation and the uneducated. It is increasingly being relegated to the background in spite of the stiff opposition of tradition and Islam.

3. Female age at marriage in Lagos is definitely higher than is usually supposed. Though husbands remain much older than wives, the difference between ages of husbands and wives will decrease with the decline of polygyny and increased female education, which was significantly associated with age at marriage. Other related factors include age, occupation, city and non-city residence before marriage. It would appear that the younger wives interviewed married earlier than the older ones, but this may merely arise from some cases of markedly older age at marriage among the latter. On the other hand, if expressed attitude could influence behaviour, it might well be that the average age at marriage will become higher than at present, since ideal preferred age was higher than actual age at marriage.

4. In view of the relatively high degree of urbanization in Lagos, actual fertility, as measured by the average number of children ever born, was certainly high by urban standards in many countries, particularly in the developed world, but not by West African standards. It need hardly be emphasized that the level and impact of urbanization on behaviour in Lagos, as in many West African cities, is still not very significant. Because most of these cities developed only recently from native towns, the grip of tradition on behaviour and way of life is still very strong.

5. The level of fertility is not as high as one would expect the fecundity of 'non-contraceptive' women entering marriage around 20 years of age would allow. In the absence of deliberate artificial control, explanation should be sought in either self-restraint such as the lactation taboo and physical separation, or in physiological impediments such as disease, malnutrition and early menopause.[10]

6. In principle, there were some salient social and economic differences in fertility. As observed in the incidence of polygyny, age at marriage and ideal family size, education, maternal age and marriage duration bore the most significant associations. Religion, age at marriage, rooms occupied, type of marriage and quality of residence were less definitely associated.

Footnotes

1. J. C. CALDWELL, 'Family Formation and Limitation in Ghana: A Study of the Residents of Economically Superior Areas' (mimeographed paper presented at the International Conference on Family Planning Programmes), Geneva, August 1965, p. 9.

2. M. FORTES, 'A Demographic Field Study in Ashanti', in F. LORIMER *et al.*, *Culture and Human Fertility*, UNESCO, 1954, pp. 283–85.
See also E. ADNER, *Divorce and Fertility: An African Study*, OUP, 1962, p. 38.

3. D. BAIRD *et al.*, 'Age and Human Reproduction', *Journal of Obstetrics and Gynaecology of the British Empire*, Vol. 65, Part 6, December 1958.

4. J. M. TANNER *et al.*, 'Age at Menarche in Nigerian School Girls with a Note on their Heights and Weights from Age 12 to 19', *Human Biology*, Vol. 34, No. 3, September 1962, p. 188.

5. D. WHITBOURNE, 'Notes on the Infant Mortality of the Colony of Lagos', *The West African Medical Journal*, Vol. IV, No. 1, July 1930.
6. P. MARIS, *Family and Social Change in an African City*, London, 1961, p. 45.
7. REV. S. JOHNSON, *The History of the Yorubas*, London, 1921, p. 103.
8. Federal Ministry of Health, Nigeria, *Statistics*, 6/31.
9. *Population Census of Lagos, 1950*, p. 13.
10. *Medical Census of Southern Nigeria*, 1931, pp. 7–9.

40 Ghana fertility survey[1]: a preliminary report

D. I. Pool

Sociology Department, University of Ghana, Ghana

Introduction

During 1965 interviewing was carried out as the first step of a survey of fertility in Ghana. This paper outlines the aims, methods and progress to date of the survey.

The need for fertility surveys in Africa cannot be over-emphasized; there is a genuine lack of studies in depth of patterns and levels of African fertility, and of the conjugal experiences contributing to these patterns and levels. Yet, with declines in mortality, high fertility has become the essential factor producing high levels of population growth. For all planning and administrative purposes, therefore, it is essential to obtain full details of factors likely to affect fertility trends. These respond to variations in levels of sterility and rates of foetal mortality, to changing patterns of age at marriage and age at first intercourse, to the degree of continuity of exposure to intercourse thereafter, to patterns of nuptiality (involving customary as well as 'ordinance' marriage, and, to use an apt West African phrase, 'befriending'), and to the employment of methods of family limitation, from induced abortion or abstention through to oral contraceptives or IUCDs.

Two factors seem particularly relevant to changes in the rate of population growth in Ghana:

1. An increase in the median age of marriage (or first continuous exposure to intercourse), in itself a concomitant of urbanization and social change, could result in declines in completed family size.
2. There may be a rise in the average number of unions, nuptial or ex-nuptial, women participate in during their reproductive span. This change, which could accompany urbanization, might result in declines in fertility if continued for a long period, or if intensified. West Indian experience has shown that women participating in temporary liaisons are exposed to intercourse for a lower proportion of their reproductive life than are women in stable monogamous unions.[2]

In Ghana, as elsewhere, there are indications that the birth rate is lower in urban than in rural areas. The urban birth rate is 40 per 1,000, while that for Ghana as a whole is 47 per 1,000.[3] This difference is partly an artifact of differential age-sex-structures, but three additional factors may be of importance. They form the basic working hypotheses for the survey, namely:

(i) that age at entry to marriage or continuous exposure to conception is higher in urban than in rural Ghana; and

(ii) that, throughout the reproductive span, years of exposure to conception are fewer among urban than among rural women, partly as a result of later entry into marriage, and partly because of the frequency with which urban women enter temporary liaisons;

(iii) a third hypothesis relating to Caldwell's work: his finding that among Ghanaian urban élites, as among such groups elsewhere, there is a growing interest in having smaller families[4]; it is hypothesized here, however, that this change is not restricted to members of higher status groups, although the lead in these matters may come from them, but is characteristic of a wide range of urban dwellers.

Regardless of whether these three hypotheses are proved or disproved, data will have been obtained relating to two general questions. First, are there likely to be declines in fertility in Ghana as a concomitant of increasing urbanization? Second, if there are to be decreases, what are the mechanisms which will bring them about?

This latter point has general implications. The relationship of demographic transitions, particularly of declines in fertility, to urbanization is often asserted, or even accepted as a truism, but seldom have the actual processes been studied. For example, as a stimulus for the practice of family limitation, what is the rôle of female participation in the labour force as against a growing realization that survivorship levels are increasing?

The final aim of the survey is more general. Each time new data become available relating to populations currently undergoing demographic transitions, theories based on the experience of so-called 'Western' populations have had to be severely modified to be of value as analytical tools: post-war decreases in levels of mortality have not followed Western antecedents; fertility declines in Asia, where these have occurred, have differed from 'Western' models, as have patterns of fertility control. Demographers still tend to think of the 'Third World' as a demographically homogeneous unit in contrast to the 'West' and the 'Socialist bloc'. Yet, is it not probable that African demographic transitions will differ as radically from those of Asia or Latin-America, as theirs, in turn, have diverged from 'Western' experience? Certainly African mortality patterns appear to be somewhat different.[5] For fertility a crucial factor may be, to restate an earlier point, considerable differences between rural and urban patterns of nuptiality and 'befriending'. Moreover, African attitudes to family limitation and desired family size will not necessarily be similar to the attitudes of those nurtured within the framework of Hindu or Buddhist philosophies and concepts. In addition, it will be interesting to determine whether the Muslim religion has as monolithic a control over its adherents' fertility, as Kirk has suggested in a recent paper.[6]

Samples

It was decided that these questions could best be studied by undertaking sample surveys throughout Ghana. These had to be sufficiently diverse to cover a wide range of rural and urban fertility patterns, and large enough to obtain significant results for small sub-samples, yet not so large that questioning in depth was impractical or supervision of interviewing impossible. The samples had to be random so that generalizations relating to Ghana as a whole could be made with some degree of confidence. Moreover, attention had to be paid to the problem encountered in obtaining women interviewers. It was also felt that a separate sample should be drawn to determine the attitude of male respondents regarding family limitation and desired family size.

Details relating to the samples are presented in Table 1. The urban random sample of female respondents is divided into two interpenetrating sub-samples, for one of which women interviewers were employed and for the other men. These two sub-samples were derived from a replicated random sample, the frame of which had been designed by Dr G. Parnicky for the malaria survey of September 1964.[7] It was particularly fortunate that this frame could be employed, for its use had several advantages: full locational details had been obtained for every dwelling, while the frame itself had been prepared recently, and thus relatively few difficulties were encountered when clusters of dwellings, termed segments by Parnicky, were being re-identified in the field. Finally, it was a random sample of the *people* of Accra, in

Table 1

Ghana Fertility Survey: Size and State of Completion of the Various Random Samples[a]

Samples	NO. OF CLUSTERS: i.e. segments (urban areas); or localities (rural areas)					NO. OF RESPONDENTS			Size of population from which the sample was selected (1960)	Sampling proportion (to date) (per cent)
	Total	Completed	Almost completed	Partly completed	Not yet begun	Approached (to date)	Interviewed	Non-respondents		
Female Respondents in Accra										
Male interviewers	38	35	1	2	—	2,003	1,830	173	n.a.	1·9
Female interviewers	13	10	2	1	—	673	635	38	n.a.	0·7
Sub-total	51	45	3	3	—	2,676	2,465	211	102,096	2·6
Rural areas	21	20	—	—	1	2,843	2,790	52	1,424,030	0·2
Total Female Respondents	72	65	3	3	1	5,518	5,255	263	n.a.	n.a.
Male Respondents in Accra	(5)[b]	n.a.	n.a.	n.a.	All	(338)	nil	n.a.	135,028	(0·25)

Notes: (a) These figures are provisional (Jan. 1966).
(b) Estimated on basis of female sample with allowance for urban sex-ratio; ten half-segments will be used.

the sense that it had been based on enumeration areas stratified by population size, then divided into segments containing roughly ten dwellings each.[8] In this way, Parnicky attempted to preclude the type of biases inherent, for example, in area sampling, for his frame took cognisance of differential densities of population. Moreover, the division into segments took account of new building since the date of the census and thus of changes in population distribution. The sample of urban males has been prepared from this same frame, for it is essential to interview males from the same households as those from which the women have come.[9]

For a number of reasons, Accra was picked to exemplify urban Ghana. The University is situated in Accra, while the availability of a carefully designed frame was an important consideration. Moreover, Accra is the largest and perhaps most 'urban' locality in Ghana. Thus, if small rural localities were also surveyed, the resulting samples would be drawn from the extremes of the rural–urban continuum and values for intermediate settlement types could be interpolated with some degree of confidence. Finally, Accra is the capital. Fertility surveys have been carried out in a

Table 2

Ghana Fertility Survey: Rural Localities[a]

Locality[b]		Local council
	Western Region	
WR 1.	Kegyina	Nzima-Evalue-Ajomoro-Gwira
WR 2.	Anyinabrim (Enyinaberemu)	Sefwi-Wiawso
WR 3.	Narkwa	Mfantsiman
WR 4.	Osai Krodua	Gomoa-Awutu-Effutu
	Eastern Region	
ER 1.	Kabu Sisi	Manya-Krobo
ER 2.	Sankubanase	E. Akim Abuakwa
ER 3.	Kwahu Ada	S. Kwahu
	Ashanti Region	
AR 1.	Dedesua	Kumasi South
AR 2.	Afrante	Kumasi North
AR 3.	Abuakwa	Amansie
	Brong-Ahafo	
BA 1.	Nyomoase	Brong-Ahafo East
BA 2.	Abrikaso	Brong-Ahafo Central
	Volta	
VR 1.	Kosamma Wawaso	Buem-Krachi
VR 2.	Ada Klu Abuadi	Ho
VR 3.	Aveme Gbohome	Kpandu
	Northern	
NR 1.	Duon	Wale
NR 2.	Balienaa	Wale
NR 3.	Sandema Awusuyeri	Builsa
NR 4.	Balungu Apoligabisi (B. Ayulgabisi)	Frafra
NR 5.	Kuloko	Kusasi
	Accra Capital Territory	
CT 1.	Damfa	Ga-Adangbe-Shai

Notes: (a) Regions defined as at time of 1960 census.
(b) Spellings as in *1960 Population Census of Ghana*, Vol. I, Accra.

number of other capitals (e.g. Ohadike's Lagos Survey, ch. 39) or else are being undertaken at present (the United Nations is surveying selected South and Central American cities). Useful and valid comparison might, therefore, be drawn with the results of these other surveys.

The rural sample was devised to obtain a random selection of Ghana women living in settlements containing fewer than 5,000 persons (termed here 'rural population'). The Regions, of 1960, were stratified by size of rural population, and on this basis 20 localities were distributed among them *pro rata*. In addition, one rural locality was allotted to Accra Capital Territory. The local councils[10] in these regions were divided into 'lots' of 25,000 population each. A council with a large rural population would have more lots, and thus a greater chance of being selected, than a council with a small population composed of only a few lots. In each Region lots were selected randomly, so that it was possible to determine the local councils from which the region's allotted number of rural localities had to be drawn, the number per region being shown in Table 2. In Wale this process led to two villages being picked from the one local council.

In the selected local councils, every locality with less than 5,000 persons was numbered serially with no weighting for size. Then one locality was randomly selected, except in Wale where two were picked. There is a bias introduced at this stage for, obviously, in most local councils there will be far more small localities than large.

For practical reasons it was preferable to sample small localities containing 100–200 females. In fact, where selected localities were larger than this, it was necessary to subdivide the village in order to keep interviewing to practical limits. However, as localities were selected with due cognisance being given to the regional distribution and differing densities of Ghana's rural populations, it may be possible to assign the data from each locality an equal weighting when generalizations are being made relating to rural Ghana as a whole. This may not be possible if it is found that there has been a redistribution of rural population since the 1960 census, or if the data for any locality are affected by seasonal changes in population size.[11]

The Questionnaire: Women Respondents

A schedule was designed that would cover every major aspect of exposure to intercourse and conception, and that would give details of the respondents' social backgrounds and experiences. Thus, questions were included to elicit five sets of data:

(a) Complete conjugal histories from puberty until the date of the interview, covering all unions, however temporary, and differentiating between monogamous and polygynous. It was not felt advisable, in view of the widely different definitions of marriage and the varied distinctions between marriage and 'befriending', to use, in an initial question, the categories 'married' or 'not married', but rather to attempt to distinguish between 'befriending/living with' a man and 'not befriending/living with'. Once it had been ascertained that the respondent was/had been involved in a union, questions were then asked to determine the nature and duration of this union.

(b) Full pregnancy histories, including, for each pregnancy, foetal outcome, survival of live-births, length of time spent breast-feeding, the period that elapsed before menstruation recurred, and the span of post-partum abstention from intercourse.

(c) Migration histories. These data are of intrinsic value, but for the fertility analysis *per se* they were collected in order that a cross-check could be maintained on the conjugal and pregnancy histories; perhaps marital separations arising from the migration of a woman might not have been elicited during the conjugal history, or the reporting of a return home to give birth to a child—a common procedure in Ghana—might have acted as a spur to remembering one or more pregnancies.

(d) The respondent's socio-economic status, her place on a continuum of social change, levels of nutrition, family background, access to mass media etc.

(e) Attitudes to, and use and knowledge of methods of family limitation, both traditional and 'new'; recognition of changing levels of survivorship, life-chances, etc.

Retrospective Recording

The fertility data have been obtained by 'retrospective recording'. The problems relating to this method will be raised below, but first it should be noted that levels and trends of differential fertility are better, and perhaps more accurately, analysed by some method of continuous vital registration or repetitive sampling. In countries for which vital registration is incomplete it is preferable to use two reconcilable sources of data relating to the same population at risk. One set is derived from the registration of events as they occur in sample areas, and the other from retrospective recording by respondents of recent events, such as those occurring during the previous three months. Because of the necessity for providing an elaborate administrative apparatus, the time taken for cross-checking and reconciling data, and the need for repeating the interviewing and for maintaining offices, these methods are both costly and time-consuming. Moreover, to obtain data on factors related to the levels of fertility (conjugal practices and exposure to intercourse at various ages), it is still imperative, from a practical point of view, to obtain certain data by retrospective recording; otherwise, to obtain complete conjugal histories the cohorts concerned would have to be observed throughout their entire life, or at least during their reproductive span.

An alternative source of data would be the census, which is also, of course, based on retrospective recording. However, census schedules must be as brief as possible, while a number of areas of demographic, social and economic research compete for the schedule, each claim for question space being supported by urgent and valid arguments. The analytical value of the census increases when two or more have been completed, and reliable data have been obtained at each enumeration.

The fertility survey that was initiated in Ghana, therefore, was intended to serve as a detailed adjunct to other sources of data. In particular, the aim has been to secure data of a type that cannot easily be obtained except by using a random sample and a lengthy questionnaire, but the results of which can be used when interpreting results obtained by other methods.

A characteristic of retrospective recording is that respondents have difficulty recalling details, and thus levels of accuracy may be less than when other methods are employed. There is no complete solution to this problem, but an investigator must do all he can to reduce memory lapses. Two methods have been employed in an attempt to combat errors of this type. Firstly, the accuracy with which an event is recalled probably declines with the passage of time after the event and also with increase in the respondent's age. Thus, older respondents were asked only a few questions, the detailed questions being reserved for women aged 15–49 years. Secondly, cross-checks were built into the questionnaires. For example, the data in the migration history acted as a cross-check on other information; the schedules were so structured that interviewers had to cross-examine in the case of 24 months or longer gaps in the combined conjugal and pregnancy histories; and it is possible to compare ages, dates etc. for inconsistencies. In the rural areas, women discussed their pregnancies rather freely, and thus there was seldom much need to probe for pregnancies, but in Accra the cross-check for gaps proved to be of some value.

Other Problems Relating to Accuracy of Data

The illiteracy of the majority of the respondents was the other major cause of possible errors. In particular, it had to be assumed that ages, dates and similar details would be reported incorrectly in a number of instances, or would have to be estimated. Interviewers were directed to differentiate between ages reported by respondents, and ages they themselves had estimated for the women. This means that, for broad age-groups, comparisons can be made between ages as reported and estimated, in addition to carrying out standard tests of accuracy for both sets of age distributions.

From inspection of the schedules, it appears that interviewers frequently had to make age estimates. Obviously, this places some limits on the value of the survey results, but, by keeping a check on whether ages had been estimated or reported, it will be possible to define the limits.

The problem of estimation is important when a study is being made on the conjugal and, particularly, the pregnancy histories. When estimates had to be made for pregnancy histories, the interviewers used the youngest child, if present during the interview, as a reference point from which to estimate dates and ages. In addition, a considerable number of illiterate respondents had written records of their children's birth dates. Moreover, for Accra in particular, it is possible to overemphasize this problem of recall, for the largest group of respondents are still only part way through their reproductive period.

The level of comprehension and experience of the respondents is, save for a few women, most unsophisticated. For this reason, a closely structured schedule was used, in which answers were elicited from which interpretations could be made during coding, but which left no scope for interviewers to interpret or explain terms to respondents. Moreover, the only quasi-technical term used in a direct question was abortion (meaning here 'induced abortion') for which word there are, anyway, equivalents in the various Ghanaian languages.

Considerable care was taken to direct interviewers to return a 'Don't know' or 'No response' where appropriate; they were instructed not to probe or to interpret for the respondent except in those few questions where the schedule specifically directed them to do so. In particular, this has meant that the attitude questions have a very high level of 'No Response' or 'Don't Know'. This is not unexpected. Moreover, if this survey were to act as a methodological baseline for other studies, it was important to determine the type of questions Ghanaian women find difficult to answer or offensive.

Non-response, lack of understanding of questions, and reluctance to answer particular questions are all factors in the survey that have yet to be analysed, but which, so it was assumed at the outset, would play an important rôle in the study. Similarly, a check was kept on certain characteristics of those women who refused or were unable to be interviewed, plus reasons for refusal or unavailability. Non-response, altogether or for particular questions, can be cross-checked with personal data which have been kept on the interviewers, so that interviewer-biases can be analysed. Furthermore, by comparing the two random interpenetrating sub-samples, sex-biases in the interviewing can be evaluated.

Refusal to co-operate altogether was a relatively uncommon occurrence as is shown in Table 1. These data suggest a rural–urban difference, but, as rural interviewers had already obtained experience in Accra, this differential may be more apparent than real.

Difficulties in obtaining the co-operation of women altogether, or non-response for particular questions may result, among other factors, from language problems. Moreover, there is scope for a high level of error unless questions are translated correctly prior to their being asked. This problem was most acute in Accra where speakers of all major languages reside. A standardized translation was made from English into four distinct vernacular languages, Ewe, Ga, Hausa and 'Twi'. The so-called, 'Twi', was largely based on Fante and Ashanti-Twi, two of the major Akan languages, which are, however, readily intelligible to most other Akan language speakers.

The other precaution was the obtaining of the services of interviewers speaking those four and other minor languages and dialects. It proved impossible to hire a Builsa interviewer from Accra, so that for Sandema Awusyeri locality a translator had to be hired from among the local people.

Conclusion

At the beginning of 1966, interviewing for the Ghana fertility survey had almost been completed and coding was under way. At the time of writing, there are no data available in a substantive form. For this reason it has been possible to discuss only the aims and methods, and to present some of the hypotheses on which the research has been based.

It is hoped that the results, in spite of all the problems encountered, particularly in terms of accuracy of reporting, will provide a fuller understanding of the variables related to levels and patterns of fertility in Ghana, and in West Africa. The survey may provide interesting new data on the factors which bring about fertility declines, following or paralleling urbanization.

Footnotes

1. This survey was initiated by the writer and financed by the Population Council as an integral part of their demographic research and training programme at the University of Ghana.
2. See JUDITH BLAKE, 'Family Instability in Jamaica', *Current Research in Human Fertility*, Milbank Memorial Fund, 1955, pp. 24–41.
3. CENTRAL BUREAU OF STATISTICS, *Memorandum on a Population Policy for Ghana*, Accra, 1965 (Duplicated).
4. J. C. CALDWELL, 'Family Formation and Limitation in Ghana: A Study of Residents of Economically Superior Urban Areas', *Background Papers: International Conference on Family Planning Programmes*, Geneva, August 1965.
5. FRANK LORIMER *et al.*, 'Demography', in ROBERT LYSTAD (ed.), *The African World: A Survey of Social Research*, London, 1965.
6. DUDLEY KIRK, 'Factors Affecting Muslim Natality', *International Conference on Family Planning Programmes*, Geneva, August 1965.
7. I wish to thank Dr Parnicky and the Central Bureau of Statistics for permitting me to use this frame.
8. When the 1960 census was being planned, enumeration areas were delimited according to a number of criteria, one of which was that they should contain about 1,000 people.
9. The survey of male attitudes, to be carried out soon, will employ a questionnaire based on parts of the schedule used for females. The male sample will be limited to 330–340 respondents.
10. Local Councils are the administrative units containing rural populations (as against *Urban* Councils).
11. Three factors must be considered:
    (a) Some difficulty was encountered in re-identifying rural enumeration areas during fieldwork. This was particularly true where settlement was dispersed (Builsa, Frafra, Kusasi, Krobo and Buem areas), and where units under the one chief had been subdivided by census enumerators. In one case, a name had been changed since 1960 (Kusasi).
    (b) Population redistribution (Krobo).
    (c) The survey coincided with cocoa-harvesting and thus with an influx or eflux of seasonal migrants, whereas the 1960 census had been taken in many areas after harvesting.

41 Survey of attitudes in Nigeria towards family planning

T. Daramola, R. D. Wright
University of Lagos Medical School, Nigeria

with

G. O. Sofoluwe

A. Adeniyi-Jones

H. Elliott

Introduction

In the past, people have tended to prepare community health programmes without adequate advance study of community needs. Consequently, considerable energy, money and manpower have been used with relatively few results. It is becoming apparent that, in order to launch a successful health programme, it is important that the people's traditions, cultures, and educational, social and economic backgrounds should be taken into consideration, as well as the mortality and morbidity patterns of the community. It was with these considerations in mind that the Department of Community Health, University of Lagos Medical School, decided to conduct a survey of family planning attitudes and practices. The major part of the study was done in the Surulere section of Lagos adjacent to the Teaching Hospital.

The major survey was conducted during July and August 1965, among a random sample of 642 Surulere mothers; three subsidiary surveys also were conducted, two in Lagos and one in Northern Nigeria. These smaller samples were drawn from respondents attending:

(a) the Institute of Child Health Clinic in Surulere, totalling 125;
(b) the Surulere Health Centre, totalling 121; and
(c) two clinics in Katsina Province in Northern Nigeria, totalling 73.

Selection Training and Supervision of Interviewers

Eleven male students from the second-year class of the University of Lagos Medical School and one from the Faculty of Medicine, Ibadan, were selected to conduct the survey. The health visitor attached to the Lagos Teaching Hospital, a social worker from the Institute of Child Health, and two members of the Department of Community Health first conducted an orientation programme in sociological and medical interviewing. Students were then selected with full consideration of the languages spoken by their respondents, one Hausa-speaking student going to the north, and the other eleven, speaking either Yoruba, Ibo or one of the other southern dialects, staying in Lagos. In the random sample survey, students were assigned to houses in pairs and each mother was interviewed by at least one student speaking her language.

Selection and Description of Sample Areas

Nine hundred and sixty-one questionnaires were completed, the selection of samples being conducted in the following manner:

GROUP 1—THE RANDOM SAMPLE

Fifty streets were selected in Surulere district by random sampling, covering only houses built before December 1964. The students were to interview families in every second house on one side of the street and to keep a record of each building visited, be it residential, educational or recreational. Surulere is a new district with a rapidly growing population, in the 1950 census estimated to be 9,372, and in the 1963 census 87,067. People in a variety of social and economic levels are to be found here, including many moved from Lagos Island during the 1958–60 relocation scheme. There are two Health Centres in Surulere, a general one with an average daily attendance of 700 people and also a dispensary for children under seven with an average daily attendance of about 600 children. The students interviewed 642 respondents in this group.

GROUP 2—INSTITUTE OF CHILD HEALTH

One hundred and twenty-five subjects were interviewed from among 227 mothers under the Institute of Child Health longitudinal study. The Institute has been observing 395 children in these families since April 1963. Some of the mothers and children have been withdrawn either by death, migration, or voluntary resignation, and new ones have been recruited. Families recruited represent different social and economic backgrounds. They include families re-housed in Surulere from the low income Isale Eko area on Lagos Island, those who still live in Isale Eko, those from the densely-populated Mushin area of Western Nigeria, and those in higher income families recruited from Surulere and nearby Yaba.

GROUP 3—SURULERE HEALTH CENTRE

The first group of subjects interviewed were selected from the ante-natal clinic in the Surulere Health Centre. All participants were in the child-bearing age, and included women who were expecting a child, nursing a young baby, or helping to bring a young baby to the clinic. Willingness to participate in the programme and ability to communicate in one of the three main Nigerian languages or in English were other criteria for selection of these subjects. The students interviewed 121 respondents in this group.

GROUP 4—NORTH

The survey was conducted in Katsina City, Northern Nigeria, with a predominantly urban population, and in Malumfashi town, with mainly a rural population. In both areas, the people are predominantly Moslems. The survey was conducted in the hospital out-patients clinic in Katsina City and in the dispensary in Malumfashi town. It is felt that this survey omitted members of the upper class since the latter do not usually attend these clinics; nevertheless, we felt that the inclusion of this sample would provide valuable data on attitudes and practices among people of a different cultural and religious background from those in Lagos. Seventy-three questionnaires were completed in this group.

Results of Data Analysis

The questionnaire was designed to elicit information regarding attitudes toward, use of, and knowledge about family planning, as well as to obtain basic demographic and socio-economic data on the families involved. I.B.M. Computer Number 1620 of the University of Lagos was used in this analysis.

ETHNIC GROUP, EDUCATION LEVEL, AND RELIGION

The random sample of 642 Surulere mothers was composed of 292 Yorubas, 218 Ibos, 126 representatives of other smaller Southern Nigerian tribes, with only four Hausas and one Fulani from the Northern Nigerian tribes. The education and literacy levels were high for both the respondents and their husbands. Almost 45 per cent of the wives and over 80 per cent of the husbands had completed primary school or gone further. Our findings indicate that about two thirds of the wives and almost 90 per cent of the husbands were literate in some language, most of them in English. Just over half the sample were Protestant religion, almost one-third Catholics and only 16 per cent Moslems, with five others professing adherence to traditional or other beliefs.

The other two smaller Lagos samples contained no representatives of the Northern tribes being otherwise roughly similar in characteristics to the larger Surulere group. The Institute of Child Health sample of 125 was predominantly Yoruba, comprising 89 Yorubas, 26 Ibos, and nine other members of Southern Nigerian tribes. The Surulere Health Centre sample of 121 comprised 41 per cent Ibos, 39 per cent Yorubas, and 19 per cent members of other Southern tribes. As with the larger sample, about half the wives and almost 80 per cent of the husbands had completed primary school or gone further. About 60 per cent of the wives in the ICH group and 70 per cent in the Health Centre group were literate in some language, with about 85 per cent of the husbands in both groups being literate. With respect to religious profession, there were some variations, the ICH group being 40 per cent Moslem, 35 per cent Protestant and 23 per cent Catholic. In the Health Centre group, almost half were Protestants, less than 30 per cent Catholics and just under 20 per cent Moslems. The most interesting variation here is in the numbers of Moslems, the higher percentage in the Institute of Child Health group probably being attributable to the fact that this sample was drawn from all over Lagos, including the older and more traditional areas, whereas fewer Moslems appear to have settled in the newer Surulere area.

The Katsina sample of 73 mothers, is in marked contrast to the three Lagos groups. Here, 32 mothers were Hausas and 24 were Fulanis, with only 16 representatives of the Southern tribes, including four Ibos and no Yorubas at all. With respect to education, two mothers and four husbands had completed primary school, one of the latter having advanced beyond the level of secondary school. Our findings indicate that 95 per cent of the mothers and 89 per cent of the husbands were illiterate. Just over three-quarters of the sample were Moslems, seven others (about 10 per cent) Christians (five Protestants and two Catholics) and another seven professed traditional beliefs.

In addition to the ethnic, educational, and religious differences between the North group on the one hand, and the three Lagos groups on the other, it should be noted that, in the Lagos samples, the educational level of the husbands was substantially higher than that of the wives, twice as many husbands as wives having completed primary school or gone further.

USE OF FAMILY PLANNING METHODS AND METHODS TRIED

Eighty-eight per cent of the random sample, 79 per cent of the Institute of Child Health group, 85 per cent of the Surulere Health Centre group, and 98·6 per cent of the North group had never tried any of the contraceptives. In all the samples 88 per cent had never used any contraceptive device, the highest being in the North where 72 out of 73 mothers had never used any method at all—the one exception having used oral pills.

Among the few people who have used contraceptives, the condom is the most commonly used (3·6 per cent random sample; 4·1 per cent Surulere Health Centre), but in the Institute of Child Health group, coitus interruptus is the method most usually employed. The second most commonly used contraceptive is oral pills (3·4 per cent random sample; 3·3 per cent Surulere Health Centre; and 1·4 per cent North). However, in the Institute of Child Health group, the condom was the second most commonly used contraceptive device.

In the random sample, rhythm is the third most commonly used contraceptive method (1·9 per cent), whereas in the Institute of Child Health group, the pessary or diaphragm (3·9 per cent) take third place. Overall, the third most commonly used method is coitus interruptus (2·5 per cent). One may note that out of 642 people interviewed in the random sample, only two (0·3 per cent) have used the coil or loop. No other person, in the Institute of Child Health, the Surulere Health Centre or in the North group, ever used this method.

A question was asked as to who were using some family planning method currently or fairly currently. Nine per cent of the random sample group, 13·6 per cent of the Institute of Child Health group and 9·1 per cent of Surulere Health Centre group answered the question in the affirmative. The rest had never used any method or had discontinued using one.

USE OF FAMILY PLANNING METHODS AND EDUCATION

Is the use of contraceptives affected by the level of education of either the respondent or her husband? Although the majority of the respondents had never used any family planning method, it is interesting to note, that out of the few respondents who used family planning methods, the majority had some secondary school education or above. Sixty-five per cent of those who used condom, 87 per cent of those using foam tablet, jelly or cream, 66 per cent of those using rhythm and all who used coitus interruptus or the coil, had a secondary school education or above. Oral pills appear to be the most used method among the uneducated, 59 per cent of these having had less than a secondary school education. The respondents' husbands' education shows a similar picture. The husbands of 87 per cent of the respondents who used the condom, a pessary or diaphragm, and of all who used coitus interruptus or the coil, had some secondary school education or above. The survey shows that the education level of either the respondent, the husband or of both is positively correlated with the use of family planning methods. In our sample, the more educated the community, the more frequently do residents apply knowledge of family planning.

ETHNIC GROUP AND USE OF FAMILY PLANNING

In the random Surulere sample, 11 per cent of the Yorubas, 11 per cent of the Ibos, 15 per cent of the minority tribes and none of the few Hausas studied used family planning methods. In Lagos it is apparent that attitude toward family planning is not correlated with the ethnic groups represented with the possible exception of the Hausas who were too small in number to be evaluated.

AGE AT FIRST MARRIAGE

In the random sample group, 47·2 per cent of the people married between 15 and 19 years and 77·9 per cent between 14 and 24 years. Similarly in the Institute of Child Health group, 40 per cent married between 15 and 19 years but 77·6 per cent married between 15 and 24 years. The North, however, shows a younger marriage age. Fifty-four per cent of this group married between 10 and 14 years and 89 per cent between 10 and 19 years. The three surveys reveal that the most popular age for marriage in Lagos is between 15 and 19 years and in the North between 10 and 14 years. No member of any group married after the age of 34 years.

AGE DIFFERENCE BETWEEN HUSBAND AND WIFE

The surveys show a contrast with regard to age differences between husbands and wives. In the North group, 34·2 per cent were of the same age as their partners. In the Lagos group, only about 15 per cent of the wives were of the same ages as their husbands.

In all samples, the majority of wives were younger than their husbands. In the random sample of 642, for example, only five respondents (0·8 per cent) were older. The husbands in the Lagos samples tended, in fact, to be considerably older than their wives. Data for the North are meagre since the majority of respondents were not in a position to provide information about their ages.

FAMILY SIZE

In all samples, first pregnancies occurred principally between the ages of 15 and 19, and the average number of pregnancies for each respondent was close to four. The numbers of surviving children per respondent average close to three, again in all four samples. This suggests a pregnancy wastage rate of one child per respondent.

In the three Lagos samples, approximately 40 per cent of the women had their first pregnancies between 15 and 19 years, whereas in the North the proportion was about 55 per cent. This is consistent with data showing an earlier age of marriage for the Northern group. It should be noted, here, that approximately 10 per cent of the women in each sample said that they had never been pregnant, and that between 4 per cent and 14 per cent in the four samples claimed never to have had any live births.

IDEAL FAMILY SIZE

In all the Lagos samples the answer to this question is similar. The ideal number of boys is three: 31·6 per cent of the random sample, 31·2 per cent of the Institute of Child Health and 33·9 per cent of Surulere Health Centre group want three boys. In the North the largest percentage of the people who responded to this question (9·5 per cent) also want three boys. However, 74 per cent in the North did not answer this question, most of those not responding saying that this was in the hands of God.

The answer regarding the number of daughters thought to be ideal shows similarity in all the samples: 37·2 per cent of the random sample group, 41·6 per cent of the Institute of Child Health group, 47·9 per cent of the Surulere Health Centre group and 12·3 per cent of the North group want two daughters. As above, 74 per cent of the North group did not answer this question. It seems clear from this survey that three boys and two daughters were the ideal numbers of children the respondents wanted.

RELATIVE IMPORTANCE OF SONS AND DAUGHTERS

When the question was asked as to whether a son or a daughter is more important, the majority in all samples stated that they were equally important. Among those who preferred one sex over the other, 35 per cent of the random group, 35 per cent of the Institute of Child Health group, 45 per cent of the Surulere Health Centre group and 41 per cent of the North group preferred boys. Of the rest, 2·7 per cent of the random group, 1·8 per cent of the Institute of Child Health group, 6·6 per cent of the Surulere Health Centre group and 6·8 per cent of the North group preferred daughters.

In another question, the respondent was asked to state one of the two most important reasons for preferring sons. Out of the 40 per cent who answered the question, the most frequent reason given was, 'To depend on the son after getting old'.

AGES OF CHILDREN WHO HAVE DIED AFTER BIRTH

In the random sample, mothers had lost on average 0·5 children. In the Institute of Child Health and Surulere Health Centre groups, the average lost was 0·6 children and in the North group 0·8 children lost. Of the respondents who lost children, two losses were the most frequently recorded. 13 per cent of the children in Lagos died (random group 12 per cent) as compared with 29 per cent of the North group. The Infant mortality in the group is 120 per 1,000 in the North.

In the random sample, 52 per cent of the respondents stated that no child had died after birth. The Institute of Child Health has the highest figure (56 per cent) of respondents who had never lost any child after birth. This is understandable in view of the clinical help the Institute gives to these mothers. It is interesting to note that the random sample, Surulere Health Centre and the North all have 52 per cent for those who have never lost any children after birth.

One may note here that one of the most important deciding factors affecting family planning is a high infant mortality rate. Until the medical services and socio-economic conditions are sufficiently improved to assure every mother that her child will have reasonable chance of survival after birth, mothers may be reluctant to use contraceptives. A Yoruba proverb says that anyone with only one child is just as if she has none for that one child may die at any time.

ABORTION AND ATTITUDE TOWARD INDUCED ABORTION

A percentage of 83·8 of the random sample stated that they had never had still births or natural abortions. The figure for the Institute of Child Health is 71·2 per cent, that for Surulere Health Centre 76·0 per cent, and for the North 80·8 per cent.

When the question on induced abortion was asked, 98·9 per cent of the random sample and 95·2 per cent of the Institute of Child Health group stated that they had never had any induced abortion, and no person in Surulere Health Centre or the North admitted having had any. In view of the fact that this is a sensitive question, the answer received may not be entirely reliable.

The Lagos samples are remarkably uniform in the percentage (about 80) who disapproved of induced abortion. In the small North group, 63 per cent disapproved. The random sample showed the lowest approval, 12·5 per cent, while the North showed the highest, 26 per cent.

NUMBER OF WIVES PER HUSBAND

A percentage of 73 of the random sample, 59 per cent of the Institute of Child Health, 69 per cent of the Surulere Health Centre, and 22 per cent of the North group stated that their husbands had one wife. A percentage of 15 of the random sample, 29 per cent of the Institute of Child Health, 16 per cent of the Surulere Health Centre, and 8 per cent of the North sample said their husbands had two wives. One may note that 53·4 per cent of the North group did not respond to the question. In the random sample, seven respondents or 1·1 per cent of the people were not married.

Knowledge of Family Planning

The respondents were requested to state in order of frequency the media through which the knowledge of family planning was brought to them. A percentage of 59·8 of the random sample stated that they had no knowledge about it at all. A percentage of 69 of the Institute of Child Health, 54 per cent of Surulere Health Centre and 34 per cent of the North had no knowledge. Among the sources of information listed, all the samples recorded friends as the commonest source: 26 per cent of the random sample, 17 per cent of the Institute of Child Health, 24 per cent of the Surulere Health Centre and 59 per cent of the North group received information about family planning from friends.

All the samples in Lagos mentioned the Health Centre as the second source of information: 6 per cent of the random sample, 11 per cent of the Institute of Child Health, and 5 per cent of the Surulere Health Centre. The North group, however, quoted radio as the second source, through which 5·5 per cent of the people received the information. In the Lagos area, radio is the third commonest source. The random sample shows 2·8 per cent of Institute of Child Health sample, 1·6 per cent of Surulere sample and 1·7 per cent of the Health Centre sample gave radio as the source. In the North the health centre is the third source, 1·4 per cent of the people receiving their information this way. No person in any of the groups reported getting information about family planning through the medium of television despite the fact that there is television service in Lagos. Only 1·7 per cent of the random sample but no one from the North obtained their information through the newspaper. When the question was asked whether the respondent ever received any family planning help from the public health personnel, 0·5 per cent stated they did very often and 0·5 per cent once in a while. In the North, no one reported receiving any such help from public health personnel.

ATTITUDES TOWARD FAMILY PLANNING METHODS

In the random sample, 75 per cent gave general approval to family planning and 25 per cent gave general disapproval. In all other samples, 71 per cent gave general approval and 22 per cent disapproved: 84 per cent Institute of Child Health, 69 per cent Surulere Health Centre and 56 per cent North approved. The samples in the Lagos area show that 23 per cent disapproved, whereas 44 per cent of the North group disapproved.

When the question was asked more specifically, 51 per cent of the Lagos groups and 25 per cent of the Northern group approved family planning methods positively, whereas only 7 per cent of the Lagos groups and 22 per cent of the North group opposed these methods positively.

The survey shows that in all the areas the majority of those interviewed approved family planning methods. Fewer people disapproved in the Lagos area than in the North group. The survey also revealed that 55 per cent of the respondents in the Lagos group and 93 per cent of the North group had not talked to their husbands about family planning. Twenty-four per cent of the husbands in the Lagos area samples and 1·4 per cent in the Northern group approved family planning strongly. In Lagos, 2·3 per cent of the husbands were strongly opposed. The numbers involved in the North group were too small to be of significance in this question.

In view of the fact that in this survey the opinions of most husbands about family planning are not known, it will be necessary to design a questionnaire primarily for the husbands. This is necessary because, in the final analysis, the opinion of the husband may be a deciding factor in determining whether a woman applies family planning knowledge.

The respondents were asked about their personal interest in family planning. Forty-nine per cent of the random sample, 58 per cent of the Institute of Child Health, 49 per cent of the Surulere Health Centre and 23 per cent of the North sample said they had very much interest. Twenty-five per cent of the random sample, 19 per cent of the Institute of Child Health, 17 per cent of Surulere Health Centre and 53 per cent of the North group indicated they had very little interest. The respondents in the Lagos area showed more personal interest, the Institute of Child Health group slightly more so than others. The North group were the least interested.

Summary

A report of the survey of attitudes toward family planning in the Surulere district is compared here with two other groups in Lagos and a group from Katsina Province in the Northern Region. Though only the first group was chosen on a random basis, some comparisons between the groups seem justified.

The report shows that Surulere is a recently established area. Seventy-five per cent of the people had come there during the previous ten years, whereas in the North 59 per cent of the people had been living there for over ten years. About 41 per cent of the people in the Surulere group graduated from secondary schools or had additional training. In the Northern group, however, only 1·4 per cent of the people had secondary school education and additional training.

The survey included major and minor ethnic groups in Nigeria, but there does not appear to be a correlation between ethnic groups and use of family planning methods. The survey shows that 88 per cent of the people in Surulere and almost 99 per cent in the North had never used any family planning methods. Of the people who used contraceptives, the condom was the most commonly used followed by oral pills. The survey indicates that the majority of those who had used a contraceptive device had secondary school education or above. The majority of the respondents in the Lagos area were 20 to 34 years old and in the Northern group 15 to 29 years old. The North showed slightly younger ages at marriage than Surulere in which 78 per cent of the people married between 15 and 24, whereas in the North 89 per cent married between 10 and 19 years. In all the series first pregnancy occurred most frequently between 15 and 19 years.

The survey shows that the average number of children born per mother was approximately 3·6 in the large random sample group and about 3·4 in the Surulere Health Centre group. For the mothers receiving more intensive care, in the Institute of Child Health group, the figure is higher, being about 4·2, whereas in the North the figure is lower, being about 2·9. The numbers of surviving children average as follows: for the random sample and Surulere Health Centre groups, about 3·0, indicating an average loss of 0·5 children per mother; for the Institute of Child Health group, slightly over 3·5, indicating a slightly higher loss of about 0·6 children per mother (possibly due to the fact that larger numbers of children are here at risk); for the North, the average number of surviving children is about two, indicating a loss of approximately one child per mother.

With respect to ideal family size, the most frequently desired number of children as reported by the mothers interviewed averaged for all four samples three boys and two girls, or a total of five children.

It is found also that those who used family planning methods are more exposed to different types of mass media. The television viewers, radio listeners and those who read books are more likely to practise family planning. Disapproval of the use of family planning methods was stronger among those who married at a younger age (under twenty-four years). Similarly, the younger the age of the individual, the less her knowledge, the less favourable her attitude and the less use of family planning.

Those who used family planning attached far greater importance to being on good terms with their spouse and less to having fewer children as a reason for use. Women are strongly influenced by their friends who practise family planning. As might be expected the use is considerably higher among the woman who do not want any more children. Those who have a fatalistic philosophy of life are less likely to practise family planning.

Although figures with respect to use of family planning methods are not high (only 12 per cent of the random sample of 642 reported using any method, for example), the most encouraging note in the entire survey was the generally favourable response toward family planning encountered in all four samples. In the random sample, 75 per cent gave general approval, and in the North, 56 per cent. This would seem to indicate that, for the majority of persons, deeply felt emotional factors in opposition to the idea of family planning are not at work, and, given sufficient education, the opening of sufficient clinics and the ready availability of contraceptive devices, one might anticipate a significant expansion in use.

42 The place of intra-uterine contraceptive devices in East Africa

George A. Saxton, Jr., M.D., M.P.H.

Department of Preventive Medicine, Makerere University College, Uganda

David M. Serwadda, M.B., Ch.B.

Kasangati Health Centre, Kampala

Anne K. Saxton, R.N.

General Secretary, Family Planning Association of Uganda, Kampala

Introduction

In the last 15 years we have seen the demographic repercussions of malaria eradication on tropical populations, especially those living on islands such as Ceylon, Zanzibar and Mauritius.[1] The rapid reduction of infant mortality rates to a fraction of their previous level creates new economic and social problems, which can result in political instability. In each case the sequence of events has been much the same, i.e. the death rate has been lowered rapidly through technological changes introduced from outside and the birth rate has remained high. The result has been a growing gap between birth and death rates. In the last two to three years we have begun to see similar demographic gaps developing in certain areas of Africa such as Pare-Taveta in northern Tanzania,[2] Kigezi in south-western Uganda[3] and in Rwanda. More recently, the number of acres of potentially productive land per capita was calculated for the countries of East Africa as follows: 4·3 in Kenya, 5·4 in Uganda and 13·5 in Tanzania.[4] In Rwanda it is estimated that there is only 0·5 acre per capita, which is the same as in India at present. These densities presented only localized problems in 1965, and, given sufficient time, adjustments could be made, such as the redistribution of land, settling underdeveloped areas, etc. However, if the populations of these countries continue to grow at the rates of the past decade, there will not be time for these adjustments and redistributions. For instance, if Kenya's population continues to grow at a rate of 3·5 per cent per year, by 1990 it will have doubled, and the acres of productive land per capita will have fallen to 2·15. Since Kenya has already suffered overpopulation in the fertile Western Highlands, is unable to educate as high a proportion of her children as she would like, and is confronted with severe unemployment problems in Nairobi, the government has decided to incorporate family planning as an integral part of national economic planning.[5] Their position is best stated by quoting from *Sessional Paper No. 10: African Socialism and its Application to Planning in Kenya* as follows: 'Immediate steps will be taken towards family planning education, because the present high rate of population growth makes extensive and intensive provision of social services more expensive, the unemployment problems more intractable, and saving for development harder than need be—thus lowering the rate of economic growth.'

Of course, much of the responsibility for the growing discrepancy between births and deaths is attributable to the medical profession. Death rates have been reduced through the combination of tsetse fly eradication, improved water-supplies and sanitation, malaria suppression and control, specific disease immunization, improved maternity and child health services—in effect, scientific medicine and public health have combined with improved socio-economic conditions to lower mortality rates at all ages more rapidly in developing countries than was ever the case in the industrialized ones. The result is higher population growth rates than have ever been recorded in previous history. This is the nature of the special population problem of the developing countries, uniquely different from the classical one of widespread high density of population developing gradually along with urbanization and industrialization. Thus, the high hopes for rapid improvement of the quality of life, including increased availability of education, medical care and well-paid jobs, would all be frustrated by the doubling every 20 years not only of the work force but also of the dependent, under 15 age group of the population.

From the clinical point of view, it is well recognized that a mother who is ill or malnourished from having babies too frequently will produce an insufficient quantity of breast milk which often results in malnutrition in her nursing infant.[6] Worse still, rapid weaning of a nursing infant because of an early subsequent pregnancy is a common custom in various parts of Africa and often results in kwashiorkor.[7] The mother's health, as well, can be seriously impaired through a rapid succession of pregnancies, leaving her with insufficient stores of iron and protein known as the 'maternal depletion syndrome'.[8]

As women in Africa nurse their babies for progressively shorter periods of time and as polygamy gives way to monogamy, new and improved methods of birth control will be increasingly important in the protection of maternal and infant health from too frequent childbearing. Consequently, if a woman asks for help in spacing her pregnancies or limiting the size of her family, it is important that the medical profession should be prepared to give her such advice, drugs and devices as seem appropriate. But how many women know how to seek such help? What are the characteristics of men and women attending family planning clinics today?

Attitudes of Men and Women

The attitudes of men and women in Uganda generally are not particularly favourable to the use of birth control. A man, on the one hand, does not remain married to a woman if she cannot bear him children, while a woman, on the other hand, feels that it is not her place to determine whether or not she will become pregnant at a given time. In a series of interviews carried out in a rural area 10 miles north of Kampala, near the Kasangati Health Centre, women said that such matters were up to God, Providence and their husbands.[9] Furthermore, one woman expressed the striking concept of a woman's body being like a machine that is meant to produce babies, and, if it stopped doing so for some time, it might get stuck and never get going again. In spite of these attitudes, the attendance of women at the family planning clinics in Kampala has been almost doubling every six months for the past two years. Obviously, the women who come to these clinics are not a representative sample of the female population of Uganda. They are a self-selected minority with a special problem, i.e. high and persisting fertility. At first, in 1963, they were mostly 'grand multips' in their late 30s seeking to stop having any more children. But after the first six months or so in 1964, younger women began to come for help with spacing their future pregnancies. In the upper half of Figure 1 it is apparent that the peak age of marriage is 18–20 years, whereas the mean age for seeking family planning is ten years later, as can be seen in the lower half of the same figure. Among women attending these clinics, 83 per cent were African, the great majority relatively sophisticated Baganda. The remainder were 11 per cent Asian and 6 per cent European.

The fertility pattern of these women is strikingly different from that reported in

Figure 1 FAMILY PLANNING CLINIC—WOMEN

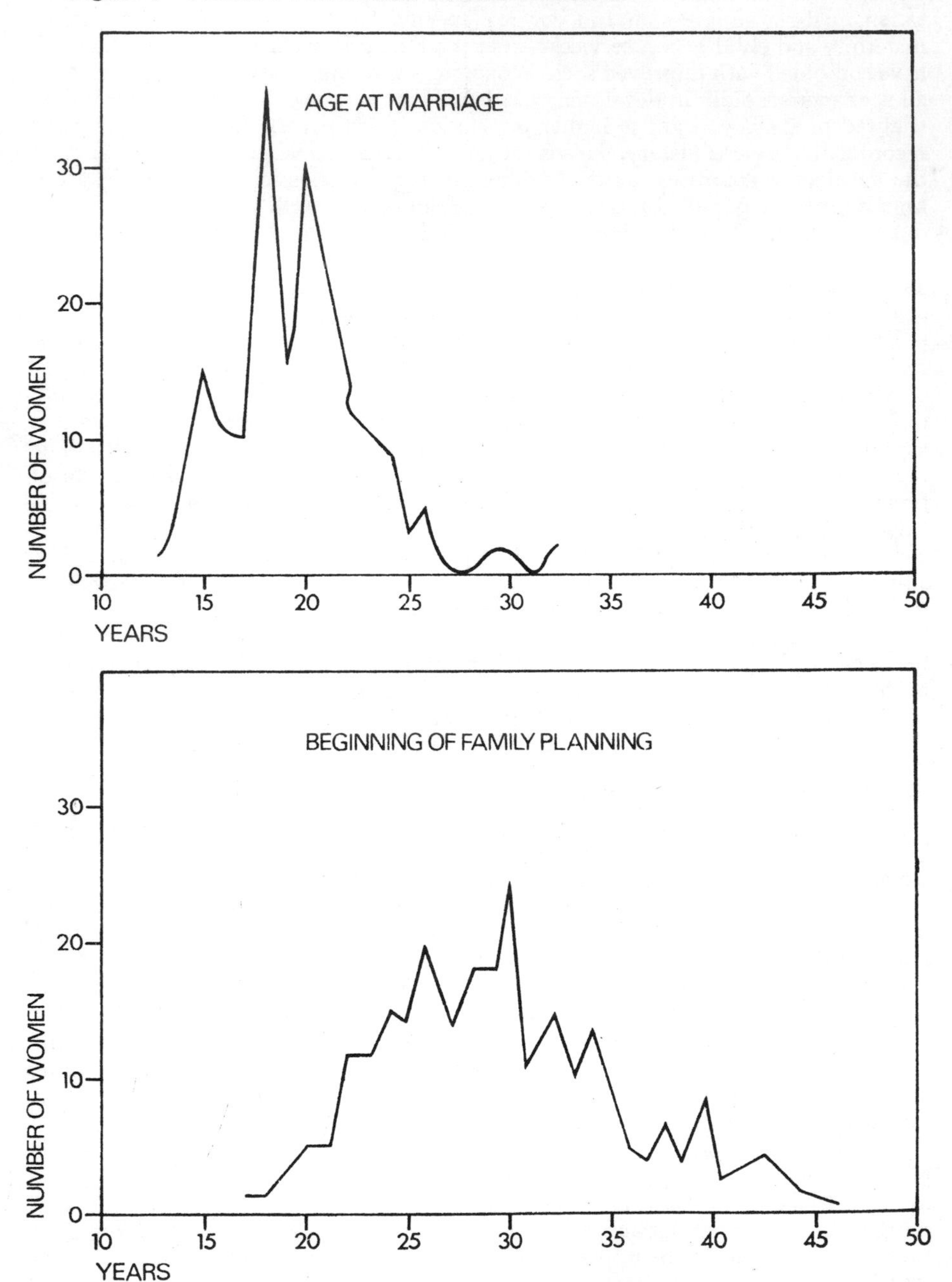

Figure 2 FERTILITY VARIATION WITH AGE AT CLINIC

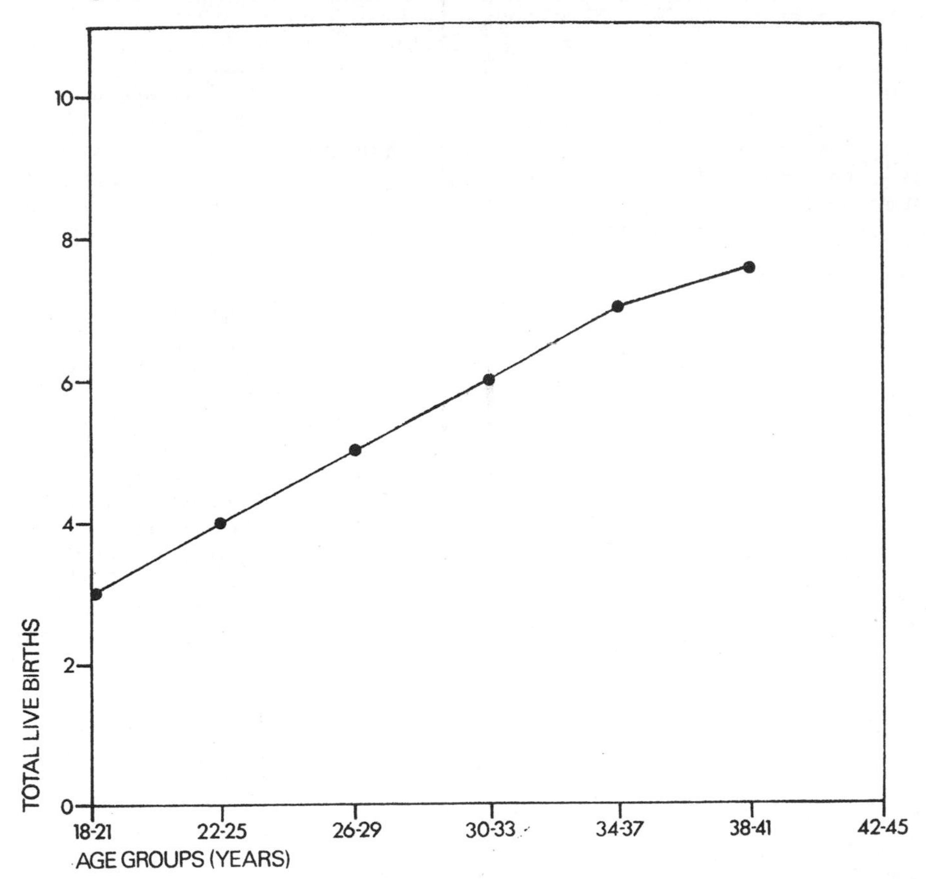

the Uganda Census of 1959. Figure 2 shows that not only is average fertility high, being 52 live births per 100 women-years at risk in marriage, but this rate persists, continuing right up into the fourth decade. In contrast, the average woman's fertility in Uganda, according to the census, declines rapidly after age 25.

Surprisingly enough, these clinic women were not highly educated. On the other hand, three-quarters of them said they were married to wage-earning men, most of whom are probably obliged to live on a fixed income. The occupations of husbands as percentages, were reported to be as follows: clerk/typists 13, teachers 12, civil servants 11, cashier/accountants 10 and doctors 10. From these data we conclude that the husband is playing a prominent rôle in the decision for the woman to start family planning.

Choice of Methods

Most of the rapid growth in attendance at family planning clinics in Kampala has developed since intra-uterine contraceptive devices (IUCDs) were included among the methods offered. Clinics were held more or less regularly from 1957 onwards, depending on when a doctor would volunteer services. The IUCDs were introduced in December 1963, and within six months one-third of women attending classes were choosing this new method and by the end of the year half were doing so. The other women chose diaphragms (22 per cent), oral pills (14 per cent) and the remaining 14 per cent chose other methods such as condoms, foam tablets or vaginal jellies. By June 1965 the proportion choosing IUCDs had risen to two-thirds. The average clinic attendance rose from 16 per month before IUCDs were being offered to 60 per month a year later, and 100 per month 18 months later. From this, it is apparent that IUCDs are enjoying growing popularity among couples living in and around Kampala. This may be because many such families lack the running water and privacy in their bedrooms required to use many methods popular among Europeans. Furthermore, the cost of insertion of an IUCD, which is effective for months or years, is only a fraction of that of diaphragm or pills over a comparable period.

History of IUCDs

Although it is generally agreed that Grafenberg (1929)[10] was the first to use intra-uterine devices for contraceptive purposes in human subjects in Germany in 1928, there is a story in North Africa that camel drivers have inserted almond size stones into the uteri of adult female camels before undertaking long journeys across the desert when pregnancy would be particularly inconvenient. Be that as it may, the metal devices of Grafenberg were associated with such a high incidence of endometritis and other complications that within five years he abandoned this approach. After the Second World War, however, the Japanese began to experiment with silk-worm gut and plastic threads as foreign bodies in the uteri for contraception. By 1950 they had developed the Ota Ring, a plastic device requiring local anaesthesia in order to permit sufficient dilation of the cervix for it to be introduced. In 1959 Dr Ishihama published a paper reporting 19,000 cases, including careful histological studies of uteri removed for other reasons in which these devices had been used for years and found no signs of malignancies developing.[11] This paper attracted the interest of two gynaecologists in New York, Dr L. Margulies (1962)[12] and Dr J. Lippes (1962),[13] who set to work devising their own plastic coils and tubes for inserting them without the necessity of dilating the cervix. The early results of their experience in private practice were so encouraging that a Co-operative International Study was organized by The Population Council in New York in 1961 in order to have this device tried in different countries around the world by fully qualified specialists in obstetrics and gynaecology. Papanicalaou smears of the cervix were required in all cases. In 1962 the Pathfinder Fund, a private foundation in Boston, Massachusetts, began to support non-specialists in various countries who were interested in using this method, in order to determine just how important it was that the procedure should be carried out by a specialist. The favourable results reported by both groups at the 2nd International Conference on Intra-uterine Contraception (1964) led the International Planned Parenthood Federation to make these devices available to all their regional and national offices for routine use without requiring special study reports or specialist qualifications. The changing point of view of conscientious doctors towards this new modification of an old form of contraception was well expressed in an editorial in *Lancet* late in 1964. It said, in part, 'Because intra-uterine devices have so long been held in disrepute, if not abhorrence, many will find it hard to adjust their minds to this form of contraception. At best they may feel it is still in its experimental phase; and, since it is obviously far from perfect, they may be inclined to urge very cautious progress—if any at all . . . But for innumerable women in developing countries, and not a few in supposedly developed ones, contraception by caps and diaphragms will be out of the question for a long time if not forever; and, even if intra-uterine devices sometimes cause pain and bleeding and can be used effectively by only 70–80 per cent of multiparous women, they will be thankfully accepted by mothers for whom the only alternative is a series of further pregnancies with all that these entail.'[14]

IUCDs in Uganda

In December 1963 the family planning clinics in Kampala began to include IUCDs among the methods offered women attending classes. During the following 18 months 300 women chose this method of contraception. However, only 250 cases will be reviewed here because the remaining 50 have too short a history for evaluation.

Written permission from both husband and wife, in the presence of a witness, is required in order to minimize misunderstandings. In general, there are two types used most commonly, the Margulies Spiral and the Lippes Loop. They are both introduced through a tube, being displaced into the uterus by a plunger. Before insertion, however, a Papanicolaou smear is taken from the cervix for examination of the exfoliative cytology. Although no gloves are worn by doctors during loading and insertion of IUCDs in many clinics, we have felt it would be wise to take this precaution. In order to avoid having to put on a clean pair of gloves for each new patient we simply wash frequently with antiseptic soap (Phisohex)—once before handling the IUCD and tube, and again after finishing with each patient.

Bimanual pelvic examination is done to rule out pre-existing pelvic infection, cervical lesions, tumours or pregnancy. An accurate menstrual history has been taken previously by the midwife in an effort to reduce the chances of interfering with an early pregnancy, though this could still occur. The face of the cervix is swabbed with an antiseptic soap (Cetavlon) and a sterile uterine sound inserted to determine the depth of the corpus uteri and confirm the presence of retroversion or anteflexion, and its degree. Then the appropriate size plastic device is taken from an antiseptic solution (Hibitane 0·075%, Cetrimide 0·75%, spirit 70%) and loaded into a straight plastic tube 4 mm. in diameter and 9 inches in length. This introducing tube is passed through the external and internal cervical os into the corpus uteri, and the IUCD is extruded by a plunger passed into the external end of the introducing tube. After this, the tube and plunger are removed. Through all this, the patient usually feels little or no pain; in rare cases one will complain of a shooting pain radiating down the leg or a vase-vagal type of reflex may occur. These symptoms have always cleared within a few minutes or on removal of the device. Re-insertion at a later date has usually been well tolerated in these cases.

The patient is then taught how to feel the plastic thread or stem protruding from the cervix so that she can check it at any time and know whether she is protected against pregnancy. This last step is particularly important because fully half of the spontaneous expulsions that occur are asymptomatic or occur during menstrual cramps, so loss of the IUCD may not be detected unless self-examination is carried out more or less regularly. In clinics where women are not taught how to do this, there is a much higher pregnancy rate than in clinics where this is done. In the Kampala series, covering 125 women-years, there has not been a known case of pregnancy occurring after an IUCD was inserted. In the large international series of 16,000 cases reported in New York (1964), there were 2·6 pregnancies per 100 women-years.[15] There may well be two to three cases of pregnancy in Kampala failing to report back to the clinic. If this were the case this method would still be far more effective than the diaphragm and cream which is reported to permit 13·8 pregnancies per 100 women-years of use. Finally, the patient returns at six weeks, six months and annually for routine checking of complaints, pelvic examination and repeat Papanicolaou smear.

Results of Follow-up

About 50 per cent of women suffer some discomfort and bleeding after the insertion of an IUCD, but these side-effects are limited to the first few days, are of little consequence in most women, and soon decrease to a tolerable level or disappear. If the intermenstrual bleeding, uterine cramps and backache do not begin to improve within a week or two it is best that the device be removed and another inserted. The patient is often the best judge of whether to remove the coil, because it is such a personal decision, depending on her subjective and domestic relationships as well as objective factors such as age and parity. It should be explained to the patient, however, that removal and re-insertion are usually painless. Insertion is a blind procedure, at best, and a better lie for the device may be obtained on re-insertion with little or no adverse side-effects.

Table 1 illustrates the comparative rates of expulsion and removal experienced by users of the different types of device. Both these events are seen to be more frequent when the large Margulies Spirals were used. By contrast, the 31 mm. Lippes Loop (Size 2D) gave the best results, with only 5 per cent expelled and 9 per cent removed

Table 1

Comparison of Types of IUCD

	Margulies spiral		Lippes loop	
	Large	Small	Hong Kong	31mm. USA
Expelled	18 (24)	2 (8)	12 (20)	6 (5)
Removed	25 (34)	8 (33)	14 (23)	10 (9)
No trouble	31 (42)	9 (59)	35 (57)	98 (86)
TOTAL	74 (100)	24 (100)	61 (100)	114 (100)

Note: Figures in brackets are percentages.

over a period of 1½–8 months follow-up. Although this is only a small series, and therefore not statistically significant, it does compare favourably with the large series (New York, 1964). Among 16,000 IUCDs of all types 14 per cent were expelled and 13 per cent were removed over a long period of follow-up. Our series is not quite comparable in terms of the type of device used or duration of follow-up. The other reports also indicated higher pregnancy rates when small Margulies Spirals or Birnberg Bows were used, which serves to emphasize the importance of inserting as large a device as can be accommodated.

Half of all expulsions occur within the first two months after insertion, making this a good time for the first return visit. There is a similar distribution of times of removal after insertion, with a median of 2·5 months. Curiously enough, these expulsions may occur for no apparent reason after more than 6–12 months of asymptomatic experience. Two-thirds of the expulsion cases request re-insertion, while 40 per cent of those requiring removal request re-insertion.

It is usually worthwhile trying a re-insertion after expulsion, because in the re-insertion cases half the IUCDs had been retained for three months when the patient was last seen in clinic and only 20 per cent had been re-expelled. There has been a comparable experience after re-insertion following removal, with 10 per cent expulsions and half of them still in place three months after re-insertion. For most women who are 'chronic expellers', it is easier to return to the clinic for a re-insertion every few months than to be bothered with other methods, if symptoms are not severe.

The complication that has worried us most from the outset has been pelvic infection. There is considerable evidence that the prevalence of pelvic inflammatory diseases in East Africa is high and one would not want to complicate these cases further by introducing a foreign body into the uterus.[16] Most of all it was feared that an IUCD might inadvertently convert a low-grade cervicitis, urethritis or endometritis into salpingitis and cause secondary sterility. However, in the first 100 women, seven cases of pelvic inflammatory disease were observed over a period of 76 women-years of follow-up, whereas only two cases have been observed so far in the next 150 women over a period of 48 women-years of follow-up. It must be noted that the normal rate of pelvic infection among 250 women in this age-range over a similar period of time is not known for comparison. Also, having had seven women develop pelvic infection among the first 100 we were then much less inclined to insert IUCDs in women with histories of low abdominal pain or discharge. We have always considered adnexal tenderness and thickening a contra-indication. However, many clinics proceed with insertion under cover of antibiotics. Finally, we were reassured by the experience of four women, who requested removal of the device in order that they could become pregnant, and who all succeeded in becoming pregnant within a few months. This was also the experience reported at the Second International Conference (1964).[16] Other contra-indications are fairly logical: pregnancy, tumours of the cervix, uterus or ovaries, history of menorrhagia or the presence of marked anaemia. It is also difficult and painful to insert in a nulliparous uterus, though it can be achieved in some cases if there are compelling reasons for using this method. In general we encourage women to use other methods early in their married lives, preferring to reserve the IUCD for multiparous women.

The examination of initial Papanicolaou smears taken before insertion of IUCDs has revealed a high prevalence of both *Trichamonas vaginalis* (38 per cent) and abnormal cytology (11 per cent Grade II or more). The Trichamonal infection seems to be comensile in that most of the women have no complaint referable to it. When they have complaints, they are treated with vaginal suppositories (Vagiflav), and, if they do not respond, systemic treatment of both husband and wife is then undertaken (Flagyl). The prevalence of *T. vaginalis* was found to be unchanged on repeat smears as compared to initial smears. Cone biopsies of the cervix were sought in ten cases with repeated and persistent abnormal cytology of Grade III or worse; of the five cases biopsied so far, four revealed carcinoma in situ. One of the biopsied cases required hysterectomy to be certain that there was not further extension. The fifth case, which was not carcinoma, did reveal severe dysplasia and is being followed closely. The relatively high number of cases of carcinoma in situ among women examined in family planning clinics is consistent with the well-established observation that women with high fertility are especially prone to develop this type of cancer. The rate per 1,000 women examined would be 12 if the present high prevalence is sustained in the future. The abnormal cytology rate of 11 per cent is 50 per cent greater than that in the obstetrical-gynaecological clinics of New Mulago Hospital (7·2 per cent). This has suggested that, from the point of view of public health, family planning clinics may be a good location for detecting carcinoma of the cervix at an early stage so that preventive surgery can be carried out.[17]

Follow-up of 120 women has permitted smears to be repeated 1–17 months after the first. Of these, 88 have remained constant and 16 have shown progression towards abnormal cytology. However, 16 others have regressed toward more normal cytology over the same period of time, under the same circumstances. In fact, five women both progressed and regressed more than one class in the course of repeated smears. In view of all this, it is felt that it is too early to be sure of the significance of these changes, especially since so little is known about the rate of progression of cervical cytology in African women who are not wearing an IUCD. At present these changes could be due simply to random variation in sampling and interpretation, plus the normal tendency for women to develop abnormal cytology with age.

Nothing conclusive can be stated until a comparable control series has been followed over a similar period of time in much larger numbers of women.

All of the foregoing discussion depends on the proportion of women who return for follow-up visits. Among the first 100 women, 93 per cent returned for at least a second visit, over a period of 10–18 months after insertion; of the second 100, 82 per cent returned over a period of 3–10 months; while only 58 per cent of the next 50 women have as yet returned over the intervening 1½–3 months since insertion. When defaulters finally return to clinic they are usually found to be asymptomatic and do not want to be bothered with being re-examined, fearing that the device might be removed for some reason. Inquiries from local hospitals have not revealed any cases consulting them that were unknown to the family planning clinics, although there must inevitably be a few.

Availability

Any registered doctor can now obtain these devices at cost through the Family Planning Associations of Uganda, Kenya or Tanzania, just as with any other contraceptive materials. Only in Kenya are they being provided through government medical services.

Summary

Plastic intra-uterine contraceptive devices (IUCDs) have been in use in Kampala, Uganda, since December 1963. A series of 250 women choosing this new method in Kampala Family Planning Clinics have been followed over a period of 18 months and the findings reported. Although half of them had minor complaints, such as uterine cramps and inter-menstrual bleeding for a few days after insertion, no serious complications have been observed. Fertility was unimpaired in four women who asked to have the device removed for a planned pregnancy. It is concluded that this new modification of an old method of contraception can be used competently by any doctor with a few months post-graduate hospital training in obstetrics and gynaecology such as is provided in most internships and residencies. In the hands of such non-specialists, three-quarters of the women having an IUCD inserted were still wearing it and wanted to keep it when last seen over 125 women-years of follow-up, and no pregnancies were known to have occurred.

Footnotes

1. R. M. TITMUS and B. ABEL-SMITH, *Social Policies and Population Growth in Mauritius*, London, 1961.
2. G. PRINGLE, *Annual Report of the East African Institute of Malaria and Vector-Borne Diseases, 1 July 1963–31 December 1964*, East African Common Services Organization, 1964.
3. J. D. TURYAGYENDA, *Uganda Journal*, Vol. 28, 1964, p. 127.
4. E. EDWARDS, personal communication, 1965.
5. Kenya Government, *African Socialism and Its Application to Planning in Kenya*, Sessional Paper No. 10 of 1963/65.
6. D. B. JELLIFFE, *Child Health in the Tropics*, London, 1964.
7. H. WELLBOURN, *Nutrition in Tropical Countries*, OUP, Nairobi, 1963.
8. D. B. JELLIFFE, *American Journal of Clinical Nutrition*, Vol. 10, 1962, p. 19.
9. V. JUNOD and F. KAMOGA, unpublished observations, 1964.
10. E. GRAFENBERG, 'Silk als Antikonzipiens', *Gehurtenregelung: Vortrage und Verhandlungen des Arztekursus*, Vols. 28–30, December, Selbstverlag, Berlin, 1928.
11. A. ISHIHAMA, *Yokoyama Medical Journal*, Vol. 10, 1959, p. 89.
12. L. C. MARGULIES, 'Intra-Uterine Contraceptive Devices', *Proceedings of First International Conference, New York*, Amsterdam, 1962.
13. J. LIPPES, 'Intra-Uterine Contraceptive Devices', *ibid.*
14. Leading Article, 'Contraceptive Intra-uterine Devices', *Lancet*, Vol. 2, 1964, pp. 945 and 958.
15. *Intra-Uterine Contraception: Proceedings of the Second International Conference, New York*, Amsterdam, 1964.
16. H. B. GRIFFITHS, *The Eugenics Review*, Vol. 55, 1963, p. 103.
17. R. R. TRUSSELL, *Association of Surgeons of East Africa*, Nairobi, 1964.

43 The Tunisian family planning programme

George F. Brown, M.D.

Population Council Representative, Tunisia

Amor Daly

Chief of Medical Service, El Menzah, Tunis, Tunisia

Introduction

The Government of Tunisia has recognized for several years the problems created by the country's rapid population growth, and has actively sought means to solve this problem. The population of Tunisia was estimated at 4·6 million in January 1965, and was growing at an estimated rate of 2·3 per cent per year. This was the product of a crude birth rate at about 46 per 1,000 and a crude death rate of about 23 per 1,000. In view of the government's programme of planned economic and social development, such a rapid rate of population growth is considered to be a major limiting factor in achieving a higher standard of living for the Tunisian people. This is especially true since the population is largely agrarian, natural resources are limited, and industry is only gradually developing.

Since Independence in 1956, the Tunisian Government has taken a number of legislative steps designed to decrease population growth. In doing this, it has reversed the pro-natalist policy established prior to independence by the French. Among the major steps have been the emancipation of women, abolition of polygyny, and limiting welfare support to only the first four children of the family. In 1961, all restrictions on contraception were removed, and importation and sale of contraceptive materials was permitted. In 1965, abortions were legalized for women with five or more living children.[1]

Tunisia embarked on a policy of planned economic development in 1962. The relationship between population growth and economic and social development became more sharply defined as goals were established for the ten-year period, 1962–71.[2] Planners based their expectations of economic growth on a decline in population growth from 2·3 to 1·7 per cent over this period. This decline was anticipated solely on the basis of improved economic and social conditions. There was no evidence, by 1965, that such a decline had started or was likely to occur in the near future. It is very likely that the population in 1971 will exceed the 4·7 million that was projected by the government's ten-year perspectives.

Discussions on family planning between the Government of Tunisia and the Ford Foundation commenced in 1962. This was the first time that a family planning programme was considered by the government as a method of decreasing the rate of population growth. Following a report by Population Council and Ford Foundation consultants, a two-year experimental programme in family planning was agreed upon in May 1963. The Ministry of Health of the Government of Tunisia administered the programme, which was supported by a Ford Foundation grant. Technical assistance was provided by the Population Council. Tunisia is thus the first country on the continent of Africa to undertake a National Family Planning Programme.

The Experimental Family Planning Programme

The programme, as originally designed,[3] was to develop a practical family planning service, based on the resources and needs of Tunisia, and to provide experience and information that would permit the Government of Tunisia to effectively expand the programme in the future. By varying the types of services offered and methods of informing the people, the most effective techniques would be developed. Development of the programme was divided into Preliminary, Operational and Evaluation phases.

PRELIMINARY PHASE

Prior to commencing the action programme, a group of Tunisian officials, including the Director of the Family Planning Programme, visited Japan, Pakistan and the USA, in order to become familiar with world-wide developments in family planning. On their return, a four-week seminar on family planning was held in Tunis in order to train doctors, paramedical personnel, health educators and social workers. Specialists in gynaecology, demography, sociology and communications, from Tunisia, the United States and Belgium participated. This seminar received nation-wide press and radio coverage, and focused national attention on family planning and population problems.

In early 1964, a social demographic sample survey of 2,175 Tunisian women was undertaken by Professor Jean Morsa of the Free University of Brussels. The survey was to provide information on attitudes, knowledge and practices of family planning in Tunisia. Preliminary results[4] indicate that a high percentage of Tunisian women of all classes favour family planning, but knowledge and use of contraceptives is extremely limited. Among women aged 30–39, 72 per cent stated that they wanted no more children. This survey, in addition to providing essential information about Tunisian attitudes toward fertility, served as a baseline for future measurements of the impact of the Family Planning Programme. A second survey is planned for 1967.

During this preliminary phase, family planning and population problems were widely discussed at all levels throughout the country. Most significantly, President Bourguiba has spoken frequently and at length in favour of family planning. Various national organizations have committed themselves to actively support family planning. This preliminary period was thus an important time for discussion, for sounding the population and for rallying support to the programme.

Certain characteristics of Tunisia have facilitated the introduction of family planning. The country is small, there are no high mountains, and roads are generally good, so that the great majority of settlements are accessible. The population is ethnically homogeneous. Government radio stations reach most of the people, as receivers are numerous and widespread. Finally, the administrative and political organization of the country enables the people to respond quickly to their leaders in such fields as rural development, campaigns against infectious diseases, and family planning problems.[4]

OPERATIONAL PHASE

The action programme commenced in June 1964. Family planning services were established in 12 Maternal and Child Health centres. The chosen centres were widely separated, to provide a wide geographic and urban–rural variation. These centres are generally well attended by mothers, and are staffed with appropriate paramedical personnel. A range of contraceptive methods was made available, and all services and supplies were provided free to clients. Publicity for these services has been entirely by word of mouth among the women who regularly attend the centres.

Three Tunis hospitals started clinical trials with the intra-uterine contraceptive device (IUCD) in June 1964. This new 'one-visit' contraceptive technique has been studied extensively in many countries[5] and has been well received by the Tunisian medical profession. Basing its decision on promising initial trials, the Ministry of Health decided to expand as rapidly as possible the clinical IUCD services through the health system. To this end, all gynaecologists and surgeons in Tunisia received training in intra-uterine contraception. By early 1965, over 70 doctors had received training in this technique, and IUCD centres were established in every hospital where competent medical personnel were available. By September 1965, 29 hospitals and Maternal and Child Health centres offered IUCD services. In many hospitals a regular IUCD clinic, one to three times a week, has been incorporated into the regular out-patient gynaecology or surgery service.

In three areas, more specialized programmes have been undertaken. In the Tunis area, the three hospital IUCD services and the three original family planning clinics in Maternal and Child Health centres have been augmented by the addition of a full-time family planning gynaecologist. This doctor makes routine weekly trips to the three centres, and to nearby towns, to perform IUCD insertions. This programme was the first attempt to bring IUCD clinics to out-patient centres on a routine basis, and it has been successful.

In a rural region, Beja, a weekly plan of visits to villages and towns from the central city of Beja was established. This programme was developed in co-operation with regional government authorities and political party workers, whose activities will be described later, providing local publicity for the visit.

A second rural region, Le Kef, has inaugurated a similar programme, also with the support of governmental workers. Women have been brought from rural areas into the central regional hospital, where IUCD insertions are performed daily. All available government vehicles are employed for transporting the women. These last two programmes have been extremely successful.

General informational support has been consistently given to the programme by the radio and the press. Repeated news broadcasts, feature stories, and interviews on family planning have appeared. As previously mentioned, family planning is a recurrent subject in President Bourguiba's speeches, which carry great influence. The effect of this support has been to keep family planning in the public eye, and to legitimize the programme.

Starting in January 1965, the Destourian Socialist Party incorporated family planning as one of its major activities. The party is highly organized on national, regional and local levels, and emphasizes close contact with the people. It interprets governmental policies to the people, and helps implement these policies regionally and locally. The activities previously described in the regions of Beja and Le Kef were supported by the Destourian Party. In Beja, regional party leaders and family planning workers planned weekly visits to small towns and villages. The visit by the medical team was extensively publicized in advance by local party workers through group meetings and individual visits. In every case this programme has met with success. In the Le Kef region, the party workers publicized family planning and arranged for transportation to the regional hospital. In both areas, channels for the medical follow-up of problem cases were established and have proven effective.

At present, evaluation of the programme is based on clinic record charts. The information in these charts has not been fully exploited as yet, and a full evaluation of this information is planned at the end of the experimental period. Table 1 summarizes clinic attendance.

While present information on the clinical programme is as yet incomplete, several observations can be made on the 18,632 women who have received family planning services. Over half these women, 11,094, chose the IUCD. Choice between methods

Table 1

Attendance at Family Planning Clinics

	Total consultations	Number of first visits	First insertions of IUCD
1964			
June	375	375	11
July	1,125	764	103
August	2,250	1,175	147
September	2,249	984	167
October	1,891	972	106
November	2,235	735	258
December	2,103	772	362
1965			
January	1,722	653	417
February	2,315	757	663
March	3,837	2,561	2,053
April	3,496	2,030	2,053
May	3,837	2,334	1,859
June	4,267	2,057	1,543
July	3,686	1,782	1,275
August*	2,850	785	680
September*	2,646	1,473	533
TOTALS	41,347	20,209	11,732

* Incomplete.

was not always available at each centre, but where a free choice was available, more than half preferred the IUCD. The average age of clients is close to 30 years, with IUCD acceptors being older than acceptors of conventional methods. The average number of living children per client is between four and five. Again, IUCD acceptors have somewhat larger families. All socio-economic levels of the population are represented in the group, but the overwhelming majority are from the poorest levels. Middle and upper classes tend to seek private services.

Among the conventional contraceptives, condoms, vaginal jellies, and vaginal aerosols have been available. In most centres, condoms have been most popular, despite the fact that it is the women who attend the clinics and receive the supplies. Less than one-half of all the women choosing conventional contraceptives are returning regularly for supplies after one year. Oral contraceptives have not been made widely available, but several gynaecologists are undertaking clinical studies on this method. Until the results of these experiences are available, oral contraceptives will not be widely used. Female sterilizations are performed on request, as are abortions for women with five or more living children. It should be emphasized that a variety of contraceptive methods is offered. A free choice between several methods is essential, as no one method is suitable for all couples.

PROGRAMME ACHIEVEMENTS

Family planning is still very new to Tunisia. The action programme is now just over one year old, and it is still too early to reach any firm conclusions. However, certain achievements are clearly evident, and others are at least suggested.

1. Family planning has been seen as necessary for Tunisian development. The Tunisian people, particularly in high governmental and medical circles, have been acquainted with population problems and with family planning. Most important of

all, the programme has proved that a national family planning programme is feasible in Tunisia and has provided the impetus for the forthcoming national campaign.

2. On the basis of the sociological survey and the results of the action programme, it has been demonstrated that a high percentage of Tunisian couples want family planning information and services.

3. The medical profession, having been convinced of the importance of family planning, has been trained and mobilized. Integration of family planning into the national health services has proved practical and desirable.

4. Government and Destourian Socialist Party workers have proved to be highly effective agents of publicity and information on family planning.

5. The programme has provided experience with the clinical use of various contraceptive methods. The IUCD has been singled out as the most widely accepted and effective method in Tunisia.

Future Plans

Resulting from the success of the experimental programme, the government of Tunisia is preparing to launch a national Family Planning Campaign, to start early in 1966. The goal is to have 120,000 women practising intra-uterine contraception within two years. It is expected that the campaign will extend beyond the two years. The broad outline of the proposed programme is as follows:

1. Present family planning services will be extended by training most or all Tunisian doctors in intra-uterine contraception. The minimum target is 200 doctors.

2. Extension of family planning services to most or all of the 52 regional hospitals and a large number of Maternal and Child Health centres, will be undertaken.

3. These services will be augmented by 13 mobile medical teams centred in each region. These teams, each consisting of doctor, midwife and assistant, will make periodic visits to towns and villages in the region.

4. The major source of information and publicity will rest with regional government and Destourian Socialist Party workers. The regional mobile medical units will co-ordinate their activities with local officials so that advance publicity and information is provided.

5. Educational and informational support will be provided by the Health Education services, the radio and television and various national organizations.

The success of the experimental programme has permitted the Tunisian Government to move rapidly into a national programme. While it is too early to predict with certainty the ultimate impact of the programme on the Tunisian birth rate, it is clear that the government is making a determined effort, based on practical experience, to achieve a decrease in the birth rate over a short period of time. It has been provisionally estimated that, if the programme goals are achieved, the birth rate may decrease by approximately 8–10 per cent between 1966 and 1968.

Footnotes

1. DALY, AMOR, 'Experience in Family Planning in the Republic of Tunisia', paper presented to the International Conference on Family Planning Programmes, Geneva, August 1965.
2. *Perspectives Décennales de Développement, 1962–71*, République Tunisienne.
3. Report on Tunisia in ***Studies in Family Planning***, No. 2, 1963, The Population Council, NY.
4. MORSA, JEAN, 'Tunisia: A Preliminary Analysis', paper presented to the International Conference on Family Planning Programmes, Geneva, August 1965.
5. TIETZE, C. and LEWIT, SARAH (eds.), 'Intra-uterine Contraceptive Devices', *Excerpta Medica*, Amsterdam, 1962.
SEGAL, S. J., SOUTHAM, A. L. and SHAFER, K. D., 'Intra-uterine Contraception', *Excerpta Medica*, Amsterdam, 1964.

44 Demographic training and research in tropical African universities

J. C. Caldwell

Department of Demography, Australian National University, Canberra, Australia

The University Situation

This paper will confine itself to tropical African universities that employ English as the medium of instruction. Thus, with the exception of Liberia and the Sudan, the title could have referred to Commonwealth universities. The subject is treated mainly in a descriptive manner. A more analytical treatment of the founding, organization and continuation of demography programmes in the area may be found elsewhere.[1]

The development of any university discipline in tropical Africa is conditioned to a considerable degree by the general development of university studies. Before the Second World War, university facilities were few, although it had been possible to obtain a Durham degree at Fourah Bay, Sierra Leone, since the mid-19th century, and it was possible to take some examinations in British degree courses at various colleges. The most marked change occurred in 1948–49 when colleges of the University of London were established to provide a wide range of tuition in Ghana, Nigeria, Uganda and the Sudan. The second important period began in 1960 and is still continuing. It has seen the conversion of university colleges into independent universities, the establishment of a considerable number of new universities and a rapid expansion of student numbers.

Included in this paper is a Table presenting in summary a survey of university activity in the areas being considered here. In some respects it is already out of date: some institutions have changed their names; it does not record the new University of Lesotho, Botswana and Swaziland nor the University of Zambia, although one of its component parts is represented. The rate of growth of student numbers during the first half of the 1960s was probably the highest in the world for an area of this size but the total numbers are still not great. By 1963 total university student numbers exceeded 10,000 for the first time in a group of countries with a total population of about 110 million.[2] Nor, because of differing histories and various degrees of national wealth, is tertiary education evenly spread. In West Africa in 1963, the number of university students per million inhabitants exceeded 300 in Liberia and Ghana and 200 in Sierra Leone. Whether it exceeded 100 in Nigeria depended on which population estimate was accepted for the country. In Central Africa, numbers ranged between 100 and 200, and Sudan also fell into this category, while in East Africa, only Uganda exceeded 100, with Kenya and Tanzania falling below. A still more distinctive pattern emerged for post-graduate education, for almost two-thirds of the 366 graduate students in Commonwealth countries were in Ghana or Nigeria, while most of the remainder were in Rhodesia. Such figures are important when considering the possible development of demographic studies, for in some universities the discipline is considered most properly placed amongst studies for higher degrees rather than for first degrees. Statistics of post-graduate students have to be treated cautiously as some universities include graduate teachers undertaking professional courses in education, while others do not. There are 18 universities or colleges in the area employing English for instruction. This paper is confined to the 15 of any size in which teaching was under way during the 1965–66 academic year and which had provided information on their activities.

The Teaching of Demography

There have been three forces encouraging either the teaching of demography or at least greater attention to demographic techniques within existing disciplines. The first is the fact that, by the time the African universities were developing, demographic studies were playing a more important rôle in various overseas universities than had been the case a generation earlier. It is not unimportant that the University Colleges of Ghana, Ibadan, Makerere and Khartoum were linked with the University of London, where the London School of Economics and Political Science had a pre-existing demography course.

The second force is that in the post-war atmosphere, of colonies developing towards independence and of newly self-governing countries, an increasing interest was taken in economic and social development and indeed in development plans. This necessitated a greater knowledge of each country's population and of the characteristics of the population. Hence a desire to hold modern censuses and the view that universities might help with the designing of such censuses and in the analysis of collected data grew together. This was partly a reflection of the change of balance occurring in the distribution of high-level technical skills in many African countries. Before the Second World War most available skill was either found in the public service or could be imported by the colonial administration from Britain. Now, a great deal of talent, in for instance such a specialized field as population mapping, can be found in the new universities or can be secured on loan through the good offices of international organizations.

The third force is the need felt in each country by those undertaking various kinds of social and economic research to organize their studies within a framework of knowledge about the numbers of people in certain areas and the characteristics of those people.

Together, these forces have produced an increasing appreciation of the value of population studies. In the replies to the *Survey of University Teaching and Research in the Field of Population*, the head of one research institute wrote that it was 'highly desirable that demographic training and research should form part of university activity in all African countries'. The head of a Department of Economics, who had been engaged in various studies of rural economies, stated, 'I regard the demographic aspects of research in African rural areas as a first priority that should precede, if possible, the more general economic type of survey', while the head of a Geography Department, who had organized a full demography course, remarked, 'I feel that demography should have a very worthy and important place in tropical African universities'.

However, demography courses as such have not as yet become established in most of the new universities. There are at present four continuing courses, one in a Sociology Department, another in a Social Anthropology Department and two in Economics Departments.[3] But these four courses are shared between only two universities.

A demography course was begun within the Sociology Department of the University of Ghana during the 1959–60 academic year, financial help and assistance in recruiting teaching staff being provided by the Population Council. In the first four years of its existence, it had to recruit four demographers in succession to keep the course alive. There were indeed short periods when the post remained vacant, but there was at least some demographic teaching in every academic year, and from 1961 students attempted the subject at every Finals examination. Tuition at the graduate

Table 1

Survey of University Teaching and Research in the field of Population in Tropical Africa (Confined to universities using English as the medium of instruction)[a]

Country and University	Department	Teaching	Research	Publications	External Research finance
Ghana					
University of Ghana (also College at Cape Coast)	African Studies	X	R	X	
	Economics	D (1964)	X	X	
	Geography	L	P	S	
	Sociology	D (1960)	D	(2)[b]	PC
	Statistics	L	D	X	
University of Science and Technology (Kumasi)	—	L	P	2	VRA
Kenya					
University College	Geography	L	P	2 (3)	
Liberia					
University of Liberia[c]	—	—	—	—	
Nigeria					
University of Ibadan	Economics	D (1964)	D	32[d]	
	Geography[c]	—	—		
	Political Science	L	R		
	Sociology	L	D		
	African Studies	X	X		
	NISER	X	X		
Ahmadu Bello University	Geography	L[e]	P, R	(2)	GKPA
University of Ife	Economic and Social Studies	S	X	X	
	Geography	S	X	X	
	African Studies	X	X	X	
University of Lagos	Business and Social Studies	—	—	—	
University of Nigeria	Geography	S	P	X	
	Agriculture	L	R	X	WHO
	Sociology and Anthropology	X	X	X	
	African Studies	X	X	X	
	Economic Development	X	X	X	
Rhodesia					
University College of Rhodesia	Sociology	L	D	12	
	Economics	L	P	4	Rockefeller Rhodesian Government
	Medicine	L	R	X	
Sierra Leone					
Fourah Bay College	Geography	D (1963)	P	X	
	Economics	L	X	X	
Sudan					
University of Khartoum	Economics and Social Studies	D	D	X	Ford
	Geography	L	P, R	X	Goldsmith
Tanzania					
University College	Economics	S	X	X	

Table 1 (*continued*)

Country and University	Department	Teaching	Research	Publications	External Research finance
Uganda Makerere University College	Sociology	D (1966)	D	5	
	Economics	X	X	X	
	Geography	X	X	X	
Zambia Rhodes-Livingstone Institute		X	D, P	23	CDF AHB Government

Notes: (a) Original survey, January 1964; information checked November–December 1964.
(b) By late 1967 this had become 16 (3).
(c) Failed to reply to original questionnaire.
(d) Estimate of publications (titles not specified).
(e) Plans or hopes for the future.

Teaching.
D = full demography course examined by at least one separate paper (year of commencement given in brackets).
S = a special series of lectures on demography constituting part of a larger course and examined with this larger course.
L = some demographic lectures or content in some course or courses.
X = no teaching of demography.
— = not known.

Research.
D = now, or in the past, a considerable research programme on population.
P = now, or in the past, a considerable amount of work on the distribution of population or population characteristics.
R = at least one piece of research on population.
X = no research on population.
— = not known.

Publications.
not in brackets = separate books or articles on population already published.
in brackets = books or articles in the process of publication.
S = several, otherwise number is given.
X = no publications.
— = not known.

Notes on External Research Finance (Research funds from other than university sources).

PC = Population Council (grants totalling $115,000 to establish teaching and research programmes at the University of Ghana).

VRA = Volta River Authority (an independent Authority established by the Government of Ghana to control the Volta Dam construction and which has set aside some money received from international and governmental sources for university research work connected with the planning of the project).

GKPA = Greater Kano Planning Authority (a local government authority financing a series of projects).

WHO = World Health Organization (a survey for yaws and smallpox control purposes is being carried out under WHO direction in Nsukka and is collecting some demographic information).

Rockefeller = Rockefeller Foundation (financed the Economic Survey of Chiweshe Reserve, 1960–61).

Rhodesian Government = (Southern) Rhodesian Government (financed the Economic Survey of Chitowa Native Purchase Area, 1963–64).

Ford	= Ford Foundation (is financing a study of fertility differentials amongst 6,000 families in different parts of the Sudan).
Goldsmith	= Goldsmith Grant (financing a small-scale survey of the water-supply and population of the Gedaref area in Sudan).
CDF	= British Government's Colonial Development and Welfare Fund (financed studies of the demographic and socio-economic structure of urban and peri-urban area in Zambia in 1956–58, and for a study of the Copperbelt in 1951–55 which aimed at providing basic data on demographic composition with a view to working out an index of urbanization).
AHB	= African Housing Board (financed a study of the household composition of African dwellings in Lusaka, Zambia, 1956–58).
Government	= Government departments (which assisted in a study of the distribution of African population in Zambia in the early 1960s).

level was offered in 1962–63 and 1963–64, the students subsequently proceeding overseas rather than taking an M.A. or M.Sc. locally. When the courses began, the University was still linked with London, and the syllabus offered has continued to bear a relation to the L.S.E. course, although with an increasing orientation towards tropical Africa as more material has become available. Demography has been offered as an alternative subject, frequently taken by the majority of students, and has been examined by a single Final Examination Paper, although it has at times been taught as a two-year course. In this case a Second Year *Population Studies* course has been followed by a Third Year one in *Techniques of Demographic Analysis*. By the 1964–65 academic year, Ghanaians who had undertaken post-graduate training in demography overseas were back in the University as staff members and there seemed little doubt about the future of teaching in the subject.

Since 1964 a somewhat similar course in demography has been offered by the Economics Department of the University of Ghana, the teaching being undertaken by a member of the Institute of Statistics. It seems likely that this course will also continue, possibly serviced by the Institute of Statistics or from demographers within the Sociology Department, if no expatriate demographer or staff member from its own students is available in the Economics Department.

In the Faculty of Economic and Social Studies of the University of Khartoum, a full demography course, similar to those already mentioned, is offered to Economics Honours students and a somewhat simplified version of the course, in combination with statistics, is provided for Social Anthropology Honours students. In addition, a course is provided in Fourth Year Economics on the Economics of Population, which includes a considerable number of lectures on population theory.

Outside the Universities of Ghana and Khartoum, demography teaching, once begun or planned, has been in considerable jeopardy. The fundamental problem has always been the difficulty of recruiting demographers to teach the syllabuses. Since the 1963–64 academic year, the Geography Syllabus of Fourah Bay College, University of Sierra Leone, has contained a full demography course, but in the year of writing it is not being taught because of the departure of the man who designed it and lectured for the first two years. However, there is a firm expectation that it will henceforth be provided in alternate years. A demography course has been in the syllabus of the Sociology Department of Uganda's Makerere University College since the 1964–65 academic year but failure to recruit a demographer has postponed teaching until 1966–67 at the earliest.

Present indications for an early extension of demography teaching look brightest in West Africa. Fourah Bay, Sierra Leone, is being advised on the establishment of a Sociology Department, and it is possible that this will contain a demography course from the outset. It would appear to an outsider that the extension of research interest in population at the University of Ibadan could easily lead to the establishment of a full teaching course.

But, quite apart from separate courses in demography, much of the simpler topics covered in such syllabuses is taught within other courses, especially those of Geography and Economics Departments. The former exist in all universities but two, and the latter in all but three. Some demography is taught within the Geography courses in universities in Nigeria (Ahmadu Bello, Nigeria, Ife and Ibadan), in Sierra Leone, in Sudan and in Ghana (Legon, Accra) and is being considered in Kenya. Such courses often give instructions on the simpler indices for measuring fertility and mortality, as well as more sophisticated techniques for analysing population distribution and migration. Some include work on population projection. All include population mapping, which increasingly covers the distribution of various demographic indices, such as child–woman ratios and age structure, as well as density, urbanization and similar measures. There is a growing tendency for the more advanced work to embrace some aspects of population theory, and to examine economic and agricultural problems posited by rapid population growth.

Besides the full demography courses offered within the Economics Departments in Ghana and the Sudan, some demography is taught within the Economics Departments in Tanzania, Nigeria (Ife), Sierra Leone and Rhodesia. Elsewhere, some work is done in the Social Anthropology Department of the University College in Rhodesia. It is often touched upon whenever problems of rural society are involved, as in some medical departments, in the Agriculture Department at Nsukka, Nigeria and the Institute of Administration at Zaria, Nigeria, which has been considering some population work.

Population Research

University research in this field displays a more even coverage of tropical Africa than is the case with teaching. A great deal is concerned with the findings of censuses or field surveys.

Of the more strictly demographic research, much of it has centred, at least until recently, around the demography programmes in the Universities of Ghana and Khartoum and around the work of what until lately was called the Rhodes–Livingstone Institute in Zambia. At the University of Ghana, the Population Council has financed a considerable body of research on fertility and mortality levels, aspects of demographic change, migration, and attitudes towards the control of family size. Work on the level of vital rates has also been undertaken in the Institute of Statistics. Only a small fraction of the findings has yet been published. In Khartoum the Ford Foundation has financed a study of differential fertility in a sample of 6,000 families. During the first half of the 1950s, the Rhodes–Livingstone Institute, financed by the British Colonial Development and Welfare Fund, undertook work on fertility in Nyasaland and later a social survey, with various demographic aspects, based on a 10 per cent sample of urban African households.[4] Much, but not all of this, has to date been analysed and published. In the second half of the 1950s, the Institute, using the same source of finance, engaged in work on the demographic and socio-economic structure of certain urban areas in Nyasaland and Northern Rhodesia.[5] Much of this work was subsequently published. Within the last two years an increasing concentration of persons interested in population phenomenon has occurred at the University of Ibadan, especially in the Population Centre, Sociology and Geography Departments, the Medical Faculty and the Nigerian Institute for Social and Economic Research (NISER). At an earlier date NISER had planned a rather ambitious demographic project but had been unable to secure funds to finance it. Such special research institutes may play an increasingly important rôle in university demographic research. Recently, both NISER and the African Studies Institute of the University of Ghana have appointed full-time demographers.

Geography Departments have undertaken research into population distribution and migration. A great deal of the work has been concerned with population mapping and the development of mapping techniques. Such mapping has been used both to assist the carrying out of censuses and to illuminate the census findings. Work of this kind has been specifically described for the Universities in Ghana, Sierra Leone, Sudan, the Eastern and Northern Regions of Nigeria, Kenya and Zambia. Work on minority groups has been undertaken, most notably on Europeans in the Universities of Khartoum and Nigeria (Nsukka). The relation between population and the environment has been studied, especially in the Sudan where it has been related to agriculture and more specifically to water supplies. In Eastern Nigeria both rural and urban settlement patterns have been examined, while in the North of the country rural economy studies involving the population aspect are under way. During the early 1960s the Rhodes–Livingstone Institute (Zambia) also was associated with population mapping projects and with the development of techniques for analysing population distribution.

At the University College in Rhodesia the economists have been active. Data on population structures and movements are being collected and analysed as part of two detailed economic surveys of rural areas. The first estimates of population movements have recently been published.

Special university institutes or departments have increasingly found that work on their problems necessitated both a study of population phenomena and a more extensive knowledge of demographic techniques. The Department of Architecture, Town Planning and Building at the University of Science and Technology in Kumasi, Ghana, is engaged in extensive studies of the 1960 census data, and in addition has been involved in survey work, with a considerable demographic component, in the area to be flooded when the Volta Dam is completed. Some of the work has already been published by the University. The College of Agriculture of the University of Nigeria (Nsukka) has co-operated with the World Health Organization in carrying out a demographic survey for medical purposes. The Institute of Administration at the Ahmadu Bello University in Northern Nigeria is considering the need for such studies as part of its work. And, as previously mentioned, the Institute of Statistics at the University of Ghana has found that many of its investigations lie wholly or partly within the field of demography.

Medical schools have also felt the need for demographic surveys in connection with public health work, and such surveys are either under way or planned in Lagos, Nigeria and Rhodesia.

Publication

Africa has no learned journal in the field of population. Thus, three major ways of presenting research findings have been found. They are publication outside the continent, presentation of papers to international conferences, and the printing of results by the university concerned either within a journal open to staff members or as a book or monograph. In surveys of university work in the population field, the universities have now supplied details of fifty publications or conference papers. Of these, ten appeared in international journals, of which *Population Studies* was the most frequently mentioned. Five appeared as essays or chapters in books on broader themes published outside Africa. Five were delivered as papers at international conferences. One was published in an African learned journal (*Central African Journal of Medicine*) and one in a government report (*East Africa Royal Commission, 1953–1955, Report*). But the majority, 28, were published by the university in which the work was done. On the whole, these latter publications are less frequently stocked by other African university libraries than are the external journals or collections of essays.

External Contacts, Finance, etc.

Demography teaching courses have been started, as presumably they will most often have to be in the future, by persons imported from universities outside Africa where demography as a study is already well established. Only at the Universities of Ghana and Khartoum could this stage be said to have passed. Demographers are at present in short supply and the chief obstacle to an expansion of teaching demography is the inability to secure staff. It is possible that this may be overcome by the help of external organizations or universities in locating suitable persons and perhaps at times with initial financial problems. It is possible that some African countries, notably Ghana and the Sudan, perhaps at some stage Nigeria, and, outside the area being considered here, the UAR, will be able to supply demographers. But most, as yet, need to keep their demographers to work for their own governments and universities.

Finance for research projects has come from three sources, from the universities themselves, from governments and from organizations outside Africa. The smaller projects, which form the majority in number, have been sustained by the universities.

Government assistance has often been given for collaborative census mapping and similar projects. Government financing of particular projects, in which it has an interest in the findings, may become more important. Before the independence of Zambia and Malawi, the British Government's Colonial Development Fund financed investigations by the Rhodes–Livingstone Institute in both countries, and it is possible that funds from Britain's new Department of Overseas Development will be used for demographic studies in some of the new countries of Africa. For some of the work, money also came from the Zambia (then Northern Rhodesia) African Housing Board. In Rhodesia, the Government has financed the Economic Survey of the Chitowa Native Purchase Area. In Ghana the Government has made available quite large sums of money for social and economic research into the problems of resettlement from the Volta Reservoir basin, as it did earlier on a smaller scale for resettlement from the Tema port area. Some of this money is used by various departments in the University of Ghana and the Kumasi University of Science and Technology, and some of the material being gathered has a demographic component. In Northern Nigeria, the Greater Kano Planning Authority is paying for the investigation by the Geography Department of Ahmadu Bello University of the rural economy of the Kano close-settled zone, a study which includes the collection of data on the demographic characteristics of the population.

Some of the larger projects are being financed from outside Africa. The Population Council has supported a demographic post at the University of Ghana since early 1960 and has financed the research programme of the post. The Ford Foundation, through the Ghana Academy of Science, supported the Social and Economic Survey of Ghana[6], which involved persons at the two Ghanaian universities as well as others outside the universities. The Foundation has also financed the differential fertility survey in the Sudan which is being directed from the Faculty of Economic and Social Studies in the University of Khartoum. In the same university a Goldsmith Grant has been used within the Department of Geography to carry out a study of water-supply and population in the Gedaref area. The Rockefeller Foundation financed the Economic Survey of the Chiweshe Reserve in Rhodesia. To date, little university research into population phenomena has been assisted by the United Nations or its agencies. However, equipment and personnel have been provided by WHO at the University of Nigeria, for the carrying out of a demographic survey of Nsukka as part of a project to eliminate smallpox.

Conclusions

Full courses in demography have become established or may become established soon in several African countries north of the equator—Ghana, Sudan, Sierra Leone, Uganda and possibly Nigeria. There are apparently no plans to date further south—Kenya, Tanzania, Zambia, Malawi, Rhodesia, Lesotho, Botswana and Swaziland. Where permanent courses are established, it is usually necessary to do so with imported personnel and to maintain a supply of such personnel until the first demographers of local origin have been sufficiently trained, perhaps both in the country and through higher degrees overseas, to secure university positions teaching the subject. Only at this stage can the subject be said to be viable. It may require external assistance with recruitment and possibly to finance the employment of expatriate staff in the formative years. There is some evidence that such demography courses are most likely to be viable either within or servicing a Department of Sociology or Social Studies.

Research in the field of demography has been somewhat more widespread than demography teaching, sometimes due to the interests of a single member of a university staff. Financial aid has been obtained in the past from a variety of sources. Such research has had, and will continue to have, a good chance of governmental support, because the findings are often in demand for planning purposes.

The relation between teaching and research has been hampered by publishing conditions. Almost certainly, no university library in the area examined here, even those where full demography courses are taught, contains half of the fifty publications on population referred to earlier. One problem is sometimes that of exchange control or other purchasing difficulties. Certainly, one form of technical aid in the field would be to assemble complete sets of such publications, as well as runs of census volumes and other government publications for the region, and to present them to all universities seriously undertaking population studies. In 1966 and 1967 the amount of available published material should increase considerably. Nevertheless, the possibility of establishing an African journal of population studies should be seriously considered. Perhaps the time is not yet opportune; the editorial offices would have to be located in a centre where demographic studies were well and soundly based and were likely to continue in this condition, and adequate publishing facilities, sufficient finance and staff with time for the task would be needed.

Footnotes

1. J. C. CALDWELL, 'Demographic Training and Research in Tropical African Universities which employ English as the medium of instruction', paper delivered at the United Nations World Population Conference, Belgrade, August–September 1965.
2. The most recent figures available are for 1963. Most are taken from the *1965 Commonwealth Universities Yearbook.*
3. Courses, as used here, implies at least one year's work leading to a full examination paper.
4. Largely the work of J. C. Mitchell and A. L. Epstein.
5. Largely the work of D. G. Bettison.
6. Subsequently published as WALTER BIRMINGHAM, I. NEUSTADT and E. N. OMABOE, *A Study of Contemporary Ghana*, Vol. I; *The Economy of Ghana*, 1966, Vol. II; *Some Aspects of Social Structure* Allen and Unwin, London, 1967.

45 Demographic training in Africa outside the universities

K. M. Jupp

Regional Statistical Adviser, Economic Commission for Africa, Addis Ababa, Ethiopia

Introduction

Demographic training in Africa outside the universities began in an organized way in the early 1960s when many newly-independent States realized that information on the size, structure and rate of growth of their populations was seriously deficient. Similar deficiencies existed in basic data on the structure and movement of national economies, and rational planning for improvement in standards of living could not be effected until more reliable estimates were available. Shortage of trained statisticians at all levels was seen as the main obstacle in carrying out the required work.

These were essentially government problems, and immediate attempts were made to solve them at a governmental level: Central Statistical Offices were established in country after country in quick succession and, beginning in 1961, plans for intensive training programmes led to the opening of a number of non-university centres, the first emphasis being on middle-level training, later supplemented by centres giving higher-level courses.

Much of the programme has been a joint venture of the United Nations and governments of member States, carried out through the Economic Commission for Africa, the biennial Conferences of African Statisticians, and through agreements with individual governments. The United Nations has made a series of such agreements with governments for the establishment and financial support of training centres which would operate on a sub-regional basis and would continue until the most urgent requirements for statisticians had been satisfied.

However, national governments have also taken the initiative in organizing training programmes and three centres were set up to supply national needs for statistical workers. Two of these three have admitted considerable numbers of students from other African countries, most of them on fellowships offered by the United Nations. Bilateral aid has also been forthcoming in a number of cases.

International co-operation has been a continuing feature of the conduct of the programme, arising largely from comparable conditions and a common preference for training in Africa close to the conditions to which general statistical procedures must be adapted. Language has presented difficulties, even within sub-regions, and it has been necessary to provide tuition in English, French and/or Arabic.

As will be seen later,[1] the non-university centres have, in the period 1961–62 to 1964–65, provided statistical training for roughly one-fifth of the statisticians holding posts in Africa in 1965; but statistical projects are expanding while statistical offices are even now understaffed, so that by 1970 the estimated government demand is for three times the number already trained outside the universities.

This is a picture of overall requirements for statisticians for government service and not for demographers or demographic statisticians. It is not possible at present to separate either the total requirements for demographers as such, or the extent to which training is meeting the requirements. However, at the middle level, where the largest numbers are needed, this is not so serious since usually specialization would occur on the job, after a general training in statistics including demography. What is more serious is:

(a) the lack of information on the adequacy of training to provide enough higher-level demographers; and

(b) the probable loss of skills acquired during middle-level training, because of lack of adequate direction once back in post, or because of lack of projects in which the skills could be further developed.

Facilities for Training in Demography

Before dealing with the demographic training available in formally established Training Centres, it is convenient to make brief reference to two supplementary sources of training:

(a) In-service training provided by national statistical offices, usually for a period of six weeks to three months, and including some treatment of demographic statistics in a general course in statistics, which by its nature has frequently to be elementary. These courses though principally intended to raise the efficiency of existing staff are used by some governments to prepare candidates for admission to one of the Training Centres.

(b) *Ad hoc* courses, such as that given in the West African Census Training Centre in Accra in 1961 for ten trainees from Nigeria, Liberia and Sierra Leone. The course lasted three months and consisted of intensive instruction and practical work in field organization and procedure, as well as in census concepts, classifications, uses and interpretation of data, etc. This is a type of training, which, whether on a national or sub-regional basis, could be used effectively for the 1970 World Census Programme. Similar provisions have been suggested on occasion for related operations, such as civil registration procedures.

TERMINOLOGY

Bearing in mind that the training courses are designed for government nominees who are almost all government officials, the question of levels of training and grades in government is constantly under discussion. To avoid the confusion which often arises between English and French practice and terminology, the following approximate equivalents are given for reference:

Higher-level statisticians	=	*Personnel de conception*
Senior Statistician	=	Ingénieur Statisticien-Economiste
Statistician	=	Ingénieur des Travaux Statistiques
Middle-level statisticians	=	*Personnel d'execution*
Statistical Officer	=	Adjoint technique
Assistant Statistical Officer	=	Agent technique

The terms 'higher' and 'middle level' have been retained in the text in preference to 'professional' and 'executive' because, though stiff, they are in such common usage that they can scarcely be avoided, and they convey the relevant distinction reasonably well.

The Training Centres

Annex I gives a summary list of Centres which provide courses on a continuing basis. Date of establishment, sub-region, language(s) of instruction, number of trainees, length and level of course are indicated, together with the emphasis given to demography in the course of instruction. In practice the arrangements are more flexible than appears in the Annex, especially in regard to the sub-regions served by the Centres.

These Centres may be divided into three categories on the basis of the emphasis given to demography and the level of training provided:

(a) Cairo and Dakar offer courses exclusively devoted to demography at the higher level, for a minimum of one academic year;

(b) Rabat[2] gives a general statistical course, at the higher level, with opportunity for almost one academic year of specialization in a number of fields, one of which is demography;

(c) Addis Ababa, Achimota (Accra), Abidjan,[3] Lagos, Rabat, Yaounde and Dar-es-Salaam offer a general statistical course at the middle level, within which demography is included as field-applied statistics.

ADMINISTRATIVE ARRANGEMENTS

Very briefly, the international Centres (Cairo, Dakar, Achimota, Addis Ababa, Dar-es-Salaam and Yaounde) operate on an arrangement whereby the United Nations provides funds for the Director, for library and laboratory equipment, fieldwork and sundry expenses as well as for fellowships for students from other countries. The host governments provide physical requirements for classrooms and hostel accommodation, clerical and administrative staff, office equipment, part-time lecturers and fellowships for their own nations. Cairo is a special case, having at present two United Nations lecturers; also a substantial proportion of the United Nations fellowships for this Centre are financed by the Population Council.

The Abidjan, Lagos and Rabat Centres were established by national governments, but the Rabat Centre, which from the start received United Nations support for lecturing staff, was recently converted into a project of the United Nations Special Fund. Abidjan receives United Nations assistance for some fellowships; Lagos too receives United Nations support (for example, the services of the Director and of some additional lecturers on an *ad hoc* basis). Bilateral assistance has been made available from EEC, FAC and USAID for fellowships at Yaounde, Abidjan and Addis Ababa.

The regions served and the language(s) of instruction shown in Annex I should not be interpreted too rigidly because flexibility has been an essential condition of meeting urgent needs. For example, trainees from any African country may be accepted in Cairo, pending the opening of the Dakar Centre, and although instruction in the Cairo Centre is mainly in English or Arabic arrangements can be made to accommodate French-speaking students. Again, both Abidjan and Yaounde admit students from West African countries.

ENTRANCE QUALIFICATIONS

The requirements apply to personnel of government statistical offices and of other government and semi-public bodies.

Cairo and Dakar: a university degree or equivalent qualification.

Rabat: the baccalaureat in mathematics or a higher academic qualification.

Other centres: a school leaving certificate with sufficient knowledge of the language of instruction in the Training Centre, basic mathematics, and/or satisfactory performance in tests or in interviews. Some Centres give a preparatory course in order to raise the candidates to the standard necessary for admission to the statistical course proper.

COMPARABILITY OF STANDARDS IN THE MIDDLE-LEVEL CENTRES

Major emphasis has been given to securing and maintaining uniformity of standards in order that the certificates issued should be accepted by countries as the basis for appointment to posts. This aim has been repeated at the regular meetings of the Directors of Statistical Training Centres, who have insisted that there be no lowering of entrance qualifications nor any substantial variation in the standard of curricula for examinations.

COURSES OF STUDY

An outline is given in Annex II of the courses of study offered at the Cairo Centre. Presumably Dakar will offer similar courses. Both Centres are expected to promote studies of special interest and utility to governments.

Annex III gives an outline of the course in demography at the Achimota Centre, as an example of the courses in middle-level Centres. Naturally the emphasis may vary from Centre to Centre but all students are expected to acquire a general understanding of the nature of demographic statistics, problems of collection and interpretation and methods of calculating the main demographic rates. In some cases, the courses are somewhat more advanced than this.

The middle-level courses last for one academic year, or approximately nine months of tuition. Again, practice varies from centre to centre, but for the most part between 15 and 20 hours of classwork is given to demography, supplemented by considerable practical work and by participation in field projects which clarify the concepts involved in data collection and the difficulties of interpretation.

Information is not available on full details of courses given at Rabat and Abidjan, but in Rabat, in the third-year course, more advanced theoretical demography is taught in the first semester while in the second semester the students specializing in demography are attached to a suitable government office to prepare a paper on their chosen theme, which must be in some way related to problems of development.

Progress to Date

The Secretariat of the Economic Commission for Africa, in a recent review of statistical manpower in Africa,[4] gives the following numbers of statisticians holding posts in 1965 and the estimated demand at the end of the five years 1966–70 (clerical grades and in-service courses are excluded):

	Higher	Middle	Total
Total in post 1965	600	1,700	2,300
Number trained in Training Centres (Cairo Demographic Centre, Rabat middle level and Lagos excluded)	112	392	504
Additional trainees required by 1970	801	1,275	2,076
From Training Centres	267	1,051	1,318
From African universities	147	130	277
From outside Africa	387	94	481

There is little point in spelling out the numerous limitations of these figures and there is no intention of minimizing them. It should be sufficient to say that losses of trained statisticians or of skills acquired during training, due to lack of opportunity for their development on the job, may more or less counterbalance the understatement in numbers trained up to 1964/65. The estimates for 1970 are for present purposes taken at face value.

The conclusions are that non-university institutions have provided about one-fifth of the higher-level staff in posts in 1965 and about one-fourth of the middle-level staff (or about one-fifth of the total of these two levels). If the estimated requirements of statistical offices in 1970 are to be met, the following *additional* non-university training must be provided in Africa in the next five years:

(a) at the higher level for 267 trainees;

(b) at the middle level for 1,051 trainees.

This is equivalent to two and a half times the numbers of higher-level staff and nearly three times those of middle-level staff trained from 1961–62 to 1964–65.

This rate of improvement will be effective in solving the total problem only if African universities and universities and other institutions outside Africa can train the large numbers (534 higher-level and 224 middle-level staff) estimated by governments to be required from these sources.

PLANS FOR EXPANSION OF TRAINING FACILITIES

These are summarized in Annex IV. For the most part the Annex refers to non-university training, but it will be noted that the summary reflects a growing tendency for training at the middle level to be associated with local universities which will continue providing statistical training when the present back-log has been met.

Conclusion

If the proposed expansion of non-university training is implemented, there will be a large number of statisticians capable of demographic work at the middle level. Whether they will be adequately used will depend on the extent to which they are placed in jobs within the government service where their training can be consolidated and developed. This will in turn depend on the availability of higher-level demographers and the implementation of programmes of demographic data collection and analysis. In view of the World Census Programme, in which most countries will participate, and the need for accurate measures of the vital rates, there is little doubt of the urgency of providing the higher-level demographers. It will continue to be necessary to find them elsewhere unless sufficient Africans are trained in Africa.

Footnotes

1. See section on Progress to date below.
2. All references to Rabat in the text should be interpreted in the light of the proposed reorganization described in Annex IV.
3. Abidjan offers the same diploma as Rabat but has been classified differently here because of the extra year available in Rabat for specialization.
4. *Report on Statistical Training and a Statistical Manpower Survey of Africa* (E/CN.14/CAS.4/9), paragraphs 18–21. The figures are based on replies from 25 countries and EACSO, and estimates for other countries. South Africa is excluded. No allowance is made here for replacing expatriates (100 higher and 100 middle level).

Annex I

African Training Centres Offering Courses in Demography (Universities excluded)

Centre	Year of establishment	Sub-region served	Language(s)	No. of trainees to 1964–65	Length of course in academic years	Level	Relative emphasis on demography
CAIRO **Demographic Research and Training Centre**	1963	N. Africa and Middle East	English Arabic French	(25 per year)	At least one	Higher	Purely demographic
DAKAR **Demographic Training and Research Centre**	Proposed for 1966	Africa other than N. Africa	French English	(20–25 per year)	At least one	Higher	Purely demographic
RABAT **Centre de Formation des Ingénieurs des Travaux Statistiques**[a]	1961	At first Morocco only; progressively internationalized	French	Year 1 – 137 2 – 93 3 – 19	Three	Higher (Ingénieur des Travaux)	Year 1 (b) Year 2 none Year 3: 1/12 of the course for one semester; remainder of year demography only, if so desired
ABIDJAN **École de la Statistique**	1961	West Africa	French	21	One	Middle (Agent technique)	(c)
				100	One	Middle (Agent technique)	(c)
					Two	Higher (Ingénieur des Travaux)	?

(a) See Annex IV for proposed reorganization of the Rabat Centre.
(b) The first-year course devotes 20 hours (plus practical work) to demography.
(c) The middle-level courses normally devote about one-third of the time to applied statistics, of which about one-sixth (say 20–25 hours) is devoted to demography. Practical work is additional.

Annex I (*continued*)

Centre	Year of establishment	Sub-region served	Language(s)	No. of trainees to 1964–65	Length of course in academic years	Level	Relative emphasis on demography
ACHIMOTA **Statistical Training Centre**	1961	West Africa	English	108	One	Middle (Assistant Statistical Officer)	(c)
ADDIS ABABA **Statistical Training Centre**	1961	Eastern and North Africa	English	77	One	Middle (Assistant Statistical Officer)	(c)
DAR-ES-SALAAM **Training Centre**	1965	Eastern Africa	English	—	One	Middle (Assistant Statistical Officer)	(c)
LAGOS **Statistical Training Centre**	1961	Nigeria	English	(about 20 per year)	One	Middle (Assistant Statistical Officer)	?
YAOUNDE **Centre International de Formation Statistique**	1961	Central Africa	French	107	One	Middle (Agent Technique)	(c)

Annex II

UNITED NATIONS NORTH AFRICAN DEMOGRAPHIC RESEARCH AND TRAINING CENTRE, CAIRO

Brief Outline of Courses

1. *Technical demography*. Sources of demographic data, rates and ratios, evaluation and adjustment of demographic data; mortality analysis, fertility analysis; analysis of reproductivity; analysis of data on marital status; migration analysis; analysis of the economically active population; population estimation; morbidity analysis; measurement of the effectiveness of contraceptives.

2. *Substantive demography*. In this course, the students will be acquainted with the previously accumulated knowledge on demographic research and the fundamental aspects of the world's population problems with special emphasis upon the region, under the following headings: World population and resources; population composition; population distribution; mortality; fertility; migration, economically active population; morbidity; dynamics of population change; population policies as factors of population change.

3. *Elementary mathematics and statistics*. Review of elementary mathematics including calculus; interpolation and graduation; collection and processing of data; frequency tables, measures of central tendency; dispersion, association, regression and correlation; elementary ideas of probability, common probability distributions; large sample theory and tests, small sample and exact tests; time series analysis; sample survey techniques; curve fitting, method of least squares.

4. *Sociology and methods of social research*. Culture and social organization; attitudes and motivations and their measurements; collection of data; sampling methods in social research; analysis and presentation of data; report writing.

5. *Economics*. Economic theory and analysis; problems of economic development in less developed countries with special reference to countries of the region; interrelationships of population growth and economic and social development.

6. *Human genetics*. Physical basis of heredity; Mendel's Laws; genetic situation in man; estimation of genetic parameters and tests of genetic hypothesis; analysis of family data; studies of blood groups, genetics and epidemiology.

7. *Physiology of reproduction and family planning*. Anatomy and physiology of male and female human reproductive organs; control of reproduction; types and limitations of family planning methods.

Brief Outline of Research Programmes

Both the members of the staff and the full-year trainees working under staff members will take part in research programmes of substantial demographic interest to countries of the region, either referring to particular countries or with a regional scope. Priorities in the research projects will be given to programmes which would be of immediate interest and utility to the governments of all countries of the region, will supplement the programmes of the Economic Commission for Africa and the African Institute for Economic Development, and will be drawn up in consultation with these agencies and in accordance with the recommendations of the United Nations Population Commission and the Economic and Social Council.

For 1963–65, the programme may consist of the following:

1. *Studies on fertility* with special reference to differential fertility in relation to education and other socio-economic variables, from case-studies or special tabulation of census data and of analysis of relation of fertility to level of living.

2. *Studies on mortality and morbidity*. Studies on health investments implied in projections of population and of mortality.

3. *Studies on internal migration and urbanization.*

4. *Assessment of the quality of the basic data* obtained from censuses, registration, and sample surveys; and estimation of basic demographic measures.

5. *Studies of demographic problems of social and economic development*. Interrelationships between demographic variables and social and economic growth; implications of population trends for investment needs in agricultural and industrial developments and for housing and urban development, and health, medical, educational and welfare facilities.

6. *Other special studies* to be worked out in co-operation with the governments of the region and the Economic Commission for Africa and which may include: projection of population and its segments (economically active, school enrolment, rural–urban), and housing.

Annex III

MIDDLE-LEVEL COURSE IN DEMOGRAPHY (ACHIMOTA)

1. *The field of demography.*

2. *Censuses.* Why they are necessary; history of censuses, census procedures and techniques; methods of enumeration; de-facto and de-jure counts; place of enumeration; collection of data —canvasser and householder methods; planning of an actual census: pre-census and post-census procedures: data processing; post-enumeration survey.

3. *Vital registration.* Vital registration systems and population registers; why West Africa lacks them; problems in setting up a vital registration system in African countries; sample techniques.

4. *Demographic rates and ratios.* Sex ratio; age composition and its influence on births and deaths; age pyramid and simple percentages; importance of age in demographic analysis; territorial distribution and density of population, child–woman ratio; crude birth rate; crude death rate; age-specific birth rate; age-specific death rate; general fertility ratio; infant death rate; growth of population—size of population—rates of growth.

5. *The life-table.* Generation and current life-tables; uses of the life-table; problems and construction of the life-table; United Nations Model Life-tables for underdeveloped area.
Migration. Urban–rural; international migration.
Health statistics. Field of health statistics and importance: morbidity statistics: sources of morbidity statistics: field surveys, hospital statistics; special statistics—mental health statistics; tuberculosis and cancer statistics; maternity and child welfare statistics.
Population projections. Mathematical methods and component method of projection.

Annex IV

SUGGESTED EXPANSION OF TRAINING FACILITIES

Recommendations have been made by the heads of statistical offices and/or by the directors of training centres to the following effect.

1. The Addis Ababa Centre should be continued at the present level for a further 4–5 years, serving, after the establishment of a proposed new centre at Cairo, mainly Ethiopia, Somalia, and Sudan.

2. A new middle-level training centre should be established in Cairo, mainly for trainees from the UAR and other Arabic-speaking countries in North Africa.

3. The Dar-es-Salaam Centre should provide a Statistical Officers' course in co-operation with the University College at Dar-es-Salaam.

4. Arrangements should be made to merge the Achimota Centre with the Institute of Statistics of the University of Ghana, where new training courses are expected to be offered (open to all African students) beginning with the 1966–67 academic year. These will comprise:

(a) the present middle-level training course;
(b) an Advanced Certificate course at the second of the higher levels; and
(c) post-graduate courses in statistics for graduates in various disciplines.

5. A course open to all Africans at the second of the higher levels (similar to that envisaged for Ghana) was being established in Nigeria by the Federal Office of Statistics in co-operation with the University of Ibadan, while the existing course at the Lagos Centre would be continued by the Federal Office of Statistics on its own as from 1966–67.

The Seventh Session of the Economic Commission (Nairobi, February 1965) proposed that the Yaounde Centre be converted into an international centre open to all Africans; the Centre is in the process of reorganization and will offer a 15 months' course at the upper middle-level (Adjoint technique) in 1965–66.

Following the recent agreement by which the Rabat Centre became a project of the UN Special Fund, it has been recommended that it be known as the Institute of Statistics and Applied Economics. It will continue to offer a middle-level course of one year's duration and a higher-level course lasting three years. The latter will be in both statistics and economics, and will be primarily but not exclusively for Moroccans. It is with the middle-level programme that Special Fund assistance will be mainly concerned.

46 Collaboration between universities and governments in demographic training and research[1]

M. I. Iro

Federal Census Office, Lagos, Nigeria

Demographic Training and Research as a Global Problem

At the second World Population Conference held in Belgrade in 1965, a session (Meeting B.8) was devoted to the promotion of demographic training and research in developing countries. The United Nations, in co-operation with national governments, has established training and research centres in Santiago (Chile), Chembur (India), the countries of ECAFE region, and Cairo (UAR). (The Cairo centre is expected to provide training for the whole of Africa.) The International Union for the Scientific Study of Population, at its meeting in Ottawa in 1963, discussed this subject at considerable length, and the Population Council has sponsored a number of projects aimed at stimulating interest in population studies. The experience of these centres and the seminar discussions on the subject form valuable background material for any student of this subject.

Since the Second World War attention has become focussed on the problem of population dynamics. Most countries have come to plan their economy, and with planning, basic data of the structure and the characteristics of the population have had to be assembled, analysed and critically evaluated. In order to assess accurately the magnitude of this problem, many of the developing countries have set up the machinery necessary to conduct censuses and investigate the problem of civil registration.

If problems of population growth and economic development are to be assessed objectively, demographers will have to be trained in various aspects of their work, including research methodology, which is essential if our knowledge of population changes is to be improved and deepened. In the present paper, an attempt is made against this background to concentrate on what can be done in Africa, where most universities have been established within the last two decades and the governments are only now beginning to be aware of the importance of quantitative data regarding the characteristics of their population for national economic and social planning.

Training and Research in Africa

It is often said that in the field of statistics, as indeed in many other scientific fields, collaboration between professional statisticians in government engaged in applied problems and theoretical statisticians in universities and research institutions leaves much to be desired. The former must carry out a specific project that is often dictated by the needs of administration, and often are fully engaged in meeting these demands as quickly and as well as possible. On the other hand, professionals in the universities and research centres have the time to give more refined and sustained attention to a limited number of problems of their own choice.

In Africa today, the study of demography as a scientific discipline is handicapped by lack of the following:

(a) personnel with sufficient knowledge of the environment and the subject;

(b) finance and personnel to conduct special surveys;
(c) basic demographic statistics either from censuses or from vital registration systems which can form a basis for analytic studies of population dynamics.

Faced with a problem of this magnitude, it appears very desirable to ensure considerable co-operation between demographers in universities and those in government. This has been to a large extent achieved in some developed countries in Europe and America. The US Bureau of Census invites experts from outside the Bureau to write census monographs and in Britain, the Chief Statistician in the Registrar-General's Office is very closely associated with demographic study in London University.

African Universities, in addition to fulfilling their basic functions as centres for learning and research, must provide skilled manpower which these countries require if they are to master modern techniques in the fields of agriculture, commerce and industry. African Governments by and large charge these institutions with the additional responsibility of training their own nationals in different fields of government activity, so that wherever possible nationals can replace expatriates and maintain high standards of efficiency. If this objective is to be accomplished, the training that is provided in African institutions should be relevant to the needs of African countries. Emphasis should be placed on particular aspects of African culture such as the response of the people and their attitude to repetitive inquiries.

Contents of Demographic Training

The study of demography is leading to new methods and techniques that call for specialized training, often spread over many years. This training can be given at undergraduate and post-graduate levels in universities, in official training centres and in research institutions. The subject can be usefully taught within the Departments of Sociology and Statistics.[2] In either case, undergraduates who aim at studying demography in depth at a later stage in life should be well acquainted with elements of sociology, including an understanding of social structure, economics, mathematics, statistics, survey methods in social investigations, demography, and mechanical aids to tabulation.[3]

Students of demography in the final year of their undergraduate courses should be able to appreciate and apply, at the elementary stage, techniques of life-tables, standardization of rates and substitution rates. They must understand that in many of the developing countries demographic statistics either from censuses or vital registration systems are defective. To cope with such situations,[4] methods of detecting and removing errors in raw data should be emphasized.

With the rapid expansion in universities, training in demography at the post-graduate level should be carried out as far as possible in local institutions, but this should be supplemented with work overseas where there is scope for more advanced work on methods of obtaining basic demographic data and other aspects of the subject, such as the interrelationship between rate of population growth, age and sex-structure, natural and human resources in economic development, levels of living and population policies.

There appears to be a strong case for some form of career guide[5] and aptitude test of candidates who are hoping to make a serious study of demography. For one thing, few demographers are engaged in full-time demographic work. Others work as economists, sociologists or statisticians. Our experience is that those who aim at making a career in statistics with demography as their major field of interest should place due emphasis on statistics rather than detailed studies of social organization.

The Nature and Extent of Collaboration between Government and Universities

At present, there are few African demographers working on African population. Many non-African demographers who work on African population live outside the continent, and the experience of some of these people is based on a limited field inquiry in one country which does not qualify them to speak of Africa as a whole, because it is not one homogeneous culture area. Nevertheless, much of the research work done by these workers has contributed immensely to our understanding of the social structure and an appreciation of the underlying problems of fundamental research in predominantly agricultural communities.[6]

CENSUS PLANNING

In many developing countries, the planning of a census is given the same importance as its execution. The type of questions and the form in which these questions should be asked, administrative problems of estimating cost, recruitment of staff, training of enumerators and supervisors and field control, the duration of the census counts, the technical merits and defects in *de facto* and *de jure* counts, the concept of households, institutional and floating population, should all be fully discussed with administrators and experts, including economists, statisticians and sociologists working in the Universities.

MAPPING

Maps are necessary to ensure that there are no omissions or duplications in enumeration areas, to provide frames for subsequent inquiries and post-enumeration surveys. The universities and Survey Departments may co-operate in providing these maps. (Economic activity maps may be better prepared by university Geography Departments.)

Special Surveys

In developing countries with scanty demographic statistics, special surveys have to be organized to provide information on vital indices. Such surveys may be conducted on a scientific sample basis or they may originate from administrative action such as studies based on in-patient/out-patient hospital records, morbidity studies, vaccination campaign programmes, etc. In the case of the former, university staff members trained in scientific sample methodology can be called upon to advise on efficient sampling design. During the analyses of survey data, the relevance of new demographic techniques, often developed by research workers in universities, may be tested.

Large-scale surveys for data collection should be organized and executed by governments calling on technical advice from universities and research institutions. Data from such surveys should be provided in such a manner that it can readily be adapted to the needs of research. Detailed analyses and studies of factors influencing economic and social change should be examined by universities. The possibility should be considered that respondents may get confused when many different agencies are collecting all sorts of information from them. If these agencies are aware of what has been done or is being done by other agencies, there will be less duplication of effort, more co-operation and improvement in research techniques and methodology.

Footnotes

1. I have benefited immensely by the suggestions and advice of the Chief Statistician to the Federal Government; the views expressed here are mine and not those of the Federal Government.
2. Some aspects of population are taught to students of Geography or Medicine. It is possible that a

university may decide to have a Department of Demography as a centralized place where courses can be given to students in different disciplines. Conflicts which arise within institutions as to the 'best' department in which to base demography do not concern us here. However, in many American Universities, Demography is mainly associated with Sociology.
3. The introduction of time-saving mechanical aids such as the computer in tabulation and processing of census or survey data requires that the demographer should have a working knowledge of these aids.
4. See *Population Studies*, March 1959: CARRIER and FARRAG, 'The reduction of errors in Census Population for statistically underdeveloped countries'.
5. This does not mean that the sky is the limit (of prospects) for demographers from developing countries. On the contrary, many demographers in these countries have to learn to adjust to other subjects (Statistics, Sociology, Economics) if they are not to remain unemployed or redundant. This view received popular support at the World Population Conference.
6. See *Population Studies*, work by C. J. Martin, C. Myburgh in East Africa.

Annex

Possible Fields of Co-operation between Universities and Governments

1. *Census data processing and programming.*
2. *Population census:*
   (a) planning and its conduct;
   (b) analyses, preparation and publication of reports.
3. *Critical examination of data from census:*
   (a) age–sex structure—methods of graduation;
   (b) population projections—mathematical and economic; component and sectoral projections (urban–rural);
   (c) projection of school enrolment population.
4. *Labour force:* determination of labour force concepts, size, analyses, projections.
5. *Life-tables, method of construction:*
   (a) complete or abridged;
   (b) working life-tables (knowledge of population working at different age-groups), double decrement tables (nuptiality and working life-tables).
6. *Migration statistics, types:*
   (a) external;
   (b) internal.

In (b) urban–rural balance in population distribution; study of frequency and streams of internal migratory movements.

7. *Vital statistics registration,* as a supplement to census statistics.
8. *Sample special studies:* morbidity, composition of households, family budgets, survey of housing needs.
9. *Population policy:* family planning; survey of types of available aids, cost and utilization of available devices.
The relationship between demographic transition and population policy.
10. *The interaction of the demographic variables on economic and social change:* age-structure and dependency, age–sex structure and the labour force, employment and unemployment; household size and housing needs, overcrowding and urban slums, etc.

Appendix

The first African Population Conference University of Ibadan, 3rd–7th January, 1966

Sponsored by the University of Ibadan in co-operation with The Population Council

Delegates to the Conference

N. O. ADDO	Institute of African Studies, University of Ghana, Ghana
S. A. AGBOOLA	Department of Geography, University of Ife, Nigeria
E. AMUCHEAZI	Institute of African Studies, University of Ibadan, Nigeria
R. G. ARMSTRONG	Institute of African Studies, University of Ibadan, Nigeria
A. F. ARYEE	Department of Sociology, University of Ghana, Ghana
T. ASUNI	Neuro-Psychiatric Centre, Aro Hospital, Abeokuta, Nigeria
C. R. BARBER	Medical School, University of Ibadan, Nigeria
K. M. BARBOUR	Department of Geography, University of Ibadan, Nigeria
O. BASSIR	Department of Biochemistry, University of Ibadan, Nigeria
J. G. C. BLACKER	The Population Investigation Committee, London School of Economics, UK
J. BOSTON	Institute of African Studies, University of Ibadan, Nigeria
J. M. BOUTE	Kinshasa, Congo
W. I. BRASS	London School of Hygiene and Tropical Medicine, UK
G. F. BROWN	Population Council Representative, Tunisia
J. C. CALDWELL	Department of Demography, Australian National University, Australia
R. CLAIRIN	Paris, France
J. I. CLARKE	Department of Geography, University of Durham, UK
A. J. COALE	Office of Population Research, Princeton University, USA
A. DALY	Ministry of Public Health, Tunisia
T. DARAMOLA	University of Lagos Medical School, Nigeria
I. S. DEMA	Department of Chemical Pathology, University of Ibadan, Nigeria
R. DESAI	Department of Sociology, Makerere University College, Uganda
K. O. DIKE	Institute of African Studies, University of Ibadan, Nigeria
R. C. DURU	Department of Geography, University of Lagos, Nigeria
G. M. EDINGTON	Department of Pathology, University of Ibadan, Nigeria
J. C. EDOZIEN	Department of Chemical Pathology, University of Ibadan, Nigeria
C. K. EICHER	Economic Development Institute, University of Nigeria, Nigeria
E. ELLIOTT	Lagos, Nigeria
J. O. N. EZE	Department of Geography, University of Nigeria, Nsukka, Nigeria
O. C. EZEAKO	Ministry of Town Planning, Enugu, Nigeria
D. FRIEDLANDER	Haifa, Israel
S. K. GAISIE	Department of Sociology, University of Ghana, Ghana
B. GIL	ILO, Geneva
D. V. GLASS	London School of Economics, UK
R. GLASS	Centre for Urban Studies, University College, London, UK
T. A. I. GRILLE	Department of Anatomy, University of Ibadan, Nigeria
D. HEAPS	Ford Foundation, Lagos, Nigeria
D. F. HEISEL	Institute for Development Studies, University College, Nairobi, Kenya
R. A. HENIN	Department of Economics, University of Khartoum, Sudan
A. HERON	University of Zambia, Zambia

T. E. HILTON	Department of Geography, University of Ghana, Ghana
U. HIMMELSTRAND	Department of Sociology, University of Ibadan, Nigeria
J. HOLZER	Institute of Statistics, University of Ghana, Ghana
A. E. IFEKWUNIGWE	Department of Paediatrics, University of Ibadan, Nigeria
M. I. IRO	Federal Census Office, Lagos, Nigeria
K. E. DE GRAFT-JOHNSON	Department of Sociology, University of Ghana, Ghana
A. ADENIYI-JONES	Public Health Department, Lagos, Nigeria
K. M. JUPP	Regional Statistical Adviser, UNECA, Addis-Ababa, Ethiopia
V. KANNISTO	Census Office, Lagos, Nigeria
D. KIRK	The Population Council, USA
D. V. RAJA-LAKSHMAN	UNESCO Field Staff, Lusaka, Zambia
T. A. LAMBO	Department of Psychiatry, University of Ibadan, Nigeria
J. B. LAWSON	Department of Obstetrics and Gynaecology, University of Ibadan, Nigeria
U. G. LISTER	Department of Obstetrics and Gynaecology, University of Ibadan, Nigeria
A. O. LUCAS	Department of Preventive Medicine, University of Ibadan, Nigeria
D. A. LURY	Department of Economics, University College, Nairobi, Kenya
A. L. MABOGUNJE	Department of Geography, University of Ibadan, Nigeria
J. MCFIE	Department of Psychiatry, University of Ibadan, Nigeria
C. M. U. MCLEAN	Medical School, University of Ibadan, Nigeria
G. R. MATTHEW	Department of Haematology, University of Ibadan, Nigeria
O. K. MITTER	Department of Mathematics, University of Nigeria, Nsukka, Nigeria
M. J. MORTIMORE	Department of Geography, Ahmadu Bello University, Zaria, Nigeria
D. NORMAN	Institute of Agricultural Research, Samaru, Zaria, Nigeria
J. O'CONNELL	Department of Political Science, University of Ibadan, Nigeria
T. O. OGUNLESI	Department of Medicine, University of Ibadan, Nigeria
A. OGUNSHEYE	Department of Extra-Mural Studies, University of Ibadan, Nigeria
J. S. OGUNTOYINBO	Department of Geography, University of Ibadan, Nigeria
P. O. OHADIKE	Department of Demography, Australian National University, Australia
G. A. AFOLABIOJO	Department of Geography, University of Ife, Nigeria
F. OKEDIJI	Department of Sociology, University of Ibadan, Nigeria
C. OKONJO	Centre for Population Studies, University of Ibadan, Nigeria
P. O. OLUSANYA	NISER, University of Ibadan, Nigeria
S. H. OMINDE	Department of Geography, University College, Nairobi, Kenya
H. M. A. ONITIRI	Director, NISER, University of Ibadan, Nigeria
D. J. OWUSU	Division of Demographic and Social Statistics, Census Office, Accra, Ghana
M. PERLMAN	Department of Economics, University of Pittsburgh, USA
D. I. POOL	Department of Sociology, University of Ghana, Ghana
R. M. PROTHERO	Department of Geography, University of Liverpool, UK
A. RAMAMURTI	Federal Office of Statistics, Ikoyi, Lagos, Nigeria
A. ROMANIUK	Faculty of Social Sciences, University of Ottawa, Canada
A. K. SAXTON	Department of Preventative Medicine, Makerere University College, Uganda
G. A. SAXTON, JR.	Department of Preventative Medicine, Makerere University College, Uganda
C. SCOTT	Regional Statistical Adviser, UNECA, Ghana
D. M. SERWADDA	Department of Preventative Medicine, Makerere University College, Uganda
A. M. EL SHAFEI	United Nations Demographic Centre, Cairo, UAR
R. K. SOM	Demographic Section, UNECA, Addis Ababa, Ethiopia
P. A. TETTEH	Faculty of Architecture, University of Science and Technology, Kumasi, Ghana
R. K. UDO	Department of Geography, University of Ibadan, Nigeria
E. U. ESSIEN-UDOM	Department of Political Science, University of Ibadan, Nigeria
E. VAN DE WALLE	Princeton University, U.S.A.
R. D. WRIGHT	University of Lagos Medical School, Lagos, Nigeria
G. B. WYATT	Department of Haematology, University of Ibadan, Nigeria
H. W. YAIDOO	Bureau of Statistics, Office of National Planning, Monrovia, Liberia
T. M. YESUFU	Faculty of Business and Social Studies, University of Lagos, Nigeria

Observers at the Conference

B. K. ADADEVOH — University of Lagos Medical School, Lagos, Nigeria
P. CALDWELL — Canberra, Australia
B. T. CHADWICK — British Council, Ibadan, Nigeria
W. J. M. EVANS — Ministry of Overseas Development, UK
A. FALODUN — Federal Manpower Board, Lagos, Nigeria
G. FERAL — Pilot Project for Rural Employment Promotion, ILO Mission, Ministry of Labour and Social Welfare, Ibadan, Nigeria
C. J. GAMBLE — The Pathfinder Fund, USA
B. C. HULL — Regional Liaison Officer, International Planned Parenthood Federation, UK
H. J. KILLICK — British Council, Ibadan, Nigeria
R. MORGAN — University of Lagos Medical School, Nigeria
Z. B. OKEDIJI — University of Lagos Medical School, Nigeria
A. OMOLULU — Department of Chemical Pathology, University of Ibadan, Nigeria
G. O. SOFOLUWE — University of Lagos Medical School, Nigeria
C. TAKES — Pilot Project for Rural Employment Promotion, ILO Mission, Ministry of Labour and Social Welfare, Ibadan, Nigeria
E. WENNER — Institute of Public Health, University College Hospital, Ibadan, Nigeria

Contributors unable to attend

C. N. EJIOGU — Department of Demography, Australian National University, Canberra, Australia
D. K. GHANSAH — Central Bureau of Statistics, Accra, Ghana
D. NORTMAN — The Population Council, USA
E. N. OMABOE — Chief Statistician, Central Bureau of Statistics, Accra, Ghana
T. E. SMITH — Institute of Commonwealth Studies, London, UK

Material referred to in the Introduction to Parts I and II but not included in the Book

Conference Papers referred to but not included in the book

Authors	Number	Title	Pages of Intro.
Addo, N. O.	CP 34	Demographic Aspects of Urban Development in Ghana in the Twentieth Century	22,333
Barber, C. R.	CP 20	Vital Statistics at Igbo Ora: A Preliminary Report on the Collection of Figures for Births and Deaths during 1964	340
ECA	CP 22	Recent Demographic Levels and Trends in Africa	8,15

CP = Conference Paper

DLs, OS, and SRs referred to but not included in the book

Author	Number	Pages of Intro.
Aryee	SR 1	II, 339,340
Blacker	DL 1	I, 5,6
Clairin	SR 11	II, 342
Coale	SR 12	II, 342
Desai	SR 7	II, 340
Eze	SR 5	II, 339
Glass	OS 4	II, 342
Jupp	OS 2a	I, 6
Kirk	OS 6	I, 8, II, 342
Mortimore	SR 6	II, 339
Okonjo	SR 4, 13	II, 339,340
Ominde	SR 8	II, 339
Owusu	SR 3	I, 5,7
El Shafei	OS 3	II, 336
El Shafei	SR 10	II, 342
Tetteh	SR 2	II, 339

DL = Discussion Leader's report
OS = Oral Statement
SR = Special Report.

Index